Towards Unde

The Qur'an

Abridged version of *Tafhīm al-Qur'ān*

SAYYID ABUL A'LĀ MAWDŪDĪ

Translated and edited by
Zafar Ishaq Ansari

For an in-depth understanding of the Qur'an please visit
www.tafhim.net
www.islamicstudies.info/tafheem.php

Sponsored by
UKIM Dawah Centre International

NOT FOR RESALE

This edition is printed by UK Islamic Mission,
Dawah Centre International, with the kind permission of
the Islamic Foundation, UK. For further enquiries please contact:

UKIM Dawah Centre International
Email: ukimdawah@gmail.com
Web: www.learnislam4free.com
Web. www.ukimdawahcentre.com

Translated and edited by Zafar Ishaq Ansari

British Library Cataloguing in Publication Data

Mawdudi, Sayyid Abul A'la, 1903–1979
Towards Understanding the Qur'an
1. Koran – Commentaries
I. Title II. Ansari, Zafar Ishaq
III. Islamic Foundation (Great Britain)
297.1'227

ISBN 13: 978-0-86037-416-9 *paperback*

We thank all those individual donors who contributed generously to
this Qur'ān project. May Allah (swt) bless and reward them
abundantly in this world and the Hereafter, Amin.

Typeset by: N. A. Qaddoura
Cover design by: Nasir Cadir

Printed and bound in India by Nutech Print Services

Contents

Contents

Contents

Transliteration Table

Arabic Consonants

Initial, unexpressed medial and final:

ء	'	د	d	ض	ḍ	ك	k
ب	b	ذ	dh	ط	ṭ	ل	l
ت	t	ر	r	ظ	z	م	m
ث	th	ز	z	ع	'	ن	n
ج	j	س	s	غ	gh	هـ	h
ح	ḥ	ش	sh	ف	f	و	w
خ	kh	ص	ṣ	ق	q	ي	y

Vowels, diphthongs, etc.

Short: َ a   ِ i   ُ u

Long: ـَا ā   ـِي ī   ـُو ū

Diphthongs: ـَوْ aw

                ـَىْ ay

Foreword

The Qur'ān is the foundation and mainstay of Islamic faith, life and culture. Islam and the Muslim *ummah* are unique in so far as their bedrock is primarily a Book – the Qur'ān. This Book gave the Muslims their distinct worldview and vision of life. Historically speaking, the Qur'ān performed the great feat of transforming a motley group of warring tribes of seventh-century Arabia into the Muslim *ummah* which soon developed into a dynamic world community with a message for humanity at large. It not only fashioned the historical personality of the Muslims but also remained the main source of their inspiration and guidance throughout the fourteen centuries of their history.

The Qur'ān encompasses the totality of God's Revelation to Muḥammad (peace be on him), the last in the distinguished series of Prophets raised for mankind's guidance. The uniqueness of the Qur'ān lies in its being the Final Revelation. It is precisely for this reason that it preserves and protects whatever was revealed prior to it. It also represents the culmination and zenith of the Divine Revelation which commenced with the birth of Adam and came to an end with the Prophet's return to the Mercy of his Lord. Being the Final Revelation, God saw to it that the ravages of time would play no havoc with it: that nothing of it would be lost, nor any part of it altered, nor anything extraneous to it find its way to it. It was God's Will that the Final Revelation should be preserved in its entirety exactly as it had been communicated to the Prophet (peace be on him) by Gabriel, and exactly as the Prophet (peace be on him) had communicated it to his contemporaries. All this was essential since this Last Book was meant to serve as a beacon light for the guidance of all humanity till the end of time.

The intrinsic value of the Qur'ān is evident to many perceiving eyes and reflecting minds. On the other hand is the heart-rending fact that human beings in large numbers are scarcely aware of the Qur'ān's message and teachings. What is more, thanks to the strong Islamophobic media that presently holds sway over the world, multitudes of people are averse to it. Quite a few Muslims regard an accumulation of external factors as responsible for creating a deep-seated prejudice against Islam and the Qur'ān. The fact, however, is that it is we Muslims who are to blame more than anyone else for the present state of affairs in so far as we have failed to give this Book its due by making it widely available in a form that would enable our fellow beings to grasp its meaning.

For a number of historical reasons, however, the interaction between the Muslims and the rest of the world, especially with the West, has been on the increase in recent times. This development can prove a turning point in history, especially if the Muslims can have the same degree of concern to make the Qur'ān's message and meaning accessible to all and sundry as they have for their mundane interests. Hence, instead of fruitlessly lamenting the sordid state of affairs of the present, vigorous efforts should be made to change it by building bridges of understanding across the religious, cultural and ethnic divide found in our world today.

The Qur'ān – uncreated Word of God though it doubtlessly is – was revealed and communicated through the medium of a human language – Arabic. No wonder its original text remains a living miracle in a variety of ways. Hence those who know Arabic have access to a whole universe of meaning which is not easy for others to reach. For it is only by reading the Qur'ān in the original that one is exposed to its true beauty and grandeur. It is only the original Arabic Qur'ān that can make one appreciate "that inimitable symphony the very sound of which moves man to tears and ecstasy,"[1] as Muhammad Marmaduke Pickthall has aptly put it. Even the best translations can never transport the Qur'ān's vast universe of meaning, or its astounding beauty and grandeur to their readers. The Qur'ān, in this sense, was always and will always remain untranslatable. Imperfect though all such translations are always bound to be, nevertheless the effort to translate the Qur'ān into other languages is absolutely essential to effectively communicate the substance of its meaning and message. Indeed it should be an ongoing activity of Muslim scholars for hopefully with the passage of time an increasingly better communication of the Qur'ān's meaning would be possible.

Now every language, including Arabic in which the Qur'ān was revealed, has its own style, diction and

---

1. Pickthall, M.M.: *The Meaning of the Glorious Koran* (New York: Mentor), p.VII.

ethos. The language of the Qur'ān is characterized by a unique mental and moral ambience: it has a distinct style, supported by a value-laden idiom, a multi-dimensional phrase-structure, a sequential inter-relatedness, all of which is expressed in a literary style of unsurpassable beauty and force. The language and style of the Qur'ān also reflect a set of values which are related to a number of concepts and ideas. All these go to make up an organic whole, a unique literary culture, and a self-sustaining spiritual and intellectual personality. In such a context it is evident that the translation needs to be really good to assist those who are not initiated to the ideas, values and spirit of this culture so that they are able to grasp the spirit and the meaning of the text. This is possible only if the translators have a good taste of the Arabic language, have remained immersed in the universe of the Qur'ānic meaning, and have the ability to express it with clarity, elegance and force.

The translations of the Qur'ān that are devoid of sympathy, understanding and reverence will fail to make their readers appreciate its message in any depth. It is unfortunate that several translations through which readers approach the Qur'ān lack empathy for the Qur'ān, and some even attempt, in our opinion, to distort and denigrate it. Even where a translation does not suffer from deliberate distortion or misrepresentation, it generally lacks an insightful understanding. Moreover, quite often these translations make a dull reading compared to the sparkling original. Since the ordinary reader of the Qur'ān is not familiar with the ethos of the Qur'ān and is not properly initiated into the culture of the Divine Word, he/she is often unable to taste its sweetness, to encompass its breadth, and fathom its depths, through many of these translations. Hence good translations in different languages, especially English, are a pressing need of the hour. It is heartening that a number of able scholars, who are respected by the Muslims as authentic spokespersons of Islam, have responded to this need of our times. Abdullah Yusuf Ali, Muhammad Marmaduke Pickthall, and Muhammad Asad are some of the most outstanding names that instantly come to mind from among a growing body of distinguished translators of the Qur'ān.

A great Muslim scholar of the twentieth century, Mawlānā Sayyid Abul A'lā Mawdūdī (1903-1979), was conscious that a fresh effort to translate and explain the Qur'ān was needed for the Urdu-reading public. In response to that he devoted several decades of his life and produced his monumental work, *Tafhīm al-Qur'ān*, which is a unique contribution to the contemporary literature on the exegesis of the Qur'ān. The uniqueness of *Tafhīm* lies in the fact that it is focused on explicating to the fullest extent possible the Guidance embodied in the Qur'ān. The Qur'ānic Guidance has to be optimally appreciated by all because it is meant to shape man's worldview and outlook on life as well as to shape the pattern of individual and collective behaviour and to mould human institutions in line with the letter and spirit of God's imperatives.

In *Tafhīm* Sayyid Mawdūdī also emphasizes that the Qur'ān is not meant for a docile, arm-chair reading. It is essentially meant for those who seek to know the Truth and after knowing it will actively engage themselves in living according to its demands and will also strive to make it prevail in their milieu. It is meant for those who are ready to change themselves and willing truly to change the world around them. It calls upon those who embrace its message not to be satisfied ever with the *status quo*, but to strive ceaselessly to improve themselves, improve their fellow-beings and improve the order of things in which they are placed.

Sayyid Mawdūdī's *magnum opus, Tafhīm al-Qur'ān*, was published in Urdu in six volumes and is spread over several thousand pages. It was felt that it should reach the vast body of English-reading public spread across the globe. Hence we arranged for its English translation which is being published under the auspices of the Islamic Foundation, Leicester, UK. Seven volumes of it have already been published. Work on the remaining volumes is under way but its completion may take several years. Hence it was considered appropriate to publish a shorter, one-volume work about the Qur'ān that would be of use to those who might not have the time or sustained interest and patience to study the voluminous work that *Tafhīm* is.

As good luck would have it, after completing *Tafhīm* Sayyid Mawdūdī himself became aware of the same need and therefore produced a one-volume edition of his work to which he gave the title *Tarjuma-'i Qur'ān-i Majīd ma' Mukhtaṣar Ḥawāshī*. Sayyid Mawdūdī added to his translation of the Qur'ān, which in itself was a landmark achievement, short notes which he considered essential for a clear understanding of the Qur'ān. These notes are by far and large an abridgement of the copious notes of his *Tafhīm*.

Sayyid Mawdūdī's translation has certain unique features. It is an interpretative translation in direct, forceful and modern Urdu which has now been rendered into forceful and modern English. In the first place, this translation conveys the meaning of the Qur'ān in a style that hopefully reflects something of the beauty, force and majesty of the Qur'ān. This translation is supported by short notes and those too in a very limited number. They primarily aim at clarifying either the background of a particular verse or elaborating a point where the uninitiated reader might require some assistance in grasping the meaning and import of a Qur'ānic verse. It is hoped that in its present form the translation with short notes accompanying it will provide a useful aid for an essential understanding of the Qur'ān. The purpose of the work is to assist those who seek to have access to the meaning of the Qur'ān but who can do so only through the medium of the English language.

Dr. Zafar Ishaq Ansari, my dear brother, life-long friend, and colleague has very ably produced the English rendering of this work. I have no hesitation in saying that Dr. Ansari has rendered the same kind of service to the English-reading public that Sayyid Mawdūdī had rendered to the Urdu-reading public. It represents a monumental achievement. I pray to Allah to bless this effort and make it a light-house for those who are stumbling in quest of the Truth of which the Qur'ān is a unique repository. May God bless all those who have contributed in one way or another to making this project see the light of day and may He amply reward them for that.

Islamabad **Khurshid Ahmad**
Muḥarram 28, 1426
March 10, 2005

Editor's Preface

Towards Understanding the Qur'ān: Abridged Version is an English rendering of *Tarjuma-'i Qur'ān-i Majīd ma' Mukhtaṣar Ḥawāshī*, a translation of the Qur'ān with short notes by Mawlānā Sayyid Abul A 'lā Mawdūdī (1903-1979), one of the most extensively read and influential Muslim scholars of the twentieth century. Though Mawdūdī was born and lived throughout his life in the South Asian Sub-continent, his writings attracted Muslims as well as a fairly large number of educated non-Muslims across the globe. These writings also greatly contributed to that complex of feeling, consciousness, and activism that has come to be characterised during the last few decades as 'Islamic resurgence'.

As a writer, Mawdūdī was both prolific and versatile. His writings, which range from small articles and tracts to voluminous books, encompass almost all significant aspects of Islam. These works were generally well-received, especially by the educated Muslim readership and his articulation of the Islamic world-view won him considerable acclaim. Mawdūdī's presentation of the socio-economic and political doctrines of Islam in particular evoked much interest and appreciation. Likewise, Mawdūdī distinguished himself by his forceful writings aimed at establishing that the principles propounded by Islam were intrinsically sound, that they were relevant for and viable in every age and clime, that they were intrinsically good and benevolent and conducive to the overall well-being of mankind.

Apart from focusing on subjects of relatively contemporaneous concern, Mawdūdī also wrote on subjects that belong to the traditionally recognized fields of Islamic scholarship such as *Ḥadīth*, *Fiqh* and *'Ilm al-Kalām*. It is the Qur'ān, however, that held for him a very special place, and one might say, overpowering fascination. He relished the Book of God beyond all measure and never ceased to look up to it at every step and turn of life for light, guidance and inspiration. In his view, the Qur'ān was not to be approached merely for *barakah* (blessing); it should rather serve as the sheet-anchor and the driving and guiding force of one's life. Hence one should let the Qur'ān shape one's intellectual outlook, mould one's character and conduct, and serve as the yardstick that should judge all things. Mawdūdī once described the Qur'ān as the 'master key', zestfully claiming that after he had found that key all locked doors were flung open and all his intellectual problems and perplexities were resolved. It was perhaps not merely a coincidence that the monthly magazine which he chose to edit and through which he disseminated his ideas for forty-six years (1933-1979) bore the appellation *Tarjumān al-Qur'ān* ("The Interpreter of the Qur'ān").

I felt greatly honoured when I was asked to render Sayyid Mawdūdī's monumental work *Tafhīm al-Qur'ān* into English. Over the years seven volumes of this work have been published by The Islamic Foundation, Leicester, UK under the title *Towards Understanding the Qur'ān*. Some time ago I was asked by my friends at the Foundation to suspend this major work for a while and devote my time and energy instead to complete the translation of the Qur'ān and the short explanatory notes that Sayyid Mawdūdī had written for his abridged, one-volume work on the Qur'ān *Tarjuma-'i Qur'ān-i Majīd ma' Mukhtaṣar Ḥawāshī* published in 1976. The idea was to make available an English translation of the Qur'ān with short explanatory notes that would meet the need of the readers of the Qur'ān who are concerned with knowing its essential teachings.

The present work represents my compliance with that request. As the readers of *Towards Understanding the Qur'ān* are aware, I had already translated up to *Sūrah* 28 (*al-Qaṣaṣ*) of the Qur'ān and this had already appeared as part of the seven volumes of the above-mentioned work published so far. For the present work, however, I reviewed that translation quite carefully and critically and modified it at quite a few places. As for the translation of the remaining *Sūrahs* – 29 to 114 – it was done afresh. I cannot thank God enough for enabling me to accomplish this task. The mere idea that I will, *inshā' Allāh*, find a place among the translators of the Qur'ān is a matter of extraordinary privilege which fills my heart with immense gratitude to the Almighty.

I must confess that before I had prepared the manuscript of the abridged one-volume work, I did not have more than a faint idea of the true value and merit of the abridged version of *Tafhīm* as a vehicle for dissemination of the Qur'ān's message. It was only after I had completed the draft of this work and read its proofs more than once – a task that made me read the text in one go – that I realized what a useful work it is. With all its merits, *Tafhīm al-Qur'ān* is a massive work and comprises something close to 4,000 pages of large-size paper in Urdu. It requires a considerable amount of sustained interest and a certain degree of academic competence to go through this significant piece of Qur'ānic scholarship, especially its copious notes. It is no wonder, therefore, that although *Tafhīm* attracted a very large readership, the abridged Urdu edition of the work prepared by Mawdūdī himself has reached a much larger readership. We hope that the abridged edition of *Tafhīm* in English will possibly also draw a very large readership and will thus be a source of enlightenment for a great number of people. The worth of the present work also lies in the fact that its short notes provide that essential explanation of the Qur'ān without which an ordinary reader's understanding of it might remain inadequate. At the same time, the notes indeed seem confined to the bare minimum so that one hardly finds anything that is not necessary for a proper understanding of the Qur'ānic teachings.

In finalizing the text of this work I have greatly benefited, as I had benefited earlier in *Towards Understanding the Qur'ān*, from the critical comments and suggestions of Ms. Suzanne Thackeray and Dr. A.R. Kidwai and it is my pleasant duty to express my profound gratitude to them. Dr. Kidwai was kind enough also to cast a second critical look at the text which helped me weed out quite a number of lapses. I greatly appreciate this important contribution of his and I am beholden to him for that. At the Foundation Mr. Naiem Qaddoura rendered valuable assistance in setting the Arabic material and page layout. Dr. Manazir Ahsan, by his constant, even if polite reminders, did not permit this writer to relax or remain indolent for long! As for my life-long friend, Khurshid Ahmad, it is no exaggeration to say that his words of appreciation, encouragement, kindness and support helped me strengthen my resolve to give this work the best of whatever I have. In a way, both *Towards Understanding the Qur'ān* and the present work are an epitome of a long, time-tested and profound friendship and camaraderie. I am thankful to all of them.

Several friends in Islamabad have also obliged me in the preparation of this work. My friend and colleague, Mr. S.M. Afzal Iqbal, Director Publishing, Administration and Finance, Islamic Research Institute, undertook the painstaking and meticulous task of culling out for this work the explanatory notes for *Sūrahs* 1-28 from the first seven volumes of *Towards Understanding the Qur'ān*. This was a very tedious task requiring meticulous care which saved me considerable time and effort. I am deeply indebted to Mr. Afzal Iqbal for the fine job he has done.

Several of my colleagues at the Islamic Research Institute have also assisted me in several ways. Mr. Amjad Mahmood and Gohar Zaman cheerfully typed and retyped the manuscript quite a number of times. Mr. Tufail Hussain Jadoon worked very hard to typeset and format the text, which was by no means an easy task. The Institute's skilled proof-readers, Mr. Muhammad Nazir and Mr. Mazhar Iqbal also worked assiduously to ensure accuracy. Dr. Muhammad Junaid Nadvi of the Centre of Islamic Studies, International Islamic University, Mr. Abdurrahman Saaleh, Editorial Assistant, *Islamic Studies* and Mr. Muhammad Akram Afzal of the Islamic Research Institute provided academic assistance. Mr. Qaiser Shahzad of the Islamic Research Institute very carefully went through the manuscript from cover to cover, perhaps more than once, and favoured me with quite a few critical comments. I feel great pleasure in acknowledging the contributions of these friends and colleagues and thanking them.

Muhammad Modassir Ali, again a colleague of mine at the Institute, worked with me on this manuscript day after day and month after month and assisted me in ways just too numerous to be counted. He critically reviewed the text over and over again, his sharp eyes and penetrating brain perceiving errors, oversights and inadequacies which had escaped my notice. His constant and critical scrutiny of the text has doubtlessly led to the improvement of the text. Apart from providing academic assistance, Modassir also contributed very significantly to technical matters pertaining to the formatting of the text, to preparing the index, and helped me with the preparation of the Glossary of Terms and Biographical Notes. Enormous is the amount of time that he has devoted to and the extent of interest he has lavished on this work of mine and most valuable is the assistance he has rendered to me in seeing this book through to completion. I do not think that mere words can ever adequately express my gratitude to him.

The responsibility for whatever mistakes, oversights or inadequacies, remain in this work despite the assistance I have received, lies squarely on my shoulders.

May Allah bless all those whose names have been mentioned above as well as those whose names could not be mentioned although they have helped and encouraged and inspired me in connection with this work in one way or another.

Islamabad   **Zafar Ishaq Ansari**
August 25, 2005

Introduction[1]

It must be said at once that this is an introduction to *Towards Understanding the Qur'ān*, and not to the Qur'ān itself. It has been written with two objectives. First, to acquaint the reader with certain matters which he should grasp at the very outset so as to achieve a more than superficial understanding of the Holy Book. Second, to clarify those disturbing questions that commonly arise in the mind of the reader during the study of the Qur'ān.

[I]

We are accustomed to reading books which present information, ideas and arguments systematically and coherently. So when we embark on the study of the Qur'ān, we expect that this book too will revolve around a definite subject, that the subject matter of the book will be clearly defined at the beginning and will then be neatly divided into sections and chapters, after which discussion will proceed in a logical sequence. We likewise expect a

---

1. Mawlānā Abul A'lā Mawdūdī wrote this 'Introduction' for his *Tafhīm al-Qur'ān*. It is being reproduced here to acquaint the readers with some of the basic ideas that inform the author's approach to understanding the Qur'ān. – Ed.

separate and systematic arrangement of instruction and guidance for each of the various aspects of human life.

However, as soon as we open the Qur'ān we encounter a hitherto completely unfamiliar genre of literature. We notice that it embodies precepts of belief and conduct, moral directives, legal prescriptions, exhortation and admonition, censure and condemnation of evil-doers, warnings to deniers of the Truth, good tidings and words of consolation and good cheer to those who have suffered for the sake of God, arguments and corroborative evidence in support of its basic message, allusions to anecdotes from the past and to signs of God visible in the universe. Moreover, these myriad subjects alternate without any apparent system; quite unlike the books to which we are accustomed, the Qur'ān deals with the same subject over and over again, each time couched in a different phraseology.

The reader also encounters abrupt transitions between one subject matter and another. Audience and speaker constantly change as the message is directed now to one and now to another group of people. There is no trace of the familiar division into chapters and sections. Likewise, the treatment of different subjects is unique. If an historical subject is raised, the narrative does not follow the pattern familiar in historical accounts. In discussions of philosophical or metaphysical questions, we miss the familiar expressions and terminology of formal logic and philosophy. Cultural and political matters, or questions pertaining to man's social and economic life, are discussed in a way very different from that usual in works of social sciences. Juristic principles and legal injunctions are elucidated, but quite differently from the manner of conventional works. When we come across an ethical instruction, we find its form differs entirely from anything to be found elsewhere in the literature of ethics.

The reader may find all this so foreign to his notion of what a book should be that he may become so confused as to feel that the Qur'ān is a piece of disorganized, incoherent and unsystematic writing, comprising nothing but a disjointed conglomeration of comments of varying lengths put together arbitrarily. Hostile critics use this as a basis for their criticism, while those more favourably inclined resort to far-fetched explanations, or else conclude that the Qur'ān consists of unrelated pieces, thus making it amenable to all kinds of interpretation, even interpretations quite opposed to the intent of God Who revealed the Book.

[II]

What kind of book, then, is the Qur'ān? In what manner was it revealed? What underlies its arrangement? What is its subject? What is its true purpose? What is the central theme to which its multifarious topics are intrinsically related? What kind of reasoning and style does it adopt in elucidating its central theme? If we could obtain clear, lucid answers to these and other related questions we might avoid some dangerous pitfalls, thus making it easier to reflect upon and to grasp the meaning and purpose of the Qur'ānic verses. If we begin studying the Qur'ān in the expectation of reading a book on religion we shall find it hard, since our notions of religion and of a book are naturally circumscribed by our range of experience. We need, therefore, to be told in advance that this Book is unique in the manner of its composition, in its theme and in its contents and arrangement. We should be forewarned that the concept of a book which we have formed from our previous readings is likely to be a hindrance, rather than a help, towards a deep understanding of the Qur'ān. We should realize that as a first step towards understanding it we must disabuse our minds of all preconceived notions.

[III]

The student of the Qur'ān should grasp, from the outset, the fundamental claims that the Qur'ān makes for itself. Whether one ultimately decides to believe in the Qur'ān or not, one must recognize the fundamental statements made by the Qur'ān and by the man to whom it was revealed, the Prophet Muḥammad (peace be on him), to be the starting point of one's study. These claims are:

1. The Lord of creation, the Creator and Sovereign of the entire universe, created man on earth (which is merely a part of His boundless realm). He also endowed man with the capacity for cognition, reflection and understanding, with the ability to distinguish between good and evil, with the freedom of choice and volition, and with the power to exercise his latent potentialities. In short, God bestowed upon man a kind of autonomy and appointed him His vicegerent on earth.

2. Although man enjoys this status, God made it abundantly plain to him that He alone is man's Lord and Sovereign, even as He is the Lord

and Sovereign of the whole universe. Man was told that he was not entitled to consider himself independent and that only God was entitled to claim absolute obedience, service and worship. It was also made clear to man that life in this world, for which he had been placed and invested with a certain honour and authority, was in fact a temporary term, and was meant to test him; that after the end of this earthly life man must return to God, Who will judge him on the basis of his performance, declaring who has succeeded and who has failed.

The right way for man is to regard God as his only Sovereign and the only object of his worship and adoration, to follow the guidance revealed by God, to act in this world in the consciousness that earthly life is merely a period of trial, and to keep his eyes fixed on the ultimate objective – success in God's final judgement. Every other way is wrong.

It was also explained to man that if he chose to adopt the right way of life – and in this choice he was free – he would enjoy peace and contentment in this world and be assigned, on his return to God, the abode of eternal bliss and happiness known as Paradise. Should man follow any other way – and he was free to do so – he would experience the evil effects of corruption and disorder in the life of this world and be consigned to eternal grief and torment when he crossed the borders of the present world and arrived in the Hereafter.

3. Having explained all this, the Lord of the Universe placed man on earth and communicated to Adam and Eve, the first human beings to live on earth, the guidance which they and their offspring were required to follow. These first human beings were not born in a state of ignorance and darkness. On the contrary, they began their life in the broad daylight of Divine Guidance. They had intimate knowledge of reality and the Law which they were to follow was communicated to them. Their way of life consisted of obedience to God (i.e. Islam) and they taught their children to live in obedience to Him (i.e. to live as Muslims).

In the course of time, however, men gradually deviated from this true way of life and began to follow various erroneous ways. They allowed true guidance to be lost through heedlessness and negligence and sometimes, even deliberately, distorted it out of evil perversity. They associated with God a number of beings, human and non-human, real as well as imaginary, and adored them as deities. They adulterated the God-given knowledge of reality, (*al-ʿilm* in the Qurʾānic terminology), with all kinds of fanciful ideas, superstitions and philosophical concepts, thereby giving birth to innumerable religions. They disregarded or distorted the sound and equitable principles of individual morality and of collective conduct (*al-Sharīʿah* in the Qurʾānic terminology) and made their own laws in accordance with their base desires and prejudices. As a result, the world became filled with wrong and injustice.

4. It was inconsistent with the limited autonomy conferred upon man by God that He should exercise His overwhelming power and compel man to righteousness. It was also inconsistent with the fact that God had granted a term to the human species in which to show their worth that He should afflict men with catastrophic destruction as soon as they showed signs of rebellion. Moreover, God had undertaken from the beginning of creation that true guidance would be made available to man throughout the term granted to him and that this guidance would be available in a manner consistent with man's autonomy. To fulfil this self-assumed responsibility God chose to appoint those human beings whose faith in Him was outstanding and who followed the way pleasing to Him. God chose these people to be His envoys. He had His messages communicated to them, honoured them with an intimate knowledge of reality, provided them with the true laws of life and entrusted them with the task of recalling man to the original path from which he had strayed.[2]

5. These Prophets were sent to different people in different lands and over a period of time covering thousands and thousands of years. They all had the same religion; the one originally revealed to man as the right way for him. All of them followed the same guidance; those principles of morality and collective life prescribed for man at the very outset of his existence. All these Prophets had the

---

2. These men were Prophets and Messengers of God. – Ed.

same mission – to call man to this true religion and subsequently to organize all who accepted this message into a community (*ummah*) which would be bound by the Law of God, which would strive to establish its observance and would seek to prevent its violation. All the Prophets discharged their missions creditably in their own time. However, there were always many who refused to accept their guidance and consequently those who did accept it and became a 'Muslim' community[3] gradually degenerated, causing the Divine Guidance either to be lost, distorted or adulterated.

6. At last the Lord of the Universe sent Muḥammad (peace be on him) to Arabia and entrusted him with the same mission that He had entrusted to the earlier Prophets. This last Messenger of God addressed the followers of the earlier Prophets (who had by this time deviated from their original teachings) as well as the rest of humanity. The mission of each Prophet was to call men to the right way of life, to communicate God's true guidance afresh and to organize into one community all who responded to his mission and accepted the guidance vouchsafed to him. Such a

---

3. That is, a group of people committed to obey the true guidance of God as revealed to His Prophets. Here the word "Muslim" is not used in the sense of followers of the last Messenger of God, Muḥammad (peace be on him), but in the wider sense, meaning all those who, at various periods, both before and after the advent of the Last Prophet, committed themselves to live in submission to God. – Ed.

community was to be dedicated to the two-fold task of moulding its own life in accordance with God's guidance and striving for the reform of the world. The Qur'ān is the Book which embodies this mission and guidance revealed by God to Muḥammad (peace be on him).

[IV]

If we remember these basic facts about the Qur'ān it becomes easy to grasp its true subject, its central theme and the objective it seeks to achieve. In so far as it seeks to explain the ultimate causes of man's success or failure the subject of the Book is MAN.

Its central theme is that concepts relating to God, the universe and man which have emanated from man's own limited knowledge run counter to reality. The same applies to concepts which have been either woven by man's intellectual fancies or which have evolved through man's obsession with animal desires. The ways of life which rest on these false foundations are both contrary to reality and ruinous for man. The essence of true knowledge is that which God revealed to man when He appointed him His vicegerent. Hence, the way of life which is in accordance with reality and conducive to human good is that which we have characterized above as 'the right way'. The real object of the Book is to call people to this 'right way' and to illuminate God's true guidance, which has often been lost either through man's negligence and heedlessness or distorted by his wicked perversity.

If we study the Qur'ān with these facts in mind it is bound to strike us that the Qur'ān does not deviate one iota from its main subject, its central theme and its basic objective. All the various themes occurring in the Qur'ān are related to the central theme; just as beads of different sizes and colour may be strung together to form a necklace. The Qur'ān speaks of the structure of the heavens and the earth and of man, refers to the signs of reality in the various phenomena of the universe, relates anecdotes of bygone nations, criticizes the beliefs, morals and deeds of different peoples, elucidates supernatural truths and discusses many other things besides. All this the Qur'ān does, not in order to provide instruction in physics, history, philosophy or any other particular branch of knowledge, but rather to remove the misconceptions people have about reality and to make that reality manifest to them.

It emphasizes that the various ways men follow, which are not in conformity with reality, are essentially false, and full of harmful consequences for mankind. It calls on men to shun all such ways and to follow instead the way which both conforms to reality and yields the best practical results. This is why the Qur'ān mentions everything only to the extent and in the manner necessary for the purposes it seeks to serve. The Qur'ān confines itself to essentials thereby omitting any irrelevant details. Thus, all its contents consistently revolve around this call.

Likewise, it is not possible fully to appreciate either the style of the Qur'ān, the order underlying the arrangement of its verses or the diversity of the subjects treated in it, without fully understanding the manner in which it was revealed.

The Qur'ān, as we have noted earlier, is not a book in the conventional sense of the term. God did not compose and entrust it in one piece to Muḥammad (peace be on him) so that he could spread its message and call people to adopt an attitude to life consonant with its teachings. Nor is the Qur'ān one of those books which discusses their subjects and main themes in the conventional manner. Its arrangement differs from that of ordinary books, and its style is correspondingly different. The nature of this Book is that God chose a man in Makkah to serve as His Messenger and asked him to preach His message, starting in his own city (Makkah) and with his own tribe (Quraysh). At this initial stage, instructions were confined to what was necessary at this particular juncture of the mission. Three themes in particular stand out:

1. Directives were given to the Prophet (peace be on him) on how he should prepare himself for his great mission and how he should begin working for the fulfilment of his task.

2. A fundamental knowledge of reality was furnished and misconceptions commonly held by people in that regard – misconceptions which gave rise to wrong orientation in life – were removed.

3. People were exhorted to adopt the right attitude toward life. Moreover, the Qur'ān also elucidated those fundamental principles which, if followed, lead to man's success and happiness.

In keeping with the character of the mission at this stage the early revelations generally consisted of short verses, couched in language of uncommon grace and power, and clothed in a literary style suited to the taste and temperament of the people to whom they were originally addressed, and whose hearts they were meant to penetrate. The rhythm, melody and vitality of these verses drew rapt attention, and such was their stylistic grace and charm that people began to recite them involuntarily.

The local colour of these early messages is conspicuous, for while the truths they contained were universal, the arguments and illustrations used to elucidate them were drawn from the immediate environment familiar to the first listeners. Allusions were made to their history and traditions and to the visible traces of the past which had crept into the beliefs, and into the moral and social life of Arabia. All this was calculated to enhance the appeal the message held for its immediate audience. This early stage lasted for four or five years, during which period the following reactions to the Prophet's message manifested themselves:

1. A few people responded to the call and agreed to join the *ummah* (community) committed, of its own volition, to submit to the Will of God.

2. Many people reacted with hostility, either from out of ignorance or egotism, or because of chauvinistic attachment to the way of life of their forefathers.

3. The call of the Prophet, however, did not remain confined to Makkah or to the Quraysh. It began to meet with favourable response beyond the borders of that city and among other tribes.

The next stage of the mission was marked by a hard, vigorous struggle between the Islamic movement and the age-old Ignorance[4] (*Jāhilīyah*) of Arabia. Not only were the Makkans and the Quraysh bent upon preserving their inherited way of life, they were also firmly resolved to suppress the new movement by force. They stopped at nothing in the pursuit of this objective. They resorted to false propaganda; they spread doubt and suspicion and used subtle, malicious insinuations to sow distrust in people's minds. They tried to prevent people from listening to the message of the Prophet. They perpetrated savage cruelties on those who embraced Islam. They subjected them to economic and social boycott, and persecuted them to such an extent that on two occasions a number of them were forced to leave home and emigrate to Abyssinia, and finally they had to emigrate *en masse* to Madīnah.

In spite of this strong and growing resistance and opposition, the Islamic movement continued to spread. There was hardly a family left in Makkah one of whose members at least had not embraced Islam. Indeed, the violence and bitterness of the enemies of Islam was due to the fact that their own kith and kin – brothers, nephews, sons, daughters, sisters, brothers-in-law and so on – had not only embraced Islam, but were even ready to sacrifice their lives for its sake. Their resistance, therefore, brought

---

4. The author uses the term "Ignorance" (*Jāhilīyah*) to denote all those world-views and ways of life which are based on the rejection or disregard of the heavenly guidance which is communicated to mankind through the Prophets and Messengers of God; the attitude of treating human life – either wholly or partly – as independent of the directives revealed by God. For this see the writings of the author, especially *Islam and Ignorance* (Lahore: 1976), and *A Short History of the Revivalist Movements in Islam*, tr. al-Ash'ari, III edition (Lahore: 1976). – Ed.

them into conflict with their own nearest and dearest. Moreover, those who had forsaken the age-old Ignorance of Arabia included many who were outstanding members of their Society. After embracing Islam, they became so remarkable for their moral uprightness, their veracity and their purity of character that the world could hardly fail to notice the superiority of the message which was attracting people of such qualities.

During the Prophet's long and arduous struggle God continued to inspire him with revelations possessing at once the smooth, natural flow of a river, the violent force of a flood and the overpowering effect of a fierce fire. These messages instructed the believers in their basic duties, inculcated in them a sense of community and belonging, exhorted them to piety, moral excellence and purity of character, taught them how to preach the true faith, sustained their spirit by promises of success and Paradise in the Hereafter, aroused them to struggle in the cause of God with patience, fortitude and high spirits, and filled their hearts with such zeal and enthusiasm that they were prepared to endure every sacrifice, brave every hardship and face every adversity.

At the same time, those either bent on opposition, or who had deviated from the right way, or who had immersed themselves in frivolity and wickedness, were warned by having their attentions called to the tragic ends of nations with whose fates they were familiar. They were asked to draw lessons from the ruins of those localities through which they passed every day in the course of their wanderings. Evidence for the unity of God and for the existence of the After-life was pointed to in signs visible to their own eyes and within the range of their ordinary experience. The weaknesses inherent in polytheism, the vanity of man's ambition to become independent even of God, the folly of denying the After-life, the perversity of blind adherence to the ways of one's ancestors regardless of right or wrong, were all fully elucidated with the help of arguments cogent enough to penetrate the minds and hearts of the audience.

Moreover, every misgiving was removed, a reasonable answer was provided to every objection, all confusion and perplexity was cleared up, and Ignorance was besieged from all sides till its irrationality was totally exposed. Along with all this went the warning of the wrath of God. The people were reminded of the horrors of Doomsday and the tormenting punishment of Hell. They were also censured for their moral corruption, for their erroneous ways of life, for their clinging to the ways of Ignorance, for their opposition to Truth and their persecution of the believers. Furthermore, these messages enunciated those fundamental principles of morality and collective life on which all sound and healthy civilizations enjoying God's approval had always rested.

This stage was unfolded in several phases. In each phase, the preaching of the message assumed ever-wider proportions, as the struggle for the cause of Islam and opposition to it became increasingly intense and severe, and as the believers encountered people of varying outlooks and beliefs. All these factors had the effect of increasing the variety of the topics treated in the messages revealed during this period. Such, in brief, was the situation forming the background to the Makkan *sūrahs* of the Qur'ān.

[V]

For thirteen years the Islamic movement strove in Makkah. It then obtained, in Madīnah, a haven of refuge in which to concentrate its followers and its strength. The Prophet's movement now entered its third stage.

During this stage, circumstances changed drastically. The Muslim community succeeded in establishing a fully-fledged state; its creation was followed by prolonged armed conflict with the representatives of the ancient Ignorance of Arabia. The community also encountered followers of the former Prophets, i.e. Jews and Christians. An additional problem was that hypocrites began to join the fold of the Muslim community; their machinations needed to be resisted. After a severe struggle, lasting ten years, the Islamic movement reached a high point of achievement when the entire Arabian peninsula came under its sway and the door was open to world-wide preaching and reform. This stage, like the preceding one, passed through various phases each of which had its peculiar problems and demands.

It was in the context of these problems that God continued to reveal messages to the Prophet. At times these messages were couched in the form of fiery speeches; at other times they were characterized by the grandeur and stateliness of majestic proclamations and ordinances. At times they had the air of instructions from a teacher; at others the style of preaching of a reformer. These messages explained how a healthy society, state and civilization could be established and the principles on which the various aspects of human life should be based.

They also dealt with matters directly related to the specific problems facing the Muslims. For example, how should they deal with the hypocrites (who were harming the Muslim community from within) and with the non-Muslims who were living under the care of the Muslim society? How should they relate to the People of the Book? What treatment should be meted out to those with whom the Muslims were at war, and how should they deal with those with whom they were bound by treaties and agreements? How should the believers, as a community, prepare to discharge their obligations as vicegerents of the Lord of the Universe? Through the Qur'ān the Muslims were guided in questions like these, were instructed and trained, made aware of their weaknesses, urged to risk their lives and property for the cause of God, taught the code of morality they should observe in all circumstances of life – in times of victory and defeat, ease and distress, prosperity and adversity, peace and security, peril and danger.

In short, they were being trained to serve as the successors of the mission of the Prophet, with the task of carrying on the message of Islam and bringing about reform in human life. The Qur'ān also addressed itself to those outside the fold of Islam, to the People of the Book, the hypocrites, the unbelievers, the polytheists. Each group was addressed according to its own particular circumstances and attitudes. Sometimes the Qur'ān invited them to the true faith with tenderness and delicacy; on other occasions, it rebuked and severely admonished them. It also warned them against, and threatened them with, punishment from God. It attempted to make them take heed by drawing their attention to instructive historical events. In short, people were left with no valid reason for refusing the call of the Prophet.

Such, briefly, is the background to the Madīnan *sūrahs* of the Qur'ān.

It is now clear to us that the revelation of the Qur'ān began and went hand in hand with the preaching of the message. This message passed through many stages and met with diverse situations from the very beginning and throughout a period of twenty-three years.

The different parts of the Qur'ān were revealed step by step according to the multifarious, changing needs and requirements of the Islamic movement during these stages. It therefore could not possibly possess the kind of coherence and systematic sequence expected of a doctoral dissertation. Moreover, the various fragments of the Qur'ān which were revealed in harmony with the growth of the Islamic movement were not published in the form of written treatises, but were spread orally. Their style, therefore, bore an oratorical flavour rather than the characteristics of literary composition.

Furthermore, these orations were delivered by one whose task meant that he had to appeal simultaneously to the mind, to the heart and to the emotions, and to people of different mental levels and dispositions. He had to revolutionize people's thinking, to arouse in them a storm of noble emotions in support of his cause, to persuade his Companions and inspire them with devotion and zeal, and with the desire to improve and reform their lives. He had to raise their morale and steel their determination, turn enemies into friends and opponents into admirers, disarm those out to oppose his message and show their position to be morally untenable. In short, he had to do everything necessary to carry his movement through to a successful conclusion. Orations revealed in conformity with the requirements of a message and movement will inevitably have a style different from that of a professorial lecture.

This explains the repetitions we encounter in the Qur'ān. The interests of a message and a movement demand that during a particular stage emphasis should be placed only on those subjects which are appropriate at that stage, to the exclusion of matters pertaining to later stages. As a result, certain subjects may require continual emphasis for months or even years. On the other hand, constant repetition in the same manner becomes exhausting. Whenever a subject is repeated, it should therefore be expressed in different phraseology, in new forms and with stylistic variations so as to ensure that the ideas and beliefs being put over find their way into the hearts of the people.

At the same time, it was essential that the fundamental beliefs and principles on which the movement was based should always be kept fresh in people's minds; a necessity which dictated that they should be repeated continually through all stages of the movement. For this reason, certain basic Islamic concepts about the unity of God and His Attributes, about the Hereafter, about man's accountability and about reward and punishment, about prophethood and belief in the revealed scriptures, about basic moral attributes such as piety, patience, trust in God and so on, recur throughout the Qur'ān. If these ideas had lost their hold on the hearts and minds of people, the Islamic movement could not have moved forward in its true spirit.

If we reflect on this, it also becomes evident why the Prophet (peace be on him) did not arrange the Qur'ān in the sequence in which it was revealed. As we have noted, the context in which the Qur'ān was revealed in the course of twenty-three years was the mission and movement of the Prophet; the revelations correspond with the various stages of this mission and movement. Now, it is evident that when the Prophet's mission was completed, the chronological sequence of the various parts of the Qur'ān – revealed in accordance with the growth of the Prophet's mission – could in no way be suitable to the changed situation. What was now required was a different sequence in tune with the changed context resulting from the completion of the mission.

Initially, the Prophet's message was addressed to people totally ignorant of Islam. Their instruction had to start with the most elementary things. After the mission had reached its successful completion, the Qur'ān acquired a compelling relevance for those who had decided to believe in the Prophet. By virtue of that belief they had become a new religious community – the Muslim *ummah*. Not only that, they had been made responsible for carrying on the Prophet's mission, which he had bequeathed to them, in a perfected form on both conceptual and practical levels. It was no longer necessary for the Qur'ānic verses to be arranged in chronological sequence. In the changed context, it had become necessary for the bearers of the mission of the Prophet (peace be on him) to be informed of their duties and of the true principles and laws governing their lives. They also had to be warned against the deviations and corruptions which had appeared among the followers of earlier Prophets.

All this was necessary in order to equip the Muslims to go out and offer the light of Divine Guidance to a world steeped in darkness.

It would be foreign to the very nature of the Qur'ān to group together in one place all verses relating to a specific subject; the nature of the Qur'ān requires that the reader should find teachings revealed during the Madīnan period interspersed with those of the Makkan period, and vice versa. It requires the juxtaposition of early discourses with instructions from the later period of the life of the Prophet. This blending of teachings from different periods helps to provide an overall view and an integrated perspective of Islam and acts as a safeguard against lopsidedness. Furthermore, a chronological arrangement of the Qur'ān would have been meaningful to later generations only if it had been supplemented with explanatory notes and these would have had to be treated as inseparable appendices to the Qur'ān. This would have been quite contrary to God's purpose in revealing the Qur'ān; the main purpose of its revelation was that all human beings – children and young people, old men and women, town and country dwellers, laymen and scholars – should be able to refer to the Divine Guidance available to them in composite form and providentially secured against adulteration. This was necessary to enable people of every level of intelligence and understanding to know what God required of them. This purpose would have been defeated had the reader been obliged solemnly to recite detailed historical notes and explanatory comments along with the Book of God.

Those who object to the present arrangement of the Qur'ān appear to be suffering from a misapprehension as to its true purpose. They sometimes almost seem under the illusion that it was revealed merely for the benefit of students of history and sociology!

[VI]

The present arrangement of the Qur'ān is not the work of later generations, but was made by the Prophet under God's direction. Whenever a *sūrah* was revealed, the Prophet summoned his scribes, to whom he carefully dictated its contents, and instructed them where to place it in relation to the other *sūrahs*. The Prophet followed the same order of *sūrahs* and verses when reciting during ritual Prayer as on other occasions, and his Companions followed the same practice in memorizing the Qur'ān. It is therefore a historical fact that the collection of the Qur'ān came to an end on the very day that its revelation ceased. The One who was responsible for its revelation was also the One who set its arrangement. The one whose heart was the receptacle of the Qur'ān was also responsible for arranging its sequence. This was far too important and too delicate a matter for anyone else to dare to become involved in.

Since Prayers were obligatory for the Muslims from the very outset of the Prophet's mission,[5] and the recitation of the Qur'ān was an obligatory part of those Prayers, Muslims were committing the Qur'ān to memory while its revelation continued. Thus, as soon as a fragment of the Qur'ān was revealed, it was memorized by some of

5. It should be noted that while the five daily Prayers were made obligatory several years after the Prophet was commissioned, Prayers were obligatory from the very outset; not a single moment elapsed when Prayers, as such, were not obligatory in Islam.

the Companions. Hence the preservation of the Qur'ān was not solely dependent on its verses being inscribed on palm leaves, pieces of bone, leather and scraps of parchment – the materials used by the Prophet's scribes for writing down Qur'ānic verses. Instead those verses came to be inscribed upon scores, then hundreds, then thousands, then hundreds of thousands of human hearts, soon after they had been revealed, so that no scope was left for any devil to alter so much as one word of them.

When, after the death of the Prophet, the storm of apostasy convulsed Arabia and the Companions had to plunge into bloody battles to suppress it, many Companions who had memorized the Qur'ān suffered martyrdom. This led 'Umar to plead that the Qur'ān ought to be preserved in writing, as well as orally. He therefore impressed the urgency of this upon Abū Bakr. After slight hesitation, the latter agreed and entrusted that task to Zayd ibn Thābit al-Anṣārī, who had worked as a scribe of the Prophet.[6]

The procedure decided upon was to try and collect all written pieces of the Qur'ān left behind by the Prophet, as well as those in the possession of his Companions.[7] When all this had been done, assistance was sought from

---

6. For an account of the early history of the Qur'ān see Ṣubḥī Ṣāliḥ, *Mabāḥith fī 'Ulūm al-Qur'ān* (Beirut: 1977), pp. 65 ff. – Ed.

7. There are authentic Traditions to the effect that several Companions had committed the entire Qur'ān, or many parts of it, to writing during the lifetime of the Prophet. Especially mentioned in this connection are the following Companions of the Prophet: 'Uthmān, 'Alī, 'Abd Allāh ibn Mas'ūd, 'Abd Allāh ibn 'Amr ibn al-'Āṣ, Sālim the mawlā of Ḥudhayfah, Mu'ādh ibn Jabal, Ubayy b. Ka'b, and Abū Zayd Qays ibn al-Sakan.

those who had memorized the Qur'ān. No verse was incorporated into the Qur'ānic codex unless all three sources were found to be in complete agreement, and every criterion of verification had been satisfied. Thus an authentic version of the Qur'ān was prepared. It was kept in the custody of Ḥafṣah (a wife of the Holy Prophet) and people were permitted to make copies of it and also to use it as the standard of comparison when rectifying the mistakes they might have made in writing down the Qur'ān.

In different parts of Arabia and among its numerous tribes there existed a diversity of dialects. The Qur'ān was revealed in the language spoken by the Quraysh of Makkah. Nevertheless, in the beginning, people of other areas and other tribes were permitted to recite it according to their own dialects and idiom, since this facilitated its recitation without affecting its substantive meaning. In the course of time, in the wake of the conquest of a sizeable part of the world outside of the Arabian peninsula, a large number of non-Arabs entered the fold of Islam. These developments affected the Arabic idiom and it was feared that the continuing use of various dialects in the recitation of the Qur'ān might give rise to grave problems. It was possible, for instance, that someone hearing the Qur'ān recited in an unfamiliar dialect might pick a fight with the reciter, thinking that the latter was deliberately distorting the Word of God. It was also possible that such differences might gradually lead to tampering with the Qur'ān itself. It was also not inconceivable that the hybridization of the Arabic language, due to the intermixture between Arabs and non-Arabs, might lead people to introduce modifications into the Qur'ānic text, thus impairing the grace of the Speech of God. As a result of such considerations, and after consultation with the Companions of the Prophet, 'Uthmān decided that copies of the standard edition of the Qur'ān, prepared earlier on the order of Abū Bakr, should be published, and that publication of the Qur'ānic text in any other dialect or idiom should be proscribed.

The Qur'ān that we possess today corresponds exactly to the edition which was prepared on the orders of Abū Bakr and copies of which were officially sent, on the orders of 'Uthmān, to various cities and provinces. Several copies of this original edition of the Qur'ān still exist today. Anyone who entertains any doubt as to the authenticity of the Qur'ān can satisfy himself by obtaining a copy of the Qur'ān from any bookseller, say in West Africa, and then have a *ḥāfiẓ* (memorizer of the Qur'ān) recite it from memory, compare the two, and then compare these with the copies of the Qur'ān published through the centuries since the time of 'Uthmān. If he detects any discrepancy, even in a single letter or syllable, he should inform the whole world of his great discovery!

Not even the most sceptical person has any reason to doubt that the Qur'ān as we know it today is identical with the Qur'ān which Muḥammad (peace be on him) set before the world; this is an unquestionable, objective, historical fact, and there is nothing in human history on which the evidence is so overwhelmingly strong and conclusive. To doubt the authenticity of the Qur'ān is like doubting the existence of the Roman Empire, the Mughals of India, or Napoleon! To doubt historical facts like these is a sign of stark ignorance, not a mark of erudition and scholarship.

[VII]

The Qur'ān is a Book to which innumerable people turn for innumerable purposes. It is difficult to offer advice appropriate to all. The readers to whom this work is addressed are those who are concerned to acquire a serious understanding of the Book, and who seek the guidance it has to offer in relation to the various problems of life. For such people we have a few suggestions to make, and we shall offer some explanations in the hope of facilitating their study of the Qur'ān.

Anyone who really wishes to understand the Qur'ān, irrespective of whether or not he believes in it, must divest his mind, as far as possible, of every preconceived notion, bias and prejudice, in order to embark upon his study with an open mind. Anyone who begins to study the Qur'ān with a set of preconceived ideas is likely to read those very ideas into the Book. No book can be profitably studied with this kind of attitude, let alone the Qur'ān which refuses to open its treasure-house to such readers.

For those who want only a superficial acquaintance with the doctrines of the Qur'ān one reading is perhaps sufficient. For those who want to fathom its depths even several readings are not enough. These people need to study the Qur'ān over and over again, taking notes of everything that strikes them as significant. Those who are willing to study the Qur'ān in this manner should do so at least twice to begin with, so as to obtain a broad grasp of the system of beliefs and practical prescriptions that it offers. In this preliminary survey, they should try to gain an overall perspective of the Qur'ān and to grasp the basic ideas which it expounds, and the system of life that it seeks to build on the basis of those ideas. If, during the course of this study, anything agitates the mind of the reader, he should note down the point concerned and patiently persevere with his study. He is likely to find that, as he proceeds, the difficulties are resolved. (When a problem has been solved, it is advisable to note down the solution alongside the problem.) Experience suggests that any problems still unsolved after a first reading of the Qur'ān are likely to be resolved by a careful second reading.

Only after acquiring a total perspective of the Qur'ān should a more detailed study be attempted. Again the reader is well advised to keep noting down the various aspects of the Qur'ānic teachings. For instance, he should note the human model that the Qur'ān extols as praiseworthy, and the model it denounces. It might be helpful to make two columns, one headed 'praiseworthy qualities', the other headed 'blameworthy qualities', and then to enter into the respective columns all that is found relevant in the Qur'ān. To take another instance, the reader might proceed to investigate the Qur'ānic point of view on what is conducive to human success and felicity, as against what leads to man's ultimate failure and perdition. An efficient way to carry out this investigation would be to note under separate headings, such as 'conducive to success' and 'conducive to failure', any relevant material encountered. In the same way, the reader should take down notes about Qur'ānic teachings on questions of belief and morals, man's rights and obligations, family life and collective behaviour, economic and political life, law and social organization, war and peace, and so on. Then he should use these various teachings to try to develop an image of the Qur'ānic teachings *vis-à-vis* each particular aspect of human life. This should be followed by an attempt at integrating these images so that he comes to grasp the total scheme of life envisaged by the Qur'ān.

Moreover, anyone wishing to study in depth the Qur'ānic viewpoint on any particular problem of life should, first of all, study all the significant strands of human thought concerning that problem. Ancient and modern works on the subject should be studied. Unresolved problems where human thinking seems to have got stuck should be noted. The Qur'ān should then be studied with these unresolved problems in mind, with a view to finding out what solutions the Qur'ān has to offer. Personal experience again suggests that anyone who studies the Qur'ān in this manner will find his problem solved with the help of verses which he may have read scores of times without it ever crossing his mind that they could have any relevance to the problems at hand.

It should be remembered, nevertheless, that full appreciation of the spirit of the Qur'ān demands practical involvement with the struggle to fulfil its mission. The Qur'ān is neither a book of abstract theories and cold doctrines which the reader can grasp while seated in a cosy armchair, nor is it merely a religious book like other religious books, the secrets of which can be grasped in seminaries and oratories. On the contrary, it is the blueprint and guidebook of a message, of a mission, of a movement. As soon as this Book was revealed, it drove a quiet, kind-hearted man from his isolation and seclusion, and placed him upon the battlefield of life to challenge a world that had gone astray. It inspired him to raise his voice against falsehood, and pitted him in a grim struggle against the standard-bearers of unbelief, of disobedience to God, of waywardness and error. One after the other, it sought out everyone who had a pure and noble soul, mustering them together under the standard of the Messenger. It also infuriated all those who by their nature were bent on mischief and drove them to wage war against the bearers of the Truth.

This is the Book which inspired and directed that great movement which began with the preaching of a message by an individual, and continued for no fewer than twenty-three years, until the Kingdom of God was truly established on earth. In this long and heart-rending struggle between Truth and falsehood, this Book unfailingly guided its followers to the eradication of the latter and the consolidation and enthronement of the former. How then could one expect to get to the heart of the Qur'ānic truths merely by reciting its verses, without so much as stepping upon the field of battle between faith and unbelief, between Islam and Ignorance? To appreciate the Qur'ān fully one must take it up and launch into the task of calling people to God, making it one's guide at every stage.

Then, and only then, does one meet the various experiences encountered at the time of its revelation. One experiences the initial rejection of the message of Islam by the city of Makkah, the persistent hostility leading to the quest for a haven of refuge in Abyssinia, and the attempt to win a favourable response from Ṭā'if which led, instead, to cruel persecution of the bearer of the Qur'ānic message. One experiences also the campaigns of Badr, of Uḥud, of Ḥunayn and of Tabūk. One comes face to face with Abū Jahl and Abū Lahab, with hypocrites and with Jews, with those who instantly respond to this call as well as those

[1]

who, lacking clarity of perception and moral strength, were drawn into Islam only at a later stage.

This will be an experience different from any so-called 'mystic experience'. I designate it the 'Qur'ānic mystic experience'. One of the characteristics of this 'experience' is that at each stage one almost automatically finds certain Qur'ānic verses to guide one, since they were revealed at a similar stage and therefore contain the guidance appropriate to it. A person engaged in this struggle may not grasp all the linguistic and grammatical subtleties, he may also miss certain finer points in the rhetoric and semantics of the Qur'ān, yet it is impossible for the Qur'ān to fail to reveal its true spirit to him.

Again, in keeping with the same principle, a man can neither understand the laws, the moral teachings, and the economic and political principles which the Qur'ān embodies, nor appreciate the full import of the Qur'ānic laws and regulations, unless he tries to implement them in his own life. Hence the individual who fails to translate the Qur'ānic precepts into personal practice will fail to understand the Book. The same must be said of any nation that allows the institutions of its collective life to run contrary to the teachings of the Qur'ān.

[VIII]

It is well known that the Qur'ān claims to be capable of guiding all mankind. Yet the student of the Qur'ān finds that it is generally addressed to the people of Arabia, who lived in the time of its revelation. Although the Qur'ān occasionally addresses itself to all mankind its contents are, on the whole, vitally related to the taste and temperament, the environment and history, and the customs and usages of Arabia. When one notices this, one begins to question why a Book which seeks to guide all mankind to salvation should assign such importance to certain aspects of a particular people's life, and to things belonging to a particular age and clime. Failure to grasp the real cause of this may lead one to believe that the Book was originally designed to reform the Arabs of that particular age alone, and that it is only people of later times who have forced upon the Book an altogether novel interpretation, proclaiming that its aim is to guide all mankind for all time.

Some might say this with no other purpose than to vent their irrational prejudice against Islam. But leaving such people aside, a word may be said to those whose critical comments are motivated by the desire to understand things better. The latter would do well to study the Qur'ān carefully, noting down any place where they find that it has propounded either some doctrine or concept, or laid down some rule for practical conduct, relevant for the Arabs alone and exclusively conditioned by the peculiarities of a certain place or time. If, while addressing the people of a particular area at a particular period of time, attempting to refute their polytheistic beliefs and adducing arguments in support of its own doctrine of the unity of God, the Qur'ān draws upon facts with which those people were familiar, this does not warrant the conclusion that its message is relevant only for that particular people or for that particular period of time.

What ought to be considered is whether or not the Qur'ānic statements in refutation of the polytheistic beliefs of the Arabs of those days apply as well to other forms of polytheism in other parts of the world. Can the arguments advanced by the Qur'ān in that connection be used to rectify the beliefs of other polytheists? Is the Qur'ānic line of argument for establishing the unity of God, with minor adaptations, valid and persuasive for every age? If the answers are positive, there is no reason why a universal teaching should be dubbed exclusive to a particular people and age merely because it happened to be addressed originally to that people and at that particular period of time. No philosophy, ideology or doctrine consists of mere abstractions and is totally unrelated to the circumstances in which it developed. Even if such an absolute abstraction were possible it would remain confined to the scraps of paper on which it was written and would fail totally to have any impact on human life.

Moreover, if one wishes to spread any intellectual, moral and cultural movement on an international scale, it is by no means essential, in fact it is not even useful, for it to start on a global scale. If one wishes to propagate certain ideas, concepts and principles as the right bases for human life, one should begin by propagating them vigorously in the country where the message originates, and to the people whose language, temperament, customs and habits are familiar to its proponents. It will thus be possible to transform the lives of the people into a practical model of the message. Only then will it be able to attract the attention of other nations, and intelligent people living elsewhere will also try to understand it and to spread it in their own lands.

Indeed, what marks out a time-bound from an eternal, and a particularistic national doctrine from a universal one, is the fact that the former either seeks to exalt a people or claims special privileges for it or else comprises ideas and principles so vitally related to that people's life and traditions as to render it totally inapplicable to the conditions of other peoples. A universal doctrine, on the other hand, is willing to accord equal rights and status to all, and its principles have an international character in that they are equally applicable to other nations. Likewise, the validity of those doctrines which seek to come to grips merely with questions of a transient and superficial nature is time-bound. If one studies the Qur'ān with these considerations in mind, can one really conclude that it has only a particularistic national character, and that its validity is therefore time-bound?

[IX]

Those who embark upon a study of the Qur'ān often proceed with the assumption that this Book is, as it is commonly believed to be, a detailed code of guidance. However, when they actually read it, they fail to find detailed regulations regarding social, political and economic matters. In fact, they notice that the Qur'ān has not laid down detailed regulations even in respect of such oft-repeated subjects as Prayers and *Zakāh* (Purifying Alms). The reader finds this somewhat disconcerting and wonders in what sense the Qur'ān can be considered a code of guidance.

The uneasiness some people feel about this arises because they forget that God did not merely reveal a Book, but that He also designated a Prophet. Suppose some laymen were to be provided with the bare outlines of a construction plan on the understanding that they would carry out the construction as they wished. In such a case, it would be reasonable to expect that they should have very elaborate directives as to how the construction should be carried out. Suppose, however, that along with the broad outline of the plan of construction, they were also provided with a competent engineer to supervise the task. In that case, it would be quite unjustifiable to disregard the work of the engineer, on the expectation that detailed directives would form an integral part of the construction plan, and then to complain of imperfection in the plan itself. (This analogy should elucidate the position of the Prophet *vis-à-vis* the Qur'ān, for he clarified and elaborated the Qur'ān, supplementing its broad general principles by giving them precise and detailed forms, and incorporating them into practical life, his own as well as that of his followers. Ed.)

The Qur'ān, to put it succinctly, is a Book of broad general principles rather than of legal minutiae. The Book's main aim is to expound, clearly and adequately, the intellectual and moral foundations of the Islamic programme for life. It seeks to consolidate these by appealing both to man's mind and to his heart. Its method of guidance for practical Islamic life does not consist of laying down minutely detailed laws and regulations. It prefers to outline the basic framework for each aspect of human activity, and to lay down certain guidelines within which man can order his life in keeping with the Will of God. The mission of the Prophet was to give practical shape to the Islamic vision of the good life, by offering the world a model of an individual character and of a human state and society, as living embodiments of the principles of the Qur'ān.

[X]

The Qur'ān is strong in its condemnation of those who indulge in schismatic squabbling after the Book of Allah has been revealed, so causing a weakening of faith;[8] yet there has been considerable disagreement over the correct interpretations of the Qur'ānic injunctions, not only among later scholars, but even among the founders of the legal schools and the Successors.[9] Indeed, disagreement can be traced back even to the times of the Companions[10] of the Prophet. One can hardly point to a single Qur'ānic verse of legal import which has received complete unanimity as regards its interpretation. One is bound to ask whether the Qur'ānic condemnation applies to all who have disagreed in this way. If it does not, then what kind of schism and disagreement does the Qur'ān denounce?

This is quite a problem and its ramifications cannot be considered at length here. The reader may rest assured that the Qur'ān is not opposed to differences of opinion within the framework of a general agreement on the fundamentals of Islam and the broad unity of the Islamic community. In addition it is not opposed to disagreement arising from an earnest endeavour to arrive at the right conclusions on a particular subject; the

---

8. See Qur'ān 2: 7; 6: 159; 42: 14; 3: 105; 8: 46. – Ed.

9. The word "Successors" has been used as the equivalent of *Tābi'ūn*, i.e. those who benefited from the Companions of the Prophet. – Ed.

10. The word "Companions" has been used as the equivalent of *Ṣaḥābah*, i.e. those who, in a state of belief, enjoyed the companionship of the Prophet (peace be on him). – Ed.

only disagreements condemned by the Qur'ān are those arising out of egotism and perversity, leading to mutual strife and hostility.

The two sorts of disagreement are different in character and give rise to different results. The first kind is a stimulus to improvement and the very soul of a healthy society. Differences of this kind are found in every society whose members are endowed with intelligence and reason. Their existence is a sign of life, while their absence only serves to demonstrate that a society is not made up of intelligent men and women but of blocks of wood. Disagreements of the second kind, however, are of an altogether different character and lead to ruin and destruction of the people among whom they arise. Far from being a sign of health, their emergence is symptomatic of a grave sickness.

The first kind of disagreement exists among scholars who are all agreed that it is their duty to obey God and His Prophet. They also agree that the Qur'ān and the *Sunnah* are their main sources of guidance. Thus, when scholarly investigation on some subsidiary question leads two or more scholars to disagree, or when two judges disagree in their judgement on some dispute, they regard neither their judgement, nor the questions on which their opinion has been expressed, as fundamentals of faith. They do not accuse those who disagree with their opinion of having left the fold of true faith. What each does is rather to proffer his arguments showing that he has done his best to investigate the matter thoroughly. It is then left to the courts (in judicial matters) and to public opinion (if the matter relates to the community at large) either to prefer whichever opinion seems the sounder, or to accept both opinions as equally permissible.

Schism occurs when the very fundamentals are made a matter of dispute and controversy. It may also happen that some scholar, mystic, *muftī*, or leader pronounces on a question to which God and His Messenger have not attached fundamental importance, exaggerating the significance of the question to such an extent that it is transformed into a basic issue of faith. Such people usually go one step further, declaring all who disagree with their opinion to have forsaken the true faith and set themselves outside the community of true believers. They may even go so far as to organize those who agree with them into a sect, claiming that sect to be identical with the Islamic community, and declaring that everyone who does not belong to it is destined to Hell-fire!

Whenever the Qur'ān denounces schismatic disagreements and sectarianism, its aim is to denounce this latter kind of disagreement. As for disagreements of the first category, we encounter several examples of these even during the life of the Prophet. The Prophet not only accepted the validity of such disagreements, he even expressed approval of them. For this kind of disagreement shows that a community is not lacking in the capacity for thought, for enquiry and investigation, for grasping or wrestling with the problems it faces. It also shows that the intelligent members of the community are earnestly concerned about their religion and how to apply its injunctions to the problems of human life. It shows too that their intellectual capacities operate within the broad framework of their religion, rather than searching beyond its boundaries for solutions to their problems. And it proves that the community is following the golden path of moderation. Such moderation preserves its unity by broad agreement on fundamentals, and at the same time provides its scholars and thinkers with full freedom of enquiry so that they may achieve fresh insights and new interpretations within the framework of the fundamental principles of Islam.

[XI]

It is not intended here to survey all the questions which may arise in the mind of a student of the Qur'ān. Many questions relate to specific *sūrahs* or verses, and they are explained in the relevant notes. This introduction confines itself to basic questions related to the understanding of the Qur'ān as a whole.

2
༺ঌ৵৽ঌ৽

Al-Baqarah [The Cow]
Madīnan Period

In the name of Allah, the Most Merciful,
the Most Compassionate

[1] *Alif, Lām, Mīm.*[1] [2] This is the Book of Allah, there is no doubt in it; it is a guidance for the pious, [3] for those who believe in the existence of that which is beyond the reach of perception,[2] who establish Prayer[3] and spend out of what We have provided them, [4] who believe in what

---

1. The names of letters of the Arabic alphabet, called *ḥurūf muqaṭṭaʻāt*, occur at the beginning of several *sūrahs* of the Qur'ān. There is no consensus among the commentators of the Qur'ān as to their precise meanings. It is obvious, however, that deriving the right guidance from the Qur'ān does not depend on grasping the meaning of these vocables.

2. *Ghayb* signifies the verities which are hidden from man's senses and are beyond the scope of man's ordinary observation and experience such as God's essence and attributes, the Angels, the process of revelation, Paradise, Hell, and so on.

3. The expression "establishment of Prayer" has a wider meaning than mere performance of Prayer. It means that the system of Prayer should be organized on a collective basis. If there is a person in a locality who prays individually but no arrangements are made for congregational Prayer, it cannot be claimed that Prayer is established in that locality.

1

❦

Al-Fātiḥah [The Opening]
Makkan Period

[1] *In the name of Allah, the Most Merciful,*
the Most Compassionate

[2] Praise[1] be to Allah, the Lord[2] of the entire Universe,
[3] the Most Merciful, the Most Compassionate; [4] the
Master of the Day of Recompense.
[5] You alone do we worship[3] and You alone do we turn
to for help. [6] Direct us on to the Straight Way, the way
of those whom You have favoured, [7] who did not incur
Your wrath, who are not astray.[4]

---

1. *Al-Fātiḥah* is actually a prayer, which God teaches to all who
embark upon the study of His Book. Its position at the beginning
signifies that anyone who wants to benefit from the Book should
first offer this prayer to the Lord of the Universe.

2. The word *Rabb* has three connotations: (i) Lord and Master,
(ii) Sustainer, Provider, Supporter, Nourisher and Guardian, and
(iii) Sovereign, He Who controls and directs. God is *Rabb* of the
Universe in all these senses.

3. *'Ibādah* is also used in three senses: (i) worship, prayer and adoration,
(ii) submission and obedience, and (iii) bondage and servitude.

4. *Al-Fātiḥah* is a prayer from man to God, and the rest of the Qur'ān
is God's response to this prayer. Man prays to God to show him
the Straight Way. In response to this prayer God offers the Qur'ān
as the true guidance, the "Straight Way," which man has sought
and prayed for.

has been revealed to you and what was revealed before you, and have firm faith in the Hereafter.

[5] Such are on true guidance from their Lord; such are the truly successful.

[6] As for those who have rejected (these truths), it is all the same whether or not you warn them, for they will not believe. [7] Allah has sealed their hearts and their hearing,[4] and a covering has fallen over their eyes. They deserve severe chastisement.

[8] There are some who say: "We believe in Allah and in the Last Day," while in fact they do not believe. [9] They are trying to deceive Allah and those who believe, but they do not realize that in truth they are only deceiving themselves. [10] There is a disease in their hearts and Allah has intensified this disease.[5] A painful chastisement awaits them for their lying. [11] Whenever they are told: "Do not spread mischief on earth," they say: "Why! We indeed are the ones who set things right." [12] They are the mischief-makers, but they do not realize it. [13] Whenever they are told: "Believe as others believe," they answer: "Shall we believe as the fools have believed?" Indeed it is they

4. This does not mean that their rejection of the Truth is a consequence of God's sealing of their hearts. What is meant is that God sealed their hearts and ears as a consequence of their decision to reject the fundamentals of faith, of their deliberate choice of a path divergent from that charted out by the Qur'ān.

5. "Disease" here refers to the disease of hypocrisy. The statement that "Allah has intensified this disease" means that He does not punish the hypocrites immediately but allows them to indulge in their hypocrisy and exult in the success of their ruses. This feeling of success intensifies their hypocrisy.

who are the fools, but they are not aware of it. [14] When they meet the believers, they say: "We believe," but when they meet their evil companions (in privacy), they say: "Surely we are with you; we were merely jesting." [15] Allah jests with them, leaving them to wander blindly on in their rebellion. [16] These are the ones who have purchased error in exchange for guidance. This bargain has brought them no profit and certainly they are not on the Right Way. [17] They are like him who kindled a fire, and when it lit up all around him, Allah took away the light (of their perception) and left them in utter darkness where they can see nothing.[6] [18] They are deaf, they are dumb, they are blind; they will never return (to the Right Way). [19] Or they are like those who encounter a violent rainstorm from the sky, accompanied by pitch-dark clouds, thunder-claps and flashes of lightning: on hearing thunder-claps they thrust their fingers into their ears in fear of death. Allah encompasses these deniers of the Truth. [20] It is as if the lightning would snatch their sight; whenever it gleams a while for them they walk a little, and when darkness covers them they halt.[7] If Allah

---

6. This means that two opposite effects emerged when a true servant of God radiated the light which made it possible to distinguish true from false and right from wrong and the Straight Way distinct from the ways of error. To those endowed with true perception, all truths became evident. But those who were almost blinded by the worship of their animal desires perceived nothing.

7. The first parable refers to those hypocrites who disbelieved completely but had become Muslims merely to further their worldly interests. The second parable refers to those who were prone to doubt and hesitation or whose faith was weak; those who believed in the Truth but not to the extent of exposing themselves to hardships for its sake.

so willed, He could indeed take away their hearing and their sight. Surely Allah is All-Powerful.

[21] O mankind, serve your Lord Who has created you as well as those before you; do so that you are saved.[8] [22] It is He Who has made the earth a resting-place for you, and the sky a canopy, and sent down water from above wherewith He brought forth fruits for your sustenance. Do not, then, set up rivals to Allah when you know (the Truth).[9]

[23] If you are in any doubt whether it is We Who have revealed this Book to Our servant, then produce just a *sūrah* like it, and call all your supporters and seek in it the support of all others save Allah. Accomplish this if you are truthful. [24] But if you fail to do this – and you will most certainly fail – then have fear of the Fire whose fuel is men and stones[10] and which has been prepared for those who deny the Truth.

[25] (O Prophet), announce glad tidings to those who believe in this Book and do righteous deeds (in accordance with its teachings), that for them are gardens beneath which rivers flow. Their fruits will have such resemblance to those of the earth that whenever they will be provided

---

8. So that you are saved from false beliefs and unrighteous conduct in this life, and from God's punishment in the Next.

9. Not to set up others as rivals to Allah means not to make anyone other than God the object of worship, service and obedience that one owes to God alone.

10. In the Next Life not only will the unbelievers become the fuel of Hell-fire, but that the same fate will befall the idol-stones they worshipped and before which they prostrated themselves.

with those fruits they will say: "It was this which was granted to us on earth before." For them there shall be pure spouses, and there they shall abide forever.

[26] Behold! Allah is not ashamed to propound the parable of a gnat, or even of something more lowly.[11] On hearing these parables the believers know that it is the truth from their Lord, while those bent on denying the Truth say: "What does Allah mean by these parables?" Thus He causes many to go astray just as He directs many to the Right Way. And He thereby causes to go astray only the transgressors,[12] [27] who break the covenant of Allah after its firm binding,[13] and cut asunder what Allah has commanded to be joined,[14] and spread mischief on earth. They are the utter losers.

---

11. Here an objection is indirectly refuted. At several places in the Qur'ān, spiders, flies, gnats and so on are mentioned in order to elucidate certain points. Opponents objected to this on the grounds that such objects were too lowly to find a place in the Book of God. They insinuated that had the Qur'ān indeed been a revelation from God it would not have mentioned such trivial objects.

12. *Fāsiq* means transgressor, disobedient.

13. The injunctions or ordinances issued by a sovereign to his servants and subjects are termed *'ahd* in Arabic since compliance with them becomes obligatory for the latter. *'Ahd* has been used here in this sense. The *'ahd* referred to here signifies God's eternal command that all human beings are obliged to render their service, obedience and worship to Him alone. "After its binding" refers to the promise made by mankind to remain faithful to the injunctions of God at the time of Adam's creation. (For details see *al-A'rāf*, 7: 172.)

14. That is, the transgressors strike their blows at those very relationships upon which the individual and collective well-being of mankind depends, relationships which God wants maintained on a sound basis.

[28] How can you be ungrateful to Allah Who bestowed life upon you when you were lifeless, then He will cause you to die and will again bring you back to life so that you will be returned to Him. [29] It is He Who created for you all that is on earth and then turned above and fashioned it into seven heavens.[15] He knows all things.

[30] Just think when your Lord said to the angels: "Lo! I am about to place a vicegerent[16] on earth," they said: "Will You place on it one who will spread mischief and shed blood while we celebrate Your glory and extol Your holiness?" He said: "Surely I know what you do not know." [31] Then Allah taught Adam the names of all things and presented them to the angels and said: "If you are right (that the appointment of a vicegerent will cause mischief) then tell Me the names of these things." [32] They said. "Glory to You! We have no knowledge except what You taught us. You, only You, are All-Knowing, All-Wise." [33] Then Allah said to Adam: "Tell them the names of these things." And when he had told them the names of all things, Allah said: "Did I not say to you that I know everything about the heavens and the earth which are

15. It is difficult to explain precisely what is meant by the "seven heavens". In all ages man has tried, with the help of observation and speculation, to conceptualize the "heavens," i.e. that which lies beyond and above the earth. As we know, the concepts that have thus developed have constantly changed. What might be broadly inferred from this statement is that either God has divided the Universe beyond the earth into seven distinct spheres, or that this earth is located in that part of the Universe which consists of seven different spheres.

16. "*Khalīfah*" or vicegerent is one who exercises the authority delegated to him by his principal.

[7]

beyond your range of knowledge and I know all that you disclose and also all that you hide?"

[34] And when We ordered the angels: "Prostrate yourselves before Adam," all of them fell prostrate, except *Iblīs*. He refused, and gloried in his arrogance and became one of the defiers.

[35] And We said: "O Adam, live in the Garden, you and your wife, and eat abundantly of whatever you wish but do not approach this tree or else you will be counted among the wrong-doers." [36] But Satan caused both of them to deflect from obeying Our command by tempting them to the tree and brought them out of the state they were in, and We said: "Get down all of you; henceforth, each of you is an enemy of the other, and on earth you shall have your abode and your livelihood for an appointed time." [37] Thereupon Adam learned from his Lord some words and repented and his Lord accepted his repentance for He is Much-Relenting, Most Compassionate.

[38] We said: "Get you down from here, all of you, and guidance shall come to you from Me: then, whoever will follow My guidance need have no fear, nor shall they grieve. [39] But those who refuse to accept this (guidance) and reject Our Signs as false are destined for the Fire where they shall abide for ever."

[40] Children of Israel![17] Recall My favour which I had bestowed on you, and fulfil your covenant with Me and

---

17. It would be pertinent to point out that the entire discourse embodied in vv. 40-121, is addressed to the Children of Israel because Jews lived in Madīnah and its vicinity in large numbers.

I shall fulfil My covenant with you, and fear Me alone. [41] And believe in the Book which I have revealed and which confirms the Scripture you already have, and be not foremost among its deniers. Do not sell My signs for a trifling gain,[18] and beware of My wrath. [42] Do not confound Truth by overlaying it with falsehood, nor knowingly conceal the Truth. [43] Establish Prayer and dispense *Zakāh* (the Purifying Alms) and bow in worship with those who bow. [44] Do you enjoin righteousness on people and forget your own selves even though you recite the Scripture? Have you no sense? [45] And resort to patience and Prayer for help. Truly Prayer is burdensome for all except the devout, [46] who realize that ultimately they will have to meet their Lord and that to Him they are destined to return.

[47] Children of Israel! Recall My favour which I bestowed upon you, exalting you above all nations.[19] [48] Fear the Day when no one shall avail another, when no intercession will be accepted, when no one will be ransomed, and no criminal will receive any help.

---

18. "Trifling gain" refers to the worldly benefits for the sake of which they were rejecting God's directives. Whatever one may gain in exchange for the Truth, be it all the treasure in the world, is trifling; the Truth is of supreme value.

19. This does not mean that their pre-eminence among nations was to last for ever; rather, it refers to that period of human history when, of all nations, only the Children of Israel possessed that knowledge of Truth which comes from God alone. At that time they were entrusted with the task of directing the nations of the world to righteousness; they were expected to serve God and to invite the rest of the world to do the same.

[49] And recall when We rescued you from the slavery of Pharaoh's people[20] who had afflicted you with dreadful suffering, slaying your males and sparing your females. That was a tremendous trial for you from your Lord.

[50] And recall when We split the sea, providing passage for you, and thus saved you and caused Pharaoh's people to drown before your very eyes.

[51] And recall when We summoned Moses for a term of forty nights,[21] and then you set up the calf as your god in his absence. You indeed committed a grave wrong. [52] Yet We pardoned you that you might be grateful.

[53] And recall (that while you were committing this wrong) We gave Moses the Scripture and the Criterion[22] that you are guided to the Right Way.

[54] And recall when (on returning with this favour) Moses said to his people: "My people! You have wronged yourselves by taking the calf for an object of worship, so turn in repentance to your Creator and kill yourselves.[23]

---

20. We have rendered *Āl-Firʿawn* as "Pharaoh's people". This includes the members of the Pharaonic family as well as the aristocracy of Egypt of the time.

21. When the Israelites reached the Sinai peninsula after their exodus from Egypt, God summoned Moses to Mount Sinai for forty days and nights so that the nation which had now achieved independence could be given law and morality.

22. "Criterion" (*furqān*) here means that understanding of religion which differentiates truth from falsehood, making each stand out distinctly.

23. That is, they should put to death those of their own number who had made the calf an object of worship and actually worshipped it.

This will be best for you in your Creator's sight." Thereupon He accepted your repentance. Indeed He is Much-Relenting, Most Compassionate.

[55] And recall when you said: "O Moses, we will not believe in you until we clearly see Allah (speaking to you)." Thereupon a tremendous thunderbolt struck you before your very eyes. [56] Then We revived you after your extinction, that you might be grateful.

[57] And We caused a cloud to comfort you with shade, and We sent down upon you manna and the quails, (saying): "Eat of the good wherewithal that We have provided you as sustenance." And by their sinning (your forefathers) did not wrong Us: it is they themselves whom they wronged.

[58] And recall when We said: "Go into this town and eat abundantly of its food; but enter the gate prostrate, saying, "Repentance".[24] We will forgive you your sins and shall bestow more favour on the doers of good." [59] Then the wrong-doers substituted another saying for that which had been given them; and so We sent down a scourge upon the wrong-doers from the heavens for their transgression.

[60] And recall when Moses prayed for water for his people and We replied: "Strike the rock with your staff." And there gushed out from it twelve springs and each

---

24. *Ḥiṭṭah* could either mean that when they entered the town they should seek God's pardon for their sins or that instead of plundering and massacring people in the wake of their conquest, they should proclaim an amnesty.

ϱ knew its drinking-place.[25] (Then you were directed):
Eat and drink of the sustenance provided by Allah, and
do not go about acting wickedly on earth, spreading
mischief."

[61] And recall when you said: "O Moses, surely we
cannot put up with one sort of food, so pray to your Lord
to bring out for us what the earth produces – its herbs
and its cucumbers and its corn and its lentils and its
garlic and its onions." Then Moses said: "Will you take a
meaner thing in exchange for what is better? Go down to
some city and there you shall get what you ask for." And
ignominy and wretchedness were pitched upon them and
they were laden with the burden of Allah's wrath. This
was because they denied the Signs of Allah and slew the
Prophets unrightfully. All this, because they disobeyed
and persistently exceeded the limits (of the Law).

[62] Whether they are the ones who believe (in the
Arabian Prophet), or whether they are Jews, Christians
or Sabians – all who believe in Allah and the Last Day,
and do righteous deeds – their reward is surely secure
with their Lord; they need have no fear, nor shall they
grieve.[26]

---

25. The number of springs was twelve because the Israelite tribes
were also twelve in number. God provided one spring for each tribe
so that they would not fight each other for water.

26. The context of the verse makes it clear that it does not seek to
enumerate in detail all the articles of faith in which one should
believe, or all the principles of conduct which one should follow
in order to merit reward from God. The aim of the verse is merely
to repudiate the illusion cherished by the Jews that, by virtue of
their being Jews, they had a monopoly of salvation. They had long

[63] And recall when We made a covenant with you and caused the Mount Sinai to tower above you, (saying): "Hold fast to the Book that We have given you, and remember the directives and commandments in it, that you be pious." [64] Then you turned away from your covenant, and had it not been for Allah's grace and mercy upon you, you would have long been utter losers.

[65] And you know the case of those of you who broke the Sabbath,[27] how We said to them: "Become apes, despised and hated." [66] And thus We made their end a warning for the people of their own time and for the succeeding generations, and an admonition to the God-fearing.

[67] And then recall when Moses said to his people: "Behold, Allah commands you to slaughter a cow." They said: "Are you jesting with us?" Moses answered: "I seek refuge in Allah that I should behave in the manner

---

entertained the notion that a special and exclusive relationship existed between them and God. They thought, therefore, that all who belonged to their group were predestined to salvation regardless of their beliefs and actions, whereas all non-Jews were predestined to serve as fuel for Hell-fire.

To clarify this misgiving the Jews are told that what really matters in God's sight is true faith and good deeds rather than formal affiliation with a certain religious community. Whoever has true faith and good deeds to his credit is bound to receive his reward, since God will judge people on the basis of merit rather than on the grounds that a person's name happens to be listed in the world as a member of one religious community or the other.

27. Sabbath, i.e. Saturday. It was laid down that the Israelites should consecrate that day for rest and worship. They were required to abstain from all worldly acts, including cooking (which they might neither do themselves, nor have their servants do for them).

of the ignorant." [68] They said: "Pray to your Lord that He make clear to us what she is like." Moses answered: "He says, she is a cow, neither old nor immature, but of an age in between the two. Do, then, what you have been commanded." [69] They said: "Pray to your Lord that He make clear to us of what colour she is." Moses answered: "He says, she is a yellow cow, with a bright colour which is pleasing to those who see!" [70] They said: "Pray to your Lord that He make clear to us what cow she is. Cows seem much alike to us, and if Allah wills, we shall be guided." [71] Moses answered: "Lo! He says, she is a cow unyoked to plough the earth or to water the tillage, one that has been kept secure, with no blemish on her!" Thereupon they cried out: "Now you have come forth with the information that will direct us aright." And they slaughtered her although they scarcely seemed to do so.[28]

[72] And recall when you killed a man and then began to remonstrate and cast the blame (of killing) upon one

---

28. Through contact with the neighbouring people, the Israelites had become infected with the attitude of sanctifying the cow; in fact they had even become accustomed to cow-worship. In order to disabuse the Jews of this, they were ordered to slaughter the cow. Their professed belief that God alone was worthy of worship could be tested only by asking them to slaughter with their own hands what they had formerly worshipped. This test was indeed a hard one since they were not fully imbued with faith. Hence, they tried to shelve the issue by resorting to enquiries about the kind of animal they were required to slaughter. But the more they enquired, the narrower the strait became for them, until the indications were as obvious as if someone had put his finger precisely on the particular animal they were required to slaughter – the animal which had for so long been an object of their worship.

another even though Allah was determined to bring to light what you were hiding. [73] Then We ordered: "Smite the corpse with a part of it." Thus does Allah bring the dead to life and thus does He show His Signs that you might understand. [74] Then (even after observing this) your hearts hardened and became like stones, or even harder. For surely there are some stones from which streams burst forth and some that split asunder and water issues out, and some that crash down for fear of Allah. Allah is not heedless of the things you do.

[75] Do you hope that these people will believe in the Message you are preaching,[29] even though a party of them has been wont to listen to the Word of Allah and after they had fully grasped it, knowingly distorted it? [76] And when they meet those who believe (in Muḥammad) they say: "We too believe in him." But in their intimate meetings they say to one another: "How foolish! Why should you intimate to them what Allah has revealed to you, for they will use it as argument against you before your Lord?" [77] Are they unaware that Allah knows all that they hide and all that they disclose? [78] Among them are also the unlettered folk who do not

---

29. This is addressed to the converts of Madīnah, who had then lately affirmed their faith in the Prophet (peace be on him). These people had some vague notions about Prophethood, Heavenly Scriptures, Angels, the After-Life, Divine Law and so on, and for this they were indebted to their Jewish neighbours. They naturally expected that those who already followed Prophets and Divine Scriptures, and who, by introducing them to these ideas had contributed to their embracing the true faith, would not only join the ranks of the true believers, but would even be amongst their vanguard.

know about the Scriptures but cherish baseless wishes and merely follow their conjectures. [79] Woe, then, to those who write out the Scriptures with their own hands and then, in order to make a trifling gain, claim: "This is from Allah." Woe to them for what their hands have written and woe to them for what they thus earn. [80] They say: "The Fire will certainly not touch us except for a limited number of days." Say (to them): "Have you received a promise from Allah – for Allah never breaks His promise – or do you attribute to Allah something about which you have no knowledge?" [81] Those who earn evil and are encompassed by their sinfulness are the people of the Fire, and there will they abide; [82] those who believe and do righteous deeds are the people of the Garden, and there will they abide.

[83] And recall when We made a covenant with the Children of Israel: "You shall serve none but Allah and do good to parents, kinsmen, orphans and the needy; you shall speak kindly to people, and establish Prayer and give *Zakāh* (Purifying Alms). And yet, except for a few of you, you turned back on this covenant, and you are still backsliders. [84] And recall when We made a covenant with you, that you shall not shed one another's blood, and shall not turn out one another from your homelands; you confirmed it, and you yourselves are witnesses to it. [85] And here you are, killing one another, turning out a party of your own from their homelands, aiding one another against them in sin and enmity, and if they come to you as captives you ransom them although the very act of expelling them was unlawful to you. Do you believe in a part of the Scripture and reject the rest? What else, then, could be the retribution of those among you

who do this than that they should live in degradation in the present life, and that on the Day of Resurrection they should be sent to the severest chastisement? Allah is not heedless of what you do. [86] These are the ones who have bought the present life in exchange for the World to Come. Their chastisement shall not be lightened, nor shall they be helped.

[87] Surely We gave Moses the Scripture and caused a train of Messengers to follow him and then sent Jesus, the son of Mary, with Clear Proofs and supported him with the spirit of holiness.[30] But is it not true that every time a Messenger brought to you something that was not to your liking, you acted arrogantly: you called some Messengers liars and killed others? [88] They say: "Our hearts are well-protected." No! The fact is that Allah has cursed them because of their denying the Truth. So, scarcely do they believe. [89] And now that there has come to them a Book from Allah, how are they treating it? Even though it confirms the Truth already in their possession, and even though they had prayed for victory against the unbelievers,[31] and yet when that Book came to them – and they recognized it – they refused to acknowledge its

---

30. The "spirit of holiness" signifies the knowledge derived through revelation. It also signifies the angel Gabriel who brought this revelation. It also denotes the holy spirit of Jesus, the spirit which God had endowed with angelic character.

31. Before the advent of the Prophet (peace be on him), the Jews were eagerly awaiting a Prophet whose coming had been prophesied by their own Prophets. In fact, the Jews used to pray for his advent so that the dominance of the unbelievers could come to an end and the age of their own dominance be ushered in.

Truth. Allah's curse be upon the unbelievers. [90] Evil indeed is what they console themselves with.[32] They deny the guidance revealed by Allah, grudging that He chose to bestow His gracious bounty (of revelation and prophethood) on some of His servants whom He willed.[33] Thus they have brought on themselves wrath after wrath, and a humiliating chastisement is in store for such unbelievers.

[91] When they are told: "Believe in what Allah has revealed," they say: "We believe only in what was revealed to us (Israel)." They deny everything else even though it be the Truth which confirms what they possess. Say (to them): "If indeed you are believers, why is it that in the past you killed the Prophets of Allah (who were from Israel)?" [92] Moses came to you with clear proofs and yet you were so wont to wrong-doing that as soon as he was gone you took to worshipping the calf. [93] Recall the covenant We made with you and caused the Mount to tower above you, stressing: "Hold to what We have given you with full strength and give heed to it." But their forefathers said: "We hear, but we disobey" – for their hearts were overflowing with love for the calf because of

---

32. Another possible rendering of the same verse is: "And how evil is that for the sake of which they had sold themselves," i.e. for the sake of which they had sacrificed their ultimate happiness and salvation.

33. They had longed for the promised Prophet to arise from among their own ranks. But when he arose among a different people, a people they despised, they decided to reject him. Their attitude bordered on saying that when God wants to raise a Prophet He should consult them and should abide by their opinion.

their unbelief. Say: "If you are people of faith, then evil are the things that your faith enjoins upon you."

[94] Say to them: "If indeed the Last Abode with Allah is yours, in exclusion of other people, then long for death if you are truthful." [95] But they shall never long for it because of the (evil) deeds they have committed; Allah is well aware of the wrong-doers. [96] You will certainly find them most eager to cling on to life, indeed even more eager than those who associate others with Allah in His Divinity. Each one of them wishes to live a thousand years although the bestowal of long life cannot remove him from chastisement. Allah sees whatever they do.

[97] Say: "Whoever is an enemy to Gabriel[34] (should know that) he revealed this (Qur'ān) to your heart by Allah's leave: it confirms the Scriptures revealed before it, and is a guidance and good tiding to the people of faith. [98] (And if this is the cause of their hostility to Gabriel, let them know) whoever is an enemy to Allah, His Angels and His Messengers and to Gabriel and Michael will surely find Allah an enemy to such unbelievers."

[99] We surely sent down to you clear verses that elucidate the Truth, (verses) which only the transgressors reject as false. [100] Is it not that every time they made a covenant with Allah a party of them set it aside? The truth is that most of them do not truly believe. [101] And whenever a Messenger from Allah came to them, confirming what

---

34. The Jews not only reviled the Prophet (peace be on him) and his followers but also God's chosen angel, Gabriel, denouncing him as their enemy, and branding him as the angel of curse rather than of blessing.

they already possessed, a party of those who had been given the Scripture flung the Book of Allah behind their backs as if they knew nothing, [102] and then followed what the evil ones falsely attributed to the Kingdom of Solomon even though Solomon had never disbelieved; it is the evil ones who disbelieved, teaching people magic. And they followed what had been revealed to the two angels in Babylon – Hārūt and Mārūt – although these two (angels) never taught it to anyone without first declaring: "We are merely a means of testing people; so, do not engage in unbelief."[35] And yet they learned from them what might cause division between a man and his wife. They could not cause harm to anyone except by the leave of Allah, and still they learned what harmed rather than profited them, knowing well that he who bought it will have no share in the World to Come. Evil indeed is what they sold themselves for. Had they but known! [103] Had they believed and been God-fearing Allah's reward would have been better! Had they but known!

---

35. There are various opinions on the interpretation of this verse. My own conclusion is that at the time when the whole Israelite nation was chained in slavery and captivity in Babylonia, God sent two angels in human form in order to test the Jews. In the same way as angels were sent to the people of Lot in the form of handsome youth (see *Sūrah Hūd* 11: 69 ff. Ed.), they were presumably sent to Israel in the form of divines who could work magic and sorcery. These angels at once began working their magical wonders but they warned the people that their presence among them was designed to test their faith, and that they ought not to jeopardize their prospects in the After-Life by practising magic. Despite the warning it seems that the Israelites had become so fond of their magical artifices that they continued to pounce upon the talismans and sorcery they taught.

[104] O you who believe! Do not say (to the Prophet): *Rāʿinā* (Lend ear to us), but say *Unẓurnā* (Favour us with your attention) and pay heed (to him).[36] A painful chastisement awaits the unbelievers. [105] The unbelievers, be they the People of the Book or those who associate others with Allah in His Divinity, do not wish that any good should be sent down upon you from your Lord. But Allah chooses for His mercy whomsoever He wills. Allah is Lord of Abounding Bounty.

[106] For whatever verse We might abrogate or consign to oblivion, We bring a better one or the like of it.[37] Are you not aware that Allah is All-Powerful? [107] Are you not aware that the dominion of the heavens and the earth

---

36. When the Jews visited the Prophet (peace be on him) they tried to vent their spite by using ambiguous expressions in their greetings and conversation. They used words which had double meanings, one innocent and the other offensive. The particular expression referred to here – which the Muslims were asked to avoid using since it lent itself to abuse – was employed by the Jews when they conversed with the Prophet (peace be on him). Whenever they wanted to request a short pause in which to finish whatever they wanted to say, they used the expression *rāʿinā*, which meant "kindly indulge us" or "kindly lend (your) ear to us." It is, however, because of the possibility of the word also being used in other meanings, some of which were evil and irreverential, that Muslims were asked to avoid it and to use instead the straightforward expression *unẓurnā*, meaning "kindly favour us with your attention" or "kindly grant us a moment to follow (what you are saying)."

37. This is in response to a doubt which the Jews tried to implant in the minds of Muslims. If both the earlier Scriptures and the Qurʾān were revelations from God, why was it – they asked – that the injunctions found in the earlier scriptures had been replaced by new ones in the Qurʾān?

belongs to Allah, and that none apart from Allah is your protector or helper?

[108] Or would you ask your Messenger in the manner Moses was asked before?[38] And whoever exchanges faith for unbelief has surely strayed from the Right Way. [109] Out of sheer envy many People of the Book would be glad to turn you back into unbelievers after you have become believers even though the Truth has become clear to them. Nevertheless, forgive and be indulgent towards them until Allah brings forth His decision. Surely Allah is All-Powerful. [110] Establish Prayer and dispense *Zakāh*. Whatever good deeds you send forth for your own good, you will find them with Allah. Surely Allah sees all that you do.

[111] They say: "None shall enter the Garden unless he be a Jew or (according to the Christians), a Christian." These are their vain desires. Say: "Bring your proof if you are speaking the truth." [112] (None has any special claim upon reward from Allah.) Whoever submits himself completely to the obedience of Allah and does good will find his reward with his Lord. No fear shall come upon them, nor shall they grieve.

[113] The Jews say: "The Christians have no basis for their beliefs," and the Christians say: "The Jews have no basis for their beliefs." They say so even though they read the Scripture. The claim of those who have no knowledge (of

---

38. The Jews, who were addicted to hair-splitting arguments, instigated the Muslims to ask the Prophet (peace be on him) a great many questions. God, therefore, cautioned the Muslims against following the example of the Jews in this matter, and admonished them against unnecessary inquisitiveness.

the Scripture) is similar. Allah will judge between them concerning their differences on the Day of Resurrection.

[114] Who is more iniquitous than he who bars Allah's places of worship, that His name be mentioned there, and seeks their destruction? It does not behove such people to enter them, and should they enter, they should enter in fear. There is degradation for them in this world and a mighty chastisement in the Next.

[115] The East and the West belong to Allah. To whichever direction you turn, you will be turning to Allah. Allah is All-Embracing, All-Knowing.

[116] They say: "Allah has taken to Himself a son." Glory to Him! Nay, whatever is in the heavens and the earth belongs to Him; to Him are all in obeisance. [117] He is the Originator of the heavens and the earth; whenever He decrees a matter He (merely) says: "Be", and it is.

[118] The ignorant say: "Why does Allah not speak to us? Why does no Sign come to us?" The same was said by people before them. Their hearts are all alike. We have made the Signs clear for people of firm faith. [119] (What greater Sign can there be than that) We sent you with the Truth as a bearer of good tidings and a warner![39] And you will not be answerable about the people of the Blazing Flame!

---

39. Why speak of other signs when the most conspicuous sign of Truth is the very person of Muḥammad (peace be on him)? Let us recall his life before the commencement of his prophethood, the conditions existing in the area where, and the people among whom, he was born, the manner in which he was brought up and spent the first forty years of his life, and then his glorious achievements as a Prophet. What further signs could we want in support of his message?

[120] Never will the Jews be pleased with you, (O Prophet), nor the Christians until you follow their way. Say: "Surely Allah's guidance, is the true guidance." Should you follow their desires disregarding the knowledge which has come to you, you shall have no protector or helper against Allah. [121] Those to whom We have given the Scripture, and who recite it as it ought to be recited, they truly believe in it;[40] and those who disbelieve in it, they are the real losers.

[122] Children of Israel! Recall My favour which I bestowed upon you and I exalted you above the nations of the world, [123] and beware of the Day when no one shall avail another, when ransom shall be accepted from no one, when no one's intercession will profit anyone, when there shall be no help from any quarter.

[124] Recall when Abraham's Lord tested him in certain matters and when he successfully stood the test, He said: "Indeed I am going to appoint you a leader of all people." When Abraham asked: "And is this covenant also for my descendants?" the Lord responded: "My covenant does not embrace the wrong-doers."[41]

---

40. This refers to the pious element among the People of the Book. Since these people read the Book with sincerity and honesty of purpose, they are inclined to accept whatever they find to be true according to it.

41. This specifies that God's promise of the conferment of leadership applied only to those of Abraham's offspring who were righteous, and that the wrong-doers were naturally excluded. The word "wrong-doer" does not merely apply to those who are unjust and cruel to human beings but also to those who are unjust with regard to the Truth.

[125] And We made this House (Ka'bah) a resort for mankind and a place of security, commanding people: "Take the station of Abraham as a permanent place for Prayer," and enjoined Abraham and Ishmael: "Purify My House for those who walk around it, and those who abide in devotion, and those who bow, and who prostrate themselves (in Prayer)."

[126] And when Abraham prayed: "O my Lord! Make this a place of security and provide those of its people that believe in Allah and the Last Day with fruits for sustenance," Allah answered, "And I shall still provide him who disbelieves with the wherewithal for this short life, and then I shall drive him to the chastisement of the Fire; that is an evil end."

[127] Recall when Abraham and Ishmael raised the foundations of the House, praying: "Our Lord! Accept this from us; You are All-Hearing, All-Knowing. [128] Our Lord! Make us submissive to You and make out of our descendants a community that submits itself to You, and show us the ways of Your worship, and turn to us in mercy. You are Much-Relenting, Most Compassionate. [129] Our Lord! Raise up in the midst of our offspring a Messenger from among them who shall recite to them Your verses, and instruct them in the Book and in Wisdom, and purify their lives. Verily, You are the Most Mighty, the Most Wise."

[130] And who but a fool would be averse to the way of Abraham? For it is We Who chose Abraham for Our mission in this world, and surely in the World to Come he shall be reckoned among the righteous. [131] Such was

Abraham that when his Lord said to him: "Submit,"[42] he said: "I have submitted to the Lord of the Universe." [132] And Abraham enjoined the same upon his children, and so did Jacob: "My children! Behold, Allah has chosen this religion for you. Remain till death in submission (to Allah)." [133] Why, were you witnesses when death came to Jacob? He asked his children: "Whom will you serve after me?" They said: "We shall serve your God, the God of your forefathers, Abraham, Ishmael and Isaac, the One God, and unto Him do we submit."

[134] Now, they were a people who passed away. Theirs is what they have earned, and yours is what you have earned. You shall not be asked concerning what they did.

[135] They say: "Be Jews," or "Be Christians." "Then you will be rightly guided." Say to them: "No, follow exclusively the way of Abraham who was not one of those who associate others with Allah in His Divinity." [136] Say: "We believe in Allah, and in what has been revealed to us and to Abraham, Ishmael, Isaac, Jacob and the descendants (of Jacob) and in what was given to Moses and Jesus and in what the other Prophets received from

---

42. The word "Muslim" signifies he who bows in obedience to God, who acknowledges God alone as his Sovereign, Lord and Master, and the only object of worship, devotion and service, who unreservedly surrenders himself to God and undertakes to live his life in accordance with the guidance that has come down from Him. Islam is the appellation which characterizes the above-mentioned belief and conduct. That belief and outlook constitute the core and kernel of the religion of all the Prophets who have appeared from time to time among different peoples and in different countries since the beginning of human life.

their Lord. We make no distinction between any of them, and we are those who submit to Allah."

[137] And then if they come to believe as you believe, they are on right guidance; and if they turn away, then quite obviously they have merely fallen into opposition to the Truth. Allah will suffice you for protection against them. He is All-Hearing, All-Knowing.

[138] Say: "Take on Allah's colour." And whose colour is better than Allah's? It is Him that we serve.

[139] Say (O Prophet): "Will you then dispute with us concerning Allah when He is our Lord and your Lord? Our deeds are for us and your deeds are for you. And it is Him that we serve exclusively." [140] Or do you claim that Abraham and Ishmael, Isaac and Jacob and the descendants (of Jacob) were "Jews" or "Christians?" Say: "Who has greater knowledge, you or Allah?" Who does greater wrong than he who conceals a testimony he has received from Allah? Allah is not heedless of the things you do. [141] Now, they were a people who passed away. Theirs is what they earned, and yours is what you earn; you shall not be questioned concerning what they did.

[142] The block-headed will say: "What has turned them away from the direction they formerly observed in Prayer?"[43] Say: "To Allah belong the East and the

---

43. After his migration to Madīnah the Prophet (peace be on him) continued to pray in the direction of Jerusalem approximately for a period between sixteen and seventeen months. Subsequently, he received the injunction to pray in the direction of the Kaʿbah.

West; He guides whomsoever He wills onto a Straight Way." [143] And it is thus that We appointed you to be the community of the middle way[44] so that you might be witnesses to all mankind and the Messenger might be a witness to you.[45] We appointed the direction which you formerly observed so that We might distinguish those who follow the Messenger from those who turn on their heels. For it was indeed burdensome except for those whom Allah guided. And Allah will never leave your faith to waste. Allah is full of gentleness and mercy to mankind.

[144] We see you oft turning your face towards the sky; now We are turning you to the direction that will satisfy you.

---

44. The Arabic expression which we have translated as "the community of the middle way" is too rich in meaning to find an adequate equivalent in any other language. It signifies that distinguished group of people which follows the path of justice and equity, of balance and moderation, a group which occupies a central position among the nations of the world so that its relationship with all is based on righteousness and justice and none receives its support in wrong and injustice.

45. What this means is that when the whole of mankind is called to account, the Prophet (peace be on him), as God's representative, will stand witness to the fact that he had communicated to the Muslims and had put into practice the teachings which expound sound beliefs, righteous conduct and a balanced system of life which he had received from on high. The Muslims, acting on behalf of the Prophet (peace be on him) after the latter's return to God's mercy, will be asked to bear the same witness before the rest of mankind, confirming that they had spared no effort in either communicating to mankind what the Prophet (peace be on him) had communicated to them, or in exemplifying in their own lives what the Prophet (peace be on him) by his own conduct, had translated into actual practice.

Turn your face towards the Holy Mosque, and wherever you are, turn your faces towards it in Prayer.[46] Those who have been granted the Scripture certainly know that this (injunction to change the direction of Prayer) is right and is from their Lord. Allah is not heedless of what they do. [145] And yet no matter what proofs you bring before the People of the Book they will not follow your direction of Prayer; nor will you follow their direction of Prayer. None is prepared to follow the other's direction of Prayer. Were you to follow their desires in disregard of the knowledge which has come to you, you will surely be reckoned among the wrong-doers. [146] Those to whom We have given the Scripture recognize the place (towards which one must turn in Prayer) as fully as they recognize their own sons,[47] this even though a group of them knowingly

46. This is the injunction concerning the change in the direction of Prayer which was revealed in Rajab or Shaʿbān 2 A.H. According to a tradition in the *Ṭabaqāt* of Ibn Saʿd, the Prophet (peace be on him) was at the house of a Companion where he had been invited to a meal. When the time of *Ẓuhr* Prayer came, the Prophet (peace be on him) rose to lead it. He had completed two *rakʿāt* and was in the third when this verse was suddenly revealed. Soon after the revelation of this verse everybody, following the Prophet's action, turned the direction of Prayer away from Jerusalem to the Kaʿbah. A public proclamation of the new injunction was then made throughout Madīnah and its suburbs. The words, "We see you oft turning your face towards the sky," and "We are turning you to the direction that will satisfy you," clearly show that even before the revelation of this injunction the Prophet (peace be on him) was looking forward to receiving an injunction of this kind.

47. "To recognize something as fully as one recognizes one's sons" is an Arabic idiom. It is used with regard to things which one knows without the least shadow of a doubt. The Jewish and Christian scholars were well aware that the Kaʿbah had been constructed

conceals the Truth. [147] This is a definite Truth from your Lord; be not, then, among the doubters.

[148] Everyone has a direction towards which he turns; so excel one another in good works. Allah will bring you all together wherever you might be, for nothing is beyond His power.

[149] From wheresoever you might come forth turn your face towards the Holy Mosque; for that indeed is the Truth from your Lord, and Allah is not heedless of what you do. [150] From wheresoever you come forth turn your faces towards the Holy Mosque, and wheresoever you may be, turn your faces towards it in Prayer so that none may have an argument against you,[48] unless they be those immersed in wrong-doing. Do not fear them, but fear only Me so that I may complete My favour[49] upon you; perhaps you will be guided to the Right Way. [151] Just as when We sent among you a Messenger of yourselves, who recites

---

by Abraham and that Jerusalem had been built by Solomon some thirteen hundred years after that, and that in the latter's time it was made the *qiblah*. This is an unquestionable historical fact and they knew it to be so.

48. Any lapse in this matter on the part of Muslims would give their opponents a weapon to use against them in their polemics. They would be able to hold Muslims up to ridicule on the grounds that they had violated what they themselves claimed to be from their Lord.

49. The "favour" here refers to the position of world leadership and guidance from which God later removed the Children of Israel and which was then conferred upon this *ummah*. The Muslims should follow the directives of God if for no other reason than that ingratitude and disobedience might divest them of the honour that has been bestowed upon them.

to you Our Signs, purifies your lives, instructs you in the Book and in Wisdom, and instructs you what you did not know. [152] So remember Me and I shall remember you; give thanks to Me and do not be ungrateful to Me for My favours.

[153] Believers! Seek help in patience and in Prayer; Allah is with those that are patient. [154] And do not say of those who are killed in the way of Allah that they are dead; they are alive even though you have no knowledge of their life. [155] We shall certainly test you by afflicting you with fear, hunger, loss of properties and lives and fruits. Give glad tidings, then, to those who remain patient; [156] those who when any affliction smites them, they say: "Verily, we belong to Allah, and it is to Him that we are destined to return." [157] Upon them will be the blessings and mercy of their Lord, and it is they who are rightly guided.

[158] Surely, al-Ṣafā and al-Marwah are the symbols of Allah. Hence, whoever performs *Ḥajj* (Full Pilgrimage) to the House (of Allah) or makes *ʿUmrah* (Minor Pilgrimage),[50] will find that it is no sin for him to ambulate between the two. And whoever does a good work voluntarily should know that Allah is Appreciative, All-Knowing.

[159] Those who conceal anything of the clear teachings and true guidance which We have sent down even though We have made them clear in Our Book, Allah curses such people and so do all the cursers, [160] except those who repent and make amends and openly declare (what

---

50. The pilgrimage to the Kaʿbah along with a set of other rites on certain fixed dates of Dhū al-Ḥijjah is known as *Ḥajj*. Pilgrimage at other times is known as *ʿUmrah*.

they had concealed). Such shall I pardon for I am Much-Relenting, Most Compassionate.

[161] As for those who disbelieved[51] and died disbelieving, surely the curse of Allah and of the angels and of all men is on them. [162] Thus shall they abide and their chastisement shall not be lightened, nor shall they be given respite.

[163] Your God is One God, there is no god but He; the Most Merciful, the Most Compassionate. [164] (To guide) those who use their reason (to this Truth) there are many Signs in the structure of the heavens and the earth, in the constant alternation of night and day, in the vessels which speed across the sea carrying goods that are of profit to people, in the water which Allah sends down from the sky and thereby quickens the earth after it was dead, and disperse over it all manner of animals, and in the changing courses of the winds and the clouds pressed into service between heaven and earth. [165] Yet there are some who take others as equals to Allah and love them as Allah alone

---

51. The original meaning of *kufr* is to conceal. This lent the word a nuance of denial and it began to be used as an antonym of *Īmān*. *Īmān* means to believe, to accept, and to recognize. *Kufr*, on the contrary, denotes refusal to believe, to deny, to reject. According to the Qur'ān, there are several possible forms of disbelief. One is to refuse either to believe in the existence of God, not to acknowledge His sovereignty, not to recognize Him as the only Lord of the Universe and of mankind and the only object of worship and adoration. The second form of disbelief is that a man might recognize the existence of God but still refuse to accept His ordinances and directives as the only source of true guidance, and as the true law for his life. The third form of disbelief is that although a man might recognize, in principle, that he ought to

should be loved; but those who (truly) believe, they love Allah more than all else. If only the wrong-doers were to perceive now – as they will perceive when they will see the chastisement – that all power belongs to Allah alone, and that Allah is severe in chastisement! [166] At that moment those who have been followed will disown their followers, and they will see the chastisement, and their resources will be cut asunder. [167] And the followers will then say: "Oh if only we might return again, we would disown them as they have disowned us?" Thus Allah will show them their works in a manner causing them bitter regrets. Never will they come out of the Fire.

[168] O people! Eat of the lawful and pure things in the earth and follow not in the footsteps of Satan. For surely he is your open enemy; [169] he only commands you to do evil and commit acts of indecency and to ascribe to Allah the things concerning which you have no knowledge (that He really is their source).

[170] And when they are told: "Follow what Allah has revealed," they say: "No, we shall follow what we

---

follow God's guidance, he refuses to believe in the Prophets who were the means of communicating God's guidance to mankind. The fourth form of disbelief is to differentiate between one Prophet and another, to accept some Prophets and reject others because of parochialism and bigotry. The fifth form of disbelief is the refusal to recognize, either totally or partially, the teachings communicated on God's behalf by the Prophets concerning beliefs, principles of morality, and laws to fashion human life. The sixth form of disbelief is that a person might theoretically accept all that he should accept but then wilfully disobeys God's ordinances and persists in this disobedience, and considers disobedience rather than obedience to God to be the true principle of life.

found our forefathers adhering to." What! Even if their forefathers were devoid of understanding and right guidance? [171] Those who have refused to follow the Way of Allah resemble cattle; when the shepherd calls them they hear nothing except shouting and crying; they are deaf, dumb and blind, and so they understand nothing.

[172] Believers! Eat of the pure things wherewith We have provided you for sustenance and give thanks to Allah if it is Him that you serve. [173] He has made unlawful to you only carrion and blood and the flesh of swine and that over which there has been pronounced the name of anyone other than Allah's. But he who is constrained (to eat of them) – and he neither covets them nor exceeds the indispensable limit incurs no sin: Allah is All-Forgiving, All-Compassionate.[52]

[174] Those who conceal anything of the Book revealed by Allah and sell it away for a trifling gain are merely filling their bellies with Fire. Allah will neither address them on the Day of Resurrection, nor shall He pronounce them "pure". A painful chastisement lies in store for them. [175] They are the ones who bought error in exchange for true guidance, and chastisement in exchange for

---

52. This verse grants permission to use prohibited things on three conditions. First, that one must be in a state of extreme compulsion, for example, one is gravely ill or so hungry and thirsty that one's very life is in danger, and a prohibited thing is all that is available to save one's life. Second, the person who consumes a prohibited thing in such a dire state of compulsion should have no inclination to violate the Law of God. Third, in consuming the prohibited thing one should not exceed the limit of bare necessity. If a few bites or a few drops are enough to save one's life, one ought not to go beyond this absolute minimum.

forgiveness. How patient they are in enduring the Fire! [176] This is so because Allah revealed the Book with the Truth, but those who disagreed concerning the Book veered far away from the Truth.

[177] Righteousness does not consist in turning your faces towards the east or towards the west; true righteousness consists in believing in Allah and the Last Day, the angels, the Book and the Prophets, and in giving away one's property in love of Him to one's kinsmen, the orphans, the poor and the wayfarer, and to those who ask for help, and in freeing the necks of slaves, and in establishing Prayer and dispensing the *Zakāh*. True righteousness is attained by those who are faithful to their promise once they have made it and by those who remain steadfast in adversity and affliction and at the time of battle (between Truth and falsehood). Such are the truthful ones; such are the God-fearing.

[178] Believers! Retribution is prescribed for you in cases of killing: if a freeman is guilty then the freeman; if a slave is guilty then the slave; if a female is guilty, then the female. But if something of a murderer's guilt is remitted by his brother this should be adhered to in fairness, and payment be made in a goodly manner.[53] This is an alleviation and a mercy from your Lord; and

---

53. This verse also makes it clear that according to the Islamic penal law the question of homicide can be settled by the mutual consent of the two parties. It is the prerogative of the heirs of the victim to forgive the murderer, and if they want to exercise this prerogative not even a judge has the authority to insist on carrying out the death sentence. In such a case, however, as the verse mentions, the murderer will be required to pay blood money.

for him who commits excess[54] after that there is a painful chastisement. [179] People of understanding, there is life for you in retribution that you may guard yourselves against violating the Law.

[180] It is decreed that when death approaches, those of you who leave behind property shall bequeath equitably to parents and kinsmen.[55] This is an obligation on the God-fearing. [181] Then if anyone alters the will after hearing it, this sin shall be upon them who alter. Surely Allah is All-Hearing, All-Knowing. [182] He who suspects that the testator has committed an error or injustice and then brings about a settlement among the parties concerned

---

54. "Excess" might consist of the attempt, on the part of the heirs of the murdered person after they have settled the matter and received blood money to take revenge for the blood of the victim. It will also be excess, and in this case it will be on the part of the murderer, if he tries to delay the payment of blood money to the heirs of the victim. They would thus be repaying the heirs of the victim with ingratitude for their kindness and goodwill.

55. This injunction relates to a period when no rules had yet been laid down for the distribution of inheritance. Thus everyone was required to make testamentary disposal of their property so as to ensure that no disputes arose in the family and no legitimate claimant to inheritance was deprived of his due share. Later on when God revealed a set of laws regarding the distribution of inheritance (see *Sūrah al-Nisā'* 4: 11 ff.), the Prophet (peace be on him) further elucidated the laws relating to inheritance and testamentary disposition by expounding three rules. First, that no person can make any will regarding his estate in favour of any of his legal heirs. The portions of the legal heirs were laid down in the Qur'ān and it was not permitted either to increase or decrease them. Second, that testamentary disposition might be made only to the extent of one-third of the estate, but no more. Third, neither a Muslim nor a non-Muslim could be each other's legal heirs.

incurs no sin. Surely Allah is Much-Forgiving, Most Compassionate.

[183] Believers! Fasting is enjoined upon you, as it was enjoined upon those before you, that you become God-fearing. [184] Fasting is for a fixed number of days, and if one of you be sick, or if one of you be on a journey, you will fast the same number of other days later on. For those who are capable of fasting (but still do not fast) there is a redemption: feeding a needy man for each day missed. Whoever voluntarily does more good than is required, will find it better for him; and that you should fast is better for you, if you only know.[56]

[185] During the month of Ramaḍān the Qur'ān was sent down as a guidance to the people with Clear Signs of the true guidance and as the Criterion (between right and wrong). So those of you who live to see that month should fast it, and whoever is sick or on a journey should fast the same number of other days instead. Allah wants ease and not hardship for you so that you may complete the number of days required, magnify Allah for what He has guided you to, and give thanks to Him.

---

56. Like most other injunctions of Islam those relating to fasting were revealed gradually. In the beginning the Prophet (peace be on him) had instructed the Muslims to fast three days in every month, though this was not obligatory. When the injunction in the present verse was later revealed in 2 A.H., a degree of relaxation was introduced: it was stipulated that those who did not fast despite their capacity to endure fasting were obliged to feed one poor person as an expiation for each day of obligatory fasting missed (see verse 184). Another injunction was revealed later (see verse 185).

[186] (O Muḥammad), when My servants ask you about Me, tell them I am quite near; I hear and answer the call of the caller whenever he calls Me. Let them listen to My call and believe in Me; perhaps they will be guided aright.

[187] It has been made lawful for you to go in to your wives during the night of the fast. They are your garment, and you are theirs. Allah knows that you used to betray yourselves and He mercifully relented and pardoned you. So you may now associate intimately with your wives and benefit from the enjoyment Allah has made lawful for you, and eat and drink at night until you can discern the white streak of dawn against the blackness of the night; then (give up all that and) complete your fasting until night sets in. But do not associate intimately with your wives during the period when you are on retreat in the mosques. These are the bounds set by Allah; do not, then, even draw near them. Thus does Allah make His Signs clear to mankind that they may stay away from evil.

[188] Do not usurp one another's possessions by false means, nor proffer your possessions to the authorities so that you may sinfully and knowingly usurp a portion of another's possessions.[57]

---

57. One meaning of this verse is that people should not try to seek illegitimate benefits by bribing magistrates. Another meaning is that when a person is aware that the property to which he lays a claim rightfully belongs to someone else, he should not file a judicial petition simply because the other party lacks the evidence to support their case or because, by trickery and cunning, the petitioner can usurp that property. It is possible that the judicial authority would decide the case in favour of the false claimant on the basis of the formal strength of the claim, but as this judicial verdict would merely be the result of the chicanery to which the claimant had resorted he would not be its rightful owner.

[189] People question you concerning the phases of the moon. Say: "They are signs to determine time for the sake of people and for the Pilgrimage." Also tell them: "True righteousness is not that you enter your houses from the back; righteousness lies in fearing Allah. So, enter your houses by their doors, and fear Allah that you might attain true success."[58]

[190] Fight in the way of Allah against those who fight against you but do not transgress, for Allah does not love transgressors. [191] Kill them whenever you confront them and drive them out from where they drove you out. (For though killing is sinful) wrongful persecution is even worse than killing.[59] Do not fight against them near the Holy Mosque unless they fight against you; but if they fight against you kill them, for that is the reward of such unbelievers. [192] Then if they desist, know well that Allah is Ever-Forgiving, Most Compassionate.

---

58. One superstitious custom of the Arabs was that once they entered the state of consecration for Pilgrimage they did not enter their houses by the door. Instead, they either leapt over the walls from the rear or climbed through windows which they had especially erected for that purpose. On returning from journeys, too, they entered their houses from the rear. In this verse this superstitious custom is denounced, as are other superstitious customs. It is emphatically pointed out that the essence of moral excellence consists of fearing God and abstaining from disobeying His commands.

59. Here the word *fitnah* is used in the sense of "persecution". It refers to a situation whereby either a person or a group is subjected to harassment and intimidation for having accepted what is right and rejected what is wrong.

[193] Keep on fighting against them until mischief ends and the way prescribed by Allah prevails. But if they desist, then know that hostility is directed only against the wrong-doers.

[194] The sacred month for the sacred month; sanctities should be respected alike (by all concerned).[60] Thus, if someone has attacked you, attack him just as he attacked you, and fear Allah and remain conscious that Allah is with those who guard against violating the bounds set by Him.

[195] Spend in the Way of Allah and do not cast yourselves into destruction with your own hands; do good, for Allah loves those who do good.

[196] Complete *Ḥajj* and *'Umrah* for Allah. And if you are prevented from doing so, then make the offering which is available to you,[61] and do not shave your heads until the offering reaches its appointed place. If any of you should have to shave your head before that because of illness, or injury to the head, then you should make redemption

---

60. From the time of Abraham three months – Dhū al-Qaʿdah, Dhū al-Ḥijjah and Muḥarram – were consecrated for *Ḥajj*, and the month of Rajab was consecrated for *'Umrah*. For the duration of these four months warfare, killing and pillage were prohibited so that people could perform Pilgrimage and return home safely. For this reason these months were called the "sacred months".

61. If any obstruction prevents a person from proceeding with the Pilgrimage and he is forced to stay behind, he should make a sacrificial offering to God of whatever is available – for example, either a camel, a cow, a goat or a sheep.

by fasting, or almsgiving, or ritual sacrifice.[62] And when you are secure,[63] then he who avails of *'Umrah* before the time of *Ḥajj* shall give the offering he can afford; and if he cannot afford the offering, he shall fast for three days during *Ḥajj* and for seven days after he returns home; that is, ten days in all. This privilege is for those whose families do not live near the Holy Mosque. Guard against violating these ordinances of Allah and be mindful that Allah is severe in chastisement.

[197] The months of *Ḥajj* are well known. Whoever intends to perform Pilgrimage in these months shall abstain from sensual indulgence, wicked conduct and quarrelling; and whatever good you do, Allah knows it. Take your provisions for the Pilgrimage; but, in truth, the best provision is piety. Men of understanding, beware of disobeying Me. [198] It is no offence for you to seek the bounty of your Lord during Pilgrimage.[64] When you hasten back from 'Arafāt then remember Allah at al-Mash'ar al-Ḥarām (i.e. al-Muzdalifah), and remember Him in the manner He has directed you, for before this you were surely in error. [199] Then press on even as

---

62. According to the *Ḥadīth*, in such a situation the Prophet (peace be on him) ordered three days of fasting, or the feeding of six poor people, or the slaughter of one sheep or goat.

63. This refers to the change in the situation when the obstacle to proceed with the Pilgrimage has been removed.

64. "Seeking the bounty of your Lord" means earning one's livelihood during the Pilgrimage.

others press on and implore Allah's forgiveness;[65] Allah is Most Forgiving, Most Merciful. [200] And when you have performed your rites remember Allah as you remember your fathers; or remember Him even more. There are some (among those that remember Allah) who say: "Our Lord, grant us what is good in this world;" such shall have no share in the Hereafter. [201] There are others who say: "Our Lord, grant us what is good in this world and what is good in the World to Come, and protect us from the chastisement of the Fire." [202] They shall have a portion from what they earned; Allah is quick in reckoning. [203] And remember Allah through the appointed days. It is no sin for him who hastens off and returns in two days, and it is no sin for him who delays the return[66] provided he has spent the days in piety. Beware of disobeying Allah and know well that to Him you all shall be mustered.

[204] Among people there is a kind whose sayings on the affairs of the world fascinate you: he calls Allah

---

65. Since the time of Abraham and Ishmael the recognized practice of the Arabs with regard to *Ḥajj* was that on the 9th of Dhū al-Ḥijjah they went from Minā to 'Arafāt, returning on the morning of the 10th to stay at Muzdalifah. Later, as the priestly monopoly of the Quraysh became well established, they claimed that it was below their dignity to go to 'Arafāt with the ordinary people of Arabia. As a mark of what they called their distinction, they only went to Muzdalifah, without going to 'Arafāt and returned from there, leaving it to the commoners to go to 'Arafāt. It is this idol of pride and vainglory which has been shattered to pieces by the present verse.

66. It was perfectly alright whether a person returned on the 12th or on the 13th of Dhū al-Ḥijjah from Minā to Makkah as long as it is during the days of *tashrīq*.

again and again to bear testimony to his sincerity; yet he is most fierce in enmity. [205] Whenever he attains authority,[67] he goes about the earth spreading mischief and laying to waste crops and human life, even though Allah (whose testimony he invokes) does not love mischief. [206] Whenever he is told: "Fear Allah," his vainglory seizes him in his sin. So Hell shall suffice for him; what a wretched resting place! [207] On the other hand, among men there is a kind who dedicates his life seeking to please Allah; Allah is Immensely Kind to such devoted servants. [208] Believers! Enter wholly into Islam[68] and do not follow in the footsteps of Satan for he is your open enemy. [209] And if you stumble in spite of the clear instructions which have come to you, then know well that Allah is Most Mighty, Most Wise. [210] Are those people (who are not following the Right Path in spite of admonition and instruction) waiting for Allah to come to them in canopies of clouds with a retinue of angels and settle the matter finally? To Allah shall all matters ultimately be referred.

[211] Ask the Children of Israel how many Clear Signs We gave them! And when a people tamper with Allah's bounty after it has been bestowed on them – then indeed Allah is severe in punishment.

---

67. The words *idhā tawallā* can also be so translated as to make the verse mean that once the sweet and apparently genuine protestations of such people are over, they engage in arrogant and destructive action.

68. God demands that man should submit, without reservation, his whole being to His will. For God does not accept the splitting up of human life into separate compartments, some governed by the teachings of Islam and others exempt from them.

[212] Worldly life has been made attractive to those who have denied the Truth. Such men deride the men of faith, but the pious shall rank higher than them on the Day of Resurrection. As for worldly livelihood, Allah grants it to whomsoever He wills without measure.

[213] In the beginning mankind followed one single way. (Later on this state ended and differences arose.) Then Allah sent forth Prophets as heralds of good tidings for the righteous and as warners against the consequences of evil-doing. He sent down with them the Book embodying the Truth so that it might judge among people in their disputes. And those who innovated divergent ways rather than follow the Truth were none other than those who had received the knowledge of the Truth and clear guidance; and they did so to commit excesses against each other. So by His leave Allah directed the believers to the Right Way in matters on which they disagreed. Allah guides whomsoever He wills onto a Straight Way.

[214] Do you suppose that you will enter Paradise untouched by the suffering endured by the people of faith who passed away before you?[69] They were afflicted by misery and hardship and were so convulsed that the Messenger and the believers with him cried out: "When

---

69. The point emphasized here is that whenever the Prophets came into the world they, and their followers, were confronted with severe resistance from those in rebellion against God. At grave risk to themselves they strove to establish the hegemony of the true faith over the false ways of life. The profession of faith has always demanded that one should strive to establish the true religion, which one had adopted as one's faith, as a living reality and that one should spare no effort in undermining the power of the Devil who seeks to resist it.

will Allah's help arrive?" They were assured: "Behold, Allah's help is close by."

[215] People ask you what they should spend. Say: "Whatever wealth you spend let it be for your parents and kinsmen, the orphans, the needy and the wayfarer; Allah is aware of whatever good you do."

[216] Fighting is ordained upon you and it is disliked by you; it may well be that you dislike a thing even though it is good for you, and it may well be that you like a thing even though it is bad for you. Allah knows and you do not know.

[217] People ask you about fighting in the holy month. Say: "Fighting in it is an awesome sin, but barring people from the Way of Allah, disbelieving in Him, and denying entry into the Holy Mosque and expelling its inmates from it are more awesome acts in the sight of Allah; and persecution is even more heinous than killing."[70] They will not cease fighting against you till they turn you from your religion if they can. (So remember well) that whoever from amongst you turns away from his religion and dies in the state of unbelief their work will go to waste in this

---

70. This relates to a certain incident. In Rajab 2 A.H. the Prophet (peace be on him) sent an expedition of eight persons to Nakhlah (which lies between Makkah and Ṭā'if). He directed them to follow the movements of the Quraysh and gather information about their plans, but not to engage in fighting. In the course of this journey they came across a trade caravan belonging to the Quraysh and ambushed it. They killed one person and captured the rest along with their belongings and took them to Madīnah. They did this at a time when the month of Rajab was approaching its end and Sha'bān was about to begin. It was, therefore, doubtful whether the attack was actually carried out in one of the sacred months, that is,

world and in the Next. They are destined for the Fire and it is there that they will abide. [218] (On the contrary) those who believed, and forsook their hearth and home and strove in the Way of Allah,⁷¹ such may rightly hope for the mercy of Allah: for Allah is All-Forgiving, All-Merciful.

[219] They ask you about wine and games of chance. Say: "In both these there is great evil, even though there is some benefit for people, but their evil is greater than their benefit."⁷² They ask: "What should we spend in the Way of Allah?" Say: "Whatever you can spare."⁷³ In this way

---

Rajab, or not. But the Quraysh, and the Jews who were secretly in league with them, as well as the hypocrites played up this affair and used it as a weapon in their propaganda campaign against the Muslims. They pointed out the contradiction between the claims of the Muslims to follow true faith on the one hand, and their not hesitating to shed blood in a sacred month on the other. This verse is addressed to these objections.

71. *Jihād* denotes exerting one's utmost to achieve something. It is not an equivalent of war, for which the Arabic word is *qitāl*. *Jihād* has a wider connotation and embraces every kind of striving in God's cause.

72. This is the first injunction concerning intoxicating drinks and gambling, and here the matter has been left merely at the expression of disapproval. The injunction commanding not to perform Prayer when one is in a state of intoxication came later, and ultimately alcohol, gambling and the like were categorically prohibited (see *al-Nisā'* 4: 43 and *al-Mā'idah* 5: 90).

73. What is being asked is how much of one's resources should be spent in charity so that Allah be pleased. The answer provided is that one should fulfil one's needs and whatever is beyond one's needs should be spent in the Way of Allah. Such spending to earn God's grace is voluntary rather than mandatory.

Allah clearly expounds His injunctions to you that you may reflect upon them, [220] both in regard to this world and the Next. They question you concerning orphans. Say: "To deal with them in the way which is to their good, that is best. And if you intermix (your expenses and living) with them, (there is no harm for) they are your brothers." Allah knows the mischievous from the righteous, and had Allah willed, He would indeed have imposed on you exacting conditions; but He is All-Powerful, Most Wise.

[221] Marry not the women who associate others with Allah in His Divinity until they believe; for a believing slavegirl is better than a (free, respectable) woman who associates others with Allah in His Divinity, even though she might please you. Likewise, do not give your women in marriage to men who associate others with Allah in His Divinity until they believe; for a believing slave is better than a (free, respectable) man who associates others with Allah in His Divinity, even though he might please you. Such people call you towards the Fire, and Allah calls you, by His leave, towards Paradise and forgiveness; and He makes His injunctions clear to people so that they may take heed.

[222] They ask you about menstruation. Say: "It is a state of impurity; so keep away from women in the state of menstruation, and do not approach them[74] until they are cleansed. And when they are cleansed, then come to them as Allah has commanded you." Truly, Allah loves those who abstain from evil and keep themselves pure.

---

74. During this period people are only required to abstain from sexual intercourse; no change is postulated in other relationships.

[223] Your wives are your tilth; go, then, into your tilth as you wish but take heed of your ultimate future and avoid incurring the wrath of Allah.[75] Know well that one Day you shall face Him. Announce good tidings to the believers.

[224] Do not swear by Allah in your oaths if they are intended to hinder you from virtue, piety and promoting the good of mankind. Surely Allah is All-Hearing, All-Knowing. [225] Allah will not take you to task for the oaths you utter in vain, but will certainly take you to task for the oaths you utter in earnest. Allah is All-Forgiving, All-Forbearing.

[226] For those who vow abstinence from their wives there is a respite of four months.[76] Then, if they go back

---

75. These words admit of two meanings. First, that one should try to maintain the continuity of the human race so that when one departs from this world there should be others to replace in performing one's tasks. Second, that one should be concerned with the quality of the coming generation, i.e., how far it is endowed with religious devotion, moral excellence and humanity.

76. In the legal terminology of Islam this is known as *īlā'*. It is obvious that harmony and cordiality do not always prevail in matrimonial life. There are occasions when strains and tensions develop, leading to discord and estrangement. But the Law of God does not approve of that discord which causes a husband and wife, who are legally tied to one another in matrimony, to remain for long alienated from one another for all practical purposes as if they had ceased to be spouses. For this kind of abnormal discord and estrangement God has fixed a limit of four months during which the spouses are required either to settle their differences, or to break the tie of wedlock so that each becomes free to contract marriage with someone with whom a harmonious matrimonial relationship appears more likely.

on their vow they will find that Allah is All-Forgiving, All-Compassionate. [227] And if they resolve on divorce, surely Allah is All-Hearing, All-Knowing.[77]

[228] Divorced women shall keep themselves in waiting for three menstrual courses and it is unlawful for them, if they believe in Allah and the Last Day, to hide whatever Allah might have created in their wombs. Should their husbands desire reconciliation during this time they are entitled to take them back into wedlock.[78] Women have the same rights against their men as men have against them; but men have a degree above them. Allah is All-Powerful, All-Wise.

[229] Divorce can be pronounced twice: then, either honourable retention or kindly release should follow.[79] (While dissolving the marriage tie) it is unlawful for you to take back anything of what you have given to your wives unless both fear that they may not be able to keep within the bounds set by Allah. Then, if they fear that they might not be able to keep within the bounds set by Allah, there

---

77. That is, if a man has abandoned his wife on unreasonable grounds, he should not feel secure from the wrath of God for God is not unaware of the excesses that he may have committed.

78. This injunction only relates to a situation where the husband has pronounced divorce once or twice. In that case the husband retains the right to revoke the divorce before the expiry of *ʿiddah* (waiting period).

79. According to this verse, a man may pronounce revocable divorce upon his wife not more than twice. Should he pronounce divorce for the third time after revoking it twice, the wife will be permanently alienated from him.

is no blame upon them for what the wife might give away of her property to become released from the marriage tie.[80] These are the bounds set by Allah; do not transgress them. Those of you who transgress the bounds set by Allah are indeed the wrong-doers.

[230] Then, if he divorces her (for the third time, after having pronounced the divorce twice), she shall not be lawful to him unless she first takes another man for a husband, and he divorces her.[81] There is no blame upon them if both of them return to one another thereafter, provided they think that they will be able to keep within the bounds set by Allah. These are the bounds of Allah which He makes clear to a people who have knowledge (of the consequences of violating those bounds).

[231] And so, when you divorce women and they reach the end of their waiting term, then either retain them in a fair manner or let them go in a fair manner. And do not retain them to their hurt or by way of transgression; whosoever will do that will indeed wrong himself. Do not take the

---

80. In the terminology of Islamic Law this is known as *khul'*, i.e. a woman's securing the annulment of her marriage through the payment of some compensation to her husband. In case of *khul'* it is permissible for the husband to reclaim the whole or part, as agreed upon, of what he had given to his wife. But in case of divorce by the husband he has no right to reclaim any part of what he had gifted to the wife.

81. What it means is that the second husband divorces her voluntarily if and when he likes. This provides no room for the sham marriage and divorce that are arranged just to make it permissible for the first husband to remarry his divorced wife.

Signs of Allah in jest and remember Allah's favour upon you. He exhorts you to revere the Book and the Wisdom that He has sent down upon you. Fear Allah, and know well that Allah has full knowledge of everything.

[232] When you divorce women and they have completed their waiting term do not hinder them from marrying other men if they have agreed to this in a fair manner. That is an admonition to everyone of you who believes in Allah and the Last Day; that is a cleaner and purer way for you. For Allah knows whereas you do not know.

[233] If they (i.e. the fathers) wish that the period of suckling for their children be completed, mothers may suckle their children for two whole years.[82] (In such a case) it is incumbent upon him who has begotten the child to provide them (i.e. divorced women) their sustenance and clothing in a fair manner. But none shall be burdened with more than he is able to bear; neither shall a mother suffer because of her child nor shall the father be made to suffer because he has begotten him. The same duty towards the suckling mother rests upon the heir as upon him (i.e. the father). And if both (the parents) decide, by mutual consent and consultation, to wean the child, there is no blame on them; if you decide to have other women suckle your children there is no blame upon you, provided you hand over its compensation in a fair manner. Fear Allah and know well that Allah sees all that you do.

---

82. This injunction applies to the condition where the couple have separated either because of divorce, or *khulʿ* or *faskh* (annulment) or *tafrīq* (repudiation as a result of judicial decision) and the woman is nursing a child.

[234] The wives of men who have died must observe a waiting period of four months and ten days;[83] when they have reached the end of the waiting term, there is no blame upon you regarding what they may do with themselves in a fair manner. Allah is well aware of what you do. [235] There is no blame upon you whether you hint at a marriage proposal to such women or keep the proposal hidden in your hearts. Allah knows that you will think of them in that connection. But do not make any secret engagement with them and speak openly in an honourable manner. Do not resolve on the marriage tie until the ordained term has come to its end. Know well that Allah knows even what is in your hearts. So, have fear of Him and know well that Allah is All-Forgiving, All-Forbearing.

[236] There is no blame upon you if you divorce your wives before you have touched them or settled a bridal gift upon them. But even in this case you should make some provision for them: the affluent, according to his means; the straitened, according to his means – a provision in fair manner. That is a duty upon the good-doers. [237] And if you divorce them before you touch them or settle a bridal gift upon them, then (give them) half of what you have settled unless either the women act leniently and forgo

---

83. The waiting period owing to the death of the husband is obligatory even for a woman with whom consummation of marriage has not taken place. A pregnant woman, however, is exempt from this. Her waiting period expires with childbirth, even if the time between the husband's death and the childbirth is less than the waiting period prescribed by Law. To observe "a waiting period" does not mean merely that the women concerned should refrain from marrying, but also from self-adornment.

their claim, or he in whose hand is the marriage tie acts leniently (and pays the full amount). If you act leniently, it is closer to God-fearing. And forget not to act gracefully with one another, for indeed Allah sees all that you do.

[238] Be watchful over the Prayers, and over praying with the utmost excellence,[84] and stand before Allah as would utterly obedient servants. [239] And even if you face the state of fear, still perform the Prayer whether on foot or riding; and when you are secure, remember Allah in the manner that He taught you, the manner that you did not know earlier.

[240] Those of you who die leaving behind your wives should make testament of one year's provision without expulsion in favour of your wives; and if they themselves depart, there shall be no blame upon you for what they may do with themselves in an honourable manner. Allah is All-Mighty, All-Wise. [241] Likewise, let there be a fair provision for the divorced women; this is an obligation on the God-fearing.

[242] Thus Allah makes His injunctions clear to you that you may understand.

---

84. The expression used here is *al-ṣalāt al-wusṭā*. The adjective *wusṭā*, in addition to signifying the middle position of the subject that it qualifies, also signifies its excellence. Hence the expression could legitimately be interpreted both in the sense of the middle Prayer as well as in the sense of the Prayer which is performed at the right time and with full devotion and attention to God, a Prayer which contains all the attributes of excellence. The commentators who favour "middle Prayer" to be the meaning of the expression take it to mean the ʿAṣr Prayer.

[243] (O Messenger), have you thought of those who went forth from their homes for fear of death even though they were in their thousands? Allah said to them: "Die!" Then He restored them to life.[85] Indeed Allah is Bounteous to mankind; but most people do not give thanks in return. [244] So fight in the Way of Allah and know well that Allah is All-Hearing, All-Knowing. [245] Who of you will lend Allah a goodly loan which He will return after multiplying it for him manifold?[86] For Allah has the power both to decrease and increase, and to Him will you be returned.

[246] (O Messenger), have you thought of what happened with the elders of the Children of Israel after Moses? They asked one of their Prophets: "Set up for us a king so that we may fight in the way of Allah." He said: "Would you possibly refrain from fighting if fighting is ordained for you?" They said: "And why would we not fight in the way of Allah when we have been torn from our homes and our children?" But when fighting was ordained for them they turned back, except a few of them. Allah is well aware of the wrong-doers.

[247] And their Prophet said to them: "Indeed Allah has sent forth Saul (Ṭālūt) as your king." They said: "By what right shall he rule over us when we are more worthy than he to dominion, for he is not very wealthy?" He said:

---

85. This refers to the exodus of the Israelites. See *Sūrah al-Māʾidah* 5: vv. 20 ff. which narrates the details of this incident.

86. "Goodly loan" signifies whatever one gives to another person selflessly, and from absolutely pure motives. God describes whatever man spends in this manner as a loan made to none other than Him, and He undertakes to repay that loan and to repay it several-fold.

"Allah has chosen him over you and has endowed him abundantly with both intellectual and physical capacities. Allah indeed has the power to bestow dominion upon whomsoever He wills. Allah is All-Resourceful, All-Knowing." [248] And their Prophet said to them: "The Sign of his dominion is that in his reign the Ark, wherein is inner peace for you, will be brought back to you, and the sacred relics left behind by the house of Moses and the house of Aaron borne by angels. Truly in that is a Sign for you, if indeed you are people of faith."

[249] When Saul (Ṭālūt) set out with his forces he said: "Allah will try you with a river, and whoever drinks of it does not belong to me; he who refrains from tasting it – unless it be just a palmful – he indeed belongs to me." Then all, except a few of them, drank their fill at the river. But as soon as Saul (Ṭālūt) and the believers with him went forth across the river, they said: "Today we have no strength to face Goliath (Jālūt) and his forces."[87] But those who believed that they were bound to meet their Lord said: "How often has a small party prevailed against a large party by the leave of Allah." Allah is with those who remain steadfast. [250] And when they went forth against Goliath (Jālūt) and his forces, they prayed: "Our Lord! Shower us with patience, and set our feet firm, and grant us victory over this unbelieving people." [251] Thereupon by Allah's leave they put the unbelievers to flight, and David killed Goliath, and Allah granted him dominion and wisdom, and imparted to him the knowledge of whatever He willed. And were it not that

---

87. These were presumably the people who had shown their impatience on the bank of the river.

Allah repelled some people with another, the earth would surely be overlaid with mischief. But Allah is Bounteous to the people of the world (and thus extirpates mischief).

[252] These are the Signs of Allah which We recite to you in Truth, for indeed you are one of those entrusted with the Message. [253] And these Messengers (who have been designated to guide people), We have exalted some of them above the others. Among them are such as were spoken to by Allah Himself, and some He exalted in other respects. And We granted Jesus, son of Mary, Clear Signs and supported him with the spirit of holiness. Had He willed, those who had seen these Clear Signs would not have fought one another thereafter. But (it was not the will of Allah to prevent people from disagreement by compulsion, hence) they differed among themselves whereby some attained faith and others denied the Truth. Yet had Allah so willed they would not have fought one another. Allah does whatever He wills.

[254] O you who believe! Spend out of what We have provided you before there comes a Day when there will be no buying and selling, nor will friendship and intercession be of any avail. Indeed those who disbelieve are the wrong-doers.

[255] Allah, the Ever-Living, the Self-Subsisting by Whom all subsist, there is no god but He. Neither slumber seizes Him, nor sleep; to Him belongs all that is in the heavens and all that is in the earth. Who is there who might intercede with Him save with His leave? He knows what lies before them and what is hidden from them, whereas

they cannot attain to anything of His knowledge save what He wills them to attain. His Dominion[88] overspreads the heavens and the earth, and their upholding wearies Him not. He is All-High, All-Glorious.

[256] There is no compulsion in religion.[89] The Right Way stands clearly distinguished from the wrong. Hence he who rejects the evil ones[90] and believes in Allah has indeed taken hold of the firm, unbreakable handle. And Allah (Whom he has held for support) is All-Hearing, All-Knowing. [257] Allah is the Guardian of those who believe, He brings them out of every darkness into light. And those who disbelieve, their guardians are the evil ones;[91] they bring them out of light into all kinds of darkness. These are destined for the Fire, and there shall they abide.

---

88. The Arabic term *kursī* signifies sovereignty, dominion and authority. This verse is generally known as the "Verse of the Throne" and it provides in one piece a knowledge of God without any parallel. No wonder it has been characterized in the *Ḥadīth* as the most excellent verse of the Qur'ān.

89. The verse means that the Islamic system, embracing belief, morals and practical conduct cannot be enforced by compulsion. These are not things to which people can be yoked forcibly.

90. Literally *ṭāghūt* (pl. *ṭawāghīt*) means anyone who exceeds his legitimate limits. In the Qur'ānic terminology, however, it refers to the creature who exceeds the limits of his creatureliness and arrogates to himself Godhead and lordship.

91. Here *ṭāghūt* (see n. 90 above) has a plural connotation. This implies that by turning away from God a man is subjected not to the tyranny of one, but to the tyranny of many *ṭawāghīt* (evil ones).

[258] Did you not consider the case of the person who remonstrated with Abraham[92] about who was Abraham's Lord just because Allah had granted him dominion? When Abraham said: "My Lord is He Who grants life and causes death," he replied: "I grant life and I cause death." Abraham said: "But surely Allah causes the sun to rise from the east; now you cause it to rise from the west." Thereupon the denier of the Truth was confounded. Allah does not direct the wrong-doers to the Right Way.

[259] Or consider him by way of example who passed by a town that was fallen down upon its turrets. He exclaimed: "How will Allah restore life to this town that is now dead?" Allah then caused him to remain dead for a hundred years and then raised him to life, and asked him: "How long did you remain in this state?" He replied: "I remained so for a day or a part of a day." Allah rejoined: "No, you have rather stayed thus for a hundred years. But look at your food and your drink, there is no deterioration in them. And look at your ass (how its entire skeleton has rotted)! And We did all this so that We might make you a token of instruction for people. And see how We will put the bones (of the ass) together and will clothe them with flesh." Thus when the reality became clear to him, he said: "I know that Allah has power over everything."

[260] And recall when Abraham said: "My Lord, show me how You give life to the dead," Allah said: "Why! Do you have no faith?" Abraham replied: "Yes, but in order that

---

92. Here the reference is to Nimrod, the ruler of the land of Abraham's birth, Iraq.

my heart be at rest."[93] He said: "Then take four birds, and tame them to yourself, then put a part of them on every hill, and summon them; they will come to you flying. Know well that Allah is All-Mighty, All-Wise."

[261] The example of those who spend their wealth in the Way of Allah is like that of a grain of corn that sprouts seven ears, and in every ear there are a hundred grains. Thus Allah multiplies the action of whomsoever He wills. Allah is Munificent, All-Knowing. [262] Those who spend their wealth in the Way of Allah and do not follow up their spending by stressing their benevolence and causing hurt, will find their reward secure with their Lord. They have no cause for fear and grief. [263] To speak a kind word and to forgive people's faults is better than charity followed by hurt. Allah is All-Sufficient, All-Forbearing. [264] Believers! Do not nullify your acts of charity by stressing your benevolence and causing hurt as does he who spends his wealth only to be seen by people and does not believe in Allah and the Last Day. The example of his spending is that of a rock with a thin coating of earth upon it: when a heavy rain smites it, the earth is washed away, leaving the rock bare; such people derive no gain from their acts of charity. Allah does not set the deniers of the Truth on the Right Way.[94] [265] The example of those who spend their wealth singlemindedly to please Allah is that of a garden on a high ground. If a heavy rain smites it, it brings forth its fruits twofold, and if there is

---

93. That is, the rest and inner peace that one attains as a result of direct personal observation.

94. Here the term *kāfir* is used in the sense of the ungrateful person who refuses to acknowledge the benevolence of his benefactor.

no heavy rain, even a light shower suffices it. Allah sees all that you do.

[266] Would any of you desire that he should have a garden of palms and vines with rivers flowing beneath it – a garden in which he has every manner of fruit – and that it should then be struck by a fiery whirlwind and be utterly burnt down at a time when old age has overtaken him, and his offspring are still too small to look after their affairs?[95] Thus does Allah make His teachings clear to you that you may reflect.

[267] Believers! Spend (in the Way of Allah) out of the good things you have earned and out of what We have produced for you from the earth, and choose not for your spending the bad things such as you yourselves would not accept or accept only by overlooking its defects. Know well that Allah is All-Munificent, Most Praiseworthy. [268] Satan frightens you with poverty and bids you to commit indecency whereas Allah promises you His forgiveness and bounty. Allah is Munificent, All-Knowing. [269] He grants wisdom to those whom He wills; and whoever is granted wisdom has indeed been granted much good. Yet none except people of understanding take heed.

---

95. It is obvious that a man does not like to see that the earnings of his lifetime are destroyed when he is stricken with age and needs them badly and is no longer in a position to earn them. How is it, then, that he can contemplate stepping into the realm of the Hereafter and finding suddenly that he is empty-handed; that he has sown nothing whose fruit he can harvest?

[270] Allah knows whatever you spend or whatever you vow (to spend).[96] The wrong-doers have none to succour them. [271] If you dispense your charity publicly, it is well; but if you conceal it and pay it to the needy in secret, it will be even better for you. This will atone for several of your misdeeds. Allah is well aware of all that you do.

[272] You are not responsible for setting these people on the Right Way; Allah sets on the Right Way whomsoever He wills. Whatever wealth you spend in charity is to your own benefit for you spend merely to please Allah. So, whatever you spend in charity will be repaid to you in full and you shall not be wronged.

[273] Those needy ones who are wholly wrapped up in the cause of Allah, and who are hindered from moving about the earth in search of their livelihood, especially deserve help. He who is unaware of their circumstances supposes them to be wealthy because of their dignified bearing, but you will know them by their countenance, although they do not go about begging of people with importunity. Whatever wealth you spend on helping them, Allah will know of it.

---

96. "Vow" means either a man's pledge to spend something or to perform some act of goodness which is not obligatory upon him provided that a particular wish of his is fulfilled. It is essential, however, that this vow, should relate to some wish which is in itself permissible and good and that the person concerned makes it to none but God and for the sake of God. It is then that such a vow will be reckoned as an act of obedience to God and its fulfilment will be worthy of reward. Otherwise such a vow will be seen as an act of disobedience and sin and its fulfilment will invite punishment from God.

[274] Those who spend their wealth by night and by day, secretly and publicly, will find that their reward is secure with their Lord and that there is no reason for them to entertain any fear or grief. [275] As for those who devour interest, they behave as the one whom Satan has confounded with his touch.[97] Seized in this state they say: "Buying and selling is but a kind of interest,"[98] even though Allah has made buying and selling lawful, and interest unlawful. Hence, he who receives this admonition from his Lord, and then gives up (dealing in interest), may keep his previous gains, and it will be for Allah to judge him.[99] As for those who revert to it, they are the people of the Fire, and in it shall they abide. [276] Allah deprives interest of all blessing, whereas He blesses charity with growth. Allah loves none who is ungrateful and persists in sin. [277] Truly the reward of those who believe and do righteous deeds and establish Prayer and pay *Zakāh*

97. The Arabs used the word *majnūn* (possessed by the *jinn*) to characterize the insane. The Qur'ān uses the same expression about those who charge interest.

98. The unsoundness of this view lies in not differentiating between the profit one gains on investment in commercial enterprises on the one hand, and interest on the other. As a result of this confusion, the proponents of this view argue that if profit on money invested in a business enterprise is permissible, why should the profit accruing on loaned money – that is interest – be deemed unlawful?

99. What is said here is not that man will be pardoned by God for the interest charged in the past, but that it is for God to judge him. The expression: "may keep his previous gain" does not signify absolute pardon from God for the interest one has realized, rather it points to the legal concession that has been made. It only means that no legal claim will be made against a person for the interest he had charged in the past.

is with their Lord; they have no reason to entertain any fear or grief.

[278] Believers! Have fear of Allah and give up all outstanding interest if you do truly believe. [279] But if you fail to do so, then be warned of war from Allah and His Messenger.[100] If you repent even now, you have the right of the return of your capital; neither will you do wrong nor will you be wronged. [280] But if the debtor is in straitened circumstance, let him have respite until the time of ease; and whatever you remit by way of charity is better for you, if only you know.[101] [281] And have fear of the Day when you shall return to Allah, and every human being shall be fully repaid for whatever (good or evil) he has done, and none shall be wronged.

---

100. This verse was revealed after the conquest of Makkah and has been placed here because of its contextual relevance. Although interest was considered objectionable even before, it had not been legally prohibited. After the revelation of this verse interest-bearing transactions became a punishable offence within the realm of Islam. On the basis of the last words of the verse, Ibn 'Abbās, Ḥasan al-Baṣrī, Ibn Sīrīn and Rabīʿ ibn Anas are of the view that pressure should be brought against anyone who charges interest within the boundaries of the Islamic State (*Dār al-Islām*) to repudiate the transaction and recant; and if he persists, he should be put to death. Others consider it sufficient to imprison such people and keep them in prison until they pledge to give up charging interest.

101. This verse is the basis of the Islamic regulation that if a person is incapable of paying off his debt, the court will force the creditors to grant him respite from payment. In fact, under certain circumstances, the court is entitled to remit a part of his debt and, in some cases, the whole of it. Muslim jurists have made it clear that a debtor's residential house, eating utensils, clothes and the tools which he uses for earning his livelihood may not be confiscated in any circumstance whatsoever for non-payment of loans.

[282] Believers! Whenever you contract a debt from one another for a known term,[102] commit it to writing. Let a scribe write it down between you justly, and the scribe may not refuse to write it down according to what Allah has taught him; so let him write, and let the debtor dictate; and let him fear Allah, his Lord, and curtail no part of it. If the debtor be feebleminded, weak, or incapable of dictating, let his guardian dictate equitably, and call upon two of your men as witnesses; but if two men are not there, then let there be one man and two women as witnesses from among those acceptable to you so that if one of the two women should fail to remember, the other might remind her. Let not the witnesses refuse when they are summoned (to give evidence). Do not show slackness in writing down the transaction, whether small or large, along with the term of its payment. That is fairest in the sight of Allah; it is best for testimony and is more likely to exclude all doubts. If it be a matter of buying and selling on the spot, it is not blameworthy if you do not write it down; but do take witnesses when you settle commercial transactions with one another. And the scribe or the witness may be done no harm. It will be sinful if you do so. Beware of the wrath of Allah. He teaches you the Right Way and has full knowledge of everything.

---

102. This is the basis of the rule that the time for the repayment of a loan should be fixed at the time when the loan is transacted.

[283] And if you are on a journey and do not find a scribe to write the document then resort to taking pledges in hand.[103] But if any of you trusts another, let him who is trusted, fulfil the trust and fear Allah, his Lord. And do not conceal what you have witnessed, for whoever conceals it, his heart is sinful. Allah has full knowledge of all that you do.

[284] All that is in the heavens and the earth belongs to Allah. Whether you disclose whatever is in your hearts or conceal it, Allah will call you to account for it, and will then forgive whomsoever He wills, and will chastise whomsoever He wills. Allah has power over everything.

[285] The Messenger believes, and so do the believers, in the guidance sent down upon him from his Lord: each of them believes in Allah, and in His angels, and in His Books, and in His Messengers. They say: "We make no distinction between any of His Messengers. We hear and obey. Our Lord! Grant us Your forgiveness; to You we are destined to return."

[286] Allah does not lay a responsibility on anyone beyond his capacity. In his favour shall be whatever good each one

---

103. It should also be noted that the purpose of taking a pledge is merely to assure the lender the return of his loan. He has no right at all to benefit from the pledged property. If, however, either cattle or beasts of burden have been pledged, they can be milked and used for transport in lieu of the fodder that one provides them during the period of custody.

does, and against him whatever evil he does. (Believers! Pray thus to your Lord): "Our Lord! Take us not to task if we forget or commit mistakes. Our Lord! Lay not on us a burden such as You laid on those gone before us. Our Lord! Lay not on us burdens which we do not have the power to bear. And overlook our faults, and forgive us, and have mercy upon us. You are our Guardian; so grant us victory against the unbelieving folk."

3

Āl ʿImrān [The House of ʿImrān]
Madīnan Period

In the name of Allah, the Most Merciful,
the Most Compassionate

[1] *Alif, Lām, Mīm.* [2] Allah, the Ever-Living, the Self-Subsisting, Who sustains the entire order of the Universe – there is no god but He.

[3] He has revealed this Book to you, setting forth the Truth and confirming the earlier Books, and He revealed the Torah and the Gospel [4] before that for the guidance of mankind; and He has also revealed the Criterion (to distinguish the Truth from falsehood). A severe chastisement lies in store for those who deny the Signs of Allah. Allah is All-Mighty; He is the Lord of Retribution.

[5] Nothing in the earth and in the heavens is hidden from Allah. [6] It is He Who fashions you in the wombs as He wills. There is no god but He; the All-Mighty, the All-Wise. [7] He it is Who has revealed the Book to you. Among them there are absolutely clear and lucid verses,[1]

---

1. The *muḥkam* verses mentioned here are those Qurʾānic verses which are embodied in clear and lucid language and whose meaning is not liable to any ambiguity and equivocation. Such

and these are the core of the Book. Others are ambiguous.[2] Those in whose hearts there is perversity, go about the part that is ambiguous, seeking mischief and seeking to arrive at its meaning arbitrarily, although none knows their true meaning but Allah. But those firmly rooted in knowledge say: "We believe in it; it is all from our Lord alone."[3] No

---

verses form the core of the Book; they are the verses which fulfil the true purpose for which the Qur'ān was revealed, and they invite the whole world to Islam. They embody admonition and instruction, refutation of erroneous doctrines as well as elucidation of the Right Way. They also contain the fundamentals of the true faith, embodying teachings relating to belief, worship and morality, and mandatory duties and prohibitions.

2. "Ambiguous" (*mutashābih*) verses are those whose meaning may have some degree of equivocation. It is obvious that no way of life can be prescribed for man unless a certain amount of knowledge explaining the truth about the universe, its origin and end, about man's position in it and other matters of similar importance, is intimated to him. It is also evident that the truths which lie beyond the range of human perception have always eluded and will continue to elude man; no words exist in the human vocabulary which either express or portray them. In speaking about such things, we necessarily resort to words and expressions that are generally employed in connection with tangible objects. In the Qur'ān, too, this kind of language is employed in relation to supernatural matters; the verses which have been characterized as "ambiguous" refer to such matters.

3. This might give rise to an unnecessary problem: How can people believe in "ambiguous" verses when the contents of these cannot be grasped? The fact is that a reasonable person will have faith that the Qur'ān is the Book of God through his reading of its clear and lucid verses, rather than by learning fanciful interpretations of the ambiguous verses. Once so convinced, he is not likely to be troubled by doubts and anxieties caused by the ambiguities of a few verses.

one derives true admonition from anything except the people of understanding. [8] They pray to Allah: "Our Lord! Do not let our hearts swerve towards crookedness after You have guided us to the Right Way, and bestow upon us Your Mercy for You are the Munificent Giver! [9] Our Lord! One Day You will surely gather all mankind together, a Day about (the coming of which) there is no doubt. Surely Allah never goes against His promise."

[10] As for the unbelievers, neither their wealth nor their offspring will avail them in the least against Allah. They shall be the fuel of the Fire. [11] (To them shall happen) the like of what happened to the people of Pharaoh, and those before them. They rejected Our signs as false, so Allah seized them for their sins. Allah indeed is severe in punishment. [12] Tell those who have disbelieved: "You shall soon be overpowered and mustered to Hell; what an evil resting place!" [13] You have already come across an instructive sign in the two hosts that encountered each other in battle (at Badr): one host fighting in the way of Allah, and the other that of unbelievers. They saw with their very eyes that one host was twice the number of the other.[4] But (the result of the battle proved that) Allah succours with His victory whomsoever He wills. In this there is surely a lesson for all who have discerning eyes.

[14] People are naturally tempted by the lure of women, children, treasures of gold and silver, horses of mark,

---

4. The actual disparity between the two armies was roughly that of three to one, but even a cursory glance was enough to tell the casual observer that the army of unbelievers was about twice as large as that of the believers.

cattle and plantations. These are the enjoyments in the life
of this world; but with Allah lies a goodly abode to return
to. [15] Say: "Shall I tell you of things better than these?
For the God-fearing there are, with their Lord, Gardens
beneath which rivers flow; there they will abide for ever,
will have spouses of stainless purity as companions, and
will enjoy the good pleasure of Allah." Allah thoroughly
observes His servants. [16] These are the ones who pray:
"Our Lord! We do indeed believe, so forgive us our sins
and keep us safe from the chastisement of the Fire;"
[17] people who are steadfast, truthful, obedient, spend
(in the way of Allah) and implore Allah's forgiveness
before daybreak.

[18] Allah Himself bears witness that there is no god but
He; and likewise do the angels and those possessed of
knowledge bear witness in truth and justice that there
is no god but He, the All-Mighty, the All-Wise. [19] The
true religion with Allah is Islam. The People of the Book
adopted many different ways rather than follow the True
Way of Islam even after the knowledge of Truth had
reached them, and this merely to commit excesses against
one another. Let him who refuses to follow the ordinances
and directives of Allah know that Allah is swift in His
reckoning. [20] But if they remonstrate with you, tell them:
"I have submitted my whole being to Allah, and so have
those who follow me." And ask the People of the Book as
well as those who follow no heavenly Scripture: "Have
you also submitted (to Allah)?" If they have submitted
to Him, they are indeed on the Right Way; but if they
turn away from submitting to Allah, then your duty is

merely to deliver the Message. Allah observes the affairs of His servants.

[21] Give those who refuse to follow the directives of Allah, who unjustly slay the Prophets, and slay those who enjoin justice, the glad tidings of a grievous chastisement. [22] These are the people whose works have gone to waste both in this world and in the World to Come. They have none to come to their help.

[23] Have you not noticed those who were given a portion of the Book? Whenever their learned men are summoned to the Book of Allah to judge the differences among them, a party of them turns away in aversion. [24] This is because they say: "The Fire of Hell shall not touch us except for a limited number of days." The false beliefs which they have forged have deluded them in their faith. [25] How, then, will they fare when We shall gather them all together to witness the Day about (the coming of) which there is no doubt, and when every human being shall be paid in full for what he has done, and none shall be wronged?

[26] Say: "O Allah, Lord of all dominion! You bestow dominion on whomever You please, and take away dominion from whomever You please, and You exalt whom You please, and abase whom You please. In Your Hand is all good. Surely You are All-Powerful. [27] You cause the night to pass into the day and the day to pass into the night. You bring forth the living out of the dead, and You bring the dead out of the living, and You grant livelihood to whomever You will beyond all reckoning."

[28] The believers may not take the unbelievers for their allies in preference to the believers. Whoever does this

has nothing to do with Allah unless he does so in order to protect himself from their wrongdoing.[5] Allah warns you to beware of Him for to Allah is the ultimate return.[6] [29] Say: "Whether you conceal what is in your hearts or disclose it, Allah knows it. Allah knows all that is in the heavens and in the earth and He has power over everything." [30] The Day is approaching when every soul shall find itself confronted with whatever good it has done and whatever evil it has wrought. It will then wish that there be a wide space between it and the Day! Allah warns you to beware of Him; He is Most Tender towards His servants.

[31] (O Messenger), tell people: "If you indeed love Allah, follow me, and Allah will love you and will forgive you your sins. Allah is All-Forgiving, All-Compassionate." [32] Say: "Obey Allah and obey the Messenger." If they

---

5. This means that it is lawful for a believer, helpless in the grip of the enemies of Islam and in imminent danger of severe wrong and persecution, to keep his faith concealed and to behave in such manner as to create the impression that he is on the same side as his enemies. A person whose Muslim identity is discovered is permitted to adopt a friendly attitude towards the unbelievers in order to save his life. If he considers himself incapable of enduring the excess to which he may be subjected, he may even state that he is not a believer.

6. One may resort to prudent concealment of faith (taqīyah) in order to save one's life. This concealment should, however, remain within reasonable limits. The most one is permitted to do is to save one's life and property without jeopardizing either the interests of Islam or the Muslim community as a whole, and without causing loss of life and property to other Muslims. One must never allow saving one's own life to lead to the propagation of unbelief at the expense of Islam and to the dominance of unbelievers over Muslims.

turn away from this then know that Allah does not love those who refuse to obey Him and His Messenger.

[33] Truly Allah chose Adam and Noah and the descendants of Abraham and of 'Imrān[7] above all mankind [34] (for His Messengership) – a people alike and the seed of one another. Allah is All-Hearing, All-Knowing [35] (He also heard) when 'Imrān's woman[8] said: "O Lord! Behold, unto You do I vow that the child in my womb is to be devoted to Your exclusive service. Accept it, then, from me. Surely You alone are All-Hearing, All-Knowing." [36] But when she gave birth to a female child, she said: "O Lord! I have given birth to a female" – and Allah knew full well what she had given birth to – "and a male is not the same as a female. I have named her Mary and commit her and her offspring to You for protection from Satan, the accursed." [37] Thereupon her Lord graciously accepted Mary and vouchsafed to her a goodly growth and placed her in the care of Zechariah. Whenever Zechariah visited her in the sanctuary, he found her provided with food. He asked her: "Mary, how did this come to you?" She said: "It is from Allah. Allah provides sustenance to whom He wills beyond all reckoning." [38] Then Zechariah prayed to his Lord: "O Lord! Grant me from Yourself out of Your grace the gift of a goodly offspring, for indeed You alone heed

---

7. 'Imrān was the father of Moses and Aaron, and has been mentioned in the Bible as Amram.

8. If "'Imrān's woman" is interpreted as the wife of 'Imrān, this 'Imrān must be different from the 'Imrān just mentioned. He would rather be the father of Mary who was probably called 'Imrān. If this expression, however, is interpreted to mean "a woman of the house of 'Imrān," it would mean that the mother of Mary belonged to that tribe.

all prayers." [39] As he stood praying in the sanctuary, the angels called out to him: "Allah gives you good tidings of John (Yaḥyā), who shall confirm a command[9] of Allah, shall be outstanding among people, utterly chaste, and a Prophet from among the righteous." [40] Zechariah exclaimed, "My Lord! How shall I have a son when old age has overtaken me and my wife is barren?" He said: "Thus shall it be;[10] Allah does what He wills." [41] Zechariah said: "O my Lord! Appoint a Sign for me." The angel said: "The Sign for you shall be that you shall not speak to people for three days except by gesture. Remember your Lord and extol His glory by night and by day."

[42] Then came the time when the angels said: "O Mary! Behold, Allah has chosen you, and has made you pure, and has exalted you above all the women in the world. [43] O Mary! Remain devout to your Lord, and prostrate yourself in worship, and bow down with those who bow down (before Him)."

[44] (O Muḥammad), We reveal to you this account from a realm which lies beyond the reach of your perception for you were not with them when they drew lots with their pens[11] about who should be Mary's guardian, and you were not with them when they disputed about it.

---

9. The "command from Allah" here signifies Jesus (peace be on him). His birth took place as the result of an extraordinary command from God and in an unusual manner, hence he is designated as "the command" or "word" from Allah.

10. Here it is being stressed that God would grant Zechariah a son despite his old age and the barrenness of his wife.

11. They drew lots to decide who should be the guardian of Mary, whose mother had consecrated her to the service of God in the Temple.

[45] And when the angels said: "O Mary! Allah gives you the glad tidings of a command from Him: his name shall be Messiah, Jesus, the son of Mary. He shall be highly honoured in this world and in the Next, and shall be one of those near stationed to Allah. [46] And he shall speak to people in the cradle and also later when he grows to maturity and shall indeed be among the righteous." [47] She said: "O my Lord! How shall I have a son when no man has ever touched me?" The angel answered: "Thus shall it be.¹² Allah creates whatever He wills. When He decides something, He merely says: "Be," and it is. [48] And He will teach him the Book, the Wisdom, the Torah, the Gospel, [49] and he will be a Messenger to the Children of Israel." (And when he came to them he said): "I have come to you with a Sign from your Lord. I will make for you from clay the likeness of a bird and then I will breathe into it and by the leave of Allah it will become a bird. I will also heal the blind and the leper, and by the leave of Allah I will bring the dead to life. I will also inform you of what things you eat and what you treasure up in your houses. Surely this is a Sign for you if you are true believers. [50] And I have come to confirm the truth of whatever there still remains of the Torah, and to make lawful to you some of the things which had been forbidden to you.¹³ I have come to you with a Sign from

12. Thus it was affirmed that a child would be born to Mary despite the fact that no man had touched her.

13. What Jesus wanted to impress upon them was that he would abolish the prohibitive innovations which had infiltrated the original Divine Law (*Sharīʿah*). These innovations were the result of the superstitions of their ignorant commoners, the legal hair-splitting of their lawyers, and the exaggerations of their world-

your Lord; so have fear of Allah and obey me. [51] Surely,
Allah is my Lord and your Lord; so serve Him alone. This
is the Straight Way."

[52] And when Jesus perceived their leaning towards
unbelief, he asked: "Who will be my helpers in the Way
of Allah?" The disciples[14] said: "We are the helpers of
Allah.[15] We believe in Allah, and be our witness that we
have submitted ourselves exclusively to Allah. [53] Our
Lord! We believe in the commandment You have revealed
and we obey the Messenger; make us, then, one of those
who bear witness (to the Truth)."

[54] Then they schemed (against the Messiah), and Allah
countered their schemes by schemes of His own. Allah is
the best of schemers. [55] (And it was part of His scheme)
when Allah said. "O Jesus! I will recall you[16] and raise you
up to Me and will purify you (of the company) of those
who disbelieve, and will set your followers above the
unbelievers till the Day of Resurrection. Then to Me shall
all of you return, and I shall judge between you regarding
whatever you differed among yourselves. [56] As for those

---

renouncing pietists. He also made it clear that in determining what
is lawful and unlawful, he would be guided by the injunctions of
God and not by the inventions of human beings.

14. The word *ḥawārī* means approximately the same as the word
anṣār in the Islamic tradition.

15. That is, they are his allies in the cause of directing people to
the Path of God.

16. The expression used is *mutawaffīka*. The original meaning of
tawaffā is to take and receive. To "seize a person's soul" constitutes
the figurative rather than the literal meaning of the word.

who disbelieved, I shall inflict a terrible chastisement on them in this world and in the Next; and they shall find none to help them." [57] But those who believe and do righteous deeds, He will reward them in full. Allah does not love the unjust.

[58] What We recite to you consists of signs and wise admonition. [59] Surely, in the sight of Allah, the similitude of the creation of Jesus is as the creation of Adam whom He created out of dust, and then said: "Be," and he was.[17] [60] This is the truth from your Lord; be not, then, among those who doubt.

[61] Tell whoever disputes with you on this matter after true knowledge has come to you: "Come! Let us summon our sons and your sons, and our women and your women, and ourselves and yourselves, and then let us pray together and invoke the curse of Allah on those who lie." [62] This is the true story. There is no god but Allah, and assuredly Allah is All-Mighty, All-Wise. [63] And if they turn their backs, truly Allah knows those who cause mischief.

[64] Say: "People of the Book! Come to a word common between us and you: that we shall serve none but Allah and shall associate none with Him in His Divinity and that some of us will not take others as lords other than Allah." And if they turn away (from accepting this call),

---

17. This means that if Jesus' miraculous birth is sufficient proof that he should be regarded either as God or the son of God then there are even stronger grounds to apply this to Adam. For, while Jesus was born without a father, Adam was born without any father and mother.

tell them: "Bear witness that we are the ones who have submitted ourselves exclusively to Allah."

[65] People of the Book! Why do you dispute with us about Abraham even though the Torah and the Gospel were not revealed until after his time? Do you not understand? [66] Behold, you are those who have severely disputed concerning matters of which you have knowledge; why are you now disputing concerning matters that you know nothing about? Allah knows it whereas you do not know. [67] Abraham was neither a Jew nor a Christian; he was a Muslim, wholly devoted to God.[18] And he certainly was not amongst those who associate others with Allah in His Divinity. [68] Surely the people who have the best claim to affiliation with Abraham are those who followed him (in the past), and presently this Prophet and those who believe in him. Allah is the Guardian of those who truly believe.

[69] A party of the People of the Book would fain lead you astray, whereas in truth they lead none astray except themselves, but that they do not realize it. [70] People of the Book! Why do you reject the Signs of Allah even though you yourselves witness them?[19] [71] People of the

---

18. The word *ḥanīf* denotes someone who turns his face away from all other directions in order to follow one particular course. We have tried to convey this sense through the expression: "a Muslim, wholly devoted to God."

19. Another rendering of this could be, "and you yourselves bear witness" to Muḥammad's prophethood. However it is translated, the sense remains the same. In fact, the impeccable purity of the life of the Prophet (peace be on him), the astounding impact of his teachings and training on the lives of his Companions, and

Book! Why do you confound the Truth with falsehood, and why do you conceal the Truth knowingly?

[72] A party of the People of the Book said: "Believe in the morning what has been revealed to those who believe, and then deny it in the evening that they may retract (from their faith)." [73] They also say among themselves: "Do not follow anyone except him who follows your faith." Say: "Surely true guidance is Allah's. It is His favour that anyone should be given the like of what you have been given in the past, and that others should have been given firm evidence to proffer against you before your Lord." Say: "Surely bounty is in the Hand of Allah; He gives it to whom He wills. Allah is All-Embracing,[20] All-Knowing. [74] He singles out for His Mercy whomever He wills. Allah is possessed of abounding bounty."

[75] There are some among the People of the Book who will restore you even if you were to entrust a treasure of gold, and among them are also others who, were you to entrust

---

the loftiness of the teachings of the Qurʾān all constituted such illustrious signs of God that it was very difficult for anyone conversant with the lives of the Prophets and the tenor of Divine Scriptures to doubt Muḥammad's prophethood.

20. The word *wāsiʿ* which is used here occurs in the Qurʾān in three contexts. The first context is the narrow-mindedness and mean outlook of certain people, in contrast to which God is not narrow. The second context is the denunciation of miserliness, meanness and niggardliness, in contrast to which God is Generous and Munificent. The third context is the ascription of finite, limited concepts to God as a result of their limited imagination, whereas the truth is that God is infinite.

one gold piece, will not restore it unless you stand over them. That is because they say: "We will not be taken to task for whatever we may do to non-Jews (*ummīs*)." Thus they falsely fix a lie upon Allah, and do so wittingly. [76] But Allah loves only those who fulfil their covenant and fear Allah. Truly Allah loves the God-fearing. [77] There shall be no share in the Life to Come for those who sell away the covenant of Allah and their oaths for a trivial gain. On the Day of Resurrection Allah will neither address them, nor look at them, nor will He purify them. A grievous chastisement awaits them.

[78] There is a party among them who twist their tongues while reciting the Book to make you think that it is part of the Book when in fact it is not. They say: "It is from Allah," when in fact it is not from Allah. They falsely fix a lie upon Allah, and do so wittingly.

[79] It does not befit a man that Allah should grant him His Book and sound judgement and prophethood, and thereafter he should say to people: "Become servants to me apart from Allah." He would rather say: "Become dedicated men of Allah, in accord with the dictates of the Book you have been teaching and studying." [80] He will never enjoin you to take the angels or Prophets for your lords. Will he enjoin upon you unbelief when you have submitted yourselves to Allah?

[81] Recall when Allah took a covenant from the Prophets: "This is the Book and the Wisdom which I have granted you. But should a Prophet come to you confirming what you already possess, you shall believe in him and shall

help him."[21] So saying, Allah asked: "Do you agree and accept to take up the burden of the covenant?" They answered: "We agree." He said: "Then bear witness; and I will be with you among the witnesses. [82] Then whosoever shall turn away from this covenant, they are the transgressors."

[83] Do they now seek a religion other than that prescribed by Allah and this despite all that is in the heavens and the earth is in submission to Him – willingly or unwillingly – and to Him all shall return? [84] Say: "We believe in Allah and what was revealed to us and what was revealed to Abraham and Ishmael and to Isaac and Jacob and his descendants, and the teachings which Allah gave to Moses and Jesus and to other Prophets. We make no distinction between any of them; and to Him do we submit." [85] And whoever seeks a way other than this way of submission – Islam – will find that it will not be accepted from him and he will be among the losers in the Life to Come.

---

21. This means that all Prophets had been asked to pledge – and the pledge of a Prophet is automatically binding upon his followers – that they would support every Prophet that God sent to preach and establish His religion, for the cause for which they had been raised. It is useful to point out that the Prophets before Muḥammad (peace be on him) had to take this pledge, and this is why every Prophet announced to his followers the coming of other Prophets in the future and directed them to support those Prophets whenever they appeared. It seems significant that there is no mention, either in the Qurʾān or in the *Ḥadīth*, that the Prophet Muḥammad (peace be on him) was asked to take such a pledge. Moreover, the Prophet (peace be on him) neither informed his followers of the advent of any future Prophet nor did he direct them to believe in the prophethood of any such Prophet. On the contrary, he has been

[86] How can Allah guide a people who once believed, and after they had received Clear Signs and affirmed that the Messenger was a true one, they lapsed into disbelief? Allah does not guide the wrong-doers. [87] The recompense for their wrong-doing is that the curse of Allah and of the angels and of all men shall be upon them. [88] Thus shall they abide. Neither shall their chastisement be lightened nor shall they be granted any respite. [89] But for those who repent and mend their ways Allah is indeed Most Forgiving, Most Compassionate. [90] Those who disbelieved after having believed and then hardened in their disbelief,[22] their (pretence to) repentance shall not be accepted. Such have utterly gone astray. [91] Truly those who embraced unbelief and died as unbelievers, not even the whole earth full of gold will be accepted from them as ransom. For such there is painful chastisement; and none shall come to their help.

[92] You shall not attain righteousness until you spend (for the sake of Allah) out of what you love. Allah knows whatever you spend.

---

pronounced *khātam al-nabīyīn* (the seal of the Prophets), meaning the last of them by the Qur'ān. Several traditions from the Prophet (peace be on him) confirm that he categorically declared that no Prophet would come after him.

22. These opponents of the Truth were not content with just rejecting the call to the Truth but stood in vehement opposition and hostility to it and spared no efforts to obstruct people from following the way of God. They created doubts, spread misgivings, sowed seeds of distrust and engaged in the worst conspiracies and machinations to frustrate the mission of the Prophet (peace be on him).

[93] All food (that is lawful in the Law revealed to Muḥammad) was lawful to the Children of Israel,[23] except what Israel made unlawful to themselves before the revelation of the Torah. Tell them: "Bring the Torah and recite any passage of it if you are truthful." [94] Those who forge lies against Allah despite this are the wrongdoers. [95] Say: "Whatever Allah has said is true. Follow, then, the way of Abraham in total devotion to Allah. He was not among those who associate others with Allah in His Divinity."

[96] Behold, the first House (of Prayer) established for mankind is the one at Bakkah: it is full of blessing and is a centre of guidance for the whole world. [97] In it there are Clear Signs[24] and the station of Abraham; whoever enters

---

23. The Jewish rabbis found no grounds to criticize the fundamental teachings of the Prophet (peace be on him) for there was no difference between the teachings of the previous Prophets and that of the Arabian Prophet on matters which constitute the core of religion. They, therefore, raised objections about the details of the religious law. The first objection was that the Prophet (peace be on him) had declared lawful a number of things which had been reckoned as unlawful since the time of the ancient Prophets. What is said here is to refute that objection. The Jews also raised the objection that the direction of Prayer had been changed from Jerusalem to the Kaʿbah. The verses that follow address this objection.

24. Here it is stressed that there are several Clear Signs which prove that the Makkan sanctuary enjoys God's blessing and has been chosen by Him as His sanctuary. Even though it is located in the middle of wide expanses of desert God has seen to it that its inhabitants enjoy a satisfactory living. Although the rest of Arabia was plunged into chaos and disorder for about two and a half thousand years, peace and tranquillity reigned in both the precincts

it becomes secure. Pilgrimage to the House is a duty owed to Allah by all who can make their way to it. As for those who refuse to follow His command, surely Allah stands in need of no one in the whole universe.

[98] Say: "People of the Book! Why do you reject the Signs of Allah when Allah is witness to all that you do?" [99] Say: "People of the Book! Why do you hinder believers from the Way of Allah, seeking that they follow a crooked way, even though you yourselves are witness to its being the Right Way?" Allah is not heedless of what you do.

[100] Believers! Were you to obey a party of those who were given the Book, they might cause you to renounce the Truth after you have attained to faith. [101] How can you disbelieve when you are the ones to whom the Signs of Allah are recited and when His Messenger is in your midst? Whoever holds fast to Allah will certainly be guided to the Straight Way.

[102] Believers! Fear Allah as He should be feared, and see that you do not die save in submission to Allah.

---

and environs of the Ka ʿbah. Thanks to the Ka ʿbah the entire Arabian peninsula enjoyed four months of peace and order every year. These were the sacred months when people went on Pilgrimage. Moreover, barely a half century before the revelation of these verses, people had seen how Abrahah, the Abyssinian invader, fell prey to God's scourge when he attacked Makkah to destroy the Ka ʿbah. At the time when the Qur ʾān was revealed, this incident was known to everybody in Arabia. Its memory was fresh and many eye-witnesses were still alive at the time of the Prophet (peace be on him).

[103] Hold fast together to the cable of Allah,[25] and be not divided. Remember the blessing that Allah bestowed upon you: you were once enemies, then He brought your hearts together, so that through His blessing you became brothers. You stood on the brink of a pit of fire and He delivered you from it. Thus Allah makes His Signs clear to you that you may be guided to the Right Way.

[104] And from amongst you there must be a party who will call people to all that is good and will enjoin the doing of all that is right and will forbid the doing of all that is wrong. It is they who will attain true success. [105] Do not be like those who fell into factions and became opposed to one another after Clear Signs had come to them. A mighty chastisement awaits them [106] on the Day when some faces will turn bright and other faces will turn dark. Those whose faces have turned dark will be told: "Did you fall into unbelief after you had been blessed with belief? Taste, then, chastisement for your unbelief." [107] And those whose faces have turned bright, they will be in the mercy of Allah, and therein they shall abide. [108] These are the messages of Allah which We recite to you in all truth, and Allah desires no wrong to the people of the world. [109] To Allah belongs all that is in the heavens and the earth, and to Allah are all matters referred for decision.

[110] You are now the best nation brought forth for mankind. You enjoin what is right and forbid what is

---

25. The expression "cable of Allah" in the verse refers to the "religion of God". The reason for use of the word "cable" (*ḥabl*) is that it both establishes a bond between man and God and joins all believers together.

wrong and believe in Allah. Had the People of the Book[26] believed, it were better for them. Some of them are believers but most of them are transgressors. [111] They will not be able to harm you except for a little hurt, and if they fight against you they will turn their backs (in flight), and then they will not be succoured. [112] Wherever they were, they were covered with ignominy, except when they were protected by either a covenant with Allah or a covenant with men.[27] They are laden with the burden of Allah's wrath, and humiliation has been pitched upon them; all this because they rejected the Signs of Allah and slew the Prophets without right, and because they wantonly disobeyed and used to transgress.

[113] Yet all are not alike among the People of the Book: there are upright people who recite the messages of Allah in the watches of the night and prostrate themselves in worship. [114] They believe in Allah and in the Last Day and enjoin what is right and forbid what is wrong, and hasten to excel each other in doing good. These are among the righteous. [115] Whatever good they do shall not go unappreciated. Allah fully knows those who are pious. [116] As for those who denied the

---

26. "People of the Book" refers here to the Children of Israel.

27. If the Jews have ever enjoyed any measure of peace and security anywhere in the world they owe it to the goodwill and benevolence of others rather than to their own power and strength. At times Muslim governments granted them havens of refuge while at others non-Muslim powers extended protection. Similarly, if the Jews ever emerged as a power it was due not to their intrinsic strength but to the strength of others. Similar is the status of the present-day Jewish state called Israel which came into being with the active support of the U.S.A., Britain and U.S.S.R.

Truth, neither their possessions nor their children will avail them against Allah. They are the people of the Fire, and therein they shall abide. [117] The example of what they spend in the life of this world is like that of a wind accompanied with frost which smote the harvest of a people who wronged themselves, and laid it to waste. It is not Allah Who wronged them; rather, it is they who wronged themselves.

[118] Believers! Do not take for intimate friends those who are not of your kind. They spare nothing to ruin you; indeed they long for you to suffer. Their hatred is clearly manifest in what they say, and what their breasts conceal is even greater. Now We have made Our messages clear to you; if only you can understand (the danger of their intimacy)! [119] Lo! It is you who love them but they do not love you even though you believe in the scriptures. When they meet you they say: "We believe," but when they are by themselves they bite their fingers in rage at you. Say: "Perish in your rage." Allah knows even what lies hidden in their breasts. [120] If anything good happens to you, they are grieved; if any misfortune befalls you, they rejoice. Yet if you remain steadfast and mindful of Allah their designs will not cause you any harm. Allah surely encompasses all that they do.

[121] (O Messenger, remind the Muslims of the occasion) when you went forth from your home at early dawn (to the battlefield of Uḥud) and placed the believers in battle arrays. Allah is All-Hearing, All-Knowing.

[122] And recall when two groups from among you were inclined to flag although Allah was their Protector;

it is in Allah that the believers should put their trust. [123] For sure Allah helped you at Badr when you were utterly weak. Beware, then, of Allah; perhaps you will be thankful.

[124] And recall when you said to the believers: "Will it not suffice you that your Lord will aid you by sending down three thousand angels?" [125] If you are steadfast and mindful of God, even though the enemy should suddenly fall upon you, your Lord will help you with five thousand marked angels. [126] Allah has reminded you of this only as a glad tiding to you and to let your hearts be at rest. Help can only come from Allah, the All-Mighty, the All-Wise. [127] (Allah provided this aid to you) in order that He may cut asunder a part of those who disbelieved or frustrate them so that they retreat in utter disappointment.

[128] (O Messenger), you have no part of the authority to decide whether He will accept their repentance or chastise them, for they surely are wrong-doers. [129] Whatever is in the heavens and the earth belongs to Allah. He forgives whom He wills, and chastises whom He wills. Allah is indeed All-Forgiving, Most Compassionate.[28]

[130] Believers! Do not devour interest, doubled and redoubled, and be mindful of Allah so that you may attain true success, [131] and do have fear of the Fire

---

28. When the Prophet was injured in the Battle of Uḥud he uttered words of imprecation against the unbelievers: "How can a people that injures its own Prophet attain salvation?" These verses are in response to that utterance.

Al 'Imrān 3: 132–40

Allah and the Messenger, that mercy be shown to you.
[133] And hasten to the forgiveness of your Lord and to
a Paradise as vast as the heavens and the earth, prepared
for the God-fearing [134] who spend in the way of Allah
both in affluence and hardship, who restrain their anger,
and forgive others. Allah loves such good-doers. [135]
These are the ones who, when they commit any indecency
or wrong themselves, instantly remember Allah and
implore forgiveness for their sins – for who will forgive
sins save Allah? – and do not wilfully persist in the wrong
they had committed. [136] They shall be recompensed
by forgiveness from their Lord and by Gardens beneath
which rivers flow; there they shall abide. How good is the
reward of those who earnestly labour! [137] Many eras
have passed before you. Go about, then, in the land and
behold the end of those who rejected (the directives and
commands of Allah), calling them lies. [138] This is a plain
exposition for mankind, and a guidance and admonition
for the God-fearing.

[139] Do not, then, lose heart or grieve: for you shall surely
gain the upper hand if you are believers. [140] If you
have suffered a wound the people opposed to you have
suffered a similar wound.[29] These are vicissitudes of time
which We deal out in turn among people so that Allah
might mark out those who truly believe and select from

---

29. This alludes to the Battle of Badr. The purpose is to point out
to the Muslims that if the unbelievers were not demoralized by
the setback they suffered at Badr then the Muslims should not be
disheartened by the setback they suffered in the Battle of Uḥud.

[89]

among you those who really bear witness (to the Truth):[30] for Allah does not love the wrong-doers, [141] and He makes men go through trials in order that He might purge the believers and blot out those who deny the Truth. [142] Did you think that you would enter Paradise even though Allah has not yet seen who among you strove hard in His Way and remained steadfast? [143] You previously longed for death (in the way of Allah): now you have faced it, observing it with your own eyes.

[144] Muḥammad is no more than a Messenger, and Messengers have passed away before him. Then, if he were to die or be slain, will you turn about on your heels? Whoever turns about on his heels can in no way harm Allah. As for the grateful ones, Allah will soon reward them.

[145] It is not given to any soul to die except with the leave of Allah, and at an appointed time. He who desires his reward in this world, We shall grant him the reward of this world; and he who desires the reward of the Other World, We shall grant him the reward of the Other World. And soon shall We reward those that are grateful.

---

30. The actual words of this verse, *wa yattakhidha minkum shuhadā'* can be interpreted in two ways. One meaning could be that God wanted to select some of them so that He could bestow upon them the honour of martyrdom. The second meaning could be that out of the hotchpotch of true believers and hypocrites of which their community was comprised at that moment, God wanted to sift those who were truly His witnesses over all mankind, i.e. those who were capable of fulfilling the responsibility of carrying out the mission assigned to them.

[146] Many were the Prophets on whose side fought a large number of people devoted to God: they neither lost heart for all they had to suffer in the Way of Allah nor did they weaken nor did they abase themselves. Allah loves such steadfast ones. [147] And all they said was this: "Our Lord! Forgive us our sins, and our excesses in our affairs, and set our feet firm, and succour us against those who deny the Truth." [148] Thereupon Allah granted them the reward of this world as well as a better reward of the World to Come. Allah loves those who do good.

[149] Believers! If you follow those who deny the Truth, they will drive you back on your heels; and you will turn about, losers. [150] But Allah is your Protector, and He is the Best of helpers. [151] We will cast terror into the hearts of those who have denied the Truth since they have associated others with Allah in His Divinity, for which He has sent down no sanction. The Fire is their abode; how bad the resting place of the wrong-doers will be!

[152] Allah surely fulfilled His promise (of succour) when you were slaying them by His leave until the moment when you flagged and quarrelled among yourselves about the matter, and disobeyed (the Prophet) after He showed you what you intensely desire; for some of you sought this world and some of you sought the Next. Thereupon, in order to put you to a test He turned you away from your foes. Still He pardoned you after that for Allah is Bounteous to those who believe.

[153] Recall when you were fleeing without casting even a side glance at anyone, and the Messenger was calling

out to you from the rear.[31] Then Allah requited you by inflicting grief after grief upon you so as to instruct you neither to grieve for the losses you might suffer or for the afflictions that might befall you. Allah knows all that you do.

[154] Then, after inflicting this grief, He sent down an inner peace upon you, a sleep which overtook some of you.[32] Those who were concerned merely about themselves, entertaining false notions about Allah – the notions of the Age of Ignorance – asked: "Have we any say in the matter?" Tell them: "Truly, all power of decision rests solely with Allah." Indeed, they conceal in their hearts what they would not reveal to you, saying: "If we had any power of decision, we would not have been slain here." Say: "Even if you had been in your houses, those for whom slaying had been appointed would have gone forth to the places where they were to be slain." All this happened so that Allah might test the thoughts you entertained in your hearts and purge your hearts of all impurities. Allah knows well what is in the breasts of men.

---

31. When subjected to a sudden two-pronged attack, the Muslims scattered; some fled to Madīnah while others climbed Mount Uḥud. Despite this, the Prophet (peace be on him) did not budge from his position. The enemy surrounded him on all sides and only a small party of ten to twelve followers was left with him. Even at that critical moment his feet remained firm and he continued to summon his fleeing followers towards himself.

32. A strange phenomenon was experienced at the time by some Muslim soldiers. Abū Ṭalḥah, who took part in the battle, states that the Muslims were seized by such drowsiness that their swords began to slip from their hands.

[155] Surely those of them who turned their backs on the day when the two armies met did so because Satan made them slip because of some of their lapses. But Allah has pardoned them; He is All-Forgiving, All-Forbearing.

[156] Believers, do not be like those who disbelieved and said to their brethren (who met some suffering) in the course of journey or fighting: "Had they remained with us, they would not have died nor been slain." Allah makes such thoughts the cause of deep regrets in their hearts. For in truth it is Allah alone Who grants life and deals death. Allah sees all that you do. [157] If you were to be slain or to die in the Way of Allah, then surely Allah's forgiveness and mercy are better than all the goods that people amass. [158] Were you to die or be slain, it is to Allah that all of you will be mustered.

[159] (O Prophet), it was thanks to Allah's mercy that you were gentle to them. Had you been rough, hard-hearted, they would surely have scattered away from you. So pardon them, and pray for their forgiveness, and take counsel from them in matters of importance. And when you are resolved on a course of action put your trust in Allah. Surely Allah loves those who put their trust (in Him). [160] If Allah helps you, none shall prevail over you, and if He forsakes you, then who can help you? It is in Allah that the believers should put all their trust.

[161] It is not for a Prophet to defraud; and whoever defrauds shall bring with him the fruits of his fraud on the Day of Resurrection, when every human being shall be paid in full what he has earned, and shall not be wronged.

[162] Is he who follows the good pleasure of Allah like him who is laden with Allah's wrath and whose abode is Hell? How evil that is for a resting place! [163] They vary greatly in rank in the sight of Allah, and Allah sees what they do. [164] Surely Allah conferred a great favour on the believers when He raised from among them a Messenger to recite to them His Signs, and to purify them, and to teach them the Book and Wisdom. For before that they were in manifest error.

[165] And how come when a calamity befell you, even though the enemy had suffered at your hands (in the Battle of Badr) twice what you have suffered, you began to ask: "How has this come about?" Say: "This calamity has been brought about by yourselves. Surely Allah has power over everything." [166] What befell you on the day when the two hosts met was by the leave of Allah, and in order that He might mark out those who believe [167] from those who are hypocrites. And when these hypocrites were asked: "Come and fight in the Way of Allah," or (at least) "defend yourselves," they answered: "If we but knew that there would be fighting, we would certainly have followed." They were then nearer to infidelity than to faith. They utter from their mouths what is not in their hearts. Allah knows well what they conceal. [168] These are the ones who stayed away, saying about their brothers: "Had they followed us, they would not have been slain." Say: "If you speak the truth then avert death when it comes to you."

[169] Think not of those slain in the Way of Allah as dead. Indeed they are living, and with their Lord they have their sustenance, [170] rejoicing in what Allah has bestowed upon them out of His bounty, jubilant that neither fear nor grief shall come upon the believers who have been left behind in the world and have not yet joined them. [171] They rejoice at the favours and bounties of Allah, and at the awareness that Allah will not cause the reward of the believers to be lost. [172] There were those who responded to the call of Allah and the Messenger after injury had smitten them.³³ There is mighty reward for all those who do good and fear Allah. [173] When people said to them: "Behold, a host has gathered around you and you should fear them," it only increased their faith and they answered: "Allah is Sufficient for us; and what an excellent Guardian He is!" [174] So they returned with a mighty favour and a great bounty from Allah having

---

33. When, after the Battle of Uḥud, the Makkan polytheists had travelled several stages of their journey, they began to say among themselves what a mistake they had made in allowing the opportunity to crush the power of Muḥammad to slip out of their hands. At one place they halted and deliberated among themselves about launching a second attack on Madīnah. They failed, however, to muster sufficient courage and carried on to Makkah. The Prophet (peace be on him), for his part, also realized that the Makkans might attack once again. The second day after the Battle of Uḥud, therefore, he gathered the Muslims and urged them to pursue the unbelievers. Even though this was a highly critical moment, those who were truly faithful girded their loins and were prepared to lay down their lives at the behest of the Prophet (peace be on him). They accompanied him to Ḥamrā' al-Asad, eight miles from Madīnah. The present verse refers to those dedicated men.

suffered no harm. They followed the good pleasure of Allah, and Allah is the Lord of great bounty.[34] [175] It was Satan who urged you to have fear of his allies. But do not fear them; fear Me, if you truly believe.

[176] Let not those who run towards unbelief grieve you; they shall not hurt Allah in the least. Allah will not provide for them any share in the Next Life. A mighty chastisement awaits them. [177] Indeed those who have purchased unbelief in exchange for faith shall not hurt Allah in the least. Theirs shall be a painful chastisement. [178] Let not the unbelievers imagine that the respite We grant them is good for them. We grant them respite so that they may grow in wickedness. A humiliating chastisement awaits them.

---

34. While returning from the Battle of Uḥud, Abū Sufyān challenged the Muslims to another encounter at Badr the following year. But when the appointed time arrived, Abū Sufyān's courage failed him on account of the famine prevailing in Makkah that year. As a face-saving device he arranged to send an agent to Madīnah who spread the rumour that tremendous war preparations were afoot among the Quraysh, and that they were trying to muster a huge army which would be too powerful to be resisted by any power in the whole of Arabia. The effect of this measure was such that when the Prophet (peace be on him) urged the Muslims to accompany him to Badr the initial response was not encouraging. Finally, the Prophet (peace be on him) publicly announced that if no one would accompany him, he would go alone. In response, fifteen hundred devotees expressed their willingness and accompanied him to Badr. As for the camp of unbelievers, Abū Sufyān did not turn up to give battle. The Prophet (peace be on him) and his Companions stayed at Badr for eight days awaiting the promised encounter. Meanwhile, they conducted business with a trade caravan which yielded them considerable profit.

[179] Allah will not let the believers stay in the state they are: He will set the wicked apart from the good. Allah is not going to disclose to you what is hidden in the realm beyond the reach of perception[35] but He chooses from among His Messengers whom He wills (to intimate such knowledge). So believe in Allah and in His Messengers; and if you believe and become God-fearing, yours will be a great reward.

[180] Those who are niggardly about what Allah has granted them out of His bounty think that niggardliness is good for them; rather, it is bad for them. What they were niggardly about will turn into a halter round their necks on the Day of Resurrection. To Allah belongs the inheritance of the heavens and the earth. Allah is well aware of what you do.

[181] Allah has heard the saying of those who said: "Allah is poor, and we are rich."[36] We shall record what they have said, and the fact of their slaying the Prophets unjustly, and we shall say to them: "Taste now the torment of the Fire. [182] That is in recompense for your own deeds." Allah does no wrong to His servants.

---

35. This means that God does not resort to revelation to provide information regarding specific persons whether they are true men of faith or hypocrites.

36. This statement was made by the Jews. When the Qurʾānic verse (*al-Baqarah* 2: 245): "Who of you will lend Allah a goodly loan?" was revealed, the Jews began to make fun of it, saying: "Look, God has now gone bankrupt and has begun to beg of His creatures for loans."

[183] To those who say: "Allah has directed us that we accept none as Messenger until he makes an offering that the fire will consume," say: "Other Messengers came to you before me with Clear Signs, and with the sign you have mentioned. So why did you slay them, if what you say is true?" [184] Now, if they give the lie to you, then other Messengers who came with Clear Signs and scriptures and the illuminating Book were also given the lie to before you. [185] Everyone is bound to taste death and you shall receive your full reward on the Day of Resurrection. Then, whoever is spared the Fire and is admitted to Paradise has indeed been successful. The life of this world is merely an illusory enjoyment.

[186] (Believers), you will certainly be put to test in regard to your properties and lives, and you will certainly hear many hurtful things from those who were granted the Book before you, and from those who have associated others with Allah in His Divinity. If you remain patient and God-fearing this indeed is a matter of great resolution. [187] Recall when Allah took a covenant from those who were given the Book: "You shall explain it to people and not hide it." Then they cast the Book behind their backs and sold it away for a trivial gain. Evil indeed is their bargain. [188] Do not think that those who exult in their misdeeds and love to be praised for what indeed they have not done, do not (even) think that they are secure from chastisement. A painful chastisement awaits them. [189] To Allah belongs the dominion of the heavens and the earth; and Allah is All-Powerful.

[190] Surely in the creation of the heavens and the earth, and in the alternation of night and day, there are Signs for people of understanding [191] – those who remember Allah while standing, sitting or (reclining) on their backs, and reflect in the creation of the heavens and the earth, (saying): "Our Lord! You have not created this in vain. Glory to You! Save us, then, from the chastisement of the Fire. [192] Our Lord! Whomsoever You cause to enter the Fire, him You indeed bring to disgrace, and there will be none to succour the wrong-doers. [193] Our Lord! We indeed heard a crier calling to the faith, saying: "Believe in your Lord"; so we did believe. Our Lord! Forgive us our sins, and wipe out our evil deeds and make us die with the truly pious. [194] Our Lord! Fulfil what You promised to us through Your Messengers, and disgrace us not on the Day of Resurrection; indeed You never go back on Your promise."

[195] Their Lord answered the prayer thus: "I will not suffer the work of any of you, whether male or female, to go to waste; each of you is from the other. Those who emigrated and were driven out from their homesteads and were persecuted in My cause, and who fought and were slain, indeed I shall wipe out their evil deeds from them and shall certainly admit them to the Gardens beneath which rivers flow." This is their reward with their Lord; and with Allah lies the best reward.

[196] (O Messenger), do not let the strutting about of the unbelievers in the land deceive you. [197] This is but a trifling and fleeting enjoyment; then their destination is

Hell – what an evil resting place! [198] But those who fear their Lord: theirs shall be the Gardens beneath which rivers flow and therein they will live forever: a hospitality from Allah. And Allah's reward is best for the truly pious. [199] Among the People of the Book some believe in Allah and what has been revealed to you, and what has been revealed to them. They humble themselves before Allah, and do not sell Allah's revelations for a trivial gain. For such their reward lies with their Lord. Allah is swift in reckoning.

[200] Believers, be steadfast, and vie in steadfastness, stand firm in your faith, and hold Allah in fear that you may attain true success.

4

Al-Nisā' [Women]
Madīnan Period

In the name of Allah, the Most Merciful,
the Most Compassionate

[1] O people! Fear your Lord Who created you from a single being and out of it created its mate; and out of the two spread many men and women. Fear Allah in Whose name you plead for rights, and heed the ties of kinship. Surely, Allah is ever watchful over you.

[2] Give orphans their property, and do not exchange the bad for the good, and do not eat up their property by mixing it with your own. This surely is a mighty sin.

[3] If you fear that you might not treat the orphans justly, then marry the women that seem good to you: two, or three, or four.[1] If you fear that you will not be able to treat

---

1. It should be noted that making polygamy lawful was not the real purpose of this verse, for polygamy was already in vogue in Arabia and the Prophet (peace be on him) himself had more than one wife when this verse was revealed. The real object of its revelation was to help solve the problem of orphaned children of Muslim martyrs, for it tells the Muslims that if they cannot give the orphans their due rights they may marry women with orphaned children.

them justly, then marry (only) one,[2] or marry from among those whom your right hands possess.[3] This will make it more likely that you will avoid injustice.

[4] Give women their bridal-due in good cheer (considering it a duty); but if they willingly remit any part of it, consume it with good pleasure.

[5] Do not entrust your properties – which Allah has made a means of support for you – to the weak of

---

2. Muslim jurists are agreed that according to this verse the maximum number of wives has been fixed at four. This verse stipulates that marrying more wives than one is permissible on the condition that one treats one's wives equitably. A person who avails himself of this permission granted by God to have a plurality of wives, and disregards the condition laid down by God to treat them equitably, has not acted in good faith with God. In case there are complaints from wives that they are not being treated equitably, the Islamic state has the right to intervene and redress such grievances. Some people who have been overwhelmed and overawed by the Christianized outlook of Westerners have tried to prove that the real aim of the Qur'ān was to put an end to polygamy (which, in their opinion, is intrinsically evil). Such arguments only show the mental bondage to which these people have succumbed. That polygamy is an evil *per se* is an unacceptable proposition, for under certain conditions it becomes a moral and social necessity. For this reason the Qur'ān has allowed those who feel the need for it to resort to polygamy. The Qur'ān has expressed its permission of polygamy in quite categorical terms. Indeed, there is not the slightest hint in the Qur'ān that could justify the conclusion that it advocates abolition of polygamy.

3. This expression denotes "slave-girls," i.e. female captives of war who are distributed by the state among individuals when no exchange of prisoners of war takes place.

understanding, but maintain and clothe them out of it, and say to them a kind word of admonition.

[6] Test the orphans until they reach the age of marriage,[4] and then if you find them mature of mind hand over to them their property, and do not eat it up by either spending extravagantly or in haste, fearing that they would grow up (and claim it). If the guardian of the orphan is rich let him abstain entirely (from his ward's property); and if he is poor, let him partake of it in a fair measure.[5] When you hand over their property to them let there be witnesses on their behalf. Allah is sufficient to take account (of your deeds).

[7] Just as there is a share for men in what their parents and kinsfolk leave behind, so there is a share for women in what their parents and kinsfolk leave behind – be it little or much[6] – a share ordained (by Allah).

4. When such people approach their majority their mental development should be watched so as to determine to what extent they have become capable of managing their own affairs.

5. The guardian is entitled to remuneration for his services. The amount of this remuneration should be one that is deemed fair by neutral and reasonable people. Moreover, the guardian is directed that he should take a fixed and known amount by way of remuneration, that he should take it openly rather than secretly, and that he should keep an account of it.

6. This verse embodies five legal injunctions. First, that women as well as men are entitled to inheritance. Second, that inheritance, however meagre it might be, should be distributed.

[8] And if other near of kin, orphans and needy are present at the time of division of inheritance give them something of it and speak to them kindly.

[9] And those who would have been fearful on account of their helpless offspring they may have behind them, let them fear Allah and say what is right. [10] Behold, those who wrongfully devour the properties of orphans only fill their bellies with fire. Soon they will burn in the Blazing Flame.

[11] Thus does Allah command you concerning your children: the share of the male is like that of two females.[7] If (the heirs of the deceased are) more than two daughters, they shall have two-thirds of the inheritance;[8] and if there is only one daughter, then she shall have half the inheritance. If the deceased has any offspring, each of his

---

Third, that the law of inheritance is applicable to all kinds of property – movable and immovable, agricultural, industrial and so on. Fourth, that the right of inheritance comes into force only after a person dies leaving some property behind him, but not while he is alive. Fifth, it implies the rule that immediate blood-relatives exclude those that are further removed. This law has been further explained in vv. 11 and 33 below.

7. Since Islamic law imposes greater financial obligations on men in respect of family life and relieves women of a number of such obligations, justice demands that a woman's share in inheritance should be less than that of a man.

8. The same applies in the case where there are two daughters. If the deceased leaves behind only daughters, and if there are two or more daughters, then they will receive two-thirds of the inheritance and the remaining one-third will go to the other heirs. But if the deceased has only one son there is consensus

parents shall have a sixth of the inheritance;[9] and if the deceased has no child and his parents alone inherit him, then one-third shall go to his mother;[10] and if the deceased has brothers and sisters, then one-sixth shall go to his mother.[11] All these shares are to be given after payment of the bequest he might have made or any debts outstanding against him.[12] You do not know which of them, your parents or your children, are more beneficial to you. But these portions have been determined by Allah, for He indeed knows everything, is cognizant of all beneficent considerations.

---

among jurists that in the absence of other heirs he is entitled to all the property; but if the deceased has other heirs, he is entitled to the property left after their shares have been distributed.

9. If the deceased leaves any issue each of his parents will receive one-sixth of the inheritance irrespective of whether the issue consists either only of daughters, only of sons or of both sons and daughters, or just one son or just one daughter. The remaining two-thirds will be distributed among the rest of the heirs.

10. If there are no other heirs than the parents, the remaining two-thirds will go to the share of the father; otherwise two-thirds will be distributed between the father and other heirs.

11. In the case where the deceased also has brothers and sisters the share of the mother will be one-sixth rather than one-third. In this case, the sixth that was deducted from the share of the mother will be added to that of the father, for in this circumstance the father's obligations are heavier. It should be noted that if the parents of the deceased are alive, the brothers and sisters will not be entitled to any share in the inheritance.

12. The mention of bequest precedes the mention of debt, but there is consensus among Muslims that the payment of debt takes precedence over the payment of bequest, i.e. if

[12] And to you belongs half of whatever has been left behind by your wives if they die childless; but if they have any children then to you belongs a fourth of what they have left behind, after payment of the bequest they might have made or any debts outstanding against them. And to them belongs a fourth of what you leave behind, if you die childless; and if you have any child then to them belongs one eighth[13] of what you have left behind, after the payment of the bequest you might have made or any debts outstanding against you. And if the man or woman (whose inheritance is to be distributed) has no heir in the direct line, but has a brother or sister, then each of these shall inherit one-sixth; but if their number is more than that then all of them shall be entitled to one-third of the inheritance,[14] after the payment of the bequest that might have been made or any debts outstanding against the deceased, providing that the bequest causes no injury.[15] This is a commandment from Allah; Allah is All-Knowing, All-Forbearing.

[13] These are the bounds set by Allah. Allah will make him who obeys Allah and His Messenger enter the

---

the deceased owes a debt and also leaves a bequest, the debt will first be paid out of the inheritance, and only then will his bequest be honoured.

13. Whether a man has one wife or several wives the share of the wife/wives is one-eighth of the inheritance when the deceased has any issue, and one-fourth when he has no issue. The share of the wives, whether one-fourth or one-eighth, will be distributed equally among them.

14. Qur'ānic commentators are agreed that the sisters and brothers mentioned here mean half-brothers and half-sisters,

Gardens beneath which rivers flow. He will abide there for ever. That is the mighty triumph. [14] And he who disobeys Allah and His Messenger and transgresses the bounds set by Him – him shall Allah cause to enter the Fire. There he will abide. A humiliating chastisement awaits him.

[15] As for those of your women who are guilty of immoral conduct, call upon four from among you to bear witness against them. And if four men do bear witness, confine those women to their houses until either death takes them away or Allah opens some way for them. [16] Punish both of those among you who are guilty of this sin, then if they repent and mend their ways, leave them alone. For Allah is ever ready to accept repentance, is All-Compassionate.[16]

[17] (And remember that) Allah's acceptance of repentance is only for those who commit evil out of ignorance and

---

i.e. those who have kinship with the deceased on the mother's side. Injunctions affecting full brothers and sisters, and half-brothers and half-sisters on the father's side are mentioned towards the end of the present *sūrah*. (See verse 176 below. Ed.)

15. Bequests which cause injury are those that entail depriving the deserving kins of their legitimate rights. Similarly, the debt which causes injury is the fake debt which one falsely admits to owing, or any other device to which one resorts merely to deprive the rightful heirs of their shares in inheritance.

16. In these two verses (15-16) the first, preliminary directives regarding punishment of unlawful sexual intercourse are stated. Later, another injunction was revealed (see *Sūrah al-Nūr* 24: 2) which laid down that both the male and female involved in this act should be given a hundred lashes.

then soon repent. It is towards such persons that Allah turns graciously. Allah is All-Knowing, All-Wise. [18] But of no avail is the repentance of those who do evil until death approaches any of them and then he says: "Now I repent." Nor is the repentance of those who die in the state of unbelief of any avail to them. For them We have kept in readiness a painful chastisement.

[19] Believers! It is not lawful for you to become heirs to women against their will.[17] It is not lawful that you should put constraint upon them so that you may take away anything of what you have given them; (you may not put constraint upon them)[18] unless they are guilty of brazenly immoral conduct. Live with your wives gracefully. If you dislike them in any manner, it may be that you dislike something in which Allah has placed much good for you. [20] And if you decide to dispense with a wife in order to take another, do not take away anything of what you might have given the first one, even if you had given her a heap of gold. Would you take it back by slandering her and committing a manifest wrong? [21] How can you take it away after each one has enjoyed the other, and they have taken a firm covenant from you?

---

17. This means that the relatives of the husband should not treat the widow of the deceased as if she were a part of the inheritance and begin imposing their will on her. Upon the death of her husband a woman becomes independent. As soon as her legally-prescribed period of waiting ends, she is free to go wherever she likes and to marry anyone she wishes to.

18. This injunction is not meant to provide people with an excuse to grab the property of their wives; instead, the purpose is to enable them to put constraint upon them if they are guilty of brazenly immoral conduct.

[22] Do not marry the women whom your fathers married, although what is past is past.[19] This indeed was a shameful deed, a hateful thing, and an evil way.[20]

[23] Forbidden to you are your mothers,[21] your daughters,[22] your sisters,[23] your father's sisters and your mother's sisters, your brother's daughters and your sister's daughters,[24] your milk-mothers, your milk-sisters,[25] the

---

19. It does not mean that if a man had married his step-mother during the days of Ignorance he can maintain the matrimonial relationship with her even after the revelation of this prohibitory injunction. What it rather means is that the children born of such previously contracted marriage will not be considered illegitimate after the promulgation of this injunction and will not be disinherited.

20. In Islamic law marrying women who fall in the prohibited degrees of marriage is a recognized criminal offence.

21. The word "mother" applies to one's step-mother as well as to one's real mother. Hence the prohibition extends to both. This injunction also includes prohibition of the grandmother, both paternal and maternal.

22. The injunction with regard to daughters also applies to grand-daughters on both the paternal and maternal sides.

23. This applies to full sisters as well as to half-sisters.

24. In all these relationships, no distinction is made between the full and step-relationships.

25. There is consensus among Muslims that if a boy or girl is breast-fed by a woman, that woman attains the status of mother, and her husband the status of father. It is forbidden to marry relatives through milk-feeding in the same way as marriage is forbidden with relatives through one's real mother and real father. Not only is the foster mother's child, who has taken suck along with the

mothers of your wives, and the stepdaughters – who are your foster-children,[26] born of your wives with whom you have consummated the marriage; but if you have not consummated the marriage with them, there will be no blame upon you (if you marry their daughters). It is also forbidden for you to take the wives of the sons who have sprung from your loins[27] and to take two sisters together in marriage,[28] although what is past is past. Surely Allah is All-Forgiving, All-Compassionate.[29] [24] Also forbidden to you are all married women (*muḥsanāt*) except those women whom your right hands have come to possess

foster child, forbidden for him but all the children of the foster mother are just like real brothers and sisters and their children are for him just like his real nephews.

26. This prohibitive restriction in regard to such girls is not based on the consideration of their having been brought up in the house of a step-father. The jurists are almost unanimous that it is prohibited to marry one's step-daughter irrespective of whether or not she has been raised in the step-father's house.

27. Like the wife of one's own son, the wives of grandsons – both paternal and maternal – are prohibited to grandfathers on both the mother's and father's side.

28. The Prophet (peace be on him) has taught that it is prohibited for a man to combine in marriage an aunt – whether maternal or paternal – with her niece. The guiding principle is that it is prohibited to have as wives two women who, if one of them were a male, would be prohibited to each other.

29. This is an assurance that God would not call them to task for such misdeeds of the *Jāhilīyah* period as combining two sisters in matrimony. For this reason if a man has two sisters as his wives, he is required to divorce one of them when he embraces Islam.

(as a result of war).[30] This is Allah's decree and it is binding upon you. But it is lawful for you to seek out all women except these, offering them your wealth and the protection of wedlock rather than using them for the unfettered satisfaction of lust. And give bridal-due of those whom you have enjoyed in wedlock as an obligation. But there is no blame on you if you mutually agree to alter the settlement after it has been made. Surely Allah is All-Knowing, All-Wise. [25] And those of you who cannot afford to marry free, believing women (*muḥṣanāt*), let them marry such believing women whom your right hands possess. Allah knows all about your faith. All of you belong to one another. Marry them, then, with the leave of their guardians, and give them their bridal-due in a fair manner that they may live in the protection of wedlock rather than be either mere objects of unfettered lust or given to secret love affairs. Then if they become guilty of immoral conduct after they have entered into wedlock, they shall be liable to half the penalty to which free women (*muḥṣanāt*) are liable.[31] This relaxation is

---

30. Women who come as captives of war, leaving their husbands behind in *Dār al-Ḥarb* (Domain of War), are not prohibited, for their marriage is nullified by virtue of their entry into *Dār al-Islām* (Domain of Islam).

31. In verses 24-5, the term *muḥṣanāt* (protected women) is used in two different meanings. First, it is used in the sense of "married women", that is, those who enjoy the protection of their husbands. Second, it is used in the sense of "women belonging to families", i.e. those who enjoy the protection of their families even though they may not be married. In the verse under discussion, the word *muḥṣanāt* is used in the latter sense, i.e. in the sense of women who enjoy the protection of their families as opposed to slave-girls.

for those of you who fear falling into sin by remaining unmarried. But if you persevere, it is better for you. Allah is All-Forgiving, All-Compassionate.

[26] Allah wants to make all this clear to you, and to guide you to the ways which the righteous have followed in the past; He will graciously turn towards you. Allah is All-Knowing, All-Wise. [27] Allah indeed wants to turn graciously towards you; but those who follow their lusts would want you to drift far away from the Right Way. [28] Allah wants to lighten your burdens, for man was created weak.

[29] Believers! Do not devour one another's possessions wrongfully; rather, let there be trading by mutual consent;³² and do not kill yourselves.³³ Surely Allah is ever Compassionate to you. [30] And whoever does this by way of transgression and injustice We shall surely

---

At the same time, the word is also used in the first meaning when slave-girls have acquired the protection accorded by the contract of marriage (*fa idhā uḥṣinna*). In that case they will be liable to the punishment laid down in this verse if they are guilty of unlawful sexual intercourse.

32. The expression "wrongfully" embraces all transactions which are opposed to righteousness and which are either legally or morally reprehensible. "Mutual consent" means that the exchange should be free of undue pressure, fraud and deception.

33. This can be considered either as complementary to the preceding statement or as an independent statement. If it is complementary, it means that to consume the property of others by wrongful means is tantamount to courting one's destruction. Taken as an independent statement, it would mean either that one should not kill others or that one should not kill oneself.

cast him into the Fire; that indeed is quite easy for Allah. [31] But if you avoid the major sins which you have been forbidden, We shall remit your (trivial) offences, and cause you to enter an honourable abode.

[32] Do not covet what Allah has conferred more abundantly on some of you than others. Men shall have a share according to what they have earned, and women shall have a share according to what they have earned. Do ask Allah for His bounty. Allah has full knowledge of everything.

[33] To everyone We have appointed rightful heirs to inherit whatever the parents and near of kin might leave behind. As to those with whom you have made a solemn covenant, give them their share. Allah watches over all things.³⁴

[34] Men are the protectors and maintainers of women³⁵ because Allah has made one of them excel over the other, and because they spend out of their possessions (to

---

34. According to the customary law of Arabia, those who concluded compacts of alliance and friendship also became mutual heirs. Likewise, an adopted son inherited from his foster-father. While abrogating this customary law, this verse reveals that inheritance goes to one's kin according to the rules for the distribution of inheritance laid down by God Himself. However, if a man has made commitments to people, he has the right to give away to them whatever he wishes during his lifetime.

35. A *qawwām* or *qayyim* is a person responsible for administering and supervising the affairs of either a person, or an organization or a system; responsible for protecting and safeguarding them and providing for the needs of those under his supervision.

support them). Thus righteous women are obedient and guard the rights of men in their absence under Allah's protection. As for women of whom you fear rebellion, admonish them, and remain apart from them in beds, and beat them.[36] Then if they obey you, do not seek ways to harm them. Allah is the Exalted, the Great. [35] If you fear a breach between the two, appoint an arbitrator from his people and an arbitrator from her people. If they both want to set things right,[37] Allah will bring about reconciliation between them. Allah is All-Knowing, All-Aware.

[36] Serve Allah and ascribe no partner to Him. Do good to your parents, to near of kin, to orphans, and to the needy, and to the neighbour who is of kin and to the neighbour

---

36. This does not mean that a man should resort to these three measures all at once, but that they may be employed if a wife adopts an attitude of obstinate defiance. So far as the actual application of these measures is concerned, there should naturally be some correspondence between the fault and the punishment that is administered. Moreover, it is obvious that wherever a light measure can prove effective one should not resort to stern measures. Whenever the Prophet (peace be on him) permitted a man to administer corporal punishment to his wife, he did so with great reluctance, and continued to express his utter distaste for it.

37. The statement: "if they both want to set things right" may be interpreted as referring either to the mediators or to the spouses concerned. Every dispute can be resolved provided the parties concerned desire reconciliation, and the mediators too are keen to remove the misunderstandings between them and to bring them together.

who is a stranger, and to the companion by your side,[38] and to the wayfarer, and to those whom your right hands possess. Allah does not love the arrogant and the boastful, [37] who are niggardly and bid others to be niggardly and conceal the bounty which Allah has bestowed upon them. We have kept in readiness a humiliating chastisement for such deniers (of Allah's bounty). [38] Allah does not love those who spend out of their wealth to make a show of it to people when in fact they neither believe in Allah nor in the Last Day. And he who has taken Satan for a companion has indeed taken for himself a very bad companion. [39] What harm would have befallen them if they had believed in Allah and the Last Day, and spent on charity what Allah had bestowed upon them as sustenance? For Allah indeed has full knowledge of them. [40] Indeed Allah wrongs none, not even as much as an atom's weight. Whenever a man does good, He multiplies it two-fold, and bestows out of His grace a mighty reward. [41] Consider, then, when We shall bring forward witnesses from every community, and will bring you, (O Muḥammad), as a witness against them all. [42] Those who disbelieved and disobeyed the Messenger will wish on that Day that the

---

38. The expression *al-sāḥib bi al-janb* (the companion by your side) embraces those with whom one has friendly relations of an abiding nature as well as those with whom one's relationship is transient: for instance, either the person who walks beside one on the way to the market or who sits beside one while buying things from the same shop or one's fellow traveller. Even this temporary relationship imposes certain claims on every refined and decent person – that he should treat the latter, as far as possible, in a kind and gracious manner and avoid causing him any discomfort.

earth were levelled with them. They will not be able to conceal anything from Allah.

[43] Believers! Do not draw near to the Prayer while you are intoxicated[39] until you know what you are saying;[40] nor when you are defiled[41] – save when you are travelling – until you have washed yourselves.[42] If you are either ill or travelling or have satisfied a want of nature or have had contact with women[43] and can find no

---

39. This is the second in the chronological sequence of injunctions concerning intoxicants. We have already come across the first injunction in *Sūrah al-Baqarah* (2: 219).

40. What is required is that while praying one should at least be conscious enough to know what one is uttering in the Prayer.

41. The term *janābah* denotes the state of major ritual impurity, which results from the act of sexual intercourse or from seminal emission (ensuing either from sexual stimulation or from a wet dream).

42. A group of jurists and Qur'ānic commentators interprets this verse to mean that one should not enter a mosque in the state of major ritual impurity (*janābah*), unless it be out of necessity. Another group thinks that the reference here is to travel. In the opinion of this group, if a traveller is in the state of major ritual impurity he may resort to *tayammum* (i.e. symbolic ablution attained through wiping the hands and face with clean earth).

43. There is disagreement as to what is meant here by the verb *lāmastum*. Several jurists are of the opinion that it signifies sexual intercourse. Abū Ḥanīfah and his school follow this view. Contrary to this, some other jurists hold that it merely signifies the act of touching. This is the opinion adopted by Shāfi'ī. Mālik is of the opinion that if a man and a woman touch each other with sexual desire, their ablution is nullified. He sees nothing objectionable, however, in the mere act of a man touching a woman's body, or vice versa, provided the act is not motivated by sexual desire.

water, then betake yourselves to pure earth, passing with
it lightly over your face and your hands.⁴⁴ Surely Allah is
All-Relenting, All-Forgiving.

[44] Have you not seen those to whom a portion of the
Book was given? They purchased error for themselves,
and wish that you too lose the Right Way? [45] Allah
knows your enemies better and Allah suffices as a
Protector, and Allah suffices as a Helper. [46] Among those
who have become Jews there are some who alter the words
from their context,⁴⁵ and make a malicious play with their
tongues and seek to revile the True Faith. They say: "We
have heard and we disobey" (*samiʿnā wa ʿaṣaynā*).⁴⁶ "Do

---

44. The detailed rules of *tayammum* are as follows: A man who
either needs to perform ablution or take a bath to attain the state
of purity for ritual Prayer may resort to *tayammum* provided water
is not available to him. Permission to resort to *tayammum*, rather
than make ablution with water or take a bath, is also extended to
invalids whose health is likely to be harmed by the use of water.

45. This signifies three things. First, that they tampered with the
text of the Scripture. Second, that they misinterpreted the Scripture
and thereby distorted the meanings of the verses of the Book. Third,
that they came and stayed in the company of the Prophet (peace
be on him) and his Companions and listened to the conversations
which took place there, then went to other people and misreported
what they had heard.

46. When God's commands are announced to such people, they
loudly proclaim: "Yes, we heard" (*samiʿnā*), but then they whisper:
"And we disobeyed" (*wa ʿaṣaynā*). Or else they pronounce *aṭaʿnā*
("we obey") with such a twist of the tongue that it becomes
indistinguishable from *ʿaṣaynā*.

hear us, may you turn dumb" (*ismaʿ ghayr musmaʿin*),[47] and "Hearken to us" (*rāʿinā*).[48] It would indeed have been better for them and more upright if they had said, "We have heard and we obey" (*samiʿnā wa aṭʿanā*) and: "Do listen to us, and look at us (with kindness)" (*wa ismaʿ wa unẓurnā*). But Allah has cursed them because of their unbelief. Scarcely do they believe.

[47] O you who have been granted the Book! Do believe in what We have (now) revealed, which confirms the revelation which you already possess. Do this before We alter countenances, turning them backwards, or lay a curse upon them as We cursed the Sabbath men. Bear in mind that Allah's command is done. [48] Surely Allah does not forgive that a partner be ascribed to Him, although He forgives any other sins for whomever He wills. He who associates anyone with Allah in His Divinity has indeed forged a mighty lie and committed an awesome sin.

[49] Have you not seen those who boast of their righteousness, even though it is Allah Who grants righteousness to whomsoever He wills? They are not

---

47. Whenever they wanted to say something to the Prophet (peace be on him) they would say, *ismaʿ* (listen), but they added to this the expression, *ghayr musmaʿin* which had several meanings. It could either be a polite expression, meaning that he was worthy of such deep respect that one should say nothing to his dislike or it could have a malicious implication, meaning that he did not deserve to be addressed by anybody. It also meant the imprecation: "May God turn you deaf."

48. For an explanation of this see *Sūrah al-Baqarah* 2: 104, n. 36 above.

wronged even as much as the husk of a date-stone (if they are not granted righteousness). [50] See how they forge lies about Allah! This in itself is a manifest sin.

[51] Have you not seen those to whom a portion of the Book was given? They believe in baseless superstitions,[49] and *ṭāghūt*[50] (false deities), and say about the unbelievers that they are better guided than those who believe.[51] [52] Such are the ones whom Allah has cursed; and he whom Allah curses has none to come to his help. [53] Have they any share in the dominion (of Allah)? Had that been so, they would never have granted people even as much as the speck on a date-stone. [54] Do they envy others for the bounty that Allah has bestowed upon them? (Let them bear in mind that) We bestowed upon the house of Abraham the Book and Wisdom, and We bestowed upon them a mighty dominion, [55] whereupon some of them believed, and others turned away. (As for those who turn away), Hell suffices for a blaze.[52] [56] Surely We shall cast

---

49. *Jibt* signifies "a thing devoid of any true basis and bereft of all usefulness." In Islamic terminology the various forms of sorcery, divination and soothsaying, in short all superstitions, are termed *jibt*.

50. For explanation see *Sūrah al-Baqarah* 2: 256, nn. 89–90 above.

51. In this verse the word "unbelievers" means those people in Arabia who associated others with God in His Divinity.

52. This is in response to the malicious remarks of the Israelites. What is being said is that they had no justified reason to feel jealous since both the Israelites and Ishmaelites were offspring of the same Abraham. Now, the leadership of the world had been promised only to those children of Abraham who followed the Book and Wisdom revealed by God. The Book and Wisdom had been sent

those who reject Our Signs into the Fire; and as often as
their skins are burnt out, We shall give them other skins
in exchange that they may fully taste the chastisement.
Surely Allah is All-Mighty, All-Wise. [57] And those who
believe and do good deeds, We shall cause them to enter
the Gardens beneath which rivers flow. There they shall
abide forever. There they shall have spouses purified
and there We shall cause them to enter a shelter with
plenteous shade.

[58] Allah commands you to deliver trusts to those worthy
of them; and when you judge between people, judge with
justice.[53] Excellent is the admonition Allah gives you.
Allah is All-Hearing, All-Seeing.

---

down earlier to the Israelites, and to their discredit, they turned
away from them. The same Book and Wisdom had now been made
available to the Ishmaelites and they had decided to receive it with
faith and gratitude.

53. Here the Muslims are forewarned against the evils which had
afflicted the Israelites. One of the fundamental mistakes committed
by the Israelites was that in the time of their decadence they
had handed over positions of trust, (i.e. religious and political
leadership), to incompetent, mean, immoral, dishonest and corrupt
persons. The result was that corruption spread throughout the
nation. The Muslims are being directed to take heed of this, and to
entrust positions of responsibility only to those who are capable of
shouldering the burden of such positions. The major weakness of
the Israelites was that they had completely lost their sense of justice.
They pursued either personal or national interests at the cost of
honesty, equity, reasonableness and good faith. After informing the
Muslims of the iniquity of the Jews, God now warns them against
committing similar injustices. They should rather declare what is
right in the face of friend and foe alike, and judge between people
with justice and equity.

[59] Believers! Obey Allah and obey the Messenger, and those invested with authority among you; and then if you were to dispute among yourselves about anything refer it to Allah and the Messenger[54] if you indeed believe in Allah and the Last Day; that is better and more commendable in the end.

[60] (O Messenger), have you not seen those who claim to believe in the Book which has been revealed to you and in the Books revealed before you, and yet desire to submit their disputes to the judgement of *ṭāghūt* (the

---

54. This verse is the cornerstone of the entire religious, social and political structure of Islam and the very first clause of the constitution of an Islamic state. It lays down the following principles as permanent guidelines:

(1) In the Islamic order of life, God alone is the focus of loyalty and obedience. A Muslim is the servant of God before anything else.

(2) Another basic principle of the Islamic order of life is obedience to the Prophet (peace be on him).

(3) In the Islamic order of life the Muslims are further required to obey their fellow Muslims invested with authority (*ūlū al-amr*). These include all those entrusted with directing Muslims in matters of common concern. Hence, persons "invested with authority" include the intellectual and political leaders of the community, as well as administrative officials, judges of the courts, tribal chiefs and regional leaders.

(4) In an Islamic order the injunctions of God and the way of the Prophet (peace be on him) constitute the basic law and paramount authority in all matters. Whenever there is any dispute among Muslims or between the rulers and the ruled the matter should be referred to the Qur'ān and the *Sunnah* and all concerned should faithfully accept the judgement that is thus arrived at.

Satanic authorities who decide independently of the law of Allah), whereas they had been asked to reject it.[55] Satan seeks to make them drift far away from the Right Path. [61] When they are told: "Come to that which Allah has revealed, and come to the Messenger," you will notice the hypocrites turning away from you in aversion. [62] But what happens when some misfortune visits them because of their own misdeeds? Then they come to you swearing by Allah, saying: "We wanted nothing but to do good and to create harmony (between the two parties)." [63] As for them, Allah knows what is in their hearts. Leave them alone, admonish them, and say to them penetrating words about themselves. [64] (And tell them that) We never sent a Messenger but that he should be obeyed by the leave of Allah. If whenever they wronged themselves they had come to you praying to Allah for forgiveness, and had the Messenger prayed for their forgiveness, they would indeed have found Allah All-Forgiving, All-Compassionate. [65] But no, by your Lord, they cannot become true believers until they seek your arbitration in all matters on which they disagree among themselves, and then do not find the least vexation in their hearts over your judgement, and accept it in willing submission. [66] Had We enjoined upon them: "Slay yourselves," or "Leave your habitations," very few of them would have done it; yet if they had done as they were admonished, it would have been better for them and would have strengthened them; [67] whereupon We would indeed

---

55. *Ṭāghūt* clearly signifies here a sovereign who judges things according to criteria other than the Law of God. It also stands for a legal and judicial system which acknowledges neither the sovereignty of God nor the paramount authority of God's Book.

grant them from Us a mighty reward, and [68] guide them to a Straight Way. [69] He who obeys Allah and the Messenger – such shall be with those whom Allah has favoured – the Prophets, those steadfast in truthfulness, the martyrs, and the righteous.⁵⁶ How excellent will they be for companions! [70] That is a bounty from Allah, and Allah suffices to know the truth.

[71] Believers! Be ever prepared to encounter (the enemy); either advance in detachments or advance in one body (as the circumstance demands).⁵⁷ [72] Among you there is such who lags behind, then if some affliction strikes you, he says: "Indeed Allah bestowed His favour upon me that I was not present with them." [73] And if a bounty from Allah is given you, he says – and says as if there never was any affection between you and him – "Oh, would that I had been with them, I would have come by a great gain." [74] Let those who seek the life of the Next World in exchange for the life of this world fight in the Way of Allah. We shall grant a mighty reward to whoever fights in the way of Allah, whether he is slain or comes out victorious. [75] How is it that you do not fight in the way of Allah and in support of the helpless – men, women and children – who pray: "Our Lord, bring us out of this land whose people are oppressors and appoint

56. This means that in the Hereafter they will be in the company of those blessed people. It does not mean, however, that any of them can ever attain the office of a Prophet by virtue of his righteous deeds.

57. This discourse was revealed after the Battle of Uḥud when the tribes living around Madīnah had been greatly emboldened by the defeat of the Muslims.

for us from Yourself, a protector, and appoint for us from Yourself a helper"?[58] [76] Those who have faith fight in the Way of Allah, while those who disbelieve fight in the way of *ṭāghūt* (Satan). Fight, then, against the fellows of Satan. Surely Satan's strategy is weak.

[77] Have you not seen those who were told: "Restrain your hands, and establish the Prayer, and pay the *Zakāh*"? But when fighting was enjoined upon them some of them feared men as one should fear Allah, or even more, and said: "Our Lord, why have You ordained fighting for us? Why did You not grant us a little more respite?" Say to them: "There is little enjoyment in this world. The World to Come is much better for the God-fearing, and you shall not be wronged even to the extent of the husk of a date-stone."[59] [78] Wherever you might be, death will overtake you even though you be in massive towers. And when some good happens to them, they say: "This is from Allah"; whereas when some misfortune befalls them, they say: "This is because of you." Say: "All is from Allah." What has happened to these people that they seem to understand nothing? [79] Whatever good happens to you is from Allah; and whatever misfortune smites you is because of your own action. We have sent you to

---

58. This refers to those wronged and persecuted men, women and children of Makkah and of other tribes in Arabia who had embraced Islam but were unable either to emigrate or to protect themselves from the wrongs to which they were subjected. These helpless people suffered many kinds of persecution and prayed to God to deliver them from their miserable state.

59. Were they to serve God's religion and spend their energy in that cause, they would surely be rewarded by Him.

mankind, (O Muḥammad), as a Messenger, and Allah is sufficient as a witness. [80] He who obeys the Messenger thereby obeys Allah; as for he who turns away, We have not sent you as a keeper over them!

[81] They say (in your presence): "We obey," but when they leave your presence a party of them meets by night to plan against what you have said. Allah takes note of all their plots. So, let them alone, and put your trust in Allah. Allah is sufficient as a Guardian. [82] Do they not ponder about the Qur'ān? Had it been from any other than Allah, they would surely have found in it much inconsistency.[60]

[83] Whenever they come upon any news bearing upon either security or causing consternation they go about spreading it, whereas if they were to convey it to either the Messenger or to those from among them entrusted with authority, it would come to the knowledge of those who are competent to investigate it.[61] But for Allah's bounty and

---

60. The Qur'ān itself is a strong, persuasive testimony to its Divine origin. It is inconceivable that any human being should compose discourses on different subjects under different circumstances and on different occasions and the collection of those discourses should then grow into a coherent, homogeneous and integrated work, no component of which is discordant with the rest. It is also inconceivable that such a work would be permeated throughout with a uniform outlook and attitude, a work manifesting remarkable consistency in the mood and spirit of its Author, a work so perfect that it would never require any change or revision.

61. This was a period of turbulence and upheaval and many rumours were rife in Madīnah. Occasionally, baseless and exaggerated reports circulated and seized the whole city and its outlying areas with alarm and consternation. At other times

mercy upon you, (weak as you were), all but a few of you would surely have followed Satan.

[84] So, (O Messenger), fight in the Way of Allah. You are responsible only for yourself. And rouse the believers to fight, for Allah may well curb the might of the unbelievers. Indeed Allah is the Strongest in power and the Most Terrible in chastisement. [85] He who intercedes in a good cause shall have a share in its good result, and he who intercedes in an evil cause shall have a share in its burden. Allah watches over everything.

[86] When you are greeted with a salutation then return it with a better one, or at least the same. Surely Allah takes good count of everything. [87] There is no god but Allah. He will certainly gather you all together on the Day of Resurrection – the Day regarding which there can be no doubt. Whose word can be truer than Allah's?

[88] What has happened to you that you have two minds about the hypocrites even though Allah has reverted them owing to the sins that they earned? Do you want to lead those to the Right Way whom Allah let go astray? And he whom Allah lets go astray, for him you can never find a way. [89] They wish that you should disbelieve just as they disbelieved so that you may all be alike. Do not, therefore, take allies from them until they emigrate in the Way of

---

some cunning enemy tried to conceal the dangers threatening the Muslims by spreading soothing reports. The common people were not aware of the far-reaching consequences of rumour-mongering. As soon as they heard something, they ran about spreading it everywhere. This rebuke is addressed to such people. They are warned against spreading rumours and are directed to convey every report they receive to responsible quarters.

Allah; but if they turn their backs (on emigration), seize them and slay them wherever you come upon them.[62] Take none of them for your ally or helper, [90] unless it be such of them who seek refuge with a people who are joined with you by a covenant,[63] or those who come to you because their hearts shrink from fighting either against you or against their own people. Had Allah so willed, He would certainly have given them power over you and they would have fought against you. If they leave you alone and do not fight against you and offer you peace, then Allah does not permit you to harm them. [91] You will also find others who wish to be secure from you, and secure from their people, but who, whenever they have any opportunity to cause mischief, plunge into it headlong. If such people neither leave you alone nor offer you peace nor restrain their hands from hurting you, seize them and slay them wherever you come upon them. It is against these that We have granted you a clear sanction.

[92] It is not for a believer to slay another believer unless by mistake. And he who has slain a believer by mistake, his atonement is to set free from bondage a believing

---

62. This is the verdict on those hypocrites who claimed to be believers but also, in fact, had their affinities with a belligerent, non-Muslim nation; they were the ones who actually participated in acts of hostility against the Islamic state.

63. The exception here does not relate to the injunction that they should not be taken as friends and supporters; it rather relates to the injunction that the believers should seize and slay them. What is meant is that if a hypocrite takes shelter among an unbelieving people with whom the Muslims have an agreement he should not be pursued into that territory.

person[64] and to pay blood-money to his (that is, the slain person's) heirs,[65] unless they forgo it by way of charity. And if the slain belonged to a hostile people, but was a believer, then the atonement is to set free from bondage a believing person. And if the slain belonged to a (non-Muslim) people with whom you have a covenant, then the atonement is to pay the blood-money to his heirs, and to set free from bondage a believing person.[66] But he who cannot (free a slave) should fast for two consecutive

---

64. Since the person killed was a believer, expiation of the sin required the emancipation of a Muslim slave.

65. The Prophet (peace be on him) has fixed the blood-money at either 100 camels, 200 oxen or 2,000 heads of cattle. If someone wished to pay this in another form the amount would be determined with reference to the market value of the animals mentioned above. For instance, for those who wished to pay blood-money in cash, the fixed amount in the time of the Prophet (peace be on him) was 800 dinars (8,000 dirhams). In the time of Caliph 'Umar the amount of blood-money was fixed at 1000 golden dinars (12,000 silver dirhams). It should be noted, however, that this amount relates to an unintentional rather than a deliberate homicide.

66. The legal injunctions embodied in this verse are as follows:

(1) If the victim was a resident of the Domain of Islam (*Dār al-Islām*), the assassin is not only required to pay blood-money but also to emancipate a slave by way of expiation.

(2) If the victim was a resident of the Domain of War (*Dār al-Ḥarb*), the assassin is only required to emancipate a slave.

(3) If the victim was a resident of a non-Muslim country which had treaty relations with an Islamic state, the assassin is required to emancipate a slave and also to pay blood-money. The amount of blood-money, however, depends on the terms stipulated in the treaty between the Muslims and the territory to which the victim belonged.

months.[67] This is the penance ordained by Allah.[68] Allah is All-Knowing, All-Wise. [93] And he who wilfully slays a believer his reward is Hell, where he will abide. Allah's wrath is against him and He has cast His curse upon him, and has prepared for him a great chastisement.

[94] Believers! When you go forth in the Way of Allah, ascertain and distinguish (between friend and foe), and do not say to him who offers you the greeting of peace: "You are not a believer." If you seek the good of this worldly life, there lies with Allah abundant gain. After all, you too were such before, but then Allah was gracious to you. Discern, then,[69] for Allah is well aware of what you do.

---

67. This means that he should observe uninterrupted fasting for the entire period. If a man breaks his fast for just one day without a legally valid reason, he will be required to resume fasting afresh.

68. This shows that what has been prescribed is an act of repentance and expiation rather than a penalty inflicted on a criminal. Penalization is essentially devoid of the spirit of repentance and of the urge to self-reform. A penalty is suffered under duress, usually with resentment, and leaves behind repugnance and bitterness. On the contrary, what God wants is that the believer who has committed a sin should wash away its stain from his soul by supererogatory worship, by acts of charity, and by a meticulous fulfilment of the duties incumbent upon him. Such a person is required to turn to God in remorse and repentance so that his sin may be forgiven and his soul secured against the recurrence of similar errors.

69. In the early days of Islam the greeting of *al-salām 'alaykum* ("peace be on you") was a distinguishing symbol of the Muslims. When a Muslim greeted another Muslim with this expression it signified that he was a member of the same community, that he was a friend and well-wisher, one who wished peace and security, from whom one need entertain no fear of hostility and towards

[95] Those believers who sit at home, unless they do so out of a disabling injury, are not the equals of those who strive in the Way of Allah with their possessions and their lives. Allah has exalted in rank those who strive with their possessions and their lives over those who sit at home; this even though to each Allah has promised some good reward, He has preferred for a mighty reward those who strive (in the Way of Allah) over those who sit at home. [96] For them are ranks, forgiveness, and favours from Him. Allah is All-Forgiving, All-Compassionate.

---

whom, in return, one should not behave with hostility. This was particularly important in those days because there were no distinctions in dress, language and so on by which the Muslims could be conclusively marked off from others.

The Muslims also encountered a strange problem on the battlefield. Whenever a Muslim was in danger of being harmed inadvertently by other Muslims during fighting, he resorted to either the Islamic greeting (*al-salām 'alaykum*) or to pronouncing the Islamic creed. "There is no god save Allah" (*lā ilāha illa Allah*) in order to indicate that he was their brother-in-faith. The Muslims, however, often suspected this to be merely a ruse of the enemy and therefore, sometimes, disregarded the utterance of the Islamic greeting or of the Islamic creed, and killed such people. The purport of the verse is that no one has the right to summarily judge those who profess to be Muslims, and to assume them to be lying for fear of their lives. At least two possibilities exist: the claim may either be true or it may be false. The truth can only be ascertained by proper investigation. While it is impossible to investigate a person's case properly during fighting, and this might enable him to save his life by lying, it is equally possible that an innocent, true believer might be put to death by mistake.

[97] While taking the souls of those who were engaged in wronging themselves,[70] the angels asked: "In what circumstances were you?" They replied: "We were too weak and helpless in the land." The angels said: "Was not the earth of Allah wide enough for you to emigrate in it?" For such persons their refuge is Hell – an evil destination indeed; [98] except the men, women, and children who were indeed too feeble to be able to seek the means of escape and did not know where to go – [99] maybe Allah shall pardon these, for Allah is All-Pardoning, Most Forgiving. [100] He who emigrates in the Way of Allah will find in the earth enough room for refuge and plentiful resources. And he who goes forth from his house as a migrant in the way of Allah and His Messenger, and whom death overtakes, his reward becomes incumbent on Allah. Surely Allah is All-Forgiving, All-Compassionate.[71]

70. The reference here is to those who, instead of going to the battlefield, stayed behind along with the unbelievers, despite no genuine disability. They were satisfied with a life made up of a blend of Islamic and un-Islamic elements, even though they had the chance to emigrate to *Dār al-Islām* and thus enjoy a full Islamic life and had also been invited by *Dār al-Islām* to emigrate, thereby ensuring the safety of their faith.

71. It should be understood clearly that it is only permissible for a person who believes in the True Faith enjoined by God to live under the dominance of an un-Islamic system on one of the following conditions. First, that the believer strives to put an end to the hegemony of the un-Islamic system and to have it replaced by the Islamic system of life, as the Prophets and their early followers did. Second, that he stays in a land where an un-Islamic system prevails because of his inability to depart from that land, but he is utterly unhappy at living under such a system.

[101] When you go forth journeying in the land, there is no blame on you if you shorten the Prayer,[72] (especially) if you fear that the unbelievers might cause you harm. Surely the unbelievers are your open enemies.

[102] (O Messenger), if you are among the believers and rise (in the state of war) to lead the Prayer for them, let a party of them stand with you to worship, keeping their arms. When they have performed their prostration, let them go behind you, and let another party who have not prayed, pray with you, remaining on guard and keeping their arms,[73] for the unbelievers love to see you heedless of your arms and your baggage so that they might swoop upon you in a surprise attack. But there shall be no blame upon you if you were to lay aside your arms if you are either troubled by rain or are sick; but remain on guard. Surely Allah has prepared a humiliating chastisement for the unbelievers. [103] When you have finished the Prayer, remember Allah – standing, and sitting, and reclining. And when you become secure, perform the regular Prayer. Prayer is enjoined upon the believers at stated times.

[104] Do not be faint of heart in pursuing these people: if you happen to suffer harm they too are suffering just as

---

72. Shortening the Prayer (*qaṣr*) while travelling in peace-time consists of praying two *rak'āt* at those appointed times when one is normally required to pray four *rak'āt*. The form of *qaṣr* during the state of war has not been specified. Prayers should, therefore, be performed as circumstances permit.

73. This injunction regarding Prayer in the state of either fear or insecurity (*khawf*) refers to the condition when an enemy attack is anticipated, but the fighting has not yet begun.

you are, while you may hope from Allah what they cannot hope for. Allah is All-Knowing, All-Wise.

[105] (O Messenger), We have revealed to you this Book with the Truth so that you may judge between people in accordance with what Allah has shown you. So do not dispute on behalf of the dishonest, [106] and seek forgiveness from Allah. Surely Allah is All-Forgiving, All-Compassionate. [107] Do not plead for those who are dishonest to themselves;⁷⁴ Allah does not love him who betrays trust and persists in sin. [108] They can hide (their deeds) from humans, but they cannot hide (them) from Allah for He is with them even when they hold nightly counsels that are unpleasing to Allah. Allah encompasses all their doings. [109] You pleaded on their behalf in this worldly life but who will plead with Allah on their behalf on the Day of Resurrection, or who will be their defender there? [110] He who does either evil or wrongs himself, and then asks for Allah's forgiveness, will find Allah All-Forgiving, All-Compassionate. [111] He who commits a sin, commits it only to his detriment. Surely Allah is All-Knowing, All-Wise. [112] But he who commits either a fault or a sin, and then casts it upon an innocent person, lays upon himself the burden of a false charge and a flagrant sin.

[113] (O Messenger), but for Allah's favour and mercy upon you, a party of them had resolved to mislead you, yet they only misled themselves, and could not have

---

74. Whoever commits a breach of trust with others in fact commits first a breach of trust with his own self.

harmed you in any way.[75] Allah revealed to you the Book
and Wisdom, and He taught you what you knew not. Great
indeed has been Allah's favour upon you.

[114] Most of their secret conferrings are devoid of good,
unless one secretly enjoins charity, good deeds, and
setting the affairs of men right. We shall grant whoever
does that seeking to please Allah a great reward. [115] As
for him who sets himself against the Messenger and
follows a path other than that of the believers even after
true guidance had become clear to him, We will let him
go the way he has turned to, and We will cast him into
Hell – an evil destination.

[116] Truly it is only associating others with Allah in
His Divinity that Allah does not forgive, and forgives
anything besides that to whomsoever He wills. Whoever
associates others with Allah in His Divinity has indeed
strayed far away. [117] Rather than call upon Him, they
call upon goddesses, and call upon a rebellious Satan[76]

---

75. Even if some people succeeded in their design to obtain from
the Prophet (peace be on him) a wrong judgement in their favour
by presenting a false account of facts, the real loss would have
been theirs rather than the Prophet's (peace be on him). For the real
culprits in the sight of God are the perpetrators of that fraud and
not the Prophet (peace be on him). Whoever obtains a judgement
in his favour by tricking the courts deludes himself into believing
that by such tricks he can bring right to his side; right remains with
its true claimant notwithstanding the judgements that might be
obtained by fraud and deception.

76. No one sets up Satan as his "god" in the sense that he makes
him the object of his ritual worship and declares him to be God
in so many words. The way to make Satan one's god is to entrust
one's reins to him and let oneself be drawn helplessly in whichever

[118] upon whom Allah has laid His curse. He said (to Allah): "I will take to myself an appointed portion of Your servants[77] [119] and shall lead them astray, and shall engross them in vain desires, and I shall command them and they will cut off the ears of the cattle,[78] and I shall command them and they will disfigure Allah's creation."[79] He who took Satan rather than Allah for his

---

direction Satan wants; the relationship between the two becomes, then, one of worshipper and worshipped. This shows that either absolute, unreserved obedience to or blind following of anybody is tantamount to worshipping him, so that whoever indulges in this kind of absolute obedience is guilty of worshipping a "god" other than the One True God.

77. This shows that Satan is determined to lay his claim to a portion of man's time, of his effort and labour, of his energies and capacities, of his material belongings, and of his offspring, and would somehow trick him into devoting a sizeable portion of all these to his cause.

78. The reference here is to a superstitious Arabian custom. It was customary among the Arabs that after a camel had given birth to five or ten young to slit her ears and let her go in the name of their deity; they considered it forbidden to put her to any work. Likewise, the male camel that had generated ten offspring was consecrated to some deity. The slitting of ears symbolized this consecration.

79. To alter God's creation in some respect does not mean changing its original form. Hence the alteration of God's creation, which is characterized as Satanic, consists in using a thing not for the purpose for which it was created by God. In other words, all acts performed in violation either of one's true nature or of the intrinsic nature of these other objects are the result of the misleading promptings of Satan. These include, for instance, sodomy, birth control, monasticism, celibacy, sterilization of either men or women, turning males into eunuchs, diverting females from the functions entrusted to them by nature and driving them to perform the functions for which men were created.

guardian has indeed suffered a manifest loss. [120] Satan makes promises to them and fills them with vain hopes, but whatever he promises them is merely delusion. [121] For these people, their abode shall be Hell and from there they shall find no way of escape. [122] But those who believe and do good, We shall cause them to enter the Gardens beneath which rivers flow. Here they will abide for ever. This is Allah's promise in truth and whose word is truer than Allah's?

[123] It is neither your fancies nor the fancies of the People of the Book which matter. Whoever does evil shall reap its consequence and will find none to protect and help him against Allah. [124] Whoever does good and believes – whether he is male or female – such shall enter the Garden, and they shall not be wronged in the slightest. [125] And whose way of life could be better than that of he who submits his whole being to Allah, does good, and follows exclusively the way of Abraham whom Allah took for a friend? [126] Whatever is in the heavens and in the earth belongs to Allah; Allah encompasses everything.

[127] They ask you to pronounce laws concerning women.[80] Say: "Allah pronounces to you concerning them, and reminds you of the injunctions which were recited to you in the Book about female orphans whom you do not give what has been ordained for them and whom you wish to marry (out of greed)," and the commandments

---

80. The actual query about women is not spelled out directly. The judgement pronounced a little later in response to that query, however, makes it abundantly clear what the query was.

relating to the children who are weak and helpless. Allah directs you to treat the orphans with justice. Allah is well aware of whatever good you do.

[128] If a woman[81] fears either ill-treatment or aversion from her husband it is not wrong for the husband and wife to bring about reconciliation among themselves (by compromising on their rights),[82] for reconciliation is better. Man is prone to selfishness, but if you do good and are God-fearing, then surely Allah is aware of the things you do. [129] You will not be able to treat your wives with (absolute) justice not even if you keenly desire to do so. (It suffices in order to follow the Law of Allah that) you do

---

81. The actual response to the query begins here. The question is how a person who had more than one wife can comply with the injunctions to be just and equitable towards all of them. Is a person obligated by Islam to feel equally towards each of his wives, to love each to an equal degree, and treat each of them equally even in respect of sexual relationship? Such questions are especially relevant with regard to a husband one of whose wives might be, say, afflicted with either sterility or permanent sickness or who is incapable of sexual intercourse. Does justice demand that if a person fails to live up to the standards of equality mentioned above he should renounce his first wife in order to marry another woman? Moreover, where the first wife is disinclined to agree to the annulment of marriage, is it appropriate for the spouses to make a voluntary accord among themselves, according to which the wife, towards whom the husband feels relatively less attracted, voluntarily surrenders some of her rights and thereby persuades her husband not to repudiate the marriage? Would such an act be against the dictates of justice?

82. It is better for the spouses to come to a mutual understanding so that the wife may remain with the same man with whom she has already spent a part of her life.

[137]

not wholly incline to one, leaving the other in suspense.[83]
If you act rightly and remain God-fearing, surely Allah
is All-Forgiving, All-Compassionate. [130] But if the two
separate, out of His plenty Allah will make each dispense
with the other. Indeed Allah is Most Bounteous, Most
Wise. [131] All that is in the heavens and all that is in the
earth belongs to Allah. We enjoined upon those who were
given the Book before you, and also yourselves, to have
fear of Allah. But if you disbelieve, then bear in mind that
all that is in the heavens and all that is in the earth belongs
to Allah. Allah is Self-Sufficient, Most Praiseworthy.
[132] To Allah belongs all that is in the heavens and all that
is in the earth; and Allah suffices for help and protection.
[133] If He wills, He has full power to remove you, O
mankind, and bring in others in your place. [134] He who
desires the reward of this world, let him know that with
Allah is the reward of this world and also of the World
to Come. Allah is All-Hearing, All-Seeing.

[135] Believers! Be upholders of justice, and bearers
of witness to Truth for the sake of Allah, even though

---

83. Some people point out that the Qur'ān in one breath stipulates
justice as the necessary condition for plurality of wives and in the
next declares it to be impossible. On this basis they conclude that
the Qur'ān has itself revoked the permission to marry more than
one wife. There is, therefore, absolutely no justification for having
a plurality of wives. Such an inference would have been justified
had the Qur'ān merely said that "You will not be able to treat
your wives with (absolute) justice." But the Qur'ānic statement is
followed by the direction: "… do not wholly incline to one, leaving
the other in suspense." This leaves no grounds at all for the blind
followers of Christian Europe to force an interpretation of their
liking on the verse.

it may be against yourselves or against your parents and kinsmen, or the rich or the poor, for Allah is more concerned with their well-being than you are. Do not, then, follow your own desires lest you keep away from justice. If you twist or turn away from (the Truth), know that Allah is well aware of all that you do.

[136] Believers! Believe in Allah and His Messenger and in the Book He has revealed to His Messenger, and in the Book He revealed before.[84] And whoever disbelieves in Allah, in His angels, in His Books, in His Messengers and in the Last Day,[85] has indeed strayed far away. [137] Allah will neither forgive nor show the Right Way to those who believed, and then disbelieved, then believed, and again disbelieved, and thenceforth became ever more intense in their disbelief. [138] Give tidings of painful chastisement to the hypocrites [139] who take the unbelievers for their allies in preference to the believers. Do they seek honour

---

84. To ask the believers to "believe" might at first sight seem strange. The fact is, however, that belief as used here has two meanings. In the first instance, belief denotes that a man has preferred to acknowledge the soundness of God's true guidance, to distance himself from the fold of those who disbelieve, and to join the camp of the believers. In the second instance, however, belief denotes firm faith, a man's believing in the Truth with all his heart, with full earnestness and sincerity. This verse is addressed to all those who are "believers" in the first sense of the term, and they are asked to transform themselves into true believers, i.e. believers in the second sense.

85. *Kufr* has two meanings. One signifies categorical rejection. The other signifies that pretence of belief even when one's heart is not fully convinced or one's conduct is flagrantly opposed to the demands of one's belief.

from them whereas honour altogether belongs to Allah alone? [140] Allah has enjoined upon you in the Book that when you hear the Signs of Allah being rejected and scoffed at, you will not sit with them until they engage in some other talk, or else you will become like them. Know well, Allah will gather the hypocrites and the unbelievers in Hell – all together. [141] These hypocrites watch you closely: if victory is granted to you by Allah, they will say: "Were we not with you?" And were the unbelievers to gain the upper hand, they will say: "Did we not have mastery over you, and yet we protected you from the believers?" It is Allah Who will judge between you on the Day of Resurrection, and He will not allow the unbelievers, in any way, to gain advantage over the believers.

[142] Behold, the hypocrites seek to delude Allah, but it is He Who has subjected them to delusion. When they rise to Prayer, they rise reluctantly, and only to be seen by people. They remember Allah but little. [143] They dangle between the one and the other (that is, faith and unbelief), and belong fully neither to these nor to those. And he whom Allah lets go astray, for him you can find no way.[86]

---

86. Here an important fact has been stated about the person who has remained undirected to the Truth despite his acquaintance with the Book of God and the life of the Prophet (peace be on him). His case is of a person who was so averse to the Truth and so infatuated with error that even God let him go forth along the same erroneous direction that he had chosen for himself, a person on whom the door of true guidance was shut and the way towards error was made smooth and easy by God. It is virtually beyond the power of human beings to direct such a person to the Truth.

[144] Believers! Do not take the unbelievers as your allies in preference to the believers. Do you wish to offer Allah a clear proof of guilt against yourselves? [145] Surely the hypocrites shall be in the lowest depth of the Fire and you shall find none to come to their help, [146] except those who repent and mend their ways and hold fast to Allah and devote their faith exclusively to Allah. Such shall be numbered with the believers and Allah will certainly bestow on the believers a great reward. [147] Why should Allah deal chastisement to you if you are grateful to Him and believe? Allah is All-Appreciative,[87] All-Knowing.

[148] Allah does not like speaking evil publicly unless one has been wronged.[88] Allah is All-Hearing, All-Knowing. [149] (Even though you have the right to speak evil if you are wronged), if you keep doing good – whether openly or secretly – or at least pardon the evil (then that is the attribute of Allah). Allah is All-Pardoning and He has all the power to chastise.

[150] There are those who disbelieve in Allah and His Messengers and seek to differentiate between Allah and His Messengers, and say: "We believe in some and deny others," and they seek to strike a way between the two. [151] It is they, indeed they, who are, beyond all doubt,

---

87. In the context of the God-man relationship, when the word *shukr* is used in respect of God, it denotes God's appreciation of man's service and obedience. When it is used in respect of man, it denotes his acknowledgement of God's benefaction and his feeling of gratitude to Him.

88. The one who has been wronged is justified in speaking out against the person who has done wrong to one.

unbelievers; and for the unbelievers We have prepared a humiliating chastisement. [152] For those who believe in Allah and His Messengers, and do not differentiate between them, We shall certainly give them their reward. Allah is All-Forgiving, All-Compassionate.

[153] The People of the Book now ask of you to have a Book come down on them from heaven; indeed they had asked of Moses even greater things than this, for they said: "Make us see Allah with our own eyes" – whereupon a thunder-bolt suddenly smote them for their wickedness. Then they took to worshipping the calf after Clear Signs had come to them. We forgave them, and conferred a manifest commandment upon Moses, [154] and We raised the Mount high above them and took from them a covenant (to obey the commandment), and ordered them: "Enter the gate in the state of prostration."[89] And We said to them: "Do not violate the law of the Sabbath," and took from them a firm covenant. [155] (They have incurred Allah's wrath) for their breaking the covenant, and their rejection of the Signs of Allah, and for slaying Prophets without right, and for saying: "Our hearts are wrapped up in covers"[90] – even though in fact Allah has sealed their hearts because of their disbelief, so that they scarcely believe – [156] and for their going so far in disbelief as uttering against Mary a mighty calumny, [157] and their saying: "We slew the Messiah,

---

89. See *al-Baqarah* 2: 58-9.

90. Whenever the Messengers of God tried to admonish the Israelites, they said point-blank that no matter what argument or evidence the former might adduce in support of their message, they would remain unmoved.

Jesus, son of Mary," the Messenger of Allah[91] – whereas in fact they had neither slain him nor crucified him but the matter was made dubious to them[92] – and those who differed about it too were in a state of doubt. They have no definite knowledge of it, but merely follow conjecture; and they surely slew him not, [158] but Allah raised him to Himself. Allah is All-Mighty, All-Wise. [159] There are none among the People of the Book but will believe in him before his death,[93] and he will be a witness against them on the Day of Resurrection. [160] Thus, We forbade them many clean things which had earlier been made lawful for them[94] for the wrong-doing of those who became Jews, for

---

91. Their criminal boldness had reached such proportions that they even attempted to put an end to the life of the person whom they themselves knew to be a Prophet, and subsequently went around boasting of this achievement. Were we to refer to *Sūrah Maryam* 19: 16-40, along with the relevant notes, it will be clear that the Jews recognized Jesus to be a Prophet. Despite this, they carried out the crucifixion of someone who, in their belief, was none other than Jesus.

92. This verse categorically states that Jesus was raised on high before he could be crucified, and that the belief of both the Jews and the Christians that Jesus died on the cross is based on a misconception. Before the Jews could crucify him God raised Jesus up to the heavens. The person whom the Jews subsequently crucified was someone else rather than Jesus, someone who for one reason or another was mistaken as Jesus.

93. The text lends itself to two meanings. We have adopted the first meaning in our translation. If we accept the alternative meaning, the verse would mean: "There is no one among the People of the Book who, before his death, will not believe in Jesus."

94. This may refer to the regulation mentioned in *Sūrah al-An'ām* 6: 146 that all beasts with claws and the fat of both oxen and sheep

their barring many from the Way of Allah, [161] and for their taking interest which had been prohibited to them, and for their consuming the wealth of others wrongfully. As for the unbelievers among them, We have prepared a painful chastisement. [162] Those among them who are firmly rooted in knowledge and the believers, they believe in what has been revealed to you and what was revealed before you. (Those who truly believe) establish the Prayer and pay *Zakāh*, firmly believe in Allah and in the Last Day, to them We shall indeed pay a great reward.

[163] (O Muḥammad), we have revealed to you as We revealed to Noah and the Prophets after him, and We revealed to Abraham, Ishmael, Isaac, Jacob and the offspring of Jacob, and Jesus and Job, and Jonah, and Aaron and Solomon, and We gave to David Psalms. [164] We revealed to the Messengers We have already told you of, and to the Messengers We have not told you of; and to Moses Allah spoke directly. [165] These Messengers were sent as bearers of glad tidings and as warners so that after sending the Messengers people may have no plea against Allah.[95] Allah is All-Mighty, All-Wise.

---

were prohibited to the Jews. It might also refer, however, to the highly elaborate set of prohibitions found in Judaic Law. To restrict the choice of alternatives in a people's life is indeed a kind of punishment for them.

95. God's purpose in raising the Prophets was to establish His argument against mankind. God did not want criminals to have any basis on which to plead that their actions were done in ignorance and that no arrangement had been made to guide man to the Truth.

[166] (Whether people believe or not) Allah bears witness that whatever He has revealed to you, He has revealed with His knowledge, and the angels bear witness to it too, though the witness of Allah is sufficient. [167] Those who denied this Truth and barred others from the way of Allah have indeed strayed far away. [168] Likewise, Allah will neither forgive those who denied the Truth and took to wrong-doing nor will He show them any other way [169] save that of Hell wherein they will abide. And that is easy for Allah.

[170] O people! Now that the Messenger has come to you bearing the Truth from your Lord, believe in him; it will be good for you. If you reject, know well that to Allah belongs all that is in the heavens and the earth. Allah is All-Knowing, All-Wise.[96]

[171] People of the Book! Do not exceed the limits in your religion,[97] and do not attribute to Allah anything except the Truth. The Messiah, Jesus, son of Mary, was only a Messenger of Allah, and His command that He conveyed

---

96. Mankind are being informed that their Lord is not at all unaware of the wickedness in which they indulge, nor does He lack the capacity to deal severely with those who violated His commands.

97. The expression "People of the Book" refers here to the Christians and the word *ghulūw* denotes the tendency to exceed the limits of propriety in supporting one doctrine or another. While the fault of the Jews was that they had exceeded the limits of propriety in rejecting and opposing Jesus, the mistake of the Christians was that they had gone beyond the proper limits in their love for and devotion to Jesus and held him to be son of God, nay God Himself.

unto Mary,[98] and a spirit from Him[99] (which led to Mary's conception). So believe in Allah and in His Messengers and do not say: "(Allah is a) trinity."[100] Give up this assertion; it would be better for you. Allah is indeed just

---

98. What is meant by sending the "command" to Mary is that God ordered Mary's womb to become impregnated without coming into contact with the human seed. In the beginning the Christians were told that this was the secret of the fatherless birth of Jesus. Later on, under the misleading influence of Greek philosophy, they equated this with the Logos, which was subsequently interpreted as the Divine attribute of speech. The next step in this connection was the development of the notion that this Divine attribute entered into the womb of Mary and assumed the physical form of Jesus. Thus there developed among the Christians the false doctrine of the Godhead of Jesus, and the false notion that out of His attributes, God had caused His attribute of Speech to appear in the form of Jesus.

99. Here Jesus himself is called "a spirit from God". The same idea is also expressed elsewhere in the Qur'ān: "And We supported him with the spirit of holiness" (*Sūrah al-Baqarah* 2: 87). The import of both verses is that God endowed Jesus with a pure, impeccable soul. He was, therefore, an embodiment of truth, veracity, righteousness, and excellence. This is what the Christians had been told about Christ. But they exceeded the proper limits of veneration for Jesus, the "spirit *from* God" became the "spirit *of* God", and the "spirit of holiness" was interpreted to mean God's own Spirit which became incarnate in Jesus. Thus, along with God and Jesus, there also developed the third person of God – the Holy Ghost.

100. It is urged that the Trinitarian doctrine, whatever its forms, should be abandoned. The fact is that Christians subscribe simultaneously to the unity and the trinity of God. The statements of Jesus on this question in the Gospels, however, are so categorical that no Christian can easily justify anything but the clear, straightforward doctrine that God is One and that there is no god but He. The Christians, therefore, find it impossible to deny that monotheism is the very core of true religion. But the original

One God. Far be it from His glory that He should have a son.[101] To Him belongs all that is in the heavens and in the earth. Allah is sufficient for a Guardian.

[172] Neither did the Messiah disdain to be a servant of Allah nor do the angels who are near-stationed to Him; and whoever disdains to serve Him, and waxes arrogant, Allah will certainly muster them all to Himself. [173] He will grant those who have believed and done good deeds their rewards in full, and will give them more out of His bounty. He will bestow upon those who have been disdainful and arrogant a painful chastisement; and they will find for themselves neither any guardian nor helper apart from Allah.

---

confusion that in Jesus the Word of God became flesh, that the Spirit of God was incarnate in him, led them to believe in the Godhead of Jesus and of the Holy Ghost along with that of God (the Father). This gratuitous assumption gave rise to an insoluble riddle: how to combine monotheism with the notion of trinity.

101. This is the refutation of the fourth extravagance in which the Christians have indulged. Even if the reports embodied in the New Testament are considered authentic, the most that can be inferred from them, (particularly those embodied in the first three Gospels), is that Jesus likened the relationship between God and His servants to that between a father and his children, and that he used to employ the term "father" as a metaphor for God. But in this respect Jesus was not unique. From very ancient times the Israelites had employed the term "father" for God. The Old Testament is full of examples of this usage. Jesus obviously employed this expression in conformity with the literary usage of his people. Moreover, he characterized God not merely as his own father but as the father of all human beings. Nevertheless, the Christians exceeded all reasonable limits when they declared Jesus to be the only begotten son of God.

[174] O people! A proof has come to you from your Lord, and We have sent down to you a clear light. [175] Allah will surely admit those who believe in Him and hold fast to Him to His mercy and bounty, and will guide them on to a Straight Way to Himself.

[176] People ask you to pronounce a ruling concerning inheritance from those who have left behind no lineal heirs (*kalālah*).[102] Say: "Allah pronounces for you the ruling: should a man die childless but have a sister,[103] she shall have one half of what he has left behind; and should the sister die childless, (but have a brother), he shall inherit her.[104] And if the heirs are two sisters, they shall have two-thirds of what he has left behind.[105] And if the

---

102. There is disagreement about the meaning of the word *kalālah*. According to some scholars, it means one who dies leaving neither issue nor father nor grandfather. According to others, it refers to those who die without issue. But the majority of jurists accept the opinion of Abū Bakr who held the former meaning to be correct. The Qur'ān also seems to support this, for here the sister of the *kalālah* has been apportioned half of the inheritance although had his father been alive, the sister would not have inherited from him at all.

103. The apportioned shares of inheritance mentioned here are those of brothers and sisters, whether related through both parents or through a common father only. Abū Bakr gave this interpretation in one of his pronouncements and none of the Companions expressed any dissent. This view is, therefore, considered to be supported by consensus (*ijmā'*).

104. This means that if there is no other legal heir the brother will receive the entire inheritance. In the presence of other heirs (such as husband), the brother will receive all the residual inheritance after the other heirs have received their apportioned shares.

105. The same also applies to more than two sisters.

heirs are sisters and brothers, then the male shall have the share of two females. Allah makes (His commandments) clear to you lest you go astray. Allah has full knowledge of everything."

5

Al-Māʾidah [The Table]
Madīnan Period

In the name of Allah, the Most Merciful,
the Most Compassionate

[1] Believers! Honour your bonds![1] All grazing beasts of
the flock are permitted to you[2] except those which are
recited to you hereinafter; but you are not allowed to hunt
in the state of *iḥrām* (the state of Pilgrim Sanctity). Indeed
Allah decrees as He wills.

[2] Believers! Neither desecrate the symbols of (devotion
to) Allah,[3] nor the holy month, nor the animals of offering,

---

1. People are asked to abide by the limitations and prohibitions
laid down in the Qurʾān.

2. The Arabic word *anʿām* (cattle) denotes camels, oxen, sheep and
goats, whereas the word *bahīmah* means all grazing quadrupeds.
The terms in which the injunction is conveyed are *bahīmat al-anʿām*
(all grazing beasts of the flock). Hence the permission is of wider
import and embraces all grazing quadrupeds of the cattle type, i.e.
those which do not possess canine teeth, which feed on plants rather
than animals, and which resemble the cattle. This implication was
elucidated by the Prophet (peace be on him) and is embodied in
a tradition in which he prohibited those beasts which kill and eat
animals. Likewise, the Prophet (peace be on him) also prohibited
birds with claws and those that feed on carrion.

3. Whatever characteristically represents either a particular doctrine,
creed, way of thought or conduct is recognized as its symbol. For

nor the animals wearing collars indicating they are for sacrifice, nor ill-treat those who have set out for the Holy House seeking from their Lord His bounty and good pleasure. But once you are free from Pilgrimage obligations, you are free to hunt. Do not let your wrath against the people who have barred you from the Holy Mosque move you to commit undue transgressions;[4] rather, help one another in acts of righteousness and piety, and do not help one another in sin and transgression. Fear Allah: Surely Allah is severe in retribution.

---

example, official flags, uniforms of the armed forces, coins, notes and stamps are symbols used by governments. Cathedrals, altars and crosses are symbols of Christianity. A special bunch of hair on the head, a special kind of bead-rosary and the temple are symbols of Hinduism. A turban, bracelet and *kirpān* (a special dagger kept by the Sikhs) are symbols of the Sikh religion. The hammer and sickle are the symbols of Communism. The followers of these ideologies are required to treat these symbols with respect. If a person insults any symbol associated with a particular ideology it is regarded as an act of hostility; and if the person concerned is himself a follower of that ideology then that insult is considered to be tantamount to abandonment of, and revolt against, it. The expression *sha'ā'ir Allāh* refers to all those rites which, in opposition to polytheism and outright unbelief and atheism, are the characteristic symbols of exclusive devotion to God.

4. The unbelievers had prevented the Muslims from visiting the Ka'bah. In fact, in violation of the ancient usage of Arabia they had even deprived them of their right to make Pilgrimage. As a result, the Muslims felt inclined to prevent the pagan tribes too from making Pilgrimage by not letting them pass along the routes to Makkah which lay close to the Islamic domains, and to attack their trading caravans during the time of Pilgrimage (*Ḥajj*). God prevented them from carrying out this plan through this revelation.

[3] Forbidden to you are carrion, blood, the flesh of swine, the animal slaughtered in any name other than Allah's, the animal which has either been strangled, killed by blows, has died of a fall, or by goring or devoured by a beast of prey – unless it be that which you yourselves might have slaughtered while it was still alive – and forbidden to you also that which was slaughtered at the altars.[5] You are also forbidden to seek knowledge of your fate by divining arrows. All these are sinful acts. This day the unbelievers have fully despaired of your religion. Do not fear them; but fear Me.[6] This day I have perfected for you your religion, and have bestowed upon you My Bounty in full measure, and have been pleased to assign for you Islam as your religion.[7] (Follow, then, the lawful and unlawful

5. The word *nuṣub* signifies all the places consecrated for offerings to others than the One True God, regardless of whether they are images of wood, stone or anything else.

6. "This day" here does not signify a particular day or a specific date. It refers to that period of time when these verses were revealed. In our usage, too, expressions like "today" or "this day" often have the sense of the "present time". "This day the unbelievers have fully despaired of your religion" refers to the fact that the Muslims' religion had developed into a full-fledged system of life, reinforced by the authority and governmental power which it had acquired. The unbelievers who had hitherto resisted its establishment had now despaired of being able to destroy Islam and of forcing the believers to return to their former state of Ignorance. The believers, therefore, no longer needed to fear other humans: they should fear God alone. They were told that they would not be treated lightly if they failed to carry out His commands, especially as there was no longer any justifiable excuse for such failure.

7. The "perfection of religion" mentioned in this verse refers to making it a self-sufficient system of belief and conduct, and an order

bounds enjoined upon you.) As for he who is driven by hunger, without being wilfully inclined to sin, surely Allah is All-Forgiving[8] All-Compassionate.

[4] They ask you what has been made lawful to them. Say that all clean things have been made lawful to you,[9] and

---

of social life providing its own answers to the questions with which man is confronted so that in no circumstance would one need to look for guidance to any extraneous source. The bounty referred to in the statement: "I have bestowed upon you My bounty in full measure," is the bounty of true guidance. The statement: "I have been pleased to assign for you Islam as your religion" means that since the Muslims had proved by their conduct and their striving that they were honest and sincere about the commitment they had made to God in embracing Islam – the commitment to serve and obey Him – He had accepted their sincerity and created the conditions in which they were no longer yoked in bondage to anyone but Him. Thus the Muslims were no longer prevented from living in submission to God because of extraneous constraints just as there were no constraints preventing them from subscribing to true beliefs.

8. See *Sūrah al-Baqarah* 2: n. 52 above.

9. The questioners wanted a list of what was lawful so that they could treat everything else as prohibited, but the Qur'ān provided them instead with a list of what is prohibited and then left them with the guiding principle that all "clean things" are lawful. This meant a complete reversal of the old religious outlook according to which everything that had not been declared lawful was considered prohibited. The lawfulness of things has been tied, however, to the stipulation of their being "clean" so that no one can argue for the lawfulness of things which are unclean. The question which arises at this point is: How are we to determine which things are clean? The answer is that everything is clean apart from those things which can be reckoned as unclean either according to any of the principles embodied in the Law or which are repellent to man's

such hunting animals as you teach, training them to hunt, teaching them the knowledge Allah has given you – you may eat what they catch for you[10] – but invoke the name of Allah on it.[11] Have fear of Allah (in violating His Law). Allah is swift in His reckoning.

[5] This day all clean things have been made lawful to you. The food of the People of the Book is permitted to you, and your food is permitted to them.[12] And permitted to

---

innate sense of good taste or which civilized human beings have generally found offensive to their natural feelings of cleanliness and decency.

10. The expression "hunting animals" signifies hounds, cheetahs, hawks and all those beasts and birds which men use in hunting. It is a characteristic of animals which have been trained to hunt that they hold the prey for their masters rather than devour it. It is for this reason that while the catch of these trained animals is lawful, that of others is prohibited.

11. Hunters should pronounce the name of God at the time of dispatching animals to the hunt. The verse under discussion makes it clear that it is necessary to pronounce the name of God while dispatching a hound to the hunt. If a man later finds the prey alive he should slaughter it. But if he does not find it alive it will still be lawful to eat it since the name of God had already been pronounced. The same rule applies with regard to shooting arrows in hunting.

12. The food of the People of the Book includes the animals slaughtered by them. The rule that "our food is lawful to them and theirs lawful to us" signifies that there need be no barriers between Muslims and the People of the Book regarding food. Muslims may eat with them and they with Muslims. But this general proclamation of permission is preceded by a reiteration of the statement: "All clean things have been made lawful to you." This indicates that if the People of the Book do not observe those principles of cleanliness and purity which are considered obligatory by the Law or if their

you are chaste women, be they from among the believers, or from among those who have received the Book before you,[13] provided you become their protectors in wedlock after paying them their bridal-due, rather than going around committing fornication and taking them as secret-companions. The work of he who refuses to follow the Way of faith will go to waste, and he will be among the utter losers in the Hereafter.

[6] Believers! When you stand up for Prayer wash your faces and your hands up to the elbows, and wipe your heads, and wash your feet up to the ankles.[14] And if you are in the state of ritual impurity, purify yourselves (by taking a bath). But if you are either ill, or travelling, or

---

food includes prohibited items, then one should abstain from eating them. If, for instance, they either slaughter an animal without pronouncing the name of God or if they slaughter it in the name of anyone other than God it is not lawful for us to eat the flesh of that animal.

13. This expression signifies the Jews and the Christians. As for non-Muslim women, Muslims may marry only Christians and Jews, and of them only those who have been characterized as *muḥsanāt* (i.e. "well-protected women".) A Muslim who avails of this permission has, however, been cautioned to guard his faith against any possible detrimental influences of his Jewish or Christian wife.

14. The explanation of this injunction by the Prophet (peace be on him) indicates that washing of the face includes rinsing one's mouth and inhaling water into the nostrils. Unless this is done the washing of the face is not considered complete. Likewise, since the ears are part of the head, "wiping the head" includes wiping one's hands over the external and internal parts of the ears as well. Moreover, before starting to wash the other parts one should first wash one's hands so that the instruments of washing are themselves clean.

have satisfied a want of nature or have had (intimate) contact with women and find no water, then have recourse to clean earth and wipe your faces and your hands therewith.[15] Allah does not want to lay any hardship upon you; rather He wants to purify you and complete His favours upon you so that you may give thanks.

[7] Remember Allah's favour upon you and His covenant which He made with you when you said: "We have heard and we obey." So do fear Allah. Allah has full knowledge even of that which is hidden in the breasts of people. [8] Believers! Be upright bearers of witness for Allah, and do not let the enmity of any people move you to deviate from justice. Act justly, that is nearer to God-fearing. And fear Allah. Surely Allah is well aware of what you do. [9] Allah has promised those who believe and do righteous deeds forgiveness from sins and a great reward. [10] As for those who disbelieve and give the lie to Our Signs, they are destined for the Blazing Flame.

[11] Believers! Remember Allah's favour upon you. When a certain people decided to stretch their hands against you,[16] He restrained their hands from you. Do fear Allah. Men of faith should put their trust only in Allah.

---

15. For explanation see *Sūrah al-Nisā'* 4: nn. 41, 43 above.

16. This alludes to the incident reported by ʿAbd Allāh ibn ʿAbbās when a group of Jews invited the Prophet (peace be on him) and a number of his close Companions to dinner. They had in fact hatched a plot to pounce upon the guests and thus undermine the very foundation of Islam. But by the grace of God the Prophet (peace be on him) came to know of the plot at the eleventh hour and did not go to that dinner.

[12] Surely Allah took a covenant with the Children of Israel, and We raised up from them twelve of their leaders,[17] and Allah said: "Behold, I am with you; if you establish Prayer and pay *Zakāh* and believe in My Prophets and help them, and lend Allah a goodly loan, I will certainly efface from you your evil deeds, and will surely cause you to enter the Gardens beneath which rivers flow. Whosoever of you disbelieves thereafter has indeed gone astray from the Right Way."[18] [13] Then, for their breach of the covenant We cast them away from Our Mercy and caused their hearts to harden. (And now they are in such a state that) they pervert words from their context and distort their meaning, and have forgotten a good portion of the teaching they were imparted, and regarding all except a few of them you continue to learn that they committed acts of treachery. Pardon them, then, and overlook their deeds. Surely Allah loves those who act benevolently.

[14] We also took a covenant from those who said: "We are Christians (*Naṣārā*)"; but they forgot a good portion of the teaching they had been imparted. Wherefore We aroused enmity and spite between them till the Day of

---

17. The word *naqīb* in Arabic denotes supervisor and censor. There were twelve tribes among the Israelites and each tribe was required to appoint one of its members as a *naqīb* so that he might look after the affairs of his fellow-tribesmen and try to prevent them from becoming victims of irreligiousness and moral corruption.

18. *Sawāʾ al-sabīl* (Right Path) is the designated highway that would lead to one's destination. Straying from the "Right Path" would take one off the highway as a result of which one might wander about and get lost.

Resurrection, and ultimately Allah will tell them what they used to do.

[15] People of the Book! Now Our Messenger has come to you: he makes clear to you a good many things of the Book which you were wont to conceal, and also passes over many things.[19] There has now come to you a Light from Allah, and a Clear Book [16] through which Allah shows to all who seek to please Him the paths leading to safety. He brings them out, by His leave, from darkness to Light and directs them on to the Straight Way.

[17] Indeed those who said: "Christ, the son of Mary, he indeed is God," were guilty of unbelief. Say, (O Muḥammad): "Who could have overruled Allah had He so willed to destroy Christ, the son of Mary, and his mother, and all those who are on earth?" For to Allah belongs the dominion of the heavens and the earth and all that is between them; He creates what He wills.[20] Allah is All-Powerful.

[18] The Jews and the Christians say: "We are Allah's children and His beloved ones." Ask them: "Why, then,

---

19. God discloses some of the dishonest and treacherous dealings of the People of the Book. He, however, discloses only those dealings which He deems necessary to strengthen the cause of the true faith and ignores the disclosure of those which are not indispensable.

20. That is, they had started believing that Jesus was God just because he was conceived without a father, although God creates whomsoever He will in the manner He pleases. Divinity cannot be claimed for anyone simply because God has created him in an extraordinary manner.

does He chastise you for your sins?" You are the same as other human beings He has created. He forgives whom He wills and chastises whom He wills. And to Allah belongs the dominion of the heavens and the earth, and all that is between them. To Him is the eventual return.

[19] People of the Book! After a long interlude during which no Messengers appeared there has come to you Our Messenger to elucidate the teaching of the true faith lest you say: "No bearer of glad tidings and no warner has come to us." For now there indeed has come to you a bearer of glad tidings and a warner. Allah is All-Powerful.[21]

[20] Remember when Moses said to his people: "My people, recall Allah's favour upon you when He raised Prophets among you and appointed you rulers, and granted to you what He had not granted to anyone else in the world. [21] My people! Enter the holy land which Allah has ordained for you;[22] and do not turn back for then you will turn about losers." [22] They answered: "Moses, therein live a ferocious people: we will not enter unless they depart from it; but if they do depart from it then we will surely enter it." [23] Two from among these men who were frightened but upon whom Allah had

---

21. The People of the Book should bear in mind that if they disregard the injunctions of God, He can chastise them as He wills, for He is All-Powerful and All-Mighty.

22. This signifies Palestine which at the time was inhabited by idolatrous and immoral groups of people. After their exodus from Egypt, God designated this land for the Israelites and commanded them to go forth to Palestine and conquer it.

bestowed His favour[23] said: "Enter upon them through the gate – for if you do enter – you will be the victors. And put your trust in Allah if indeed you are people of faith." [24] Nevertheless they said: "O Moses! Never shall we enter it as long as they are there. Go forth, then, you and your Lord, and fight both of you. As for us, we will remain sitting here." [25] Thereupon Moses said: "My Lord! I have control over none but my own self and my brother; so make a distinction between us and the transgressing people." [26] Allah said: "This land will now be forbidden to them for forty years and they will remain wandering about on the earth. Do not grieve over the condition of these transgressing people."[24]

[27] Narrate to them in all truth the story of the two sons of Adam. When both of them made an offering and it was accepted from one of them and was not accepted from the other, the latter said: "I will surely kill you." Thereupon the former said: "Allah only accepts offerings from the God-fearing. [28] Even if you stretch forth your hand against me to kill me, I will not stretch forth my hand

---

23. One of these holy men was Joshua, son of Nūn, who succeeded the Prophet Moses as his caliph. The other was Caleb, who became the right-hand man of Joshua. When after their 40-year wandering the Israelites entered Palestine these two were the only Companions of Moses who were alive.

24. The purpose of referring to this event becomes clear if we reflect upon the context. The purpose seems to be to bring home to the Israelites that the punishment to which they would be subjected if they adopted a rebellious attitude towards Muḥammad (peace be on him) would be even more severe than the one to which people were subjected in the time of Moses.

to kill you.[25] Surely, I fear Allah, the Lord of the entire Universe. [29] I would desire that you be laden with my sin and with your own sin, and thus become among the inmates of the Fire. That indeed is the right recompense of the wrong-doers." [30] At last his evil soul drove him to the murder of his brother, and he killed him, whereby he himself became one of the losers. [31] Thereupon Allah sent forth a raven who began to scratch the earth to show him how he might cover the corpse of his brother. So seeing he cried: "Woe unto me! Was I unable even to be like this raven and find a way to cover the corpse of my brother?" Then he became full of remorse at his doing.[26]

[32] Therefore We ordained for the Children of Israel that he who slays a soul unless it be (in punishment) for murder or for spreading mischief on earth shall be as if he had slain all mankind; and he who saves a life shall be as if he had given life to all mankind. And indeed again and again did Our Messengers come to them with

---

25. This does not mean that his brother assured him that when the latter stepped forward to kill him he would keep his hands tied and instead of defending himself he would stretch out his neck to be cut down. What this statement amounts to is an assurance on his part that even though his brother was intent on killing him, he himself had no such intention towards his brother.

26. The purpose of mentioning this particular incident is to subtly reproach the Jews for the plot they had hatched to assassinate the Prophet (peace be on him) and some of his illustrious Companions (see n. 16 above). The resemblance between the two incidents is evident. These people wanted to kill the Prophet (peace be on him) out of sheer jealousy. The errant son of Adam also killed his brother and did so for the same reason.

clear directives, yet many of them continued to commit excesses on earth.

[33] Those who wage war against Allah and His Messenger, and go about the earth spreading mischief[27] – indeed their recompense is that they either be done to death, or be crucified, or have their hands and feet be cut off from the opposite sides or they be banished from the land. Such shall be their degradation in this world; and a mighty chastisement lies in store for them in the World to Come [34] except for those who repent before you have overpowered them. Know well that Allah is All-Forgiving, All-Compassionate.[28]

---

27. The word "land" here signifies either the country or territory wherein the responsibility of establishing law and order has been undertaken by an Islamic state. The expression "to wage war against Allah and His Messenger" denotes war against the righteous order established by the Islamic state. According to Islamic jurists the people to whom reference has been made here are organized and armed bands of criminals who commit robbery and indulge in plunder.

28. If they give up subversion and abandon their activities to disrupt or overthrow the righteous order, and if their subsequent conduct shows that they have indeed become peace-loving, law-abiding citizens of good character, they need not be subjected to the punishments mentioned here even if any of their former crimes against the state should come to light. If their crimes include violation of the rights of others they may not be absolved of their guilt. If, for instance, they have either killed a person, or seized someone's property or committed any other crime against human life or property they will be tried according to the criminal law of Islam. They will, however, not be accused of either rebellion and high treason or of waging war against God and His Messenger.

[35] Believers! Fear Allah and seek the means to come near to Him,[29] and strive hard in His Way; maybe you will attain true success. [36] For those who disbelieved – even if they had all that is in the earth, and the like of it with it and they had offered it all as ransom from chastisement on the Day of Resurrection, it will not be accepted of them. A painful chastisement lies in store for them. [37] They will wish to come out of the Fire, but they will not. Theirs will be a long-lasting chastisement.

[38] As for the thief – male or female – cut off the hands of both.[30] This is a recompense for what they have done, and an exemplary punishment from Allah. Allah is All-Mighty, All-Wise. [39] But he who repents after he has committed wrong, and makes amends, Allah will graciously turn to him.[31] Truly Allah is All-Forgiving, All-Compassionate.

---

29. People are urged to solicit all means which might bring them close to God and enable them to please Him.

30. The injunction is to cut off one not both hands. There is consensus among jurists that in the event of the first theft the right hand should be cut off. Theft is applicable only to acts involving the seizure by stealth of someone else's property. The punishment of cutting off a hand should, however, not be applied in cases where the value of the article stolen is less than that of a shield. In the time of the Prophet (peace be on him) its value was ten dirhams. Moreover, there are several things the theft of which would not necessitate cutting off a hand. For instance, theft of fruit, vegetables, food, a bird, paltry things, an item from the public treasury, etc. will not warrant cutting off a hand.

31. Forgiveness on the part of God does not mean that the hand of the thief should not be cut off. It rather means that he who repents and becomes righteous by purging his soul of the sin of stealing will be spared the wrath of God, Who will remove the stain of that sin

[40] Do you not know that to Allah belongs the dominion of the heavens and the earth? He chastises whom He wills and forgives whom He wills. Allah is All-Powerful.

[41] O Messenger! Do not be grieved on account of those who vie with one another in disbelieving, even though they be those who say with their mouths: "We believe," but their hearts have no faith; or they be Jews who have their ears eagerly turned to falsehood and spy for other people who did not chance to come to you, who pervert the words of Allah, taking them out of their proper context in order to distort their meaning. They say to people: "If such and such teaching is given to you, accept it; if you are not given that, then avoid it."[32] You can be of no avail to him whom Allah wills to fall into error.[33] Those

---

from him. But if after his hand has been cut off the person concerned does not purge himself of evil intent and continues to nurture the same impure feelings which had led to his stealing and thus to the cutting off of his hand, it is evident that even though his hand has been severed from his body, stealing remains ingrained in his soul. The result will be that he will continue to merit God's wrath as he did before his hand was cut off. The Qur'ān, therefore, directs the thief to seek pardon from God and to try to reform himself. Judicial punishment does not automatically purify a person's soul. Purity of soul can be achieved only by repentance and turning to God.

32. This refers to the Jews who went about telling the ignorant masses that they should follow the teachings of the Prophet (peace be on him) only if they conformed to Jewish teachings.

33. God's will to put someone to the test means that God confronts him in whom He sees the growth of evil with opportunities to commit evils so that he might go through the struggle between good and evil within himself. If the person is not yet fully inclined towards evil, his latent potentialities to resist evil are revived. But if he has

are the ones whose hearts Allah does not want to purify. For them there is degradation in this world and a mighty chastisement in the Next.

[42] They are listeners of falsehood and greedy devourers of unlawful earnings. If they come to you (for your judgement), you may either judge between them or turn away from them. And were you to turn away from them they shall not be able to harm you; and were you to judge between them judge with justice. Surely Allah loves the just.³⁴ [43] Yet how will they appoint you a judge when they have the Torah with them, wherein there is Allah's judgement – and still they turn away from it? The fact is, they are not believers.

[44] Surely We revealed the Torah, wherein there is Guidance and Light. Thereby did Prophets – who had submitted themselves (to Allah) – judge for the Judaized

---

become excessively inclined towards evil, and goodness has been totally crushed from within his being, then every such test is bound to entangle him still more tightly in evil. His well-wisher will now be powerless to rescue him.

34. Until then the Jews had not become full-fledged subjects of the Islamic state. Their relations with that state were simply based on agreements. They were, therefore, not legally bound to submit their disputes either to the Prophet (peace be on him) for adjudication or to the judges appointed by him. But in cases where it seemed detrimental to their interests to have their disputes settled according to their own religious law they approached the Prophet (peace be on him) in the hope that the Prophet would give a different ruling and they would thereby escape the application of their own religious law.

folk; and so did the scholars and jurists.[35] They judged by the Book of Allah for they had been entrusted to keep it and bear witness to it. So, (O Jews), do not fear human beings but fear Me, and do not barter away My signs for a trivial gain. Those who do not judge by what Allah has revealed are indeed the unbelievers.

[45] And therein We had ordained for them: "A life for a life, and an eye for an eye, and a nose for a nose, and an ear for an ear, and a tooth for a tooth, and for all wounds, like for like. But whosoever foregoes it by way of charity, it will be for him an expiation." Those who do not judge by what Allah has revealed are indeed the wrong-doers.

[46] And We sent Jesus, the son of Mary, after those Prophets, confirming the truth of whatever there still remained of the Torah. And We gave him the Gospel wherein is Guidance and Light, and which confirms the truth of whatever there still remained of the Torah, and a Guidance and Admonition for the God-fearing. [47] Let the followers of the Gospel judge by what Allah has revealed therein, and those who do not judge by what Allah has revealed are the transgressors.[36]

---

35. *Rabbānī* = religious scholars, theologians. *Aḥbār* = religious jurists.

36. Here three verdicts are issued against those who do not judge in accordance with the Law revealed by God. The first is that they are *kāfir* (unbelievers); the second, that they are *ẓālim* (wrong-doers); and the third, that they are *fāsiq* (transgressors). This clearly means that anyone who, in disregard of God's commandments and of the laws revealed by Him, pronounces judgements according to man-made laws – whether made by himself or by others – is an unbeliever, a wrong-doer and a transgressor. A man who is convinced that the

[48] Then We revealed the Book to you, (O Muḥammad), with Truth, confirming whatever of the Book was revealed before, and protecting and guarding over it.[37] Judge, then, in the affairs of men in accordance with the Law that Allah has revealed, and do not follow their desires in disregard of the Truth which has come to you. For each of you We have appointed a Law and a way of life. And had Allah so willed, He would surely have made you one single

---

injunctions of God are right but makes judgements contrary to them in practice is not an unbeliever in the sense that he ceases to be a member of the Islamic community, but he is guilty of adulterating his faith by blending it with *kufr*, *ẓulm* and *fisq*. In the same manner, those who deviate from the injunctions of God in all matters are unbelievers, wrong-doers and transgressors. For those who are obedient in some respects and disobedient in others, the blending of faith and submission to God with the opposite attributes of unbelief, wrong-doing and transgression in their lives will be exactly in proportion to the mixture of their obedience to, and their deviation from, God's commands.

37. This points to a fact of major significance. It could also have been said that the Qur'ān confirms all those parts of the earlier Scriptures which are still extant in their true and original form. But the sense has been conveyed by employing the word "the Book" rather than "the previous Books". This expression indicates that the Qur'ān and all those Books sent down by God at various times and in different languages in reality constitute one and the same Book. Their Author is one and the same; their aim and purpose are the same; their teaching is the same; and the knowledge which they seek to impart to mankind is the same. The difference between these Books lies in their modes of expression, and this was necessarily so since they were addressed to different audiences. To say that the Qur'ān is *muhaymin* on *al-kitāb* means that it preserves all the true teachings of the earlier books of Divine provenance; that it has secured them from loss.

community; instead, (He gave each of you a Law and a way of life) in order to test you by what He gave you. Vie, then, with one another in good works. Unto Allah is the return of all of you; and He will then make you understand the truth concerning the matters on which you disagreed. [49] Therefore, judge between them, (O Muḥammad), by what Allah has revealed and do not follow their desires, and beware lest they tempt you away from anything of what Allah has revealed to you. And if they turn away, then know well that Allah has indeed decided to afflict them for some of their sins. For surely many of them are transgressors. [50] (If they turn away from the Law of Allah) do they desire judgement according to the Law of Ignorance?[38] But whose judgement can be better than Allah's for those who have certainty of belief?

[51] Believers! Do not take Jews and Christians for your allies. They are the allies of each other. And among you he who takes them for allies, shall be regarded as one of them. Allah does not guide the wrong-doers.

[52] Indeed you see that those afflicted with the disease of hypocrisy race towards them, saying: "We fear lest some misfortune overtakes us." And it may happen that

---

38. The word *jāhilīyah* (literally "ignorance") is used as an antonym of Islam. Islam is the way of *'ilm* (true knowledge), since it is God Himself Who has shown this way and His knowledge embraces everything. In contrast is the way that diverges from Islam – the way of Ignorance (*jāhilīyah*). The pre-Islamic period in Arabia is designated as *jāhilīyah* because this was the era when human beings derived their norms from either superstitious beliefs, conjectures and imagination or from their desires. Whenever such an attitude is adopted, it is bound to be designated as Ignorance.

Allah will either bring you a decisive victory or bring about something else from Himself and then they will feel remorseful at their hypocrisy which they have kept concealed in their breasts, [53] while those who believe will exclaim: "Are these the self-same people who solemnly swore by Allah that they were with you?" All their acts have gone to waste and now they are the losers.

[54] Believers! If any of you should ever turn away from your faith, remember that Allah will raise up a people whom He loves and who love Him; a people humble towards the believers, and firm towards the unbelievers;[39] who will strive hard in the way of Allah and will not fear the reproach of the reproacher. This is the favour of Allah which He grants to whom He wills. Allah is All-Resourceful, All-Knowing.

[55] Only Allah, His Messenger, and those who believe and who establish Prayer, pay *Zakāh*, and bow down

---

39. To be "humble towards the believers" signifies that a person should never use his strength against the believers. His native intelligence, shrewdness, ability, influence, wealth, physical prowess, should not be used either for suppressing, persecuting or causing harm to the Muslims. Among themselves, the Muslims should always find him gentle, merciful, sympathetic and mild-tempered. On the contrary, to be "firm towards the unbelievers," means that a believer, by virtue of the intensity of his faith, the sincerity of his conviction, strict adherence to his principles, his strength of character and his insight and perspicacity born of faith, should be firm as a rock in his dealing with the opponents of Islam, so that they find it impossible to dislodge him. There should be no doubt in their minds that the believer would rather lay down his life than compromise his position as regards his principles by yielding to external pressures.

(before Allah) are your allies. [56] All those who accept Allah and His Messenger and the believers as their allies should remember that the party of Allah will be triumphant.

[57] Believers! Do not take for your allies those who make a mockery and sport of your faith, be they those given the Book before you or other unbelievers. Fear Allah if you indeed believe. [58] And when you are called to pray, they take it for a mockery and sport.⁴⁰ That because they are a people who do not understand. [59] Say to them: "People of the Book! Do you hate us for anything else except that we believe in Allah, and in the teaching which has been revealed to us and in the teaching which was revealed before? Indeed most of you are transgressors." [60] Then say to them: "Shall I tell you about those whose retribution with Allah will be even worse? They are the ones whom Allah has cursed, and have incurred His wrath and some of whom were changed into apes and swine, and who served the false deities." Such have an even worse rank and have strayed farther away from the Right Path.

[61] Whenever they come to you they say: "We believe," whereas in fact they come disbelieving, and go away disbelieving, and Allah knows all that they hide. [62] You will see many of them hastening towards sin and transgression and devouring unlawful earnings. Evil indeed is what they do. [63] Why is it that their scholars and jurists do not forbid them from sinful utterances and

---

40. When they hear the call to Prayer the unbelievers make fun of it by mimicry; they pervert its words to ridicule it, and utter disparaging and taunting remarks about it.

devouring unlawful earnings? Indeed they have been contriving evil.

[64] The Jews say: "The Hand of Allah is fettered."[41] It is their own hands which are fettered,[42] and they stand cursed for the evil they have uttered. No, His hands are outspread; He spends as He wills. Surely the Message that has been revealed to you from your Lord has increased many of them in their insurgence and unbelief, and so We have cast enmity and spite among them until the Day of Resurrection. And as often as they kindle the fire of war, Allah extinguishes it; and they go about trying to spread mischief on earth, whereas Allah does not love those who spread mischief.

[65] Had the People of the Book only believed and been God-fearing, We should surely have effaced from them their evil deeds and caused them to enter the Gardens of Bliss. [66] Had the People of the Book observed the Torah and the Gospel and all that had been revealed to them from their Lord, sustenance would have been showered over them from above and would have risen from beneath their feet. Some among them certainly keep to the Right Path, but many of them do things that are evil.

[67] O Messenger! Deliver what has been revealed to you from your Lord, for if you fail to do that, you have not fulfilled the task of His messengership. Allah will certainly

---

41. To say that someone's hands are tied, in Arabic usage, means that he is niggardly, that something prevents him from being generous and bountiful.

42. They accused God of miserliness from which they themselves suffered and for which they had become notorious.

protect you from the evil of men. Surely Allah will not guide the unbelievers (to succeed against you). [68] Say to them: "People of the Book! You have no solid ground to stand on unless you establish the Torah and the Gospel and all that had been revealed to you from your Lord." Indeed the Message revealed to you from your Lord will lead to the aggravation of insurgence and unbelief in many of them. So do not grieve for those who disbelieve. [69] (Know well, none has an exclusive claim to the Truth.) For all those who believe in Allah and in the Last Day and do good deeds – whether they are Muslims or Jews or Sabaeans or Christians – neither fear shall fall upon them, nor shall they have any reason to grieve.[43]

[70] We took a covenant from the Children of Israel and sent to them many Messengers. But whenever any Messenger brought to them something that did not suit their desires, they gave the lie to some of them and killed the others, [71] thinking that no harm would come from it. Thus they became blind and deaf (to the Truth). Thereafter Allah turned towards them in gracious forgiveness; but many of them became even more deaf and blind (to the Truth). Allah sees all that they do.

[72] And surely they disbelieved when they said: "Christ, the son of Mary, is indeed God"; whereas Christ had said: "Children of Israel! Serve Allah, Who is your Lord and my Lord." Allah has forbidden Paradise to those who associate anything with Him in His Divinity and their refuge shall be the Fire. No one will be able to help such wrong-doers.

---

43. For further explanation see *Sūrah al-Baqarah* 2: 62, n. 26 above.

[73] Those who said: "Allah is one of the Three," certainly they disbelieved, for there is no god save the One God. And if they do not give up this claim, all who have disbelieved among them shall be subjected to painful chastisement. [74] Will they not, then, turn to Allah in repentance, and ask for His forgiveness? Allah is All-Forgiving, All-Compassionate.

[75] The Messiah, son of Mary, was no more than a Messenger, before whom many Messengers have passed away; and his mother adhered wholly to truthfulness, and they both ate food (as other mortals do). See how We make Our signs clear to them; and see where they are turning away![44]

[76] Say: "Do you serve, instead of Allah, that which has no power either to harm or benefit you, whereas Allah alone is All-Hearing, All-Knowing?" [77] Say: "People of the Book! Do not exceed the proper limits in your religion at the cost of Truth, and do not follow the caprices of the people who strayed before, and caused others to go astray, and strayed far away from the Right Path."

---

44. In these few words the Christian doctrine of the Divinity of Jesus Christ is repudiated. The true nature of the Messiah is clear from the indications given here: he was merely a human being, he was one born from the womb of a woman, who had a known genealogy, who possessed a physical body, who was subject to all the limitations of a human being and had all the attributes characteristic of human beings. Jesus slept, ate, felt the discomfort of heat and cold and was so human that he was even tested by Satan. How could any reasonable person believe that such a being was either God or a partner or associate of God in His Godhead?

[78] Those of the Children of Israel who took to unbelief have been cursed by the tongue of David and Jesus, the son of Mary, for they rebelled and exceeded the bounds of right. [79] They did not forbid each other from committing the abominable deeds they committed.[45] Evil indeed was what they did. [80] And now you can see many of them taking the unbelievers (instead of the believers) for their allies. Indeed they have sent forth evil for themselves. Allah is angry with them, and they shall abide in chastisement. [81] For had they truly believed in Allah and the Messenger and what was sent down to him, they would not have taken the unbelievers (instead of believers) for their allies. But many of them have altogether rebelled against Allah.

[82] Of all people you will find the Jews and those who associate others with Allah in His Divinity to be the most hostile to those who believe; and you will surely find that of all people they who say: "We are Christians," are closest to feeling affection for those who believe. This because there are worshipful priests and monks among them, and because they are not arrogant. [83] And when they hear what has been revealed to the Messenger you see that their eyes overflow with tears because of the Truth that they recognize and they say: "Our Lord! We do believe;

---

45. The corruption of any nation begins with the corruption of a few individuals. If the collective conscience of that nation is alive, the pressure of public opinion keeps the people in check and prevents the nation as a whole from becoming corrupted. But if instead of censuring such individuals, the nation leaves them free to behave corruptly, the corruption that was originally confined to a few persons continues to spread till it engulfs the whole nation. It was this which ultimately caused the degeneration of Israel.

write us down, therefore, with those who bear witness (to the Truth). [84] And why should we not believe in Allah and the Truth which has come down to us when we do fervently desire that our Lord should include us among the righteous?" [85] So Allah rewarded them for these words with the Gardens beneath which rivers flow so that they would abide there forever. Such is the reward of the people who do good. [86] Those who disbelieved and gave the lie to Our Signs are rightfully the inmates of the Blazing Flame.

[87] Believers! Do not hold as unlawful the good things which Allah has made lawful to you,[46] and do not exceed the bounds of right. Allah does not love those who transgress the bounds of right. [88] And partake of the lawful, good things which Allah has provided you as sustenance, and refrain from disobeying Allah in Whom you believe.

[89] Allah does not take you to task for the oaths you utter vainly, but He will certainly take you to task for the oaths you have sworn in earnest. The expiation (for breaking such oaths) is either to feed ten needy persons with more or less the same food as you are wont to give to your

---

46. This verse embodies two directives. The first is that man should not arrogate to himself the authority to proclaim things either lawful or unlawful according to his own wishes. Only that which God has held to be lawful is lawful, and only that which God has declared unlawful is unlawful. If human beings were to declare certain things either lawful or unlawful on their own authority, they would not be following the law of God but their own laws. The second directive is that they should not adopt the course of world-renunciation and abstention from worldly pleasures as the Christian monks, Hindu mendicants, Buddhist *bhikshus* and illuminationist mystics did.

families, or to clothe them, or to set free from bondage the neck of one man; and he who does not find the means shall fast for three days. This shall be the expiation for your oaths whenever you have sworn (and broken them), and do keep your oaths. Thus does Allah make clear to you His commandments; maybe you will be grateful.

[90] Believers! Intoxicants, games of chance, idolatrous sacrifices at altars, and divining arrows are all abominations, the handiwork of Satan. So turn wholly away from it that you may attain to true success.[47] [91] By intoxicants and games of chance Satan only desires to create enmity and hatred among you, and to turn you away from the remembrance of Allah and from Prayer. Will you, then, desist? [92] Obey Allah and obey the Messenger, and beware. But if you turn away, then know well that Our Messenger had merely to deliver the Message clearly.

[93] There will be no blame on those who believe and do righteous deeds for whatever they might have partaken (in the past) as long as they refrain from the things prohibited, and persist in their faith and do righteous deeds, and continue to refrain from whatever is forbidden and submit

---

47. Two injunctions had already been revealed concerning the prohibition of intoxicants. (See *Sūrah al-Baqarah* 2: 219 and *Sūrah al-Nisā'* 4: 43.) Before the revelation of the last injunction, the Prophet (peace be on him) had warned people that intoxicants were highly displeasing to God. Hinting at the possibility of their being prohibited, he counselled people to dispose of intoxicants if they had any. A little later the present verse was revealed and the Prophet (peace be on him) then proclaimed that those who had intoxicants should neither consume nor sell them; instead, they should destroy them. No sooner than this proclamation was made that intoxicating liquors were poured into the streets of Madīnah.

to Divine commandments, and persevere in doing good, fearing Allah. Allah loves those who do good.

[94] Believers, Allah will surely try you with a game which will be within the range of your hands and lances so that He might mark out those of you who fear Him, even though He is beyond the reach of perception. A painful chastisement awaits whosoever transgresses the bounds set by Allah after His firm warning. [95] Believers! Do not kill game while you are in the state of Pilgrim Sanctity.[48] Whoever of you kills it wilfully there shall be a recompense, the like of what he has killed in cattle – as shall be judged by two persons of equity among you – to be brought to the Ka'bah as an offering, or feed the needy as an expiation, or its equivalent in fasting in order that he may taste the grievousness of his deed. Allah has pardoned whatever has passed; but Allah will exact a penalty from him who repeats it. Allah is All-Mighty. He is fully capable of exacting retribution.

[96] The game of the water and eating thereof are permitted to you as a provision for those of you (who are settled) and for those on a journey; but to hunt on land

---

48. When a person is in the state of Pilgrim Sanctity (*iḥrām*) it is prohibited for him both to hunt and to assist in hunting animals. Indeed, even if an animal has been hunted for him by someone else he may not eat it. However, if someone hunts an animal for himself and makes a gift of it to such a person, there is no harm in his eating it. There is, however, an exception to this injunction against killing animals when one is in the state of *iḥrām*, and that is with regard to harmful animals. Snakes, scorpions, mad dogs and such other animals which cause injury to human beings may be killed even by those in the state of *iḥrām*.

while you are in the state of Pilgrim Sanctity is forbidden for you. Beware, then, of disobeying Allah to Whom all of you shall be mustered.

[97] Allah has appointed the Ka'bah, the Sacred House, as a means of support for (the collective life of) people, and has caused the holy month (of Pilgrimage), and the animals of sacrificial offering and their distinguishing collars to assist therein. This is so that you may know that Allah is aware of all that is in the heavens and all that is in the earth; and that Allah has knowledge of everything. [98] Know well that Allah is severe in retribution, and that Allah is also All-Forgiving, All-Compassionate. [99] The Messenger is bound only to deliver the Message, whereafter Allah knows well all that you disclose and all that you conceal. [100] (O Messenger), say to them: "The bad things and the good things are not equal, even though the abundance of the bad things might make you pleased with them.[49] People of understanding, beware of disobeying Allah; maybe you will attain true success."

[101] Believers! Do not ask of the things which, if made manifest to you, would vex you; for,[50] if you should ask about them while the Qur'ān is being revealed, they will

---

49. This verse enunciates a standard of evaluation and judgement quite distinct from the standards employed by superficial people. For the latter, a hundred dollars would be worth more than five dollars, since the figure hundred is more than five. But according to this verse, if those hundred dollars have been earned in a manner entailing the disobedience of God, the entire amount becomes unclean. If, on the contrary, a man earns five dollars while obeying God then this amount is clean; and anything which is unclean, whatever its quantity, cannot be worth that which is clean.

be made manifest to you. Allah has pardoned whatever happened in the past. He is All-Forgiving, All-Forbearing. [102] Indeed some people before you had asked such questions and in consequence fell into unbelief.

[103] Allah has neither appointed (cattle consecrated to idols such as) *Baḥīrah, Sā'ibah Waṣīlah* nor *Ḥām;*[51] but those who disbelieve forge lies against Allah and of them most have no understanding (and therefore succumb to such superstitions). [104] When they are asked: "Come to what Allah has revealed, and come to the Messenger,"

---

50. People used to ask the Prophet (peace be on him) many questions which were of no practical relevance to either religious or day-to-day affairs. Hence they were given this directive.

51. Here is a mention of some of the superstitious practices of the Arabs of the *Jāhilīyah* period. *Baḥīrah* was the name of a female camel which had already borne five young, the last of which was a male. The practice was to slit the ear of such a camel and then let her loose. Thereafter no one could ride her, use her milk, slaughter her or shear her hair. She was entitled to graze and drink water wherever she liked. *Sā'ibah* was the name of either a male or female camel which had been let loose after consecration as a mark of gratitude in fulfilment of a vow taken for either the recovery from some ailment or delivery from some danger. In the same way the female camel which had given birth ten times, and each time to a female, was let loose. As for *Waṣīlah* if the first kid born to a goat was a male, it was slaughtered in the name of the deities; but if it was a female, it was kept by the owners for themselves. If twins were born and one of them was a male and the other a female goat, the male was not slaughtered but rather let loose in the name of the deities. This male goat was called *waṣīlah*. There was also another category known as *hām*: If the young of camels in the second degree of descent had become worthy of riding they were let loose. Likewise, if ten offspring had been borne by a female camel she was also let loose and called *hām*.

they reply: "The way of our forefathers suffices us." (Will they continue to follow their forefathers) even though their forefathers might have known nothing, and might have been on the wrong way?

[105] Believers, take heed as regards your own selves. If you are rightly-guided, the error of he who strays will not harm you.[52] To Allah will all of you return; then He will let all of you know what you did.

[106] Believers! When death approaches you, let two persons of equity[53] among you act as witnesses when you make your bequest; or let two of those from others than yourselves act as witnesses if you are on a journey when the affliction of death befalls you. Then if any doubt occurs you shall detain both of them (in the mosque) after the Prayer, and they shall swear by Allah: "We shall

---

52. What is stressed here is that rather than occupying oneself unduly with examining faults in the belief and conduct of others, one should pay greater attention to a critical examination of one's own conduct. This verse, however, in no way means that a person should be occupied only with his own salvation and should remain unconcerned with the reform of others. Abū Bakr removed this misconception in one of his sermons when he remarked: "You recited this verse but interpret it erroneously. I have heard the Messenger of Allah (peace be on him) say that when people see corruption but do not try to change it, and when they see a wrong-doer commit wrong but do not prevent him from doing so, it is not unlikely that God's chastisement will seize them all. By God, it is incumbent upon you that you bid what is good and forbid what is evil or else God will grant power over you to those who are the worst among you. They will greatly chastise you and then when your righteous ones pray to God, their prayers will not be answered."

53. That is, pious, straightforward and trustworthy Muslims.

neither sell our testimony in return for any gain even though it concerns any near of kin nor shall we conceal our testimony which we owe to Allah, for then we should become among the sinners." [107] Then if it is discovered later that the two are guilty of such sin, then two others shall stand in their place from among those against whom the two had sinfully deposed, and swear by Allah: "Our testimony is truer than the testimony of the other two, and we have not transgressed in our statement; for then indeed we would become sinners." [108] Thus it is more likely that they will either bear the right testimony or else they will at least fear that their oaths may be rebutted by other oaths. Have fear of Allah and pay heed. Allah does not direct the disobedient to the Right Way.

[109] The Day when Allah will gather together the Messengers and say: "What answer were you given?"[54] They will reply: "We have no real knowledge of it. You alone fully know all that lies beyond the reach of perception." [110] Imagine, then, when Allah will say: "Jesus, son of Mary, recall My favour upon you and your mother, and when I strengthened you with the spirit of holiness so that you talked to people in the cradle and also when you became of age; and when I taught you the Book and Wisdom, and the Torah and the Gospel; and when, by My leave, you fashioned from clay the likeness of a bird and you breathed into it, and by My leave it became a bird; and you healed, by My leave, the blind by birth and the leprous; and when, by My leave, you caused the dead to come to life.[55] And recall when

---

54. On the Day of Judgement the Prophets will be asked: what was the response of the people of the world to their call?

I restrained the Israelites from you when you came to them with clear proofs whereupon those of them who disbelieved said: "This is nothing but plain magic." [111] And recall when I revealed to the disciples to believe in Me and in My Messenger, they said: "We do believe, and we bear witness that indeed we are the ones who submit to Allah." [112] Also recall[56] when the disciples asked: "Jesus, son of Mary, has your Lord the power to send down to us a repast from the heaven?" Thereupon Jesus said: "Fear Allah if you do indeed have faith." [113] They said: "We desire to partake of it that our hearts be satisfied and we know that you did speak the truth to us, and that we are its witnesses." [114] Jesus, son of Mary, then prayed: "O Allah, our Lord, send down to us a repast from the heavens that shall be a festival for the first of us and for the last of us and a Sign from You. And provide us with sustenance for You are the Best Provider of sustenance." [115] Allah said: "I shall indeed send it down to you; then I shall afflict whoever among you disbelieves with a chastisement wherewith I will afflict none (else) in the world." [116] And imagine when thereafter Allah will say: "Jesus, son of Mary, did you

55. That is, with God's command Jesus restored people to life from the state of death.

56. Since the disciples have been mentioned here, the continuity of the subject is interrupted for a moment in order to introduce another incident connected with the disciples. This clearly shows that Jesus' direct disciples considered him merely a human being and a servant of God; they did not entertain any notion that their master was either God or God's partner or son. Jesus, too, had presented himself to them as a servant of God and made no claim to having Divine status or authority.

say to people: 'Take me and my mother for gods beside Allah?',⁵⁷ and he will answer: "Glory to You! It was not for me to say what I had no right to. Had I said so, You would surely have known it. You know all what is within my mind whereas I do not know what is within Yours. You, indeed You, fully know all that is beyond the reach of perception. [117] I said to them nothing except what You commanded me, that is: "Serve Allah, my Lord and your Lord. I watched over them as long as I remained among them; and when You did recall me, then You Yourself became the Watcher over them. Indeed, You are witness over everything. [118] If You chastise them, they are Your servants; and if You forgive them, You are the All-Mighty, the All-Wise," [119] Thereupon Allah will say: "This day truthfulness shall profit the truthful. For them are Gardens beneath which rivers flow. There they will abide for ever. Allah is well-pleased with them, and they well-pleased with Allah. That indeed is the mighty triumph."

[120] To Allah belongs the dominion of the heavens and the earth and all that is in them and He has full power over everything.

---

57. The Christians were not content merely with deifying Jesus and the Holy Spirit. They even turned Mary, the mother of Jesus, into a full-fledged object of worship. The Bible does not contain even the remotest suggestion that Mary was in any way either divine or superhuman. During the first three centuries after the Messiah, such a concept was totally alien to Christian thinking. Towards the end of the third century of the Christian era, however, some theologians of Alexandria employed, for the first time, the expression "Mother of God" in connection with Mary. Subsequently, belief in Mary's Divinity and the practice of Mariolatry spread among Christians.

6
❦

Al-An'ām [Livestock]
Makkan Period

In the name of Allah, the Most Merciful,
the Most Compassionate

[1] All praise is due for Allah alone, Who created the heavens and the earth, and brought into being light and darkness, and yet those who have rejected the call of the Truth ascribe others to be equals to their Lord. [2] He it is Who has created you out of clay, and then decreed a term (of life), and has also appointed another term, a term determined with Him.[1] Yet you are in doubt! [3] And He it is Who is the One True God in the heavens and the earth. He knows your deeds – both secret and open – and knows fully whatever good or evil you do.

[4] Yet every time a Sign of their Lord comes to them, they run away from it, [5] and thus they gave the lie to the Truth that has now come to them. Soon they will come upon some news concerning what they had

---

1. This alludes to the Hour of Judgement when all human beings, regardless of the time in which they lived, will be brought back to life and summoned to render their account before their Lord.

[184]

mocked at.[2] [6] Have they not seen how many a people We have destroyed before them? People whom We had made more powerful in the earth than you are and upon whom We had showered abundant rains, from the heavens and at whose feet We caused the rivers to flow? And then (when they behaved ungratefully) We destroyed them for their sins, and raised other peoples in their place.

[7] (O Messenger), had We sent down to you a book inscribed on parchment, and had they even touched it with their own hands, the unbelievers would still have said: "This is nothing but plain magic." [8] They also say: "Why has no angel been sent down to this Prophet?"[3] Had We sent down an angel, the matter would surely have long been decided and no respite would have been granted them. [9] Had We appointed an angel, We would have sent him down in the form of a man – and thus We would have caused them the same doubt which they now entertain.

[10] And indeed before your time, (O Muḥammad), many a Messenger has been scoffed at; but those who mocked at them were encompassed by the Truth they had scoffed at.

---

2. The allusion here is to the Migration (*Hijrah*) and the numerous victories destined to follow it in quick succession. When this allusion was made, the unbelievers could not have guessed what kind of news they would receive, and even the Muslims could not have imagined the developments that were about to unfold.

3. The unbelievers said that if Muḥammad (peace be on him) had indeed been endowed with prophethood, an angel should have been sent down from heaven to announce that he was the Messenger of God, and that people would be punished if they did not follow his directives.

[11] Say: "Go about journeying the earth, and behold the end of those who gave the lie (to the Truth)."

[12] Ask them: "To whom belongs all that is in the heavens and on the earth?" Say: "Everything belongs to Allah." He has bound Himself to the exercise of Mercy (and thus does not instantly chastise you for your disobedience and excesses). Surely He will gather you all together on the Day of Resurrection the coming of which is beyond doubt; but those who have courted their own ruin are not going to believe.

[13] And to Him belongs all that dwells in the night and the day. He is All-Hearing, All-Knowing. [14] Say: "Shall I take for my Guardian anyone other than Allah, the Originator of the heavens and earth; He Who feeds and Himself is not fed?" Say: "Surely I have been commanded to be the first among those who submit (to Allah) and not to be one of those who associate others with Allah in His Divinity (even though others may do so)." [15] Say: "Surely do I fear, if I disobey my Lord, the chastisement of an awesome Day." [16] Whosoever has been spared chastisement on that Day, Allah has bestowed His Mercy upon him. That is the manifest triumph. [17] Should Allah touch you with affliction, there is none to remove it but He; and should He touch you with good, He has the power to do everything. [18] He has the supreme hold over His servants. He is All-Wise, All-Aware.

[19] Ask them: "Whose testimony is the greatest?" Say: "Allah is the witness between me and you; and this Qur'ān was revealed to me that I should warn you thereby and also whomsoever it may reach." Do you indeed testify

that there are other gods with Allah?[4] Say: "I shall never testify such a thing." Say: "He is the One God and I am altogether averse to all that you associate with Him in His Divinity." [20] Those whom We have given the Book recognize this just as they recognize their own offspring; but those who have courted their own ruin will not believe. [21] And who could be more wrong-doing than he who either foists a lie on Allah or gives the lie to His Signs? Surely such wrong-doers shall not attain success.

[22] On the Day when We shall gather them all together, We shall ask those who associated others with Allah in His Divinity: "Where, now, are your partners whom you imagined (to have a share in the Divinity of Allah)?" [23] Then they will be able to play no mischief but will say (falsely): "By Allah, our Lord, we associated none (with You in Your Divinity)." [24] Behold, how they will lie against themselves and how their forged deities will forsake them!

[25] And of them there are some who appear to pay heed to you, but upon their hearts We have laid coverings so they do not understand; and in their ears, there is heaviness (so they do not hear). Even if they were to witness every Sign, they would still not believe in it so much so that

---

4. In order to bear witness to something, mere guesswork and imagination are not enough. What is required is knowledge on the basis of which a person can state something with full conviction. Hence, the question means: Did they really have knowledge of anyone other than God who could lay claim to man's worship and absolute service on the grounds that He was the Omnipotent Sovereign, and the One whose will prevailed throughout the Universe?

when they come to you, they dispute with you and those who disbelieve contend: "This is nothing but fables of the ancient times." [26] As for others, they prevent them from embracing the Truth; and they themselves flee from it (so as to harm you). But they court their own ruin, although they do not realize it. [27] If you could but see when they shall be made to stand by the Fire! They will plead: "Would that we were brought back to life? Then we would not give the lie to the Signs of our Lord and would be among the believers." [28] No! They will say this merely because the Truth which they had concealed will become obvious to them; or else if they were sent back, they would still revert to what was forbidden to them. (So this plea of theirs would be a lie too) for they are just liars. [29] They say now: "There is nothing but the life of this world, and we shall not be raised from the dead." [30] If you could but see when they will be made to stand before their Lord. He will say: "Is not this the Truth?" They will say: "Yes indeed, by our Lord." Whereupon He will say: "Then taste the chastisement for your denying the Truth."

[31] Those who consider it a lie that they will have to meet Allah are indeed the losers so much so that when that Hour comes to them suddenly they will say: "Alas for us, how negligent we have been in this behalf." They will carry their burden (of sins) on their backs. How evil is the burden they bear! [32] The life of this world is nothing but a sport and a pastime,⁵ and the life of the Hereafter is

---

5. This does not mean that earthly life has nothing serious about it and that it has been brought into being merely as a sport and pastime. What this observation means is that as compared with the true and abiding life of the Hereafter, earthly life *seems* as if it were

far better for those who seek to ward off their ruin. Will you, then, not understand?

[33] (O Muḥammad), We know indeed that the things they say grieve you, though in truth it is not you whom they give the lie to, but it is the Signs of Allah that these wrong-doers reject.[6] [34] Messengers before you have been given the lie to, and they endured with patience their being given the lie to and being persecuted until the time when Our help reached them. None has the power to alter the words of Allah. Indeed some account of the Messengers has already reached you. [35] Nevertheless, if their turning away grieves you, then

---

a sport, a transient pastime with which to amuse oneself before turning to serious business. Earthly life has been likened to a sport and pastime for another reason as well. Since the Ultimate Reality is hidden during the course of worldly life, the superficially-minded ones who lack true perception of things encounter many a thing which causes them to fall a prey to misconceptions. As a result of these misconceptions such persons indulge in a variety of actions which are so blatantly opposed to reality that their life seems to consist merely of sport and pastime.

6. The fact is that before the Prophet Muḥammad (peace be on him) began to preach God's Message, his people regarded him as truthful and trustworthy and had full confidence in his veracity. Only after he began to preach God's Message did they call him a liar. Even during this period none dared to say that the Prophet (peace be on him) had ever been guilty of untruthfulness in personal matters. Not even his worst enemies ever accused him of lying in any matter. When they did accuse him of falsehood, they did so in respect of his prophetic mission. Abū Jahl, for instance, was one of his staunchest enemies. According to a tradition from 'Alī, Abū Jahl once said to the Prophet (peace be on him): "We do not disbelieve you. We do not believe in your Message."

seek – if you can – either a way down into the earth or a ladder to the heavens, and try to bring to them some Sign. Had Allah so willed, He would have gathered them all to the true guidance. Do not, then, be among the ignorant.⁷ [36] Only those who listen can respond to the call of the Truth;⁸ as for the dead, Allah will raise them and then to Him they will be returned.

[37] And they say: "Why has no miraculous Sign been sent down to him from his Lord?" Say: "Surely Allah has the power to send down a Sign, but most of them do not know.⁹ [38] There is no animal that crawls on the earth and no bird that flies with its two wings but are communities like you. We have neglected nothing in the Book (of Decree). Then to their Lord will they all be mustered.

---

7. Don't trouble yourself about showing them the Signs that would convince them of the Truth and make them accept the true faith. Had it been required that all people should be driven to embrace the Truth, there would have been no need to send Prophets and to direct the believers to engage in struggle against the unbelievers.

8. "Those who hear" refers to those whose consciences are alive, who have not atrophied their intellect and reason, who have not closed their hearts to the Truth out of irrational prejudice and mental adamance. In contrast to such people are those who are characterized as "dead" – who blindly follow the old, familiar, beaten tracks, and can never deviate from the ways they have inherited, even when these ways are plainly at variance with the Truth.

9. The word *āyah* here signifies a tangible miracle. The purpose of the verse is to point out that the reason for not showing a miraculous Sign is not God's powerlessness. The true reason is something else which those people in their immaturity have failed to comprehend.

[39] Those who gave the lie to Our Signs are deaf and dumb and blunder about in darkness. Allah causes whomsoever He wills to stray in error, and sets whomsoever He wills on the Straight Way."[10] [40] Say: "What do you think if some chastisement of Allah or the Hour suddenly overtakes you: do you cry to any other than Allah? Answer, if you speak the truth. [41] Lo, it is to Him alone that you cry and then, if He so wills, He removes the distress for which you had cried to Him. Then you forget the partners you had set up with Allah."[11]

[42] And We indeed sent Messengers to other nations before you and then seized those nations with misfortune and hardship so that they might humble themselves (before Us). [43] But when misfortune befell them from

---

10. God's act of misguiding a man consists in not enabling him who cherishes his ignorance to observe the signs of God. The fact is that if a biased person – one who does not really cherish the Truth – were to observe the Signs of God, he might still fail to perceive it. Indeed, all those things which cause misconception and confusion would probably continue to alienate him from it. God's act of true guidance consists in enabling a seeker after the Truth to benefit from the sources of true knowledge so that he constantly discovers sign after sign, leading him ultimately to the Truth.

11. This Sign is ingrained in man's soul. When either some great calamity befalls a man or when death starkly stares him in the face, it is only to God that he turns for refuge. On such occasions even the staunchest polytheists forget their false gods and cry out to the One True God, and even the most rabid atheists stretch out their hands in prayer to Him. This phenomenon is mentioned here in order to draw an instructive lesson. It shows that devotion to God and monotheism are ingrained in the human soul. No matter how overlaid this truth might be, some day it shakes off man's heedlessness and ignorance and manifests itself with full force.

Us why did they not humble themselves? Their hearts had hardened and Satan had made their deeds seem fair to them. [44] So, when they forgot what they had been reminded of, We opened the gates of all things so that while they rejoiced in what they had been granted We suddenly seized them and they were plunged into utter despair. [45] Thus the last remnant of those wrong-doing people was cut off. All praise be to Allah, the Lord of the entire Universe, (for having punished them so).

[46] Say (O Muḥammad): "What do you think? If Allah should take away your hearing and your sight and seal your hearts¹² – who is the god, other than Allah, who could restore them to you?" Behold, how We put forth Our Signs in diverse forms, and yet they turn away from them. [47] Say: "If the chastisement of Allah were to overtake you suddenly or openly shall any except the wrong-doing people be destroyed?" [48] We do not send Messengers except as bearers of glad tidings and warners. So, he who believes in their Message and mends his conduct need have no fear and need not grieve, [49] whereas those who give the lie to Our Signs, chastisement will visit them for their transgression.

[50] (O Muḥammad)! Say: "I do not say to you that I have the treasures of Allah; nor do I have knowledge of what is beyond the reach of perception; nor do I say to you that I am an angel. I only follow what is revealed to me." Then ask them: "Are the blind and the seeing alike?" Do you not then reflect?

---

12. The expression "sealing of hearts" means rendering people incapable of thinking and understanding things correctly.

[51] And warn with this (revealed message) those who fear that they shall be mustered to their Lord, that there will be none apart from Allah to act as their protector and intercessor; then maybe they will become God-fearing. [52] And do not drive away those who invoke their Lord in the morning and the evening, seeking His pleasure all the time. You are by no means accountable for them just as they are by no means accountable for you. If you still drive them away, you will become among the wrong-doers. [53] Thus We have made some of them a means to test others[13] so that they should say: "Are these the ones among us upon whom Allah has bestowed His Favour?" Yes, does Allah not know well who are the thankful? [54] And when those who believe in Our Signs come to you, say to them: "Peace be upon you. Your Lord has made Mercy incumbent upon Himself so that if anyone of you does a bad deed out of ignorance and thereafter repents and makes amends, surely you will find Him All-Forgiving, All-Compassionate."[14] [55] Thus do We clearly set forth Our Signs that the way of the wicked might become distinct.

---

13. By enabling the poor and the indigent, the people who have a low station in society to take the lead in believing, God has put those who wax proud on account of their wealth, power and pelf to a severe test.

14. Several of those who came to believe in the Prophet (peace be on him) had committed many serious sins before they embraced Islam. Even though their lives had altogether changed following their conversion, the opponents continued to play up the weaknesses and misdeeds of their past life. The Prophet (peace be on him) is asked to comfort such persons and to tell them that God does not punish those who sincerely repent for their sins and mend their ways.

[56] Say, (O Muḥammad): "I have been forbidden to serve those whom you call upon other than Allah." Say: "I do not follow your desires, for were I to do that, I would go astray and would not be of those who are rightly-guided." [57] Say: "I take stand upon a Clear Evidence from my Lord and it is that which you have given the lie to. What you desire to be hastened is not within my power. Judgement lies with Allah alone. He declares the Truth, and He is the Best Judge." [58] Say: "If what you demand so hastily were in my power, the matter between me and you would have long been decided. But Allah knows best how to judge the wrong-doers. [59] He has the keys to the realm of the Unseen which none knows but He. And He knows what is on the land and in the sea; there is not a leaf which falls that He does not know about and there is not a grain in the darkness of the earth or anything green or dry which has not been recorded in a Clear Book. [60] He recalls your souls by night, and knows what you do by day, and then He raises you back each day in order that the term appointed by Him is fulfilled. Then to Him you will return, whereupon He will let you know what you have been doing. [61] And He alone holds sway over His servants and sets guardians over you till death approaches any of you and Our deputed angels take his soul, neglecting no part of their task. [62] Then all are restored to Allah, their True Protector. Behold, His is the judgement. He is the swiftest of those who take account."

[63] Ask them, (O Muḥammad): "Who is it that delivers you from dangers in the deep darknesses of the land and the sea, and whom do you call upon in humility and in the secrecy of your hearts? To whom do you pray: If He

will but save us from this distress, we shall most certainly be among the thankful?" [64] Say: "Allah delivers you from this and from every distress, and yet you associate others with Allah in His Divinity."[15] [65] Say: "It is He Who has the power to send forth chastisement upon you from above you, or from beneath your feet, or split you into hostile groups and make some of you taste each other's violence. Behold, how We set forth Our Signs in diverse forms, so that they may understand the Truth." [66] Your people have denied it even though it is the Truth. Say: "I am not a guardian over you.[16]

---

15. That God alone possesses all power and authority and has full control over the things which cause benefit or harm to people, that He alone holds the reins of their destiny are facts to which there is ample testimony in man's own life. For instance, whenever man is faced with a really hard time, and when the resources upon which he normally falls back seem to fail him, he instinctively turns to God. In spite of such a clear sign, people set up partners to God without any shred of evidence that anyone other than God has any share in His power and authority. The anomaly is that even though they are nourished by resources that God alone has created, they acknowledge others than Him to be their lords. Even though they have been delivered from insecurity and stress by His grace and mercy, they consider others rather than God to be their protectors and helpers. Even though they were God's born slaves, it is to others that they devote their worship. Even though it is God alone Who relieves their distress and to Whom they cry out in adversity for deliverance, no sooner are they out of immediate danger than they extol others as their rescuers, and it is to them rather than to the One True God that they pay homage and make offerings.

16. A Prophet is neither required to compel people to see what they are not prepared to see nor to force into their hearts what they fail to comprehend. It is not a Prophet's task to chastise people for failing to see and comprehend the Truth.

[67] Every tiding has its appointed time; you yourselves will soon know (the end)."

[68] When you see those who are engaged in blasphemy against Our Signs, turn away from them until they begin to talk of other things; and should Satan ever cause you to forget, then do not remain, after recollection, in the company of those wrong-doing people. [69] For those who are God-fearing are by no means accountable for others except that it is their duty to admonish them; maybe they will shun evil. [70] Leave alone those who have made a sport and a pastime of their religion and whom the life of the world has beguiled. But continue to admonish them (with the Qur'ān) lest a man should be caught for what he has himself earned, for there shall neither be any protector nor intercessor apart from Allah; and though he may offer any conceivable ransom it shall not be accepted from him, for such people have been caught for the deeds that they have themselves earned. Boiling water to drink and a painful chastisement to suffer for their unbelief is what awaits them.

[71] Ask them, (O Muḥammad): "Shall we invoke, anything apart from Allah, that can neither benefit nor harm us, and thus be turned back on our heels after Allah has guided us? Like the one whom the evil ones have lured into bewilderment in the earth, even though he has friends who call him to true guidance, saying, "Come to us." Say: "Surely Allah's guidance is the only true guidance, and we have been commanded to submit ourselves to the Lord of the entire Universe, [72] and to establish Prayer, and to have fear of Him. It is to Him that all of you shall be gathered. [73] And He it is Who has

created the heavens and the earth in Truth;[17] and the very day He will say: "(Let there) be (resurrection)" and it will be. His Word is the Truth and His will be the dominion on the day the Trumpet is blown. He knows that which

---

17. It has been asserted again and again in the Qur'ān that God created the heavens and the earth "in Truth". This covers a wide range of meanings:

First, that the heavens and the earth have not been created just for the fun of it. This state of existence is not a theatrical farce. This world is not a child's toy with which to amuse oneself as long as one wishes before crushing it to bits and throwing it away. Creation is rather an act of great seriousness. A great objective motivates it, and a wise and benevolent purpose underlies it. Hence, after the lapse of a certain stage it is necessary for the Creator to take full account of the work that has been done and to use those results as the basis for the next stage.

Second, it means that God has created this entire system of the universe on solid foundations of Truth. The whole of the universe is based on justice, wisdom and truth. Hence, there is no scope in the system for falsehood to take root and prosper. The phenomenon of the prosperity of falsehood which we observe is to be ascribed to the will of God, Who grants the followers of falsehood the opportunity, if they so wish, to expend their efforts in promoting unrighteousness, injustice and untruth. In the end, however, the earth will throw up all the seeds of untruth that have been sown, and in the final reckoning every follower of falsehood will see that the efforts he devoted to cultivating and watering this precious tree have all gone to waste.

Third, it means that God has founded the universe on the basis of right, and it is on account of being its Creator that He governs it. His Command in the Universe is supreme since He alone has the right to govern it, the Universe being nothing but His creation. No one else has any right to enforce his will.

is hidden and that which is evident, He is the All-Wise, the All-Aware."[18]

[74] And recall when Abraham said to his father, Āzar: "Do you take idols for gods? I see you and your people in obvious error." [75] And thus We showed Abraham the kingdom of the heavens and the earth, so that he might become one of those who have sure faith. [76] Then, when the night outspread over him, he beheld a star, and said: "This is my Lord." But when it went down, he said: "I do not love the things that go down." [77] Then, when he beheld the moon rising, he said: "This is my Lord!" But when it went down, he said: "Were that my Lord did not guide me, I surely would have become among the people who have gone astray." [78] Then when he beheld the sun rising, he said: "This is my Lord. This is the greatest of all." Then, when it went down, he said: "O my people! Most certainly I am quit of those whom you associate with Allah in His Divinity.[19] [79] Behold, I have turned my face in exclusive devotion to the One Who originated the heavens and the earth, and I am certainly not one of

---

18. *Ghayb* signifies all that is hidden from, and is beyond the ken of man's knowledge. *Shahādah*, as opposed to *ghayb*, signifies that which is manifest and thus can be known by man.

19. Here some light is thrown on the mental experience through which Abraham passed in the beginning and which led him to an understanding of the Truth before prophethood was bestowed on him. This experience shows how a right-thinking and sound-hearted person who had opened his eyes in a purely polytheistic environment and had received no instruction in monotheism, was ultimately led to discover the Truth by careful observation of, and serious reflection on, the phenomena of the Universe.

those who associate others with Allah in His Divinity."
[80] His people remonstrated with him whereupon
Abraham said: "Do you remonstrate with me concerning
Allah Who has guided me to the right way? I do not fear
those whom you associate with Allah in His Divinity. Only
that which my Lord wills, indeed that alone will come
by. My Lord embraces all things within His knowledge.
Will you not take heed?[20] [81] Why should I fear those
whom you have associated (with Allah in His Divinity)
when you do not fear associating others with Allah in His
Divinity – something for which He has sent down to you
no authority. Then, which of the two parties has better title
to security? Tell us, if you have any knowledge! [82] Those
who believe and did not tarnish their faith with wrong-
doing for them there is security, and it is they who have
been guided to the right way."

[83] That was Our argument which We gave to Abraham
against his people. We raise in ranks whom We will. Truly
your Lord is All-Wise, All-Knowing.

[84] And We bestowed upon Abraham (his offspring) Isḥāq
(Isaac) and Ya'qūb (Jacob) and each of them did We guide
to the Right Way as We had earlier guided Noah to the
Right Way; and (of his descendants We guided) Dā'ūd
(David) and Sulaymān (Solomon), Ayyūb (Job), Yūsuf
(Joseph), Mūsā (Moses) and Hārūn (Aaron). Thus do We
reward those who do good. [85] (And of his descendants

---

20. The word used here is *tadhakkur*, which conveys the sense that
somebody who had been either heedless or negligent of something
suddenly wakes up to its true meaning. Hence this translation of
afalā tatadhakkarūn.

We guided) Zakarīyā (Zechariah), Yaḥyā (John), 'Īsā (Jesus) and Ilyās (Elias): each one of them was of the righteous. [86] (And of his descendants We guided) Ismā'īl (Ishmael), al-Yasa' (Elisha), Yūnus (Jonah), and Lūṭ (Lot). And each one of them We favoured over all mankind. [87] Likewise We elected for Our cause and guided on to a Straight Way some of their forefathers and their offspring and their brethren. [88] That is Allah's guidance wherewith He guides those of His servants whom He will. But if they ever associate others with Allah in His Divinity, then all that they had done would have gone to waste. [89] Those are the ones to whom We gave the Book, and judgement and prophethood.[21] And if they refuse to believe in it now, We will bestow this favour on a people who do believe in it. [90] (O Muḥammad), those are the ones Allah guided to the Right Way. Follow, then, their way, and say: "I ask of you no reward (for carrying on this mission); it is merely an admonition to all mankind."

[91] They did not form any proper estimate of Allah when they said: "Allah has not revealed anything to any man." Ask them: "The Book which Moses brought as a light and guidance for people and which you keep in bits and scraps – some of which you disclose while the rest you conceal, even though through it you were taught that

---

21. Here the Prophets are mentioned as having been endowed with three things: first, the revealed guidance embodied in the Book; second, *ḥukm*, i.e. the correct understanding of the revealed guidance, the ability to apply its principles to the practical affairs of life, the God-given ability to arrive at right opinions regarding human problems; and third, prophethood, the office by virtue of which they are enabled to lead human beings in the light of the guidance vouchsafed to them.

which neither you nor your forefathers knew – who was it who revealed it?"²² Say: "Allah!" – and then leave them to sport with their argumentation. [92] (Like that Book) this too is a Book which We have revealed, one full of blessing, confirming what was revealed before it so that you might warn the people of the Mother of Cities (Makkah) and those around it. Those who believe in the Hereafter believe in it, and are ever-mindful of their Prayers. [93] Who can be more unjust than he who foists a lie on Allah or says: "Revelation has come to me" when in fact nothing was revealed to him, and who says: "I will produce the like of what Allah has revealed?" If you could but see the wrong-doers in the agonies of death, and the angels stretching out their hands (saying): "Yield up your souls! Today you will be recompensed with the chastisement of humiliation for the lie you spoke concerning Allah, and for you waxing proud against His Signs." [94] (And Allah will say): "Now you have come to Us all alone even as We had created you in the first instance, and you have left behind all that We had bestowed upon you in the world. We do not see with you your intercessors whom you imagined to have a share with Allah in your affairs. You have now been cut off from one another and all those whom you imagined (to be Allah's associates in your affairs) have vanished from you."

---

22. The revelation of the Torah to Moses (peace be on him) is adduced by way of evidence since the Jews, to whom this response is addressed, believed that it was revealed. It is obvious that their recognition of the Torah as the Book revealed to Moses negated their standpoint that God had never revealed anything to any human being. Their belief in the Torah at least proved that revelation to man is possible, and that it had actually taken place.

[95] Truly it is Allah Who causes the grain and the fruit-kernel to sprout.[23] He brings forth the living from the dead and brings forth the dead from the living.[24] Such is Allah. So whither are you tending in error? [96] It is He Who causes the dawn to split forth, and has ordained the night for repose, and the sun and the moon for reckoning time. All this is determined by Allah the Almighty, the All-Knowing. [97] It is He Who has made for you the stars that you may follow the right direction in the darkness of the land and the sea. We have indeed spelled out Signs[25] for the people who have knowledge. [98] It is He Who created you out of a single being, and appointed for each of you a place of stay (in life) and a resting place (after death) and a resting place, We have indeed spelled out Our Signs for those who can understand. [99] It is He Who has sent down water from the heavens, and thereby We have brought vegetation of every kind, and out of this We have brought forth green foliage and then from it close-packed ears of corn, and out of the palm-tree – from the sheath of it – thick-clustered dates, hanging down with heaviness, and gardens of vines, and the olive tree, and

---

23. The one who causes the seed-grain to split open under the surface of the earth and then makes it grow and appear on the surface as a plant is none other than God.

24. To "bring forth the living from the dead" means creating living beings out of dead matter. Likewise, "to bring out the dead from the living" means to remove the lifeless elements from a living organism.

25. By "signs" are meant all that support the proposition that there is only One God, that is, no one has either the attributes of God or any share in His authority or can rightfully claim any of the rights which exclusively belong to Him.

the pomegranate – all resembling one another and yet so different. Behold their fruit when they bear fruit and ripen! Surely, in all this there are Signs for those who believe. [100] And yet, some people have come to associate the *jinn* with Allah in His Divinity,[26] even though it is He Who created them; and in ignorance they impute to Him sons and daughters. He is Holy and Exalted far above that which they attribute to Him. [101] He is the Originator of the heavens and the earth. How can He have a son when He has had no mate? He has created everything and He has full knowledge of all things. [102] Such is Allah, your Lord. There is no god but He – the Creator of all things. Serve Him alone – for it is He Who is the Guardian of everything. [103] No visual perception can encompass Him, even though He encompasses all visual perception. He is the All-Subtle, the All-Aware.

[104] The lights of clear perception have now come to you from your Lord. Then, he who chooses to see clearly, does so to his own good; and he who chooses to remain blind, does so to his own harm. I am not your keeper.[27]

---

26. Because of man's imaginativeness and superstitious disposition, he has often associated other invisible beings with God in His governance of the Universe and in the making and marring of man's destiny. He has believed, for example, that there was a deity of rain and another of vegetation; a god of wealth and another of health, and so on. Such absurd beliefs are found among all polytheistic nations of the world.

27. Even though this statement is from God, it is expressed through the mouth of the Prophet (peace be on him). This is similar to what we find in *Sūrah al-Fātiḥah*. Though the statement is God's, it is expressed as a statement of His servants (men of faith). The

[105] Thus do We make Our Signs clear in diverse ways that they might say: "You have learned this (from somebody)"; and "We do this in order that We make the Truth clear to the people of knowledge." [106] (O Muḥammad), follow the revelation which has come to you from your Lord, other than Whom there is no god, and turn away from those who associate others with Allah in His Divinity. [107] Had Allah so willed they would not have associated others with Him in His Divinity; and We have not appointed you a watcher over them, and you are not their guardian. [108] Do not revile those other than Allah whom they invoke, because they will revile Allah in ignorance out of spite. For We have indeed made the deeds of every people seem fair to them. Thereafter, they will return to their Lord and He will inform them of what they have done.

[109] They swear by Allah with their most solemn oaths that if a Sign comes to them, they will certainly believe in it. Say: "Signs are in Allah's power alone. What will make you realize that even if those Signs were to come, they would still not believe?"[28] [110] We are turning their

---

statement "I am not your keeper" signifies that the task of the Prophet is confined to carrying the light of true guidance to others and then it is up to them either to use it to perceive the Reality or to keep their eyes closed. The Prophet (peace be on him) is not required to compel those who deliberately kept their eyes shut to open them, forcing them to see what they did not wish to see.

28. These words are addressed to the Muslims. Driven by the restless yearning to see people embrace Islam – a yearning which they sometimes expressed in words – they wished some miracle to happen, a miracle that would lead their erring brethren to the true faith.

hearts and eyes away from the Truth even as they did not believe in the first instance – and We leave them in their insurgence to stumble blindly. [111] Even if We had sent angels down to them and the dead had spoken to them, and even if We had assembled before them all the things, face to face, they would still not believe unless it be Allah's will that they believe. Most of them behave in utter ignorance. [112] And so it is that against every Prophet We have set up the evil ones from among human beings and *jinn*, some of them inspire others with specious speech only by way of delusion. Had it been your Lord's will, they would not have done it. Leave them alone to fabricate what they will, [113] so that the hearts of those who do not believe in the Life to Come might incline towards this attractive delusion, and that they may be well pleased with it and might acquire the evils that they are bent on acquiring.[29] [114] Shall I look upon anyone apart from Allah for judgement when it is He Who has revealed to you the Book in detail?[30] And those whom We gave the Book (before you) know that this (Book) has been revealed in Truth by your Lord. Do not, then, be among the doubters. [115] The Word of your Lord is perfect in truthfulness and justice; no one can change His words. He is the All-Hearing, the All-Knowing.

---

29. What the verses 110–113 convey is that the Law of God does not envisage man receiving guidance as a matter of course in the manner that a tree bears fruit or the human skull grows hair. Rather, God has sent human beings to the world to put them to a test which leaves them free to either choose the right path or the wrong one. If a person chooses the wrong path God does not compel him to righteousness.

30. The implied speaker in this sentence is the Prophet (peace be on him) and the words are addressed to the Muslims.

[116] (O Muḥammad), if you obey the majority of those who live on earth, they will lead you away from Allah's Path. They only follow idle fancies, indulging in conjecture. [117] And your Lord knows well those who stray from His Path, and also those who are rightly-guided.

[118] If you believe in the Signs of Allah, eat (the flesh) of that over which Allah's name has been pronounced. [119] And how is it that you do not eat of that over which Allah's name has been pronounced even though He has clearly spelled out to you what He has forbidden you unless you are constrained to it. Many indeed say misleading things without knowledge, driven merely by their desires. But your Lord knows well the transgressors. [120] Abstain from sin, be it open or secret. Indeed those who commit sins shall surely be requited for all they have done. [121] Do not eat of (the animal) over which the name of Allah has not been pronounced (at the time of its slaughtering), for that is a transgression. And behold, the evil ones do (indeed) inspire doubts and objections into the hearts of their friends so that they might dispute with you; but if you obey them, you will surely turn into those who associate others with Allah in His Divinity.

[122] He who was dead and whom We raised to life, and We set a light for him to walk among people – is he like the one steeped in darkness out of which he does not come out?[31] Thus have their own doings been made to seem fair to the unbelievers. [123] We have appointed the leaders of the wicked ones in every land to weave their plots; but

---

31. The question is: "There are some who have been able to attain genuine consciousness of their true human nature and

in truth they plot only to their own harm, without even realizing it.

[124] Whenever there comes to them a Sign from Allah, they say: "We will not believe until we are given what was given to the Messengers of Allah." Allah knows best where to place His Message. Soon shall these wicked ones meet with humiliation and severe chastisement from Allah for all their evil plotting.

[125] So whomsoever Allah wills to guide, He opens his breast for Islam; and whomsoever He wills to let go astray, He causes his breast to become strait and constricted, as if he were climbing towards the sky. Thus Allah lays the abomination (of aversion from Islam) on those who do not believe[32] [126] even though this Way is the Straight Way of your Lord, and We have distinguished its Signs to those who heed to the Admonition. [127] Theirs shall be an abode of peace with their Lord – their Protector – in recompense for all they have done.

[128] And on the Day when He shall muster them all together, He will say (to the *jinn*): "O assembly of *jinn*, you have seduced a good many of mankind." And their

---

who, by dint of their knowledge of the Truth, can clearly distinguish the Straight Way from the numerous crooked ways of life. How can we expect such people to live like those who lack true consciousness and who keep on stumbling in the darkness of ignorance and folly?"

32. It is clear from this verse that God constricts the breast with regard to Islam of those who disbelieve and are disinclined to accept the true faith. God does not desire to direct such people to the Right Way.

companions from among the humans will say: "Our Lord! We did indeed benefit from one another and now have reached the term which You had set for us." Thereupon Allah will say: "The Fire is now your abode, and therein you shall abide." Only those whom Allah wills shall escape the Fire. Surely your Lord is All-Wise, All-Knowing. [129] In this manner We shall make the wrong-doers the friends of one another (in the Hereafter) because they earned (evil in the world) together. [130] (Then Allah will also ask them): "O assembly of *jinn* and mankind! Did there not come to you Messengers from among yourselves, relating to you My Signs, and warning you of the encounter of this Day (of Judgement) of yours?" They will say: "Yes, we bear witness against ourselves." They have been deluded by the life of this world, and they will bear witness against themselves that they had disbelieved. [131] (They will be made to bear this witness to show that) it is not the Way of your Lord to destroy cities unjustly while their people were unaware of the Truth.

[132] Everyone is assigned a degree according to his deed. Your Lord is not heedless of what people do. [133] Your Lord is Self-Sufficient, full of compassion. If He wills, He can put you away and cause whomever He wills to succeed you just as He has produced you from the seed of another people. [134] Surely what you have been promised shall come to pass; and you do not have the power to frustrate (Allah). [135] Say, (O Muḥammad): "O people! Work in your place; and I too am at work. Soon you will know in whose favour the ultimate decision will be. Surely the wrong-doers will not prosper."

[136] They assign to Allah a portion out of the produce and cattle that He has created, saying out of their fancy: "This is for Allah" – so they deem – "and this is for the associates (of Allah) whom we have contrived." Then, the portion assigned to the beings whom they have set up as associates (of Allah) does not reach Allah, but the portion assigned to Allah reaches the beings they set up as associates (of Allah).[33] How evil are their judgements!

[137] And, likewise, the beings supposed to have a share in Allah's Divinity have made the slaying of their offspring seem lawful to many of those who associate others with Allah in His Divinity[34] so that they may ruin them and

33. This is a subtle sarcasm at the trickery to which the polytheists resorted when they divided the offerings between God and those whom they had set up as His partners. By one device or another they increased the share of the false deities, which only showed that their hearts lay with those sham partners of God rather than with God Himself.

It is instructive to recall those tricks. If, while they were apportioning God's share of cereals and fruits, anything belonging to His share fell out of its place, it used to be added to the portion earmarked for the share of God's partners. On the contrary, if any part of the partners' share fell out or got mixed up with the portion earmarked for God, they meticulously returned it to where it belonged. Likewise, they were in need of consuming out of the apportioned shares they would use the one that belonged to God but refrain from touching the one earmarked for the false deities for fear lest some calamity should befall them.

34. The word "associate" is used here in a different sense from that implied in verse 136. There it meant the deities whose blessing or intercession are considered helpful in obtaining good fortune. They therefore gave thanks to those deities even as they gave thanks to God for the benefactions that they enjoyed. However, in the present

confound them regarding their faith.[35] If Allah had so willed, they would not have done that. Leave them alone to persist in their fabrication.

[138] They say: "These animals and these crops are sacrosanct: none may eat of them save those whom we will" – imposing interdictions of their own contriving.

---

verse the word "associate" refers to those humans who had made the killing of their own children lawful and the evil ones who had made them regard this callous custom as legitimate, nay even a desirable act.

It is pertinent to recall that three forms of infanticide were practised among the Arabs, and the Qur'ān alludes to each:

(1) Girls were put to death either to forestall the intrusion of a son-in-law, to prevent them from falling into the hands of enemies in the event of an outbreak of tribal feuding or to stop them from becoming a source of disgrace for other possible reasons.

(2) Both male and female children were killed if parents thought they would not be able to support them and that they would thus become an unendurable burden.

(3) Children of both sexes were placed as sacrificial offerings on the altars of the deities in order to gratify them.

35. In *Jāhilīyah*, the Age of Ignorance, the Arabs both identified themselves with Abraham and Ishmael and were quite convinced that they were indeed the followers of Abraham and Ishmael. They therefore considered their religion to be the one that had been prescribed by God. The fact, however, was that over the course of centuries a number of innovations had overlaid the religion preached by Abraham and Ishmael. These innovations, which had been introduced by their religious leaders, the tribal chiefs and the elders of noted families, had become hallowed with the passage of time, and were considered an integral part of their original religion. This rendered the entire religious tradition of the Arabs unauthentic in the sight of the people of Arabia themselves.

And they declare that it is forbidden to burden the backs of certain cattle, and these are the cattle over which they do not pronounce the name of Allah. All these are fabrications against Allah, and He will soon requite them for all that they fabricate.

[139] They say: "What is within the bellies of such and such cattle is exclusively for our males and is forbidden to our females; but if it be born dead, they all may share in it." He will soon requite them for all that they (falsely) attribute to Allah. He is All-Wise, All-Knowing.

[140] Those who slew their children out of folly and ignorance, and forbade the sustenance that Allah has provided them, falsely ascribing that to Allah, are utter losers; they have gone astray, and are certainly not among those guided to the Right Way.

[141] It is He Who has brought into being gardens – the trellised and the untrellised – and the palm trees, and crops, all varying in taste, and the olive and pomegranates, all resembling one another and yet so different. Eat of their fruits when they come to fruition and pay His due on the day of harvesting, and do not exceed the proper limits, for He does not love those who exceed the proper limits. [142] And of the cattle (He has made) some for burden, and some whose flesh you eat and whose skins and hair you use to spread on the ground.[36] Eat of the sustenance that Allah has provided you and do not follow in the footsteps of Satan, for surely he is your open enemy.

---

36. That is, their skins and hair are used for preparing coverings for the floor.

[143] These are eight couples, two of sheep, two of goats. Now ask them: "Is it either the two males that Allah has forbidden or the two females, or what the wombs of the two females may contain? Tell me about this on the basis of sure knowledge, if you speak the truth." [144] And likewise, of camels there are two, and of oxen there are two. Ask them: "Is it either the two males that He has forbidden or the two females, or that which the wombs of the two females may contain? Or were you present when Allah enjoined this commandment on you?" Who, then, would be more unjust than he who fabricates a lie against Allah that he may lead people astray without knowledge. Surely Allah never guides such a wrong-doing folk.

[145] Tell them (O Muḥammad!): "I do not find in what has been revealed to me anything forbidden for anyone who wants to eat unless it be carrion, outpoured blood and the flesh of swine, all of which is unclean; or that which is profane having been slaughtered in a name other than that of Allah.[37] But whosoever is constrained to it by necessity – neither desiring to disobey nor exceeding the limit of necessity – to such your Lord is surely All-Forgiving, All-Compassionate." [146] And to those who had Judaized We have forbidden all beasts with claws, and the fat of oxen and sheep except the fat which is either on their backs or their entrails, or that which sticks to the bones. Thus did

---

37. This does not mean that besides these no other eatables have been forbidden by the *Sharī'ah*. What it implies is that the forbidden does not consist of the things that people have made unlawful for themselves but the ones that God has made unlawful. The point is further elucidated in nn. 2 and 9, *Sūrah al-Mā'idah* (5: 1 and 4).

We requite them for their rebellion.[38] Surely We state the Truth. [147] Then if they give you the lie, say: "Your Lord is the Lord of unbounded Mercy; but His punishment shall not be averted from the guilty folk."

[148] Those who associate others with Allah in His Divinity will now surely say: "Had Allah willed, neither we nor our forefathers would have associated others with Allah in His Divinity, nor would we have declared anything (which Allah did not forbid) as forbidden."[39] Even so those who had lived before them gave the lie (to the Truth) until they tasted Our chastisement. Tell them: "Have you any sure knowledge that you can produce before us? In fact you are only following idle fancies and are merely conjecturing." [149] Then say to them: "(As against your argument) Allah's is the conclusive argument. Surely, had He willed, He would have guided you all to the Truth."[40]

---

38. See *Sūrah Āl 'Imrān* (3: 93) and *Sūrah al-Nisā'* (4: 160).

39. Their apology for their crimes and misdeeds would be that which has always been advanced by criminals and wrong-doers – an apology based on the assumption of absolute determinism. They would plead that when they associated others with God in His Divinity, or unwarrantedly regarded certain things as prohibited, they did so because those acts had been willed for them by God. Had He not so willed, they would not have been able to do what they did. Hence, since they were doing everything according to the will of God, everything was proper. If anyone was to blame, it was God and not they. They were under compulsion to do what they did, for the ability to do otherwise lay beyond their power.

40. The argument which they put forward, viz. "If Allah had willed, we would not have associated others with Allah in His Divinity,"

[150] Say to them: "Call your witnesses to testify that Allah forbade such and such." Then if they do testify, neither testify with them[41] nor follow the desires of those who have given the lie to Our Signs and who do not believe in the Hereafter and set up equals to their Lord.

[151] Say to them, (O Muḥammad): "Come, let me recite what your Lord has forbidden:[42]

> (i)   that you associate nothing with Him;
>
> (ii) and do good to your parents;
>
> (iii) and do not slay your children out of fear of poverty. We provide you and will likewise provide them with sustenance;
>
> (iv) and do not even draw near to things shameful[43] – be they open or secret;

does not embody the whole truth. The whole truth is that "had He willed, He would have guided you all to the Truth." In other words, they were not prepared to take the Straight Way of their own choice and volition. As it was not God's intent to create them with inherent right guidance like the angels, they would be allowed to persist in the error they had chosen for themselves.

41. A person who is conscious that he should testify only to that which he knows, can never testify to this. But if some people are brazen enough to feel no compunction in bearing false witness, then at least the believers should not become their partners in lying.

42. The restrictions which have shackled your lives are not those imposed by God. The ones prescribed by God are as follows.

43. The word *fawāḥish* applies to all those acts whose abominable character is self-evident. In the Qur'ān all extra-marital sexual relationships, sodomy, nudity, false accusations of unchastity, and taking as one's wife a woman who had been married to one's father, are specifically reckoned as "shameful deeds". According to *Ḥadīth*, theft, taking intoxicating drinks and

(v) and do not slay the soul sanctified by Allah except in just cause; this He has enjoined upon you so that you may understand;

[152] (vi) and do not even draw near to the property of the orphan in his minority except in the best manner;

(vii) and give full measures and weight with justice, We do not burden anyone beyond his capacity;

(viii) when you speak, be just, even though it concerns a near of kin;

(ix) and fulfil the covenant of Allah.[44] That is what He has enjoined upon you so that you may take heed.

[153] (x) This is My Way – that which is Straight; follow it, then, and do not follow other paths lest they scatter you from His Path. This is what He has enjoined upon you, so that you may beware."

[154] Then We gave to Moses the Book, completing the benediction of Allah upon the one who acts righteously, spelling out every thing clearly, a guidance and a mercy, that they may believe in their meeting with their Lord.[45]

---

begging have been characterized as *fawāḥish*, as several other brazenly indecent acts. Man is required to abstain from them both openly and in secret.

44. "Covenant of Allah" signifies commitment to God, as well as commitments between one human being and another which automatically take place the moment a person is born onto God's earth and in human society.

45. To believe in "meeting with the Lord" signifies the conviction that one is answerable to God, which leads one to adopt a responsible behaviour in life.

[155] And likewise We revealed this Book – a blessed one. Follow it, then, and become God-fearing; you may be shown Mercy. [156] (You may no longer) say now that the Book was revealed only to two groups of people before us and that we had indeed been unaware of what they read. [157] Nor may you claim that: "Had the Book been revealed to us, we would have been better guided than they." Surely clear evidence has come to you from your Lord, which is both a guidance and a mercy. Who, then, is more unjust than he who gave the lie to the Signs of Allah and turned away from them? And We shall soon requite those who turn away from Our Signs with a severe chastisement for having turned away. [158] What, do they wait either for the angels to appear before them or for your Lord to come unto them or for some Clear Signs[46] of your Lord to appear before them? When some Clear Signs of your Lord will appear, believing will be of no avail to anyone who did not believe before, or who earned no good deeds through his faith. Say: "Wait on; we too are waiting."

[159] Surely you have nothing to do with those who have made divisions in their religion and have split into factions. Their matter is with Allah and He will indeed tell them (in time) what they have been doing. [160] Whoever will come to Allah with a good deed shall have ten times as much, and whoever will come to Allah with an evil deed, shall be requited with no more than the like of it. They shall not be wronged.

---

46. That is, either tokens of the approach of the Day of Reckoning or God's scourge or any other Sign that will uncover the Truth, after which there will be no reason left for testing people.

[161] Say: "As for me, my Lord has guided me on to a
Straight Way, a right religion, the way of Abraham who
adopted it in exclusive devotion to Allah, and he was not
of those who associated others with Allah in His Divinity."
[162] Say: "Surely my Prayer, all my acts of worship,[47]
and my living and my dying are only for Allah, the Lord
of the whole Universe. [163] He has no associate. Thus
have I been bidden, and I am the foremost of those who
submit themselves (to Allah)." [164] Say: "Shall I seek
someone other than Allah as Lord when He is the Lord of
everything?" Everyone will bear the consequence of what
he does, and no one shall bear the burden of another.[48]
Thereafter your return will be to your Lord, whereupon
He will let you know what you disagreed about. [165] For
He it is Who has appointed you vicegerent over the earth,
and has exalted some of you over others in rank that He
may try you in what He has bestowed upon you. Indeed
your Lord is swift in retribution, and He is certainly All-
Forgiving, All-Compassionate.

---

47. The Arabic word *nusuk* used here signifies ritual sacrifice as
well as other forms of devotion and worship.

48. Every person is responsible for whatever he does; and no one
is responsible for the deeds of others.

7

Al-Aʿrāf [The Heights]
Makkan Period

In the name of Allah, the Most Merciful,
the Most Compassionate

[1] *Alif. Lām. Mīm. Ṣād.* [2] This is a Book revealed to you. Let there be no qualm in your heart about it.¹ (It has been revealed to you) that you may thereby warn (the unbelievers), and that it may serve as a reminder to the believers.

[3] (O people), follow what has been revealed to you from your Lord and follow no masters other than Him. Little are you admonished.

[4] How many a township have We destroyed! Our scourge fell upon them at night, or when they were taking midday rest. [5] And when Our scourge fell upon them their only cry was: "We are indeed transgressors."

[6] So We shall call to account those to whom Messengers were sent, and We shall call to account the Messengers (to see how dutifully they conveyed the Message, and how people responded to it). [7] Then We shall narrate to them

---

1. The Prophet (peace be on him) is directed to preach his Message without fear or hesitation, and to disregard his opponents' response.

with knowledge the whole account. For surely We were not away from them. [8] The weighing on that Day will be the true weighing:² those whose scales are heavy will prosper, [9] and those whose scales are light will be the losers, for they are the ones who have been iniquitous to Our signs.

[10] We assuredly established you in the earth and arranged for your livelihood in it. Little do you give thanks.

[11] We initiated your creation, then We gave you each a shape, and then We said to the angels: "Prostrate yourselves before Adam." They all prostrated themselves except *Iblīs*: he was not one of those who fell prostrate.³

[12] Allah said: "What prevented you from prostrating yourself when I commanded you to do so?" He said: "I am better than he. You created me from fire, and him You created from clay." [13] Allah said: "Then get you down from here. It does not behove you to be arrogant here. So

_____

2. This means that when the Balance is fixed on the Day of Judgement, "truth" and "weight" will be identical. The more truth one has to one's credit, the more the weight in one's scale; and vice versa. One will be judged solely on the basis of this weight. In other words, no consideration other than *truth* will enter into the calculation.

3. This does not mean that *Iblīs* was one of the angels. When the angels employed for managing the affairs of the earth were ordered to bow down before Adam it meant that all the creatures under the control of the angels should also submit to Adam. Of all these creatures *Iblīs* was the one who declared that he would not bow down before Adam.

be gone. You will be among the humiliated."⁴ [14] Satan replied: "Give me respite till the Day they shall be raised." [15] Allah said: "You are granted respite." [16] Satan said: "Since You have caused me to come to this end, I shall surely sit in ambush for them on Your Straight Path. [17] Then I will come upon them from the front and from the rear, and from their right and from their left. And You will not find most of them thankful." [18] Allah said: "Go away from here – disgraced and banished. I shall fill the Hell with all those that follow you. [19] O Adam! Live you and your spouse in the Garden and both of you eat from it wherever you will, but never approach this tree or you shall become wrong-doers."

[20] But Satan made an evil suggestion to both of them that he might reveal to them their shame that had remained hidden from them. He said: "Your Lord has forbidden you to approach this tree only to prevent you from becoming angels or immortals." [21] And he swore to them both: "Surely I am your sincere well-wisher." [22] Thus Satan brought about their fall by deceit. And when they tasted of the tree, their shame became visible to them, and both began to cover themselves with leaves from the Garden. Then their Lord called out to them: "Did I not forbid you from that tree, and did I not warn you that Satan is your open enemy?" [23] Both cried out: "Our Lord! We

---

4. Implicit in the Qur'ānic expression (*ṣāghirūn*) is the idea of contentment with one's disgrace and indignity, for *ṣāghir* is he who invites disgrace and indignity upon himself. Now, Satan was a victim of vanity and pride, which could only bring upon him disgrace and indignity. Satan's degradation was, therefore, self-inflicted.

have wronged ourselves. If You do not forgive us and do not have mercy on us, we shall surely be among the losers."[5] [24] Allah said: "Go down; you are enemies one of the other. For you there is dwelling and provision on the earth for a while." [25] He continued: "You shall live there, and there shall you die, and from it you shall be raised to life."

[26] O Children of Adam! Indeed We have sent down to you a garment which covers your shame and provides protection and adornment. But the finest of all is the garment of piety. That is one of the signs of Allah so that they may take heed. [27] Children of Adam! Let not Satan deceive you in the manner he deceived your parents out of Paradise, pulling off from them their clothing to reveal to them their shame. He and his host surely see you from whence you do not see them. We have made satans the guardians of those who do not believe.

---

5. This shows that modesty and bashfulness are inherent in human nature. The primary manifestation of this instinct is seen in the sense of shame that one feels when one is required to expose the private parts of one's body in the presence of others. The very first stratagem adopted by Satan in his bid to lead man astray from the Right Path consisted of undermining man's sense of modesty, to direct him towards lewdness and make him sexually deviant. Man is naturally drawn towards lofty ideals such as the attainment of an exalted spiritual station. Satan, therefore, was forced to present himself as man's sincere well-wisher and to promise him a more elevated position than the present one. This shows that the quality in man that distinguishes him from Satan is that on committing sin he repents and seeks God's forgiveness. In contrast, what brought disgrace and indignity upon Satan was that after disobeying he became adamant in transgression and resorted to rebellion.

[28] And when such people commit an indecent act they say: "We found our fathers doing that, and Allah has enjoined it on us."[6] Say: "Surely Allah never enjoins any indecency. Do you say things regarding Allah that you do not know?" [29] Say to them (O Muḥammad): "My Lord enjoins justice; and that you set your faces aright at the time of every Prayer; and that you call upon Him, exclusively dedicating your faith to Him. You shall return to Him as you were created." [30] A party He has guided to the Right Way, and for another party straying is justly its due for they have taken satans, rather than Allah, as their guardians, for they think that they are rightly-guided.

[31] Children of Adam! Take your adornment at every time of Prayer;[7] and eat and drink without going to excesses. For Allah does not like those who go to excess.

[32] Say (O Muḥammad): "Who has forbidden the adornment which Allah has brought forth for His creatures or the good things from among the means of

---

6. This refers to the pre-Islamic Arabian practice of circumambulating the Ka'bah in stark nakedness. Many of the people of those days circumambulated during *Ḥajj* in a state of nakedness. The women were even more shameless than men. They considered it a ritual which had both religious sanction and merit.

7. The word *zīnah* which occurs in this verse refers to full and proper dress. While performing Prayer people are required not only to cover the private parts of their body but also to wear a dress that serves the two-fold purpose of covering the body and giving a decent appearance. One dresses up decently to meet a respectable person. In the same way one should put on a fine dress at the time of Prayer (when one goes, as it were, to meet one's Lord).

sustenance?" Say: "These are for the enjoyment of the believers in this world, and shall be exclusively theirs on the Day of Resurrection." Thus do We clearly expound Our revelations for those who have knowledge.

[33] Tell them (O Muḥammad): "My Lord has only forbidden indecent acts, whether overt or hidden; all manner of sin;[8] wrongful transgression;[9] and (He has forbidden) that you associate with Allah in His Divinity that for which He has sent down no sanction; and that you ascribe to Allah things of which you have no sure knowledge that they are from Him."

[34] For every community there is an appointed term; and when its term arrives, they cannot delay it by a moment, nor can they hasten it. [35] Children of Adam! If Messengers come to you from amongst yourselves, rehearsing to you My Signs, then those who shun disobedience and mend their ways shall have nothing to fear, nor shall they grieve. [36] And those who reject Our revelations as false and arrogantly turn away from them, they shall be the inmates of Hell; and there they shall abide. [37] Who is more unjust than he who invents a falsehood, ascribing it to Allah, or who rejects His revelation as false? Their full portion of God's Decree shall reach them,[10] until Our deputed angels come to them to

---

8. The word *ithm* denotes negligence, dereliction of duty. Here it implies being slack in obeying the Lord.

9. That means to exceed the limits set by God and to enter an area which has been declared out of bounds for man.

10. All persons, whether good or bad, have been granted a definite term in this world which they will spend and obtain their share of worldly happiness and misery.

take charge of their souls, and say: "Where are the deities now, those whom you invoked besides Allah?" They will say: "They are all gone away from us." And they shall bear witness against themselves that they were unbelievers. [38] Allah will say: "Enter the Fire of Hell and join the groups of *jinn* and humans that have gone before you." As a group enters Hell, it will curse the one that went before it, and when all are gathered there, the last of them shall say of the first: "Our Lord! These are the ones who led us astray. Let their torment be doubled in Hell-Fire." He will answer: "Each will have a doubled torment; although you do not know."[11] [39] Then the preceding ones will say to the succeeding ones: "You were in no way superior to us; taste, then, this torment for your deeds."

[40] Surely the gates of Heaven shall not be opened for those who reject Our Signs as false and turn away from them in arrogance; nor shall they enter Paradise until a camel passes through the eye of a needle. Thus do We reward the guilty ones. [41] Hell shall be their bed, and also above them their covering. Thus do We reward the wrong-doers. [42] As for those who believe and do good, We do not impose upon any of them a burden beyond his capacity. They are the people of Paradise. And there they shall abide. [43] We shall strip away all rancour from their hearts, and rivers shall flow beneath them, and they shall say: "All praise be to Allah Who has guided us on to this.

---

11. The torment resulting from wrong-doing, to which is added the punishment for being an evil influence on others. The punishment for one's own sins is doubled by the crime of leaving behind a legacy of sins which one's followers will indulge in.

Had it not been for Allah, Who granted us right guidance, we would not be on the Right Path. Surely the Messengers of our Lord came down with the Truth." Then a voice will cry out to them: "This is the Paradise which you are made to inherit as a reward for your deeds."

[44] And the people of Paradise shall cry to the people of Hell: "Surely we have found our Lord's promise to us to be true; have you also found true what your Lord had promised you?" "Yes", they shall answer; and a herald shall cry out among them: "Allah's curse be upon the wrong-doers; [45] upon those who hinder people from the path of Allah and seek to make it crooked, and disbelieve in the Hereafter."

[46] And between the two there will be a barrier, and on the Heights will be some other people who will recognize each person by his mark and will cry out to the people of Paradise: "Peace be to you." These will be the ones who had not yet joined them in Paradise, though they long to do so.[12] [47] And when the eyes of the people of the Heights will be turned towards the people of Hell they will say: "Our Lord! Do not cast us with the wrong-doing people." [48] And the people of the Heights will cry out to the prominent people (of Hell) whom they would recognize by their marks: "Neither your host nor the riches of which you were proud availed you. [49] Are these (people of

---

12. The people of *A'rāf* (Heights) will be the people who are neither righteous enough to enter Paradise nor wicked enough to be cast into Hell. They will, therefore, dwell at a place situated between the two and will look forward to God's Mercy to be allowed to enter Paradise.

Paradise) not the ones about whom you swore that Allah shall grant them no part of His mercy?" To such it will be said: "Enter Paradise. You have no cause to fear, nor shall you grieve."

[50] And the people of the Fire will cry out to the people of Paradise: "Pour out some water on us or throw at us something of what Allah has bestowed upon you." They will reply: "Allah has forbidden both of these to the deniers of the Truth, [51] who had made their religion a sport and play, and who were beguiled by the life of the world. So on that Day We shall forget them in the manner they forget their meeting of this Day with Us and persisted in denying Our revelations."

[52] Surely We have brought them a Book which We expounded with knowledge; a guidance and a mercy to those who believe. [53] Are they waiting for the fulfilment of its warning? On the Day that warning is fulfilled, those that have neglected it before will say: "The Messengers of Our Lord did indeed bring forth the Truth. Are there any intercessors who will now plead on our behalf; or, can we be restored to life that we might perform differently from that which we did?" They surely ended in utter loss, and the lies they had fabricated failed them.

[54] Surely your Lord is none other than Allah, Who created the heavens and the earth in six days,[13] and then

---

13. The word "day" in the above verse has been used either in the usual sense of the twenty-four hour unit of time, or in a more general sense of "period" of time.

ascended His Throne,[14] Who causes the night to cover the day and then the day swiftly pursues the night, Who created the sun and the moon and the stars making them all subservient to His command. Lo! His is the creation and His is the command.[15] Blessed is Allah,[16] the Lord of the whole Universe. [55] Call upon your Lord with humility and in secret. Surely He does not love the transgressors. [56] And do not make mischief in the earth after it has been set in order,[17] and call upon Him with fear and longing. Surely Allah's mercy is close to those who do good.

[57] And it is He Who sends forth winds as glad tidings in advance of His mercy, and when they have carried a heavy-laden cloud We drive it to a dead land, then We send down rain from it and therewith bring forth fruits of every kind. In this manner do We raise the dead that you may take heed. [58] As for the good land, vegetation comes forth in abundance by the command of its Lord,

---

14. It is quite difficult to fully appreciate the exact nature of the Qur'ānic statement: that (Allah) ascended the Throne. This is a figurative expression whose precise meaning cannot be established.

15. God is not merely the sole creator but also the only One Who commands and governs. It is not true to imagine that after creating He has detached Himself from His creation, leaving it to the care of others who might rule over it as they please.

16. To say that God is full of *barakah* means that His goodness knows no bounds; that endless beneficence emanates from Him.

17. Do not corrupt, by your perversity and folly, the right order of human life that has been established in hundreds and thousands of years by the efforts of God's Prophets and reformers.

whereas from the bad land, only poor vegetation comes forth. Thus do We expound Our Signs in diverse ways for a people who are grateful.

[59] Indeed We sent forth Noah to his people,[18] and he said: "O my people! Serve Allah, you have no other god than Him. Indeed I fear for you the chastisement of an awesome Day." [60] The leading people of his nation replied: "We see that you are in palpable error." [61] He said: "O my people! There is no error in me, but I am a Messenger from the Lord of the Universe. [62] I convey to you the messages of my Lord, give you sincere advice, and I know from Allah that which you do not know. [63] Do you wonder that admonition should come to you from your Lord through a man from amongst yourselves that he may warn you, that you may avoid evil and that mercy may be shown to you?" [64] But they charged him with falsehood. Thereupon We delivered Noah and those who were with him in the Ark, and caused those who rejected Our signs as false to be drowned. Surely they were a blind folk.

[65] And to 'Ād We sent forth their brother Hūd.[19] He said: "O my people! Serve Allah, you have no other god than He. Will you, then, not avoid evil?" [66] The unbelievers among the leading men of his people said: "Indeed we

---

18. The people of Noah inhabited the land presently known as Iraq.

19. The people of 'Ād lived mainly in the Aḥqāf region which lies between Ḥijāz, Yemen and Yamāmah. It was from there that the people of 'Ād spread to the western coast of Yemen and established their hegemony in 'Umān, Ḥaḍramawt and Iraq.

see you in folly, and consider you to be a liar." [67] He said: "O my people! There is no folly in me; rather, I am a Messenger from the Lord of the Universe. [68] I convey to you the messages of my Lord, and I give you sincere advice. [69] Do you wonder that an exhortation should come to you from your Lord through a man from amongst yourselves that he may warn you? And do call to mind when He made you successors after the people of Noah and amply increased you in stature. Remember, then, the wondrous bounties of Allah[20] that you may prosper." [70] They said: "Have you come to us that we should worship none other than Allah and forsake all whom our forefathers were wont to worship? Then bring upon us the scourge with which you have threatened us if you are truthful!" [71] Hūd warned them: "Surely punishment and wrath from your Lord have befallen upon you. Do you dispute with me about mere names that you and your forefathers have concocted[21] and for which Allah has sent down no sanction? Wait, then, and I too am with you among those who wait." [72] Then We delivered Hūd and his companions by Our mercy, and We utterly cut off the last remnant of those who gave the lie to Our signs and would not believe.

---

20. The word *ālā'* used in the above verse stands for bounties, wondrous works of nature, and praiseworthy qualities.

21. They had appointed for themselves gods of rain, and gods of wind, and gods of wealth, and health. But none of these enjoys Godhead. These titles are merely empty words, bereft of the qualities attributed to them. All argumentation aimed at justifying these titles amounts to a lot of sound and fury about nothing.

[73] And to Thamūd We sent forth their brother, Ṣāliḥ.[22] He said to them: "O my people! Serve Allah, you have no other god than He. Truly there has come to you a clear proof from your Lord. This she-camel from Allah is a Divine portent for you.[23] So leave her alone to pasture on Allah's earth, and touch her with no evil lest a painful chastisement should seize you. [74] And call to mind when after 'Ād He made you their successors and gave you power in the earth so that you took for yourselves palaces in its plains and hewed out dwellings in the mountains. Remember, then, the wondrous bounties of Allah and do not go about creating mischief in the land.

[75] The haughty elders of his nation said to those believers who had been oppressed: "Do you know that Ṣāliḥ is one sent forth with a message from his Lord?" They replied: "Surely we believe in the message with which he has been sent." [76] The haughty ones remarked: "Most certainly we disbelieve in that which you believe."

[77] Then they hamstrung the she-camel,[24] disdainfully disobeyed the commandment of their Lord, and said:

---

22. The Thamūd lived in the north-western part of Arabia which is still called al-Ḥijr. In the present time there is a station on the Ḥijāz railway between Madīnah and Tabūk. This is called Madā'in Ṣāliḥ, which was the capital town of Thamūd and was then known as al-Ḥijr, the rock-hewn city. It survives to this day.

23. From the details of this story that can be gleaned from the Qur'ān one learns that the Thamūd themselves had asked the Prophet Ṣāliḥ to produce some sign which would support his claim to be God's Messenger. Responding to it, Ṣāliḥ pointed to the she-camel.

24. Although the she-camel was killed by an individual, as we learn also from *Sūrahs al-Qamar* (54) and *al-Shams* (91), the whole nation

---

"O Ṣāliḥ! Bring upon us the scourge with which you threatened us if you are truly a Messenger (of Allah)." [78] Thereupon a shocking catastrophe seized them so that they lay prostrate in their dwellings. [79] And Ṣāliḥ left them, saying: "O my people! I conveyed to you the message of my Lord and gave you good advice; but you have no liking for your well-wishers."

[80] And remember when We sent Lot (as a Messenger) to his people and he said to them:[25] "Do you realize that you practise an indecency of which no other people in the world were guilty of before you? [81] You approach men lustfully in place of women. You are a people who exceed all bounds." [82] Their only answer was: "Banish them from your town. They are a people who pretend to be pure." [83] Then We delivered Lot and his household save his wife who stayed behind, [84] and We let loose a shower (of stones) upon them.[26] Observe, then, the end of the evil-doers.

was considered guilty since it stood at the killer's back. He was a mere tool for carrying out the collective will of the nation. The whole nation was therefore held guilty.

25. The Prophet Lot was a nephew of the Prophet Abraham. God bestowed prophethood upon him and assigned to him the mission of reforming his misguided people who inhabited the land which is situated either somewhere near the Dead Sea, or presently lies submerged under it.

26. The "rainfall" in the verse does not refer to the descent of water from the sky. It rather refers to the volley of stones that rained upon them, as stated at other places in the Qurʾān.

[85] And to Midian²⁷ We sent forth their brother Shuʿayb. He exhorted them: "O my people! Serve Allah, you have no god other than He. Indeed a clear proof has come to you from your Lord. So give just weight and measure and diminish not to people their things, and make no mischief on the earth after it has been set in good order. That is to your own good, if you do truly believe.²⁸ [86] And do not lie in ambush by every path (of life) seeking to overawe or to hinder those who believe from the path of Allah, nor seek to make the path crooked. Remember, how you were once few, and then He multiplied you, and keep in mind what was the end of the mischief-makers. [87] And if there are some among you who believe in the message that I bear while some do not believe, have patience till Allah should judge between us. He is the best of those who judge."

[88] The haughty elders of his nation said: "O Shuʿayb! We shall certainly banish you and your companions-in-faith from our town, or else you shall return to our faith." Shuʿayb said: "What, even though we abhor (your faith)? [89] If we return to your faith after Allah has delivered us from it we would be fabricating a lie against Allah;

---

27. The territory of Madyan (Midian) lay to the north-west of Ḥijāz and south of Palestine on the coast of the Red Sea and the Gulf of ʿAqaba, and a part of the territory stretched to the northern border of the Sinai Peninsula. The Midianites were traders and their towns were situated at the crossroads of the trade routes from Yemen through Makkah and Yanbuʿ to Syria along the Red Sea coast, and from Iraq to Egypt.

28. This clearly shows that the people concerned claimed to be believers.

nor can we return to it again unless it be by the will of Allah, our Lord. Our Lord has knowledge of all things, and in Allah do we put our trust. Our Lord! Judge rightly between us and our people, for You are the best of those who judge."

[90] The disbelieving elders of his nation said: "Should you follow Shuʿayb, you will be utter losers."[29] [91] Thereupon a shocking catastrophe seized them, and they remained prostrate in their dwellings. [92] Those who had charged Shuʿayb with lying became as though they had never lived there; it is they who became utter losers. [93] Shuʿayb then departed from his people, and said: "O my people! Surely I conveyed to you the message of my Lord, and gave you sincere advice. How, then, can I mourn for a people who refuse to accept the Truth?"

[94] Never have We sent any Prophet to a place without trying its people with adversity and hardship that they may humble themselves. [95] Then We changed adversity into ease until they thrived and said: "Our forefathers had also seen both adversity and prosperity." So We suddenly seized them without their even perceiving it.[30]

---

29. Such attitudes have not, however, been confined to the tribal chiefs of Shuʿayb. People who stray away from truth, honesty and righteousness, regardless of their age and clime, have always found in honesty a means of great loss. People of warped mentalities in every age have always believed that trade, politics, and other worldly pursuits can never flourish unless they resort to dishonest and immoral practices. The pursuit of truth, in their view, spells one's material doom.

30. After narrating individually the stories of how various nations responded to the Message of their Prophets, the Qurʾān now spells

[96] Had the people of those towns believed and been God-fearing, We would certainly have opened up to them blessings from the heavens and the earth; but they gave the lie (to their Prophets) and so We seized them for their deeds. [97] Do the people of those towns feel secure that Our punishment will not come upon them at night while they are asleep? [98] Or, do the people of those towns feel secure that Our punishment will not come upon them by day while they are at play? [99] Do they feel secure against Allah's design? None can feel secure against Allah's design[31] except the utter losers.

[100] Has it not, then, become plain to those who have inherited the earth in the wake of the former generations that, if We had so willed, We could have afflicted them for their sins, (they, however, are heedless to the basic facts and so) We seal their hearts so that they hear nothing.

---

out the general rule which has been operative throughout the ages. First, before the appearance of a Prophet in any nation, conditions that would be conducive to the acceptance of his Message were created. This was usually done by subjecting the nations concerned to a variety of afflictions and punishments so that they should incline to heed the words of warning and to turn to God in humility. But if the people continued to refrain from embracing the Truth they were subjected to another kind of test – that of affluence. This last test signalled the beginning of their destruction. Rolling in abundant wealth and luxury in spite of their refusal to heed the moral admonition of their Prophet, they thought that there was no God above them Who could call them to account. This made them arrogant and vain, leading them to being punished by God.

31. The expression *makr* signifies a secret design of which the victim has no inkling until the decisive blow is struck. Until then, the victim is under the illusion that everything is in good order.

[101] To those (earlier) communities – some of whose stories We relate to you – there had indeed come Messengers with clear proofs, but they would not believe what they had once rejected as false. Thus it is that Allah seals the hearts of those who deny the Truth. [102] We did not find most of them true to their covenants; indeed, We found most of them to be transgressors.

[103] After them We sent forth Moses to Pharaoh³² and his nobles with Our Signs, but they treated Our Signs iniquitously. Observe, then, what happened to the mischief-makers!

[104] And Moses said: "O Pharaoh! I am a Messenger from the Lord of the Universe. [105] It behoves me to say nothing about Allah except what is true. I have come to you with a Clear Sign of having been sent from your Lord. So let the Children of Israel go with me." [106] Pharaoh said: "If you have brought a Sign, then bring it forth if you are truthful." [107] Thereupon Moses threw his rod, and suddenly it was a veritable serpent. [108] Then he drew out his hand, and it appeared luminous to all beholders. [109] The elders of Pharaoh's nation said: "Surely this person is a skilful magician [110] who seeks to drive you out from your land.³³ What would you have us do?"

---

32. Pharaoh literally means "the offspring of the sun-god". The ancient Egyptians called the sun Ra, worshipped it as their supreme deity, and Pharaoh – Ra's physical manifestation and representative – was named after it. This was not the name of any individual but the title of Egyptian kings, like Czar and Chosroes, the titles of the Russian and Iranian kings, respectively.

33. Moses' claim to prophethood implied the call to total change, obviously including political change. For if a person lays claim

[111] Then they advised Pharaoh: "Put off Moses and his brother for a while, and send forth heralds to your cities [112] to summon every skilful magician to your presence." [113] And the magicians came to Pharaoh and said: "Shall we indeed have a reward if we win?" [114] Pharaoh replied: "Certainly, and you shall be among those who are near to me." [115] Then they said: "O Moses, will you (first) throw your rod, or shall we throw?" [116] Moses said: "You throw." So when they threw [their rods], they enchanted the eyes of the people, and struck them with awe, and produced a mighty sorcery. [117] Then We directed Moses: "Now you throw your rod." And lo! it swallowed up all their false devices.

[118] Thus was the Truth established, and their doings were shown to be false. [119] Pharaoh and his comrades were defeated and put to shame, [120] and the magicians flung themselves prostrate, [121] saying: "We believe in the Lord of the whole Universe, [122] the Lord of Moses and Aaron."³⁴

---

to be God's Messenger, it implies that people should obey him unreservedly. For God's Messengers are not sent to the world to obey other human beings and live in subordination to them as that would be inconsistent with their position as Prophets; they rather ask others to accept them as their leaders and rulers. It is this which explains why Pharaoh and his coterie felt threatened by an all-out revolution – political, economic and social – when Moses came forth with his call and they apprehended that if he succeeded they would lose their political power.

34. Thus God turned the tables on Pharaoh and his courtiers. They had arranged the magic show in the hope that it would convince the people that Moses was just a sorcerer, and thus make them sceptical about his claim to prophethood. But the actual outcome was quite

[123] Pharaoh said: "What, do you believe before you have my permission? Surely this is a plot you have contrived to drive out the rulers from the capital. So you shall see, [124] I shall cut off your hands and feet on the opposite sides, and then crucify you all."

[125] They replied: "We shall surely return to our Lord. [126] Will you punish us just because we believed in the Signs of our Lord when they came to us? Our Lord! Shower us with perseverance and cause us to die as those who have submitted (to You)."[35]

---

the opposite. The sorcerers who had been assembled were defeated. Not only that, it was also unanimously acknowledged that the signs displayed by Moses in support of his claim were not feats of magic. Rather, his signs manifested the might of God, the Lord of the Universe, and hence could not be overcome by magic.

35. Faced with utter failure Pharaoh finally resorted to branding the whole magic tournament as a conspiracy concocted by Moses and his accomplice sorcerers. Under threat of death and physical torture he asked the sorcerers to confess that they had acted in collusion with Moses. This last move by Pharaoh was ineffectual. For the sorcerers readily agreed to endure every torture, clearly proving thereby that their decision to accept Moses' message reflected their sincere conviction and that no conspiracy was involved. The tremendous and instantaneous change which took place in the characters of the sorcerers as a result of belief is also of significance. The sorcerers had come all the way from their homes with the purpose of vindicating their ancestral faith and receiving pecuniary reward from Pharaoh for overcoming Moses. However, the moment true faith illumined their hearts, they displayed such resoluteness of will and love for the Truth that they contemptuously turned down Pharaoh's offer, and demonstrated their full readiness to endure even the worst punishments for the sake of the truth that had dawned upon them.

[127] The elders of Pharaoh's nation said: "Will you leave alone Moses and his people to spread mischief in the land, and forsake you and your gods?" Pharaoh replied: "We will kill their male children and spare their female ones.[36] For indeed we hold irresistible sway over them."

[128] Moses said to his people: "Seek help from Allah and be steadfast. The earth is Allah's, He bestows it on those of His servants He chooses.[37] The end of things belongs to the God-fearing." [129] The people of Moses replied: "We were oppressed before your coming to us and after it." Moses said: "Your Lord will soon destroy your enemy and make you rulers in the land. Then He will see how you act."

[130] We afflicted the people of Pharaoh with hard times and with poor harvest that they may heed. [131] But whenever prosperity came their way, they said: "This is our due." And whatever hardship befell them, they attributed it to the misfortune of Moses and those who followed him. Surely, their misfortune had been decreed by Allah – but most of them do not know that. [132] And they said to Moses: "Whatever Sign you might produce

---

36. There were two periods of persecution. The first was during the reign of Rameses II and took place before Moses' birth, whereas the second period of persecution started after Moses was designated a Prophet. Common to both periods is the killing of the male issue of Israelites while the female was spared. It was a calculated design to rob the Israelites of their identity and to bring about their forcible assimilation.

37. Nowadays some people pick out for special attention the words "The earth is Allah's" and ignore the next part of the statement, viz. "He bestows it on those of His servants He chooses."

before us in order to enchant us, we are not going to believe you." [133] Then We afflicted them with a great flood and locusts, and lice, and frogs, and blood. All these were distinct Signs and yet they remained haughty. They were a wicked people. [134] Each time a scourge struck them they said: "O Moses! Pray for us to your Lord on the strength of the prophethood He has bestowed upon you. Surely, if you remove this scourge from us, we will truly believe in you, and will let the Children of Israel go with you." [135] But when We removed the scourge from them until a term – a term which they were bound to reach – they at once broke their promise. [136] So We inflicted Our retribution on them, and caused them to drown in the sea because they gave the lie to Our Signs and were heedless of them. [137] And We made those who had been persecuted inherit the eastern and western lands which We had blessed.[38] Thus your Lord's gracious promise was fulfilled to the Children of Israel, for they had endured with patience; and We destroyed all that Pharaoh and his people had wrought, and all that they had built.

[138] And We led the Children of Israel across the sea; and then they came upon a people who were devoted to the worship of their idols. They said: "O Moses, make for us a god even as they have gods."[39] Moses said: "You are

---

38. The Israelites were made the inheritors of Palestine. It is the land of Palestine and Syria about which the Qur'ān says at several places that blessing was bestowed on it by God.

39. Though the Israelites were Muslims they had imbibed these influences during the centuries of living together with the idolatrous people of Egypt.

indeed an ignorant people." [139] The way these people follow is bound to lead to destruction; and all their works are vain. [140] Moses said: "Should I seek any god for you other than Allah although it is He Who has exalted you above all?" [141] And call to mind when We delivered you from Pharaoh's people who perpetrated on you a terrible torment, putting your males to death and sparing your females. Surely in it there was an awesome trial for you from your Lord.

[142] And We appointed for Moses thirty nights, to which We added ten, whereby the term of forty nights set by his Lord was fulfilled. And Moses said to Aaron, his brother: "Take my place among my people, act righteously, and do not follow the path of those who create mischief." [143] And when Moses came at Our appointment, and his Lord spoke to him, he said: "O my Lord! Reveal Yourself to me, that I may look upon You!" He replied: "Never can you see Me. However, behold this mount; if it remains firm in its place, only then will you be able to see Me." And as soon as his Lord unveiled His glory to the mount, He crushed it into fine dust, and Moses fell down in a swoon. And when he recovered, he said: "Glory be to You! To You I turn in repentance, and I am the foremost among those who believe." [144] He said: "O Moses! I have indeed preferred you to others by virtue of the Message I have entrusted to you and by virtue of My speaking to you. Hold fast, therefore, to whatever I have granted you, and give thanks."

[145] And We ordained for Moses in the Tablets all manner of admonition, and instruction concerning all things, and said to him: "Hold to these, with all your strength, and

bid your people to follow them in accord with their best understanding. I shall soon show you the habitation of the wicked. [146] I shall turn away from My Signs those who, without any right, behaved haughtily in the earth. Even if they may witness each and every Sign, they shall not believe therein. And even if they see the Right Path, they shall still not follow it; but if they see the path of error, they shall choose it for their path. This is because they rejected Our signs and were heedless to them. [147] Vain are the deeds of those who reject Our signs as false and to the meeting of the Hereafter as false. Shall they be recompensed, except according to their deeds?"

[148] And in the absence of Moses his people made the image of a calf from their ornaments, which lowed. Did they not observe that it could neither speak nor give them any guidance? And still they made it an object of worship. They were indeed wrong-doing.[40] [149] And when they were afflicted with remorse and realized that they had fallen into error, they said: "If our Lord does not have mercy on us and does not pardon us, we shall be among the losers." [150] And when Moses returned to his people, full of wrath and sorrow, he said: "Vile is the course you have followed in my absence. Could you not patiently wait for the decree of your Lord?" And he threw down the Tablets (of the Law) and took hold of his brother's head,

---

40. Their cow-worship was another manifestation of the Israelites' slavish attachment to the Egyptian traditions at the time of the Exodus. It is well-known that cow-worship was widespread in Egypt. The Israelis were so deeply influenced by this practice that no sooner had their Prophet left than they made for themselves the image of a calf to worship.

dragging him to himself. Aaron said: "My mother's son, the people overpowered me and almost killed me. So let not my enemies gloat over me, and do not number me among the wrong-doing folk." [151] Thereupon Moses said: "O Lord! Bestow forgiveness upon me and my brother and admit us to Your Mercy, for You are Most Merciful of the Merciful." [152] In reply they were told: "Verily those who worshipped the calf will certainly incur indignation from their Lord, and will be abased in the life of this world. Thus do We recompense those who fabricate lies. [153] As for those who do evil, and later repent and have faith, such shall find their Lord All-Forgiving, All-Compassionate after (they repent and believe)."

[154] And when the anger of Moses was stilled, he took up the Tablets again, the text of which comprised guidance and mercy to those who fear their Lord. [155] And out of his people Moses singled out seventy men for Our appointment.[41] Then, when a violent shaking seized them, he addressed his Lord: "Had You willed, O my Lord, You could have destroyed them and me long ago. Will You destroy us for the misdeeds of the fools amongst us? That was nothing but a trial from You whereby You mislead whom You will and guide whom You will. You alone are our Guardian. Forgive us, then, and have mercy upon us. You are the best of those who forgive. [156] And ordain for us what is good in this world and in the World to Come for to You have we turned." He replied: "I afflict

41. Moses was summoned for the second time to Mount Sinai along with seventy chiefs of his nation in order that they might seek pardon for their calf-worship and renew their covenant with God.

whomsoever I wish with My chastisement. As for My Mercy, it encompasses everything. I will show Mercy to those who abstain from evil, pay *Zakāh*, and have faith in Our Signs."

[157] (Today this Mercy is for) those who follow the *ummī* Prophet,[42] whom they find mentioned in the Torah and the Gospel that they have. He enjoins upon them what is good and forbids them what is evil. He makes the clean things lawful to them and prohibits all corrupt things and removes from them their burdens and the shackles that were upon them.[43] So those who believe in him and assist him, and succour him and follow the Light which has been sent down with him, it is they who shall prosper. [158] (Say, O Muḥammad): "O people! I am Allah's Messenger to you all – of Him to Whom belongs the dominion of the heavens and the earth. There is no god but He. He grants life and deals death. Have faith, then, in Allah and in His Messenger the *ummī* Prophet who believes in Allah and His words; and follow him so that you may be guided aright."

---

42. Reference to the Prophet (peace be on him) in this verse as *ummī* is significant as the Israelites branded all other nations as Gentiles (*ummīs*). Steeped in racial prejudice, they did not consider members of other nations as their equals, let alone accept any person not belonging to them as a Prophet. The Qurʾān also states the Jewish belief that they would not be taken to task for whatever they might do to non-Jews. (See *Āl ʿImrān* 3: 75.) Employing the same term which they themselves had used, the Qurʾān tells them that their destiny was linked with the *ummī* Prophet. By obeying him they would become deserving of God's Mercy. As for disobedience to the Prophet (peace be on him), it would continue to arouse God's wrath which had been afflicted upon them for centuries.

[159] Among the people of Moses there was a party who guided others in the way of the Truth and established justice in its light. [160] And We divided them into twelve tribes, forming them into communities. When his people asked Moses for water We directed him: "Smite the rock with your rod." Then twelve springs gushed forth from the rock and every people knew their drinking-places. And We caused thick clouds to provide them shade, and sent down upon them manna and quails, saying: "Eat of the clean things that We have provided you." They wronged not Us, but it was themselves that they wronged.

[161] And recall when it was said to them: "Dwell in this town and eat plentifully of whatever you please, and say: 'Repentance,' and enter the gate prostrate. We shall forgive you your sins and shall bestow further favours on those who do good." [162] Then the wrong-doers among them substituted another word in place of the one told to them. So We sent upon them a scourge from the sky as a punishment for their wrong-doing.

[163] And ask the people of Moses concerning the town situated along the sea:⁴⁴ how its people profaned the

---

43. The Israelites had fettered their lives by undue restrictions which had been placed on them by the legal hair-splitting of their jurists, the pietistic exaggerations of their spiritual leaders, the introduction of superstitions and self-contrived laws and regulations by their masses. The Prophet (peace be on him), by relieving them of every unnecessary burden and releasing them from every unjustified restriction, in fact liberated their shackled lives.

44. Most scholars identify this place with Eilat, Eilath or Eloth. The seaport called Elat which has been built by the present state of Israel (which is close to the Jordanian seaport of 'Aqaba), stands on the same site.

Sabbath when fish came to them breaking the water's surface on Sabbath days, and it would not come to them on other than Sabbath days. Thus did We try them because of their disobedience. [164] And recall when a party of them said: "Why do you admonish a people whom Allah is about to destroy or punish severely?" They said: "We admonish them in order to be able to offer an excuse before Your Lord, and in the hope that they will guard against disobedience." [165] Then, when they forgot what they had been exhorted, We delivered those who forbade evil and afflicted the wrong-doers with a grievous chastisement because of their evil-doing. [166] And when they persisted in pursuing that which had been forbidden We said: "Become despised apes."[45]

---

45. This shows that the people in that town were of three categories. One, those who flagrantly violated God's commands. Two, those who were silent spectators to such violations and discouraged those who admonished the criminals, pleading that their efforts were fruitless. Three, those who, moved by their religious commitment, actively enjoined good and forbade evil so that the evil-doers might make amends. In so doing, they were prompted by a sense of duty to bring back the evil-doers to the Right Path, and if the latter did not respond to their call, they would at least be able to establish before their Lord that for their part they had fulfilled their duty to admonish the evil-doers. So, when the town was struck by God's punishment, only the people belonging to the last category were spared for they had displayed God-consciousness and performed the duties incumbent upon them. As for the people of the other two categories, they were reckoned as transgressors and were punished in proportion to their crimes. But the punishment of transforming the persistent evil-doers into apes was confined only to the people of the second category.

[167] And recall when your Lord proclaimed that He would continually set in authority over them, till the Day of Judgement, those who would ruthlessly oppress them. Surely, your Lord is swift in chastising; and yet He is All-Forgiving, All-Merciful.

[168] And We dispersed them through the earth in communities – some were righteous, others were not – and We tested them with prosperity and adversity that they may revert (to righteousness). [169] Then others succeeded them who inherited the scriptures, and yet kept themselves occupied in acquiring the goods of this world and kept saying: "We shall be forgiven." And when there comes to them an opportunity for acquiring more of those goods, they seize it. Was not the covenant of the Book taken from them that they would not ascribe to Allah anything but the Truth? And they have read what is in the Book and know that the abode of the Hereafter is better for the God-fearing.[46] Do you not understand? [170] Those who hold fast to the Book and establish Prayer – We shall not allow the reward of such righteous people to go to waste. [171] And recall when We shook the mountain over them as though it were a canopy, and they thought that it was going to fall over them, and We said: "Hold firmly to that which We have given you, and remember what is in it, that you may guard against evil."

[172] And recall, (O Prophet), when your Lord brought forth descendants from the loins of the sons of Adam,

---

46. The above verse has two renderings. It may be either translated as above or it may be rendered thus: "For the righteous, only the home in the Hereafter is the best."

and made them witnesses against their own selves, asking them: "Am I not your Lord?" They said: "Yes, we do testify."[47] We did so lest you should claim on the Day of Resurrection: "We were unaware of this." [173] Or say: "(It was our forefathers) before us who associated others with Allah in His Divinity; we were merely their offspring who followed them. Would You destroy us for the deeds of the unrighteous?" [174] Thus do We expound the Signs[48] that they may turn back (to the Right Path).

[175] And recite to them, (O Muḥammad), the story of the man to whom We gave Our Signs and who turned away from them; then ultimately Satan caught up with him and he was led astray. [176] Now, had We so willed We could indeed have exalted him through those Signs, but he clung to earthly life and followed his carnal desires. Thus his parable is that of the dog who lolls out his tongue whether you attack him or leave him alone.[49] Such is the parable of those who reject Our Signs as false.

---

47. This event, according to several traditions, took place at the time of the creation of Adam. Apart from the prostration of the angels before Adam and the proclamation that man would be God's vicegerent on earth, all the future progeny of Adam were gathered and were endowed with both existence and consciousness in order to bear witness to God's lordship.

48. "Signs" here refer to the imprints made by the knowledge of the Truth on the human heart which help in the cognition of the Truth.

49. According to commentators this statement is applicable to numerous people belonging to the times of the Prophet (peace be on him) as well as ancient times, though the identity of the particular person referred to here has not been revealed. However, this applies to any person who bears such character. God likens him to a dog

Narrate to them these parables that they may reflect. [177] Evil is the example of the people who reject Our Signs as false and perpetrate wrong against their own selves. [178] He whom Allah guides, he alone is rightly guided; and he whom Allah lets go astray – it is they who are the losers. [179] And certainly We have created for Hell many of the *jinn* and mankind; they have hearts with which they fail to understand; and they have eyes with which they fail to see; and they have ears with which they fail to hear. They are like cattle – indeed, even more astray. Such are utterly heedless.⁵⁰

[180] Allah has the most excellent names. So call on Him by His names and shun those who distort them. They shall soon be requited for their deeds.⁵¹ [181] And of those whom We have created there is a party who guide people through the Truth and act justly according to it. [182] As for those who reject Our Signs as false, We shall lead them, step by step, to their ruin without their even perceiving it.

---

who lolls out his tongue and salivates all the time testifying to his insatiable greed and avarice. The basis of this metaphor is the same for which a person blinded by worldly greed is called a dog of the world.

50. Even though God has bestowed upon people the faculties of observation, hearing and reasoning, some people do not use them properly. Thus, because of their own failing, they end up in Hell.

51. The "most excellent names" used of God express His greatness and paramountcy, holiness, purity, and the absoluteness of His attributes. The commitment of *ilḥād* in naming God mentioned in the verse consists of choosing names which are below His majestic dignity and inconsistent with the reverence due to Him; names which ascribe evil or defect to God, or reflect false notions about Him.

[183] And (for this purpose) I shall grant them respite. My design is incontrovertible.

[184] Have they not pondered that their companion (i.e. the Prophet Muḥammad) is not afflicted with insanity?[52] He is only a plain warner. [185] Have they not observed the kingdom of the heavens and the earth, and all that Allah has created, and that their term of life might have drawn near? After this warning from the Prophet, what will it be that will make them believe? [186] For those whom Allah lets go astray, there is no guide; and He will leave them to stumble blindly in their transgression.

[187] They ask you concerning the Hour, when will its coming be? Say: "The knowledge of it is with my Lord alone: none but He will disclose it at its time. That will weigh heavily on the heavens and the earth, and it shall come upon you all too suddenly." They ask you, as if you are eagerly inquisitive about it. Say to them: "The knowledge of it lies with none except Allah. But most

---

52. The word "companion" here refers to the Prophet (peace be on him), who was born, brought up, and grew into youth, in short, spent his whole life including his old age in their midst. Before the advent of his prophethood, Muḥammad (peace be on him) was known to all the Quraysh as good-natured and of sound mind. However, as he started calling people to accept the Message of God, they immediately dubbed him insane. Now it is obvious that they were not attributing insanity to him as regards his pre-prophetic life. The charge of insanity, therefore, was levelled against the Message he began to preach when he was designated a Prophet. The Qur'ān, therefore, asks them to give serious thought to the teachings of the Prophet (peace be on him) and to see if there is anything that is inconsistent with sanity, or is meaningless and irrational.

people are unaware of this reality." [188] Tell them (O Muḥammad): "I have no power to benefit or harm myself except as Allah may please. And had I knowledge of the Unseen, I should have amassed all kinds of good, and no evil would have ever touched me. I am merely a warner and the herald of glad tidings to those who have faith."

[189] It is He – Allah – Who created you from a single being, and out of it He made its mate, that he may find comfort in her. And when he covers her, she bears a light burden and goes about with it. Then, when she grows heavy, they pray to their Lord: "If You bestow upon us a healthy child, we will surely give thanks." [190] But when He bestows upon them a healthy child, they attribute to Him partners in what Allah had bestowed upon them.[53] Exalted is Allah above that which they associate with Him. [191] Do they associate (with Allah in His Divinity) those who can create nothing; rather, they themselves are created? [192] They have no power to help others, nor can they help themselves. [193] And if you call them

---

53. God holds absolute power over the entire process leading to man's birth. No one has the power to change the form of His creation if He caused a woman to give birth to an animal or to some odd creature, or to a physically or mentally handicapped baby. This fact is equally acknowledged by monotheists and polytheists that in the final stage of pregnancy, people are inclined to turn to God and pray for the birth of a sound and healthy baby. However, when the prayer is granted and a sound and healthy baby is born as a result of God's will, man makes offerings at the altars of false gods, goddesses, or saints. Occasionally, the names given to the child also indicate that man feels grateful to others than God and regards the child as a gift from others rather than God.

to True Guidance, they will not follow you. It is all the same for you whether you call them to True Guidance or keep silent.[54] [194] Those whom you invoke other than Allah are creatures like you. So invoke them and see if they answer your call, if what you claim is true. [195] Have they feet on which they can walk? Have they hands with which they can grasp? Have they eyes with which they can see? Have they ears with which they can hear? Say (O Muḥammad): "Invoke all those to whom you ascribe a share in Allah's Divinity, then scheme against me and grant me no respite. [196] My Guardian is Allah Who has revealed the Book, and it is He Who protects the righteous. [197] Those whom you invoke other than Allah, they can neither help themselves nor you. [198] If you were to call them to True Guidance, they will not hear; and you observe them looking at you whereas they have no power to see."

[199] (O Prophet!) Show forgiveness, enjoin what is good, and avoid the ignorant. [200] And if it happens that a prompting from Satan should stir you up, seek refuge with Allah. He is All-Hearing, All-Knowing. [201] If the God-fearing are instigated by any suggestion of Satan, they instantly become alert, whereafter they clearly perceive the Right Way. [202] As for their brethren (the satans), they draw them deeper into error and do not relax in their efforts.

---

54. As to the false gods set up by the polytheists, what is the extent of their power? Not only do they not have the power to guide others, they do not even have the power to follow others or even to answer the call of their devotees.

[203] (O Prophet), when you do not produce before them any miracle, they say: "Why do you not choose for yourself a miracle?" Say to them: "I follow only what is revealed to me by my Lord. This is nothing but a means of insight into the Truth, and Guidance and Mercy from your Lord to the people who believe." [204] So when the Qur'ān is recited, listen carefully to it, and keep silent so that you may be shown mercy.

[205] And remember, (O Prophet), your Lord in your heart with humility and fear and without raising your voice; remember Him in the morning and evening, and do not become of those who are negligent. [206] (The angels) who are near to your Lord, never turn away from His service out of arrogance; they rather glorify Him and prostrate themselves before Him.[55]

---

55. Whoever recites or hears this verse should fall in prostration. There are fourteen verses in the Qur'ān after reciting which one is required to perform prostration.

8

Al-Anfāl [The Spoils]
Madīnan Period

In the name of Allah, the Most Merciful,
the Most Compassionate

[1] They ask you concerning the spoils of war.¹ Tell them: "The spoils of war belong to Allah and the Messenger. So fear Allah, and set things right among you, and obey Allah and His Messenger if you are true believers."²
[2] The true believers are those who, when Allah's name is mentioned, their hearts quake, and when His verses are recited to them their faith grows, and who put their

---

1. The word *anfāl*, which is the plural of *nafl*, stands for that which is extra, that which is over and above what is obligatory. If this extra is from the servant, it denotes that additional service which he voluntarily renders over and above what is obligatory. On the other hand, when this extra is from the master, it denotes the additional reward which the master awards his servant over and above what he is entitled to. The word *anfāl* used here implies the spoils of the Battle of Badr. What is being conveyed here by using the word *anfāl*, is, in fact, that all wrangling about spoils is out of place since it concerns not what they are entitled to, but the additional rewards that they will receive from God.

2. The clarification was occasioned by the fact that prior to the revelation concerning the distribution of the spoils of the battle different groups of the believers had started laying claim to their respective shares in the booty.

trust in their Lord, [3] who establish Prayer and spend out of what We have provided them. [4] Such indeed are true believers. They have high ranks with their Lord and forgiveness for their sins and an honourable sustenance. [5] (Now with regard to the spoils the same situation exists as when) your Lord brought you forth from your home in a righteous cause while a party among the believers was much averse to it. [6] They disputed with you about the Truth after that had become evident, as if they were being driven to death with their eyes wide open.

[7] And recall when Allah promised you that one of the two hosts would fall to you,³ and you wished that the one without arms should fall into your hands. But Allah sought to confirm the Truth by His words and to annihilate the last remnant of the unbelievers [8] so that He might prove the Truth to be true and the false to be false, however much the evil-doers might dislike it.

[9] And recall when you implored your Lord for help and He responded to you: "I will indeed reinforce you with a thousand angels, coming host after host." [10] Allah meant this as glad tidings and in order that your hearts may be set at rest. For every help comes from Allah alone. Surely Allah is All-Mighty, All-Wise.

[11] And recall when Allah brought on you drowsiness, giving you a feeling of peace and security (coming) from Him,⁴ and He sent down rain upon you from the sky

---

3. This refers to the trading caravan of the Quraysh returning from Syria, or the Quraysh army from Makkah advancing on Madīnah.

4. In the Battle of Uḥud the Muslims passed through a similar experience. (See *Āl ‘Imrān* 3: 154 above.)

that He might thereby cleanse you and take away the pollution of Satan from you and strengthen your hearts and steady your feet.

[12] And recall when your Lord inspired the angels: "I am certainly with you. So make firm the feet of those who believe. I will cast terror into the hearts of those who disbelieve. So strike at their necks and strike at every pore and tip."[5] [13] This is because they defied Allah and His Messenger. Whoever defies Allah and His Messenger must know that Allah is severe in punishment. [14] That is your punishment (from Allah).[6] So taste this punishment, and know that the chastisement of the Fire awaits the unbelievers.

[15] Believers, whenever you encounter a hostile force of unbelievers, do not turn your backs to them in flight. [16] For he who turns his back on them on such an occasion – except that it be for tactical reasons, or turning

---

5. In recounting the events of the Battle of Badr, the Qur'ān aims to explain the significance of the word *al-anfāl* (spoils of war). In the opening verse of the *sūrah* the Muslims were told that they should not deem the spoils to be a reward for their toil. Rather, the spoils should constitute a special reward granted to the Muslims by God, to Whom the spoils rightfully belong. The events recounted here support this. The Muslims could reflect on the course of events and see for themselves to what extent the victory they had achieved was due to God's favour, and to what extent it was due to their own efforts. Therefore, it was for God and not the Muslims to decide how the spoils should be distributed.

6. Here the discourse is suddenly directed to the unbelievers who were routed at Badr.

to join another company – he shall incur the wrath of Allah and Hell shall be his abode. It is an evil destination.

[17] So the fact is that it was not you, but it was Allah Who killed them; and it was not you when you threw (sand at them), but it was Allah Who threw it,[7] (and the believers were employed for the task) that He might cause the believers to successfully pass through this test. Allah is All-Hearing, All-Knowing. [18] This is His manner of dealing with you. As for the unbelievers, Allah will surely undermine their designs. [19] (Tell the unbelievers): "If you have sought a judgement, then surely a judgement has come to you.[8] And if you desist from disobedience, it is all the better for you. But if you revert to your mischief, We will again chastise you; and your host, howsoever numerous, will never be of any avail to you. Know well, Allah is with the believers."

[20] Believers! Obey Allah and His Messenger and do not turn away from him after you hear his command. [21] And do not be like those who say: "We hear," though they do not hearken.

---

7. This refers to the occasion when the armies of the Muslims and the unbelievers stood face to face in the Battle of Badr and were on the verge of actual fighting. At that moment, the Prophet (peace be on him) threw a handful of dust at the enemy saying: "May their faces be scorched." So saying the Prophet (peace be on him) made a gesture and the Muslims started their charge. The incident is being recalled to emphasize that though the dust was thrown by the Messenger (peace be on him), it was in fact the hand of God that struck.

8. Before marching out from Makkah the unbelievers held the covering of the Ka'bah and prayed: "O God! Grant victory to the better of the two parties."

[22] Indeed the worst kind of all beasts in the sight of Allah are the people who are deaf and dumb and who do not understand. [23] And had Allah known any good in them He would surely have made them hear; but (considering what they are) even if He made them hear, they would have surely turned away in aversion.

[24] Believers! Respond to Allah, and respond to the Messenger when he calls you to that which gives you life. Know well that Allah stands between a person and his heart, and it is to Him that all of you shall be mustered. [25] And guard against the mischief that will bring punishment not only to the wrong-doers among you.⁹ Know well that Allah is severe in punishment. [26] And recall when you were few in number and deemed weak in the land, when you were fearful lest people do away with you. And then He provided you refuge, strengthened you with His help, and provided you sustenance with good things that you may be grateful. [27] Believers! Do not be unfaithful to Allah and the Messenger, nor be knowingly unfaithful to your trusts.¹⁰ [28] Know well that your belongings and your children are but a trial, and

---

9. This refers to those widespread social evils whose baneful effects are not confined only to those addicted to them, but which affect even those who put up with the evils just by dint of bearing to live in an evil society.

10. "Trusts" embrace all the responsibilities which are imparted to someone because he is trusted. These might consist of obligations arising out of an agreement or a collective covenant. It might also consist of the secrets of a group. It might also consist of personal or collective property, or any office or position which might be bestowed upon a person by the group.

that there lies a mighty reward with Allah. [29] Believers! If you fear Allah He will grant you a criterion[11] and will cleanse you of your sins and forgive you. Allah is the Lord of abounding bounty.

[30] And recall how those who disbelieved schemed against you to take you captive, or kill you, or drive you away.[12] They schemed and Allah also schemed. Allah is the best of those who scheme. [31] And when Our verses are recited to them, they say: "We have heard. We could, if we willed, compose the like of it. They are nothing but fables of the ancient times." [32] And also recall when they said: "O Allah! If this indeed be the Truth from You, then rain down stones upon us from heaven, or bring upon us a painful chastisement." [33] But Allah was not to chastise them while you are in their midst; nor was Allah going to chastise them while they sought His forgiveness. [34] But why should Allah not chastise them now when

---

11. "Criterion" signifies that which enables one to distinguish the true from the false, the real from the fake. This is the shade of meaning conveyed by the Qur'ānic term *"furqān"*. If a man is God-fearing and tries his best to refrain from acts which displease God, God will create in him the ability to discern for himself at every step which attitude is proper and which is not; which is the path of truth and leads one to God, and which is false and leads one to Satan.

12. This refers to the situation when the Quraysh became certain that Muḥammad (peace be on him), too, would migrate to Madīnah. They realized that once he left Makkah he would be beyond their reach and they would be confronted with a formidable threat. So they convened a council to decide on a decisive course of action to thwart the menace posed by the Muslims.

they are hindering people from the Holy Mosque, even though they are not even its true guardians? For its true guardians are none but the God-fearing, though most of them do not know that. [35] Their Prayer at the House is nothing but whistling and hand-clapping. Taste, then, the chastisement for your denying the Truth. [36] Surely those who deny the Truth spend their wealth to hinder people from the Way of Allah. They will continue to so spend until their efforts become a source of intense regret for them, and then they will be vanquished, and then these deniers of the Truth will be driven to Hell, [37] so that Allah may separate the bad from the good, and join together all those who are bad into a pile, one upon another, and cast them into Hell. They, it is they, who are the losers.

[38] (O Prophet), tell the unbelievers that if they desist from evil, their past deeds shall be forgiven and if they revert to their past ways, then it is well known what happened with the people of the past.

[39] And fight against them until the mischief ends and the way prescribed by Allah – the whole of it – prevails. Then, if they give up mischief, surely Allah sees what they do. [40] But if they turn away, then know well that Allah is your Protector – an excellent Protector and an excellent Helper.

[41] Know that one-fifth of the spoils that you obtain[13] belongs to Allah and to the Messenger and to the near

---

13. This verse lays down the law for distributing the spoils of war. Spoils of war, as mentioned earlier, essentially belong to God and His Messenger. (See verse 1 above.) They alone have the right to dispose of them.

of kin, to the orphans and the needy, and the wayfarer. This you must observe if you truly believe in Allah and in what We sent down on Our servant on the day when the true was distinguished from the false, the day on which the two armies met in battle.[14] Allah has power over all things.

[42] And recall when you were encamped at the nearer end of the valley (of Badr) and they were at the farther end and the caravan was below you (along the seaside). Had you made a mutual appointment to meet in an encounter, you would have declined. But the encounter was brought about so that Allah might accomplish what He had decreed, and that he who was to perish should perish through a clear proof, and who was to survive might survive through a clear proof. Surely Allah is All-Hearing, All-Knowing.

[43] And recall when Allah showed them to you in your dream to be few in number.[15] And had He showed them to you to be numerous, you would have flagged and disagreed with one another about fighting them. But Allah saved you. Surely Allah knows what is hidden in the breasts.

---

14. This refers to the support and help from God on the occasion of the Battle of Badr which brought about victory for the Muslims, and won them the spoils of battle.

15. This refers to the time when the Prophet (peace be on him) was leaving Madīnah along with the Muslims, or was on his way to Badr for the encounter with the Quraysh and did not have any definite information about the strength of the enemy. In a dream, however, the Prophet (peace be on him) had a vision of the enemy. On the basis of that vision, the Prophet (peace be on him) estimated that the enemy was not too powerful.

[44] And recall when He made them appear to be few in your eyes when you met them in the battle just as He lessened you in their eyes so that Allah might accomplish what had been decreed. To Allah are all matters referred for decision.

[45] Believers! When you encounter a host in battle, stand firm and remember Allah much that you may triumph. [46] And obey Allah and His Messenger, and do not quarrel with one another lest you should lose courage and your power depart. Be steadfast;[16] surely Allah is with those who remain steadfast. [47] And be not like those who came forth from their homes exulting, with a desire to be seen by people as full of strength, and hindering others from the Way of Allah. Allah encompasses all that they do.

[48] And recall when Satan made their works seem fair to them and said: "None shall overcome you today, and I am your supporter." But when the two armies faced each other, he turned on his heels, and said: "Surely I am quit of you for I behold that which you do not.

---

16. The believers were asked to exercise self-restraint. They were required to refrain from haste, panic, consternation, greed and uncalled-for enthusiasm. They were counselled to proceed cool-headedly and to take well-considered decisions. They were also asked not to relent an inch even in the face of grave dangers; refrain from acting rashly under provocation; to desist from taking hasty action out of impatience. They were also asked to exercise control over themselves lest they were tempted by worldly gains. All these instructions are implicit in the Qur'ānic directive of "steadfastness" given to the Muslims. God extends all help and support to those who exercise "steadfastness" (*ṣabr*) in the above sense.

Indeed I fear Allah, and Allah is stern in punishment."
[49] And recall when the hypocrites and those whose
hearts were diseased said: "Their faith has deluded these
(believers)."[17] But he who puts his trust in Allah shall find
Allah All-Mighty, All-Wise. [50] And if you could only see
when the angels took away the souls of the unbelievers,
striking them on their faces and backs, saying: "Taste
the torment of burning. [51] This is your punishment for
what your hands have wrought. Allah is not unjust in the
least to His creatures." [52] Their case is like that of the
people of Pharaoh and those before them. They denied
the signs of Allah and so Allah seized them for their sins.
Surely Allah is All-Powerful, Most Stern in retribution.
[53] This happened because Allah is not one to change the
favour which He has bestowed upon a people until they
have changed their attitude. Surely Allah is All-Hearing,
All-Knowing. [54] Their case is like that of the people of
Pharaoh and those before them: they rejected the signs
of their Lord as false and so We destroyed them for their
sins, and caused the people of Pharaoh to drown. For all
of them were wrong-doers.

---

17. Observing that a small band of resourceless Muslims was
getting ready to confront the powerful Quraysh, the hypocrites
as well as those who were heedless of God and cared only
for worldly interests, often tended to say to one another that
the religious passion of the Muslims had driven them to utter
fanaticism and zealotry. They were sure that the Muslims would
face a total rout on the battlefield. They were puzzled by how the
Prophet (peace be on him), in whom the Muslims believed, had
cast such a spell over them that they were altogether incapable of
rational calculation and were hence rushing straight into the very
mouth of death.

[55] Surely the worst moving creatures in the sight of Allah are those who definitively denied the Truth and are therefore in no way prepared to accept it, [56] (especially) those with whom you entered into a covenant and then they broke their covenant time after time, and who do not fear Allah.[18] [57] So if you meet them in war, make of them a fearsome example for those who follow them[19] that they may be admonished. [58] And if you fear treachery from any people (with whom you have a covenant) then publicly throw their covenant at them.[20] Allah does not love the treacherous. [59] Let not the deniers of the Truth be deluded that they will gain any advantage. Surely they can never overcome Us!

---

18. This refers especially to the Jews. After arriving in Madīnah, the Prophet (peace be on him) concluded a treaty of mutual co-operation and good neighbourliness with them. But in spite of that they were actively hostile towards the Prophet (peace be on him) and the Muslims. This is evident from the fact that they lost no time after the Battle of Badr to incite the Quraysh to wreak vengeance upon the Muslims.

19. The verse makes it lawful for Muslims to feel absolved of the obligations of a treaty with a people who, despite that alliance, threw the obligations of the treaty overboard and engaged in acts of hostility against the Muslims. It would even be lawful for the Muslims to engage in hostilities against them. Likewise, if the Muslims are engaged in hostilities against a people and the non-Muslims who are bound in treaties of alliance or friendship with the Muslims array themselves on the side of the enemy and fight against the Muslims, it would be lawful for the Muslims to treat them as enemies and kill them.

20. This means that the Muslims should publicly announce that the treaty stands annulled as it is being violated by them.

[60] Make ready for an encounter against them all the forces and well-readied horses you can muster[21] so that you may overawe the enemies of Allah and your own enemies and others besides them of whom you are unaware but of whom Allah is aware. Whatever you may spend in the cause of Allah shall be fully repaid to you, and you shall not be wronged.

[61] If they incline to peace, incline you as well to it, and trust in Allah. Surely He is All-Hearing, All-Knowing. [62] And should they seek to deceive you, Allah is sufficient for you. He it is Who strengthened you with His succour and the believers [63] and joined their hearts. Had you given away all the riches of the earth you could not have joined their hearts, but it is Allah Who joined their hearts. Indeed He is All-Mighty, All-Wise. [64] O Prophet! Allah is sufficient for you and the believers who follow you.

[65] O Prophet! Rouse the believers to fighting. If there be twenty of you who persevere, they shall vanquish two hundred; and if there be of you a hundred, they shall vanquish a thousand of those who disbelieve, for they are a people who lack understanding.[22] [66] Allah has

---

21. Muslims should be equipped with military resources and should have a standing army in a state of preparedness in order that it may be used when needed. Never should it happen that the Muslims are caught unawares and have to hurriedly look around right and left to build up their defences and collect arms and supplies in order to meet the challenge of the enemy. For then it might be too late and the enemy might have accomplished its purpose.

22. What is nowadays called morale has been described as "understanding" in the Qur'ān. The word in this context refers to the one who is fully cognizant of his objective, who is quite

now lightened your burden for He found weakness in you. So if there be a hundred of you who persevere, they shall vanquish two hundred; and if there be a thousand of you they shall, by the leave of Allah, vanquish two thousand.[23] Allah is with those who persevere.

[67] It behoves not a Prophet to take captives until he has sufficiently suppressed the enemies in the land. You merely seek the gains of the world whereas Allah desires (for you the good) of the Hereafter. Allah is All-Mighty, All-Wise. [68] Had there not been a previous decree from Allah, a stern punishment would have afflicted you for what you have taken. [69] So eat that which you have obtained – for it is lawful and clean – and fear Allah.[24] Surely Allah is Ever Forgiving, Most Merciful.

---

clear in his mind that the cause for which he has staked his life is much more valuable than his own life, and hence if that cause is left unrealized, his life will lose all its worth and meaning. Such a conscious, committed person actually becomes many times more powerful than he who fights without any consciousness of his cause, even though the two might be comparable in physical strength.

23. This does not mean that since the faith of Muslims had declined, their ten times superiority over the unbelievers had been reduced to twice only. What it means is that ideally a Muslim is ten times stronger than an unbeliever. However, since the Muslims had not as yet been thoroughly trained and had not reached the desired level of maturity in their understanding, they are asked not to feel uneasy at least at challenging an enemy which is twice as strong. It should be borne in mind that the Qur'ānic directive was given in 2 A.H./624 C.E. when most of the Muslims, being recent converts to Islam, had undergone little training.

24. The preliminary instructions about war given in *Sūrah Muḥammad* (47: 4) before the Battle of Badr had allowed ransom for

[70] O Prophet! Say to the captives in your hands: "If Allah finds any goodness in your hearts He will give you that which is better than what has been taken away from you, and He will forgive you. Allah is Ever Forgiving, Most Merciful." [71] But if they seek to betray you, know that they had already betrayed Allah. Therefore He made you prevail over them. Allah is All-Knowing, All-Wise.

[72] Surely those who believed and migrated and strove hard in the way of Allah with their possessions and their lives, and those that sheltered and helped them – they alone are the true allies of one another. And those who believed but did not migrate (to *Dār al-Islām*), you are under no obligation of alliance unless they migrate.[25] And should they seek help from you in the matter of religion,

---

release of prisoners of war. But the permission pre-supposed the crushing of the enemy's might before the vanquished were taken prisoners. Their capture at Badr and the acceptance of ransom for their release, though lawful, fell short of the stipulation that the enemy be completely crushed before any prisoners were taken and the spoils of war were collected. God disapproved of this negligence on the part of Muslims. If they had strictly followed the command of God and chased the fleeing enemy the Quraysh could have been dealt a death blow once and for all.

25. The Arabic word *walāyah* denotes the relationship of kinship, support, succour, protection, friendship, and guardianship. In the context of the present verse the word signifies the relationship of mutual support between the Islamic state and its citizens, and among the citizens themselves. Thus, this verse lays down that in a political and constitutional sense, only those Muslims who live within the territorial boundaries of the Islamic state will enjoy the privileges of *walāyah* (guardianship) of the Islamic state. As for Muslims who are settled in a non-Islamic state, they are excluded

it is incumbent on you to provide help unless it be against a people with whom you have a pact.[26] Allah is cognizant of all that you do. [73] And those who disbelieve, they are allies of one another; and unless you act likewise, there will be oppression in the world and great corruption.[27]

[74] Those who believe and have migrated and strove in the way of Allah, and those who gave them refuge and help – it is they who are the true believers. Theirs shall be forgiveness and honourable sustenance.

---

from its political and constitutional guardianship. The non-existence of a *walāyah* relationship has numerous legal implications which cannot be spelled out here.

26. The Muslims living outside the Islamic state have no political bond with the Islamic state. This verse, however, does emphasize that those Muslims are not free of the bond of religious brotherhood. If Muslims living in a non-Islamic state are persecuted and seek help from the Islamic state or its citizens, it is incumbent upon the latter to help the persecuted Muslims. While helping one's brethren-in-faith the Muslims are expected to act scrupulously. This help should be rendered without violating international obligations and with due regard to the requirements of moral propriety. If the Islamic state happens to be bound in a treaty relationship with a nation which inflicts wrong on Muslims, the oppressed Muslims will not be helped in a manner which is inconsistent with the moral obligations incumbent on the Islamic state as a result of that treaty.

27. The world would become full of mischief and disorder if the Muslims of *Dār al-Islām* (a) failed to help one another; (b) failed to provide political support and protection to the Muslims who have settled down in non-Islamic states and have not migrated to *Dār al-Islām*; (c) failed to help the Muslims living under oppression in territories outside *Dār al-Islām* when they ask for it, and (d) failed to sever their friendly ties with the unbelievers.

[75] And those who believed afterwards and migrated and strove along with you: they belong to you. But those related by blood are nearer to one another according to the Book of Allah.[28] Allah has knowledge of everything.

---

28. The purpose of the verse is to make it clear that the basis of inheritance is blood relationship and marriage rather than the mere bond of Islamic brotherhood. This statement finds an elaboration in the saying of the Prophet (peace be on him) that only Muslim relatives will inherit one another. The law does not countenance inheritance between Muslims and non-Muslims.

9

Al-Tawbah [Repentance]
Madīnan Period

[1] This is a declaration of disavowal¹ by Allah and His Messenger to those who associate others with Allah in His Divinity and with whom you have made treaties:² [2] "You may go about freely in the land, for four months, but know well that you will not be able to frustrate Allah,

---

1. The first discourse (verses 1–37] was revealed in 9 A.H./631 C.E. at a time when the Prophet (peace be on him) had already sent Abū Bakr as leader of the Pilgrims to perform the Ḥajj. The Prophet (peace be on him) dispatched ʿAlī to Makkah and directed him to not only recite the verses concerned publicly in the presence of the Ḥujjāj (Pilgrims) but also to make the following proclamation on the occasion: (i) that no one who refuses to accept Islam would enter Paradise; (ii) that no polytheist would henceforth be allowed to perform Ḥajj; (iii) that naked circumambulation around the Kaʿbah – a pre-Islamic Arabian practice – would henceforth be forbidden; (iv) that the treaties concluded between the Prophet (peace be on him) and the unbelievers which were still in force since the other party had not broken them, would be honoured until the expiry of their terms. Accordingly ʿAlī made these announcements on the 10th of Dhū al-Ḥijjah, 9 A.H.

2. The Qurʾān had already laid down the rule: "If you fear treachery from any group, then publicly throw their covenant at them" [8: 58] and publicly terminate the treaty. This Qurʾānic principle also applied to those tribes that, despite their treaties,

and that Allah will bring disgrace upon those who deny
the Truth."

[3] This is a public proclamation by Allah and His Messenger
to all people on the day of the Great Pilgrimage:³ "Allah
is free from all obligation to those who associate others
with Allah in His Divinity; and so is His Messenger. If you
repent, it shall be for your own good; but if you turn away,
then know well that you will not be able to frustrate Allah.
So give glad tidings of a painful chastisement to those
who disbelieve. [4] In exception to those who associate
others with Allah in His Divinity are those with whom
you have made treaties and who have not violated their
treaties nor have backed up anyone against you. Fulfil
your treaties with them till the end of their term. Surely
Allah loves the pious."

[5] But when the sacred months expire⁴ slay those who
associate others with Allah in His Divinity wherever you

had constantly conspired against and were openly hostile to Islam
whenever the opportunity presented itself. The public annulment of
the treaties presented the polytheists with three alternatives. They
could either come out into the open and engage in conflict with
the Islamic state which would have led to their total extinction.
They could flee from Arabia or they could embrace Islam and
submit themselves, and the lands which they controlled, to the
Islamic state.

3. *Al-Ḥajj al-Akbar* (the day of Greater Pilgrimage) is in contrast
to *al-Ḥajj al-Aṣghar* (that is, ʿUmrah or Minor Pilgrimage). The
Pilgrimage performed on the appointed dates in the month of Dhū
al-Ḥijjah is called "the Greater Pilgrimage".

4. The expression "sacred months" refers to the four months
of respite granted to the polytheists. Since it was not lawful for

find them; seize them, and besiege them, and lie in wait for them. But if they repent and establish the Prayer and pay *Zakāh*, leave them alone.⁵ Surely Allah is All-Forgiving, Ever-Merciful. [6] And if any of those who associate others with Allah in His Divinity seeks asylum, grant him asylum that he may hear the Word of Allah, and then escort him to safety for they are a people who do not know.

[7] How can there be a covenant with those who associate others with Allah in His Divinity be binding upon Allah and His Messenger, excepting those with whom you made a covenant near the Sacred Mosque?⁶ Behave in a straight manner with them so long as they behave with you in a straight manner for Allah loves the God-fearing. [8] How can there be any covenant with the other polytheists for were they to prevail against you, they will respect neither kinship nor agreement. They seek to please you with their tongues while their hearts are averse to you, and most of them are wicked. [9] They have sold the revelations of Allah for a paltry price and have firmly hindered people from His Path. Evil indeed is what they have done. [10] They neither have any respect for kinship nor for agreement in respect of the believers. Such are indeed transgressors. [11] But if they repent and

---

Muslims to attack the polytheists during those months, they were characterized as "*ḥurum*" (sacred, prohibited).

5. Apart from a disavowal of unbelief and polytheism, the Muslims are required to establish Prayers and pay *Zakāh*. Without these, their claim that they had abandoned unbelief and embraced Islam would have no credence.

6. This alludes to the Kinānah, Khuzāʿah and Ḍamrah tribes.

establish Prayer and give *Zakāh* they are your brothers in faith.[7] Thus do We expound Our revelations to those who know. [12] But if they break their pledges after making them and attack your faith, make war on the leaders of unbelief that they may desist, for they have no regard for their pledged words.[8]

[13] Will you not fight against those who broke their pledges and did all they could to drive the Messenger away and initiated hostilities against you? Do you fear them? Surely Allah has greater right that you should fear Him, if you are true believers. [14] Make war on them. Allah will chastise them through you and will humiliate them. He will grant you victory over them, and will soothe the bosoms of those who believe, [15] and will remove rage from their hearts, and will enable whomsoever He wills

---

7. This reiterates the statement that if the repentance of the unbelievers is not accompanied by the establishment of Prayers and the payment of *Zakāh*, then they would not be considered as part of the Islamic fraternity merely on the grounds of their repentance. But if they fulfil the requisite conditions, it would no longer be permissible for Muslims to fight against them, and their lives and properties would become sacred. Moreover, they would be entitled to enjoy equal rights in the Islamic society. They would be treated like other Muslims in all social and legal matters. Also they would not be discriminated against in any way, nor would any obstacles be placed before them to impede their progress in achieving what they might be capable of achieving.

8. Pledges here mean their acceptance of Islam and their oath of allegiance to it. What it implies is that if, having accepted Islam, they commit apostasy the Muslims should make war on them. In dealing with apostates Abū Bakr acted on the directive set forth in this verse.

to repent.[9] Allah is All-Knowing, All-Wise. [16] Do you imagine that you will be spared without being subjected to any test? Know well that Allah has not yet determined who strove hard (in His cause), and has not taken any others instead of His Messenger and the believers as his trusted allies? Allah is well aware of all that you do.

[17] It does not become those who associate others with Allah in His Divinity to visit and tend Allah's mosques while they bear witness of unbelief against themselves. All their works have gone to waste. They shall abide in the Fire. [18] It only becomes those who believe in Allah and the Last Day and establish Prayer and pay *Zakāh* and fear none but Allah to visit and tend the mosques of Allah. These are likely to be guided aright. [19] Do you consider providing water to the Pilgrims and tending the Sacred Mosque equal in worth to believing in Allah and the Last Day and striving in the cause of Allah?[10] The two are not equal with Allah. Allah does not direct the wrong-doing folk to the Right Way. [20] The higher rank with Allah is for those who believed and migrated and strove in His cause with their belongings and their persons. It is they who are triumphant. [21] Their Lord gives them glad tidings of mercy from Him and of His

---

9. The Muslims were apprehensive that the Prophet's annulment of an agreement would enrage the polytheists and plunge the land into a blood-bath. God assured them that their fear was misplaced and that the outcome would be contrary to what they apprehended.

10. This proclaimed the decision that the custodianship of the Ka'bah and the Sacred Mosque around it would no longer be with the polytheists. The polytheists of the Quraysh did not deserve the honour merely because they had been tending the Pilgrims.

good pleasure. For them await Gardens of eternal bliss. [22] Therein they shall abide forever. Surely with Allah a mighty reward awaits them.

[23] Believers, do not take your fathers and your brothers for your allies if they choose unbelief in preference to belief. Whosoever of you takes them as allies those are wrong-doers. [24] Tell them, (O Prophet): "If your fathers and your sons and your brothers and your wives and your tribe and the riches you have acquired and the commerce of which you fear a slackening, and the dwellings that you love, if they are dearer to you than Allah and His Messenger and striving in His cause, then wait until Allah brings about His decree. Allah does not guide the evil-doing folk."

[25] Surely Allah has succoured you before on many a battlefield, and (you have yourselves witnessed His succour to you) on the day of Ḥunayn[11] when your numbers made you proud, but they did you no good, and the earth, for all its vastness, constrained you, and

---

11. Allusion is made here to the Battle of Ḥunayn which took place in Shawwāl 8 A.H./630 C.E. in the Ḥunayn valley, about one year before the revelation of this verse. In this battle the Muslim army consisted of twelve thousand people, so far the strongest Muslim army. The army of the unbelievers was much smaller. Yet the archers of the Hawāzin tribe put up a very tough fight and routed the Muslim army. Only the Prophet (peace be on him) and a handful of intrepid Companions stood their ground. This enabled the Muslim army to reconsolidate its position and eventually win the battle. Had the outcome of the battle been different, the Muslims would have lost much more by this defeat than what they had gained by the conquest of Makkah.

you turned your backs in retreat. [26] Then Allah caused His tranquillity to descend upon His Messenger and upon the believers, and He sent down hosts whom you did not see, and chastised those who disbelieved. Such is the recompense of those who deny the Truth. [27] Then (after so chastising the unbelievers), Allah enables, whomsoever He wills, to repent.[12] Allah is All-Forgiving, All-Merciful.

[28] Believers, those who associate others with Allah in His Divinity are unclean. So, after the expiry of this year, let them not even go near the Sacred Mosque.[13] And should you fear poverty, Allah will enrich you out of His bounty, if He wills. Surely Allah is All-Knowing, All-Wise.

[29] Those who do not believe in Allah and the Last Day – even though they were given the scriptures, and who do not hold as unlawful that which Allah and His Messenger have declared to be unlawful, and who do not follow the true religion – fight against them until they pay tribute out of their hand and are utterly subdued.[14]

12. This alludes to the fact that all the unbelievers who lost the Battle of Ḥunayn later embraced Islam.

13. The polytheists were not only forbidden to perform *Hajj*, but also to enter the precincts of the Sacred Mosque.

14. The purpose for which the Muslims are required to fight is not, as one might think, to compel the unbelievers into embracing Islam. Rather, its purpose is to put an end to the suzerainty of the unbelievers so that the latter are unable to rule over people. The authority to rule should only be vested in those who follow the True Faith; unbelievers who do not follow this True Faith should live in a state of subordination. Anybody who becomes convinced

[30] The Jews say: "Ezra ('Uzayr) is Allah's son," and the Christians say: "The Messiah is the son of Allah." These are merely verbal assertions in imitation of the sayings of those unbelievers who preceded them. May Allah ruin them. How do they turn away from the Truth? [31] They take their rabbis and their monks for their lords apart from Allah,[15] and also the Messiah, son of Mary, whereas they were commanded to worship none but the One True God. There is no god but He. Exalted be He above those whom they associate with Him in His Divinity. [32] They seek to extinguish the light of Allah by blowing through their mouths; but Allah refuses everything except that He will perfect His light howsoever the unbelievers might abhor it.

---

of the Truth of Islam may accept the faith of his/her own volition. The unbelievers are required to pay *jizyah* (poll tax) in return for the security provided to them as the *dhimmīs* ("Protected People") of an Islamic state. *Jizyah* symbolizes the submission of the unbelievers to the suzerainty of Islam.

15. As reported in a tradition, 'Adī b. Ḥātim, a Christian convert to Islam, once requested the Prophet (peace be on him) to explain the import of the following Qur'ānic statement: "They (i.e. the Jews and Christians) take their priests and monks as lords apart from Allah." In reply the Prophet (peace be on him) asked him: "Is it not so that you consider unlawful whatever your priests declare to be unlawful, and consider lawful whatever your priests declare to be lawful?" 'Adī confirmed that such was the practice of the Jews and Christians. Thereupon the Prophet (peace be on him) told him that doing so amounted to "taking them as lords apart from Allah". This means, according to the Qur'ān, that those who declare things to be lawful or unlawful without any sanction in the Book of God, in fact place themselves in the position of God. Similarly, those who accept the right of such persons to make laws according to their will also take them as their lords.

[33] He it is Who has sent His Messenger with the guidance and the True Religion that He may make it prevail over all religions, howsoever those who associate others with Allah in His Divinity might detest it.[16] [34] Believers! Many of the rabbis and monks wrongfully devour mankind's possessions and hinder people from the Way of Allah. And there are those who amass gold and silver and do not spend it in the Way of Allah. Announce to them the tidings of a painful chastisement [35] on a Day when they shall be heated up in the Fire of Hell, and their foreheads and their sides and their backs shall be branded with it, (and they shall be told): "This is the treasure which you hoarded for yourselves. Taste, then, the punishment for what you have hoarded."

[36] Surely the reckoning of months, in the sight of Allah, is twelve months, laid down in Allah's decree on the

---

16. The word used in the verse is *al-dīn*. In Arabic this word signifies a way of life to which one subjects oneself because of one's belief that he who prescribed it enjoys supreme authority and is worthy of obedience. The verse makes it clear that the purpose of the Prophets was to establish the supremacy of the Guidance and the Right Way revealed to them by God and make them prevail over all other systems of life. In other words, a Prophet is never sent with a sanction to let the way of life revealed to him be subjected to other ways of life. Nor is a Prophet sent to be content to live at the sufferance of the false ways of life which might hold sway. Since a Prophet is the representative of the Lord of the Universe, he seeks to make the Right Way prevail. If any other way of life continues to exist, it should be satisfied with the concessions made to it by Islam. For example, the rights granted to the *dhimmīs* to enjoy the protection offered by Islam in lieu of *jizyah*. The opposite of this should not happen, i.e. the unbelievers should not be dominant and the believers should lead the life of *dhimmīs* instead.

day when He created the heavens and the earth; and out of these months four are sacred.¹⁷ That is the true ordainment. Do not, therefore, wrong yourselves, with respect to these months. And fight all together against those who associate others with Allah in His Divinity in the manner that they fight against you all together, and know well that Allah is with the God-fearing.¹⁸ [37] The intercalation (of sacred months) is an act of gross infidelity which causes the unbelievers to be led further astray. They declare a month to be lawful in one year and forbidden in another year in order that they may conform to the number of months that Allah has declared as sacred, and at the same time make lawful what Allah has forbidden.¹⁹ Their foul acts seem fair to them. Allah does not direct those who deny the Truth to the Right Way.

---

17. The sacred four months alluded to here are the months of Dhū al-Qaʿdah, Dhū al-Ḥijjah and Muḥarram for *Ḥajj* (Major Pilgrimage) and Rajab for *ʿUmrah* (Minor Pilgrimage).

18. The Muslims are told that they are free to fight in the sacred months if the unbelievers attack them. If the unbelievers fight unitedly against the Muslims in disregard of the sacred months, the Muslims may also unitedly fight against them. (For an explanation of this verse, see *al-Baqarah* 2: 194.)

19. *Nasīʾ* was practised by the Arabs in two ways:

(1) In order to shed blood or to plunder, or to satisfy a blood vendetta, they declared a sacred month to be an ordinary one, and compensated for this violation later on by declaring one of the ordinary months to be sacred.

(2) With a view to harmonizing the lunar calendar with the solar calendar the Arabs used to add a month to the lunar calendar. Their purpose in so doing was to ensure that the *Ḥajj* dates should consistently fall in the same season

[38] Believers![20] What is amiss with you that when it is said to you: "March forth in the cause of Allah," you cling heavily to the earth? Do you prefer the worldly life to the Hereafter? Know well that all the enjoyment of this world, in comparison with the Hereafter, is trivial. [39] If you do not march forth, Allah will chastise you grievously and will replace you by another people, while you will in no way be able to harm Him. Allah has power over everything. [40] It will matter little if you do not help the Prophet, for Allah surely helped him when the unbelievers drove him out of his home and he was but one of the two when they were in the cave, and when he said to his companion: "Do not grieve. Allah is with us."[21] Then Allah caused His tranquillity to descend upon him, and supported him with hosts you did not see, and

so that they were spared the hardship and inconvenience resulting from the observation of the lunar calendar for the fixation of *Ḥajj* dates. As a result of this practice, *Ḥajj* was performed once on its appointed date, the days on which the 9th and 10th of Dhū al-Ḥijjah truly fell, and then for the next thirty-three years it was performed on days which were fictitiously declared to be 9th and 10th of Dhū al-Ḥijjah. The year the Prophet (peace be on him) performed the Farewell Pilgrimage the *Ḥajj* fell on the due dates. Since then *nasī'* stands abolished.

20. This verse marks the beginning of the second discourse of the *sūrah* comprising verses 38-72. It was revealed during the preparations for the Tabūk expedition.

21. This refers to the time when the unbelievers had resolved to kill the Prophet (peace be on him). The night he was to be assassinated the Prophet (peace be on him) left Makkah and secluded himself in a cave known as Thawr. Three days later he migrated to Madīnah. Only Abū Bakr was with him in the cave.

He humbled the word of the unbelievers. As for Allah's Word, it is inherently uppermost. Allah is All-Powerful, All-Wise.

[41] March forth whether light or heavy, and strive in the way of Allah with your belongings and your lives. That is best for you if you only knew it.

[42] Were it a gain at hand or a short journey, they would have surely followed you, but the distance seemed too far to them.[22] Still they will swear by Allah: "If only we could, we would surely have gone forth with you." They merely bring ruin upon themselves. Allah knows well that they are liars.

[43] (O Prophet), may Allah forgive you! Why did you give them leave to stay behind before it became clear to you as to who were truthful and who were liars? [44] Those who believe in Allah and the Last Day will never ask your leave to be excused from striving (in the cause of Allah) with their belongings and their lives. Allah fully knows the God-fearing. [45] It is only those who do not believe in Allah and the Last Day, and whose hearts are filled with doubt that seek exemption from striving (in the cause of Allah). They keep tossing to and fro in their doubt.

---

22. The idea of marching across vast stretches of desert to reach Tabūk appeared quite arduous for a number of reasons. Because of the prospect of an armed encounter with a power as mighty as that of the Romans; because the journey was to take place in the blazing heat of summer; and because the harvesting season was just at hand, and this was of great importance that year when famine conditions prevailed.

[46] Had they truly intended to march forth to fight, they would have certainly made some preparation for it. But Allah was averse to their going forth, so He made them lag behind, and they were told: "Stay behind with those that are staying behind." [47] Had they gone forth with you, they would have only added to your trouble, and would have run about in your midst seeking to stir up sedition among you, whereas there are among you some who are prone to lend ears to them. Allah knows well the wrong-doers. [48] Surely they sought even earlier to stir up sedition, and turned things upside down to frustrate you until the Truth came and the decree of Allah appeared, however hateful this may have been to them.

[49] And among them is he who says: "Grant me leave to stay behind, and do not expose me to temptation." Lo! They have already fallen into temptation. Surely Hell encompasses the unbelievers.

[50] If good fortune befalls you, it vexes them; and if an affliction befalls you, they turn away in jubilation and say: "We have taken due care of our affairs in good time." [51] Say: "Nothing will befall us except what Allah has decreed for us; He is our Protector." Let the believers, then, put all their trust in Allah.

[52] Tell them: "What you await to befall upon us is nothing but one of the two good things![23] And what we await for you is that Allah visit you with chastisement from Him or chastise you at our hands. So continue waiting; we too shall wait with you."

---

23. That is, loss of life in the Way of God or victory.

[53] Tell them: "Whether you spend your money willingly or unwillingly, it shall not find acceptance (with Allah) for you are an evil-doing folk." [54] Nothing prevents that their expendings be accepted except that they disbelieve in Allah and His Messenger, and whenever they come to the Prayer they do so lazily, and whenever they spend they do so grudgingly. [55] Let neither their riches nor their children excite your admiration. Allah only wants to chastise them through these things in the present life, and to cause them to die while they are unbelievers.

[56] They swear by Allah that they are part of you whereas they are certainly not part of you. They are merely a people who dread you. [57] If they could find any shelter or any cavern, or any retreat, they would turn around and rush headlong into it.

[58] (O Prophet), some of them find fault with you in the distribution of alms.[24] If they are given something of it they are pleased, and if they are given nothing they are angry. [59] Would that they were content with what Allah and His Messenger gave them, and were to say: "Allah suffices for us, and Allah will give us out of His bounty and so will His Messenger. It is to Allah alone that we turn with hope." [60] The alms are meant only for the poor and the needy[25] and those who are in charge

---

24. That is, the *Zakāh* collections.

25. The Qur'ānic term *faqīr* (the poor) applies to those who depend for their subsistence on others. As for the *masākīn*, they are those who are in greater distress than the ordinary poor people.

thereof, those whose hearts are to be reconciled,[26] and to free those in bondage,[27] and to help those burdened with debt, and for expenditure in the Way of Allah[28] and for the wayfarer.[29] This is an obligation from Allah. Allah is All-Knowing, All-Wise.

---

26. The expression *ta'līf al-qalb* whencefrom the expression *al-mu'allafat qubūbihim* is derived means to win the hearts of people. The rule embodied in this verse is that *Zakāh* funds may be used to calm down those who are actively engaged in hostile activities against Islam, or to win over the support of those who are in the unbelievers' camp. *Zakāh* may also be used for securing the loyalty of those converts to Islam about whom it might be legitimately feared that if no consideration is shown to them they may revert to unbelief. It would be lawful that stipends or lump sum amounts are paid to such persons on a regular or temporary basis in order to secure either their support and backing for Islam, or preferably their conversion to it, or at least to neutralize such persons even if they remain in the opposite camp.

27. That is, emancipation of slaves.

28. The expression "in the Way of Allah" has a wide and general connotation and encompasses all good deeds which please God. Some authorities, therefore, believe that *Zakāh* may be spent on all good purposes. But the truth of the matter is – and this is also the view of a great majority of past scholars – that "in the Way of Allah" stands for *jihād* in the Way of Allah. This expression signifies the struggle launched with a view to overthrowing ungodly systems and replacing them by the Islamic system of life. All those who participate in this struggle may be given assistance from *Zakāh* funds, whether it be for journey expenses, for providing means of transport, for arms and equipment or for other goods relating to warfare. Such assistance may be provided even to those who are otherwise well off and need no financial assistance in connection with their own living.

29. A traveller, though otherwise rich, is entitled to receive help out of *Zakāh* funds if he needs such help during his journey.

[61] And of them there are some who distress the Prophet, saying: "He is all ears." Tell them: "He listens for your good. He believes in Allah and trusts the believers, and is a mercy for those of you who believe. A painful punishment lies in store for those who cause distress to the Messenger of Allah."

[62] They swear by Allah to please you, while it is Allah and His Messenger whose pleasure they should seek if they truly believe. [63] Are they not aware that Hell Fire awaits whosoever opposes Allah and His Messenger, and in it he shall abide? That surely is the great humiliation.

[64] The hypocrites are afraid lest a *sūrah* should be revealed concerning them intimating to the believers what lay hidden in their hearts. Tell them (O Prophet): "Continue your mockery if you will. Allah will surely bring to light all that whose disclosure you dread." [65] Should you question them what they were talking about, they would certainly say: "We were merely jesting and being playful."[30] Tell them: "Was it Allah and His

---

30. When preparations for the Tabūk expedition were under way, the hypocrites used to scoff at the Prophet (peace be on him) and the Muslims. They did so with the idea of demoralizing the Muslims engaged in *jihād* preparations. Many such reports are recorded in the traditions. Of these, one goes thus: "Some hypocrites were talking idly in their private meeting. One of them said: 'Do you think that fighting against the Roman warriors is like the mutual fight among the Arabs? I am sure that no sooner than the war breaks out you will find these (Muslim) warriors tied by ropes.' To this another added: 'It will be much better if, apart from that, each one of them is whipped a hundred times as well.' On seeing the Prophet (peace be on him) busy in *jihād* preparations, a hypocrite derisively told another: 'Just look at this man! He is out to conquer the Roman and Syrian fortresses!'"

revelation and His Messenger that you were mocking?" [66] Now, make no excuses. The truth is, you have fallen into unbelief after having believed. Even if We were to forgive some of you, We will surely chastise others because they are guilty.

[67] The hypocrites, be they men or women, are all alike. They enjoin what is evil, and forbid what is good, and withhold their hands from doing good. They forgot Allah, so Allah also forgot them. Surely the hypocrites are wicked. [68] Allah has promised Hell-Fire to the hypocrites, both men and women, and to the unbelievers. They shall abide in it: a sufficient recompense for them. Allah has cursed them, and theirs is a lasting torment. [69] Your ways are like the ways of those who have gone before you. They were mightier than you in power, and more abundant in riches and children. They enjoyed their lot for a while as you have enjoyed your lot, and you also engaged in idle talk as they did. Their works have come to naught in this world, and in the Hereafter they are surely the losers. [70] Have they not heard the accounts of those who came before them – of the people of Noah and 'Ād and Thamūd, and the people of Abraham and the dwellers of Madyan (Midian), and the cities that were overturned?[31] Their Messengers came to them with Clear Signs. Then, it was not Allah Who caused them any wrong; they rather wronged themselves.

[71] The believers, both men and women, are allies of one another. They enjoin good, forbid evil, establish Prayer, pay *Zakāh*, and obey Allah and His Messenger. Surely Allah

---

31. This refers to the areas where the people of Lot lived.

will show mercy to them. Allah is All-Mighty, All-Wise. [72] Allah has promised the believing men and believing women Gardens beneath which rivers flow. They shall abide in it. There are delightful dwelling places for them in the Gardens of Eternity. They shall, above all, enjoy the good pleasure of Allah. That is the great achievement.

[73] O Prophet![32] Strive against the unbelievers and the hypocrites, and be severe to them. Hell shall be their abode; what an evil destination! [74] They swear by Allah that they said nothing blasphemous whereas they indeed blasphemed,[33] and fell into unbelief after believing, and also had evil designs which they could not carry into effect.[34] They are spiteful against Muslims for no other

---

32. This marks the beginning of the third discourse of the *sūrah* (comprising verses 73-129), which was revealed after the expedition to Tabūk.

33. There is no certainty about what constitutes the "word of unbelief" mentioned in the above verse. However, there are references in traditions to the many blasphemous utterances of the hypocrites. For example, a hypocrite is reported to have told his Muslim relatives: "If the message delivered by him (the Prophet, peace be on him) is really genuine, then we are worse than donkeys." According to another report, during the expedition to Tabūk when a she-camel of the Prophet (peace be on him) went astray and the Muslims set about searching for it, a group of hypocrites made much fun of the incident, saying to one another: "Just look at this man! He brings us news about the heavens but cannot tell where his she-camel is!"

34. This alludes to the conspiracies contrived by the hypocrites during the expedition to Tabūk. One of these, according to traditionists, was that the hypocrites had planned to throw the Prophet (peace be on him) into a ravine during his return from Tabūk. Another conspiracy hatched by the hypocrites was that

reason than that Allah and His Messenger have enriched them through His bounty! So, if they repent, it will be to their own good. But if they turn away, Allah will sternly punish them in this world and in the Hereafter. None in the world will be able to protect or help them.

[75] Some of them made a covenant with Allah: "If Allah gives us out of His bounty, we will give alms and act righteously." [76] Then, when He gave them out of His bounty, they grew niggardly and turned their backs (upon their covenant). [77] So He caused hypocrisy to take root in their hearts and to remain therein until the Day they meet Him because they broke their promise with Allah and because they lied. [78] Are they not aware that Allah knows what they conceal and what they secretly discuss, and that Allah has full knowledge even of all that is beyond the reach of perception. [79] He also knows (the rich that are niggardly) who taunt the believers that voluntarily give alms, they scoff at those who have nothing to give except what they earn through their hard toil. Allah scoffs at them in return. A grievous chastisement awaits them. [80] (O Prophet), it is all the same whether or not you ask for their forgiveness. Even if you were to ask forgiveness for them seventy times, Allah shall not forgive them. That is because they disbelieved in Allah and His Messenger; and Allah does not bestow His Guidance on such evil-doing folk.

[81] Those who were allowed to stay behind rejoiced at remaining behind and not accompanying the Messenger

---

they secretly decided that as soon as the news would come that the Muslim army had been defeated by the Romans, they would install ʿAbd Allāh ibn Ubayy as the ruler of Madīnah.

of Allah. They were averse to striving in the Way of Allah with their belongings and their lives and told others: "Do not go forth in this fierce heat." Tell them: "The Hell is far fiercer in heat." Would that they understand! [82] Let them, then, laugh little, and weep much at the contemplation of the punishment for the evil they have committed. [83] Then if Allah brings you face to face with a party of them, and they ask your leave to go forth (to fight in the Way of Allah), tell them: "You shall not go forth with me, and shall never fight against any enemy along with me. You were well-pleased to remain at home the first time, so now continue to remain with those who have stayed behind."

[84] Do not ever pray over any of them who dies, nor stand over his grave. They disbelieved in Allah and His Messenger and died in iniquity. [85] Let not their riches or their children excite your admiration. Through these Allah seeks to chastise them in this world, and that their lives will depart them while they are unbelievers.

[86] And whenever any *sūrah* is revealed enjoining: "Believe in Allah and strive (in His Way) along with His Messenger," the affluent among them ask you to excuse them, saying: "Leave us with those who will sit back at home." [87] They were content to stay behind with the womenfolk. Their hearts were sealed, leaving them bereft of understanding. [88] But the Messenger and those who shared his faith strove with their belongings and their lives. It is they who shall have all kinds of good. It is they who shall prosper. [89] Allah has prepared for them Gardens beneath which rivers flow. There shall they abide. That is the supreme triumph.

[90] Many of the bedouin Arabs came with excuses, seeking leave to stay behind. Thus those who were false to Allah and His Messenger in their covenant remained behind. A painful chastisement shall befall those of them that disbelieved.

[91] There is no blame on the weak nor on the sick nor on those who have nothing to enable them to join (the struggle in the Way of Allah) if they stay behind provided that they are sincere to Allah and to His Messenger.[35] There is no cause for reproach against those who do good. Allah is All-Forgiving, Ever Merciful. [92] Nor can there be any cause for reproach against those who, when they came to you asking for mounts to go to the battlefront, and when you said that you had no mounts for them, they went back, their eyes overflowing with tears, grieving that they had no resources to enable them to take part in fighting. [93] But there are grounds for reproach against those who seek leave to stay behind even though they are affluent. They are the ones who were content to be with the womenfolk who stay behind. Allah has set a seal on their hearts, leaving them bereft of understanding.

[94] They will put up excuses before you when you return to them. Tell them: "Make no excuses. We will not believe you. Allah has already informed us of the truth about

35. This makes it clear that even those who are otherwise apparently exempt from *jihād* are in fact not automatically so on grounds of physical disability, sickness or indigence. They are exempt only when these disabilities are combined with their true loyalty to God and His Messenger. If someone lacks this loyalty, he cannot be pardoned for the simple reason that when it became obligatory for him to wage *jihād* he was sick or indigent.

you. Allah will observe your conduct, and so will His
Messenger; then you will be brought back to Him Who
knows alike what lies beyond perception and what lies in
the range of perception and will let you know what you
have done." [95] When you return to them they will surely
swear to you in the name of Allah that you may leave them
alone. So do leave them alone; they are unclean. Hell shall
be their home, a recompense for what they did. [96] They
will swear to you in order to please you. But even if you
become pleased with them, Allah will not be pleased with
such an evil-doing folk.

[97] The bedouin Arabs surpass all in unbelief and
hypocrisy and are most likely to be unaware of the
limits prescribed by Allah in what He has revealed
to His Messenger.[36] Allah is All-Knowing, All-Wise.
[98] And among the bedouin Arabs there are such as

---

36. The word *al-A'rāb*, as we have explained earlier, signifies
the Bedouin – whether of the desert or the countryside – in the
vicinity of Madīnah. For a long time they had followed a policy
of opportunism with regard to the conflict between Islam and
unbelief. However, as Islam established its sway over the greater
part of Hijāz and Najd and the power of the tribes hostile to Islam
began to weaken, they saw that their interests lay in entering the
fold of Islam. Of them, only a minority embraced Islam out of
their conviction and with the readiness to fulfil its demands. In the
above verse the Qur'ān refers to this attitude of the Bedouin who,
compared with the town dwellers, were relatively more prone to
hypocrisy and unbelief. Town dwellers fare better since they have
the opportunity to meet learned and pious people and thus gain
some knowledge of religion and its requirements. The Bedouin,
however, tend to engross themselves in the pursuit of their bread
and butter alone, leaving them no time available for higher pursuits.
At the end of the day they are no more than economic brutes, and as

regard whatever they spend (in the Way of Allah) as a fine and wait for some misfortune to befall you. May ill fortune befall them! Allah is All-Hearing, All-Knowing. [99] And among the bedouin Arabs are those who believe in Allah and the Last Day, and regard their spending (in the Way of Allah) as a means of drawing near to Allah and of deserving the prayers of the Messenger. Indeed, this shall be a means of drawing near to Allah. Allah will surely admit them to His mercy. Allah is All-Forgiving, Ever Merciful.

[100] And of those who led the way – the first of the Emigrants (*Muhājirūn*) and the Helpers (*Anṣār*), and those who followed them in the best possible manner – Allah is well-pleased with them and they are well-pleased with Allah. He has prepared for them Gardens beneath which rivers flow; therein they will abide forever. That is the supreme triumph.

[101] As for the bedouin Arabs around you, some are hypocrites; and so are some of the people of Madīnah who have become inured to hypocrisy. You do not know them, but We know them. We will inflict double chastisement on them, and then they shall be returned to an awesome suffering.

[102] There are others who have confessed their faults. They intermixed their good deeds with evil. It is likely that Allah will turn to them in mercy, for Allah is All-Forgiving, Ever Merciful. [103] (O Prophet)! "Take alms

such are in greater peril of remaining ignorant of the True Religion and the limits prescribed by God. Verse 122 suggests a remedy for the situation.

out of their riches and thereby cleanse them and bring about their growth (in righteousness), and pray for them. Indeed your prayer is a source of tranquillity for them." Allah is All-Hearing, All-Knowing. [104] Are they not aware that it is Allah Who accepts the repentance of His servants and accepts their alms, and that it is Allah Who is Oft-Relenting, Ever Merciful? [105] And tell them, (O Prophet): "Keep working: Allah will behold your works and so will His Messenger and the believers; and you shall be brought back to Him Who knows that which is beyond the reach of perception and that which is within the reach of perception. He will then declare to you all that you have been doing."

[106] There are others in whose regard Allah's decree is awaited: whether He will chastise them or relent towards them. Allah is All-Knowing, All-Wise.

[107] Then there are others who have set up a mosque to hurt the True Faith, to promote unbelief, and cause division among believers, and as an ambush for one who had earlier made war on Allah and His Messenger. They will surely swear: "We intended nothing but good," whereas Allah bears witness that they are liars. [108] Never stand therein. Surely a mosque founded from the first day on piety is more worthy that you should stand in it for Prayer. In it are people who love to purify themselves, and Allah loves those that purify themselves.[37] [109] Is he,

---

37. At that time there were two mosques in Madīnah: the mosque of Qubā which was situated on the outskirts of the town, and the Prophet's Mosque which was in the heart of Madīnah. There was, therefore, hardly any need for another mosque. The

then, who has erected his structure on the fear of Allah and His good pleasure better, or he who erects his structure on the brink of a crumbling bank, so that it crumbles down with him into the Hell-Fire? Allah does not bestow His Guidance on the wrong-doing folk. [110] And the structure which they have erected will ever inspire their hearts with doubts unless it be that their very hearts are cut into pieces. Allah is All-Knowing, All-Wise.

[111] Surely Allah has purchased of the believers their lives and their belongings and in return has promised that they shall have Paradise.[38] They fight in the Way of Allah, and slay and are slain. Such is the promise He has made incumbent upon Himself in the Torah, and the Gospel, and the Qur'ān. Who is more faithful to his promise than

---

hypocrites, knowing that there was no convincing justification for a new mosque, began to put forward flimsy pleas saying that such a mosque was necessary because of the difficulties of praying congregationally, five times a day, and particularly at night in cold and rainy weather; that this was especially difficult for the old and the disabled who lived at some distance from the Mosque of the Prophet (peace be on him). They thus secured the permission to construct this mosque and started using it as a centre for hatching conspiracies. They wanted to inveigle the Prophet (peace be on him) into inaugurating the mosque. But God forewarned him of their intentions and the Prophet (peace be on him) razed the Ḍirār mosque to the ground on his return from Tabūk.

38. When a man has true faith it involves a commitment to devote himself sincerely to God and thus attain His reward in return for that commitment. This two-way commitment has been described as a "transaction". What this means is that faith is in fact a contract according to which man places all that he has – his life, his wealth – at the disposal of God; he "sells" them to God. In return, he accepts God's promise of Paradise in the Next Life.

Allah? Rejoice, then, in the bargain you have made with Him. That indeed is the mighty triumph. [112] Those who constantly turn to Allah in repentance,[39] who constantly worship Him, who celebrate His praise, who go about the world to serve His cause,[40] who bow down to Him, who prostrate themselves before Him, who enjoin what is good and forbid what is evil, and who keep the limits set by Allah. Announce glad tidings to such believers.

[113] After it has become clear that they are condemned to the Flaming Fire, it is not for the Prophet and those who believe to ask for the forgiveness of those who associate others with Allah in His Divinity even if they be near of kin. [114] And Abraham's prayer for the forgiveness of his father was only because of a promise which he had made to him. Then, when it became clear to him that he was an enemy of Allah, he dissociated himself from him. Surely Abraham was most tender-hearted, God-fearing, forbearing.

[115] It is not Allah's way to cause people to stray in error after He has guided them until He has made clear to them what they should guard against. Surely Allah knows everything. [116] Indeed Allah's is the Kingdom of the heavens and the earth. He it is Who confers life

---

39. The word *tā'ibūn* used in the above verse may be translated literally as "those who turn to God in repentance". However, the context in which this word occurs indicates that repentance is a recurring characteristic of believers, implying that far from repenting once, they constantly turn to God in repentance. We have tried to convey this nuance in the translation of the verse.

40. Another translation can be "those who fast".

and causes death. You have no protector or helper apart from Allah.

[117] Surely Allah has relented towards the Prophet, and towards the *Muhājirūn* (Emigrants) and the *Anṣār* (Helpers) who stood by him in the hour of hardship, although the hearts of a party of them had well-nigh swerved.⁴¹ (But when they gave up swerving from the Right Course and followed the Prophet), Allah relented towards them. Surely to them He is the Most Tender, the Most Merciful. [118] And He also relented towards the three whose cases had been deferred. When the earth, for all its spaciousness, became constrained to them, and their own beings became a burden to them, and they realized that there was no refuge for them from Allah except in Him; He relented towards them that they may turn back to Him. Surely, it is Allah Who is Much Forgiving, Ever Merciful.⁴²

41. This refers to some sincere and devoted Companions who initially shrank from *jihād*. However, being genuine believers and true lovers of Islam, they were able to overcome their initial reluctance and fear.

42. The three Companions referred to in this verse are those who stayed behind – Ka'b b. Mālik, Hilāl b. Umayyah and Murārah b. Rabī'. All the three had firm belief in Islam and had repeatedly proved their sincerity and made many sacrifices. Notwithstanding their illustrious services to the cause of Islam in the past, they were reproached severely for having slacked off in their duty to join the *jihād* to which all the able-bodied Muslims had been summoned. After his return from Tabūk, the Prophet (peace be on him) asked all Muslims to sever their ties with these three. Forty days later even their wives were asked to part company with them. The anguish they then suffered in Madīnah – their home town – has

[119] Believers! Have fear of Allah and stand with those that are truthful. [120] It did not behove the people of Madīnah and the bedouin Arabs around them that they should refrain from accompanying the Messenger of Allah and stay behind and prefer their own security to his. For whenever they suffer from thirst or weariness or hunger in the Way of Allah, and whenever they tread a place which enrages the unbelievers (whenever anything of this comes to pass), a good deed is recorded in their favour. Allah does not cause the work of the doers of good to go to waste. [121] Likewise, each amount they spend, be it small or large, and each journey they undertake, shall be recorded in their favour so that Allah may bestow upon them reward for their good deeds.

[122] It was not necessary for the believers to go forth all together (to receive religious instruction), but why did not a party of them go forth that they may grow in religious understanding, and that they may warn their people when they return to them, so that they may avoid (erroneous attitudes)?[43]

---

been graphically set forth in the above verse. After having undergone the tormenting social boycott for a full fifty days, they were eventually pardoned by God.

43. This did not necessitate the *en masse* migration of the Bedouins to Madīnah in quest of knowledge. If just a few drawn from each desert village and tribe had visited Madīnah to study Islam, and tried to create an awakening and consciousness among their people upon their return, the situation could have been remedied. Replacement of ignorance with enlightenment of faith would have cured them of hypocrisy which had prevented them from fulfilling their obligations as Muslims despite having embraced Islam.

[123] Believers! Fight against the unbelievers who live around you;⁴⁴ and let them find in you sternness.⁴⁵ Know that Allah is with the God-fearing. [124] And whenever a new *sūrah* is revealed some of the hypocrites ask the believers (in jest): "Whose faith has increased because of this?" As for those who believe, it will certainly increase their faith, and they are joyful over that. [125] But those whose hearts are affected with the disease (of hypocrisy), every new *sūrah* added a fresh abomination to their abomination. They remained unbelievers till their death. [126] Do they not see that they are tried every year once or twice?⁴⁶ Yet they neither repent nor take heed. [127] And whenever a *sūrah* is revealed, they glance at each other as though saying: "Is anyone watching?" Then they slip away. Allah has turned away their hearts for they are a people who are bereft of understanding.

[128] There has come to you a Messenger of Allah from among yourselves, who is distressed by the losses you sustain, who is ardently desirous of your welfare and is tender and merciful to those that believe. [129] Yet, if they should turn away, then tell them: "Allah is sufficient for me; there is no god but He. In Him I have put my trust. He is the Lord of the Mighty Throne."

---

44. On reading the verse in conjunction with the succeeding passage it appears that the reference is to fighting against those whose hypocrisy was clearly established and whose interaction with different sections of the Islamic population had caused much damage.

45. The lenient policy adopted towards the hypocrites so far should now be given up.

46. Not a year passes when the claim of the hypocrites to be believers is not tested once or twice and invariably found to be hollow.

10
❦

Yūnus [Jonah]
Makkan Period

In the name of Allah, the Most Merciful,
the Most Compassionate

[1] *Alif. Lām. Ra'.* These are the verses of the Book overflowing with wisdom.

[2] Does it seem strange to people that We should have revealed to a man from among themselves, directing him to warn the people (who are engrossed in heedlessness), and to give good news to the believers that they shall enjoy true honour and an exalted status with their Lord? (This seemed so strange that) the deniers of the Truth said: "This man is indeed a plain sorcerer!"[1]

[3] Surely your Lord is Allah, Who created the heavens and the earth in six days, then established Himself on the Throne (of His Dominion), governing all affairs of

---

1. The Prophet (peace be on him) was called a sorcerer in the sense that whosoever embraced Islam was so impressed by the Word of God (the Qur'ān) and the Prophet's own preaching was so forceful that he continued to support them even at the risk to his life, at the cost of his relationship with his kindred among the unbelievers, and braved many privations in this regard.

the Universe. None may intercede with Him except after obtaining His leave. Such is Allah, your Lord; do therefore serve Him. Will you not take heed?

[4] To Him is your return. This is Allah's promise that will certainly come true. Surely it is He Who brings about the creation of all and He will repeat it so that He may justly reward those who believe and do righteous deeds, and those who disbelieve may have a draught of boiling water and suffer a painful chastisement for their denying the Truth.

[5] He it is Who gave the sun radiance and the moon light, and determined the stages (for the waxing and waning of the moon) that you may learn the calculation of years and the reckoning of time. Allah has created all this with a rightful purpose (rather than out of play). He expounds His Signs for the people who know. [6] Surely in the alternation of the night and the day and in all that Allah has created in the heavens and the earth there are Signs for the people who seek to avoid (error of outlook and conduct).²

[7] Surely those who do not expect to meet Us, who are gratified with the life of the world and are well-pleased with it, and are heedless of Our signs, [8] their abode shall be the Fire in return for their misdeeds.

---

2. Those who will be able to benefit from God's Signs are those (i) who liberate themselves from prejudices and seek knowledge with the help of the natural endowments bestowed upon them by God, and (ii) who are keen not to fall into error, and earnestly seek to follow the Right Way.

[9] Surely those who believe (in the Truths revealed in the Book) and do righteous deeds their Lord will guide them aright because of their faith. Rivers shall flow beneath them in the Gardens of Bliss. [10] Their cry in it will be: "Glory be to You, Our Lord," and their greeting: "Peace"; and their cry will always end with: "All praise be to Allah, the Lord of the entire Universe."

[11] Were Allah to hasten to bring upon people (the consequence of) evil in the way people hasten in seeking the wealth of this world, their term would have long since expired. (But that is not Our Way.) So We leave alone those who do not expect to meet Us that they may blindly stumble in their transgression. [12] And (such is man that) when an affliction befalls him, he cries out to Us, reclining and sitting and standing. But no sooner than We have removed his affliction, he passes on as though he had never cried out to Us to remove his affliction. Thus it is that the misdeeds of the transgressors are made fair-seeming to them. [13] Surely We destroyed the nations before you[3] (which had risen to heights of glory in their times) when they indulged in wrong-doing and

---

3. In Arabic the word *qarn*, which occurs in the above verse, usually denotes "the people of a given age". However, the word in its several usages in the Qur'ān, connotes a "nation" which, in its heyday, was ascendant in the world. When it is said that a certain nation was "destroyed" this does not necessarily mean its total annihilation. When any such nation suffers the loss of its ascendancy and leadership, when its culture and civilization become extinct, when its identity is effaced, in fact, when such a nation disintegrates and its component parts become assimilated into other nations, then it is fair to say that it has suffered destruction.

refused to believe even when their Messengers brought Clear Signs to them. Thus do We recompense the people who are guilty. [14] Now We have appointed you as their successors in the earth to see how you act.

[15] And whenever Our clear revelations are recited to them, those who do not expect to meet Us say: "Bring us a Qur'ān other than this one, or at least make changes in it." Tell them, (O Muḥammad): "It is not for me to change it of my accord. I only follow what is revealed to me. Were I to disobey my Lord, I fear the chastisement of an Awesome Day." [16] Tell them: "Had Allah so willed, I would not have recited the Qur'ān to you, nor would Allah have informed you of it. I have spent a lifetime among you before this. Do you, then, not use your reason?[4] [17] Who, then, is a greater wrong-doer than he who forges a lie against Allah or rejects His Signs as false? Surely the guilty shall not prosper."

[18] They worship, beside Allah, those who can neither harm nor profit them, saying: "These are our intercessors with Allah." Tell them, (O Muḥammad): "Do you inform Allah of something regarding whose existence in the

---

4. The Prophet (peace be on him) was no stranger to the people of Makkah. He was born in their city. He lived his life among them right from his childhood and reached his middle age in their midst. Being quite familiar with the whole of his life as well as his moral character could they truly ascribe the authorship of the Qur'ān to him or think that he would make such an utterly false claim; or could they expect that after having composed it himself, he would lay claim that it was revealed to him by God?

heavens or on the earth He has no knowledge?[5] Holy is He and exalted far above what they associate with Him in His Divinity."

[19] Once all human beings were but a single community; then they disagreed (and formulated different beliefs and rites). Had it not been that your Lord had already so ordained, a decisive judgement would have been made regarding their disagreements.[6]

[20] They say: "Why was a Sign not sent down upon the Prophet from His Lord?" Tell (such people): "The realm of the Unseen belongs to Allah. Wait, then; I shall wait along with you."

[21] No sooner than We bestow Mercy on a people after hardship has hit them than they begin to scheme against Our Signs.[7] Tell them: "Allah is swifter in scheming. Our

---

5. To say that something is not known to God amounts to saying that it does not exist. For, quite obviously, all that exists is known to God. The above verse thus subtly points out the non-existence of any intercessors on behalf of the unbelievers in so far as God does not know that there exist any such in the heavens or on earth who would intercede on their behalf. That being so, who are those intercessors about whose existence and whose power of intercession with God the unbelievers wanted to inform the Prophet (peace be on him)?

6. If God had not already ordained that the matter would be resolved on the Day of Judgement a decision would have been given here and now.

7. The unbelievers were subjected by God to hardship to make them realize that none of their deities had any power to deliver them from

angels are recording all your intriguing." [22] He it is Who enables you to journey through the land and the sea. And so it happens that when you have boarded the ships and they set sail with a favourable wind, and the passengers rejoice at the pleasant voyage, then suddenly a fierce gale appears, and wave upon wave surges upon them from every side, and people believe that they are surrounded from all directions, and all of them cry out to Allah in full sincerity of faith: "If You deliver us from this we shall surely be thankful." [23] But no sooner than He delivers them than they go about committing excesses on the earth, acting unjustly. O mankind! The excesses you commit will be of harm only to yourselves. (Enjoy, if you will), the fleeting pleasure of this world; in the end you shall all return to Us, and then We shall tell you what you have been doing. [24] The example of the life of this world (which has enamoured you into becoming heedless to Our signs) is that of water that We sent down from the sky which caused the vegetation of the earth, sustaining human beings and cattle, to grow luxuriantly. But when the earth took on its golden raiment and became well adorned and the owners believed that they had full control over their lands Our Command came upon them by night or by day, and We converted it into a stubble as though it had not blossomed yesterday. Thus do We expound the Signs for a people who reflect. [25] (You are being lured by this ephemeral world)

their hardship for the power to do so lay with God alone. But once the hardship was over, they reverted to their unbelief, attributing their deliverance to their deities whom they considered to be their intercessors with God.

although Allah calls you to the Abode of Peace[8] and guides whomsoever He wills to a Straight Way. [26] For those who do good there is good reward and more besides; neither gloom nor humiliation shall cover their faces. They are the people of the Garden and in it they shall abide. [27] Those who do evil deeds, the recompense of an evil deed is its like, and humiliation shall spread over them and there will be none to protect them from Allah. Darkness will cover their faces as though they were veiled with the dark blackness of night. These are the people of the Fire and in it they shall abide. [28] And the Day when We shall muster them all together, We shall say to those who associated others with Allah in His Divinity: "Keep to your places, you and those whom you associated with Allah." Then We shall remove the veil of foreignness separating them.[9] Those whom they had associated with Allah will say: "It was not us that you worshipped. [29] Allah's witness suffices between you and us that (even if you worshipped us) we were totally unaware of your worshipping us." [30] Thereupon everyone shall taste the recompense of his past deeds. All shall be sent back to Allah, their true Lord, and then all the falsehoods they had fabricated will have forsaken them.

---

8. God calls man to the path which would ensure for him his entry into the "Abode of Peace" in the Hereafter. The expression *Dār al-salām* which literally means the "Abode of Peace," stands for Paradise, whose inhabitants shall be secure against every calamity, loss, sorrow or suffering.

9. It will become quite clear as to what distinguishes one group from the other. The polytheists will come to know those they considered to be their gods, and the false deities will also come to know those who had worshipped them.

[31] Ask them: "Who provides you with sustenance out of the heavens and the earth? Who holds mastery over your hearing and sight? Who brings forth the living from the dead and the dead from the living? Who governs all affairs of the Universe?" They will surely say: "Allah." Tell them: "Will you, then, not shun (going against reality)?" [32] Such, then, is Allah, your true Lord. And what is there after Truth but error? How, then, are you being turned away?[10] [33] Thus the word of your Lord is fulfilled concerning the transgressors that they shall not believe.

[34] Ask them: "Is there any among those whom you associate with Allah in His Divinity who brings about the creation of all beings in the first instance and will then repeat it?" Tell them: "It is Allah Who brings about the creation of all beings and will then repeat it." How are you, then, being misled?

[35] Ask them: "Are there among those whom you associate with Allah in His Divinity any who can guide to the Truth?" Say: "It is Allah alone Who guides to the Truth." Then, who is more worthy to be followed – He

---

10. Addressing the generality of the unbelievers, the Qur'ān inquires: "How, then, are you, being turned away?" The question that is posed here makes it clear that it is not the unbelievers themselves who are guilty of turning away, rather they are being made to turn away from the Right Way and that this is happening under the influence of some person or group engaged in misleading people. It is for this reason that in effect people are being asked: "Why should they go about blindly following those who are out to mislead them? Why should they not use their brains and think for themselves why they are being turned in a direction which is contrary to reality?"

Who guides to the Truth, or he who cannot find the Right Way unless others guide him to it? What is wrong with you? How ill do you judge!

[36] Most of them only follow conjectures;[11] and surely conjecture can be no substitute for the Truth. Allah is well aware of whatever they do.

[37] And this Qur'ān is such that it could not be composed by any unless it be revealed from Allah. It is a confirmation of the revelation made before it and a detailed exposition of the Book. Beyond doubt it is from the Lord of the entire Universe.

[38] Do they say that the Messenger has himself composed the Qur'ān? Say: "In that case bring forth just one *sūrah* like it and call on all whom you can, except Allah, to help you, if you are truthful." [39] In fact they arbitrarily rejected as false whatever they failed to comprehend and whose final sequel was not apparent to them. Likewise, had their predecessors rejected the Truth, declaring it falsehood. Do observe, then, what was the end of the wrong-doers. [40] Of those some will believe and others will not. Your Lord fully knows the mischief-makers.

---

11. Those who, in disregard of God's Guidance, invented religions, developed philosophies and prescribed laws to govern human life did not do this on the basis of any definite knowledge that they possessed; rather, it was the result of their conjecture and fancy. Likewise, those who followed their religious and worldly leaders did so not because they fully knew and fully understood all that the latter espoused. Rather, they followed those leaders merely on the gratuitous assumption that whatever was being taught by those great people, and whatever had been recognized as "right" by their own forefathers, must indeed be true.

[41] And if they reject you as false, tell them: "My deeds are for myself and your deeds for yourselves. You will not be held responsible for my deeds, nor I for your deeds."[12]

[42] Of them some seem to give heed to you; will you, then, make the deaf hear even though they understand nothing?[13] [43] And of them some look towards you; will you, then, guide the blind, even though they can see nothing? [44] Surely Allah does not wrong people; they rather wrong themselves. [45] (But today they are oblivious of everything except enjoyment of worldly life.) And on the Day when He will muster all people together, they will feel as though they had been in the world no more than an hour of the day to get acquainted with one another. (It will then become evident that) those who called the lie to meeting with Allah were the utter losers and were not rightly directed. [46] Whether We let you see (during your lifetime) some of the chastisement with which We threaten them, or We call you to Us (before the

---

12. Since every individual is himself accountable for his deeds, there is no point in engaging in unnecessary discussions which are often actuated by obduracy. For if the Prophet (peace be on him) was indeed inventing lies, he would bear the evil consequence of such an action. On the other hand, if his opponents were denying the Truth, their action will not hurt the Prophet (peace be on him), but rather hurt themselves.

13. In its most elementary sense even animals are possessed of the faculty of hearing. But "hearing" in its true sense is applicable only when the act of hearing is accompanied with the attention required to grasp the meaning of what one hears, and with the readiness to accept it if it is found reasonable.

chastisement strikes them), in any case they are bound to return to Us. Allah is witness to all that they do.

[47] A Messenger is sent to every people;[14] and when their Messenger comes, the fate of that people is decided with full justice; they are subjected to no wrong.

[48] They say: "If what you promise is true, when will this threat be fulfilled?" [49] Tell them: "I have no power to harm or benefit even myself, except what Allah may will. There is an appointed term for every people; and when the end of their term comes, neither can they defer it for an hour, nor can they bring it an hour before." [50] Tell them: "Did you consider (what you would do) were His chastisement to fall upon you suddenly by night or by day? So why are the culprits seeking to hasten its coming? [51] Is it only when this chastisement has actually overtaken you that you will believe in it? (And when the

---

14. The Qur'ānic expression *ummah* is not to be taken in the narrow sense in which the word "nation" is used. The word *ummah* embraces all those who receive the Message of a Messenger of God after his advent. Furthermore, this word embraces even those among whom no Messenger is physically alive, provided that they have received his Message. All those who, after the advent of a Messenger, happen to live in an age when the teachings of that Messenger are extant or at least it is possible for people to know what he had taught, constitute the *ummah* of that Messenger. Besides, all such people will be subject to the law mentioned here. In this respect, all human beings who happen to live in the age which commences with the advent of Muḥammad (peace be on him) onwards are his *ummah* and will continue to be so as long as the Qur'ān is available in its pristine purity. Hence the verse does not say: "Among every people there is a Messenger." It rather says: "There is a Messenger for every people."

chastisement will surprise you), you will try to get away from it, although it is you who had sought to hasten its coming." [52] The wrong-doers will then be told: "Suffer now the abiding chastisement. How else can you be rewarded except according to your deeds?"

[53] They ask you if what you say is true? Tell them: "Yes, by my Lord, this is altogether true, and you have no power to prevent the chastisement from befalling." [54] If a wrong-doer had all that is in the earth he would surely offer it to ransom himself. When the wrong-doers perceive the chastisement, they will feel intense remorse in their hearts. But a judgement shall be made with full justice about them. They shall not be wronged. [55] Indeed all that is in the heavens and the earth belongs to Allah. And most certainly Allah's promise will be fulfilled, though most people are not aware of it. [56] He it is Who gives life and causes death, and to Him shall you all be returned.

[57] Mankind! Now there has come to you an exhortation from your Lord, a healing for the ailments of the hearts, and a guidance and mercy for those who believe. [58] Tell them, (O Prophet): "Let them rejoice in Allah's Grace and Mercy through which this (Book) has come to you. It is better than all the riches that they accumulate. [59] Did you consider that the sustenance[15] which Allah had sent down for you of your own accord you have declared

---

15. The word *rizq* is often used in daily parlance to denote "eatables". However, in Arabic it is used in a broad sense, and covers all the things that are granted to man by God in this world for his use.

some of it as unlawful and some as lawful?"[16] Ask them: "Did Allah bestow upon you any authority for this or do you forge lies against Allah?"[17] [60] Think how those who invent lies against Him will be treated on the Day of Judgement? Allah is bountiful to people yet most of them do not give thanks.

[61] (O Prophet), whatever you may be engaged in – whether you recite any portion of the Qur'ān, or whatever else all of you are doing – We are witnesses to whatever you may be occupied with. Not even an atom's weight on the earth or in the heavens escapes your Lord, nor is there anything smaller or bigger than that, except that it is, on record in a Clear Book. [62] Surely the friends of Allah have nothing to fear, nor shall they grieve – [63] the ones who believe and are God-fearing. [64] For them are glad tidings in this world and in the Hereafter. The words of Allah shall not change. That is the supreme triumph. [65] (O Prophet), let not the utterances of the opponents distress you. Indeed all honour is Allah's. He is All-Hearing, All-Knowing.

---

16. They arrogate to themselves the authority to lay down the limits that are lawful and those that are unlawful. In fact God, Who has conferred upon them their *rizq*, alone has the authority to set these limits.

17. "Lies invented against God" may mean any of the following: claiming that God has delegated the authority to frame laws for man; saying that it is not for God to make law and prescribe limits for him; ascribing to God what man himself has made lawful and unlawful, but is unable to cite from any revealed book any basis for his assertion.

[66] Verily whoever dwells in the heavens or the earth belongs to Allah. Those who invoke others instead of Allah, associating them with Him in His Divinity, only follow conjectures and are merely guessing. [67] It is Allah alone Who has made the night that you may rest in it, and has made the day light-giving. Surely in it there are signs for those who give heed (to the call of the Messenger).

[68] They say: "Allah has taken a son." Glory be to Him. He is self-sufficient! His is all that is in the heavens and all that is in the earth. Have you any authority to support (that Allah has taken a son)? Do you ascribe to Allah something of which you have no knowledge? [69] Tell them, (O Muḥammad): "Indeed those who invent lies against Allah will never prosper. [70] They may enjoy the life of this world, but in the end they must return to Us, and then We shall cause them to taste severe chastisement for their disbelieving."

[71] Narrate to them the story of Noah when he said to his people: "My people! If my living in your midst and my effort to shake you out of heedlessness by reciting to you the revelations of Allah offend you, then remember that I have put all my trust in Allah. So draw up your plan in concert with those whom you associate with Allah in His Divinity, leaving no part of it obscure, and then put it into effect against me, and give me no respite. [72] When you turned your back on my admonition (what harm did you cause me)? I had asked you for no reward, for my reward lies only with Allah, and I am commanded to be of those who totally submit (to Him)." [73] But they rejected Noah, calling him a liar. So We saved him and those who were with him in the Ark, and made them successors (to the

authority in the land), and drowned all those who had rejected Our signs as false. Consider, then, the fate of those who had been warned (and still did not believe).

[74] Then We sent forth after him other Messengers, each one to his people. They brought to them Clear Signs, but they were not such as to believe in what they had rejected earlier as false. Thus do We seal the hearts of those who transgress.

[75] Then, after them, We sent forth Moses and Aaron to Pharaoh and his chiefs with Our signs, but they waxed proud. They were a wicked people. [76] And when the Truth came to them from Us, they said: "Indeed this is plain sorcery." [77] Moses said: "Do you say this about the Truth after it has come to you? Is this sorcery? You call this sorcery although sorcerers never come to a happy end."[18] [78] They replied: "Have you come to turn us away from the way of our forefathers that the two of you might become supreme in the land? We shall never accept what the two of you say." [79] And Pharaoh said (to his men): "Bring every skilled sorcerer to me." [80] And when the sorcerers came Moses said to them: "Cast whatever you wish to cast."

---

18. In view of the apparent similarity between sorcery and miracle the Israelites hastily branded Moses (peace be on him) a sorcerer. In relegating Moses to the role of a sorcerer, however, these simpletons ignored the fact that the character and conduct as well as the motives of the activity of sorcerers are entirely different from those of the Prophets. Is it consistent with the known character of a sorcerer that he should fearlessly make his way to the court of a tyrant, reproach him for his error, and summon him to devote himself exclusively to God and to strive for his self-purification?

[81] Then when they had cast (their staffs and ropes), Moses said: "What you have produced is sheer sorcery. Allah will certainly reduce it to naught. Surely Allah does not set right the work of the mischief-makers. [82] Allah vindicates the Truth by His commands, howsoever much the guilty might detest that."

[83] None but a few youths of Moses' people accepted him,[19] fearing that Pharaoh and their own chiefs would persecute them. Indeed Pharaoh was mighty in the land; he was among those who exceed all limits.[20]

[84] Moses said: "My people! If you believe in Allah and are truly Muslims then place your reliance on Him alone."

---

19. The word *dhurriyah* used in this verse literally means "offspring". We have, however, rendered this into English as "a few youths". We have preferred this translation because the Qur'ān employed this particular expression so as to convey the idea that it was a few youths – male and female – who had the courage of their convictions to embrace and champion the Truth in those perilous times whereas their parents and the more elderly members of the community were unable to do so. The older segment of the population was too deeply concerned with its material interests, too engrossed in worldliness, and too eager to enjoy a secure life to stand up for the Truth when that seemed to invite all kinds of peril. Instead, this older generation tried to persuade the young ones to stay away from Moses for the simple reason that it would invite the wrath of Pharaoh upon them and upon others.

20. The word *musrifīn* has been used to refer to those who, in order to achieve their objectives, are not deterred from using any means, howsoever evil they may be. Such people do not mind committing injustice, or indulging in acts of moral turpitude. They are also wont to go to any extent in pursuing their desires. Once they have something in mind, they simply know no bounds.

[85] They replied:[21] "We place our reliance on Allah. Our Lord! Do not make us a trial for the oppressors, [86] and deliver us, through Your Mercy, from the unbelievers."

[87] And We directed Moses and his brother: "Prepare a few houses for your people in Egypt, and make your houses a direction for them to pray, and establish Prayer,[22] and give glad tidings to the people of faith."

[88] Moses prayed: "Our Lord! You bestowed upon Pharaoh and his nobles splendour and riches in the world. Our Lord! Have You done this that they may lead people astray from Your Path? Our Lord! Obliterate their riches and harden their hearts that they may not

---

21. This was the reply of the youths who came forward to support Moses (peace be on him). It is evident from the context that the ones who said: "We place our reliance on Allah" were not the "wrong-doing folk" (mentioned in the present verse) but the "youths" (mentioned in verse 83 above).

22. Perhaps because of the oppression prevailing in Egypt, and because the faith of the Israelites had become quite weak, congregational Prayer had become defunct among both the Israeli and Egyptian Muslims. The abandonment of congregational Prayer was a major cause of the disintegration of their collective entity and the virtual extinction of their religious life. That is why Moses (peace be on him) was directed to re-establish congregational Prayer and to construct or acquire a few houses in Egypt specifically for that purpose. The directive to "make your houses a direction for people to pray" suggests, in my opinion, that these prayer-houses should become pivotal points for the entire people. That the directive to "establish Prayer" immediately follows this statement means that rather than offer Prayers at different places, they should congregate in the houses set aside for Prayers and perform it collectively.

believe until they observe the painful chastisement."[23]
[89] Allah responded: "The prayer of the two of you is accepted. So keep steadfast, and do not follow the path of the ignorant."

[90] And We led the Children of Israel across the sea. Then Pharaoh and his hosts pursued them in iniquity and transgression until Pharaoh cried out while he was drowning: "I believe that there is no god but Allah in Whom the Children of Israel believe, and I am also one of those who submit to Allah." [91] (Thereupon came the response): "Now you believe, although you disobeyed earlier and were among the mischief-makers. [92] We shall now save your corpse that you may serve as a sign of warning for all posterity; although many men are heedless of Our signs."

[93] We settled the Children of Israel in a blessed land and provided them with all manner of good things. They only disagreed among themselves after knowledge (of the Truth had) come to them. Surely your Lord will judge

---

23. This prayer was made by the Prophet Moses (peace be on him) during his very last days in Egypt. Moses resorted to this prayer when, although Pharaoh and his nobles had witnessed a series of Signs betokening the Truth, and even though Moses (peace be on him) had made the Truth all too patently clear to them, they still obdurately persisted in their hostility. Moses' prayer that God may "obliterate their riches and harden their hearts" is a prayer that Prophets are wont to make at a time when they are faced with opposition like that mentioned above. The prayer is substantially in accord with God's own judgement against those who obdurately oppose the Truth – that they may never be enabled to have faith.

among them on the Day of Resurrection concerning their disagreements.

[94] Now, if you are in doubt concerning what We have revealed to you, then ask those who have been reading the Book before you. It is the Truth that has come to you from your Lord, so never become one of those who doubt, [95] nor reject the Signs of Allah as false, for then you shall be among the utter losers.[24]

[96] Surely those against whom the word of your Lord has been fulfilled[25] will not believe [97] even if they witness every single Sign that might come to them until they are face to face with the painful chastisement. [98] Did it ever happen that the people of a town believed on seeing God's chastisement and its believing profited them? (There is no such instance) except of the people of Yūnus. When they believed We granted them reprieve from a humiliating

---

24. Though this admonition is apparently addressed to the Prophet Muḥammad (peace be on him), in point of fact it is directed at those who entertained doubts about the Prophet's Message. Reference is made to the People of the Book because the Arabs were not commonly conversant with the Scriptures. But so far as the People of the Book were concerned, there were doubtlessly some pious religious scholars among them who were in a position to corroborate that the Qur'ānic Message was essentially the same as that delivered by the earlier Prophets.

25. The statement that "the word of your Lord has been fulfilled" refers to those who are not interested in seeking the Truth; who, by dint of their apathy, bigotry, stubbornness, excessive worldliness and total unconcern about the After-life, make their hearts immune to the Truth. God's judgement about such persons is that they will not be blessed with faith.

chastisement in this world,[26] and We let them enjoy themselves for a while.

[99] Had your Lord so willed, all those who are on earth would have believed. Will you, then, force people into believing? [100] No one can believe except by Allah's leave, and Allah lays abomination on those who do not use their understanding.

[101] Tell them: "Observe carefully all that is in the heavens and the earth." But no Signs and warnings can avail those who are bent on not believing. [102] What are they waiting for except to witness the repetition of the days of calamity that their predecessors witnessed? Tell them: "Wait; I too am waiting with you. [103] Then, (when Allah's wrath falls upon the wicked), We save our Messengers and also those who believe. It is incumbent on Us to deliver the believers."

[104] (O Prophet), tell them: "O people! If you are still in doubt concerning my religion, know that I do not serve those whom you serve beside Allah. I only serve Allah Who will cause (all of) you to die. I have been commanded to be one of those who believe, [105] and to adhere exclusively and sincerely to the true faith,[27] and

---

26. The view of the Qur'ān commentators is that since the Prophet Jonah (peace be on him) had left his station without obtaining God's permission to do so and since the Assyrians repented and sought pardon from God as soon as they saw the Signs of God's impending punishment, God pardoned them.

27. The actual words of the verse suggest that one should focus one's attention on the true faith, that one ought not to waver and let one's attention wander, that one ought to refrain from occasionally

not to be one of those who associate others with Allah in His Divinity. [106] Do not call upon any apart from Allah, upon those who have no power to benefit or hurt you. For if you call upon others than Allah you will be reckoned among the wrong-doers. [107] If Allah afflicts you with any hardship, none other than He can remove it; and if He wills any good for you, none can avert His Bounty. He bestows good upon whomsoever of His servants He wills. He is All-Forgiving, All-Merciful."

[108] Tell them (O Muḥammad): "O people! Truth has come to you from your Lord. Whosoever, then, follows the True Guidance does so for his own good; and whosoever strays, his straying will be to his own hurt. I am no custodian over you. [109] And follow, (O Prophet), whatever is revealed to you, and remain patient until Allah brings forth His judgement. He is the Best of those who judge."

---

moving a step forward and then taking another step backward, or turning alternately left and right. What one is rather required to do is to keep moving straight ahead on the path to which one has been directed. This is clear and forceful enough in itself. However, the Qur'ān does not stop at that. It adds the condition that the attention should be the one characterized by exclusive and sincere devotion to the One True God.

11

Hūd
Makkan Period

In the name of Allah, the Most Merciful,
the Most Compassionate

[1] *Alif. Lām. Rā'.* This is a Divine Command¹ whose contents have been made firm and set forth in detail; (a Command) from One Who is All-Wise, All-Aware [2] that you may worship none but Allah. Verily I have come to you as a warner and a bearer of good news from Him [3] that you may seek forgiveness of your Lord and turn to Him in repentance whereupon He will grant you a fair enjoyment of life until an appointed term,² and

---

1. In keeping with the context, the word *kitāb* has here been rendered as "Divine Command". The word *kitāb* in its Arabic usage denotes not only book or inscription, but also writ and command. There are several instances in the Qur'ān of the use of the word in the latter sense.

2. During the term appointed for you in this world God will lavish upon you His bounties, confer a variety of benedictions, provide a life of prosperity, grant peace and tranquillity, and cause you to live honourably rather than in ignominy and disgrace.

will bestow favour on everyone who merits favour.³ But should you turn away (from the Truth), I fear for you the chastisement of an Awesome Day. [4] Unto Allah is your return, and He has power to do everything.

[5] Lo! They fold up their breasts that they may conceal themselves from him.⁴ Surely when they cover themselves up with their garments Allah still knows well what they cover and what they reveal. Indeed He even knows the secrets hidden in the breasts of people. [6] There is not a single moving creature on earth except that Allah is responsible for providing its sustenance. He knows where it dwells and where it will permanently rest. All this is recorded in a Clear Book.

[7] And He it is Who created the heavens and the earth in six days – and (before that) His Throne was upon the water⁵ – that He may test you, who of you is better in

---

3. The more a person excels in moral conduct and good deeds, the higher will be the status that God will confer upon him. God deals with His creatures in such a way that anyone who deserves a reward is fully granted that reward.

4. If the unbelievers of Makkah saw him somewhere they would turn their faces away or try to hide themselves. They made every effort to avoid any encounter with the Prophet (peace be on him).

5. We are not in a position to state with certainty the meaning of the word "water" used in the verse. Does it mean the "water" in the sense known to us by that word? Or has it been used metaphorically to refer to matter in its liquid form before it assumed its present form? As for the statement that God's "Throne was upon water," it means – as far as we have been able to grasp – that God's kingdom was over water.

conduct.⁶ If you were to say, (O Muḥammad): "All of
you will surely be raised after death," then those who
disbelieve will certainly say: "This is nothing but plain
sorcery."⁷ [8] And were We to put off the chastisement
from them for a determined period, they will cry out:
"What withholds Him from chastising?" Surely when
the day of the chastisement comes, nothing will avert
it and the chastisement which they had ridiculed shall
encompass them.

[9] If We ever favour man with Our Mercy, and thereafter
take it away from him, he becomes utterly desperate,
totally ungrateful. [10] And if We let him taste favour after
harm has touched him, he says: "All my ills are gone," and
he suddenly becomes exultant and boastful, [11] except
those who are patient and act righteously. Such shall have
Allah's forgiveness and a great reward.

[12] (O Messenger), let it not happen that you omit (to
expound) a portion of what was revealed to you. And
do not be distressed that they will say: "Why was a
treasure not bestowed upon him?" or "Why did no angel
accompany him?" For you are merely a warner, whereas
Allah has control over everything.

[13] Do they say: "He has invented this Book himself?"
Say: "If that is so, bring ten *sūrahs* the like of it of your

---

6. The purpose of creation was to create man and then put him
to a test.

7. That is: "It is not possible for people to be raised after their
death. We are being subjected to enchantment to believe what is
unbelievable."

composition, and call upon all (the deities) that you can to your help other than Allah. Do so if you are truthful." [14] Then if (your deities) do not respond to your call for help feel assured that this Book was revealed with the knowledge of Allah, and that there is no god but He. Will you, then, surrender (to this truth)?

[15] Those who merely seek the present world and its adornment, We fully recompense them for their work in this world, and they are made to suffer no diminution in it concerning what is their due. [16] They are the ones who shall have nothing in the Hereafter except Fire. (There they shall came to know) that their deeds in the world have come to naught, and that whatever they have done is absolutely useless.

[17] Can it happen that he who enjoyed a clear evidence from his Lord[8] – which is subsequently followed by a witness from Him (in his support),[9] and prior to that was the Book of Moses revealed as a guide and a mercy – (would even such a person deny the Truth in

---

8. There is ample evidence in man's own self, let alone in the structure of the heavens and the earth and in the order that prevails in the Universe to prove that God is the only creator, master, lord and sovereign of the Universe. This evidence referred to above also inclines man to believe that the present life will be followed by another one in which man will be required to render an account of his deeds and wherein he will be requited for his performance in the life of this world.

9. The "witness from Him" is the Qur'ān which confirms the natural and rational evidence that God is the Reality whose signs are manifest in man's own self and in his surroundings.

the manner of those who adore the life of this world)? Rather, such persons are bound to believe in it. The Fire shall be the promised resort of the groups of people that disbelieve. So be in no doubt about it for this indeed is the Truth from your Lord although most people do not believe.

[18] And who is a greater wrong-doer than he who invents a lie against Allah?[10] Such persons will be set forth before their Lord and the witnesses will testify: "These are the ones who lied against their Lord." Lo! Allah's curse be upon the wrong-doers;[11] [19] upon those who bar people from the Way of Allah, and seek in it crookedness, and disbelieve in the Hereafter. [20] They had no power to frustrate Allah's plan on earth, nor did they have any protectors against Allah. Their chastisement will be doubled. They were unable to hear, nor could they see. [21] They caused utter loss to themselves, and all that they had invented failed them. [22] Doubtlessly they shall be the greatest losers in the Hereafter. [23] As for those who

10. To invent a lie against God consists of stating that beings other than God also have a share with God in His Godhead, that like God they too are entitled to be served and worshipped by God's creatures. Inventing a lie against God also consists of stating that God is not concerned with providing guidance to His creatures, that He did not raise Prophets for that purpose, and that He rather left human beings free to behave as they pleased. Inventing a lie against God also consists of stating that God created human beings by way of jest and sport and that He will not have them render an account to Him, and that He will not requite them for their deeds.

11. Such a proclamation would be made on the Day of Judgement when such iniquitous people will be presented before their Lord.

believed and acted righteously and dedicated themselves totally to their Lord – they are the people of Paradise, and there they shall abide forever. [24] The example of the two parties is that one is blind and deaf, and the other capable of seeing and hearing. Can the two be equal? Will you, then, not heed?

[25] (Such were the circumstances) when We sent forth Noah to his people. (He said): "I have been sent to you to warn you plainly [26] that you may worship none but Allah or else I fear for you the chastisement of a Grievous Day." [27] The elders among Noah's own people, who had refused to follow him, responded: "We see you as merely a human being like ourselves. Nor do we find among those who follow you except the lowliest of our folk, those who follow you without any proper reason. We see nothing in you to suggest that you are any better than us. Rather, we believe you to be liars." [28] Noah said: "My people! If I base myself on a clear evidence from my Lord – and I have also been blessed by His Mercy to which you have been blind – how can we force it upon you despite your aversion to it? [29] My people! I seek no recompense from you. My recompense is only with Allah. Nor will I drive away those who believe. They are destined to meet their Lord. But I find you to be an ignorant people. [30] My people! Were I to drive the people of faith away, who will protect me from (the chastisement of) Allah? Do you not understand even this much? [31] I do not say to you that I possess Allah's treasures, nor that I have access to the realm beyond the ken of perception, nor do I claim to be an angel, nor do I say regarding those whom you look upon with disdain that Allah will not bestow any good

upon them. Allah knows best what is in their hearts. Were I to say so I would be one of the wrong-doers."

[32] They said: "O Noah! Surely you have disputed with us and have prolonged your dispute. Now bring upon us the chastisement that you threaten us with; do so, if you are truthful." [33] Noah said: "Only Allah will bring it upon you if He so wills, and you will be utterly unable to frustrate that. [34] If I want to give you good advice it will not profit you if Allah Himself has decided to let you go astray.[12] He is your Lord, and to Him will you be returned."

[35] (O Muḥammad), do they say that he himself has forged this Message? Tell them: "If I have forged this, the guilt of it will fall upon me, but I am not responsible for the crimes you are committing."

[36] It was revealed to Noah that no more of your people, other than those who already believe, will ever come to believe. So do not grieve over their deeds, [37] and build the Ark under Our eyes and Our direction. And do not supplicate Me concerning those who have engaged in wrong-doing. They are doomed to be drowned.

[38] As Noah was building the Ark, whenever the elders of his nation passed by him, they would scoff at him.

---

12. Such was their obduracy, mischievousness and absolute disregard for righteous behaviour that quite understandably God should decide not to direct them to the Right Way and let them, as they wished, stumble in error. Once God had made such a decision no one's effort to direct them to the Right Way – not even the Prophet's – could be of any avail.

He said: "If you scoff at us, we too scoff at you in like manner. [39] You will come to know who will be struck by a humiliating chastisement, and who will be subjected to an unceasing torment."[13]

[40] Thus it was until Our Command came to pass and the oven boiled over.[14] We said: "Take into the Ark a pair of every species; and take your own family except those

13. This fascinating story illustrates how man can be deluded by the appearance of things. When the Prophet Noah (peace be on him) was busy building the Ark on a tract of land far from any sea or river, it must have appeared a very silly thing to do. Noah's people would surely have laughed at him, mocking at the old fellow's apparently senile plan. They may even have called it an adventure of sailing on the Ark across dry land! At that moment it would have simply been inconceivable for anyone to think that the Ark would one day indeed sail on that very tract of land as it became flooded with water. The same act would, however, have been perceived quite differently by anyone who really knew what was going to happen, who knew that soon enough a ship would indeed be a necessity for anyone who wished to move around. Such a person could only have laughed at the ignorance and stupid complaisance of his people. Noah (peace be on him), who knew these things well, would often have said to himself: "How stupid are these people! God's chastisement is just about to afflict them, and I have been warning them of this. That moment has all but come and they even see me making an effort to escape the impending chastisement. Is it not strange that they remain totally unperturbed? Not only that, but they look upon me as an utter lunatic."

14. Commentators on the Qur'ān have offered different explanations of this incident. In our view the correct position is the one deducible from the text of the Qur'ān that the place from which the Flood began was a particular oven. It is from beneath it that a spring of water burst forth. This was followed by both a heavy downpour and by a very large number of springs which gushed forth.

who have already been declared (as unworthy);[15] and also take everyone who believes." But those who, along with him, had believed were indeed just a few. [41] Noah said: "Embark in it. In the name of Allah is its sailing and its anchorage. My Lord is Ever Forgiving, Most Merciful."

[42] The Ark sailed along with them amid mountain-like waves. Noah, spotting his son at a distance, called out to him: "My son, embark with us, and do not be with the unbelievers." [43] The son replied: "I will go to a mountain for refuge and it will save me from the water." Noah said: "None can save anyone today from the Command of Allah except those on whom He may have Mercy." Thereupon a wave swept in between the two and he was drowned.

[44] And the Command was given: "Earth! Swallow up your water"; and: "Heavens! Abate!" So the water subsided, the Command was fulfilled, and the Ark settled on Mount Jūdī,[16] and it was said: "Away with the wrong-doing folk!"

[45] And Noah called out to his Lord, saying: "My Lord! My son is of my family. Surely Your promise is true, and You are the Best of those who judge." [46] In response Noah was told: "Most certainly he is not of your family;

---

15. Information that some members of Noah's family were unbelievers and so were unworthy of God's Mercy had already been given. Noah (peace be on him) had been directed not to accommodate them in the Ark.

16. Mount Jūdī is situated to the northeast of the Island of Ibn 'Umar in Kurdistan and is known by this name.

verily he is of unrighteous conduct.[17] So do not ask of Me for that concerning which you have no knowledge. I admonish you never to act like the ignorant ones."

[47] Noah said: "My Lord! I take refuge with You that I should ask You for that concerning which I have no knowledge.[18] And if You do not forgive me and do not show Mercy to me, I shall be among the losers."

[48] It was said: "Noah! Disembark, with Our peace, and with blessings upon you and upon those who are with you. There are also people whom We shall allow to enjoy themselves for a while, and then a painful chastisement from Us shall afflict them."

[49] We reveal to you these accounts of matters that are beyond the reach of perception. Neither you nor your people knew about them before this. Be patient, then. Surely, the good end is for the God-fearing.[19]

---

17. The import of this Qur'ānic verse may best be appreciated by analogy to the limbs on a person's body. A limb may become rotten and a physician may decide to remove it by surgical operation. Now, the patient may ask his doctor not to amputate because it is a part of his body. The natural reply of the physician would be that the rotten limb was not truly a part of his body. Likewise, when a righteous father is told about his unworthy son that he is of unrighteous conduct it is tantamount to saying that the trouble he had taken to raise the son had gone to waste and he should be considered a spoilage.

18. That is, ask God for something I am not sure it is right to pray for.

19. The Prophet Muḥammad (peace be on him) is consoled by the statement that in the same way that Noah (peace be on him) and his righteous people ultimately succeeded, so will he and his

[50] And to 'Ād We sent their brother Hūd. He said: "My people! Serve Allah: you have no god but He. (In attributing partners to Allah) you have merely been fabricating lies. [51] My people, I seek no reward from you for my work. My reward lies only with Him Who created me. Do you not understand anything? [52] My people! Ask your Lord for forgiveness and turn to Him in repentance. He will shower abundant rains upon you from the heaven, and will add strength to your strength. Do not turn away as those given to guilt."

[53] They said: "O Hūd! You have not brought to us any clear evidence, and we are not going to forsake our gods merely because you say so. We are not going to believe you. [54] All we can say is that some of our gods have afflicted you with evil."[20]

Hūd said: "Indeed I take Allah as my witness, and you too to be my witnesses that I have nothing to do with your associating with Allah [55] others than Him in His Divinity. So conspire against me, all of you, and give me no respite. [56] I have put my trust in Allah, Who is my Lord and your Lord. There is no moving creature but that He holds it by its forelock. Surely, My Lord is on the Straight Path. [57] If you, then, turn away (from the Truth),

---

Companions. So the believers should not feel heart-broken by their ephemeral suffering. Instead, they should persevere, with courage and fortitude, in their struggle for the cause of the Truth.

20. The unbelievers presumably thought that because of his sacrilegious behaviour towards some saint or deity, the Prophet Hūd (peace be on him) had been smitten with madness. Consequently, both words of abuse and stones were hurled at him even though he had once enjoyed much esteem and respect of his people.

know that I have delivered the Message with which I was sent to you. Now my Lord will set up another people in place of you and you shall in no way be able to harm Him. Surely my Lord keeps a watch over everything."

[58] And when Our Command came to pass, We delivered Hūd, together with those who shared his faith, out of Our Mercy. We delivered them from a woeful chastisement.

[59] Such were 'Ād. They repudiated the Signs of their Lord, disobeyed His Messengers, and followed the bidding of every tyrannical enemy of the Truth. [60] They were pursued by a curse in this world, and so will they be on the Day of Judgement. Lo, 'Ād disbelieved in the Lord. Lo, ruined are 'Ād, the people of Hūd.

[61] And to Thamūd We sent their brother Ṣāliḥ. He said: "My people! Serve Allah; you have no god but He. He brought you into being out of the earth, and has made you dwell in it. So ask Him to forgive you, and do turn towards Him in repentance. Indeed My Lord is near, responsive to prayers."²¹

---

21. This verse is aimed at removing a major misconception which had been prevalent among the polytheists. This misconception is in fact one of the major reasons which prompted people to associate others with God in His Divinity. Such people fell prey to the false belief that God is well above the reach of ordinary human beings. This belief spread further because many clever people found it quite profitable to propagate such a notion. No wonder, many people felt that God could only be approached through powerful intermediaries and intercessors. The only way that a person's prayer could reach God and be answered by Him was to approach Him through one of the holy men. It was, therefore, considered necessary to grease the palm of the religious functionaries who

[62] They said: "O Ṣāliḥ! Until now you were one of those among us in whom we placed great hopes. Now, would you forbid us to worship what our forefathers were wont to worship? Indeed we are in disquieting doubt about what you are calling us to."

[63] Ṣāliḥ said: "My people! What do you think? If I had a clear evidence from my Lord, and then He also bestowed His Mercy upon me, who will rescue me from the punishment of Allah if I still disobey Him? You can only make me lose even more. [64] My people! This she-camel of Allah is a Sign for you. So let her pasture on Allah's earth, and do not hurt her or else some chastisement – which is near at hand – shall overtake you."

---

supposedly enjoyed the privilege of conveying a man's offerings and prayers to the One on high. This misconception gave birth to a pantheon of small and large deities and to intercessors who were supposed to act as intermediaries between man and God. The Prophet Ṣāliḥ (peace be on him) strikes at the root of this ignorant system, and totally demolishes its intellectual infrastructure. This he does by emphasizing two facts: that God is extremely close to all His creatures and that He answers their prayers. Thus he refutes many misconceptions about God: that He is far away, altogether withdrawn from human beings, and that He does not answer their prayers if they were to directly approach Him. On the contrary, everyone can find Him just beside himself. Everyone can whisper to Him. Everyone can address his prayers to God. God answers the prayers of all His creatures directly. The fact is that God's court with all its majesty is just around everyone's corner, so close to one's threshold, and always open to all. How silly it is, therefore, for people to search for intercessors and intermediaries.

[65] But they slaughtered her. Thereupon Ṣāliḥ warned them: "Enjoy yourselves in your homes for a maximum of three days. This is a promise which shall not be belied."

[66] Then, when Our Command came to pass, We saved Ṣāliḥ and those who shared his faith by Our Mercy, from the disgrace of that day. Truly Your Lord is All-Strong, All-Mighty. [67] And the Blast overtook those who were wont to do wrong, and then they lay lifeless in their homes [68] as though they had never lived there before.

Oh, verily the Thamūd denied their Lord! Oh, the Thamūd were destroyed.

[69] Indeed Our messengers came to Abraham, bearing glad tidings. They greeted him with "peace", and Abraham answered back to them "peace", and hurriedly brought to them a roasted calf.[22] [70] When he perceived that their hands were not stretching to it[23] he mistrusted them, and felt afraid of them. They said: "Do not be afraid. We have been sent to the people of Lot." [71] And Abraham's wife was standing by and on hearing this she laughed. And We gave her the good news of (the birth of) Isaac, and after Isaac, of Jacob.

---

22. This shows that the angels visited the Prophet Abraham (peace be on him) in the human form and that initially they did not disclose their identity. The Prophet Abraham (peace be on him), therefore, thought that they were strangers and immediately arranged a good meal for them.

23. As soon as Abraham (peace be on him) noticed that his guests were disinclined to eat, he realized that they were angels.

[72] She said: "Woe is me![24] Shall I bear a child now that I am an old woman and my husband is much too age-stricken? This is indeed strange!" [73] They said: "Do you wonder at Allah's decree? Allah's Mercy and His blessings be upon you, O people of the house. Surely, He is Praise-worthy, Glorious."

[74] Thus when fear had left Abraham and the good news had been conveyed to him, he began to dispute with Us concerning the people of Lot.[25] [75] Surely Abraham was forbearing, tender-hearted and oft-turning to Allah. [76] Thereupon (Our angels) said to him: "O Abraham! Desist from this, for indeed your Lord's command has come; and a chastisement which cannot be averted is about to befall them."

---

24. This expression does not, in any way, suggest that Sarah, instead of feeling happy, considered this prediction the foreboding of a calamity. In point of fact the expression is an exclamation to which women, in particular, resort to in a state of wonder and amazement.

25. The word "dispute" here expresses the nexus of affection and endearment between Abraham (peace be on him) and God. Perusal of this verse brings to one's mind Abraham's persistent pleading to God that He may spare Lot's people His chastisement. To this God replied that since they were totally devoid of all good and had exceeded all reasonable limits, they did not deserve any leniency. Yet Abraham (peace be on him) continued to plead for them and presumably submitted that if there was even the least bit of good left in them, their chastisement be deferred so that this good may come to the fore.

[77] And when Our messengers came to Lot, he was perturbed by their coming and felt troubled on their account, and said: "This is a distressing day."[26] [78] And his people came to him rushing. Before this they were wont to commit evil deeds. Lot said: "My people! Here are my daughters; they are purer for you.[27] Have fear of Allah and do not disgrace me concerning my guests. Is there not even one right-minded person in your midst?" [79] They said: "Surely you already know that we have nothing to do with your daughters. You also know well what we want." [80] He said: "Would that I had the strength to set you straight or could seek refuge in some powerful support." [81] Thereupon the angels said: "O Lot! We indeed are messengers of your Lord. And your people will in no way be able to hurt you. So depart with your family in a part of the night and let none of you turn around excepting your wife (who shall not go); for what will befall them shall also befall her. In the morning their promised hour will come. Is not the morning near?"

---

26. The angels had come to Lot (peace be on him) in the form of handsome young boys. Lot (peace be on him) was unaware that they were angels. He also felt quite disturbed, therefore, at the sight of the visiting young boys. His reaction was natural in view of the known degeneration and unabashed perversity prevalent among his people.

27. One should not misunderstand the statement and think this to be an invitation to Lot's people to indulge in illegitimate sex with his daughters. For the very next part of his remark, viz. "they are purer for you," excludes all justification for such a misunderstanding. The whole thrust of Lot's statement was that if they wished to satisfy their sex-urge, they should do so in the natural and legitimate manner as laid down by God as there was no dearth of women in their society.

[82] And when Our Command came to pass, We turned the town upside down, and rained on it stones of baked clay, one on another, [83] marked from your Lord.[28] Such punishment is not far from the wrong-doers.

[84] And to (the people of) Midian We sent their brother Shuʿayb. He said: "My people! Serve Allah; you have no god but He. And do not diminish the measure and weight. Indeed I see that you are prospering now, but I fear for you the chastisement of an encompassing day in the future. [85] My people! Give full measure and weight with justice, do not diminish the goods of others, and do not go about creating corruption in the land. [86] The gains that Allah lets you retain are better for you, if you indeed believe. In any case, I have not been appointed a keeper over you."

[87] They replied: "O Shuʿayb! Does your Prayer enjoin upon you that we should forsake the deities whom our forefathers worshipped, or that we should give up using our wealth as we please? Do you fancy that you, and only you, are forbearing and rightly-directed?"

[88] Shuʿayb said: "My people! What do you think? If I stand on clear evidence from my Lord, and He has also provided me a handsome provision from Himself[29] –

---

28. This implies that each stone had been earmarked for a specific act of destruction or for a particular offender.

29. If his Lord had granted Shuʿayb knowledge of reality and also a livelihood that was pure and lawful and when God had lavished His favours upon Shuʿayb, how could it be appropriate for him to act ungratefully towards God by legitimizing their erroneous beliefs and acts of corruption?

(should I still be ungrateful to Him and share your error and iniquity)? Nor do I desire to act contrary to what I admonish you. I desire nothing but to set things right as far as I can. My succour is only with Allah. In Him have I put my trust, and to Him do I always turn. [89] My people! Let not your opposition to me lead you to guilt that would bring upon you the chastisement that struck earlier the people of Noah, and the people of Hūd, and the people of Ṣāliḥ. And the land of the people of Lot is not far from you! [90] Seek the forgiveness of your Lord and turn to Him in repentance. Surely my Lord is Ever Merciful, Most Loving."

[91] They said: "O Shuʿayb! We do not understand much of what you say. Indeed we see you weak in our midst. Were it not for your kinsmen, we would surely have stoned you for you have no strength to overpower us."

[92] Shuʿayb said: "My people, are my kinsmen mightier with you than Allah that you (hold the kinsmen in awe while) you cast Allah behind your back? Surely my Lord encompasses all that you do. [93] My people! Go on working according to your way and I will keep working (according to mine). Soon you will come to know who will be afflicted by a humiliating chastisement, and who will be proved a liar. And I too shall watch with you."

[94] And when Our Command came to pass, We delivered Shuʿayb and those who shared his faith out of Our Mercy, and the Blast seized those who were engaged in wrongdoing, so they lay lifeless in their homes [95] as though they had never dwelt in them before. Lo, (the people of) Midian, were done away with as were the Thamūd!

[96] And indeed We sent Moses, with Our Signs and with a clear authority, [97] to Pharaoh and his nobles. But they obeyed the command of Pharaoh even though Pharaoh's command was not rightly-directed. [98] He shall stand at the head of his people on the Day of Resurrection, and will bring them down to the Fire. What a wretched destination to be led to! [99] They were pursued by a curse in this world and so will they be on the Day of Resurrection. What an evil reward will they receive!

[100] That is an account of some towns which We recount to you. Of them some are still standing and some have been mown down. [101] We did not wrong them; it is rather they who wronged themselves. And when the Command of your Lord came to pass, the gods whom they had called upon instead of Allah did not avail them in the least. They added nothing to them except ruin.

[102] Such is the seizing of your Lord that when He does seize the towns immersed in wrong-doing, His seizing is painful, terrible. [103] Surely in that is a Sign for him who fears the chastisement of the Hereafter. That will be a Day when all people shall be mustered together. That will be a Day when whatever happens shall be witnessed by all. [104] Nor shall We withhold it except till an appointed term. [105] And when the appointed Day comes, no one shall even dare to speak except by the leave of Allah. Then some will be declared wretched, others blessed. [106] As for the wretched, they shall be in the Fire, and in it they shall sigh and groan.

[107] They shall abide in it as long as the heavens and the earth last,[30] unless your Lord should will otherwise. Surely your Lord does whatsoever He wills. [108] And as for those who are blessed, they shall abide in the Garden as long as the heavens and the earth last, unless your Lord should will otherwise. They shall enjoy an unceasing gift.

[109] (O Prophet), have no doubt about what they worship. For they worship what their fathers worshipped before. And (yet) We shall grant them their due portion in full, diminishing of it nothing.

[110] And We certainly gave Moses the Book before, and there arose disagreements about it (even as there are disagreements now about the Book revealed to you). Had it not been for a decree that had already gone forth from your Lord, the matter disputed among them would have long been decided. Indeed they are in a disquieting doubt about it. [111] Surely your Lord will recompense all to the full for their deeds. For indeed He is well aware of all what they do. [112] So, (O Muḥammad), remain steadfast in following the Right Way and let those with you who have returned with you (to the fold of faith and obedience), follow the Right Way as you were commanded, and do not exceed the proper limits of (devotion to Allah). For certainly He is aware of all that you do. [113] And do not incline towards the wrong-doers lest the Fire seize you and then you have none to protect you against Allah; and then you will not be helped from anywhere.

---

30. These words are used figuratively to convey the idea of perpetuity.

[114] And establish the Prayer at the two ends of the day and in the first hours of the night.[31] Indeed the good deeds drive away the evil deeds. This is a Reminder to those who are mindful of Allah. [115] And be patient; for indeed Allah never lets the reward of those who do good go to waste.

[116] Why were there no righteous persons among the generations that passed away before you who would forbid others from causing corruption on earth? And if such were there, they were only a few whom We had saved from those generations, or else the wrong-doers kept pursuing the ease and comfort which had been conferred upon them, thus losing themselves in sinfulness. [117] And your Lord is not such as would wrongfully destroy human habitations while their inhabitants are righteous. [118] Had your Lord so willed, He would surely have made mankind one community. But as things stand, they will not cease to differ among themselves and to follow erroneous ways [119] except for those on whom your Lord has Mercy. And it is for this (exercise of freedom of choice) that He has created them. And the word of your Lord was fulfilled: "Indeed I will fill the Hell, with *jinn* and mankind, altogether."

[120] (O Muḥammad), We narrate these anecdotes of Messengers to you that We may strengthen your heart through them. In these anecdotes come to you the Truth,

---

31. The "two ends of the day" refer to the morning and the sunset. Similarly, the "first hours of the night" refer to the time of the "'Ishā'" Prayer. For details of Prayer times see *Banī Isrā'īl* 17: 78; *Ṭā' Hā'* 20: 130, and *al-Rūm* 30: 17-18.

and an Exhortation, and a Reminder for the believers. [121] As for those who are bent on not believing, tell them: "Work according to your way and we are working according to ours. [122] And do wait for the end of things; we too are waiting. [123] All that is hidden in the heavens and the earth lies within the power of Allah. To Him are all matters referred for judgement. So do serve Him and put in Him all your trust. Your Lord is not heedless of what you do."

12
◈◈◈◈

Yūsuf [Joseph]
Makkan Period

In the name of Allah, the Most Merciful,
the Most Compassionate

[1] *Alif. Lām. Rā'.* These are the verses of a Book that clearly expounds the truth. [2] We have revealed it as a Recitation[1] in Arabic that you may fully understand. [3] (O Muḥammad), by revealing the Qur'ān to you We narrate to you in the best manner the stories of the past although before this narration you were utterly unaware of them.

[4] Call to mind when Joseph said to his father: "My father! I saw (in a dream) eleven stars and the sun and the moon: I saw them prostrating themselves before me." [5] His father said: "My son! Do not relate your dream to your brothers lest they hatch a plot to harm you.[2] Indeed

---

1. The word "Qur'ān" is a derivative of the Arabic verb *qara'a* meaning "he read". The appellation "Qur'ān" with reference to a book suggests that it is something that is meant to be read or recited over and over again by all, by the élite and commoners alike.

2. This is a reference to Joseph's ten brothers who were born of his stepmothers. He also had a real brother who was younger than him. Jacob (peace be on him) was well aware that the stepbrothers were jealous of Joseph. He was also aware that the brothers, lacking the scruples of righteous people, would not hesitate to use any means, howsoever vile, to achieve their selfish designs. Jacob (peace be on

Satan is man's open enemy. [6] (As you have seen in the dream), so will your Lord choose you (for His task) and will impart to you the comprehension of the deeper meaning of things³ and will bestow the full measure of His favour upon you and upon the house of Jacob even as He earlier bestowed it in full measure upon your forefathers, Abraham and Isaac. Surely your Lord is All-Knowing, All-Wise."

[7] Verily in the story of Joseph and his brothers there are many signs for those who inquire (about the truth). [8] And call to mind when the brothers of Joseph conferred together and said: "Surely Joseph and his brother⁴ are dearer to our father than we are, although we are a group of so many. Our father is clearly mistaken. [9] So either kill Joseph or cast him into some distant land so that your father's attention may become exclusively yours. And after so doing become righteous." [10] Thereupon one of them said: "Do not kill Joseph, but if you are bent upon doing something, cast him down to the bottom of some dark pit, perhaps some caravan passing by will take him out of it."

him), therefore, thought it necessary to warn Joseph (peace be on him) about them. As for Joseph's dream, its meaning was clear. Jacob was the sun; his wife, the stepmother of Joseph, was the moon; and his eleven sons were the eleven stars.

3. The Qur'ānic expression *ta'wil al-aḥādīth* does not simply signify explanation of the true meaning of dreams, as people are wont to believe. What it really signifies is that God would bless Joseph with the capacity to grasp complicated matters, to understand the true nature of things.

4. This refers to Benjamin, Joseph's true brother, who was younger than him by a few years.

[11] After so deciding they said to their father: "Why is it that you do not trust us regarding Joseph although we are his true well-wishers?" [12] Send him out with us tomorrow that he may enjoy himself[5] and play while we will be there, standing guard over him." [13] Their father answered: "It grieves me indeed that you should take him with you for I fear that some wolf might eat him up while you are negligent of him." [14] They said: "Should a wolf eat him, despite the presence of our strong group, we would indeed be a worthless lot!" [15] So when they went away with Joseph and decided to cast him in the bottom of the dark pit, We revealed to Joseph: "Surely a time will come when you will remind them of their deed. They know nothing about the consequence of what they are doing." [16] At nightfall they came to their father weeping [17] and said: "Father! We went racing with one another and left Joseph behind with our things, and then a wolf came and ate him up. We know that you will not believe us howsoever truthful we might be." [18] And they brought Joseph's shirt, stained with false blood. Seeing this their father exclaimed: "Nay (this is not true); rather your evil souls have made it easy for you to commit a heinous act. So I will bear this patiently, and in good grace. It is Allah's help alone that I seek against your fabrication."

[19] And a caravan came, and they sent their water drawer to draw water. As he let down his bucket in the well he (observed Joseph) and cried out: "This is good news. There is a boy." They concealed him, considering him as part of their merchandise, while Allah was well aware

---

5. He may move about and pluck and eat fruit in the forest.

of what they did. [20] Later they sold him for a paltry sum – just a few dirhams; they did not care to obtain a higher price.

[21] The man from Egypt who bought him said to his wife: "Take good care of him, possibly he might be of benefit to us or we might adopt him as a son." Thus We found a way for Joseph to become established in that land and in order that We might teach him to comprehend the deeper meaning of things. Allah has full power to implement His design although most people do not know that. [22] And when Joseph reached the age of maturity, We granted him judgement and knowledge. Thus do We reward those who do good.

[23] And it so happened that the lady in whose house Joseph was living, sought to tempt him to herself, and one day bolting the doors she said: "Come on now!" Joseph answered: "May Allah grant me refuge! My Lord[6] has provided an honourable abode for me (so how can I do something so evil)? Such wrong-doers never prosper." [24] And she advanced towards him, and had Joseph

---

6. The translators as well as the commentators of the Qur'ān interpret the expression "my lord" as referring to the person in whose employ Joseph was at that time. In other words, Joseph said that he could not betray his "lord" – i.e. the chief who had treated him so well. What this meant is that in view of the official's kindness to Joseph, his indulgence in illegitimate sex with the wife of the chief was absolutely out of the question. However, it seems altogether unbecoming of a Prophet that he should abstain from a sin out of consideration for some human being rather than out of consideration for God. If we turn to the Qur'ān, there is not a single instance in which a Prophet would have called anyone other than God his *rabb* ("lord").

not perceived a sign from his Lord he too would have advanced towards her.[7] Thus was Joseph shown a sign from his Lord that We might avert from him all evil and indecency, for indeed he was one of Our chosen servants. [25] Then both of them rushed to the door, each seeking to get ahead of the other, and she tore Joseph's shirt from behind. Then both of them found the husband of the lady at the door. Seeing him she said: "What should be the punishment of him who has foul designs on your wife except that he should be imprisoned or subjected to painful chastisement?" [26] Joseph said: "It is she who was trying to tempt me to herself." And a witness belonging to her own household testified (on grounds of circumstantial evidence): "If his shirt is torn from the front, then she is telling the truth and he is a liar. [27] But if his shirt is torn from behind, then she has lied, and he is truthful."[8] [28] So when the husband saw Joseph's shirt torn from behind he exclaimed: "Surely, this is one of the tricks of you women; your tricks are indeed great.

---

7. The word *burhān* denotes an argument or proof. *Burhān* from the Lord signifies the argument inspired by God to arouse Joseph's conscience and convince him that it is not at all appropriate for him to accept the woman's invitation to illegitimate enjoyment. Now, what was the "argument" to which reference has been made in the present verse? That argument has already been mentioned in the previous verse: "My Lord has provided an honourable abode for me (so how can I do something so evil)? Such wrong-doers never prosper."

8. The whole point of this statement is that if the shirt was rent from the front, it indicated that Joseph had taken the initiative in advancing towards the lady and that the latter had resisted his amorous advances. However, if Joseph's shirt was rent from the back, that showed the opposite, viz. that it was the lady who had

[29] Joseph, disregard this. And you – woman – ask forgiveness for your sin, for indeed it is you who has been at fault."

[30] And some ladies in the city began to say: "The chief's[9] wife, violently in love with her houseboy, is out to tempt him. We think she is clearly mistaken." [31] Hearing of their sly talk the chief's wife sent for those ladies, and arranged for them a banquet, and got ready couches, and gave each guest a knife. Then, while they were cutting and eating the fruit, she signalled Joseph: "Come out to them." When the ladies saw him they were so struck with admiration that they cut their hands, exclaiming: "Allah preserve us. This is no mortal human. This is nothing but a noble angel!" [32] She said: "So now you see! This is the one regarding whom you reproached me. Indeed I tried to tempt him to myself but he held back, although if he were not to follow my order, he would certainly be imprisoned and humiliated." [33] Joseph said: "My Lord! I prefer imprisonment to what they ask me to do. And if You do not avert from me the guile of these women, I will succumb to their attraction and lapse into ignorance." [34] Thereupon his Lord granted his prayer, and averted their guile from him. Surely He alone is All-Hearing, All-Knowing.

---

made the advances while Joseph had tried to run away from her. This statement also contains a subtle suggestion which needs to be pointed out. The fact that only Joseph's shirt was mentioned implies that there were no traces of any violence on the body or dress of the lady. Had Joseph been guilty of making any advances, traces of his violent advances would clearly have been visible.

9. 'Azīz was not his name. It was also not the title of any office, but was used for a person holding a position of high authority in Egypt.

[35] Then it occurred to them to cast Joseph into prison for a while even though they had seen clear signs (of Joseph's innocence and of the evil ways of their ladies).[10]

[36] And with Joseph two other slaves entered the prison. One of them said: "I saw myself pressing wine in a dream"; and the other said: "I saw myself carrying bread on my head of which the birds were eating." Both said: "Tell us what is its interpretation; for we consider you to be one of those who do good." [37] Joseph said: "I will inform you about the interpretation of the dreams before the arrival of the food that is sent to you. This knowledge is part of what I have been taught by my Lord. I have renounced the way of those who do not believe in Allah, and who deny the Hereafter, [38] and I have adopted the way of my forefathers – Abraham and Isaac and Jacob. It is not for us to associate any with Allah in His Divinity. It is out of Allah's grace upon us and upon mankind (that He did not require of us to serve any other than Allah), and yet most people do not give thanks. [39] Fellow-prisoners! Is it better that there be diverse lords, or just Allah, the One, the Irresistible? [40] Those whom you serve beside Him are merely idle names that you and your fathers have fabricated, without Allah sending down any sanction for them. All authority to govern rests only with Allah. He has commanded that you serve none but Him. This is the Right Way of life, though most people are altogether unaware. [41] Fellow-prisoners! (This is the interpretation of your

---

10. This shows that sending innocent persons to prison in disregard of the due process of justice and without caring to establish their guilt or innocence is one of the accepted practices of rulers from olden days. In this regard, the evil forces of today are no better than those of four thousand years ago.

dreams): one of you will serve wine to his lord (the king of Egypt).[11] As for the other, he will be crucified and birds will eat of his head. The question concerning what you asked has thus been decided."

[42] And Joseph said to the one of the two prisoners who he knew would be set free: "Mention me in your lord's presence." But Satan caused him to forget mentioning this to his lord (the ruler of Egypt) and so Joseph languished in prison for several years.

[43] And once[12] the king said: "I have dreamt that there are seven fat cows and seven lean cows are devouring them, and there are seven fresh green ears of corn and seven others dry and withered. My nobles! Tell me what is the interpretation of this dream, if you are well-versed in interpretation of dreams." [44] They said: "These are confused dreams, and we do not know the interpretation of such dreams."

[45] Then of the two prisoners, the one who had been set free, now remembered, after the lapse of a long period, what Joseph had said. He said: "I will tell you the interpretation of this dream; just send me (to Joseph in prison)."

---

11. While studying this verse if one were to refer to verse 23 one would see that when Joseph had used the expression: "My Lord (*Rabbī*)" he meant God. But when he told the slave of the King that he would serve wine to his lord (*rabb*) he meant the king because the slave regarded the latter as his lord and master.

12. Omitting a few years of Joseph's life in prison, the thread of the narrative is picked up again. It is connected with the stage which marks the worldly rise of Joseph.

[46] Then he went to Joseph and said to him: "Joseph, O truthfulness incarnate,[13] tell the true meaning of the dream in which seven fat cows are devoured by seven lean ones; and there are seven green ears of corn and seven others dry and withered so that I may return to the people and they may learn."[14] [47] Joseph said: "You will cultivate consecutively for seven years. Leave in the ears all that you have harvested except the little out of which you may eat. [48] Then there will follow seven years of great hardship in which you will eat up all you have stored earlier, except the little that you may set aside. [49] Then there will come a year when people will be helped by plenty of rain and they will press (grapes)."

[50] The king said: "Bring this man to me." But when the royal messenger came to Joseph he said: "Go back to your master and ask him about the case of the women who had cut their hands. Surely my Lord has full knowledge of their guile." [51] Thereupon the king asked the women: "What happened when you sought to tempt Joseph?" They said: "Allah forbid! We found no evil in him." The chief's wife said: "Now the truth has come to light. It was I who sought to tempt him. He is indeed truthful."

---

13. In Arabic usage the word *ṣiddīq*, which occurs in this verse, denotes the highest degree of truthfulness and veracity. The use of the word shows how deeply that person had been influenced by Joseph's character. The impression seems to have been a very profound one since it endured for a very long time.

14. One of the two prisoners asked Joseph to interpret the dream in order that his true worth might be recognized and so that it might also be realized that a big mistake had been committed by having a person of his standing imprisoned. This, he thought, would also enable him to fulfil the promise he had made to Joseph in prison.

[52] Joseph said: "I did this so that he [i.e. the chief] may know that I did not betray him in his absence, and that Allah does not allow the design of the treacherous to succeed. [53] I do not seek to acquit myself; for surely one's self prompts one to evil except him to whom my Lord may show mercy. Verily my Lord is Ever Forgiving, Most Merciful."

[54] The king said: "Bring him to me. I will select him exclusively for my own service." So when Joseph spoke to him the king said: "You are now one of established position, fully-trusted by us." [55] Joseph said: "Place me in charge of the treasures of the land. I am a good keeper and know my task well."

[56] Thus did We establish Joseph in the land so that he could settle wherever he pleased.[15] We bestow favour, out of Our Mercy, on whomsoever We please, and We do not cause the reward of those who do good to go to waste. [57] Surely the reward of the Hereafter is better for those who believe and act in a God-fearing way.

[58] And Joseph's brothers came to Egypt and presented themselves before him.[16] He recognized them, but they did not know him. [59] And when he had prepared for them their provisions, Joseph said: "Bring to me your

---

15. This means that now that Egypt was under Joseph's control, he could call every part of it his own. Joseph could go without any let or hindrance to any part of Egypt that he wanted. The above verse, thus, describes the total sway, the all-pervasive authority Joseph held over Egypt. The earlier commentators of the Qur'ān have understood this verse in this way. For instance, Ibn Jarīr al-Ṭabarī, citing Ibn Zayd, has explained this verse to mean that God put Joseph in charge of everything in Egypt. Joseph was free to do

other brother from your father. Do you not see that I give full measure and am most hospitable? [60] If you do not bring him to me, you shall have no corn from me; and do not even attempt to come close to me."[17] [61] They said: "We will surely try to prevail over our father to send him. Be sure we shall do so." [62] And Joseph said to his servants: "Put surreptitiously in their packs the goods they had given in exchange for corn." Joseph did so expecting that they would find it when they returned home. Feeling grateful for this generosity, they might be inclined to return to him.

[63] When they returned to their father they said: "Father! We have been denied further supply of corn. So send with

whatever he wished since the whole land was under his control. Such was his authority that had he wanted, he could even have placed himself above Pharaoh. Al-Ṭabarī also quotes a statement from Mujāhid, one of the earliest leading Qur'ān commentators, that the Egyptian king had embraced Islam at the hands of Joseph.

16. Once again the events of some seven or eight years have been skipped over and the narration has been resumed from the point of describing the migration of the Israelites to Egypt.

17. It will be recalled that food rationing was in force in Egypt at that time and each individual was entitled to a specified quantity of grain and no more. As we know, the ten brothers had come with the purpose of obtaining grain, and would naturally have asked for a share on behalf of their father and their eleventh brother. This presumably provided Joseph with grounds reasonable enough to make his point. He could possibly have accepted that there was a valid reason for their father not to come to Egypt, for he was old and blind but there was no such reason in respect of their brother. Joseph might have said that trusting their word he would permit them to receive the full supply of grain on this occasion, but if they failed to bring their stepbrother the next time, they would not be trusted any longer and would receive no grain at all.

us our brother that we may bring the supplies. We shall be responsible for his protection." [64] The father said: "Shall I trust you with regard to him as I had trusted you earlier with regard to his brother? Allah is the Best Protector and is the Most Merciful." [65] And when they opened their things they found that their goods had been given back to them. Thereupon they cried: "Father! What else would we desire? Look, even our goods have been given back to us, so we shall go now and bring supplies for our family, we shall protect our brother, and bring another camel-load of corn. That additional supply will be easily secured." [66] Their father said: "I shall never send him with you until you give me a solemn promise in the name of Allah that you will bring him back to me, unless you yourselves are surrounded." Then after they had given him their solemn promise, he said. "Allah watches over what we have said." [67] And he enjoined them: "My sons! Do not enter the city by one gate;¹⁸ rather enter it by different gates. I can be of no help to you against Allah. Allah's command alone prevails. In Him have I put my trust and in Him should all those who have faith put their trust." [68] And it so happened that when they entered the city (by many gates) as their father had directed them, this precautionary measure proved ineffective against Allah's will. There was an uneasiness in Jacob's soul which he so tried to remove. Surely he was possessed of knowledge owing to the knowledge that We bestowed upon him. But most people do not know the truth of the matter.

---

18. Jacob might have feared that if his sons entered in a group during a period of famine, they might be mistaken for wild tribesmen looking for loot and plunder.

[69] When they presented themselves before Joseph, he took his brother aside to himself and said: "Verily I am your own brother Joseph; so do not grieve over the manner they have treated you."[19]

[70] Then, while Joseph was having their provisions loaded, he put his drinking-cup in his brother's saddlebag. And then a herald cried: "Travellers, you are thieves." [71] Turning back they asked: "What have you lost?" [72] The officials said: "We have lost the king's cup." (And their chief added): "He who brings it shall have a camel-load of provisions, I guarantee that." [73] They said: "By Allah, you certainly know that we did not come to act corruptly in this land, nor are we those who steal." [74] The officials said: "If you are lying, what will be the penalty for him who has stolen?" [75] They replied: "He in whose saddlebag the cup is found, he himself shall be its recompense." Thus do we punish the wrong-doers. [76] Then Joseph began searching their bags before searching his own brother's bag. Then he brought forth the drinking-cup from his brother's bag. Thus did We contrive to support Joseph. He had no right, according to the religion of the king (i.e. the law of Egypt), to take his brother, unless Allah so willed.[20] We exalt whomsoever We

---

19. Benjamin might have told Joseph of the maltreatment meted out to him by his stepbrothers. Joseph might also have comforted Benjamin, saying that from then onwards he would stay with him and that he would not allow him to return with his cruel stepbrothers. It is quite likely that at this point the two brothers might have jointly worked out a plan that would enable Benjamin to remain behind in Egypt. The two brothers did not, however, wish to disclose this plan as Joseph (peace be on him) wanted certain things to stay concealed at least for a while.

will over others by several degrees. And above all those who know is the One Who truly knows.

[77] They said: "No wonder that he steals for a brother of his stole before." But Joseph kept his reaction to himself without disclosing the truth to them. He merely said to himself: "You are an evil lot. Allah knows well the truth of the accusation that you are making against me (to my face)."

[78] They said: "O powerful chief (al-'azīz)![21] His father is an age-stricken man, (and in order that he may not suffer) seize one of us in his stead. We indeed consider you an excellent person." [79] Joseph said: "Allah forbid that we should seize any except him with whom we found our

---

20. Usually translators and commentators of the Qur'ān consider the verse to mean the following: "Joseph could not have apprehended his brother according to the law of the land." Such an understanding of the verse is wrong. For, what would prevent Joseph from arresting a thief under the king's law? In fact, there has never been any state on earth which prevented the arrest of a thief. Therefore, it would be right to say that it would have been unbecoming of Joseph, a Prophet of God, to act according to the law of the king. He, therefore, asked his brothers about their own law and arrested his brother under the Abrahamic law.

21. In the above verse the title *'azīz* (literally the "powerful one") has been used for Joseph. In view of this usage, some Qur'ān commentators are of the opinion that Joseph was appointed to the same office that had been held earlier by Zelicha's husband. We have already noted that the word *'azīz* was not the specific appellation of any particular office. It was used in the sense of "incumbent of power".

good.²² Were we to do so, we would surely be one of the wrong-doers."

[80] Then, when they had despaired of Joseph they went to a corner and counselled together. The eldest of them said: "Do you not know that your father has taken a solemn promise from you in the name of Allah, and you failed in your duty towards Joseph? So I will not depart from this land until my father permits me, or Allah pronounces His judgement in my favour. He is the best of those who judge."

---

22. Joseph's circumspection is noteworthy. When the cup was found in Benjamin's saddlebag, Joseph did not charge him with stealing. Joseph, according to the Qur'ān, used the expression "with whom we found our good". In Islamic terminology, such an expression is termed *tawriyah*. The term denotes "covering up" or "concealing" some fact.

One may resort to *tawriyah* in a situation when there remains no other alternative to save a victim from his oppressor, or to ward off a serious mischief other than resorting to a statement or device which conceals the true facts. Faced with a difficult situation such as the one mentioned above, a pious person would refrain from lying, but he might well resort to an ambiguous statement or to a device aimed at concealing facts so as to ward off wrong. Now let us consider how in this particular instance Joseph fulfilled all the conditions of a permissible *tawriyah*. First, he put the drinking cup in Benjamin's saddlebag with the latter's full consent. He did not, however, direct the servants to charge Benjamin with stealing. When the servants charged the brothers with theft, Joseph simply stood up and without uttering a word searched their belongings. Subsequently, when Joseph's brothers requested him to detain any of them in place of Benjamin, he simply responded by saying that they themselves had suggested that only the person with whom the stolen good was found should be detained. Now since the cup was found in Benjamin's saddlebag he could be detained. For, by what right could anyone else be detained?

[81] So go back to your father and tell him: "Father! Your son has certainly been guilty of stealing. We did not see him stealing but testify according to what we know, and obviously we had no power to keep watch over that what is altogether hidden from us. [82] You may inquire of the dwellers of the city where we were, and of the people of the caravan with whom we travelled. We are altogether truthful in what we say."

[83] The father heard the narration and said: "(All that is untrue). But your souls have made it easy for you to engage in a heinous act.²³ So, I will be graciously patient even at this. Allah may well bring them all back to me. He is All-Knowing, All-Wise." [84] Then he turned his back to them, and said: "O my grief for Joseph!" His eyes whitened with grief and he was choked up with sorrow trying to suppress his grief. [85] The sons said: "By Allah! You will continue to remember Joseph until you will either consume yourself with grief, or will die." [86] He said: "I will address my sorrow and grief only to Allah, and I know from Allah what you do not know. [87] My sons! Go and try to find out about Joseph and his brother and do not despair of Allah's mercy. Verily only the unbelievers despair of Allah's mercy."

---

23. Jacob said that it was not at all difficult for his sons to accuse Benjamin – whose character and conduct he knew to be excellent – of stealing a cup. Such behaviour on their part did not surprise him. For in the past, they had deliberately caused their brother Joseph to be lost. Not only that, they had felt no compunction in bringing back his shirt with false bloodstains in order to reinforce their claim that Joseph had been eaten up by a wolf. And now they were telling Jacob, with equal ease of conscience, that Benjamin had committed theft.

[88] On going to Egypt they presented themselves to Joseph and said to him: "O chief! We and our family are struck with distress and have brought only a paltry sum. So give us corn in full measure, and give it to us in charity. Allah rewards those who are charitable." [89] When Joseph heard this (he could not hold himself and said): "Do you remember what you did to Joseph and his brother when you were ignorant?" [90] They exclaimed: "Are you indeed Joseph?" He said: "Yes, I am Joseph and this is my brother. Allah has surely been gracious to us. Indeed whoever fears Allah and remains patient, Allah does not allow the reward of such people to go to waste." [91] They said: "We swear by Allah! Indeed Allah has chosen you in preference to us and we were truly guilty." [92] He replied: "No blame lies with you today. May Allah forgive you. He is the Most Merciful of all those that are merciful. [93] Take this shirt of mine and throw it over my father's face. He will regain his sight. And bring to me all your family."

[94] And as the caravan set out (from Egypt), their father said (in Canaan): "Indeed I smell the fragrance of Joseph. I say so although you may think that I am doting." [95] They said: "Surely you are still in your same old craze."

[96] And when the bearer of good news came he threw Joseph's shirt over Jacob's face, whereupon he regained his sight, and said: "Did I not tell you that I know from Allah what you do not know?" [97] They said: "Father! Pray for the forgiveness of our sins; we were truly guilty." [98] He said: "I shall pray to my Lord for your forgiveness, for He, and indeed He alone, is Ever Forgiving, Most Merciful."

[99] And when they went to Joseph, he took his parents aside and said (to the members of his family): "Enter the city now, and if Allah wills, you shall be secure."

[100] And after they had entered the city, Joseph raised his parents to the throne beside himself, and they (involuntarily) bowed in prostration before him.[24] Joseph said: "Father! This is the fulfilment of the vision I had before – one that My Lord has caused to come true. He was kind to me when He rescued me from the prison, and brought you from the desert after Satan had stirred discord between me and my brothers. Certainly my Lord is Subtle in the fulfilment of His will; He is All-Knowing, All-Wise. [101] My Lord! You have bestowed dominion upon me and have taught me to comprehend the depths

24. The use of the term *sajdah* (prostration) in the above verse has given rise to considerable misconception. This misconception reached such heights that some people interpreted the verse to justify prostration before kings and saints, calling it "prostration of greeting" or "prostration of respect" as distinguished from "prostration of worship". Since in Islam prostration is associated with worship, some scholars resorted to an altogether novel explanation. They contended that it was only the prostration of worship, provided it was directed to any other than God, which was prohibited in the earlier versions of Divine Law. As for prostration which did not signify any worship, it was permissible even in respect of persons other than God. They claimed that it is only in the *Sharīʿah* of the Prophet Muḥammad (peace be on him) that all forms of prostration directed to anyone other than God are forbidden. What lies at the core of all this confusion is the word *sajdah* (prostration) as used in the verse. It has been taken in the technical sense in which it has come to be used in Islam as meaning putting one's feet, knees and forehead on the ground. However, the true meaning of *sajdah* is "to bow" and in the above verse the word has been used exactly in that sense.

of things. O Creator of heavens and earth! You are my Guardian in this world and in the Hereafter. Cause me to die in submission to You, and join me, in the end, with the righteous."

[102] (O Muḥammad), this is part of news from the Unseen that We reveal to you for you were not present with them when Joseph's brothers jointly resolved on a plot. [103] And most of the people, howsoever you might so desire, are not going to believe. [104] You do not seek from them any recompense for your service. This is merely an admonition to all mankind.

[105] How many are the signs in the heavens and the earth which people pass by without giving any heed! [106] And most of them believe in Allah only when they associate others with Him in His Divinity. [107] Do they, then, feel secure that an overwhelming chastisement shall not visit them, and the Hour shall not suddenly come upon them without their even perceiving it? [108] Tell them plainly: "This is my way: I call you to Allah, on the basis of clear perception – both I and those who follow me. Allah – Glory be to Him – is free of every imperfection. I have nothing to do with those who associate others with Allah in His Divinity."

[109] The Messengers whom We raised before you, (O Muḥammad), and to whom We sent down revelations, were only human beings, and were from among those living in earthly habitations. Have these people not travelled in the earth that they may observe the end of their predecessors? Certainly the abode of the Hereafter is much better for those (who accepted the call of the

Messengers and) acted in a God-fearing manner. Will you still not act with good sense? [110] (It also happened with the earlier Messengers that for long they preached and people paid no heed) until the Messengers despaired of their people, and the people also fancied that they had been told lies (by the Messengers), then suddenly Our help came to the Messengers. And when such an occasion comes We rescue whom We will; as for the guilty, Our chastisement cannot be averted from them.

[111] Certainly in the stories of the bygone people there is a lesson for people of understanding. What is being narrated in the Qur'ān is no fabrication; it is rather confirmation of the Books that preceded it, and a detailed exposition of everything,[25] and a guidance and mercy for people of faith.

---

25. "A detailed exposition of everything" refers to a detailed exposition of all that is necessary for man's guidance. This does not encompass everything in a literal sense. Some people misunderstand the purpose of this verse and consider "everything" to include even such matters as detailed knowledge of forestry, medicine, mathematics and all other branches of learning. They feel perplexed when they do not find information regarding all arts and sciences in the Qur'ān. On the other hand, some people are prepared to go to any length to prove the availability of all conceivable details of everything in the Scripture.

13

Al-Ra'd [Thunder]
Makkan Period

In the name of Allah, the Most Merciful,
the Most Compassionate

[1] *Alif. Lām. Mīm. Rā'.* These are the verses of the Divine Book. Whatever has been revealed to you from your Lord is the truth, and yet most (of your) people do not believe.

[2] It is Allah Who has raised the heavens without any supports that you could see,[1] and then He established Himself on the Throne (of Dominion). And He it is Who has made the sun and the moon subservient (to a law), each running its course till an appointed term. He governs the entire order of the universe and clearly explains the signs[2] that you may be firmly convinced about meeting your Lord.

---

1. In other words, the heavens were raised without anything perceptible to support them. There is nothing tangible in space which holds the virtually infinite number of heavenly bodies together. Nevertheless, there is a force – an imperceptible one – which keeps each heavenly body exactly where it belongs and regulates its orbit. This force also prevents these immense bodies from colliding with the earth or with each other.

2. There are many signs which indicate that the information about the ultimate truths provided by the Prophet (peace be on him) is indeed fully reliable. If one looks around with open eyes there are

[3] He it is Who has stretched out the earth and has placed in it firm mountains and has caused the rivers to flow. He has made every fruit in pairs, two and two, and He it is Who causes the night to cover the day. Surely there are signs in these for those who reflect.

[4] And on the earth there are many tracts of land neighbouring each other. There are on it vineyards, and sown fields, and date palms: some growing in clusters from one root, some standing alone. They are irrigated by the same water, and yet We make some excel others in taste. Surely there are signs in these for a people who use their reason.

[5] And were you to wonder, then wondrous indeed is the saying of those who say: "What! After we have been reduced to dust, shall we be created afresh?" They are the ones who disbelieved in their Lord;[3] they are the ones who shall have shackles around their necks.[4] They shall be the inmates of the Fire, wherein they will abide for ever.

---

innumerable signs spread across the heavens and the earth which testify to the truths which the Qur'ān invites people to accept.

3. The unbelievers' denial of the After-Life amounts to denying God, to denying His power, and to denying His wisdom. For they do not simply call into question that human beings will be resurrected. Implicit in their rejection of the After-life is the idea that God either lacks the power to create human beings afresh, or the wisdom to recognize the need to do so.

4. The Qur'ānic statement that "they are the ones who shall have shackles around their necks," means that they are prisoners of their ignorance and obduracy, prisoners of their lusts, and prisoners of uncritical adherence to their ancestral ways. It is because of all this that they have become incapable of thinking independently.

[6] They challenge you to hasten the coming of evil upon them before the coming of any good,[5] although people who followed a like course before had met with exemplary punishment (from Allah). Verily your Lord is forgiving to mankind despite all their wrong-doing. Verily your Lord is also severe in retribution.

[7] Those who refused to believe in you say: "Why has no (miraculous) sign been sent down upon him from his Lord?" You are only a warner, and every people has its guide.

[8] Allah knows what every female bears; and what the wombs fall short of (in gestation), and what they may add. With Him everything is in a fixed measure. [9] He knows both what is hidden and what is manifest. He is the Supreme One, the Most High.

[10] It is all the same for Him whether any of you says a thing secretly, or says it loudly, and whether one hides oneself in the darkness of night, or struts about in broad daylight. [11] There are guardians over everyone, both before him and behind him, who guard him by Allah's command. Verily Allah does not change a people's condition unless they change their inner selves. And when Allah decides to make a people suffer punishment, no

---

They are too strongly bound by their prejudices to appreciate that the Hereafter is inevitable. They continue to deny it despite the fact that reason and common sense require that the present life be followed by another.

5. That is, they are demanding that God's chastisement might hastily smite them.

one can avert it. Nor can any be of help to such a people against Allah.

[12] He it is Who causes you to see lightning that inspires you with both fear and hope, and He it is Who whips up heavy clouds. [13] The thunder celebrates His praise and holiness,[6] and the angels, too, celebrate His praise for awe of Him. He hurls thunderbolts, striking with them whom He wills while they are engaged in disputation concerning Allah. He is Mighty in His contriving.

[14] To Him alone should all prayer be addressed,[7] for those to whom they do address their prayers beside Him are altogether powerless to respond to them. The example of praying to any other than Allah is that of a man who stretches out his hands to water, asking it to reach his mouth, although water has no power to reach his mouth.

---

6. The thunder of the clouds shows that it is God Who causes the winds to blow, vapours to rise, heavy clouds to accumulate, the lightning to flash, and the clouds to bring about the downpour which provides His creatures with water. All this shows that God's wisdom and power are absolute; that He is perfect and free from all defect; that none shares with Him in His Godhead. For those who are not appreciative of their distinct humanity and thus look upon the thunder in the manner of brutes hold that thunder is no more than a deafening sound from the clouds. But those who have ears that are capable of heeding the truth realize that thunder proclaims God's unity.

7. To "address all prayer to God" signifies one's calling upon God to come to one's aid. People ought to do so because the power needed to fulfil man's purposes and to remove his difficulties and distress lies with God alone. Hence, it is quite appropriate to address all prayers to Him, and to Him alone.

The prayers of the unbelievers are a sheer waste. [15] All that is in the heavens and the earth prostrates itself, whether willingly or by force, before Allah;[8] and so do their shadows in the morning and in the evening.[9]

[16] Ask them: "Who is the Lord of the heavens and the earth?" Say: "Allah." Tell them: "Have you taken beside Him as your patrons those who do not have the power to benefit or to hurt even themselves?" Say: "Can the blind and the seeing be deemed equals? Or can light and darkness be deemed equals?" If that is not so, then have those whom they associate with Allah in His Divinity ever created anything like what Allah did so that the question of creation has become dubious to them? Say: "Allah is the creator of everything. He is the One, the Irresistible."

[17] Allah sends down water from the heavens and the river-beds flow, each according to its measure, and the torrent carries along a swelling scum. In like manner, from that metal which they smelt in the fire to make ornaments and utensils, there arises scum like it. Thus does Allah depict truth and falsehood. As for the scum, it passes away as dross; but that which benefits mankind abides on the earth. Thus does Allah explain (the truth) through examples.

---

8. Prostration refers to bowing down in obeisance, to carrying out a command, and to lowering oneself in submission to someone.

9. The prostration of shadows before God refers to the falling of the shadows on the earth: to the west, in the morning, and in the afternoon to the east. This symbolizes the subjection of those objects to God's will and command.

[18] There is good reward for those who respond to the call of their Lord. And those who do not respond to their Lord, (a time will come when) they shall offer all they have – even if they have all the riches of the world and the like of it besides to redeem themselves (from the chastisement of Allah). They will be subjected to a severe reckoning and Hell shall be their refuge. What a wretched resting place it is!

[19] He who knows that the Book which has been sent to you from your Lord is the Truth, is he like him who is blind to that truth? It is only people of understanding who take heed: [20] those who fulfil their covenant with Allah and do not break their compact after firmly confirming it; [21] who join together the ties which Allah has bidden to be joined; who fear their Lord and dread lest they are subjected to severe reckoning; [22] who are steadfast in seeking the good pleasure of their Lord; who establish Prayer and spend both secretly and openly out of the wealth We have provided them, and who ward off evil with good. Theirs shall be the ultimate abode [23] – the Ever-lasting Gardens which they shall enter and so shall the righteous from among their fathers, and their spouses, and their offspring. And angels shall enter unto them from every gate, and say: [24] "Peace be upon you. You merit this reward for your steadfastness." How excellent is the ultimate abode! [25] As for those who break the covenant of Allah after firmly confirming it, who cut asunder the ties that Allah has commanded to be joined, and who create corruption in the land: Allah's curse shall be upon them and theirs shall be a wretched abode (in the Hereafter).

[26] Allah grants the provision to whomsoever He wills abundantly and grants others in strict measure. They exult in the life of the world, although compared with the Hereafter, the life of the world is no more than temporary enjoyment.

[27] Those who have rejected (the message of Muḥammad) say: "Why has no sign been sent down upon him from his Lord?" Tell them: "Allah lets go astray those whom He wills, and guides to Himself those who turn to Him." [28] Such are the ones who believe (in the message of the Prophet) and whose hearts find rest in the remembrance of Allah. Surely in Allah's remembrance do hearts find rest. [29] So those who believe (in the message of the Truth) and do good are destined for happiness and a blissful end.

[30] Thus have We sent you as a Messenger[10] to a community before which many other communities have passed away that you may recite to them whatever We have revealed to you. And yet they deny the Lord of Mercy. Say to them: "He is my Lord, there is no god but Him. In Him I have placed all my trust and to Him I shall return."

[31] And what would have happened were a Qur'ān to be revealed wherewith mountains could be set in motion, or the earth cleft, or the dead made to speak? (To show such signs is not at all difficult for) everything rests

---

10. That is to say that the Prophet (peace be on him) was sent without any signs of the kind which the unbelievers had asked for.

entirely with Allah.[11] So, do not the people of faith (still
look forward to such a sign in response to the demand
of the unbelievers and) despair as a result of knowing
that had Allah so willed, He could have guided all to the
Truth.[12] Misfortune continues to afflict the unbelievers
on account of their misdeeds, or to befall on locations
close to their habitation. This will continue until Allah's
promise (of chastisement) is fulfilled. Indeed Allah does
not go back upon His promise. [32] Surely the Messengers
before you were ridiculed, but I always initially granted
respite to those who disbelieved, and then I seized
them (with chastisement). Then, how awesome was My
chastisement!

[33] Is it, then, in regard to Him Who watches over the
deeds of every person that they are acting blasphemously
by setting up His associates? Tell them: "Name those
associates (if Allah Himself has made them His associates)!
Or are you informing Allah of something the existence of
which He does not even know?" Or do people arbitrarily
utter empty words? Indeed, their foul contriving has been

---

11. The true reason for not showing miraculous signs was not that
God had no power to do so but because this was inconsistent with
God's scheme of things. For the true purpose of that scheme was
not so much to drive some people into affirming the prophethood
of some Prophet, but to help them attain true guidance. Such a
purpose can only be achieved by reforming people's outlook and
re-orienting their thinking pattern.

12. Had the purpose merely been that people should believe
without understanding and without being rationally convinced
then perhaps God did not have to show miraculous signs. That
purpose could have been achieved by simply creating all human
beings as born believers.

made to seem fair to the unbelievers[13] and they have been barred from finding the Right Way. Whomsoever Allah lets go astray will have none to guide him. [34] They shall suffer chastisement in the life of the world, and surely the chastisement of the Hereafter is even more grievous. None has the power to shield them from (the chastisement of) Allah. [35] And such will be the Paradise promised to the God-fearing: rivers will flow beneath it, its fruits will be eternal, and so will be its blissful shade. That is the ultimate destiny of the God-fearing while Fire is the destiny of the unbelievers.

[36] Those upon whom We bestowed the Scriptures earlier rejoice at the Book revealed to you, while there are also some among different groups that reject part of it. Tell them: "I have only been commanded to serve Allah and not to associate anyone with Him. To Him do I call, and to Him is my return." [37] And it is with the same directive that We revealed to you this Arabic Writ. Were you indeed to follow the vain desires of people after the true knowledge has come to you, none will be your supporter against Allah, and none will have the power to shield you from His punishment.

---

13. The association of others with God in His Divinity by the unbelievers has been branded as a "foul contriving". For the celestial bodies or angels or spirits or saints which are said to be God's associates in His attributes, powers and rights have never made any such claims. They do not ask the unbelievers to worship or bow down before them. It is merely a contriving of some unscrupulous human beings who, in order to establish their own control over ordinary people and to usurp their earnings, have invented false gods and have misled people into becoming their devotees. This enabled them to exploit people under the claim that they were the authorized representatives of those so-called gods.

[38] We indeed sent many Messengers before you and We gave them wives and children;[14] and no Messenger had the power to produce a miraculous sign except by the command of Allah. Every age has its own (revealed) Book. [39] Allah effaces whatever He wills and retains whatever He wills. With Him is the Mother of the Book.[15]

[40] (O Prophet), whether We make you see a part of the punishment that We have threatened them with come to pass during your life-time, or We take you away before that happens, your duty is no more than to convey the Message, and it is for Us to make a reckoning. [41] Do they not see that We are advancing in the land, diminishing it by its borders on all sides?[16] Allah judges, and no one

---

14. This is the answer to another objection hurled at the Prophet (peace be on him). The unbelievers decried him for being one like ordinary mortals in so far as his life was also encumbered with such worldly concerns as those relating to spouse and children. They were at a loss to appreciate how someone was God's Messenger who could also have the sexual urge that would prompt him to marry, whereas the Quraysh prided themselves on being the descendants of the Prophets Abraham and Ishmael.

15. The expression *Umm al-Kitāb* ("Mother of the Book") which occurs in the verse refers to that "Original Book" which is the source of all heavenly scriptures.

16. The opponents are reminded that Islam's influence was spreading to every nook and cranny of Arabia. This naturally meant the shrinking of the unbelievers' influence and the growing pressure upon them. Did these facts not indicate that they were heading towards their doom? What God says here, viz. "We are advancing in the land," is a very subtle and refined way of indicating the direction of the change which was then taking place. Since Islam is from God, Who supports the propounders of that message, the spread of Islam has been characterized as the advance of God Himself.

has the power to reverse His judgement. He is swift in reckoning. [42] Those who lived before them also devised many a plot, but the master plot rests with Allah. He knows what everyone does. The deniers of the truth will soon come to know whose end is good.

[43] The unbelievers claim that you have not been sent by Allah. Tell them: "Allah is sufficient as a witness between me and you; and so also do those who know the Scriptures."

14

Ibrāhīm [Abraham]
Makkan Period

In the name of Allah, the Most Merciful,
the Most Compassionate

[1] *Alif. Lām. Rā'.* This is a Book which We have revealed to you that you may bring forth mankind from every kind of darkness into light, and direct them, with the leave of their Lord, to the Way of the Mighty, the Innately Praiseworthy,[1] [2] (to the Way of) Allah to Whom belongs all that is in the heavens and all that is in the earth.

Woe be to those who reject the Truth for a severe chastisement, [3] to those who have chosen the life of the world in preference to the Hereafter, who hinder people from the Way of Allah, and seek to make it crooked. They have gone far astray.

[4] Never have We sent a Messenger but he has addressed his people in their language that he may fully expound his Message to them. (And after the Message is expounded), Allah lets go astray whomsoever He wills, and guides to

---

1. The word used here is *ḥamīd* which is synonymous with *maḥmūd* (the praised one). There is, however, a subtle difference in their meaning. The word *maḥmūd* is used for anyone who is praised. The word *ḥamīd,* which has been used here, signifies one who innately deserves praise regardless of whether anyone actually praises him or not.

the Right Way whomsoever He wills. He is the All-Mighty, the All-Wise.

[5] We indeed sent Moses with Our Signs, saying: "Lead your people out of all kinds of darkness into light, and admonish them by narrating to them anecdotes from the Days of Allah."² Verily in it there are great Signs for everyone who is patient and gives thanks (to Allah).³

[6] And call to mind when Moses said to his people: "Remember Allah's favour upon you when He delivered you from Pharaoh's people who afflicted you with a grievous chastisement, slaughtering your sons, while letting your women live. In it there was a terrible trial from your Lord." [7] Also call to mind when your Lord proclaimed: "If you give thanks, I will certainly grant you more; but if you are ungrateful for My favours, My chastisement is terrible." [8] Moses said: "Were you to disbelieve – you and all those who live on earth – Allah is still Self-Sufficient, Innately Praiseworthy."

---

2. The word *ayyām*, as a technical term, signifies events of great historical significance. The expression *Ayyām Allāh* (literally, "the Days of Allah") refers to those major events in human history which show that God treated the nations and major personalities of the past according to their deeds, punishing or rewarding them on that account.

3. These signs are found everywhere. However, not everyone can derive the right conclusions from them. It is only people who possess certain qualities who can fully appreciate those signs and, thus, benefit from them. Such people are those who, when they are put to any test by God, observe patience and fortitude. When they are blessed with God's favours, they are fully appreciative of them and are inclined to give thanks to God.

[9] Have the accounts of your predecessors not reached you:[4] the people of Noah, the ʿĀd, the Thamūd, and those who came after them – they whose number is not known to any except Allah? Their Messengers came to them with Clear Signs, but they thrust their hands in their mouths,[5] and said: "We do surely reject the Message you have brought, and we are in disquieting doubt about what you are summoning us to." [10] Their Messengers said: "Can there be any doubt about Allah, the Creator of the heavens and the earth? He invites you that He may forgive you your sins and grant you respite till an appointed term." They replied: "You are only a human being like ourselves. You seek to prevent us from serving those whom our forefathers have been serving all along. If that is so, produce a clear authority for it." [11] Their Messengers told them: "Indeed we are only human beings like yourselves, but Allah bestows His favour on those of His servants whom He wills. It does not lie in our power to produce any authority except by the leave of Allah. It is in Allah that the believers should put their trust. [12] And why should we not put our trust in Allah when it is indeed He Who has guided us to the ways of our life? We shall surely continue to remain steadfast in face of your persecution. All those who have to put trust, should put their trust only in Allah."

4. This marks the conclusion of the Prophet Moses' speech. Hereafter, the discourse turns directly to the unbelievers of Makkah.

5. The expression has been used to signify both flat rejection of the Prophets' Message and even a sense of astonishment at being asked to believe in it.

[13] Then the unbelievers told their Messengers: "You will have to return to the fold of our faith⁶ or else we shall banish you from our land." Thereupon their Lord revealed to them: "We will most certainly destroy these wrong-doers, [14] and will then cause you to settle in the land as their successors. That is the reward for him who fears to stand for reckoning and holds My threat in awe." [15] They sought Our judgement. And (thanks to that judgement) every obstinate tyrant opposed to the Truth was brought to naught. [16] Hell is before him and he shall be made to drink of the oozing pus, [17] which he will gulp but will scarcely swallow, and death will come upon him from every quarter, and yet he will not be able to die. A terrible chastisement lies ahead in pursuit of him.

[18] This is the example of those who disbelieve in their Lord: their works are like ashes upon which the wind blows fiercely on a tempestuous day. They shall find no reward for their deeds. That indeed is the farthest point in straying. [19] Do you not see that Allah created the heavens and the earth in Truth? Were He to will, He could

---

6. The expression "return to the fold of our faith" does not imply that before being designated to the office of prophethood, the Prophets belonged to the fold of unbelievers. In fact, the verse can be fully appreciated if we bear in mind that before designation to their office, Prophets live a relatively quiet life. For prior to that designation, they preach no specific religious doctrines. Nor do they engage in refuting the religious doctrines that are generally accepted by their people. As a result, people are commonly inclined to think that they too are an integral part of their religious fold. Hence, when Prophets embark on teaching true religious doctrines, they are charged by their people with having renounced their ancestral faith. The fact, however, is that they were never a part of the fold of those unbelievers.

take you away and bring a new creation. [20] That is not at all difficult for Allah.

[21] Then all of them will appear exposed before Allah, and the weak ones will say to the haughty ones: "We merely followed you. Will you, then, protect us from Allah's chastisement?" They will say: "Had Allah shown us the Way to our salvation, we would surely have also guided you. Now it is all the same whether we cry or suffer patiently, we have no escape."

[22] After the matter has been finally decided Satan will say: "Surely whatever Allah promised you was true; as for me, I went back on the promise I made to you. I had no power over you except that I called you to my way and you responded to me. So, do not blame me but blame yourselves. Here, neither I can come to your rescue, nor can you come to mine. I disavow your former act of associating me in the past with Allah.[7] A grievous chastisement inevitably lies ahead for such wrong-doers."

[23] As for those who had believed and did good in the world, they shall be admitted to the Gardens beneath which rivers flow. There, with the leave of Allah, they shall abide forever, and will be greeted with: "Peace". [24] Do you not see how Allah has given the example of a good

---

7. Obviously no one professes, at the doctrinal level, that Satan is a partner of God in His Divinity. Nor does anyone worship Satan. In fact, so far as verbal expressions go, people generally curse Satan. Ironically, the same people who curse him, also follow his ways, at times consciously, and at other times unconsciously. It is precisely this which has been termed as associating Satan with God in His Divinity.

word? It is like a good tree, whose root is firmly fixed, and whose branches reach the sky, [25] ever yielding its fruit in every season with the leave of its Lord. Allah gives examples for mankind that they may take heed. [26] And the example of an evil word is that of an evil tree, uprooted from the surface of the earth, wholly unable to endure. [27] Thus, through a firm word, Allah grants firmness to the believers both in this world and in the Hereafter. As for the wrong-doers, Allah lets them go astray. Allah does whatever He wills.

[28] Did you not see those who have exchanged Allah's favour with ingratitude to Him, causing their people to be cast in the abode of utter perdition [29] Hell, wherein they shall roast? How wretched a place to settle in! [30] They have set up rivals to Allah that they may lead people astray from His way. Tell them: "Enjoy for a while. You are doomed to end up in the Fire!"

[31] (O Prophet), tell those of My servants who believe that they should establish Prayer and spend out of what We have provided them with, both secretly and openly, before there arrives the Day when there will be no bargaining, nor any mutual befriending.

[32] It is Allah Who created the heavens and the earth, Who sent down water from the heaven and thereby brought forth a variety of fruits as your sustenance, Who subjected for you the ships that they may sail in the sea by His command, Who subjected for you the rivers, [33] Who subjected for you the sun and the moon and both of them are constant on their courses, Who subjected for you the

night and the day,[8] [34] and Who gave you all that you asked Him for.[9] Were you to count the favours of Allah you shall never be able to encompass them. Verily man is highly unjust, exceedingly ungrateful.

[35] And call to mind when Abraham prayed: "My Lord! Make this city secure, and keep me and my sons away from worshipping the idols. [36] My Lord! They have caused many people to go astray. Now, if anyone follows my way, he is from me; and if anyone follows a way opposed to mine, then surely You are Ever-Forgiving, Most Merciful." [37] "Our Lord! I have made some of my offspring settle in a barren valley near Your Sacred House! Our Lord! I did so that they may establish Prayer. So make the hearts of people affectionately inclined to them, and provide them with fruits for their sustenance that they may give thanks. [38] Our Lord! Surely You know all that we conceal and all that we reveal, and nothing in the earth or in the heaven is hidden from Allah. [39] All praise be to Allah Who, despite my old age, has given me Ishmael

8. The Qur'ānic statement "God has subjected for you the night and the day" is often misunderstood. Some think that it means that the forces of nature have been placed under the control of man. Such an assumption leads people to develop a variety of odd ideas. Some even go so far as to say that to achieve mastery over the heavens and the earth is the true end of man's existence. However, what the Qur'ānic statement means by the subjection of the natural phenomena is simply that God has bound them to laws which are beneficial for mankind.

9. That is, God provided man with everything that his nature called for. He also provided all that was needed for man's sustenance, and made available, in plenty, the resources that would ensure his survival and growth.

and Isaac. Surely my Lord hears all prayers. [40] My Lord! Enable me and my offspring to establish Prayer, and do accept, our Lord, this prayer of mine. [41] Our Lord! Forgive me and my parents[10] and the believers on the Day when the reckoning will take place."

[42] Do not think Allah is heedless of the evil deeds in which the evil-doers are engaged. He is merely granting them respite until a Day when their eyes shall continue to stare in horror, [43] when they shall keep pressing ahead in haste, their heads lifted up, their gaze directed forward, unable to look away from what they behold, their hearts utterly void. [44] (O Muḥammad), warn mankind of the Day when a severe chastisement shall overtake them, and the wrong-doers will say: "Our Lord, grant us respite for a short while; we shall respond to Your call and will follow Your Messengers." (But they will be clearly told): "Are you not the same who swore earlier that they shall never suffer decline?" [45] You said so even though you had lived in the dwellings of those who had wronged themselves (by sinning), and you were aware how We dealt with them, and We had even explained to you all this by giving examples. [46] Indeed the unbelievers contrived their plan, but it is in Allah's power to nullify their plan, even though their plans were such that would move even mountains.

---

10. Abraham included his father in this prayer for forgiveness on account of the promise the former had made at the time of leaving his homeland: "I will pray to my Lord for your forgiveness" (*Maryam* 19: 47). However, when he later realized that his father was God's enemy, he recanted. (See *al-Tawbah* 9: 114.)

[47] So, do not think, (O Prophet), that Allah will go back upon His promise to His Messengers. Surely Allah is Mighty, Lord of retribution. [48] (Do warn them of the) Day when the heavens and the earth shall be altogether changed;[11] when all will appear fully exposed before Allah, the One, the Irresistible! [49] On that Day you shall see the guilty ones secured in chains; [50] their garments shall be black as if made out of pitch, and flames of the Fire shall cover their faces [51] so that Allah may requite each person for his deeds. Allah is swift in reckoning.

[52] This is a proclamation for all mankind that they may be warned by it, and that they may know that their God is none but the One True God, and that men of understanding may take heed.

---

11. The present verse as well as several allusions to the subject at different places in the Qur'ān indicate that the present heavens and earth will not be totally destroyed. It seems that it is only the present physical order of things that will be disrupted. Between the first and the second blowing of the Trumpet there will be a time gap the duration of which is known only to God. During this intervening period the present form of the heavens and the earth will be transformed. A new physical order will be created along with a different set of natural laws. This will mark the advent of the Hereafter. Also, with the second blowing of the Trumpet, all human beings created since Adam till the Day of Judgement will be resurrected and will be made to stand before God. This is what the Qur'ān calls *ḥashr* ("the gathering").

15
❦

Al-Ḥijr [The Rock]
Makkan Period

In the name of Allah, the Most Merciful,
the Most Compassionate

[1] *Alif. Lām. Rā'.* These are the verses of the Book, and a Clear Qur'ān.[1]

[2] Soon will the time come when the unbelievers will wish they were Muslims. [3] Leave them to eat and enjoy life and let false hopes amuse them. They will soon come to know. [4] Whenever We destroyed a town, a definite term had previously been decreed for it. [5] No people can outstrip the term for its destruction nor can it delay it.

[6] They say: "O you to whom the Admonition[2] has been revealed,[3] you are surely crazed. [7] Why do you not bring

---

1. The Qur'ān is characterized by its clarity. The purpose of this characterization is to emphasize that the Qur'ān has set out its teachings in lucid terms, rendering them understandable.

2. The term "Admonition" has been used to signify the Book of God. This characterization is quite apt since the whole of the Qur'ān consists of admonition and good counsel. All the earlier scriptures were based on admonition, and so is the Qur'ān. (Literally, *dhikr* means to remind, to caution, to tender good advice.)

3. The unbelievers referred to the Qur'ān as "admonition" by way of sarcasm. They did not believe that it was a revelation from God

down angels upon us if you are indeed truthful?" [8] We
do not send down the angels (in frivolity); and when We
do send them down, We do so with Truth; then people
are granted no respite.⁴ [9] As for the Admonition, indeed
it is We Who have revealed it and it is indeed We Who
are its guardians.

[10] (O Muḥammad), certainly We did send Messengers
before you among the nations which have gone by.
[11] And whenever a Messenger came to them, they
never failed to mock him. [12] Even so We make a way
for it (that is, the Admonition) in the hearts of the culprits
(like a hot rod);⁵ [13] they do not believe in it. This has
been the wont of people of this kind from ancient times.

---

to the Prophet Muḥammad (peace be on him). Had they so believed,
they would not have called him "crazed". If this element of sarcasm
is borne in mind, it is easy to appreciate what was meant by saying:
"O you to whom the Admonition has been revealed!"

4. Angels are not dispatched to a people merely to entertain them.
Hence, it makes no sense that whenever a people ask God to send
angels down to the earth, God accepts it forthwith. Instead, angels
are sent down to a people after a definitive decision has been made
by God to destroy them. The statement that "angels are sent down
in truth" implies that they descend in order to wipe out falsehood
and replace it with the truth. In other words, they are sent down
with God's decree to destroy a people and make sure that the decree
is fully enforced.

5. The Arabic word *salaka* literally means to penetrate, to put
something into another as thread is put into a needle. What the
verse, therefore, means is that so far as the believers are concerned,
when "the Admonition" penetrates their hearts, it provides them
with peace of mind and spiritual nourishment. On the contrary,
when it penetrates the hearts of the unbelievers, they feel as if it
was a hot, burning rod.

[14] If We were even to open for them a way to the heavens, and they could continually climb up to it in broad daylight, [15] they would still have said: "Surely our eyes have been dazzled; rather, we have been enchanted."

[16] We have indeed set constellations[6] in the heavens and have beautified them for the beholders, [17] and have protected them against every accursed satan [18] save him who may eavesdrop,[7] and then a bright flame pursues him.[8]

---

6. In Arabic the word *burūj* is used to denote a fort or palace, or a strong, fortified building. Reflection over the content of the present verse and the verse which immediately follows leads one to think that perhaps the reference here is to the heavenly spheres, which have been separated from each other by means of fortified boundaries. In this sense, we are inclined to consider *burūj* as signifying "fortified heavenly spheres".

7. Here reference is made to those satans who try to obtain information regarding matters belonging to the realm beyond the ken of sense-perception, and convey it to their friends. They in fact possess no means of obtaining such information. The universe has not been laid open to them to roam as they please and gain access to Divine secrets. They do try to obtain information by eaves-dropping. But in actual fact they are able to lay their hands on nothing.

8. The Qur'ānic expression *shihāb mubīn* means "bright flame". (Elsewhere the Qur'ān uses the expression *shihāb thāqib* – literally, "the flame that penetrates the darkness".) What the Qur'ān means by this expression is not necessarily that it is a meteor. It might in fact be referring to some cosmic rays, or possibly to some other kind of rays not yet known to us. At the same time, it is also possible that the expression might indeed refer to the meteors which we occasionally observe shooting across the sky and then falling to the earth. They might be the impediments which prevent the free movements of satans in the outer space.

[19] As for the earth, We have stretched it out and have cast on it firm mountains, and have caused to grow in it everything well-measured. [20] And We have provided sustenance for you on it and also for those of whom you are not the providers. [21] There is nothing except that its treasuries are with Us and We do not send it down except in a known measure. [22] We send fertilizing winds, and then cause rain to descend from the sky, providing you abundant water to drink even though you could not have stored it up for yourselves. [23] It is indeed We Who grant life and cause death and it is We who shall be the sole Inheritors of all.[9] [24] Surely We know those of you who have passed before and those who will come later. [25] Indeed your Lord will gather them all together. Surely He is All-Wise, All-Knowing.

[26] Surely We brought man into being out of dry ringing clay which was wrought from black mud,[10] [27] while We had brought the *jinn* into being before out of blazing

---

9. God alone will ultimately inherit all since all beings except God Himself are destined to pass away. Men have been granted the opportunity to make use of their possessions only temporarily. A day will come when they will leave everything behind in the world. Then ultimately everything will revert to God's treasury.

10. The Qur'ān here clearly refutes the doctrine that it was after a process of evolution involving many stages of animal existence that he entered the stage of humanity. The Qur'ānic statement is, therefore, in direct conflict with the opinions that are currently being expressed by some commentators on the Qur'ān who, under the influence of the Darwinian theory of evolution, are striving to lend support to that theory with arguments drawn from the Qur'ān. They do so in spite of the fact that the Qur'ān envisages that man was directly created out of elements derived from the earth.

fire.[11] [28] Recall when your Lord said to the angels: "I will indeed bring into being a human being out of dry ringing clay wrought from black mud. [29] When I have completed shaping him and have breathed into him of My Spirit, then fall you down before him in prostration." [30] So, the angels – all of them – fell down in prostration, [31] except *Iblīs*; he refused to join those who prostrated. [32] The Lord inquired: "*Iblīs*! What is the matter with you that you did not join those who prostrated?" [33] He said: "It does not behove of me to prostrate myself before a human being whom You have created out of dry ringing clay wrought from black mud." [34] The Lord said: "Then get out of here; you are rejected, [35] and there shall be a curse upon you till the Day of Recompense." [36] *Iblīs* said: "My Lord! Grant me respite till the Day when they will be resurrected." [37] Allah said: "For sure you are granted respite [38] until the day of a known time." [39] *Iblīs* said: "My Lord! In the manner You led me to error, I will make things on earth seem attractive to them and lead all of them to error, [40] except those of Your servants whom You have singled out for Yourself." [41] Allah said: "Here is the path that leads straight to Me.[12] [42] Over My true

---

11. *Samūm* denotes blazing wind. Used in conjunction with *nār*, the word suggests intense heat. This explains the Qur'ānic statements which mention the *jinn* to have been brought into being out of fire.

12. The Qur'ānic expression may be translated in two ways. One possible meaning is: "Here is the path that leads straight to Me." We have understood the verse to mean so and this is reflected in our translation. Another meaning, however, could be: "This is the right way which I have taken upon Myself to keep under My protection."

servants you will be able to exercise no power, your power will be confined to the erring ones, those who choose to follow you.[13] [43] Surely Hell is the promised place for all of them."

[44] There are seven gates in it, and to each gate a portion of them has been allotted.[14] [45] As for the God-fearing, they shall be amid gardens and springs. [46] They will be told: "Enter it in peace and security." [47] And We shall purge their breasts of all traces of rancour; and they shall be seated on couches facing one another as brothers. [48] They shall face no fatigue in it, nor shall they ever be driven out of it.

[49] (O Prophet), declare to My servants that I am indeed Ever Forgiving, Most Merciful. [50] At the same time, My chastisement is highly painful.

---

13. The other meaning could be: "You will have no power over My servants (i.e. mankind) to force them to disobedience. However, those who have fallen into error and have decided to follow you out of their own volition, they will be allowed to do so. We will not forcefully prevent them from proceeding in that direction."

14. The gates of Hell will correspond to the kind of error and sin which a person commits, making him deserving of being cast into Hell. Some people deserve being cast into Hell because of polytheism; some because of hypocrisy; some because of excessive self-indulgence; some because of their injustice and oppression and the harm they have done to other human beings. There are still others who deserve to be cast into Hell on the basis that they propagated some outrageously misleading doctrines, or caused unbelief to prevail, or worked to spread corruption and shameful immorality. The nature of his predominant sin will determine the gate through which the guilty will enter Hell.

[51] And tell them about Abraham's guests. [52] When they came to Abraham they said: "Peace be upon you!"

He replied: "Indeed we feel afraid of you." [53] They said: "Do not feel afraid, for we give you the good news of a wise boy."[15] [54] Abraham said: "What, do you give me this tiding though old age has smitten me? Just consider what tiding do you give me!" [55] They said: "The good tiding we give you is of truth. Do not, therefore, be of those who despair." [56] Abraham said: "Who despairs of the Mercy of his Lord except the misguided?" [57] He added: "What is your errand O sent ones?" [58] They said: "Verily we have been sent to a guilty people [59] excepting the household of Lot. We shall deliver all of them, [60] except his wife (about whom Allah says that) We have decreed that she shall be among those who stay behind."

[61] So when the envoys came to the household of Lot, [62] he said: "Surely you are an unknown folk." [63] They said: "Nay, we have brought to you that concerning which they have been in doubt. [64] We truly tell you that we have brought to you the Truth. [65] So set out with your family in a watch of the night, and keep yourself behind them, and no one of you may turn around, and keep going ahead as you have been commanded." [66] And We communicated to him the decree that by the morning those people will be totally destroyed.

[67] In the meantime the people of the city came to Lot rejoicing. [68] He said: "These are my guests, so do not

---

15. This alludes to the prophecy about the birth of Isaac (peace be on him), which has been clearly stated in *Hūd*. (See *Hūd* 11: 71.)

disgrace me. [69] Have fear of Allah, and do not humiliate me." [70] They replied: "Did we not forbid you again and again to extend hospitality to all and sundry?" [71] Lot exclaimed in exasperation: "If you are bent on doing something, then here are my daughters."[16]

[72] By your life, (O Prophet), they went about blindly stumbling in their intoxication. [73] Then the mighty Blast caught them at sunrise, [74] and turned the land upside down, and rained down stones of baked clay.

[75] There are great Signs in this for those endowed with intelligence. [76] The place (where this occurred) lies along a known route.[17] [77] Verily there is a Sign in this for the believers.

[78] And the people of Aykah[18] were also wrong-doers. [79] So We chastised them. The desolate locations of both communities lie on a well-known highway.[19]

[80] Surely the people of al-Ḥijr also rejected the Messengers, calling them liars. [81] We also gave them Our Signs, yet they turned away from them.

---

16. This point has been elaborated in *Hūd*, nn. 26 and 27 above.

17. This devastated piece of land lies on the route from the Ḥijāz to Syria and Iraq to Egypt. The caravans that pass by this region witness traces of the devastation. In fact, some of these traces can be observed even today.

18. The people of Aykah were the people of the Prophet Shu'ayb (peace be on him). As to the word Aykah, it was the former name of the city called Tabūk.

19. The territory of the Midianites also lies on the route from the Ḥijāz to Palestine and Syria.

[82] They used to hew out houses from the mountains and lived in security. [83] Then the Blast caught them in the morning [84] and whatever they had been earning proved of no avail.

[85] We have not created the heavens and the earth and all that is in between them except with Truth. Surely the Hour will come. So, (O Muḥammad), do graciously overlook them (despite their misdeeds). [86] Your Lord is indeed the Creator of all, the All-Knowing. [87] We have indeed bestowed on you the seven oft-repeated verses[20] and the Great Qur'ān. [88] Do not even cast your eyes towards the worldly goods We have granted to different kinds of people, nor grieve over the state they are in, but turn your loving attention to the believers instead, [89] and clearly tell the unbelievers: "I am most certainly a plain warner," [90] even as We had sent warning to those who had divided their religion into fragments; [91] those who had split up their Qur'ān into pieces.[21] [92] By your Lord, We will question them all [93] concerning what they have been doing.

---

20. The vast majority of Muslim scholars, are agreed that the expression refers to *al-Fātiḥah*. The famous *Ḥadīth* collection of al-Bukhārī mentions two traditions which show that the Prophet (peace be on him) himself clarified that the "seven oft-repeated verses" signified *al-Fātiḥah*.

21. The reference here is to the Jews. They split up their Qur'ān into pieces. This means that they split up their Scripture, which was like the Qur'ān, into pieces by believing in certain parts of it and not believing in others.

[94] (O Prophet), proclaim what you are commanded, and pay no heed to those who associate others with Allah in His Divinity. [95] Surely We suffice to deal with those who scoff at you, [96] those who set up another deity alongside Allah. They shall soon come to know.

[97] We certainly know that their statements sorely grieve you. [98] When (you feel so) glorify your Lord with His praise and prostrate yourself before Him, [99] and worship your Lord until the last moment (of your life) that will most certainly come.

16

Al-Naḥl [The Bee]
Makkan Period

In the name of Allah, the Most Merciful,
the Most Compassionate

[1] Allah's judgement[1] has (all but) come; do not, then, call for its speedy advent. Holy is He, and far above their associating others with Him in His Divinity. [2] He sends down this spirit[2] (of prophecy) by His command through His angels on any of His servants whom He wills, (directing them): "Warn people that there is no deity but Me; so hold Me alone in fear." [3] He created the heavens and the earth with Truth. Exalted is He above whatever they associate with Allah in His Divinity.

---

1. The advent and enforcement of the judgement is near. In our opinion, the "judgement" refers to the Prophet Muḥammad's migration from Makkah. This seems to be evident from the fact that soon after the revelation of this *sūrah* he was directed to migrate to Madīnah. On studying the Qur'ān, it would appear that a Prophet is asked, as a last resort, to migrate when all his efforts to reform his people have failed, and his people persist in rejection and unbelief. Hence, when a Prophet is to migrate, the fate of his people is sealed. Therefore, either God's scourge smites them, or they are destroyed at the hands of that Prophet and his followers.

2. The "spirit" mentioned here is the spirit of prophecy. The Messenger is infused with it, and it animates all that he says or does.

[4] He created man out of a mere drop of fluid, and lo! he turned into an open wrangler.³ [5] He created the cattle. They are a source of clothing and food and also a variety of other benefits for you. [6] And you find beauty in them as you drive them to pasture in the morning and as you drive them back home in the evening; [7] and they carry your loads to many a place which you would be unable to reach without much hardship. Surely your Lord is Intensely Loving, Most Merciful. [8] And He created horses and mules and asses for you to ride, and also for your adornment. And He creates many things (for you) that you do not even know about.⁴ [9] It rests with Allah alone to show you the Right Way, even when there are many crooked ways. Had He so willed, He would have (perforce) guided you all aright.

[10] He it is Who sends down water for you from the sky out of which you drink and out of which grow the plants on which you pasture your cattle, [11] and by virtue of which He causes crops and olives and date-palms and grapes and all kinds of fruit to grow for you. Surely in this there is a great Sign for those who reflect.

---

3. The Qur'ānic statement lends itself to two possible interpretations. It seems that both are at once correct. The verse states that although God created man from a mere drop of semen, he is quite argumentative and is prone to marshal proofs in support of his opinions. Another meaning is that although man was created by God from a mere drop of semen, he became so arrogant that he wrangles even with God.

4. God has yoked many a thing to man's service, making it beneficial to him. Man, however, is not even aware of all these things and the services which they render him.

[12] He has subjected for you the night and the day and the sun and the moon and the stars have also been made subservient by His command. Surely there are Signs in this for those who use their reason. [13] And there are also Signs for those who take heed in the numerous things of various colours that He has created for you on earth.

[14] And He it is Who has subjected the sea that you may eat fresh fish from it and bring forth ornaments from it that you can wear. And you see ships ploughing their course through it so that you may go forth seeking His Bounty[5] and be grateful to Him.

[15] And He has placed firm mountains on the earth lest it should move away from you, and has made rivers and tracks that you may find your way, [16] and He has set other landmarks in the earth. And by the stars too do people find their way.

[17] Is then the One Who creates like the one who does not create? Will you not, then, take heed? [18] For, were you to count the favours of Allah, you will not be able to count them. Surely Allah is Ever Forgiving, Most Merciful. [19] Allah knows all that you conceal and all that you disclose.

[20] Those whom they call upon beside Allah have created nothing; rather, they themselves were created;

---

5. The expression "seeking the bounty of your Lord" means earning a living by lawful means.

[21] they are dead, not living. They do not even know when they will be resurrected.[6]

[22] Your God is the One God. But the hearts of those who do not believe in the Hereafter are steeped in rejection of the Truth, and they are given to arrogance. [23] Surely Allah knows all that they conceal and all that they disclose. He certainly does not love those who are steeped in arrogance.

[24] When they are asked: "What is it that your Lord has revealed?"[7] They answer: "They are merely tales of olden times!" [25] (They say so) that they may bear the full weight of their burdens on the Day of Resurrection and also of the burdens of those whom they misled on account of their ignorance. What a heavy burden are they undertaking to bear! [26] Surely many people before them had plotted in a similar manner to (vanquish the Truth), but Allah uprooted the whole structure of their plot from its foundations so that the roof fell in upon them, and the chastisement (of Allah) visited them from unknown directions. [27] And again, on the Day of Resurrection, He will bring them to disgrace, and say: "Tell Me, now, where are those to whom you ascribed a share in My Divinity, and for whose sake you disputed (with the upholders of the Truth)?" Those who were endowed with knowledge

6. The words of this verse make it quite plain that the false gods whose Godhead is being denied and refuted here are human beings who at some stage in the past were consigned to graves. This is so because angels are very much alive and not dead and the question of resurrection of idols made of wood and stone does not arise.

7. As the news about the Prophet's call spread all around, people asked the Makkans wherever they went about him and the Qur'ān and its contents.

(in the world) will say: "Surely today humiliation and misery shall be the lot of the unbelievers"; [28] the same unbelievers who, when the angels seize them and cause them to die while they are engaged in wrong-doing, they will proffer their submission saying: "We were engaged in no evil." (The angels will answer them): "Surely Allah knows well all that you did. [29] Go now, and enter the gate of Hell, and abide in it for ever." Evil indeed is the abode of the arrogant.

[30] And when the God-fearing are asked: "What has your Lord revealed?" they answer: "Something excellent!" Good fortune in this world awaits those who do good; and certainly the abode of the Hereafter is even better for them. How excellent is the abode of the God-fearing: [31] everlasting gardens that they shall enter; the gardens beneath which rivers shall flow, and where they shall have whatever they desire! Thus does Allah reward the God-fearing, [32] those whose souls the angels seize while they are in a state of purity, saying: "Peace be upon you. Enter Paradise as a reward for your deeds."

[33] (O Muhammad), are they waiting for anything else than that the angels should appear before them, or that your Lord's judgement should come? Many before them acted with similar temerity. And then what happened with them was not Allah's wrong-doing; they rather wronged themselves. [34] The evil consequences of their misdeeds overtook them and what they mocked at overwhelmed them.

[35] Those who associate others with Allah in His Divinity say: "Were Allah to will so, neither we nor our forefathers would have worshipped any other than Him, nor would

we have prohibited anything without His command." Their predecessors proffered similar excuses. Do the Messengers have any other duty but to plainly convey the Message? [36] We raised a Messenger in every community (to tell them): "Serve Allah and shun the Evil One." Thereafter Allah guided some of them while others were overtaken by error. Go about the earth, then, and observe what was the end of those who rejected the Messengers, calling them liars. [37] (O Muḥammad), howsoever eager you may be to show them the Right Way, Allah does not bestow His guidance on those whom He lets go astray; and in fact none will be able to help them.

[38] They swear most solemnly in the name of Allah and say: "Allah shall not raise to life any who dies." (Yes, He will do so); that is a promise by which He is bound, even though most people do not know that. [39] (That is bound to happen in order that) He may make clear to them the reality regarding the matters on which they differ and that the unbelievers may realize that they were liars. [40] (As for the possibility of resurrection, bear in mind that) whenever We do will something, We have to do no more than say: "Be", and it is.

[41] As for those who have forsaken their homes for the sake of Allah after enduring persecution, We shall certainly grant them a good abode in this world; and surely the reward of the Hereafter is much greater.[8] If they

---

8. This is an allusion to those who migrated to Abyssinia under the pressure of persecution from the Makkan unbelievers. They migrated when this persecution had assumed unbearable proportions.

could but know (what an excellent end awaits) [42] those who remain steadfast and put their trust in their Lord.

[43] (O Muḥammad), whenever We raised any Messengers before you, they were no other than human beings; (except that) to them We sent revelation. So ask those who possess knowledge[9] if you do not know. [44] We raised the Messengers earlier with Clear Signs and Divine Books, and We have now sent down this Reminder upon you that you may elucidate to people the teaching that has been sent down for them,[10] and that the people may themselves reflect.

[45] Do those who have been devising evil plans (against the mission of the Messenger) feel secure that Allah will not cause the earth to swallow them up or that chastisement will not come upon them from a direction that they will not even be able to imagine; [46] or that He will not suddenly seize them while they are going about to and fro and they will be unable to frustrate His design, [47] or that He will not seize them when they are apprehensive of the impending calamity? Surely your Lord is Most Compassionate, Most Merciful.

---

9. They are directed to ask all those knowledgeable persons acquainted with the teachings of the scriptures: were the Prophets any other creature rather than human beings?

10. The Book was revealed to the Prophet Muḥammad (peace be on him) so that he might elucidate the teachings embodied in the Qur'ān – the "Admonition". He was required to elucidate those teachings not merely by word of mouth. He was also required to do so by his conduct. This in itself is proof of the fact that *Ḥadīth* is the authentic elucidation of the Qur'ān.

[48] Do the people not see how the objects Allah has created cast their shadows right and left, prostrating themselves in utter submission to Allah?[11] [49] All living creatures and all angels in the heavens and on the earth are in prostration before Allah; and never do they behave in arrogant defiance. [50] They hold their Lord, Who is above them, in fear, and do as they are bidden.

[51] Allah has commanded: "Do not take two gods;[12] for He is but One God. So fear Me alone." [52] His is whatever is in the heavens and the earth, and obedience to Him inevitably pervades the whole universe.[13] Will you, then, hold in awe any other than Allah?

[53] Every bounty that you enjoy is from Allah; and whenever any misfortune strikes you, it is to Him that you cry for the removal of your distress. [54] But as soon as He removes the distress from you, some of you associate others with their Lord in giving thanks, [55] that they may show ingratitude for the bounties We bestowed upon

---

11. The shadow of every physical object, be it a mountain or tree or animal or human being testifies to the fact that everything is subject to a universal law. All are characterized by subservience to the Lord of the universe and none has any share of His Divinity. That something casts a shadow indicates its materiality. And materiality, in turn, is a proof of its being a creature bound in servitude to God.

12. The negation of two gods naturally includes the negation of more than two gods as well.

13. In other words, obedience to God is the axis around which the whole system of the universe revolves.

them. So enjoy yourselves for a while, soon you will come to know (the truth).

[56] They set apart for those, whose reality they do not even know, a portion of the sustenance We have provided them. By Allah, you will surely be called to account for the lies that you have invented!

[57] They assign daughters to Allah[14] – glory be to Him – whereas they assign to themselves what they truly desire![15] [58] When any of them is told about the birth of a female his face turns dark, and he is filled with suppressed anger, [59] and he hides himself from people because of the bad news, thinking: should he keep the child despite disgrace, or should he bury it in dust? How evil is their estimate of Allah![16] [60] Those who do not believe in the Hereafter deserve to be characterized with evil attributes whereas Allah's are the most excellent attributes. He is the Most Mighty, the Most Wise.

[61] Were Allah to take people to task for their wrong-doing, He would not have spared even a single living creature on the face of the earth. But He grants them respite until an appointed term. And when that term arrives, they have no power to delay it by a single moment, nor to hasten it.

---

14. In the pantheon of Arabia, goddesses outnumbered gods. These goddesses were conceived to be the daughters of God. Likewise, angels were also considered to be God's daughters.

15. That is, sons.

16. On the one hand, they considered it a matter of shame to have daughters, and on the other, they had no compunction in saying that God had daughters.

[62] They assign to Allah what they dislike for themselves and their tongues utter a sheer lie in stating that a happy state awaits them. Without doubt the Fire awaits them and it is to it that they shall be hastened.

[63] By Allah, (O Muḥammad), We sent Messengers to other communities before you but Satan made their evil deeds attractive to them (so they paid no heed to the call of the Messengers). The same Satan is their patron today and they are heading towards a painful chastisement. [64] We have sent down the Book that you may explain to them the truth concerning what they are disputing and that the Book may serve as a guidance and mercy for those who believe in it.

[65] Allah sends down water from the heaven, and thereby He instantly revives the earth after it lay dead.[17] Verily there is a sign in it for those who have ears.

---

17. Man witnesses an instructive spectacle every year. He observes that during the course of each year a time comes when the earth turns altogether barren, becoming bereft of every sign of life and fertility. One does not even see a blade of grass, nor plants or leaves, nor vines or flowers, nor even insects. Then suddenly the rainy season sets in. The very first shower causes life to well up from the depths of the earth. Innumerable roots that lay crushed under layer upon layer of earth are suddenly revived, causing the plants which had appeared on the surface a year ago and had then withered away, to make their appearance once again. Likewise, innumerable insects, every trace of which had been destroyed by the heat of summer, make their reappearance. People observe this spectacle year after year – that life is followed by death and death by life. Despite all this, when the Prophet (peace be on him) tells people that God will restore them to life after death, they are struck with surprise.

[66] Surely there is a lesson for you in the cattle: We provide you to drink out of that which is in their bellies between the faeces and the blood – pure milk – which is a palatable drink for those who take it.

[67] And out of the fruits of date-palms and grapes you derive intoxicants as well as wholesome sustenance.[18] Surely there is a sign for those who use reason.

[68] Your Lord inspired[19] the bee, saying: "Set up hives in the mountains and in the trees and in the trellises that people put up, [69] then suck the juice of every kind of fruit and keep treading the ways of your Lord which have been made easy." There comes forth from their bellies a drink varied in colours, wherein there is healing for men. Verily there is a sign in this for those who reflect.

[70] Allah has created you, and then He causes you to die. Some of you have your lives prolonged to an abject old age, when one loses all knowledge after having acquired it. Allah is All-Knowing, All-Powerful.

[71] Allah has favoured some of you with more worldly provisions than others. Then those who are more favoured do not give away their provisions to their slaves lest they

---

18. The verse quite subtly suggests that wine does not constitute "wholesome sustenance". This is a hint of its unlawfulness.

19. The Qur'ānic term *waḥy* literally means making a veiled or subtle suggestion which is comprehended only by the concerned party. It is for this reason that the term was also used to convey the concepts of *ilqā'*, "putting something in someone's heart," and *ilhām* or inspiration (i.e. teaching something under the veil of secrecy).

become equal sharers in it. Do they, then, deny the favour of Allah?[20]

[72] And Allah has given you spouses from your kind, and has granted you through your spouses, sons and grandsons, and has provided you wholesome things as sustenance. (After knowing all this), do they still believe in falsehood[21] and deny Allah's bounty, [73] and worship

20. This verse has been grossly misinterpreted in recent times. According to people, the true purpose of the verse is to tell those who have been granted ample worldly provisions to return them to their servants and slaves so as to make them equal sharers of those provisions. It is contended that if they fail to do so, they will be guilty of denying God's favour. The fact of the matter is that the context in which this verse occurs renders any discussion of economic matters quite out of place. The discourse is in fact devoted to emphasizing God's unity and refuting polytheism. The preceding verses are directed to the above subject, and the same discussion continues. It would be quite odd if an economic principle were suddenly enunciated at this point in the midst of a discussion devoted to quite another subject matter. If one bears in mind the correct context of the verse, it can be easily appreciated that what is being said here is something quite different. Here, people are first reminded of an actual fact of life. They are told that they do not share their wealth – even though it has been bestowed upon them by God – with their slaves and servants. In view of this, how can they justify that they should associate God's helpless servants with Him in giving thanks for the favour conferred upon them by God alone? How can they consider these creatures of God equal to Him in respect of both rights and authority?

21. To charge the unbelievers that they "believe in falsehood" means that they subscribe to beliefs which are totally baseless and devoid of all truth. They subscribe, for instance, to the belief that it is gods, goddesses, *jinn* and saints of the past who have full powers to make or mar people's destiny, to respond to their invocations,

instead of Allah, those helpless beings who have no control over providing them any sustenance from the heavens and the earth; do you worship those who have no power to do anything of this sort? [74] So do not strike any similitudes to Allah.[22] Allah knows whereas you do not know.

[75] Allah sets forth a parable: There is one who is a slave and is owned by another and has no power over anything; and there is one whom We have granted good provision Ourselves, of which he spends both secretly and openly. Can they be equal? All praise be to Allah.[23] But most of them do not even know (this simple fact).

[76] Allah sets forth another parable: There are two men, one of whom is dumb and has no power over anything; he is a burden to his master, and wheresoever his master

---

to bless them with offspring and the means for their livelihood, to effectively help them in any litigation and in preventing them falling prey to disease.

22. The command "not to strike any similitudes to Allah" amounts to warning people not to conceive of Him in the image of worldly sovereigns. They tend to conceive in Him the image of a worldly ruler who is surrounded in his palace by courtiers, officers and servants. Using this as their analogy, they think that God is also helplessly surrounded by angels, saints and other chosen ones. In the same way as a worldly sovereign cannot be approached directly without having to go through intermediaries, so it is in the case of God.

23. With regard to their response, the Prophet thanks God that despite their obduracy the polytheists were unable to say that the two were equal, and thus failed to find any fault with the basic premise of monotheism.

directs him, he fails to bring forth any good. Can such a person be the equal of one who enjoins justice and himself follows the Right Way?

[77] Allah has full knowledge of the truths beyond the reach of perception both in the heavens and the earth; and the coming of the Hour will take no more than the twinkling of an eye; it may take even less. Indeed Allah has power over everything.

[78] Allah has brought you forth from your mothers' wombs when you knew nothing, and then gave you hearing, and sight and thinking hearts so that you may give thanks.

[79] Have they never noticed the birds how they are held under control in the middle of the sky, where none holds them (from falling) except Allah? Surely there are signs in this for those who believe.

[80] Allah has made your houses a repose, and has provided you with the skins of the cattle for your habitation which are light to handle both when you travel and when you camp;[24] and out of their wool and their fur and their hair He has given you furnishings and goods for use over a period of time. [81] And Allah has provided shade for you out of some of the things He has created; and He has provided you with shelters in the mountains, and has given you coats that protect you from heat as well as coats that protect you in battle. Thus does He complete His favour upon you that you may submit to Him.

---

24. This refers to a tent of skin which is quite a common feature in Arabia.

[82] But if they turn away, your only duty is to clearly deliver the message of the truth. [83] They are aware of the favours of Allah, and yet refuse to acknowledge them. Most of them are determined not to accept the Truth.

[84] (They are heedless of) the Day when We shall raise a witness from each community and then the unbelievers will neither be allowed to plead[25] nor will they be asked to repent and seek pardon. [85] Once the wrong-doers have beheld the chastisement, neither will it be lightened for them nor will they be granted any respite. [86] And when those who associated others with Allah in His Divinity will see those to whom they ascribed this share, they will say: "Our Lord! These are the beings to whom we ascribed a share in Your Divinity and whom we called upon instead of You," whereupon those beings will fling at them the words: "You are liars."[26] [87] On that Day they will offer their submission and all that they had fabricated will have vanished. [88] As for those who disbelieved and barred others from the way of Allah, We shall add further chastisement to their chastisement for all the mischief they did.

---

25. This does not mean that people will not be allowed to explain their conduct. What the verse means is that the wrong-doing of the unbelievers will be established by incontrovertible and undeniable evidence. It will leave them no room to explain away or defend their conduct.

26. What they will deny is that they neither knew nor expressed their consent, nor did they ask them to call upon them rather than upon God.

[89] (O Muḥammad), warn them of the coming of a Day when We shall bring forth a witness against them from each community and We shall bring you forth as a witness against them all; (and it is for that purpose that) We sent down the Book to you which makes everything clear, and serves as a guidance and mercy and glad tidings to those who have submitted to Allah.

[90] Surely Allah enjoins justice, kindness and the doing of good to kith and kin, and forbids all that is shameful, evil and oppressive. He exhorts you so that you may be mindful. [91] And fulfil the covenant which you have made with Allah and do not break your oaths after having firmly made them, and after having made Allah your witness. Surely Allah knows all that you do. [92] And do not become like the woman who, after having painstakingly spun her yarn, caused it to disintegrate into pieces. You resort to oaths as instruments of mutual deceit so that one people might take greater advantage than another although Allah puts you to the test through this. Surely on the Day of Resurrection He will make clear the Truth concerning the matters over which you differed. [93] Had Allah so willed, He would have made you all one single community. However, He lets go astray whomsoever He wills and shows the Right Way to whomsoever He wills. Surely you shall be called to account regarding what you did.

[94] Do not make your oaths a means of deceiving one another or else your foot may slip after having been firm, and you may suffer evil consequences because of hindering people from the way of Allah. A mighty

chastisement awaits you.[27] [95] Do not barter away the covenant of Allah for a paltry gain. Verily that which is with Allah is far better for you, if you only knew. [96] Whatever you have is bound to pass away and whatever is with Allah will last. And We shall surely grant those who have been patient their reward according to the best of what they did. [97] Whosoever acts righteously – whether a man or a woman – and embraces belief, We will surely grant him a good life; and will surely grant such persons their reward according to the best of their deeds.

[98] Whenever you read the Qur'ān seek refuge with Allah from Satan, the accursed.[28] [99] Surely he has no power over those who have faith and who place their trust in their Lord. [100] He has power only over those who take him as their patron and who, under his influence, associate others with Allah in His Divinity.

---

27. This verse emphatically admonishes the believers to adhere to righteous conduct. At times, those who are otherwise intellectually convinced that Islam is sound, may observe the misbehaviour and corruption of Muslims and this may deter them from joining the fold of Islam. This because they did not find the Muslims with whom they came into contact any better in their moral conduct than the unbelievers.

28. This does not simply mean that before starting to recite the Qur'ān one should simply utter the words: "I seek refuge with Allah from Satan, the accursed." Seeking refuge with God against Satan should not merely involve a man's tongue, but also his heart. The one who fails to find guidance in the Qur'ān will get it from nowhere else. If someone is so unfortunate that he derives erroneous doctrines from the Qur'ān nothing in the world will rescue him from misguidance and doctrinal error.

[101] Whenever We replace one verse by another verse – and Allah knows what He should reveal – they are wont to say: "You are nothing but a fabricator (who has invented the Qur'ān)." The fact is that most of them are ignorant of the Truth. [102] Tell them: "It is the spirit of holiness that has brought it down, by stages, from your Lord[29] so that it might bring firmness to those who believe, and guidance to the Right Way, and give glad tidings of felicity and success to those who submit to Allah."

[103] Surely We know well that they say about you: "It is only a human being who teaches him," (notwithstanding) that he whom they maliciously hint at is of foreign tongue, while this (Qur'ān) is plain Arabic speech. [104] Surely Allah will not enable those who do not believe in the signs of Allah to be directed to the Right Way, and a painful chastisement awaits them. [105] (It is not the Prophet who invents lies), it is rather those who do not believe in the signs of Allah who invent lies.[30] They are liars.

[106] Except for those who were forced to engage in infidelity to Allah after believing the while their hearts

---

29. The Qur'ānic expression *"Rūḥ al-Qudus"* literally means "holy spirit" or the "spirit of holiness". This appellation is exclusively used for the angel Gabriel. By preferring to use this appellation rather than his proper name, the Qur'ān emphasizes that the message of the Qur'ān has been conveyed through the spirit which is free from all human weaknesses and imperfections. The Qur'ān was communicated to the Prophet (peace be on him) by one who is fully trustworthy so that there is no danger of his tampering with God's message.

30. Alternatively, this verse may be translated as follows: "It is only those who do not believe in the signs of Allah who invent lies".

remained firmly convinced of their belief, the ones whose hearts willingly embraced disbelief shall incur Allah's wrath and a mighty chastisement lies in store for them.[31] [107] That is because they love the life of this world more than the Hereafter; and Allah does not guide those who are ungrateful to Allah for His favours. [108] They are the ones upon whose hearts and hearing and eyes Allah has set a seal. They are utterly steeped in heedlessness. [109] No doubt they shall be losers in the Hereafter.[32] [110] And surely your Lord will be Most Forgiving and Most Merciful towards those who left their homes after they were pesecuted, and who thereafter struggled hard and remained constant. [111] Allah's judgement will come about them all on the Day when everyone shall come pleading in his defence, and everyone shall be fully requited for his deeds and none shall be wronged in the least.

---

31. This verse concerns those Muslims who, at that time, were being severely persecuted and were being forced under torture to revert to unbelief. Such believers are being assured that if under such unendurable pressure, and out of the desire to save their lives, they are sometimes inclined to indicate that they no longer believe in Islam, they will be pardoned by God provided their hearts remain secure from all false doctrines. However, if they not only declare their verbal dissociation from Islam, but become convinced even in their hearts that it was some other religious doctrine rather than Islam which was true, they will not be able to escape God's punishment.

32. These statements were made about those who, finding that the path of faith was difficult, recanted and rejoined the ranks of their people – the unbelievers and the polytheists.

[112] Allah sets forth the parable of (the people of) a town who were secure and content and whose sustenance came in abundance from every quarter. But then the people of the town showed ingratitude towards Allah for His bounties, so Allah afflicted them with hunger and fear in punishment for their evil deeds. [113] Most certainly a Messenger came to them from among them; but they rejected him, calling him a liar. Therefore chastisement seized them while they engaged in wrong-doing.[33]

[114] So eat out of the lawful and good sustenance that Allah has bestowed upon you, and thank Allah for His bounty, if it is Him that you serve. [115] Allah has forbidden you only carrion, and blood, and the flesh of swine; also any animal over which the name of any other than Allah has been pronounced. But whoever eats of them under compelling necessity – neither desiring it nor exceeding the limit of absolute necessity – surely for such action Allah is Much Forgiving, Most Merciful. [116] And do not utter falsehoods by letting your tongues declare: "This is lawful" and "That is unlawful,"[34] thus fabricating lies against Allah. Surely those who fabricate

---

33. It is Ibn ʿAbbās's opinion that the town referred to in the parable is Makkah itself. As for the hunger and fear mentioned in the verse (i.e. verse 112), this possibly refers to the famine that held the Makkans in its grip for quite some time after the advent of the Prophet (peace be on him).

34. The verse categorically lays down that no one other than God has the authority to declare something lawful or otherwise. In other words, God alone is the Law-Maker. If anyone else makes bold to declare on his own certain things to be lawful and others unlawful, he certainly goes beyond his legitimate limits. No such statements

lies against Allah will never prosper. [117] Brief is their enjoyment of the world, and thereafter they shall suffer a painful chastisement.

[118] We have already recounted to you what We prohibited to the Jews. In so doing We did not wrong them; it is they who wronged themselves. [119] But to those who commit evil out of ignorance and then repent and amend their ways, thereafter your Lord will be Much Forgiving, Most Merciful. [120] Indeed Abraham was a whole community by himself, obedient to Allah, exclusively devoted to Him. And he was never one of those who associated others with Allah in His Divinity. [121] He rendered thanks to Allah for His bounties so that Allah chose him (for His favours) and directed him to the Right Way. [122] We bestowed good upon him in this world, and in the Hereafter he shall certainly be among the righteous. [123] Then We revealed to you: "Follow the way of Abraham with exclusive devotion to Allah. He was not one of those who associated others with Allah in His Divinity." [124] As for the Sabbath, it was made incumbent only on those who differed about its laws. Certainly your

---

may be made unless one can demonstrate that such opinions are based on God's commands. By arrogating the right to declare things lawful or unlawful, one becomes guilty of inventing lies against God. For anyone who declares certain things to be lawful and others unlawful is guilty of any one of the following: He will either claim that his declarations of lawful and unlawful are in accordance with God's own declarations. Alternatively, he will claim that God has withdrawn His own prerogative to give man the Law which he might follow, and has, thereby, now delegated it to man himself. In either case, the statement is false and is tantamount to inventing lies against God.

Lord will judge on the Day of Resurrection between them regarding the matters they disputed.

[125] (O Prophet), call to the way of your Lord with wisdom and goodly exhortation, and reason with them in the best manner possible. Surely your Lord knows best who has strayed away from His path, and He also knows well those who are guided to the Right Way. [126] If you take retribution, then do so in proportion to the wrong done to you. But if you can bear such conduct with patience, indeed that is best for the steadfast. [127] And bear with patience, (O Muḥammad) – and your patience is only because of the help of Allah – and do not grieve over them, nor feel distressed by their evil plans. [128] For surely Allah is with those who hold Him in fear and do good.

17

Banī Isrā'īl [Children of Israel]
Makkan Period

In the name of Allah, the Most Merciful,
the Most Compassionate

[1] Holy is He Who carried His servant by night from the Holy Mosque (in Makkah) to the farther Mosque (in Jerusalem) whose surroundings We have blessed that We might show him some of Our Signs.¹ Indeed He alone is All-Hearing, All-Seeing.

---

1. This is an allusion to the event known as *Mi'rāj* (ascension) and *Isrā'* (night journey). According to most traditions – and especially the authentic ones – this event took place one year before *Hijrah*. Detailed reports about it are found in the works of *Ḥadīth* and *Sīrah* and have been narrated from as many as twenty-five Companions. The Qur'ān here only mentions that the Prophet (peace be on him) was taken from the Ka'bah to the Mosque in Jerusalem. However, *Ḥadīth* reports give copious details of the onward journey from Jerusalem to the highest point in the heavens and the experience of the Divine Presence. What was the nature of this journey? Did it take place while the Prophet (peace be on him) was asleep or while he was awake? Did he actually undertake a journey in the physical sense or did he have a spiritual vision while remaining in his own place? These questions, in our view, have been resolved by the text of the Qur'ān itself. The opening statement: "Holy is He Who carried His servant by night from the Holy Mosque to the farther Mosque ..." (verse 1) itself indicates that it was an extraordinary event which took place by dint of the infinite power

[2] We gave Moses the Book, and made it a source of guidance for the Children of Israel, commanding: "Take no other Guardian beside Me."² [3] You are the descendants of those whom We carried (in the Ark) with Noah. He was truly a thankful servant. [4] Then We clearly declared to the Children of Israel in the Book:³ "Twice you will make mischief in the land and will commit transgression." [5] So, when the occasion for the first of the transgressions arrived, We raised against you some of Our creatures who were full of might, and they ran over the whole of your land.⁴ This was a promise that was

of God. For quite obviously, to be able to perceive the kind of things mentioned in connection with the event either in a dream or by means of intuition is not so wondrous that it should be prefaced by the statement: "Holy is He Who carried His servant by night…"; a statement which amounts to proclaiming that God was free from every imperfection and flaw. Such a statement would make absolutely no sense if the purpose of it was merely to affirm that God had the power to enable man to have either visions in the course of a dream, or to receive information intuitively. In our view, the words of the verse clearly indicate that the event, far from being merely a spiritual experience or a dream vision, was an actual journey, and the observation in question was a visual observation.

2. The word *wakīl* signifies one upon whom a person totally relies; one in whom full trust is reposed; one to whose care one entrusts one's affairs, to whom one looks for guidance and support.

3. The word "Book" here does not specifically signify the Torah. Rather, it stands for the heavenly Scripture as such. On several occasions the Qur'ān uses the term *al-Kitāb* in the sense of heavenly Scripture as such rather than in the sense of one particular Book.

4. This alludes to the terrible destruction suffered by the Israelites at the hands of the Assyrians and Babylonians.

bound to be fulfilled. [6] Then We granted you an upper hand against them, and strengthened you with wealth and children, and multiplied your numbers. [7] Whenever you did good, it was to your own advantage; and whenever you committed evil, it was to your own disadvantage. So, when the time of the fulfilment of the second promise arrived, (We raised other enemies that would) disfigure your faces and enter the Temple (of Jerusalem) as they had entered the first time, and destroy whatever they could lay their hands on.⁵ [8] Your Lord may well show Mercy to you, but if you revert to your evil behaviour, We shall revert to chastising you. We have made Hell a prison for those who are thankless of Allah's bounties.

[9] Verily this Qur'ān guides to the Way that is the Straightmost. To those who believe in it, and do righteous works, it gives the good news that a great reward awaits them, [10] and warns those who do not believe in the Hereafter that We have prepared for them a grievous chastisement.

[11] Man prays for evil in the manner he ought to pray for good. Man is ever hasty.⁶

---

5. This refers to the Romans who destroyed Jerusalem completely and drove the Israelites out of Palestine. Since then they remained dispirited and dispersed throughout the world for nearly two thousand years.

6. This is in response to the foolish demands that the unbelievers of Makkah occasionally made upon the Prophet (peace be on him). Again and again they asked him to bring upon them the punishment of which he had so often warned them. This particular statement follows the preceding verse which promises a large reward for those

[12] We have made night and day as two signs. We made the sign of the night devoid of light, and made the sign of the day radiant that you may seek the bounty of your Lord and know the computation of years and numbers. Thus We have expounded everything in detail to keep everything distinct from the other.

[13] We have fastened every man's omen to his neck.[7] On the Day of Resurrection We shall produce for him his scroll in the shape of a wide open book, (saying): [14] "Read your scroll; this Day you suffice to take account of yourself."

[15] He who follows the Right Way shall do so to his own advantage; and he who strays shall incur his own loss.

---

who believe and do good and a painful chastisement for those who do not believe in the After-Life, and is intended to jolt the persons concerned into recognizing their folly. For, instead of asking for good, they were asking for God's punishment. Do they have no idea at all of the havoc that God's punishment wreaks upon those who are smitten by it?

Implicit in this statement is a subtle warning to the Muslims as well. Irked by constant persecution at the hands of the unbelievers the Muslims sometimes prayed that God's scourge might seize the unbelievers. They did so without realizing that there were many among the unbelievers who would embrace Islam and uphold its cause all across the world at one time or another in the future. Hence, it was deemed necessary to point out that man is impatient; that he is prone to ask for whatever he is immediately in need of and which he wants to have forthwith. However, in the course of time, it becomes evident to him that had his prayer been answered instantly, it would have been no good for him.

7. The causes that lead a man to his ultimate salvation or perdition, to his perpetual happiness or unending misery, lie within himself.

No one shall bear another's burden.[8] And never do We punish any people until We send a Messenger (to make the Truth distinct from falsehood).

[16] When We decide to destroy a town We command the affluent among them, whereupon they commit sins in it, then the decree (of chastisement) becomes due against them and thereafter We destroy that town utterly.[9] [17] Many a generation has been destroyed by Our command since Noah's time. Your Lord is well aware and fully observant of the sins of His servants.

[18] If anyone desires immediate benefits, (We hasten to grant whatever benefits We will in the present life to whomsoever We please, but thereafter We decree for him Hell wherein he shall burn, condemned and rejected. [19] But he who desires the Hereafter and strives for it in the manner he should, and is a true believer, his striving

---

8. The statement made here emphasizes that every man has been encumbered with moral responsibility, that each person is accountable to God in his personal capacity, that no one shares this accountability with any other.

9. The essence of the matter, as embodied in the present verse, is that what truly brings about a society's destruction is corruption of its affluent sections, the corruption of its upper classes. When a nation is close to its doom, its wealthy and influential sections blatantly resort to all kinds of evil practices, to injustice and oppression, to wickedness and mischief, and this leads to its destruction. Hence, if a people truly care about their collective well-being, they should ensure that its political power and riches do not pass on to those that are unworthy of them, to those that are conspicuously iniquitous, to those that are altogether incapable of judiciously using political and economic power.

will come to fruition.[10] [20] To all of these as well as those We shall provide the wherewithal of this life in the present world by dint of your Lord's Bounty; and from none shall the Bounty of your Lord be withheld. [21] See, how We have exalted some above others in this world,[11] and in the Life to Come they will have higher ranks and greater degrees of excellence over others.

10. He who seeks success in the Hereafter will receive full reward for his efforts towards that end, a reward that will fully correspond to that effort.

11. It is quite evident even during the course of this life that the seekers of the Hereafter are perceptibly better than those who seek the good of this worldly life alone. Quite obviously, the superiority of the former does not consist in the fact that they eat tastier food, or clothe themselves in more attractive garments, or dwell in more splendid houses, or go about in impressive vehicles, or enjoy any other trappings of material progress and prosperity. The true cause of their superiority is essentially their moral excellence. Regardless of whether the worldly possessions of people of the former category are abundant or meagre, it is certain that they earned them by honest and fair means. This is in sharp contrast to the predicament of those who exclusively seek the good of this world. For scarcely anything prevents them from employing illegitimate means to achieve their worldly objectives. Similarly, the people who essentially seek the success of the Hereafter, can also be distinguished by the manner in which they spend their earnings: they spend them with moderation. They allocate a part of their earnings to discharge their obligations to their kith and kin. They also devote a part of their earnings to assisting the needy and the indigent, as well as to other charitable purposes with a view to pleasing God. In sharp contrast to this, the people who seek nothing but worldly prosperity, are intent upon self-indulgence, upon satisfying their lusts in every conceivable way, whether legitimate or illegitimate. In sum, the life of the former group of people is distinct from and superior in all respects.

[22] Do not set up any other god with Allah lest you are rendered humiliated and helpless.

[23] Your Lord has decreed:

    (i) Do not worship any but Him;

    (ii) Be good to your parents; and should both or any one of them attain old age with you, do not say to them even "fie" neither chide them, but speak to them with respect, [24] and be humble and tender to them and say: "Lord, show mercy to them as they nurtured me when I was small." [25] Your Lord is best aware of what is in your hearts. If you are righteous, He will indeed forgive those who relent and revert (to serving Allah).

[26] (iii) Give to the near of kin his due, and also to the needy and the wayfarer.

    (iv) Do not squander your wealth wastefully, [27] for those who squander wastefully are Satan's brothers, and Satan is ever ungrateful to his Lord.

[28] (v) And when you must turn away from them – (that is, from the destitute, the near of kin, the needy, and the wayfarer) – in pursuit of God's Mercy which you expect to receive, then speak to them kindly.

[29] (vi) Do not keep your hand fastened to your neck nor outspread it, altogether outspread, for

you will be left sitting rebuked, destitute.[12]
[30] Certainly Your Lord makes plentiful the
provision of whomsoever He wills and straitens
it for whomsoever He wills. He is well-aware
and is fully observant of all that relates to His
servants.

[31] (vii) Do not kill your children for fear of want. We
will provide for them and for you. Surely killing
them is a great sin.

[32] (viii) Do not even approach fornication for it is an
outrageous act, and an evil way.

[33] (ix) Do not kill any person whom Allah has forbidden
to kill, except with right. We have granted the
heir of him who has been wrongfully killed the
authority to (claim retribution);[13] so let him not
exceed in slaying.[14] He shall be helped.[15]

---

12. "To keep one's hand fastened to one's neck" is an Arabic
idiom that denotes miserliness, and "to outspread it, altogether
outspread," denotes extravagance.

13. That "We have granted the heir of him who has been wrongfully
killed the authority to demand *qiṣāṣ* (retribution)" means that
the heir of someone who has been murdered is entitled to claim
retribution for that crime.

14. There are many ways in which one can overstep the legitimate
bounds of "slaying," and all of them are prohibited. For instance,
swayed by vengefulness, a wronged person may kill others than
the actual culprit, or subject the culprit to torture, mutilation of his
corpse, or even kill him after he has taken blood-money.

15. As the Islamic state had not been established when this verse
was revealed, who will "help" the heir is not specified. However,
after the Islamic state was established, it was made clear that

[34] (x) And do not even go near the property of the orphan – except that it be in the best manner – till he attains his maturity.

(xi) And fulfil the covenant, for you will be called to account regarding the covenant.

[35] (xii) Give full measure when you measure, and weigh with even scales. That is fair and better in consequence.

[36] (xiii) Do not follow that of which you have no knowledge.[16] Surely the hearing, the sight, the heart – each of these shall be called to account. [37] (xiv) Do not strut about in the land arrogantly. Surely you cannot cleave the earth, nor reach the heights of the mountains in stature.

[38] The wickedness of each of that is hateful to your Lord.[17] [39] That is part of the wisdom your Lord has revealed to you. So do not set up any deity beside Allah

---

"helping" the legal heir was neither the responsibility of the slain person's tribe nor of that tribe's allies. Instead, the responsibility fell upon the Islamic state and its judicial system. Individuals or groups were no longer entitled to seek retribution for murder on their own; rather, they were required to approach the Islamic state to bring the murderer to justice.

16. The purpose of this Qur'ānic verse is that people should be guided by knowledge rather than conjecture, and this both in their individual and collective lives.

17. Infraction of any of the commands mentioned above is disapproved of by God.

lest you are cast into Hell, rebuked and deprived of every good.[18] [40] What, has your Lord favoured you with sons and has taken for Himself daughters from among the angels? You are indeed uttering a monstrous lie.

[41] We have expounded (the Truth) in diverse ways in this Qur'ān that they might take it to heart but all this only aggravates their aversion. [42] Say, (O Muḥammad): "Had there been other gods with Him, as they claim, they would surely have attempted to find a way to the Lord of the Throne. [43] Holy is He and far above all that they say. [44] The seven heavens, the earth, and all that is within them give glory to Him.[19] There is nothing but gives glory to Him with His praise, though you do not understand their hymns of praise. He is Most Forbearing, Exceedingly Forgiving."

[45] When you recite the Qur'ān, We place a hidden barrier between you and those who do not believe in the Hereafter; [46] and We place a covering on their hearts so that they do not comprehend it, and We cause a heaviness in their ears;[20] and when you mention your Lord, the Only True Lord, in the Qur'ān, they turn their backs in

---

18. Although here the discourse is ostensibly addressed to the Prophet (peace be on him), the purpose of the discourse on such occasions is to provide directives to all human beings.

19. The Universe and all that there is in it bear ample testimony to the fact that its Creator, Master and Lord is free from every blemish, weakness and fault; He is far too exalted to have anyone as an associate or partner in His Godhead.

20. When a man denies the Hereafter, it naturally leads to his heart being sealed, and his ears becoming incapable of heeding the Message of the Qur'ān. For, the very cornerstone of the Qur'ānic

aversion.[21] [47] We are well aware of what they wish to hear when they listen to you and what they say when they confer in whispers, when the wrong-doers say: "You are only following one who is bewitched."[22] [48] Just see how strange are the things they invent about you. They have altogether strayed, and are unable to find the right way.

Message to man is that he should not be deceived by the external manifestations of this worldly life. What is true and what is false is not going to be determined in this world but will be made manifest in the Hereafter. Good deed is that which will earn a reward in the Hereafter regardless of the hardship to which it may subject its doer in this world. Wrong is the deed that will incur punishment in the Hereafter irrespective of how enjoyable and beneficial it may be in the present life. But the person who does not believe in the Hereafter will scarcely pay attention to this Qurʾānic message.

21. The unbelievers of Makkah found that the Prophet (peace be on him) regarded God as the only true Lord, to the exclusion of all other deities. It was, therefore, intolerable for them that the Prophet (peace be on him) should talk only about God. They were astonished that a person should believe that God – and He alone – possessed virtually everything – full knowledge of the realm beyond the ken of sense-perception, absolute power to do as He pleased, and total control over everything. It was inconceivable to them that someone should pay no heed to the saints by dint of whose grace people were granted offspring, the sick were healed, sagging businesses began to flourish, and all wishes were fulfilled.

22. This is an allusion to conversations among the leaders of the Makkan unbelievers. They were wont, surreptitiously, to listen to the Qurʾān and then consult with one another as to how they could effectively refute it. At times they suspected that some among their ranks were gradually succumbing to the spell of the Qurʾān. Whenever they became aware of this they approached the persons concerned and tried to dissuade them from taking the Prophet (peace be on him) seriously, arguing that he was under a magic spell and thus was given to saying crazy things.

[49] They say: "When we are turned to bones and particles (of dust), shall we truly be raised up as a new creation?" [50] Tell them: "(You will be raised afresh even if) you turn to stone or iron, [51] or any other form of creation you deem hardest of all (to recreate from)." They will certainly ask: "Who will bring us back (to life)?" Say: "He Who created you in the first instance." They will shake their heads at you[23] and inquire: "When will that be?" Say: "Perhaps that time might have drawn near; [52] on the Day when He will call you and you will rise praising Him in response to His call, and you will believe that you had lain in this state only for a while."[24]

[53] Tell My servants, (O Muḥammad), to say always that which is best.[25] Verily it is Satan who sows discord among people. Satan indeed is an open enemy to mankind. [54] Your Lord knows you best. He will have mercy on

23. The gesture referred to here consists of shaking one's head up and down, something one resorts to either to express amazement or derision.

24. The period between a person's death and resurrection on the Last Day will appear as if no longer than, say, a few hours. One will assume that one has just had a brief sleep and been woken by the din and noise of the Day of Reckoning.

25. In their discussions with the unbelievers and polytheists, in fact with all opponents of their faith, Muslims should refrain from losing their temper. Even in the face of provocation from their opponents, they should never utter a word that is contrary to the truth; nor should they lose their temper at the vulgarities which are flung at them by their opponents, nor be provoked to the point of paying back their opponents in the latters' own coins. Instead, they should keep their composure and say only that which is balanced and true and is in keeping with the grace and dignity of the faith which they seek to uphold.

you if He wills and chastise you if He wills.[26] We have not sent you, (O Muḥammad), as an overseer over them.

[55] Your Lord knows all who dwell in the heavens and the earth. We have exalted some Prophets over others, and We gave the Psalms to David.

[56] Tell them: "Call upon those whom you fancy to be (your helpers) instead of Him! They have no power to remove any affliction from you, nor can they shift it (to any other)."[27] [57] Those whom they call upon are themselves seeking the means of access to their Lord, each trying to be nearer to Him. They crave for His Mercy and dread His chastisement.[28] Surely your Lord's punishment is to be feared.

---

26. The believers should never go about bragging that they are going to enter Paradise, or cockily name other persons or groups as the ones destined to enter Hell. For it is God alone Who has the authority to decide such matters. It is He alone Who fully knows about all human beings, about all things both apparent and hidden which took place before or which will take place in the future. It is He alone Who will judge, He alone Who will decide, to whom He should show Mercy and whom He should punish. All that a human being can say, enunciating the teachings of the Qur'ān, is what kind of people deserve Mercy, and what kind deserve punishment. No one has the right to categorically say that a particular person will be either chastised or pardoned by God.

27. This clearly shows that not only prostrating oneself before someone other than God, but also praying to and invoking anyone other than God amounts to associating others with God in His Divinity, i.e. to polytheism.

28. The actual words used in the verse make it clear that the polytheists' deities and objects of prayer were angels and saints of the past rather than idols made of stone.

[58] There is not a town but We shall destroy it or upon which We shall inflict severe chastisement before the Day of Resurrection. This is written down in the Eternal Book (of Allah).

[59] Nothing hindered Us from sending Our Signs except that the people of olden times rejected them as lies.[29] We publicly sent the she-camel to the Thamūd to open their eyes but they wronged her. We never send Our Signs except to cause people to fear. [60] And recall when We said to you, (O Muḥammad), that your Lord encompasses these people; and that We have made that vision that We have shown you,[30] and the tree accursed in the Qur'ān,[31] but as a trial for people.[32] We go about warning them, but each warning leads them to greater transgression.

---

29. This is in response to the unbelievers' demand that Muḥammad (peace be on him) produce Signs in support of his claim to prophethood. It is pointed out that once people witness a miracle and still refuse to believe it, they inevitably invite God's chastisement upon themselves. Such people are not spared total destruction. If God is not sending his Signs it is purely out of Mercy. Is it then not sheer folly for people to continuously ask God for miracles? For if they do not care to accept the Truth even after witnessing miracles, then they are bound to meet the calamitous end of nations like the Thamūd.

30. This is an allusion to the Ascension. The word *ru'yā* is not used here as a synonym of dream; rather, it signifies seeing something with one's own eyes.

31. According to the Qur'ān, *zaqqūm* is the name of the tree that will grow in the depths of Hell and the inmates of Hell will be obliged to eat of it. To describe *zaqqūm* as an accursed tree suggests its remoteness from God's Mercy.

32. God enabled the Prophet (peace be on him) to witness a number of things in the course of the Ascension. This was in order that

[61] And recall when We asked the angels to prostrate themselves before Adam; all prostrated themselves except *Iblīs*, who said: "Shall I prostrate myself before him whom You created of clay?" [62] He then continued: "Look! This is he whom You have exalted above me! If you will grant me respite till the Day of Resurrection I shall uproot the whole of his progeny except only a few." [63] Thereupon He retorted: "Be gone! Hell shall be the recompense – and a most ample one – of whosoever of them who follows you. [64] Tempt with your call all whom you wish. Muster against them all your forces – your cavalry and your foot soldiers; share with them riches and offspring, and seduce them with rosy promises – and Satan's promise is nothing but a deception – [65] but know well that you will have no power against My servants. Your Lord suffices for them to place their trust in."

[66] Your Lord is He Who steers your vessels across the seas that you may seek of His Bounty. He is ever Merciful towards you. [67] When a calamity befalls you

---

people might learn certain truths for sure through no less truthful and trustworthy a person than the Prophet (peace be on him) who could report to them the truths that he had witnessed at first hand. This was done in order to help people follow the Right Way as a result of their having fully dependable knowledge of the Truth. However, far from taking any heed of all this, the unbelievers launched a campaign of ridicule against the Prophet (peace be on him). For example, they had been told by the Prophet (peace be on him) that their wilful disregard of the distinction between legitimate and illegitimate earning would lead them to live upon *zaqqūm*. Rather than this producing a healthy response from them, the unbelievers made fun of the Prophet, saying, in effect: "Look at this man! In one breath he says that Hell is a pit of blazing fire, and in the next, that trees grow in it."

on the sea, all those whom you invoke forsake you except Him. But when He delivers you safely to the shore you turn away from Him, for man is indeed most thankless. [68] Do you, then, feel secure against His causing you to be swallowed up by a tract of the earth, or letting loose a deadly whirlwind charged with stones towards you, and there you will find none to protect you? [69] Or do you feel secure that He will not cause you to revert to the sea, and let a tempest loose upon you and then drown you for your ingratitude whereupon you will find none even to inquire of Us what happened to you? [70] Indeed, We honoured the progeny of Adam, and bore them across land and sea and provided them with good things for their sustenance, and exalted them above many of Our creatures. [71] Then think of the Day We shall summon every community with its leader. Those who are given their Record in their right hand shall read the Record of their deeds and shall not be wronged a whit. [72] Whoever lived in this world as blind shall live as blind in the Life to Come; rather, he will be even farther astray than if he were (just) blind.

[73] (O Muḥammad), they had all but tempted you away from what We have revealed to you that you may invent something else in Our Name. Had you done so, they would have taken you as their trusted friend. [74] Indeed, had We not strengthened you, you might have inclined to them a little, [75] whereupon We would have made you taste double (the chastisement) in the world and double (the chastisement) after death, and then you would have found none to help you against Us.

[76] They were bent upon uprooting you from this land and driving you away from it. But were they to succeed,

they would not be able to remain after you more than a little while.

[77] This has been Our Way with the Messengers whom We sent before you. You will find no change in Our Way.

[78] Establish Prayer from the declining of the sun to the darkness of the night;[33] and hold fast to the recitation of the Qur'ān at dawn, for the recitation of the Qur'ān at dawn is witnessed.[34] [79] And rise from sleep during the night as well[35] – this is an additional Prayer for you. Possibly your Lord will raise you to an honoured position.[36]

[80] And pray: "My Lord! Cause me to enter wherever it be, with Truth, and cause me to exit, wherever it be, with Truth, and support me with authority from Yourself."[37]

---

33. This refers to four Prayers, from *Ẓuhr* to *'Ishā'*.

34. The expression *qur'ān al-fajr* means recitation of the Qur'ān in the *Fajr* Prayer. The statement that "*qur'ān al-fajr* is witnessed" means that it is witnessed by angels because recitation of the Qur'ān in *Fajr* Prayer has a significance of its own.

35. The word *tahajjud* means to rouse oneself from sleep. To perform *tahajjud* at night signifies the act of rising from sleep during the night and then praying.

36. Here it is proclaimed that God will bestow upon the Prophet (peace be on him) an exalted position in both the present world and the Next. It will be a position of eminence, one which will evoke universal appreciation and praise.

37. The prayer here consists of asking God either to endow him with authority, or to aid him by causing some governmental authority to be his supporter such that he might restore righteousness, stem the tide of lewdness and sin, and make God's law of justice prevail in a world steeped in corruption.

[81] And proclaim: "The Truth has come, and falsehood has vanished. Surely falsehood is ever bound to vanish."

[82] What We are sending down in the course of revealing the Qur'ān is a healing and a grace for those who have faith; but it adds only to the ruin of the wrong-doers. [83] Whenever We bestow favours upon man, he arrogantly turns away and draws aside; and whenever evil visits him, he is in utter despair. [84] Say, (O Prophet): "Each one acts according to his own manner. Your Lord knows well who is best-guided to the Right Path."

[85] They ask you about "the spirit". Say: "The spirit descends by the command of my Lord, but you have been given only a little knowledge."[38] [86] Had We willed, We could take away what We have revealed to you, then you would find none to help you in recovering it from Us. [87] (Whatever you have received) is nothing but grace from your Lord. Indeed His favour to you is great.

---

38. It is generally assumed that the word *rūḥ* here signifies "life". Some people had asked the Prophet (peace be on him) about the essence of life. In response, they are told that it comes by the command of God. The context of the verse makes it quite clear that the word *rūḥ* here signifies either revelation or the spirit of prophethood. At different points in the Qur'ān when such a statement is made, recourse is had to more or less the same words. See for example, *al-Naḥl* (16: 2), *al-Mu'min* (40: 15) and *al-Shūrā* (42: 52). Among the early scholars, Ibn 'Abbās, Qatādah and Ḥasan al-Baṣrī interpret the verse along similar lines. In *Rūḥ al-Ma'ānī* the opinion of Ḥasan al-Baṣrī and Qatādah has been quoted in the following words: "The *rūḥ* (here) stands for Gabriel, and the question (in the context of which it arose was) in fact how he (i.e. Gabriel) came down and how he conveyed revelation to the heart of the Prophet (peace be on him)."

[88] Say: "Surely, if mankind and *jinn* were to get together to produce the like of this Qur'ān, they will never be able to produce the like of it, howsoever they might help one another."

[89] We have explained things for people in this Qur'ān in diverse ways to make them understand the Message, yet most people obstinately persist in unbelief. [90] They said: "We shall not accept your Message until you cause a spring to gush forth for us from the earth; [91] or that there be a garden of palms and vines for you and then you cause rivers to abundantly flow forth through them; [92] or cause the sky to fall on us in pieces as you claimed, or bring Allah and the angels before us, face to face; [93] or that there come to be for you a house of gold, or that you ascend to the sky – though we shall not believe in your ascension (to the sky) – until you bring down a book for us that we can read." Say to them, (O Muḥammad): "Holy is my Lord! Am I anything else than a human being, who bears a Message (from Allah)?"

[94] Whenever Guidance came to people, nothing prevented them from believing except that they said: "Has Allah sent a human being as a Messenger?" [95] Say: "Had angels been walking about in peace on the earth, We would surely have sent to them an angel from the heavens as Messenger."

[96] Tell them, (O Prophet): "Allah suffices as a witness between me and you. Allah is well aware and fully observes everything pertaining to His servants."

[97] Whomsoever Allah guides is rightly guided; and whomsoever Allah lets go astray, you shall find none –

apart from Him – who could protect him. We shall muster them all on the Day of Resurrection, on their faces – blind and dumb and deaf. Hell shall be their refuge. Every time its Fire subsides, We will intensify for them its flame. [98] That will be their recompense because they disbelieved in Our Signs and said: "What, when we shall be reduced to bones and particles (of dust), shall we be raised again as a new creation?" [99] Have they not perceived that Allah, Who has created the heavens and the earth, has the power to create the like of them? He has fixed a term for them about which there is no doubt. And yet the wrong-doers obstinately persist in unbelief.

[100] Tell them, (O Prophet): "Even if you owned the treasures of my Lord's Mercy you would have held them back for fear of spending them." Man is indeed ever niggardly.[39]

[101] We granted Moses nine clear signs.[40] Ask the Children of Israel about that: when these signs came forth, Pharaoh said to him: "Moses, I think that you are bewitched." [102] Moses replied: "You know well that no one but

---

39. One of the psychological reasons why the Makkan polytheists were unable to affirm the prophethood of Muḥammad (peace be on him) was that such an affirmation clearly implied an acceptance of the Prophet's greatness. Such an attitude is understandable since people are generally disinclined to recognize the greatness of their contemporaries. In view of this common shortcoming, it is being pointed out here that those who are so predisposed to niggardliness will hardly act with liberality if they are given the keys to God's infinite treasures.

40. The nine clear signs of God to which this verse alludes are specifically mentioned in *al-Aʿrāf* (see verses 107-33).

the Lord of the heavens and the earth has sent these as eye-opening proofs.[41] I truly think, O Pharaoh, that you are indeed doomed." [103] At last Pharaoh decided to uproot Moses and the Children of Israel from the land, but We drowned him together with all who were with him; [104] and thereafter We said to the Children of Israel: "Now dwell in the land, but when the promised time of the Hereafter comes, We shall bring you all together."

[105] We have sent down the Qur'ān with the Truth, and it is with the Truth that it has descended. And We have not sent you but to proclaim good news and to warn. [106] We have revealed the Qur'ān in parts that you may recite it to people slowly and with deliberation; and (for that reason) We have revealed it gradually (to suit particular occasions). [107] Tell them, (O Prophet): "Whether you believe in it, or do not believe," but when it is recited to those who were given the knowledge before its revelation, they fall down upon their faces in prostration [108] and say: "Glory be to our Lord. Surely the promise of our Lord was bound to be fulfilled." [109] And they fall down upon their faces, weeping, and their humility increases when (the Qur'ān) is recited to them.

---

41. The Prophet Moses (peace be on him) made this statement to emphasize the fact that the calamities which befell people could only be from God. There was widespread famine across the land. Frogs in large numbers infested a vast area, covering hundreds of thousands of square miles. Food stocks in the barns throughout the land were eaten up by weevils. Calamities such as these could not be the result of some magician's sorcery, or the manifestation of some human being's extraordinary power. A magician can only bewitch a crowd of people confined to a specific place. Even then his tricks have nothing to do with reality and are mere illusions.

[110] Say to them (O Prophet!): "Call upon Him as Allah or call upon Him as *al-Raḥmān*; call Him by whichever name you will, all His names are beautiful.[42] Neither offer your Prayer in too loud a voice, nor in a voice too low; but follow a middle course."[43] [111] And say: "All praise be to Allah Who has neither taken to Himself a son, nor has He any partner in His kingdom, nor does He need anyone, out of weakness, to protect Him." So glorify Him in a manner worthy of His glory.

---

42. This is in response to the polytheists' objection to calling God by the name *al-Raḥmān*. They claimed that while they were familiar with the appellation Allah, there seemed no justification for using the appellation *al-Raḥmān*. Their objection was based on their unfamiliarity with this word as a personal name of God.

43. According to Ibn ʿAbbās, when the Prophet Muḥammad (peace be on him) or his Companions offered Prayers in Makkah or recited the Qurʾān, the unbelievers often made noises and even hurled abuse at them. The believers were, therefore, counselled neither to recite in such a loud voice that would attract the attention of the unbelievers who might interrupt their Prayers, nor to recite in a voice inaudible even to people close by. During the Madīnan period of the Prophet's life when the situation altogether changed, there was no need to follow this injunction. However, whenever Muslims are faced with the kind of circumstances which they encountered during the Makkan period of the Prophet's life, they should follow the directive laid down here.

18
❀

Al-Kahf [The Cave]
Makkan Period

In the name of Allah, the Most Merciful,
the Most Compassionate

[1] Praise be to Allah Who has revealed to His servant the Book devoid of all crookedness; [2] an unerringly Straight Book, meant to warn of a stern punishment from Allah, and to proclaim, to those who believe and work righteous deeds, the tiding that theirs shall be a good reward [3] wherein they shall abide for ever; [4] and also to warn those who say: "Allah has taken to Himself a son," [5] a thing about which they have no knowledge, neither they nor their ancestors. Dreadful is the word that comes out of their mouths. What they utter is merely a lie.

[6] (O Muḥammad), if they do not believe in this Message, you will perhaps torment yourself to death with grief, sorrowing over them. [7] Surely We have made all that is on the earth an embellishment for it in order to test people as to who of them is better in conduct. [8] In the ultimate, We shall reduce all that is on the earth to a barren plain.

[9] Do you think that the people of the Cave and the Inscription¹ were one of Our wondrous signs? [10] When

---

1. The young men who, in order to protect their Faith, had taken refuge in a cave at which an epitaph was later erected.

those youths sought refuge in the Cave and said: "Our Lord! Grant us mercy from Yourself and provide for us rectitude in our affairs."

[11] We lulled them to sleep in that cave for a number of years [12] and then roused them so that We might see which of the two parties could best tell the length of their stay.

[13] We narrate to you their true story. They were a party of young men who had faith in their Lord, and We increased them in guidance[2] [14] and strengthened their hearts when they stood up and proclaimed: "Our Lord is the Lord of the heavens and the earth. We shall call upon no other god beside Him; (for if we did so), we shall be uttering a blasphemy." [15] (Then they conferred among themselves and said): "These men, our own people, have taken others as gods beside Him: why do they not bring any clear evidence that they indeed are gods? Who can be more unjust than he who foists a lie on Allah? [16] And now that you have dissociated yourselves from them and from whatever they worship beside Allah, go and seek refuge in the Cave. Your Lord will extend His mercy to you and will provide for you the means for the disposal of your affairs."

---

2. According to traditions these young men were among the earliest followers of Jesus (peace be on him) and among the subjects of the Roman Empire who at the time were unbelievers and hostile to those who believed in the One True God.

[17] Had you seen[3] them in the Cave it would have appeared to you that when the sun rose, it moved away from their Cave to the right; and when it set, it turned away from them to the left, while they remained in a spacious hollow in the Cave. This is one of the Signs of Allah. Whomsoever Allah guides, he alone is led aright; and whomsoever Allah lets go astray, you will find for him no guardian to direct him. [18] On seeing them you would fancy them to be awake though they were asleep; and We caused them to turn their sides to their right and to their left, and their dog sat stretching out its forelegs on the threshold of the Cave. Had you looked upon them you would have certainly fled away from them, their sight filling you with terror.

[19] Likewise, We roused them in a miraculous way that they might question one another.[4] One of them asked: "How long did you remain (in this state)?" The others said: "We remained so for a day or part of a day." Then they said: "Your Lord knows better how long we remained in this state. Now send one of you to the city with this coin of yours and let him see who has the best food, and let him buy some provisions from there. Let him be cautious and not inform anyone of our whereabouts. [20] For if they should come upon us, they will stone us to death or

---

3. In the course of this narration, mention of the youths' collective decision to take refuge in a cave in this mountainous region such that they might avoid being subjected to lapidation or compelled apostasy has been omitted.

4. The manner in which these youths were roused from their long slumber was no less wondrous than the manner in which they were made to sleep, beyond the reach of the whole world.

force us to revert to their faith whereafter we shall never prosper." [21] Thus did We make their case known to the people of the city[5] so that they might know that Allah's promise is true, and that there is absolutely no doubt that the Hour will come to pass. But instead of giving thought to this, they disputed with one another concerning the People of the Cave, some saying: "Build a wall over them. Their Lord alone knows best about them."[6] But those who

5. When one of those youths went to the city to buy food, a world of change had already taken place. Pagan Rome had long since been Christianized. Perceptible changes were evident in the language, culture, civilization and dress of the people; in sum, almost everything had changed. Similarly, this young man from the cave, who in fact belonged to a period about two centuries earlier, also struck everybody as an oddity since his overall demeanour, his dress, and his language were all antiquated. So, when he presented a coin dating from the time of Decius, the shopkeeper was simply baffled and looked at him with dazed eyes. In the course of investigations it was discovered that the youth was one of the followers of Jesus Christ who had fled some two centuries ago for fear of his faith. This news instantly spread among the Christians of the city. A huge crowd of people, accompanied by government officials, therefore, soon went to the cave. On realizing that they had been awakened from a sleep which had lasted for three* hundred years, the People of the Cave greeted their fellow-Christians, and then lay down to rest and breathed their last.

6. The context indicates that this statement was made by a group of righteous Christians. They were of the opinion that the People of the Cave should be left to lie in the positions in which they were found and that the mouth of the cave should be sealed off by erecting a wall against the side of the cave. In other words, it was not right to go about investigating about them for their Lord knew best who they were, what their status was, and what treatment should rightly be meted out to them.

* The original mentions two hundred years which is an obvious oversight. See verse 25 – Editor's note.

prevailed over their affairs said: "We shall build a place of worship over them."7

[22] Some will say concerning them: "They were three and their dog, the fourth"; and some will say: "They were five, and their dog, the sixth" – all this being merely guesswork; and still others will say: "They were seven, and their dog, the eighth."8 Say: "My Lord knows their number best. Only a few know their correct number. So do not dispute concerning their number, but stick to what is evident, and do not question anyone about them."9 [23] And10 never say about anything: "I shall certainly

7. This happened because by that time common Christians had come under the influence of polytheistic ideas. They now had deities to worship in place of the old idols.

8. This shows that at the time of the revelation of the Qur'ān, approximately three hundred years after the incident, a number of stories were in circulation among the Christians about the People of the Cave. It also shows that no authentic version of the incident was available in all its details. We note, however, that the Qur'ān does not contradict the third statement mentioned here which says that the People of the Cave numbered seven. Hence, there is some basis for believing that their actual number was indeed seven.

9. The purpose of the statement is to emphasize the fact that the number of the People of the Cave is not a matter of much consequence.

10. We believe this to be a parenthetical statement which is thematically linked to the preceding verse. The preceding verse states that God alone knows the exact number of the People of the Cave and that it is pointless to try to ascertain their true number. At this stage, before proceeding to the next point, both the Prophet (peace be on him) and the believers are directed not to make categorical statements as to what they would do on the morrow. For no one knows what they will in fact be able to do.

do this tomorrow" [24] unless Allah should will it. And should you forget (and make such a statement), remember your Lord and say: "I expect my Lord to guide me to what is nearer to rectitude than this." [25] They remained in the Cave for three hundred years; and others added nine more years. [26] Say: "Allah knows best how long they remained in it,[11] for only He knows all that is hidden in the heavens and the earth. How well He sees; how well He hears! The creatures have no other guardian than Him; He allows none to share His authority."

[27] (O Prophet), recite to them from the Book of your Lord what has been revealed to you for none may change His words; (and were you to make any change in His words) you will find no refuge from Him. [28] Keep yourself content with those who call upon their Lord, morning and evening, seeking His pleasure, and do not let your eyes pass beyond them. Do you seek the pomp and glitter of the world? Do not follow him[12] whose heart We have caused to be heedless of Our remembrance, and who follows his desires, and whose attitude is of excess.

[29] And proclaim: "This is the Truth from your Lord. Now let him who will, believe; and let him who will,

---

11. The period of stay of the People of the Cave is variously speculated, as indeed is their number. There is, however, no need to research the matter. God alone knows how long they remained in that state.

12. That is, one ought not to follow a person who is heedless of God, nor submit to him, nor accept his command. Here the word "obedience" means all this, having been used in its widest, most comprehensive sense.

disbelieve. We have prepared a Fire for the wrong-doers whose billowing folds encompass them. If they ask for water, they will be served with a drink like dregs of oil that will scald their faces. How dreadful a drink, and how evil an abode! [30] As for those who believe and do good We shall not cause their reward to be lost. [31] They shall dwell in the Gardens of Eternity, beneath which streams flow. There they will be adorned with bracelets of gold,[13] will be arrayed in green garments of silk and rich brocade, and will recline on raised couches. How excellent is their reward, and how nice their resting-place!"

[32] (O Muḥammad), propound a parable to them. There were two men of whom We bestowed upon one of the two vineyards, surrounding both of them with date-palms and putting a tillage in between. [33] Both the vineyards yielded abundant produce without failure and We caused a stream to flow in their midst [34] so the owner had fruit in abundance and he said to his neighbour, while conversing with him: "I have greater wealth than you and I am stronger than you in numbers." [35] Then he entered his vine-yard and said, wronging himself: "Surely, I do not believe that all this will ever perish.

---

13. In ancient times kings used to wear bracelets of gold. This has been mentioned with regard to the People of Paradise to emphasize that the believers will be clothed in regal attire as a mark of honour. In the Hereafter even those unbelievers who are highly placed in this world, including kings, will be made to suffer humiliation. On the contrary, righteous believers – even if they had occupied humble positions in this world – will be shown the honour usually reserved for kings.

[36] Nor do I believe that the Hour of Resurrection will ever come to pass. And even if I am returned to my Lord, I shall find a better place than this." [37] While conversing with him his neighbour exclaimed: "Do you deny Him Who created you out of dust, then out of a drop of sperm, and then fashioned you into a complete man? [38] As for myself, Allah alone is my Lord, and I associate none with my Lord in His Divinity. [39] When you entered your vineyard, why did you not say: 'Whatever Allah wills shall come to pass, for there is no power save with Allah!'¹⁴ If you find me less than yourself in wealth and children [40] it may well be that my Lord will give me something better than your vineyard, and send a calamity upon your vineyard from the heavens and it will be reduced to a barren waste, [41] or the water of your vineyard will be drained deep into the ground so that you will not be able to seek it out." [42] Eventually all his produce was destroyed and he began to wring his hands in sorrow at the loss of what he had spent on it, and on seeing it fallen down upon its trellises, saying: "Would I had not associated anyone with my Lord in His Divinity." [43] And there was no host, beside Allah, to help him, nor could he be of any help to himself. [44] (Then he knew) that all power of protection rests with Allah, the True One. He is the best to reward, the best to determine the end of things.

[45] (O Prophet), propound to them the parable of the present life: it is like the vegetation of the earth which flourished luxuriantly when it mingled with the water

---

14. Whatever God alone wills comes to pass, for man does not have the power to make things happen according to his wishes. Whatever man does is only by God's aid and support.

that We sent down from the sky, but after that the same vegetation turned into stubble which the winds blew about. Allah alone has the power over all things. [46] Wealth and children are an adornment of the life of the world. But the deeds of lasting righteousness are the best in the sight of your Lord in reward, and far better a source of hope. [47] Bear in mind the Day when We shall set the mountains in motion and you will find the earth void and bare. On that Day We shall muster all men together, leaving none of them behind. [48] They shall be brought before your Lord, all lined up, and shall be told: "Now, indeed, you have come before Us in the manner We created you in the first instance, although you thought that We shall not appoint a tryst (with Us)." [49] And then the Record of their deeds shall be placed before them and you will see the guilty full of fear for what it contains, and will say: "Woe to us! What a Record this is! It leaves nothing, big or small, but encompasses it." They will find their deeds confronting them. Your Lord wrongs no one.

[50] And recall when We said to the angels: "Prostrate yourselves before Adam"; all of them fell prostrate, except *Iblīs*. He was of the *jinn* and so disobeyed the command of his Lord.[15] Will you, then, take him and his progeny as your guardians rather than Me although they are

---

15. This means that Satan did not belong to the species of angels (as sometimes people fancy). Instead, he was a *jinn*. That is why it was possible for him to disobey God's command. The nature of angels is so constituted that they can never disobey God. In contrast to angels, the *jinn* – like human beings – are invested with free-will. They are not *inherently* obedient; instead, they have the freedom to choose between belief and unbelief, between obedience and disobedience.

your open enemies? What an evil substitute are these wrong-doers taking! [51] I did not call them to witness the creation of the heavens and the earth, nor in their own creation. I do not seek the aid of those who lead people astray.[16]

[52] What will such people do on the Day when the Lord will say: "Now call upon all those whom you believed to be My partners?" Thereupon they will call upon them, but they will not respond to their call; and We shall make them a common pit of doom, [53] and the guilty shall behold the Fire and know that they are bound to fall into it, and will find no escape from it.

[54] And surely We have explained matters to people in the Qur'ān in diverse ways, using all manner of parables. But man is exceedingly contentious. [55] What is it that prevented mankind from believing when the guidance came to them, and from asking forgiveness of their Lord, except that they would like to be treated as the nations of yore, or that they would like to see the scourge come upon them face to face?

[56] We raise Messengers only to give good news and to warn. But the unbelievers resort to falsehood in order to rebut the truth with it, and scoff at My revelations and My warnings.

---

16. The verse puts a straight question to man: "What right do the satans have to be obeyed and served by mankind?" For, far from having any share in the creation of the heavens and the earth, they were themselves created by God.

[57] Who is more wicked than the man who, when he is reminded by the revelations of his Lord, turns away from them and forgets (the consequence of) the deeds wrought by his own hands? We have laid veils over their hearts lest they understand the message of the Qur'ān, and We have caused heaviness in their ears. Call them as you may to the Right Path, they will not be ever guided aright.

[58] Your Lord is All-Forgiving, full of mercy. Had He wished to take them to task for their doings, He would have hastened in sending His scourge upon them. But He has set for them a time-limit which they cannot evade.

[59] All the townships afflicted with scourge are before your eyes. When they committed wrong, We destroyed them. For the destruction of each We had set a definite term.

[60] (And recount to them the story of Moses) when Moses said to his servant: "I will journey on until I reach the point where the two rivers meet, though I may march on for ages."[17] [61] But when they reached the point where the two rivers meet, they forgot their fish, and it took its way

---

17. No authentic information is available as to where and when this journey of Moses took place and which were the two rivers on the confluence of which this incident took place. When we reflect over the details of the story we feel that the incident belongs to the period Moses lived in Egypt and the conflict with the Pharaoh was in progress. The two rivers alluded to appear to be the Blue Nile and the White Nile at the convergence of which Khartoum is located. The evidence in support of this assumption has been presented in the course of my exegesis of *Sūrah al-Kahf* 18: 60 in *Towards Understanding the Qur'ān*, ed. and tr. Z. I. Ansari, (Leicester: The Islamic Foundation, 1995], Vol. V, n. 57, pp. 116 ff.

into the sea, as if through a tunnel. [62] When they had journeyed further on, Moses said to his servant: "Bring us our repast. We are surely fatigued by today's journey." [63] The servant said: "Did you see what happened? When we betook ourselves to the rock to take rest, I forgot the fish – and it is only Satan who caused me to forget to mention it to you – so that it made its way into the sea in a strange manner." [64] Moses said: "That is what we were looking for."[18] So the two turned back, retracing their footsteps, [65] and there they found one of Our servants upon whom We had bestowed Our mercy, and to whom We had imparted a special knowledge from Ourselves.[19]

[66] Moses said to him: "May I follow you that you may teach me something of the wisdom which you have been taught?" [67] He answered: "You will surely not be able to bear with me. [68] For how can you patiently bear with something you cannot encompass in your knowledge?" [69] Moses replied: "You shall find me, if Allah wills, patient; and I shall not disobey you in anything." [70] He said: "Well, if you follow me, do not ask me concerning anything until I myself mention it to you."

[71] Then the two went forth until, when they embarked on the boat, he made a hole in it, whereupon Moses exclaimed: "Have you made a hole in it so as to drown

---

18. Moses exclaimed that it was precisely the disappearance of the fish in the sea that was the indicator of the place where he would encounter the person whom he wanted to meet.

19. According to authentic traditions, this person was called Khiḍr.

the people in the boat? You have certainly done an awful thing." [72] He replied: "Did I not tell you that you will not be able to patiently bear with me?" [73] Moses said: "Do not take me to task at my forgetfulness, and do not be hard on me."

[74] Then the two went forth until they met a lad whom he slew, whereupon Moses exclaimed: "What! Have you slain an innocent person without his having slain anyone? Surely you have done a horrible thing." [75] He said: "Did I not tell you that you will not be able to patiently bear with me?" [76] Moses said: "Keep me no more in your company if I question you concerning anything after this. You will then be fully justified."

[77] Then the two went forth until when they came to a town, they asked its people for food, but they refused to play host to them. They found in that town a wall that was on the verge of tumbling down, and he buttressed it, whereupon Moses said: "If you had wished, you could have received payment for it." [78] He said: "This brings me and you to a parting of ways. Now I shall explain to you the true meaning of things about which you could not remain patient. [79] As for the boat it belonged to some poor people who worked on the river, and I desired to damage it for beyond them lay the dominion of a king who was wont to seize every boat by force. [80] As for the lad, his parents were people of faith, and we feared lest he should plague them with transgression and disbelief, [81] and we desired that their Lord should grant them another in his place, a son more upright and more tender-hearted. [82] As for the wall, it belonged to two orphan boys in the city, and under it there was a treasure that

belonged to them. Their father was a righteous man and your Lord intended that they should come of age and then bring forth their treasure as a mercy from your Lord; I did not do this of my own bidding. This is the true meaning of things with which you could not keep your patience."[20]

[83] (O Muḥammad), they ask you about Dhū al-Qarnayn. Say: "I will give you an account of him."

[84] We granted him power in the land and endowed him with all kinds of resources. [85] He set out (westwards) on an expedition, [86] until when he reached the very limits where the sun sets,[21] he saw it setting in dark turbid

---

20. What is clear in this story is that the three acts performed by Khiḍr were in compliance with God's own command. It is also evident that two of his acts were such as are never allowed under any of God's revealed laws: No man is authorized, even on the basis of some inspiration (*ilhām*), to either damage the boat belonging to another person under the plea that it would at some later stage be confiscated by a usurper, or to kill a boy for the reason that he would grow up to be an unbeliever or commit excesses. The conclusion is therefore inescapable that Khiḍr performed these acts not under any Divine law revealed as an imperative for man but in accordance with God's cosmic laws. Divine commands of this nature are carried out through a kind of creature other than man. The very nature of this story shows that God directed Moses to this creature of His – Khiḍr – in order that he might get some idea of the kinds of exigencies that sometimes necessitate things to happen in a manner incomprehensible to man. The fact that God has described Khiḍr as His servant is not sufficient for us to assume that he is a human being. At several places in the Qur'ān, including *Sūrah al-Anbiyā'* 21: 26 and *Sūrah al-Zukhruf* 43: 19 the word "servant" has been used for angels.

21. That is, to the extreme limits of land in the west.

waters;[22] and nearby he met a people. We said: "O Dhū al-Qarnayn, you have the power to punish or to treat them with kindness." [87] He said: "We will chastise him who does wrong, whereafter he will be returned to his Lord and He will chastise him grievously. [88] But as for him who believes and acts righteously, his will be a goodly reward and we shall enjoin upon him only mild commands."

[89] Then he set out on another expedition [90] until he reached the limit where the sun rises[23] and he found it rising on a people whom We had provided no shelter from it. [91] Thus was the state of those people, and We encompassed in knowledge all concerning Dhū al-Qarnayn.

[92] Then he set out on another expedition [93] until when he reached a place between the two mountains, he found beside the mountains a people who scarcely understood anything. [94] They said: "O Dhū al-Qarnayn, Gog and Magog[24] are spreading corruption in this land. So shall

---

22. That is, at sunset it appeared that the sun was setting in the blackish muddy water of the sea.

23. That is, to the extreme limits of land in the east.

24. Gog and Magog were the wild peoples who inhabited the north-eastern region of Asia. From time to time they carried out predatory raids against civilized lands, pouring over both Asia and Europe like tidal waves. The *Book of Ezekiel* states that their land was comprised of Meshech (presently Moscow) and Tubal (presently Tubalsek). The Jewish historian, Josephus, identifies them with the Scythians who inhabited the area lying north and east of the Black Sea. According to Jerome, the Magog lived to the north of Caucasia, near the Caspian Sea.

we pay you taxes on the understanding that you will set up a barrier between us and them?" [95] He answered: "Whatever my Lord has granted me is good enough. But help me with your labour and I will erect a rampart between you and them. [96] Bring me ingots of iron." Then after he had filled up the space between the two mountain-sides, he said: "(Light a fire) and ply bellows." When he had made it (red like) fire, he said: "Bring me molten copper which I may pour on it." [97] Such was the rampart that Gog and Magog could not scale, nor could they pierce it. [98] Dhū al-Qarnayn said: "This is a mercy from my Lord: but when the time of my Lord's promise shall come, He will level the rampart with the ground. My Lord's promise always comes true."

[99] And on that Day[25] We shall let some of them surge like waves against others, and the Trumpet shall be blown. Then We shall gather them all together. [100] That will be the Day We shall place Hell before the unbelievers [101] whose eyes had become blind against My admonition and who were utterly disinclined to hear it.

[102] Do the unbelievers, then, believe that they can take any of My creatures as their guardians beside Me? Verily We have prepared Hell to welcome the unbelievers.

[103] Say, (O Muḥammad): "Shall We tell you who will be the greatest losers in respect of their works? [104] It will

---

25. "On that Day" refers to the Day of Resurrection. Dhū al-Qarnayn had alluded to the Day of Resurrection as a day that is bound to come about because God had so decided. What is being said here is in that context and is an addition to the statement made by Dhū al-Qarnayn (see verse 98 above).

be those whose effort went astray in the life of the world
and who believe nevertheless that they are doing good.
[105] Those are the ones who refused to believe in the
revelations of their Lord and that they are bound to meet
Him. Hence, all their deeds have come to naught, and We
shall assign no weight to them on the Day of Resurrection.
[106] Hell is their recompense for disbelieving and their
taking My revelations and My Messengers as objects of
jest. [107] As for those who believe and do good works,
the Gardens of Paradise shall be there to welcome them;
[108] there they will abide for ever, with no desire to be
removed from there."

[109] Say: "If the sea were to become ink to record the
Words of my Lord, indeed the sea would be all used up
before the Words of my Lord are exhausted, and it would
be the same even if We were to bring an equal amount
of ink."[26]

[110] Say (O Muḥammad): "I am no more than a human
being like you; one to whom revelation is made: 'Your
Lord is the One and Only God.' Hence, whoever looks
forward to meet his Lord, let him do righteous works, and
let him associate none with the worship of his Lord."

---

26. The term *kalimāt* ("Words") here signifies God's marvellous
acts, and the excellent and wondrous manifestations of His power
and wisdom.

19

Maryam [Mary]
Makkan Period

*In the name of Allah, the Most Merciful,
the Most Compassionate*

[1] *Kāf. Hā'. Yā'. 'Ayn. Ṣād.* [2] This is an account of the mercy of your Lord to His servant Zechariah [3] when he cried to his Lord in secret.

[4] He said: "Lord! My bones have grown feeble and my head is glistening with age; yet, never have my prayers to You, my Lord, been unfruitful. [5] I fear evil from my kinsmen after I am gone; and my wife is barren, so grant me an heir out of Your special grace, [6] one that might be my heir and the heir of the house of Jacob; and make him, Lord, one that will be pleasing to You. [7] (He was told): "Zechariah, We bring you the good news of the birth of a son whose name shall be Yaḥyā (John), one whose namesake We never created before." [8] He said: "My Lord! How can I have a boy when my wife is barren and I have reached an extremely old age?" [9] He answered: "So shall it be."¹ Your Lord says: "It is easy for Me," and then added: "For beyond doubt, I created you earlier when you were nothing." [10] Zechariah said: "Lord, grant me

---

1. The angel tells Zechariah that notwithstanding his old age and his wife's barrenness he will be blessed with a son.

a Sign." Said He: "Your Sign is that you shall not be able to speak to people for three nights, though you will be otherwise sound." [11] Thereupon Zechariah came out from the sanctuary and directed his people by gestures to extol His glory by day and by night.

[12] "O John! Hold the Book with all your strength."[2] We had bestowed wisdom[3] upon him while he was still a child; [13] and We also endowed him with tenderness and purity, and he was exceedingly pious [14] and cherishing to his parents. Never was he insolent or rebellious. [15] Peace be upon him the day he was born, and the day he will die, and the day he will be raised up alive.

[16] (O Muḥammad), recite in the Book the account of Mary, when she withdrew from her people to a place towards the east;[4] [17] and drew a curtain, screening herself from people[5] whereupon We sent to her Our spirit and he appeared to her as a well-shaped man. [18] Mary exclaimed: "I surely take refuge from you with the Most Compassionate Lord, if you are at all God-fearing."

---

2. The Qur'ānic narrative does not mention certain details of John's story – his birth under God's special command, and his attainment of youth.

3. The word *ḥukm* connotes the power of making the right decision, the ability to apply the principles of faith to changing circumstances, and the capacity to comprehend the teachings of the faith both in letter and spirit. It also connotes the ability to arrive at correct judgements and to have the authority from God to judge things.

4. That is, in the eastern part of Bayt al-Maqdis (Jerusalem).

5. That is, she went into seclusion for the purpose of religious devotion.

[19] He said: "I am just a message-bearer of your Lord, I have come to grant you a most pure boy." [20] Mary said: "How can a boy be born to me when no man has even touched me, nor have I ever been unchaste?" [21] The angel said: "Thus shall it be.[6] Your Lord says: 'It is easy for Me; and We shall do so in order to make him a Sign[7] for mankind and a mercy from Us. This has been decreed.' "

[22] Then she conceived him and withdrew with him to a far-off place. [23] Then the birth pangs drove her to the trunk of a palm-tree and she said: "Oh, would that I had died before this and had been all forgotten."[8] [24] Thereupon the angel below her cried out: "Grieve not, for your Lord has caused a stream of water to flow beneath you. [25] Shake the trunk of the palm-tree towards yourself and fresh and ripe dates shall fall upon you. [26] So eat and drink and cool your eyes; and if you see any person say to him: 'Verily I have vowed a fast to the Most Compassionate Lord, and so I shall not speak to anyone today.' "

[27] Then she came to her people, carrying her baby. They said: "O Mary! You have committed a monstrous thing.

---

6. That is, you will bear a son though no man has touched you.

7. That is, we want this child to be a living miracle.

8. If one remembers the gravity of the situation, it is easy to grasp that she did not utter these words because of intense labour pains. Rather, what tormented her was the awkward situation in which she found herself, and she did not know how she was going to come out of it. That is why she left her mother and other family members during pregnancy to live alone at a distant location.

[28] O sister of Aaron!⁹ Your father was not an evil man, nor was your mother an unchaste woman." [29] Thereupon Mary pointed to the child. They exclaimed: "How can we speak to one who is in the cradle, a mere child?" [30] The child cried out: "Verily I am Allah's servant.¹⁰ He has granted me the Book and has made me a Prophet [31] and has blessed me wherever I might be and has enjoined upon me Prayer and *Zakāh* (purifying alms) as long as I live; [32] and has made me dutiful to my mother.¹¹ He has not made me oppressive, nor bereft of God's blessings. [33] Peace be upon me the day I was born and the day I will die, and the day I will be raised up alive."¹²

---

9. In accordance with Arabic idiom, it may be taken to mean that she was a member of Aaron's house. For according to the known Arabic linguistic tradition, a person is referred to as the brother of the tribe to which he belongs. What enraged the public was that the apparently scandalous incident involved a girl who belonged to the most highly pious Israelite family – the house of Aaron.

10. This was the Sign referred to in verse 21 above. The new-born baby began to speak while yet in the cradle which made it manifest that he was not the result of any sin but a miracle wrought by God. *Sūrah Āl 'Imrān* 3: 46 and *Sūrah al-Mā'idah* 5: 110 also mention Jesus as uttering these words as a new-born baby in his cradle.

11. It is significant here that Jesus is not mentioned as one who is dutiful to his parents, but rather as one who is only dutiful to his mother. This itself suggests that he did not have a father. An evidence which further corroborates this is that Jesus is invariably referred to in the Qur'ān as "Jesus, son of Mary".

12. The "Sign" referred to above (see verse 21 above) is the person of the Prophet Jesus (peace be on him) who was presented as a miracle before the Israelites. Thereafter, when that same child had attained maturity and claimed to be a Prophet, those people not only refused to recognize him as a Prophet but turned into his sworn enemies

[34] This is Jesus, the son of Mary; and this is the truth about him concerning which they are in doubt. [35] It does not befit Allah to take for Himself a son. Glory be to Him! When He decrees a thing He only says: "Be" and it is.[13]

[36] (Jesus had said): "Indeed Allah is my Lord and your Lord, so serve Him alone. This is the Straight Way." [37] But different parties began to dispute with one another. A dreadful woe awaits on that great Day for those that reject the Truth. [38] How well shall they hear and how well shall they see on the Day they come to Us! But today the evil-doers are in manifest error. [39] (O Muḥammad), warn those who are steeped in heedlessness and are obstinately rejecting the truth that the Day shall come when things will be finally decided and they shall be left with utter remorse. [40] Ultimately, We shall inherit the earth and whatever is on it; to Us shall they be returned.

[41] (O Muḥammad), recite in the Book the account of Abraham. Most surely he was a man of truth, a Prophet. [42] (And remind people) when he said to his father: "Father! Why do you worship that which neither sees nor hears, and which can be of no avail to you? [43] Father, a knowledge that has not reached you has come to me. So follow me that I may guide you to a Straight Way. [44] Father, do not serve Satan, for Satan has indeed

---

and did not hesitate to accuse his venerable mother of adultery. Then God inflicted upon them a punishment more severe than that suffered by any other people.

13. This is yet another argument to show that the Christian belief in Jesus being God's son is false. A miraculous birth by itself is no reason for the child to be considered God's son.

been a persistent rebel against the Most Compassionate Lord. [45] Father, I fear that a punishment from the Most Compassionate Lord might strike you and you may end up as one of Satan's companions?" [46] The father said: "Abraham, have you turned away from my gods? If you do not give this up, I shall stone you to death. Now begone from me forever." [47] Abraham answered: "Peace be upon you. I shall seek pardon for you from my Lord. My Lord has always been kind to Me. [48] I shall withdraw from you and all that you call upon beside Allah. I shall only call upon my Lord. I trust the prayer to my Lord will not go unanswered." [49] Thereupon Abraham dissociated himself from his people and the deities they worshipped instead of Allah, and We bestowed upon him Isaac and Jacob and made each of them a Prophet; [50] and We bestowed on them Our mercy, and granted them a truly lofty renown.

[51] And recite in the Book the account of Moses. He was a chosen one, a Messenger, a Prophet.[14] [52] We called out

---

14. The word *rasūl* literally means "the one sent". Lexicographers disagree as to the exact meaning of the word *nabī*. Some consider it to mean someone who brings news. Others consider it to denote height and elevation. In sum, when someone is called *rasūl* and *nabī* it either means a "Messenger of high standing," or a "Messenger who brings news from God". So far as the two words – *nabī* and *rasūl* – are concerned, they are generally used in the Qur'ān as equivalents. There are, however, also instances where the two words are employed in such manner as distinguishes between a Prophet and a Messenger in respect of their status or the nature of their mission. For instance, in *Sūrah al-Ḥajj* it is said: "Never did We send a Messenger or a Prophet before you except …" (*al-Ḥajj* 22: 52). This clearly indicates that the Messenger and the Prophet represent two distinct entities. As a result, commentators on the Qur'ān have

to him from the right side of the Mount, and We drew him near to Us by communing to him in secret, [53] and out of Our mercy We appointed his brother Aaron, a Prophet (that he may assist him).

[54] And recite in the Book the account of Ishmael. He was ever true to his promise, and was a Messenger, a Prophet. [55] He enjoined his household to observe Prayer and to give *Zakāh* (purifying alms); and his Lord was well pleased with him.

[56] And recite in the Book the account of Idrīs. He was a man of truth, a Prophet; [57] and We exalted him to a lofty position.

[58] These are the Prophets upon whom Allah bestowed His favour from the seed of Adam, and from the seed of those whom We carried (in the Ark) with Noah, and from the seed of Abraham and Israel. They were those whom We guided and chose (for an exalted position). They were such that when the words of the Most Compassionate

---

engaged in serious discussions about the nature of these differences between a Prophet and a Messenger. The fact, however, remains that these scholars have failed to persuasively establish the precise nature of any difference between a Messenger and a Prophet. All that can be said with certainty is that while every Messenger is a Prophet, every Prophet does not enjoy the status of a Messenger. In other words, the word *rasūl* ("Messenger") is used for those great figures who had been assigned duties of greater significance than those assigned to mere Prophets. This point is further corroborated by a tradition. According to this tradition, Muḥammad (peace be on him) was asked about the number of Messengers. He replied that they were 313 or 315 in number, whereas when asked about the number of Prophets, he mentioned their number to be 124,000.

Lord were recited to them, they fell down in prostration, weeping.

[59] They were succeeded by a people who neglected the Prayers and pursued their lusts. They shall presently meet with their doom, [60] except those who repent and believe and act righteously. Such shall enter Paradise and shall not be wronged at all. [61] Theirs shall be everlasting Gardens which the Most Compassionate Lord has promised His servants in a realm which is beyond the ken of perception. Surely His promise shall be fulfilled. [62] They shall not hear in it anything vain; they shall hear only what is good; and they shall have their provision in it, morning and evening. [63] Such is the Paradise which We shall cause those of Our servants who have been God-fearing to inherit.

[64] (The angels will say): "(O Muḥammad!) We descend not except by the command of your Lord.¹⁵ To Him belongs all that is before us and all that is behind us, and all that is inbetween. Your Lord is not forgetful in the least. [65] He is the Lord of the heavens and the earth and all that is in between. Serve Him, then, and be constant in serving Him. Do you know anyone that might be His compeer?"

[66] Man is prone to say: "Shall I be raised to life after I die?" [67] Does man not remember that We created him

---

15. The speakers here are the angels though what they say is the word of God. The angels tell the Prophet (peace be on him) that they descend not by their own will but by the command of God whenever He pleases.

before when he was nothing? [68] By your Lord, We will surely muster them and the devils together. Then We will surely bring them all, on their knees, around Hell, [69] and then We will draw aside from each party those who were most rebellious against the Most Compassionate Lord, [70] and then We shall know well all those most worthy to be cast in Hell. [71] There is not one of you but shall pass by Hell. This is a decree which your Lord will fulfil. [72] Then We shall deliver those that feared Allah and leave the wrong-doers there on their knees.

[73] When Our clear revelations are recited to those who deny the Truth they are wont to say to those who have faith: "Which of the two groups has a better status and whose assemblies are grander?"[16] [74] How numerous are the peoples We destroyed before them – those that were more resourceful and grander in outward appearance! [75] Say: "The Most Compassionate Lord grants respite to those who stray into error, until they behold what they had been threatened with, either God's chastisement (in the world) or the Hour (of Resurrection)" – then they fully know whose station is worse, and who is weaker in hosts! [76] (On the contrary), Allah increases in guidance those

---

16. This was a fallacious argument which the unbelievers often put forward, claiming that it was they rather than the believers upon whom God's bounties were lavished. They would audaciously ask: "Who has more stately houses to live in – the believers or us? Who enjoy higher standards of living – the believers or us? Whose assemblies are more splendid and grandiose – the believers' or ours?" How is it then possible, they would ask, that those who suffered such a miserable lot are the followers of the truth whilst those who prosper are the followers of falsehood?

who follow the Right Way. Lasting acts of righteousness are better in the sight of your Lord as reward and conducive to a better end.

[77] Have you seen him who rejected Our signs and said: "Surely I shall continue to be favoured with riches and children." [78] Has he obtained knowledge of the Unseen, or has he taken a covenant with the Most Compassionate Lord? [79] By no means! We shall write down all what he says; and We shall greatly prolong his chastisement, [80] and We shall inherit all the resources and hosts of which he boasts, and he will come to Us all alone.

[81] They have taken other gods instead of Allah that they may be a source of strength for them. [82] By no means! They shall soon deny their worship and shall become their adversaries instead.

[83] Do you not see that We have sent devils upon the unbelievers who greatly incite them (to oppose the Truth)? [84] Therefore, do not hasten (in seeking a scourge against them). We are counting their days. [85] The Day shall soon come when We shall bring together the God-fearing to the Most Compassionate Lord, as honoured guests; [86] and We shall drive the guilty ones to Hell as a thirsty herd. [87] On that Day none will have the power to intercede for them except those who received a sanction from the Most Compassionate Lord.

[88] They claim: "The Most Compassionate Lord has taken a son to Himself." [89] Surely you have made a monstrous statement. [90] It is such a monstrosity that heavens might well-nigh burst forth at it, the earth might

be cleaved, and the mountains fall [91] at their ascribing a son to the Most Compassionate Lord. [92] It does not befit the Most Compassionate Lord that He should take a son. [93] There is no one in the heavens and the earth but he shall come to the Most Compassionate Lord as His servant. [94] Verily He encompasses them and has counted them all. [95] On the Day of Resurrection each one of these will come to Him singly.

[96] Indeed, the Most Compassionate Lord will soon create enduring love for those who believe and do righteous works.[17] [97] Therefore, We have revealed the Qur'ān in your tongue and made it easy to understand that you may give glad tidings to the God-fearing and warn a contentious people. [98] How numerous are the peoples that We destroyed before them! Do you now perceive any one of them, or hear even their whisper?

---

17. The believers throughout Makkah were at that time subjected to the most abject humiliation. Here they are being told that that situation will not endure. Soon they will become God's favourites, the heroes of all mankind, on account of their moral excellence. People will involuntarily be attracted to them. They will simply adore them, bowing to them in respect. As for their opponents, they are doomed to ignominy. A leadership which rests on sin and transgression, on arrogance and trickery, can never win the hearts of people; the most that it can do is to force them into outward obedience. Conversely, those who invite people to the right way and are themselves invested with honesty, veracity, sincerity and good morals, are bound to win over the hearts of all concerned in the end even if they might provoke some revulsion at the outset. It is simply impossible for those who lack honesty and sincerity to impede their path for long.

20
🙶🙶🙶

Ṭā' Hā'
Makkan Period

In the name of Allah, the Most Merciful,
the Most Compassionate

[1] *Ṭā' Hā'* [2] We did not reveal the Qur'ān to you to cause you distress; [3] it is only a reminder for him who fears Allah;¹ [4] a revelation from Him Who created the earth and the high heavens. [5] The Most Compassionate Lord is settled on the Throne (of the Universe). [6] To Him belongs all that is in the heavens and all that is in the earth, and all that is in between, and all that is beneath the soil. [7] Whether you speak out aloud (or in a low voice), He knows what is said secretly, and even that which is most hidden. [8] Allah – there is no god but He. His are the most excellent names.

---

1. God did not reveal the Qur'ān in order that the Prophet (peace be on him) might suffer by trying to accomplish something that was impossible to achieve. The Prophet (peace be on him) was not required to make those who had consciously decided not to accept the Truth believe in it. Nor was he required to imbue faith in people whose hearts had been sealed against the acceptance of that faith. The Qur'ān was revealed simply as a reminder and as an admonition so that those who feared God might take heed.

[9] Has the story of Moses reached you? [10] When he saw a fire² and said to his family: "Hold on! I have just perceived a fire; perhaps I will bring a brand from it for you, or I will find some guidance at the fire about the way to follow."³

[11] When he came to it, a voice called out: "Moses! [12] Verily I am your Lord! Take off your shoes. You are in the sacred valley, Ṭuwā! [13] I Myself have chosen you; therefore, give ear to what is revealed. [14] Verily I am Allah. There is no god beside Me. So serve Me and establish Prayers to remember Me. [15] The Hour of Resurrection is coming. I have willed to keep the time of its coming hidden so that everyone may be recompensed in accordance with his effort. [16] Let him who does not believe in it and follows his lust not turn your thought away from it, lest you are ruined. [17] And what is in your right hand, O Moses?" [18] Moses answered: "This is my staff. I lean on it (when I walk), and with it I beat down leaves for my flock, and I have many other uses for it." [19] He said: "Moses, throw it down."

---

2. This happened when the Prophet Moses (peace be on him), after his years of exile in Midian, was on his way back to Egypt accompanied by his wife whom he had married there.

3. It appears that this occurred at night in winter. Moses (peace be on him) was crossing the southern part of the Sinaitic peninsula when he saw a fire at some distance. He decided to venture over to the place where he saw the fire in the hope that he would either be able to obtain some fire that would keep his family warm during the night, or at least gain directions for the journey ahead. Ironically, he went to that spot expecting to find something ordinary and commonplace – the way to his destination in this world, only to find a way that was far more valuable – the way of success and felicity in the Hereafter.

[20] So he threw it down, and lo! it was a rapidly moving snake. [21] Then He said: "Seize it and have no fear. We shall restore it to its former state. [22] And place your hand in your armpit, it will come forth shining white,[4] without blemish. This is another Sign of Allah, [23] for We shall show you some of Our greatest Signs. [24] And go to Pharaoh now for he has transgressed all bounds." [25] Moses said: "Lord! Open my breast for me; [26] and ease my task for me, [27] and loosen the knot from my tongue [28] so that they may understand my speech; [29] and appoint for me, from my household, someone who will help me bear my burden – [30] Aaron, my brother. [31] Strengthen me through him [32] and let him share my task [33] that we may abundantly extol Your glory; [34] and may remember You much. [35] Verily, You have always watched over us." [36] He said: "Moses, your petition is granted. [37] We have again bestowed Our favour upon you. [38] Recall, when We indicated to your mother through inspiration: [39] 'Put the baby into a chest and then throw him in the river. The river will throw him up on the shore, and then an enemy of Mine and an enemy of his will take him.' And I spread My love over you in order that you might be reared in My sight. [40] Recall, when your sister went along, saying: 'Shall I direct you to one who will take charge of him?'[5] Thus We brought you

---

4. Although Moses' hand would become as bright as the sun, this would happen without causing him any harm.

5. That is, she was walking along the river bank keeping an eye on the chest. Then, when the people from the House of Pharaoh picked up the child and looked for a nurse for it, she went up and told them this.

back to your mother so that her heart might be gladdened and she might not grieve. Moses, recall when you slew a person. We delivered you from distress and made you go through several trials. Then you stayed for several years among the people of Midian, and now you have come at the right moment as ordained. [41] I have chosen you for My service. [42] So go forth, both you and your brother, with My Signs, and do not slacken in remembering Me. [43] Go both of you to Pharaoh, for he has transgressed all bounds, [44] and speak to him gently, perhaps he may take heed or fear (Allah)."

[45] The two said:[6] "Lord! We fear he may commit excesses against us, or transgress all bounds." [46] He said: "Have no fear. I am with you, hearing and seeing all. [47] So, go to him, and say: 'Behold, both of us are the Messengers of your Lord. Let the Children of Israel go with us, and do not chastise them. We have come to you with a sign from your Lord; and peace shall be for him who follows the true guidance. [48] It has been revealed to us that chastisement awaits those who called the lie to the truth and turned away from it.' "

[49] Pharaoh said:[7] "Moses! Who is the Lord of the two of you?" [50] He said: "Our Lord is He Who gave everything

---

6. It would appear that this incident relates to the time when Moses had already reached Egypt and when Aaron had begun to assist him in his mission. Presumably before proceeding to Pharaoh, both Moses and Aaron had made known to God their fears about the evil that might befall them.

7. The story resumes from the time the two brothers reach Pharaoh's court.

its form and then guided it."[8] [51] Pharaoh asked: "Then, what is the state of the former generations?"[9] [52] Moses said: "Its knowledge is with my Lord, recorded in the Book. My Lord does not err, nor does He forget."[10] [53] He[11] it is Who spread the earth for you; and made in

---

8. All that exists in the world, whatever its shape, is the creation of God alone. Now God did not simply create each thing on a certain pattern and leave it at that; rather, He taught each created being how it should function and fulfil the purpose for which it had been created. It is God Who gave sight to the eyes and hearing power to the ears and Who taught the fish to swim and the birds to fly. In sum, He not only created but also provided guidance to everything in the universe as to how it should function.

9. Pharaoh here points out that if it is God, as Moses claims, Who has created everything to perfection and Who guides it to perform its assigned role, and if there really is no Lord other than God, then this also clearly means that the ancestors of yore who had worshipped deities other than God were in error. Were they really in error and deserved God's punishment? Were they all – their venerable ancestors – dumb, stupid people?

10. Pharaoh's intent was probably to arouse the prejudice and hostility of his audience against Moses, and through them, the prejudice and hostility of the people at large. Instead, Moses replied with the utmost wisdom, saying something which was at once true but which also frustrated Pharaoh's evil designs. He pointed out that howsoever their ancestors might have behaved, they had completed their terms of life and returned to God. The record of all their acts during their lives was with God Who knew well all that they did and Who was also well aware of the motives behind those acts. It was for God, and God alone, to judge them. Indeed He alone has the requisite knowledge to do so.

11. It would appear that Moses' response concludes with the end of verse 52. The passage which follows, i.e. from verse 53 to verse 55, consists of an admonition.

it paths for you, and sent down water from the sky, and then through it We brought forth many species of diverse plants. [54] So eat yourself and pasture your cattle. Surely there are many Signs in this for people of understanding. [55] From this very earth We created you and to the same earth We shall cause you to return, and from it We shall bring you forth to life again.

[56] Indeed We showed Pharaoh Our Signs, all of them, but he declared them to be false and rejected them. [57] He said: "Have you come to us to drive us out of our land by your sorcery? [58] We shall confront you with a sorcery like your own. So appoint a day when both of us might meet face to face in an open space; an appointment which neither we nor you shall fail to keep." [59] Moses said: "The appointment to meet you is on the Day of the Feast and let all people come together before noon."[12] [60] Pharaoh went back and concerted all his stratagem and returned for the encounter. [61] (At the time of the encounter) Moses said to them: "Woe to you!

---

12. Pharaoh commanded his magicians to perform their wondrous feats, turning rods and ropes into serpents and the like. He fully believed that once such feats had been performed, Moses' miracles would lose all their effect. So when Pharaoh himself suggested an encounter between Moses and the magicians, Moses was able to seize this opportunity to demonstrate the difference between sorcery and miracle. Hence Moses readily agreed, further adding that instead of fixing a special time and place for that purpose, the national festival that was about to take place be availed since it would attract people from all over the country. Moses preferred the encounter to take place in front of all those who were expected to attend the festival, and during broad daylight, so that there would remain no ambiguity concerning the question in dispute.

Do not invent falsehoods against Allah[13] lest He destroy you with a scourge. Surely those who invent lies shall come to grief."

[62] Thereupon they wrangled among themselves about the matter and conferred in secret.[14] [63] Some of them said: "These two are magicians, who want to drive you out of your land with their magic and to destroy your excellent way of life. [64] So muster all your stratagem and come forth in a row. Whoever prevails today shall triumph."

[65] The magicians said: "Moses, will you throw down or shall we be the first to throw?" [66] Moses replied: "No, let it be you to throw first." Then suddenly it appeared to Moses, owing to their magic, as if their ropes and staffs

---

13. The people concerned were asked not to fabricate a lie against God, to refrain from calling Moses' miracle a feat of magic, and from calling a true Messenger of God a magician, one given to lying.

14. This shows that they had begun to feel weakened from within. They realized that what Moses had performed was not magic. Hence, they faced Moses in the encounter with considerable trepidation and reluctance, and when the encounter began, their resolve simply dissipated. They probably disagreed among themselves about whether the encounter should take place on the occasion of the great national festival, which would be attended by a large number of people from all parts of the land, and which would also take place in broad daylight enabling all to witness it. Some people in Pharaoh's rank seem to have been opposed to the idea, thinking that if they suffered a public defeat and people became aware of the difference between miracles and magic, then it would be extremely difficult to avoid a crushing defeat.

were running. [67] So Moses' heart was filled with fear.[15]
[68] We said to him: "Have no fear; for it is you who will
prevail. [69] And throw down what is in your right hand;
it will swallow up all that they have wrought. They have
wrought only a magician's stratagem. A magician cannot
come to any good, come whence he may." [70] Eventually
the magicians were impelled to fall down prostrate[16]
and said: "We believe in the Lord of Moses and Aaron."
[71] Pharaoh said: "What! Did you believe in Him even
before I permitted you to do so? Surely, he must be your
chief who taught you magic. Now I will certainly cut

---

15. It would appear that no sooner had Moses (peace be on him)
said: "throw" than the magicians instantly threw their rods and
ropes towards him, momentarily making Moses feel as if hundreds
of serpents were speeding towards him. There is nothing strange
about the fact that such a spectacle would have momentarily
stunned Moses. For a human being remains a human being even
if he is a Prophet. It is worth noting that the Qur'ān here indicates
that even Prophets are vulnerable to magical effects just like any
other human being. Magicians do not have the power to deprive
a Messenger of God of his Messengership. But it is nevertheless
possible that magic might temporarily have some effect on the
human powers of a Messenger. This refutes the position of those
who, when they come across the traditions which mention that
the Prophet Muḥammad (peace be on him) was affected by magic,
find the idea of a Messenger of God being affected by magic so
outrageous that they not only reject the particular *ḥadīth* in question,
but also go so far as to deny the authenticity of the whole corpus
of *Ḥadīth*.

16. When Pharaoh's magicians observed the miraculous impact
of Moses' rod, they were readily convinced that it was a genuine
miracle, and had nothing to do with magic. Instantly and
involuntarily, they fell down in prostration, as if someone had
forcibly thrown them to the ground.

off your hands and your feet on opposite sides, and will
crucify you on the trunks of palm-trees, and then you will
come to know which of us can inflict sterner and more
lasting torment." [72] The magicians answered: "By Him
Who has created us, we shall never prefer you to the
Truth after manifest Signs have come to us. So decree
whatever you will. Your decree will pertain, at the most,
to the present life of the world. [73] We believe in our Lord
that He may forgive us our sins and also forgive us the
practice of magic to which you had compelled us. Allah is
the Best and He alone will abide." [74] The truth is that[17]
Hell awaits him who comes to his Lord laden with sin;
he shall neither die in it nor live. [75] But he who comes
to Him with faith and righteous works shall be exalted
to high ranks, [76] and shall live for ever in everlasting
Gardens beneath which rivers flow. Such will be the
reward of those who purify themselves.

[77] Most certainly We revealed[18] to Moses: "Proceed with
My servants in the night and strike for them a dry path
in the sea. Have no fear of being overtaken, nor be afraid
of treading through the sea."

[78] Pharaoh pursued them with his hosts, but they were
fully overwhelmed by the sea. [79] Pharaoh led his people
astray; he did not guide them aright.

---

17. This remark is from God and supplements the magicians'
statement. The style of the sentence makes it quite evident that it
could not have been made by the magicians.

18. After describing this encounter between Moses and the magicians,
detailed information of the incidents which occurred during the
Israelites' long stay in Egypt are omitted. The story resumes from the
time Moses was commanded by God to take the Israelites out of Egypt.

[80] Children of Israel![19] We saved you from your enemy and made a covenant with you on the right side of the Mount and sent down on you manna and quails, [81] saying: "Partake of the good things that We have provided for you, but do not transgress lest My wrath fall upon you; for he upon whom My wrath falls is ruined. [82] But I am indeed Most Forgiving to him who repents and believes and does righteous works and keeps to the Right Way."

[83] "But, O Moses, what has made you come in haste from your people?"[20] [84] He said: "They are close behind me, and I hastened to You, Lord, that You may be pleased with me."

[85] Said He: "Verily We tested your people in your absence and the Sāmirī led them astray."[21]

[86] Moses returned to his people full of wrath and grief, and said: "My people! Has your Lord not made good an excellent promise He made to you?[22] And has a long

---

19. Here, details of how the Israelites crossed the sea and arrived at the foot of Mount Sinai are omitted. These details are, however, mentioned in *al-A'rāf* 7: 136–47.

20. It appears from this sentence that Moses' eagerness for an encounter with God meant that he went ahead of his people. Before the caravan of people could reach the right side of Mount Sinai, Moses had already left on his solo journey and stood in God's presence.

21. That is, the Sāmirī made a golden calf and set it up as an object of worship for the people.

22. The Israelites had received all the bounties promised to them by their Lord. In other words, God enabled them to leave Egypt in safety. He also liberated them from bondage; He annihilated their enemies

time passed since those promises were fulfilled? Or was it to incur the wrath of your Lord that you broke your promise with me?" [87] They answered: "We did not break our promise with you out of our own volition; but we were laden with the load of people's ornaments, and we simply threw them down[23] (into the fire), and the Sāmirī[24] also threw down something, [88] and brought out of there (from the molten gold) the effigy of a calf that lowed." The people cried out: "This is your deity and the deity of Moses, whom Moses has forgotten." [89] Did they not see that it did not return a word to them, and had no power either to hurt them or to cause them any benefit? [90] Certainly Aaron had said to them even before (the return of Moses): "My people, you were fallen into error because of the calf. Surely your Lord is Most Compassionate; so follow me and obey my command." [91] But they answered: "By no means shall we cease to worship it until Moses returns to us."

---

and provided them with food and shelter when they were in the desert and when they occupied the mountainous region. Had these promises not been fulfilled? God had promised to grant them law and Guidance. Did this not amount to promising them a mighty good?

23. This was the excuse offered by those who had been lured by the Sāmirī. Their contention was that they had simply thrown away their jewellery without intending to make a calf from the same that they would then worship. Nor had they any idea what people intended to do with their jewellery. Whatever happened after that was such that they were involuntarily pushed towards polytheism.

24. If one reads carefully the words: "… and we threw them down" (verses 87-91) one will appreciate that at this point the statement of the Israelites comes to an end. Whatever details follow are from God rather than from the Israelites.

[92] (After rebuking his people) Moses turned to Aaron and said: "Aaron! What prevented you, when you saw them going astray, [93] from following my way? Have you disobeyed my command?"[25] [94] Aaron answered: "Son of my mother! Do not seize me with my beard, nor by (the hair of) my head. I feared that on returning you might say: 'You sowed discord among the Children of Israel, and did not pay heed to my words.'"[26] [95] Moses said: "What,

---

25. "Command" here refers to Moses' directive to Aaron when he delegated the leadership of the Israelites to Aaron in his absence as he headed to the Mount. According to the Qur'ān: "And Moses said to Aaron his brother: 'Take my place among my people, act righteously, and do not follow the path of those who create mischief' " (*al-A'rāf* 7: 142).

26. Aaron's reply does not mean that the maintenance of unity in the ranks of the people was of greater importance than their adherence to the Truth. Nor that unity, even if it had been brought about by common acceptance of polytheism, is preferable to national disunity even if it is caused by distinguishing between Truth and falsehood. If anyone interprets this verse in this sense, it would be nothing short of distorting the Qur'ānic message. For a better understanding of the point made by Aaron the following verse should be read in conjunction with it: "My mother's son, the people overpowered me and almost killed me. So let not my enemies gloat over me, and do not number me among the wrong-doing folk" (*al-A'rāf* 7: 150). On reading both the verses together, the picture that emerges is that Aaron tried his best to prevent his people from falling into calf-worship, but they reacted with great hostility towards him and were even intent on killing him. Fearing that civil strife might break out before Moses returned, Aaron remained silent. He did so lest Moses might rebuke him, complaining as to why he had not waited for him; if he was not in a position to control things, why had he let things escalate to the extent that the situation got totally out of hand?

then, is your case, O Sāmirī?" [96] He answered: "I saw what the people did not see. So I took a handful of dust from the trail of the Messenger, and I flung it (into the fire). Thus did my mind prompt me."[27] [97] Moses said: "Be gone, then. All your life you shall cry: 'Untouchable.'[28] There awaits a term for your reckoning that you cannot fail to keep. Now look at your god that you devotedly adored: We shall burn it and scatter its remains in the sea. [98] Your God is none else than Allah, beside Whom there is no god. His knowledge embraces everything."

[99] (O Muḥammad), thus do We recount to you the events of the past, and We have bestowed upon you from Ourself an admonition. [100] He who turns away from it will surely bear a heavy burden on the Day of Resurrection, [101] and will abide under this burden for ever. Grievous shall be the burden on the Day of Resurrection, [102] the Day when the Trumpet shall be sounded and We shall muster the sinners, their eyes turned blue with terror. [103] They shall whisper among themselves: "You stayed on the earth barely ten days." [104] We know well what

---

27. The term "Messenger" could have been used by the Sāmirī to denote Moses, which demonstrates just how crafty he was. For such a statement, suggesting that even Moses' footprint could produce miracles, such as the emergence of the golden calf, was designed to flatter the Prophet Moses (peace be on him).

28. Not only was the Sāmirī branded as an outcast prohibited from maintaining any social relations, he was also directed to constantly announce his outcast status so that everyone knew that he could not be touched – in the same way that everyone avoided contact with lepers.

they will say to one another: We also know that even the most cautious in his estimate will say: "You lived in the world no more than a day." [105] They ask you concerning the mountains: "Where will they go?" Say: "My Lord will scatter them like dust, [106] and leave the earth a levelled plain [107] in which you shall find no crookedness or curvature. [108] On that Day people shall follow straight on to the call of the summoner, no one daring to show any haughtiness. Their voices shall be hushed before the Most Compassionate Lord, so that you will hear nothing but a whispering murmur. [109] On that Day intercession shall not avail save of him whom the Most Compassionate Lord permits, and whose word of intercession is pleasing to Him. [110] He knows all that is ahead of them and all that is behind them, while the others do not know. [111] All faces shall be humbled before the Ever-Living, the Self-Subsisting Lord, and he who bears the burden of iniquity will have failed; [112] but whosoever does righteous works, being a believer, shall have no fear of suffering wrong or loss."

[113] (O Muḥammad), thus have We revealed this as an Arabic Qur'ān[29] and have expounded in it warning in diverse ways so that they may avoid evil or become heedful.

---

29. That is, the Qur'ān abounds in good teachings and sound counsel.

[114] Exalted is Allah, the True King![30] Hasten not with reciting the Qur'ān before its revelation to you is finished, and pray: "Lord! Increase me in knowledge."[31]

[115] Most certainly We had given Adam a command before, but he forgot. We found him lacking in firmness of resolution.[32] [116] Recall when We said to the angels: "Prostrate yourselves before Adam"; all prostrated themselves save *Iblīs*. He refused. [117] Then We said: "Adam! He is an enemy to you and to your wife. So let him not drive both of you out of Paradise and plunge you into affliction, [118] (for in Paradise) neither are you hungry nor naked, [119] nor face thirst or scorching heat." [120] But Satan seduced him, saying: "Adam! Shall I direct you to a tree of eternal life and an abiding kingdom?" [121] Then the two of them ate the fruit of that tree and

---

30. Such statements are usually made in the Qur'ān while winding up a discourse, the purpose being to conclude with a celebration of God's glory. The context and the style here indicate that the current discourse has come to an end and that a new one starts with verse 115: "Most certainly We had given Adam a command before …."

31. Evidently, while receiving the revelation, the Prophet (peace be on him) had repeated the words of the message in order to fully retain them in his memory. This was bound to distract him from receiving the message for his mental concentration would have been affected. It was necessary, therefore, that the Prophet (peace be on him) should be apprised of the right manner of receiving the revelation, be directed not to try to memorize the revelation before the process of receiving it was over.

32. Adam did not disobey God out of pride and deliberate rebelliousness. His fault rather lay in not paying sufficient attention to God's directive, in being forgetful and weak in his resolve.

their shameful parts became revealed to each other, and they began to cover themselves with the leaves from the Garden.[33] Thus Adam disobeyed his Lord and strayed into error. [122] Thereafter his Lord exalted him, accepted his repentance, and bestowed guidance upon him,[34] [123] and said: "Get down, both of you, (that is, man and Satan), and be out of it; each of you shall be an enemy to the other. Henceforth if there comes to you a guidance from Me, then whosoever follows My guidance shall neither go astray nor suffer misery. [124] But whosoever turns away from this Admonition from Me shall have a straitened life;[35] We shall raise him blind on the Day of Resurrection," [125] where-upon he will say: "Lord! Why have You raised me blind when I had sight in the world?" [126] He will

33. In other words, as Adam and Eve disobeyed God, they were deprived of the comforts and amenities automatically available to them in Paradise under the special scheme of things obtaining there. They were first deprived of clothing. Later, the arrangement to provide food, water and shelter without any effort on their part was discontinued.

34. Unlike Satan, however, Adam was not banished from a state of grace. God did not let him remain in the state into which he had fallen as a result of his disobedience; instead, He pulled him out of the morass into which he had become enmeshed, pardoned him and selected him for a special service to His cause.

35. This does not mean that all those who are unrighteous will necessarily face poverty. What is meant is that such people will be unable to find peace and contentment. Someone may be a millionaire, and yet his life will be plagued by discontent and restlessness. Likewise, even the ruler of a vast empire may be intensely unhappy and suffer much mental agony. For it is quite possible that the success of such persons was brought about by blatantly evil means with the result that they suffer great mental anguish. Such persons will always remain in conflict with their conscience and everything around them will deprive them of true peace and happiness.

say: "Even so it is. Our Signs came to you and you ignored them. So shall you be ignored this Day." [127] Thus do We requite him who transgresses and does not believe in the signs of your Lord (during the life of the world); and surely the punishment of the Hereafter is even more terrible and more enduring.

[128] Did they not find any guidance in the fact that We destroyed many nations in whose ruined dwelling-places they now walk about? Surely there are many Signs in them for people endowed with wisdom.

[129] Were it not for a word already gone from your Lord, the decree (of their destruction) would have come to pass. [130] So bear patiently with what they say. Glorify your Lord, praising Him before sunrise and before sunset, and in the watches of the night, and glorify Him and at the ends of the day[36] that you may attain to happiness.[37]

---

36. "Glorify your Lord, praising Him before sunrise and before sunset" means the observance of Prayer. This verse also indicates the timings of Prayer: *Fajr* Prayer is before sunrise, *'Aṣr* Prayer before sunset, and *'Ishā'* and *Tahajjud* Prayers in the hours of the night. As to the "ends of the day," they can, at most, be three in number: in the morning, a little past midday, and in the evening. Hence "the sides of the day" refer to *Fajr*, *Ẓuhr* and *Maghrib* Prayers.

37. There are two possible meanings of this verse and it is quite probable that both of them are meant. In one sense, the verse urges the Prophet (peace be on him) to feel contented with his present state wherein he has to endure a number of unpalatable things for the sake of his mission. According to the alternative meaning of the verse, the Prophet (peace be on him) is urged to do as he was directed because his efforts would soon bear fruit and this would gladden his heart.

[131] Do not turn your eyes covetously towards the embellishments of worldly life that We have bestowed upon various kinds of people to test them. But the clean provision[38] bestowed upon you by your Lord is better and more enduring. [132] Enjoin Prayer on your household, and do keep observing it. We do not ask you for any worldly provision; rather, it is We Who provide you, and ultimately the pious will end up the best.

[133] They ask: "Why does he not bring us a (miraculous) sign from his Lord?" Has there not come to them a Book containing the teachings of the previous scriptures?[39] [134] Had We destroyed them through some calamity before his coming, they would have said: "Our Lord! Why did You not send any Messenger to us that we might have followed Your signs before being humbled and disgraced?" [135] Tell them, (O Muḥammad): "Everyone is waiting for his end. Wait, then, and you will soon know who are the people of the Right Way, and are rightly-guided."

---

38. We have translated the word *rizq* here as meaning "clean provision". For any unlawful earning cannot be a clean provision from God.

39. It was nothing short of a miracle that a person from among them, an unlettered person, had come forth with a Book which embodied the quintessence of the Scripture teachings. Not only did it bring together all the guidance embodied in the Scriptures, it also explained their content in such a manner that could now be comprehended by people of even ordinary understanding.

21

Al-Anbiyā' [The Prophets]
Makkan Period

In the name of Allah, the Most Merciful,
the Most Compassionate

[1] The time of people's reckoning has drawn near, and yet they turn aside in heedlessness. [2] Whenever any fresh admonition comes to them from their Lord they barely heed it and remain immersed in play, [3] their hearts being set on other concerns.

The wrong-doers whisper to one another: "This person is no more than a mortal like yourselves. Will you, then, be enchanted by sorcery while you see?"

[4] He said: "My Lord knows well all that is spoken in the heavens and the earth. He is All-Hearing, All-Knowing."[1]

[5] They say: "Nay, these are confused dreams; nay, he has forged it; nay, he is a poet. So let him bring us a sign,

---

1. The Prophet (peace be on him) did not respond to this false propaganda nor to the vicious whispering campaign against him, except in so far as he said that God hears and knows all that they said, be it loudly or in whispers. Never did the Prophet (peace be on him) stoop to the level of his opponents, hurling at them the abominations they hurled at him.

even as the Messengers of the past were sent with signs."
[6] Not one township that We destroyed before them
believed. Would they, then, believe?

[7] (O Muḥammad), even before you We never sent any
other than human beings as Messengers, and to them
We sent revelation. Ask the People of the Book if you do
not know. [8] We did not endow the Messengers with
bodies that would need no food; nor were they immortals.
[9] Then We fulfilled the promise We had made to them:
We rescued them and those whom We wished, and We
destroyed those who exceeded all bounds.

[10] We have bestowed upon you a Book that mentions
you. Do you not understand?²

[11] How many a wrong-doing town did We shatter
and then raise up another people. [12] Then, when they
perceived Our chastisement they took to their heels and
fled. [13] (They were told): "Flee not, but return to your
comforts and to your dwellings. You are likely to be

2. The Qur'ān should have been familiar material to them for its
discourse centred on the human psyche and on human affairs;
on man's nature, on his beginning and end. Additionally, the
Qur'ānic discourse is replete with signs which are drawn from
man's own environment and which point to the Truth. The Qur'ān
also concerns itself with elucidating the difference between good
and evil found in human conduct, and the human conscience
bears ample testimony to the truth of that distinction. There is
nothing enigmatic or complicated in the Qur'ān that would make
it incomprehensible to the human mind.

questioned."³ [14] They said: "Woe to us; surely we were wrong-doers." [15] They did not cease to cry this until We reduced them to stubble, still and silent.

[16] We did not create in sport the heavens and the earth and all that lies between the two. [17] Had it been Our will to find a pastime, We would have found one near at hand; if at all We were inclined to do so.⁴ [18] Nay, We hurl the Truth at falsehood so that the Truth crushes falsehood, and lo! it vanishes. Woe to you for what you utter!

[19] To Him belongs whosoever dwells in the heavens and on earth. Those (angels) that are with Him neither disdain to serve Him out of pride, nor do they weary of it.⁵ [20] They glorify Him night and day, without flagging.

---

3. This verse is rich in meaning and may be interpreted variously. It may, for instance, be taken to mean that the unbelievers are being urged to look carefully at the punishment so that they can describe it to others in the future. According to a variant view, they are being told: "Revert to your life of pomp and ceremony for maybe your courtiers will still stand in awe of you and ask you for your orders. Maintain your councils and committees, for the world may possibly approach you, seeking to benefit from your wise counsels."

4. Had God intended creation to be merely for sport, surely He Himself would have engaged in it. In which case, He would certainly not have brought into being a creature endowed with feeling, consciousness and a sense of responsibility. Nor would God have placed him in a state where he would be engaged in a constant tug-of-war between right and wrong. God could have done much better if the purpose was merely to entertain Himself!

5. Angels do not find it unpalatable at all to serve God. Serving Him is not a drudgery which they carry out with a heavy heart and which eventually wearies them.

[21] Have they taken earthly gods who are such that they raise up the dead to life?

[22] Had there been any gods in the heavens and the earth apart from Allah, the order of both the heavens and the earth would have gone to ruins. Glory be to Allah, the Lord of the Throne, Who is far above their false descriptions of Him. [23] None shall question Him about what He does, but they shall be questioned.

[24] Have they taken gods other than Him? Say, (O Muḥammad): "Bring forth your proof! Here is the Book with admonition for those of my time and there are also scriptures with admonition for people before me." But most people do not know the Truth, and have, therefore, turned away from it. [25] Never did We send any Messenger before you to whom We did not reveal: "There is no god but Me. So serve Me alone."

[26] They say: "The Most Compassionate Lord has taken to Himself a son." Glory be to Him! Those whom they so designate are only His honoured servants. [27] They do not outstrip Him in speech and only act as He commands. [28] He knows whatever is before them and whatsoever is remote from them and they do not intercede except for him, intercession on whose behalf pleases Him, and they stand constantly in awe of Him. [29] And if anyone of them were to claim: "Indeed I am a god apart from Him," We shall recompense both with Hell. Thus do We recompense the wrong-doers.

[30] Did the unbelievers (who do not accept the teaching of the Prophet) not realize that the heavens and the earth

were one solid mass, then We tore them apart, and We made every living being out of water? Will they, then, not believe (that We created all this)? [31] And We placed firm mountains on earth lest it should sway with them, and We made wide paths in them that they may find their way; [32] and We made the sky a secure canopy; and yet they turn away from these Signs. [33] It is He Who created the night and the day, and the sun and the moon. Each of them is floating in its orbit.[6]

[34] (O Muḥammad), We did not grant everlasting life to any human being even before you. If you were to die, will they live for ever? [35] Every living being shall taste death and We shall subject you to ill and good by way of trial, and to Us shall all of you be eventually sent back.

[36] When the unbelievers see you they make you an object of fun, saying: "Is he the one who mentions your gods?" They say so, and yet they reject with disdain the very mention of the Most Compassionate Lord.

[37] Man is hasty by nature. I shall certainly show you My Signs. Do not ask Me to be hasty. [38] They say: "(Tell us) when will the threat of punishment come to pass if you are truthful?" [39] If only the unbelievers knew of

---

6. The word used here is *falak* which is a familiar term in Arabic for sky. Since the verse says that each is floating in its *falak*, two points clearly emerge. First, that all the heavenly bodies are not floating in one and the same orbit; rather each has its own orbit. Second, an orbit is not something static with a planet fixed on to it. It rather seems to be something fluid, something seemingly vacuous, like space where if any heavenly bodies move, their movement gives the impression of floating.

the Hour when they shall not be able to keep off the Fire from their faces, nor from their backs; nor shall they be helped. [40] That will suddenly come upon them and stupefy them. They shall not be able to ward it off, nor shall they be granted any respite. [41] Other Messengers before you were also mocked, but those who scoffed at the Messengers were overtaken by the same scourge that they had scoffed at.

[42] Tell them, (O Muḥammad): "Who protects you, during the night or the day from the Most Compassionate Lord?" And yet they turn away from the Admonition of their Lord. [43] Do they have any gods who would protect them against Us? They have no power even to help themselves; nor do they enjoy Our support. [44] Nay, We generously provided them and their fathers, and they enjoyed Our provision for long. Do they not see that We are now advancing into their territory, diminishing it from different sides?7 Is it they, then, who will triumph?" [45] Tell them: "I only warn you by the Revelation." But the deaf do not hear the cry when they are warned. [46] Were only the slightest whiff from your Lord's punishment to touch

---

7. There are innumerable manifestations of God's power throughout the universe. Such manifestations include famines, epidemics, floods, earthquakes, and spells of severe cold and heat. From time to time any of these calamities can suddenly strike and can result in the death of thousands, even hundreds of thousands, the devastation of whole towns, the destruction of flourishing crops, and the ruination of prosperous businesses. In short, material resources shrink, sometimes in one direction, sometimes in another; and the situation can become so bad that despite his best efforts, man finds himself unable to prevent the losses caused by such disasters.

them, they would cry out: "Woe to us; we were indeed wrong-doers."

[47] We shall set up just scales on the Day of Resurrection so that none will be wronged in the least. (We shall bring forth the acts of everyone), even if it be the weight of a grain of mustard seed. We shall suffice as Reckoners.

[48] Surely We had granted to Moses and Aaron the Criterion (between right and wrong), and Light and Admonition for the good of the God-fearing, [49] for those who fear their Lord without seeing Him and dread the Hour (of Reckoning). [50] This is a Blessed Admonition that We have revealed. Are you, then, going to reject it?

[51] Surely We had bestowed wisdom upon Abraham even earlier, and We knew him well. [52] Recall, when he said to his father and his people: "What are these images to which you are devoutly clinging?" [53] They answered: "We found our fathers worshipping them." [54] He said: "Certainly you and your fathers have all been in manifest error." [55] They said: "Are you expressing your true ideas before us or are you jesting?" [56] He said: "Nay, but your Lord is the Lord of the heavens and the earth which He created and to that I bear witness before you. [57] By Allah, I shall certainly carry out my plan against your gods after you are gone." [58] Then he broke them all into pieces, sparing only the supreme one among them that they may possibly return to him. [59] (When they saw the idols in this state) they said: "Who has done this to our gods? Surely he is one of the wrong-doers." [60] Some of them said: "We heard a youth called Abraham speak (ill) of them." [61] The others said:

"Bring him, then, before the eyes of the people that they may see (what will be done to him)." [62] (On Abraham's arrival) they said: "Abraham, are you he who has done this to our gods?" [63] He answered: "Rather it was this supreme one who has done it. So ask them, if they can speak."[8] [64] Thereupon they turned to their (inner) selves and said (to themselves): "Surely it is you who are the wrong-doers." [65] Then their minds were turned upside down, and they said: "You know well that they do not speak." [66] Abraham said: "Do you, then, worship beside Allah a thing that can neither benefit you nor hurt you? [67] Fie upon you and upon all that you worship beside Allah. Do you have no sense?" [68] They said: "Burn him, and come to the support of your gods, if you are going to do anything." [69] We said: "O fire, become coolness and safety for Abraham."[9] [70] They had sought to do

---

8. Abraham was not making a statement; he was merely presenting an argument that would enable his detractors to realize the truth of the matter. His statement had a clear purpose – to make his opponents recognize that their deities were absolutely powerless so that nothing could be expected of them. Whenever a person makes a statement while trying to drive home his point, he cannot be called a liar even when his statement is objectively incorrect. For, he does not intend to convey something that is contrary to fact, and make his audience believe about something incorrect to be true. The speaker's purpose is quite evident both to him and to his audience – it is simply to establish a point.

9. The words of the verse as well as the context indicate that Abraham's opponents did indeed carry out their threat. They prepared a pit of fire and threw Abraham into it, but God commanded the fire to become cool, thus preventing Abraham from suffering any harm. This is one of the miracles mentioned in the Qur'ān.

evil to him, but We caused them to be the worst losers, [71] and We saved him and Lot and brought him to the land upon which We had bestowed Our blessings for all the people of the world. [72] And We bestowed upon him Isaac and Jacob as an additional gift,[10] making each of them righteous. [73] And We made them into leaders to guide people in accordance with Our command, and We inspired them to good works, and to establish Prayers and to give *Zakāh*. They worshipped Us alone.

[74] We bestowed upon Lot sound judgement and knowledge, and We delivered him from the city that was immersed in foul deeds. They were indeed a wicked people, exceedingly disobedient. [75] And We admitted him into Our mercy. Verily he was of the righteous.

[76] We bestowed the same favour upon Noah. Recall, when he cried to Us before; We accepted his prayer and delivered him and his household from the great distress [77] and We helped him against a people who rejected Our signs as false. They were indeed an evil people and so We drowned them all.

[78] We bestowed the same favour upon David and Solomon. Recall, when they gave judgement regarding a tillage into which the sheep of some people had strayed at night, and We were witnesses to their judgement. [79] We guided Solomon to the right verdict, and We had granted each of them judgement and knowledge. We made the mountains and the birds celebrate the praise of Allah with David. It was We Who did all this. [80] It was We Who

---

10. Not only was Abraham's son, Isaac, invested with prophethood, but, later on also his grandson, Jacob.

taught him the art of making coats of mail for your benefit so that it may protect you from each other's violence. Do you, then, give thanks? [81] And We subdued the strongly raging wind to Solomon which blew at his bidding towards the land We blessed. We know everything. [82] And We subdued many devils who dived (into the sea) for him and carried out other jobs besides that. We kept watch over all of them.

[83] We bestowed (the same wisdom, judgement and knowledge) upon Job. Recall, when he cried to his Lord: "Behold, disease has struck me and You are the Most Merciful of those that are merciful." [84] We accepted his prayer and removed the affliction from him, and We not only restored to him his family but as many more with them as a mercy from Us and as a lesson to the worshippers.

[85] And (We bestowed the same favour) upon Ishmael, Idrīs and Dhū al-Kifl, for they were all steadfast. [86] And We admitted them into Our mercy, for they were of the righteous.

[87] And We bestowed Our favour upon Dhū al-Nūn.[11] Recall, when he went forth enraged,[12] thinking We have

---

11. Reference is made here to the Prophet Jonah (peace be on him). At some places in the Qur'ān he is mentioned by his proper name and at others only his title, "Dhū al-Nūn" (the man of the fish) is used. This title does not mean that he was engaged in catching or selling fish, but rather indicates the fish which, with God's leave, devoured him, as has been described in *al-Ṣāffāt* 37: 142.

12. Angry with his people, Jonah suddenly left them. He did so before receiving God's command to emigrate – a command that

no power to take him to task. Eventually he cried out in the darkness:[13] "There is no god but You. Glory be to You! I have done wrong." [88] Thereupon We accepted his prayer, and rescued him from grief. Thus do We rescue the believers.

[89] And We bestowed favour upon Zechariah, when he cried to his Lord: "Lord! Leave me not solitary (without any issue). You are the Best Inheritor." [90] So We accepted his prayer and bestowed upon him John, and We made his wife fit (to bear a child). Verily they hastened in doing good works and called upon Us with longing and fear, and humbled themselves to Us.

[91] And also recall the woman who guarded her chastity:[14] We breathed into her of Our spirit, and made her and her son a Sign to the whole world.

[92] Verily this community of yours is a single community, and I am your Lord; so worship Me. [93] But they tore asunder their faith into many parts. But to Us they are bound to return. [94] Then whosoever does righteous works, while believing, his striving will not go unappreciated. We record them all for him. [95] It has been ordained against every town that We ever destroyed that they shall not return (to enjoy a new lease of life) [96] until Gog and Magog are let loose, and begin swooping from every mound,

---

would have provided him with the necessary justification for relinquishing the duties he had been assigned.

13. Darkness here refers to the darkness in the belly of the fish, further compounded by the darkness of the sea.

14. This is an allusion to Mary.

[97] and the time for the fulfilment of the true promise of Allah[15] draws near, whereupon the eyes of those who disbelieved will stare in fear, and they will say: "Woe to us, we were indeed heedless of this; nay, we were wrong-doers." [98] (They will be told): "Verily you and the gods you worshipped beside Allah are the fuel of Hell. All of you are bound to arrive there.[16] [99] Had these indeed been gods they would not have gone there. But (as it is), all of you shall ever abide in it." [100] There they shall groan with anguish and the din and noise in Hell will not let them hear anything. [101] But for those whom We had decided to favour with good reward, they shall be kept far removed from Hell. [102] They shall not hear even a whisper of it, and they shall live for ever in the delights which they had desired. [103] The Hour of the Great Terror shall not grieve them, and the angels shall receive them saying: "This is your Day which you had been promised."

[104] On that Day We shall roll up the heavens like a scroll for writing. Even as We originated the creation first so We shall repeat it. This is a promise binding on Us; and so We shall do. [105] Surely We wrote in the Psalms, after

---

15. That means, the time of Resurrection.

16. According to some reports, one of the chiefs who ascribed Divinity to others than the One True God objected to the import of this verse, saying that it implied that not only their deities but also Jesus, Ezra and the angels would be cast into Hell as they too had been worshipped by people. The Prophet Muḥammad (peace be on him) thereupon affirmed: "Yes, everyone who preferred that he be worshipped besides God, will be in the company of his worshippers (in Hell)."

the exhortation, that the earth shall be inherited by My righteous servants.[17] [106] Herein, surely, is a message for those devoted to worship.

[107] We have sent you forth as nothing but mercy to people of the whole world. [108] Say: "It is revealed to me that your God is only One God. Will you, then, submit to Him?" [109] If they turn away, say to them: "I have warned you all alike; and I cannot say whether what you have been promised is near or distant. [110] Indeed He knows what you say loudly and what you hide. [111] I think that this [reprieve] is possibly a trial for you, an opportunity to enjoy yourselves until an appointed time."

[112] The Messenger said: "My Lord! Judge with truth. Our Compassionate Lord alone is our support against your (blasphemous) utterances."

---

17. To understand this verse, see *Sūrah al-Zumar* 39: 73, 74.

22

Al-Ḥajj [The Pilgrimage]
Madīnan Period

*In the name of Allah, the Most Merciful,
the Most Compassionate*

[1] O mankind, fear the (wrath of) your Lord! Indeed, the earthquake of the Hour (of Judgement) will be an awesome thing. [2] On the Day when you witness it, the suckling woman shall utterly neglect the infant she suckles, and every pregnant woman shall cast her burden, and you will see people as though they are drunk, when they are not drunk; but dreadful shall be Allah's chastisement.

[3] Among people there are some who wrangle about Allah without knowledge and follow every rebellious devil, [4] although it is decreed about him that he shall lead into error whosoever takes him for a friend, and will direct him to the torment of the Fire. [5] O mankind! If you have any doubt concerning Resurrection, then know that it is surely We Who created you from dust, then from a drop of sperm, then from a clot of blood, then from a little lump of flesh, some of it shapely and other shapeless. (We are rehearsing this) that We may make the reality clear to you. We cause (the drop of sperm) that We please to remain in the wombs till an appointed time. We bring you forth as infants (and

nurture you) that you may come of age. Among you is he that dies (at a young age) and he who is kept back to the most abject age so that after once having known, he reaches a stage when he knows nothing. You see the earth dry and barren and then no sooner than We send down water upon it, it begins to quiver and swell and brings forth every kind of beauteous vegetation. [6] All this is because Allah, He is the Truth, and because He resurrects the dead, and because He has power over everything, [7] (all of which shows that) the Hour shall surely come to pass – in this there is no doubt – and Allah shall surely resurrect those that are in graves.

[8] And among people are those that wrangle about Allah without knowledge, without any true guidance, and without any scripture to enlighten them. [9] They wrangle arrogantly, intent on leading people astray from the Way of Allah. Such shall suffer disgrace in this world and We shall cause them to taste the chastisement of burning (in the Next). [10] That is the outcome of what your own hands have wrought, for Allah never wrongs His creatures.

[11] And among people is he who worships Allah on the borderline;[1] if any good befalls him, he is satisfied; but if a trial afflicts him, he utterly turns away. He will incur the loss of this world and the Hereafter. That indeed

---

1. This alludes to those whose allegiance to the true faith is peripheral; to those who, rather than be at the centre, prefer to sit on the fence. These are like reluctant soldiers who, being on the periphery, are ready to throw in their lot with the winning party, be it their own or the enemy's.

is a clear loss. [12] He invokes, instead of Allah, those who can neither harm nor benefit him. That indeed is straying far away. [13] He invokes those that are more likely to cause him harm than benefit. Such is surely an evil patron, and an evil associate. [14] (In contrast) Allah will assuredly cause those who believe and act righteously to enter Gardens beneath which rivers flow. For, most certainly, Allah does whatever He pleases. [15] Anyone who fancies that Allah will not support him in this world and in the Hereafter, let him reach out to heaven through a rope, and then make a hole in the sky and see whether his device can avert that which enrages him.

[16] Even so We have revealed the Qur'ān with Clear Signs. Verily Allah guides whomsoever He wills.

[17] On the Day of Resurrection Allah will most certainly judge among those who believe, and those who became Jews, and Sabaeans, and Christians, and Magians, and those who associate others with Allah in His Divinity. Surely Allah watches over everything. [18] Have you not seen that all those who are in the heavens and all those who are in the earth prostrate themselves before Allah; and so do the sun and the moon, and the stars and the mountains, and the trees, and the beasts, and so do many human beings, and even many of those who are condemned to chastisement? And he whom Allah humiliates, none can give him honour. Allah does whatever He wills.

[19] These two groups (the believers and unbelievers) are in dispute about their Lord.[2] As for those that disbelieve, garments of fire have been cut out for them; boiling water shall be poured down over their heads, [20] causing (not only) their skins but all that is in their bellies as well to melt away. [21] There shall be maces of iron to lash them. [22] Whenever they try, in their anguish, to escape from Hell, they will be driven back into it, (and shall be told): "Now taste the torment of burning." [23] (On the other hand), Allah will cause those who believed and acted righteously to enter the Gardens beneath which rivers flow. They shall be decked in them with bracelets of gold and pearls and their raiment shall be of silk. [24] They were guided (to accept) the pure word; they were guided to the Way of the Praiseworthy (Lord).

[25] Indeed those who disbelieve and who (now) hinder people from the Way of Allah and hinder them from the Holy Mosque which We have set up (as a place of worship) for all people,[3] equally for those who dwell therein and for those who come from outside, (they

---

2. The groups that contend about God are very many. Nevertheless, the present verse divides them into two broad categories. One consists of those who accept the teachings of the Prophets and adopt the right attitude in serving God. The other consists of those who do not accept the teachings of the Prophets, reject the Truth, and embrace unbelief. The essence of this latter attitude remains one and the same regardless of how numerous the disagreements among the exponents of such an attitude are, or the extent to which the different versions of unbelief vary from one to another.

3. That is, they prevent the Prophet Muḥammad (peace be on him) and his Companions from performing *Ḥajj* and *ʿUmrah*.

surely deserve punishment). Whosoever deviates therein from the Right Way and acts with iniquity, We shall cause him to taste a painful chastisement.

[26] Call to mind when We assigned to Abraham the site of the House (Ka'bah), directing him: "Do not associate aught with Me" and "Keep My House pure for those who walk around it, and for those who stand and who bow down and who prostrate themselves (in worship), [27] and publicly proclaim Pilgrimage for all mankind so that they come to you on foot and mounted on lean camels from every distant point [28] to witness the benefits in store for them, and pronounce the name of Allah during the appointed days over the cattle that He has provided them. So eat of it and feed the distressed and the needy. [29] Thereafter, let them tidy up and fulfil their vows and circumambulate the Ancient House."

[30] Such (was the purpose of building the Ka'bah). Whosoever, then, venerates Allah's sanctities will find it to be good for him in the sight of his Lord. Cattle have been made lawful for you[4] except those mentioned to

---

4. The statement that "Cattle have been made lawful to you except those mentioned to you (as unlawful)" is made for two purposes. First, that the Quraysh and the polytheists of Arabia considered *baḥīrah*, *sā'ibah*, *waṣīlah* and *ḥām* among the animals that were inviolable. (For further explanation of this see *al-Mā'idah* 5: 103, n. 51 – Ed.) It was, therefore, made clear that no sanctity was attached to them; that it was lawful to slaughter all cattle, including these. Second, since the hunting of animals is forbidden in the state of *iḥrām*, it was necessary to clarify that slaughtering cattle and eating them is not forbidden. The main purpose of this above verse, then, is to make these clarifications.

you (as unlawful). So shun the abomination of idols and shun all words of falsehood. [31] Become exclusively devoted to Allah, ascribing Divinity to none other than Him. Whoso ascribes Divinity to aught beside Allah, it is as though he fell down from the sky whereafter either the birds will snatch him away, or the wind will sweep him to a distant place (causing him to be shattered to pieces).⁵

[32] Such is the fact. And whoso venerates the sanctity of all that have been ordained as symbols of Allah surely does so because it is part of the true piety of the hearts.⁶

---

5. The word "sky" in this parable stands for the natural state of man wherein he is the servant of none except God and his nature recognizes no other doctrine than this, i.e. the doctrine of pure monotheism. When a man embraces the guidance brought by the Prophets, it helps him adhere to monotheism on the grounds of knowledge and sound insight and this carries him to even greater heights. On the other hand, when someone embraces polytheism or atheism, he falls away from this natural state and is then confronted with either of the following two situations. First, that Satan and those who are out to misguide others, those who are metaphorically called "birds" in the above account, pounce upon him, each trying to snatch him away. Second, that he is carried to and fro by his lusts, emotions and fancies, all of which are likened in the above verse to the wind, with the result that he is ultimately hurled into some abysmal ditch.

6. That someone "venerates" the symbols of God is indicative of his inner piety. It shows that he is possessed of some degree of God-consciousness which prompts him to revere God's symbols.

[33] You may derive benefit (from sacrificial animals) until an appointed time.[7] Thereafter their place (of sacrifice) is near the Ancient House.

[34] For every people We have laid down a ritual of sacrifice (– although the purpose of the ritual is the same –) that they pronounce the name of Allah over the cattle He has provided them.[8] Your Lord is One God; so submit yourselves to Him alone. And give, (O Prophet), glad tidings to those that humble themselves (before Allah), [35] whose hearts shiver whenever Allah is mentioned, who patiently bear whatever affliction comes to them, who establish Prayer, and who spend (for good purposes) out of what We have provided them.

---

7. The preceding verse sets out a general directive: that the symbols of God should be revered, characterizing such reverence as a manifestation of inner piety. The present statement, which follows the previous one, seeks to rectify a common misunderstanding. Sacrificial animals are, as we know, one of God's symbols. The Arabs of the time considered it sacrilegious to use them for riding or employ them to transport goods or consume their milk *en route* the House of God. The present verse removes this misconception and affirms that one may benefit from them according to one's need.

8. This verse brings out two fundamental truths. First, that sacrificial offering has always been an integral part of the system of worship in all versions of Divine Law. The other point emphasized in this verse is that what really matters is that sacrifice be truly made for the sake of God rather than with an obsessive concern with the legal minutiae of the act. Whilst details of sacrificial offering have varied in different times, lands, and communities, the common denominator, however, has always been the spirit and purpose of sacrifice.

[36] We have appointed sacrificial camels among the symbols of (devotion to) Allah. There is much good in them for you. So make them stand (at the time of sacrifice) and pronounce the name of Allah over them,[9] and when they fall down on their sides[10] (after they are slaughtered), eat and also feed them who do not ask and those who ask. Thus have We subjected these animals that you may give thanks. [37] Neither their flesh reaches Allah nor their blood; it is your piety that reaches Him. He has subjected these animals (to you) that you may magnify Allah[11] for the guidance He has bestowed upon you. Give glad tidings, (O Prophet), to those who do good.

[38] Surely Allah defends those who believe. Certainly Allah has no love for the perfidious, the thankless.

---

9. That is, pronounce the name of God while slaughtering them. The camel is made to stand and is slaughtered by piercing a spear into its throat. This is termed "*naḥr*".

10. "Falling down on their sides" does not simply mean that the sacrificial animal's body touches the ground when it falls down after slaughter. It also means that this body becomes still when it ceases to wreathe with pain and dies.

11. That is, one should sincerely acknowledge God's greatness and paramountcy, and this should be reflected in one's deeds. Here, once again, we find reference to the objective of the rite of sacrifice. Sacrifice has been made obligatory not only to express man's gratitude to God for making the cattle subservient to him; it has also been instituted in order that man may fully remember, both in thought and deed, the Lordship of God Who subjected the cattle, whom He created, to man's control. This should enable man to avoid falling prey to the illusion that he is the true master of whatever he happens to possess.

[39] Permission (to fight) has been granted to those for they have been wronged.[12] Verily Allah has the power to help them: [40] those who were unjustly expelled from their homes for no other reason than their saying: "Allah is Our Lord." If Allah were not to repel some through others, monasteries and churches and synagogues and mosques wherein the name of Allah is much mentioned, would certainly have been pulled down. Allah will most certainly help those who will help Him.[13] Verily Allah is Immensely Strong, Overwhelmingly Mighty. [41] (Allah will certainly help) those who, were We to bestow authority on them in the land, will establish Prayers, render *Zakāh*, enjoin good, and forbid evil. The end of all matters rests with Allah.

[42] (O Prophet), if they give the lie to you, then before them the people of ʿĀd and Thamūd, also gave the lie (to the Prophets), [43] and so too did the people

---

12. This *sūrah* contains the very first verse in which Muslims were allowed to engage in fighting (*qitāl*) in the way of God. The present verse, however, simply grants Muslims the *permission* to fight. It was only later that they were *commanded* to fight. The verses embodying this command are 2: 190-193, 216 and 224. There was only a short lapse of time between the granting of permission to fight and the command to do so. To the best of our knowledge, such permission was granted in Dhū al-Hijjah 1 A.H., while the command was given a little before the Battle of Badr, either in Rajab or Shaʿbān 2 A.H.

13. That those who summon mankind to monotheism, strive to establish the true faith, and seek to promote righteousness in place of evil are helpers of God is a recurrent theme in the Qurʾān. This is so because the above-mentioned tasks are God's, and those who exert themselves in the performance of these tasks, thereby become His helpers.

of Abraham and the people of Lot; [44] and so did the dwellers of Midian, and Moses too was branded a liar. Initially I granted respite to the unbelievers for a while and then seized them. How dreadful was My punishment! [45] How many towns have We destroyed because their people were steeped in iniquity: so they lie fallen down upon their turrets! How many wells lie deserted; and how many towering palaces lie in ruins! [46] Have they not journeyed in the land that their hearts might understand and their ears might listen? For indeed it is not the eyes that are blinded; it is rather the hearts in the breasts that are rendered blind.

[47] They ask you to hasten the punishment. Allah shall most certainly not fail His promise; but a Day with your Lord is as a thousand years of your reckoning.[14] [48] How many towns did I respite at first though they were steeped in iniquity, and then I seized them! To Me are all destined to return.

[49] Say (O Muḥammad): "O people! I have been sent to you only as a plain warner (before the Doom strikes you)." [50] So those who believe and act righteously shall be granted forgiveness and an honourable sustenance, [51] whereas those who strive against Our

---

14. It is preposterous to think that the consequences of obeying or disobeying God's injunctions can be observed instantly. If a nation is warned that a certain pattern of behaviour it follows will prove catastrophic, it is absurd for them to retort that they have persisted with that line of conduct for the last ten, twenty, or fifty years, and still no calamity has befallen them. For it often takes not days, months or years, but centuries for the consequences of a people's behaviour to become fully evident.

Signs, seeking to profane them, they are the friends of the Fire!

[52] Never did We send a Messenger or a Prophet before you (O Muḥammad), but that whenever he had a desire, Satan interfered with that desire. Allah eradicates the interference of Satan and strengthens His Signs. Allah is All-Knowing, All-Wise. [53] (He does this) in order that He may make the evil caused by Satan a trial for those in whose hearts there is sickness (of hypocrisy), whose hearts are hard (and vitiated). Surely these wrong-doers have gone too far in their dissension. [54] (He also does this) in order that those endowed with knowledge may know that it is the Truth from your Lord and that they may have faith in it and their hearts may humble themselves before Him. Verily Allah always directs those that believe to the Right Way.[15]

---

15. That is, God made Satan's evil designs a means of testing people so that those who are righteous may be distinguished from those who are evil. In the nature of things, those whose minds have been corrupted derive wrong conclusions from such things and this in turn becomes a means of misleading them. As for those whose minds are straight, these very things lead them to confirm the truthfulness of God's Prophets and His Books. The result is that these people are led to believe that all these are no more than Satan's mischiefs. They know that the Prophets' call is essentially to nothing other than truth and righteousness. Had this not been so, Satan would not have carried on so desperately.

The specific stage through which the mission of the Prophet (peace be on him) was then passing misled many of those who were concerned only with appearances. Such people, therefore, behaved as though the Prophet had failed in his mission. For what people could observe was simply that the person who wished his people to believe in him, virtually found no other way after thirteen years of striving than to bid farewell to his homeland with only a

[55] The unbelievers will not cease to be in doubt about it until the Hour suddenly comes upon them, or the chastisement of an ominous day overtakes them. [56] On that Day all sovereignty shall be Allah's and He will judge among them. Then those who believed and acted righteously shall be in Gardens of Bliss. [57] A humiliating chastisement awaits those who disbelieved and denied Our Signs. [58] As for those who migrated in the way of Allah, whereafter they were slain, or died, Allah will certainly grant them a goodly provision. Indeed, Allah is the Best of all those who provide. [59] He will surely admit them to a resort which will please them. Most certainly Allah is All-Knowing, Most Forbearing. [60] That indeed is so, as for him who retaliates in proportion to the excess committed against him, and is thereafter again subjected to transgression, Allah will surely aid him. Verily Allah is All-Pardoning, All-Forgiving.

[61] So shall it be because it is Allah Who causes the night to emerge out of the day and causes the day

---

handful of followers. When people considered the Prophet's claim that he was God's Messenger and that he enjoyed God's support in this regard, or when they considered the proclamation of the Qur'ān that the unbelievers who reject a true Prophet are seized with God's scourge, they were inclined to doubt the veracity of both the Prophet and the Qur'ān. In this way the detractors of the Prophet (peace be on him) were encouraged to let their tongues loose, so much so that they started mocking him, saying in effect: "Where is God's support that you so much talk about? What has happened to God's scourge against which you have been warning us?" The preceding verses contain a response to these questions, as indeed do the present ones.

to emerge out of the night and Allah is All-Hearing, All-Seeing. [62] So shall it be because Allah, He is the Truth, and all whom they invoke instead of Him are false. Allah is Most High, All-Great. [63] Do you not see that Allah sends down water from the sky whereby the earth turns green? Verily Allah is Subtle, All-Aware.[16] [64] To Him belongs all that is in the heavens and all that is in the earth. Surely Allah – He alone is Self-Sufficient, Praiseworthy. [65] Have you not seen how Allah has subjected to you all that is in the earth, and the vessels that sail in the sea by His command, and it is He Who holds back the sky that it may not fall on earth except by His leave? Surely Allah is Most Gentle, Ever Compassionate to people. [66] And it is He Who has endowed you with life and it is He who causes you to die, and it is He Who will then resurrect you. Man is indeed extremely prone to denying the Truth.[17]

[67] For every people We have prescribed a way of worship which they follow. So, (O Muḥammad), let

---

16. God is All-Hearing and All-Seeing; He is neither blind nor deaf to what happens in the world. He, therefore, visits with His scourge the unbelieving and the tyrannous; He rewards with His favours those who believe and do righteous deeds; He metes out justice to those who are wronged; and He helps with His succour the followers of the Truth who fight against tyranny with all their might.

17. This refers to deliberate denial of the Truth expounded by the Prophets.

them not dispute with you concerning this,[18] and call them to Your Lord. You are certainly on the Straight Way. [68] And if they dispute with you, say: "Allah knows well what you do. [69] Allah will judge among you on the Day of Resurrection concerning matters about which you disagreed." [70] Are you not aware that Allah knows all that is in the heaven and the earth? Surely it is all preserved in a Book. Indeed that is easy with Allah.

[71] Instead of Allah they worship those concerning whom He has revealed no sanction and concerning whom they have no true knowledge. None shall be able to help such evil-doers. [72] When Our Signs are plainly recited to them, you will perceive utter repugnance on their faces and it all but seems as if they will soon pounce upon those who recite Our Signs to them. Say: "Shall I tell you what is worse than that? The Fire with which Allah has threatened those who disbelieve. That is truly an evil end."

[73] O people, a parable is set forth: pay heed to it. Those who call upon aught other than Allah shall never be able to create even a fly, even if all of them were to come together to do that. And if the fly were to snatch away anything from them, they would not be able to

---

18. The earlier Prophets prescribed a particular way (*mansak*) for their communities. In like manner, the Prophet Muḥammad (peace be on him) also prescribed a particular way for his community. No one is entitled to dispute this because this is the only way that is suitable for the present age.

recover that from it. Powerless is the supplicant; and powerless is he to whom he supplicates. [74] They have not formed a true estimate of Allah. Indeed, Allah is All-Powerful, All-Mighty.

[75] Allah chooses Messengers from among angels and from among human beings (to convey His command). Allah is All-Hearing, All-Seeing. [76] He knows all that is before them and that which is hidden from them. And it is to Allah that all affairs are returned.

[77] Believers, bow down and prostrate yourselves before Your Lord and serve Your Lord and do good that you may prosper. [78] Strive in the cause of Allah in a manner worthy of that striving. He has chosen you (for His task), and He has not laid upon you any hardship in religion. Keep to the faith of your father Abraham. Allah named you Muslims earlier and even in this (Book), that the Messenger may be a witness over you, and that you may be witnesses over all mankind. So establish Prayer, and pay *Zakāh*, and hold fast to Allah. He is your Protector. What an excellent Protector; what an excellent Helper!

23
❧

Al-Mu'minūn [The Believers]
Makkan Period

In the name of Allah, the Most Merciful,
the Most Compassionate

[1] The believers have indeed attained true success:
[2] those who, in their Prayers, humble themselves;
[3] who avoid whatever is vain and frivolous; [4] who
observe *Zakāh*; [5] who strictly guard their private parts[1]
[6] save from their wives, or those whom their right
hands possess;[2] for with regard to them they are free from
blame – [7] As for those who seek beyond that, they are
transgressors – [8] who are true to their trusts and their
covenants, [9] and who guard their Prayers. [10] Such
are the inheritors [11] that shall inherit Paradise; and in
it they shall abide for ever.

---

1. This means two things. First, that the believers cover the private
parts of their body; that is, they shun nudity. Second, that they
guard their chastity and modesty; that they are not unfettered in
the exercise of their sex urges.

2. That means the slave-girls, who are captured in war and are
given in the possession of a person by the Islamic state in case there
is no exchange of prisoners of war.

[12] We created man out of the extract of clay, [13] then We made him into a drop of life-germ, then We placed it in a safe depository, [14] then We made this drop into a clot, then We made the clot into a lump, then We made the lump into bones, then We clothed the bones with flesh, and then We caused it to grow into another creation.³ Thus Most Blessed is Allah, the Best of all those that create. [15] Thereafter you are destined to die, [16] and then on the Day of Resurrection you shall certainly be raised up.

[17] We have indeed fashioned above you seven paths.⁴ Never were We unaware of the task of creation.⁵

---

3. Though all this happens in the creation of animals as well, by this process of creation God has shaped man into a special creature different from animals.

4. It probably means the orbit of the seven planets. Since man at that time knew only of seven planets, hence only those orbits are mentioned. This statement does not mean that there are no other orbits.

5. Alternatively, this verse can be rendered as follows: "We were never (nor are) oblivious of the creatures." The idea expressed here is that it is quite evident from everything that God has created that it has neither been created without purpose nor is the creation of any devoid of skill. On the contrary, God's creation conforms to a well-considered plan, with the result that all parts of His creation reveal a high degree of mutual harmony and coordination. Purposiveness is also evident from every aspect of this vast universe which conclusively points to the wisdom of its Creator.

Alternatively, if the verse is understood in the second sense (namely "We were never oblivious of the creatures"), it would mean that God has never been negligent of the needs of any of His creatures, nor has He ever been unaware of the state they are

[18] We sent down water from the sky in right measure, and caused it to stay in the earth, and We have the power to cause it to vanish (in the manner We please). [19] Then through water We caused gardens of date-palms and vines to grow for you wherein you have an abundance of delicious fruits and from them you derive your livelihood. [20] And We also produced the tree which springs forth from Mount Sinai,[6] containing oil and sauce for those that eat.

[21] And indeed there is also a lesson for you in cattle. We provide you with drink out of what they have in their bellies; and you have many other benefits in them: you eat of them, [22] and are carried on them and also on ships.

[23] We sent Noah to his people, and he said: "My people! Serve Allah; you have no deity other than He. Do you have no fear?" [24] But the notables among his people had refused to believe, and said: "This is none other than a mortal like yourselves who desires to attain superiority over you. Had Allah wanted (to send any Messengers) He would have sent down angels. We have heard nothing like

---

in. The result is that God has never allowed anything to go in a direction opposed to His plans, nor has He ever been negligent in providing for the natural requirements of anything. God has always been mindful of all His creation, be it a tiny particle or the leaf of a tree, or anything else.

6. This alludes to olive, the most important product in all the lands around the Mediterranean Sea. The olive tree is mentioned here in association with Mount Sinai. This presumably is because the original region of the olive tree is Mount Sinai which in turn is the most prominent place in that region.

this in the time of our forebears of old (that humans were sent as Messengers). [25] He is a person who has been seized with a little madness; so wait for a while (perhaps he will improve)." [26] Noah said: "My Lord! Come to my help at their accusation that I am lying." [27] Thereupon We revealed to him, saying: "Build the Ark under Our eyes and according to Our revelation. And when Our command comes to pass and the oven boils over, take on board a pair each from every species, and also take your household except those of them against whom sentence has already been passed and do not plead to Me on behalf of the wrong-doers. They are doomed to be drowned. [28] And then when you and those accompanying you are firmly seated in the Ark, say: "Thanks be to Allah Who has delivered us from the wrong-doing people." [29] And say: "My Lord! Make my landing a blessed landing, for You are the Best of those Who can cause people to land in safety."

[30] There are great Signs in this story; and surely We do put people to test.

[31] Then, after them, We brought forth another generation; [32] and We sent among them a Messenger from among themselves, saying: "Serve Allah; you have no god other than He. Do you have no fear?" [33] The notables among his people who had refused to believe and who denied the meeting of the Hereafter, and those whom We had endowed with ease and comfort in this life, cried out: "This is no other than a mortal like yourselves who eats

what you eat and drinks what you drink. [34] If you were to obey a human being like yourselves, you will certainly be losers. [35] Does he promise you that when you are dead and are reduced to dust and bones, you will be brought forth to life? [36] Far-fetched, utterly far-fetched is what you are being promised. [37] There is no other life than the life of the world. We shall live here and here shall we die; and we are not going to be raised again. [38] This man has forged a mere lie in the name of Allah and we shall never believe what he says." [39] The Messenger said: "My Lord! Come to my help at their accusing me of lying." [40] He answered: "A short while, and they shall be repenting." [41] Then a mighty blast quite justly overtook them, and We reduced them to a rubble. So away with the wrong-doing folk!

[42] Then, after them, We brought forth other generations. [43] No nation can outstrip its term, nor can it put it back. [44] Then We sent Our Messengers in succession. Whenever a Messenger came to his people they rejected him, calling him a liar. Thereupon, We made each people to follow the other (to its doom), reducing them to mere tales (of the past). Scourged be the people who do not believe!

[45] Then We sent Moses and his brother Aaron with Our Signs and a clear authority [46] to Pharaoh and to his chiefs, but they behaved superciliously and they were haughty. [47] They said: "Shall we put faith in two mortals like ourselves when their people are slaves to us?" [48] So they rejected them, calling them liars, and

they too eventually became of those that were destroyed.
[49] And We gave Moses the Book that people might be
guided by it.

[50] And We made Mary's son, and his mother, a Sign,
and We gave them refuge on a lofty ground, a peaceful
site with springs flowing in it.

[51] Messengers! Partake of the things that are clean, and
act righteously. I know well all that you do. [52] This
community of yours is one community, and I am your
Lord; so hold Me alone in fear.

[53] But people later cut up their religion into bits, each
group rejoicing in what they have. [54] So leave them
immersed in their heedlessness till an appointed time.

[55] Do they fancy that Our continuing to give them
wealth and children (means) that [56] We are busy
lavishing on them all kinds of good? Nay, they do not
perceive the reality of the matter. [57] Surely those who
stand in awe for fear of their Lord, [58] who have full
faith in the Signs of their Lord; [59] who associate none
with their Lord in His Divinity, [60] who give, whatever
they give in charity, with their hearts trembling at the
thought that they are destined to return to their Lord;
[61] it is these who hasten to do good works and vie in
so doing with one another. [62] We do not lay a burden
on anyone beyond his capacity. We have a Book with Us
that speaks the truth⁷ (about everyone); and they shall

---

7. The "Book" here means the record of deeds that is being
compiled separately for each individual.

in no wise be wronged. [63] Nay, their hearts are lost in ignorance of all this; and their deeds too vary from the way (mentioned above). They will persist in these deeds [64] until We seize with Our chastisement those of them that are given to luxuriant ways. They will then begin to groan. [65] "Put a stop to your groaning now! Surely no help shall be provided to you from Us. [66] My Signs were rehearsed to you and you turned back on your heels and took to flight, [67] behaving arrogantly, and making fun, and talking nonsense (about the Book in your nightly chats)."

[68] Did they never ponder over this Word (of God)? Or has he (to wit, the Messenger) brought something the like of which did not come to their forefathers of yore? [69] Or is it that they were unaware of their Messenger and were therefore repelled by him for he was a stranger to them? [70] Or do they say that there is madness in him? Nay, he has brought them the Truth and it is the Truth that most of them disdain. [71] Were the Truth to follow their desires, the order of the heavens and the earth and those who dwell in them would have been ruined. Nay, the fact is that We have brought to them their own remembrance; and yet it is from their own remembrance that they are turning away.

[72] Are you asking them for something? What Allah has given you is the best. He is the Best of providers. [73] You are calling them to a Straight Way, [74] but those who do not believe in the Hereafter are ever prone to deviate from the Right Way.

[75] Were We to be merciful to them and remove from them their present afflictions,[8] they would persist in their transgression, blindly wandering on. [76] (They are such) that We seized them with chastisement (and yet) they did not humble themselves before their Lord, nor do they entreat [77] until We opened upon them the door of a severe chastisement. Then lo, in this state they become utterly despaired of any good.

[78] It is He Who has endowed you with the faculties of hearing and sight and has given you hearts (to think). Scarcely do you give thanks. [79] It is He Who has dispersed you all around the earth, and it is unto Him that you shall all be mustered. [80] It is He Who gives life and causes death, and He holds mastery over the alternation of night and day. Do you not understand this? [81] Nay, but they say the like of what their predecessors of yore had said. [82] They say: "Is it that when we are dead and have been reduced to dust and bones, shall we then be raised up again? [83] We were promised such things and so were our forefathers before us. All these are no more than tales of the past."

[84] Ask them: "Whose is the earth and those who are in it? Tell us if you know" [85] They will surely say: "Allah's." Say: "Then why do you not take heed?" [86] Ask them: "Who is the Lord of the seven heavens, the Lord of the

---

8. This alludes to the hardship and suffering experienced by the Makkans as a result of the famine that raged for some years after the advent of Muḥammad (peace be on him) as a Prophet.

Great Throne?" [87] They will surely say: "Allah." Say: "Will you not, then, fear (Allah)?" [88] Ask them: "Say, if you indeed know, to whom belongs the dominion over all things; (Who is it) that grants asylum, but against Whom no asylum is available?" [89] They will surely say: "(The dominion over all things) belongs to Allah." Say: "Whence are you then deluded?" [90] We have brought before them the Truth, and there is no doubt that they are lying.[9] [91] Never did Allah take unto Himself any son,[10]

---

9. Their assertion that aught other than the One True God partakes of Divinity (that is, shares with God any of His attributes or authority, or His rights *vis-à-vis* His creatures) is a lie. They also lie when they say that there will be no After-Life. This lie can even be shown to be so by virtue of their own statements. For, on the one hand, they themselves conceded that God is the Lord of the heavens and the earth, and that He has absolute control over everything in the universe. On the other, they contend that Godhead is not exclusively God's but rests with others too – with those who are bound to be His creatures and servants and, thus, are under His omnipotent control. Quite evidently these two positions totally contradict each other. The same applies to the unbelievers' contention regarding the After-Life. On the one hand, they concede that God has created both human beings and this enormous Universe. On the other hand, they contend that God lacks the power to resurrect those whom He had once created. Such an assertion is most patently irrational. Thus, both their doctrines, polytheism and denial of the After-Life, are altogether inconsistent with their own stated positions.

10. This statement should not be regarded as one that simply refutes the Christian doctrine that Jesus was the son of God. It also refutes similar doctrines held by other religious groups. The Arab polytheists of the time also claimed that their deities were God's offspring. Most polytheists the world over have in one way or another succumbed to this error.

nor is there any god other than He. (Had there been any other gods) each god would have taken his creatures away with him, and each would have rushed to overpower the other. Glory be to Allah from all that they characterize Him with! [92] He knows both what is visible and what is not visible. Exalted is Allah above all that they associate with Him.

[93] Pray, (O Muḥammad): "My Lord, if You should bring the scourge of which they had been warned in my presence, [94] then do not include me, my Lord, among these wrong-doing people."[11] [95] Surely We are able to show you what We warn them against.

[96] (O Muḥammad)! Repel evil in the best manner. We are well aware of all that they say about you. [97] And pray: "My Lord! I seek Your refuge from the suggestions of the evil ones; [98] I even seek Your refuge, my Lord, lest they should approach me."

[99] (They shall persist in their deeds) until when death comes to anyone of them he will say: "My Lord, send me back to the world [100] that I have left behind. I am likely to do good." Nay, it is merely a word that he is uttering.

---

11. This, of course, does not mean that there was any danger that the Prophet (peace be on him) would become one of the wrong-doers. Nor was there any possibility that he would succumb to iniquity if he did not make the prayer mentioned here. Rather, the point that is being stressed is that God's punishment is something to be dreaded. God's punishment is so horrendous that even the righteous should seek refuge from it.

There is a barrier[12] behind all of them (who are dead) until the Day when they will be raised up. [101] And then no sooner the Trumpet is blown than there will remain no kinship among them that Day, nor will they ask one another. [102] It will be an Hour when those whose scales are heavy, they alone will attain success; [103] and those whose scales are light, those will be the ones who will have courted loss. They will abide in Hell. [104] The Fire shall scorch their faces, exposing their jaws. [105] "Are you not those to whom My revelations were recited, and you dubbed them as lies?" [106] They will say: "Our Lord! Our misfortune prevailed over us. We were indeed an erring people. [107] Our Lord! Take us out of this. Then if we revert (to evil-doing) we shall indeed be wrong-doers." [108] Allah will say: "Away from Me; stay where you are and do not address Me. [109] You are those that when a party of My servants said: 'Our Lord, we believe, so forgive us, and have mercy on us, for You are the Best of those that are merciful,' [110] you made a laughing-stock of them and your hostility to them caused you to forget Me, and you simply kept laughing. [111] Lo! I have rewarded them this Day for their steadfastness, so that they, and they alone, are triumphant." [112] Then Allah will ask them: "For how many years did you stay on earth?" [113] They will say: "We stayed for a day or part of

---

12. The word *barzakh* is an Arabized form of the Persian word *pardah* (signifying a barrier). According to this verse, there is presently a barrier between those who are dead and the present world. This barrier prevents the dead from returning to life, and so they will stay where they are till the Day of Judgement.

a day. Ask of those who keep count of this." [114] He will say: "You stayed only for a while, if you only knew that. [115] Did you imagine that We created you without any purpose, and that you will not be brought back to Us?"

[116] So, exalted be Allah, the True King! There is no god but He, the Lord of the Great Throne. [117] He who invokes any other god along with Allah – one for whom he has no evidence[13] – his reckoning is with his Lord alone. Indeed, these unbelievers shall not prosper.

[118] And say, (O Muḥammad): "My Lord, forgive us and have mercy on us, for You are the Best of those that are merciful."

---

13. An alternative rendering of the above verse could be: "He who invokes any other god along with Allah has no sanction to do so."

24

Al-Nūr [The Light]
Madīnan Period

*In the name of Allah, the Most Merciful,
the Most Compassionate*

[1] This is a *sūrah* which We have revealed, and which
We have made obligatory; We have revealed in it clear
instructions[1] so that you may take heed.

[2] Those who fornicate – whether female or male – flog
each one of them with a hundred lashes.[2] And let not
tenderness for them deter you from what pertains to
Allah's religion, if you do truly believe in Allah and

---

1. Whatever has been said in this *sūrah* is not in the nature of
recommendations or suggestions that may or may not be followed
by a person, depending on his own will. They are, instead,
categorical commands which must be followed. If someone believes
in and wants to submit himself to God, it is imperative that he acts
in conformity with these commands.

2. The preliminary command about punishment for adultery
occurred in *Sūrah al-Nisā'* 4: 15. Here the categorical punishment
is being laid down. The punishment will apply where either of
the partners is unmarried. As also alluded to in *al-Nisā'* 4: 25 and
confirmed by many traditions, the practice of the Prophet (peace
be on him), the Rightly-Guided Caliphs, and the consensus of the
Ummah, the punishment will be *rajm* (stoning to death) where the
partners found guilty of adultery happen to be married.

the Last Day; and let a party of believers witness their punishment.³

[3] Let the fornicator not marry any except a fornicatress or idolatress and let the fornicatress not marry any except a fornicator or an idolater. That is forbidden to the believers.⁴

[4] Those who accuse honourable women (of unchastity)⁵ but do not produce four witnesses, flog them with eighty

---

3. This means that the punishment should be carried out publicly. This would, on the one hand, arouse in the culprit a feeling of shame and on the other serve as a lesson to others.

4. A befitting match for a person who is guilty of unlawful sexual intercourse and who does not subsequently repent, could only be either a woman who does not mind unlawful sexual relations or a polytheist. A believing woman of good moral character cannot be a good match for such a dissolute person. It is in fact prohibited for believers to wilfully give their daughters in marriage to such persons. Therefore, as far as those women who are guilty of unlawful sex and who do not repent thereafter are concerned, it is in men of the same character or polytheists that they will find appropriate spouses. In fact it is not only inappropriate but also forbidden for a good-charactered believer to marry a woman who is known to be morally dissolute, especially in matters pertaining to sex. It is obvious then that this injunction applies to those men and women who persist in their evil ways. As for those who repent and mend their ways after some lapse, this verse is not applicable to them. For those who repent and subsequently mend their ways can no longer be treated as tainted with the guilt of unlawful sexual intercourse.

5. That is, accusing chaste women of adultery. The injunction also applies to chaste men if they are accused of adultery. This is termed *qadhaf* in the *Sharīʿah* terminology.

lashes, and do not admit their testimony ever after. They are indeed transgressors, [5] except those of them that repent thereafter and mend their behaviour. For surely Allah is Most Forgiving, Ever Compassionate.[6]

[6] As for those who accuse their wives (of unchastity),[7] and have no witnesses except themselves: the testimony of such a one is that he testify, swearing by Allah four times, that he is truthful (in his accusation), [7] and a fifth time, that the curse of Allah be on him if he be lying (in his accusation). [8] And the punishment shall be averted from the woman if she were to testify, swearing by Allah four times that the man was lying, [9] and a fifth time that the wrath of Allah be on her if the man be truthful (in his accusation).[8] [10] Were it not for Allah's Bounty and His Mercy unto you and that Allah is much prone to accept repentance and is Wise, (you would have landed yourselves into great difficulty on the question of unsubstantiated accusation of your spouses).

---

6. The jurists are agreed that the punishment for *qadhaf* does not lapse even if the accuser repents. They are also agreed that the repenter will not be regarded as a sinner and God will forgive him. But opinion is divided over the question whether the testimony of the repenter will be legally admissible. The Ḥanafīs are of the opinion that it will not be, while Shāfiʿī, Mālik and Aḥmad ibn Ḥanbal are in favour of accepting it.

7. That is, accuse them of adultery.

8. This is termed *liʿān* in the *Sharīʿah* terminology. Recourse to *liʿān* cannot be had privately but in a court of law. Both husband and wife can demand *liʿān*. If either of them avoids taking the oaths after *liʿān* has been demanded he/she will be put in prison until he/she agrees to follow the *liʿān* procedure. On the completion of the procedure they become unlawful for each other forever.

[11] Surely those who invented this calumny[9] are a band from among you. Do not deem this incident an evil for you; nay, it is good for you.[10] Every one of them has accumulated sin in proportion to his share in this guilt; and he who has the greater part of it[11] shall suffer a mighty chastisement. [12] When you heard of it, why did the believing men and women not think well of their own folk[12] and say: "This is a manifest calumny?" [13] Why did they not bring four witnesses in support of their accusation? Now that they have brought no witnesses, it is indeed they who are liars in the sight of

9. The verses from here up to 26 deal with the incident known as "calumny". The victim of the slander was 'Ā'ishah who had been accused of adultery. The slanderers propagated their calumny to an extent that it even influenced some Muslims.

10. This is intended to comfort the Prophet (peace be on him). He is being assured that this malicious campaign of slander, which had been engineered by the hypocrites, is bound to boomerang upon them. They, themselves, thought that this would be a significant blow to the Prophet. In point of fact, however, it was destined to hurt the enemies of the Prophet and to prove ultimately useful for his cause.

11. This is an allusion to 'Abd Allāh ibn Ubayy who had concocted the calumnious allegation and who was the master mind behind the slander campaign.

12. Alternatively, this may be translated as "why did the believing men and women not think well of their own folk." Both translations seem equally sound. But the one adopted here is more meaningful. It purports to pose the question as to why did not each of them pause to think that if he/she was ever faced with the kind of situation encountered by 'Ā'ishah would he/she commit adultery?

Allah.[13] [14] Were it not for Allah's Bounty and His Mercy unto you in the world and in the Hereafter a grievous chastisement would have seized you on account of what you indulged in. [15] (Just think, how wrong you were) when one tongue received it from another and you uttered with your mouths something you knew nothing about. You deemed it to be a trifle while in the sight of Allah it was a serious matter.

[16] And why, no sooner than you had heard it, did you not say: "It becomes us not even to utter such a thing? Holy are You (O Allah)! This is a mighty calumny." [17] Allah admonishes you: If you are true believers, never repeat

---

13. There should be no misunderstanding at this stage that the charge was rejected just on the grounds that it was not substantiated by the evidence of witnesses. Nor are Muslims being asked to regard that charge as a calumnious slander merely on the grounds that it was not borne out by the testimony of four witnesses. Such a misunderstanding could arise if one fails to grasp the nature of the incident. The accusers had not levelled the allegation because they themselves, or any others, had observed the monstrosity which they claimed had taken place. They built up such a serious charge merely on the grounds that 'Ā'ishah, who had been left behind, was subsequently brought back by Ṣafwān on his camel. No sensible person can even consider that 'Ā'ishah's being left behind was part of some prearranged scheme. Anyone who contrived such a scheme would not have committed the obvious mistake of appearing with 'Ā'ishah in broad daylight to rejoin the caravan which had by then pitched camp. The actual chain of events itself points to the innocence of both 'Ā'ishah and Ṣafwān. In such circumstances if any charge could have been so levelled it would have been only on the grounds of first-hand observation of the incident. For there was absolutely no *prima facie* basis, no circumstantial evidence, to support such a serious charge.

the like of what you did. [18] Allah clearly expounds to you His instructions. Allah is All-Knowing, All-Wise.

[19] Verily those who love that indecency should spread among the believers deserve a painful chastisement in the world and the Hereafter. Allah knows, but you do not know. [20] Were it not for Allah's Bounty and His Mercy unto you, and that Allah is Most Forgiving and Wise, (the evil that had been spread among you would have led to terrible consequences).

[21] Believers! Do not follow in Satan's footsteps. Let him who follows in Satan's footsteps (remember that) Satan bids people to indecency and evil. Were it not for Allah's Bounty and His Mercy unto you, not one of you would have ever attained purity. But Allah enables whomsoever He wills to attain purity. Allah is All-Hearing, All-Knowing.

[22] Let those among you who are bounteous and resourceful not swear to withhold giving to the kindred, to the needy, and to those who have forsaken their homes in the cause of Allah; rather, let them forgive and forbear. Do you not wish that Allah should forgive you? Allah is Ever Forgiving, Most Merciful.[14]

---

14. This verse alludes to the fact that one of the Muslims who, because of their simplicity, had become affected by the calumny of the slanderers was one of the relatives of Abū Bakr whom the latter used to help financially. Emotionally hurt by his conduct, Abū Bakr vowed that he would no more support him. God did not approve that a person like Abū Bakr should be unforgiving rather than forbearing.

[23] Those that accuse chaste, unwary, believing women, have been cursed in the world and the Hereafter, and a mighty chastisement awaits them. [24] (Let them not be heedless of) the Day when their own tongues, their hands, and their feet shall all bear witness against them as to what they have been doing. [25] On that Day Allah will justly requite them, and they will come to know that Allah – and He alone – is the Truth, the One Who makes the Truth manifest. [26] Corrupt women are for corrupt men, and corrupt men for corrupt women. Good women are for good men, and good men for good women. They are innocent of the calumnies people utter. There shall be forgiveness for them and a generous provision.

[27] Believers![15] Enter not houses other than your own houses until you have obtained the permission of the inmates of those houses and have greeted them with peace. This is better for you. It is expected that you will observe this. [28] Then if you find no one in them, do not enter until you have been given permission (to enter).[16] And if you are told to go back, then do go back.

---

15. The injunctions at the beginning of the *sūrah* were meant to eradicate an evil if it raised its head in society. The commands now being given are of a fundamental nature meant to prevent the rise of evils by rooting out their causes through a process of social reform and regulation of day-to-day conduct.

16. It is not permissible to enter someone's house unless the master of the house has granted prior permission to do so. It would be proper, however, for a visitor to enter a house if the master of the house were absent providing such permission had been granted. Nevertheless, it would not be proper for a visitor to enter a house without obtaining due permission from the master.

This is a purer way for you.[17] Allah knows all what you do. [29] However, it is not blameworthy for you if you enter houses that are uninhabited but wherein there is something of use to you.[18] Allah is well aware of what you disclose and what you conceal.

[30] (O Prophet), enjoin believing men to cast down their looks[19] and guard their private parts. That is purer for them. Surely Allah is well aware of all what they do.

---

17. A person should not feel offended if someone declines to meet him. For a person is perfectly within his rights to decline meeting someone or to excuse himself from such a meeting if he is preoccupied with something else.

18. This refers to public places such as hotels, guesthouses, shops and other places which everyone is entitled to enter without obtaining any specific permission to do so.

19. The words used here are *yaghuḍḍū min abṣārihim*. Literally the word *ghaḍḍ* denotes reducing or lowering something. The words *ghaḍḍ al-baṣar*, therefore, are usually translated as "lowering one's gaze" or "keeping one's gaze downwards". This Qur'ānic directive does not mean, however, that one should always gaze, quite literally, downwards. What it really means is that one should not look thoroughly at a certain thing; that one should not allow one's eyes to be unfettered in looking. In other words, one should avoid looking at things which it is improper to look at. This may be achieved either by avoiding looking at something by turning one's gaze away or by lowering it. Once again, the words *min abṣārihim* signify that some, rather than every kind of looking, needs to be avoided. It becomes evident from the context that this directive is addressed to those men who focus their gaze on women, or who cast their glances at other's private parts, or who intentionally look at obscene objects.

[31] And enjoin believing women to cast down their looks and guard their private parts and[20] not reveal their adornment except that which is revealed of itself, and to draw their veils over their bosoms, and not to reveal their adornment save to their husbands, or their fathers, or the fathers of their husbands,[21] or of their own sons, or the sons of their husbands,[22] or their brothers,[23] or the sons of their brothers, or the sons of their sisters,[24] or the women with whom they associate,[25] or those that are in

---

20. It should be noted that the demands that the Divine Law makes on women, (as mentioned in this verse), are not just what is expected of men, i.e. avoiding to look at what is improper to look at and guarding one's private parts. It also demands of women more than what it requires men to do. This clearly shows that women are not equated with men as far as this matter is concerned.

21. The word *ābā'* used in this verse covers one's father, both maternal and paternal grandfathers and great-grandfathers. A woman may, therefore, appear before these elders of either her own family or of her husband's family in the same manner as she may appear before both her father and father-in-law.

22. The word *abnā'ihinna* ("their sons") covers, apart from their own sons, their grandsons and great-grandsons, i.e. those born both of one's sons and daughters. Furthermore, no distinction is made between one's own sons and one's stepsons. A woman may appear freely before the children of her stepsons as she may appear before her own children and grandchildren.

23. "Brothers" here covers both real and stepbrothers.

24. This refers to a woman's nieces and nephews, whether they are born of her brother or sister, and whether those brothers and sisters are real or are stepbrothers and stepsisters.

25. This by itself shows that a Muslim woman should not display her attractions before immoral and immodest women.

their bondage, or the male attendants in their service free of sexual interest,[26] or boys that are yet unaware of illicit matters pertaining to women. Nor should they stamp their feet on the ground in such manner that their hidden ornament becomes revealed. Believers, turn together, all of you, to Allah in repentance that you may attain true success.

[32] Marry those of you that are single, (whether men or women), and those of your male and female slaves that are righteous. If they are poor, Allah will enrich them out of His Bounty. Allah is Immensely Resourceful, All-Knowing. [33] Let those who cannot afford to marry keep themselves chaste until Allah enriches them out of His Bounty. And write out a deed of manumission for such of your slaves that desire their freedom in lieu of payment[27] – if you see any good in them[28] – and give them out of the wealth that Allah has given you.[29] And do not

26. That is, as they are in a state of subservience there is no room to suspect that they would dare harbour evil designs regarding the women of the household.

27. When a slave, whether male or female, asks his/her master to enter into a manumission agreement and the master accepts the offer, the terms of the agreement should be recorded.

28. "Goodness" here embraces the following two points: first, that the slave should have the ability to pay the amount required for his manumission by his earnings; second, that the slave should be known for his honesty and trustworthiness so that an agreement might be made with him.

29. The masters are directed to remit at least a part of the amount which the slaves are required to pay according to the manumission agreement. Muslims in general are also directed that they should

compel your slave-girls to prostitution[30] for the sake of the benefits of worldly life the while they desire to remain chaste.[31] And if anyone compels them to prostitution, Allah will be Most Pardoning, Much Merciful (to them) after their subjection to such compulsion.

[34] Verily We have sent down for you revelations which clearly expound true guidance, and examples of those who passed away before you, and an admonition for those who fear (Allah).

[35] Allah is the Light of the heavens and the earth.[32] His Light (in the Universe) may be likened to a niche wherein is a lamp, and the lamp is in the crystal which shines in star-like brilliance. It is lit from (the oil) of a blessed olive tree that is neither eastern nor western. Its oil well nigh glows forth (of itself) though no fire touched it: Light

---

generously help those who ask them for money required for their manumission. A part of the *Zakāh* in the Public Treasury should be spent on assisting the slaves who have entered into manumission agreements so that they might become free.

30. In the pre-Islamic days of Ignorance the Arabs would force their slave-girls into prostitution and take their earnings. Islam prohibited prostitution in absolute terms.

31. If a slave-girl indulges in prostitution of her own accord, she will herself be responsible for her actions. The law will take its course and she will be brought to book. However, if her master compels her into prostitution, it is the master who will be held accountable.

32. What is meant by this statement is that God alone is the main cause for the existence of all that exists, while all else is mere darkness.

upon Light.[33] Allah guides to His Light whom He wills.
Allah sets forth parables to make people understand.
Allah knows everything. [36] (Those who are directed to
this Light are found) in houses which Allah has allowed
to be raised and wherein His name is to be remembered:
in them people glorify Him in the morning and in the
evening, [37] people whom neither commerce nor striving
after profit diverts them from remembering Allah, from
establishing Prayer, and from paying *Zakāh*; people who
dread the Day on which all hearts will be overturned
and eyes will be petrified; [38] (people who do all this
so) that Allah may reward them in accordance with the
best that they did; indeed He will bestow upon them
more out of His Bounty, for Allah grants whomsoever He
wills beyond all measure. [39] But for those who deny the
Truth, their deeds are like a mirage in the desert, which

---

33. In this parable, God is likened to a lamp, whereas the crystal
signifies the curtain by which He has concealed Himself from His
creatures. The purpose behind this curtain is not concealment;
it is rather because of the pressure to break out into the open.
Thus, the inability of creatures to observe God is not because of
the opaqueness of the curtain or its being covered with darkness.
Rather, our failure to observe God is because of the fact that the
light passing through this transparent curtain is so intense and
all-encompassing that those with limited faculties of vision fail to
perceive it. The statement that this lamp is lit from the oil of an
olive tree, "neither eastern nor western," provides an impressive
image of the perfection and intensity of the light of the lamp. In the
past, light was mostly obtained from lamps lit by olive oil, and the
brightest lamp was one which was lit from the oil of the olive tree
situated in an open and elevated place. Similarly, the statement that
"its oil well nigh glows forth (of itself) though no fire touched it,"
again reinforces the effect of the intense brightness of the lamp.

the thirsty supposes to be water until he comes to it only to find that it was nothing; he found instead that Allah was with Him and He paid his account in full. Allah is swift in settling the account. [40] Or its similitude is that of depths of darkness upon an abysmal sea, covered by a billow, above which is a billow, above which is cloud, creating darkness piled one upon another; when he puts forth his hand, he would scarcely see it. He to whom Allah assigns no light, he will have no light.

[41] Do you not see that all that is in the heavens and the earth, even the birds that go about spreading their wings in flight, extol His glory? Each knows the way of its prayer and of its extolling Allah's glory. Allah is well aware of whatever they do. [42] Allah's is the dominion of the heavens and the earth and to Him are all destined to return.

[43] Do you not see that it is Allah Who gently drives the clouds, then He joins them together and then turns them into a thick mass and thereafter you see rain-drops fall down from its midst? And then He sends down hail from the heaven – thanks to the mountains[34] – and causes it to smite whom He wills and averts it from whom He wills. The flash of His lightning almost takes away the sight. [44] It is Allah Who alternates the night and the day. Surely there is a lesson in it for those that have sight.

---

34. This statement may refer to snow-laden clouds which have figuratively been called the mountains of heaven. It could, however, also mean in quite literal terms the mountains of the earth which rise high in the sky. As a result, the winds there occasionally become so cold that they freeze the clouds. This, in turn, leads to hailstorms.

[45] Allah has created every animal from water. Of them some move on their bellies, some move on two legs and some on four. Allah creates whatever He wills. Surely Allah has power over everything.

[46] Verily We have sent down revelations that clearly explain the Truth. Allah guides whomsoever He wills to a Straight Way.

[47] They say: "We believe in Allah and the Messenger, and we obey," but thereafter a faction of them turns away (from obedience). These indeed are not believers. [48] When they are called to Allah and His Messenger that he (that is, the Messenger) may judge (the disputes) among them, a faction of them turns away. [49] However if the right is on their side they come to him (professing) their submissiveness. [50] Do their hearts suffer from the disease (of hypocrisy)? Or have they fallen prey to doubts? Or do they fear that Allah and His Messenger will wrong them? Nay, the truth is that they themselves are wrong-doers. [51] When those that believe are called to Allah and His Messenger in order that he (that is, the Messenger) may judge their disputes among them, nothing becomes them but to say: "We hear and we obey." Such shall attain true success. [52] Those who obey Allah and His Messenger and fear Him and avoid disobeying Him: such, indeed, shall triumph.

[53] (The hypocrites) solemnly swear by Allah: "If you order us, we shall surely go forth (and fight in the cause of Allah)." Tell them: "Do not swear. The state of your obedience is known. Allah is well aware of all that you do." [54] Say: "Obey Allah and obey the Messenger. But

if you turn away, then (know well) that the Messenger is responsible for what he has been charged with and you are responsible for what you have been charged with. But if you obey him, you will be guided to the Right Way. The Messenger has no other responsibility but to clearly convey (the command)."

[55] Allah has promised those of you who believe and do righteous deeds that He will surely bestow power on them in the land even as He bestowed power on those that preceded them, and that He will firmly establish their religion which He has been pleased to choose for them, and He will replace with security the state of fear that they are in. Let them serve Me and associate none with Me in My Divinity.[35] Whoso thereafter engages in unbelief,[36] such indeed are the ungodly. [56] Establish Prayer and pay *Zakāh* and obey the Messenger so that mercy may be shown to you. [57] Do not even imagine that those who disbelieve can render Allah powerless in the land. Their abode is the Fire; what an evil abode!

[58] Believers! At three times let those whom your right hands possess and those of your children who have not yet reached puberty ask leave of you before entering your

35. Some people tend to interpret vicegerency in the narrow sense of mere power, of dominance and hegemony. With this false assumption, they infer that whoever is in power is *ipso facto* the vicegerent of God, whereas what has been said is that vicegerency will be conferred upon those who are righteous.

36. Here *kufr* may imply ingratitude after having attained vicegerency, or it may mean resorting to hypocrisy: that is, though he may be a Muslim in appearance he is devoid of true faith.

quarters: before the Morning Prayer and when you take off your clothes at noon, and after the Night Prayer. These are the three times of privacy for you. If they come to you at other times then there is no sin for them nor for you, for you have to visit one another frequently. Thus does Allah clearly explain His directives to you. Allah is All-Knowing, All-Wise. [59] And when your children attain puberty let them ask leave to come to you like their elders used to ask leave. Thus does Allah clearly explain to you His Signs. He is All-Knowing, All-Wise.

[60] The women who are past their youth (and can no longer bear children) and do not look forward to marriage will incur no sin if they cast off their outer garments without displaying their adornment. But if they remain modest, that is still better for them. Allah is All-Hearing, All-Knowing.

[61] There is no blame on the blind nor any blame on the lame nor any blame on the sick nor on yourselves that you eat in your own houses, or your fathers' houses, or your mothers' houses, or your brothers' houses, or the houses of your sisters, or the houses of your fathers' brothers or the houses of your fathers' sisters, or in the houses of your mothers' brothers, or in the houses of your mothers' sisters or in the houses whose keys you possess, or the house of a friend. There is no blame if you eat together or separately. But when you enter such houses, greet each other with a salutation appointed by Allah, a salutation that is blessed and good. Thus, does Allah expound His signs to you in order that you will act with understanding.

[62] The true believers are only those who sincerely believe in Allah and in His Messenger and who, whenever they are with him on some common errand, they do not go away until they have asked leave of him. Verily those who ask leave of you, it is they who truly believe in Allah and His Messenger. So if they ask your leave in connection with some of their affairs, give leave to those whom you will, and ask Allah for forgiveness on their behalf. Surely Allah is Much Forgiving, Ever Merciful.

[63] (Muslims!) Do not make the calling of the Messenger among you as your calling one another. Allah knows well those of you who surreptitiously steal away, taking shelter behind one another. Let those who go against the order (of the Messenger) beware lest a trial or severe punishment afflict them. [64] Lo! Whatsoever is in the heavens and the earth belongs to Allah. He is well aware of your ways. And the Day when they will be returned to Him, He will tell them all what they did. Allah knows everything.

25
❧❧❧

Al-Furqān [The Criterion]
Makkan Period

In the name of Allah, the Most Merciful,
the Most Compassionate

[1] Most blessed is He Who sent down this Criterion on His servant, to be a warner to all mankind; [2] He to Whom belongs the kingdom of the heavens and the earth; Who has taken to Himself no son nor has He taken any partner in His kingdom; Who created everything and then determined its destiny. [3] Yet people have taken, instead of Him, other deities; those that create nothing but are themselves created; who do not have the power to hurt or benefit even themselves; who have no power over death, nor over life, nor over the resurrection of the dead.

[4] Those who disbelieve in the Message of the Prophet say: "This (Criterion) is nothing but a lie which he has forged with the help of others." Such have indeed resorted to a grievous wrong and sheer falsehood. [5] They say: "These are merely fairy tales of the ancients which he has got inscribed and they are then recited to him morning and evening." [6] Say to them (O Muḥammad): "It is He Who knows the secrets of the heavens and the earth Who has sent down this Book. Indeed, He is Most Forgiving, Most Compassionate."

[7] They say: "What sort of a Messenger is this: he eats food and walks about in the markets? Why was an angel not sent down to him so that he may remain with the Messenger and warn those that do not believe in him? [8] Why was a treasure not bestowed upon him, or a garden whereof he might obtain his sustenance?" The evil-doers say: "You are simply following a bewitched man." [9] See what specious arguments they put forth before you: they are so strayed that they will not find their way to anything sound. [10] Most blessed is He Who, if He wills, can grant you even better than what they propose: Gardens beneath which rivers flow, and stately mansions.

[11] Nay, the truth is that it is the Hour to which they give the lie.[1] We have kept a Blazing Fire ready for him who denies the Hour. [12] When it sees them from a place afar, they will hear its raging and roaring, [13] and when they are flung, chained together, into a narrow place in it, they will fervently call there for annihilation. [14] (They will then be told): "Do not call for a single annihilation, but for many an annihilation."

[15] Ask them: "Is this state better or the Garden of Eternity which the God-fearing have been promised?" It shall be their recompense and the end-point of their journey; [16] the Garden wherein whatever they desire will be fulfilled. In it they shall abide for ever. This is a promise whose fulfilment Your Lord has made incumbent on Himself.

---

1. That is, the Hour of Resurrection.

[17] On the Day when He will muster together all the unbelievers as well as the deities that they worship beside Allah, and He will ask them: "Was it you who caused these servants of Mine to stray away, or did they themselves stray away from the Right Path?" [18] They will say: "Glory be to You! It did not behove us to take any other than You as our guardians, but You lavished the pleasures of life upon them and their forefathers until they forgot the Admonition and became doomed to destruction." [19] Thus will those deities give the lie to all what you now say,[2] and you will not be able to avert your doom, nor obtain any succour. We shall cause whoever of you commits wrong to taste an enormous chastisement.

[20] (O Muḥammad), We never sent any Messengers before you but they ate food and walked about in the markets. We made some of you a means to test each by the other[3] to see whether you remain patient.[4] Your Lord is All-Seeing.

---

2. It is clear from the context that what is meant by "deities" here are not idols or objects like sun or moon, etc., but angels and saints whom the unbelievers have set up as deities in this world.

3. The Messenger and the believers are a means by which to test the unbelievers, and *vice versa*.

4. Once the underlying wisdom behind making the unbelievers a test for the believers and *vice versa* is grasped, the believers should be patient and appreciate that the hardships to which they are exposed is a very useful way of achieving the lofty purpose for which they are working. Are they, then, ready to suffer the injuries that the test inevitably entails?

[21] Those who do not look forward to meet Us say: "Why should angels not be sent to us, or why do we ourselves not observe our Lord?" Surely they are too proud of themselves and have gone beyond all limits in their rebellion. [22] On that Day – the Day when they will behold angels – there will be no good news for those immersed in evil, and they will cry out: "We seek refuge (in Allah)." [23] And We shall turn to their deeds and shall reduce them to scattered dust. [24] On that Day it is the inmates of Paradise that will be graced with a better abode and a fairer resting place. [25] On that Day the sky shall be rent asunder by a cloud and a whole cavalcade of angels will be made to descend. [26] On that Day the true kingdom will belong only to the Merciful Lord. That will be a hard day for those that deny the Truth; [27] a Day when the wrong-doer will bite his hands, saying: "Would that I had stood by the Messenger! [28] Woe is me! Would that I had not taken such a one for a friend! [29] He led me astray from the Admonition that had come to me. Satan proved to be a great betrayer of man." [30] And the Messenger will say: "My Lord! My own people had made this Qur'ān an object of laughter."

[31] (O Muḥammad), thus did We make for every Prophet enemies from among those immersed in evil. Your Lord suffices you as a Guide and a Helper.

[32] Those who disbelieve say: "Why was the Qur'ān not revealed to him all at once?" It was revealed thus that We may fully impress it on your mind; (and for the same end) We have revealed it gradually (according to a scheme) in fragments. [33] (This was also done so that) whenever they put any strange question to you, We sent its right answer

and explained the matter in the best manner. [34] Those who shall be mustered in the Hell upon their faces, their stand is the worst and their way most erroneous.

[35] Verily We granted Moses the Book[5] and appointed his brother Aaron with him as his helper [36] and said to him: "Go the two of you to the people who have given the lie to Our Signs." Thereafter We utterly destroyed them. [37] (The same happened with) the people of Noah: when they gave the lie to the Messengers We drowned them and made of them a Sign of warning for all mankind. We have kept ready a painful chastisement for the wrong-doers. [38] And in like manner were the ʿĀd and the Thamūd destroyed and the people of al-Rass[6] and many a nation in the centuries in between. [39] We warned each (of them) by examples (of the nations so destroyed in the past), and We totally annihilated each of them. [40] They have surely passed by the town which was rained upon

---

5. Here "the Book" most probably does not refer to the Torah which was given to Moses after the Israelites' exodus from Egypt. It refers, instead, to the whole body of guidance which was given to Moses after his designation as a Prophet until the exodus. These include the statements made by Moses in Pharaoh's court and the various instructions given to him by God during his struggle with Pharaoh. These are mentioned several times in the Qur'ān. But presumably these are not included in the Torah which begins with the Ten Commandments that were given to Moses on stone tablets on Mount Sinai.

6. The people of Rass were the people who had slain their Prophet by casting him into, or hanging him over, a well. It is also worth noting that in Arabic the word *rass* literally means an old or dry well.

by an evil rain.[7] Have they not seen it? Nay; but they do not believe in being raised up after death.

[41] Whenever they see you they take you for nothing else but an object of jest, saying: "Is this whom Allah has sent as a Messenger? [42] Had we not firmly persevered in our devotion to them (he had almost) led us astray from our gods." But soon, when they see the chastisement, they will come to know who had strayed too far from the Right Way.

[43] Have you ever considered the case of him who has taken his carnal desire for his god? Can you take responsibility for guiding him to the Right Way? [44] Do you think that most of them hear or understand? For they are merely like cattle; nay, even worse than them.

[45] Have you not seen how your Lord spreads the shade? If He will, He could have made it stationary; instead, We have made the sun its pilot.[8] [46] So (as the sun rises), We gradually roll up that shade unto Us.[9]

---

7. This refers to the habitation of the Prophet Lot. As for the "evil rain", this is the rain of stones which is mentioned on many occasions in the Qur'ān.

8. The word *dalīl* has been used here in exactly the same sense in which the word "pilot" is used in English. In seafaring terminology, *dalīl* is the person who guides the boats. To say that the sun is a *dalīl* of the shade means that the lengthening and shortening of the shade is dependent on the rise and decline of the sun.

9. To "roll up that shade unto Us" means to cause a thing to vanish, to drive it out of existence, for whatever vanishes or becomes extinct returns to God. From Him everything issues and to Him everything ultimately returns.

[47] It is Allah Who has made night a garment for you, and sleep the repose (of death), and has made day the time of rising to life.

[48] And He it is Who sends forth the winds as glad tidings, heralding His Mercy. Then We send down pure water from the sky [49] that We may revive through it a dead land and give it for drink to many cattle and human beings from among Our creation. [50] We present this wondrous phenomenon to them over and over again that they may learn a lesson from it. But most people simply decline everything except disbelief and ingratitude.

[51] Had We so willed, We would have raised up in every town a warner.[10] [52] So, (O Prophet), do not follow the unbelievers but engage in a mighty striving against them with this Qur'ān.

[53] And He it is Who has joined the two seas: one sweet and palatable and the other saltish and bitter; and He has set a barrier and an insurmountable obstruction between the two that keeps them apart.[11]

---

10. It was not beyond God's power to do so. Had He so willed, He would have raised a Prophet in every nook and corner of the world. But He did not do so and instead raised a Prophet for the whole world. Just like one sun is enough for the whole earth, this one sun of guidance was deemed sufficient for the whole of humanity.

11. This happens wherever a large river flows into the sea. There are springs of sweet water at several locations in different seas where the sweet water remains separate from the salty water of the sea. For example, near Bahrain and at other places in the Persian Gulf there are springs of sweet water under the sea from which people have drawn sweet water for ages.

[54] And He it is Who has created man from water and then produced from him two sorts of kindred: by descent and by marriage. Your Lord is All-Powerful.

[55] And yet people worship deities other than Allah that can neither benefit them nor hurt them. Besides, the unbeliever is ever prone to come to the support of everyone who rebels against his Lord.

[56] We have not sent you, (O Muḥammad), except as a bearer of good tidings and a warner.[12] [57] Say to them: "I ask of you no reward for my work. My only reward is that whoever so wills may follow the way leading to His Lord."

[58] (O Muḥammad), put your trust in Him Who is Ever-Living, Who will never die, and glorify Him with His praise. He suffices as the Knower of the sins of His servants, [59] He Who created the heavens and the earth and all that is in between them in six days, and then ascended the Throne; the Merciful One. Ask concerning Him the one who knows.

[60] When they are told: "Prostrate yourselves before the Merciful One," they say: "What is the Merciful One? Shall we prostrate ourselves before whomsoever you command us to prostrate?" This even further increases their aversion.

---

12. It is not part of a Prophet's task to reward the believers or to punish the unbelievers. A Prophet is not appointed to force people to believe. His responsibility is no more than to give good tidings to those who would accept the Truth and warn those who would adamantly persist in their evil ways, thereby inviting God's punishment.

[61] Most blessed is He Who set a constellation in the heavens, and placed in it a great lamp and a shining moon. [62] He it is Who has appointed night and day to succeed one another (as a Sign) for him who desires to take heed, or desires to be thankful.

[63] The true servants of the Merciful One are those who walk on the earth gently[13] and when the foolish ones address them, they simply say: "Peace to you"; [64] who spend the night prostrating themselves before their Lord and standing; [65] who entreat: "Our Lord! Ward off from us the chastisement of Hell, for its chastisement is one that clings. [66] Verily it is a wretched abode and resting-place." [67] (The true servants of the Merciful One are) the who are neither extravagant nor niggardly in their spending but keep the golden mean between the two; [68] who invoke no other deity along with Allah, nor take any life – which Allah has forbidden – save justly; who do not commit unlawful sexual intercourse – and whoso does that shall meet its penalty; [69] his torment shall be doubled for him on the Day of Resurrection, and he will abide in it in ignominy – [70] unless he repents and believes and does righteous works. For such, Allah will change their evil deeds into good deeds. Allah is Ever Forgiving, Most Compassionate. [71] Whosoever repents and does good, he returns to Allah in the manner that he should. [72] (The true servants of the Merciful One) are those who do not bear witness to any falsehood and who, when they pass by frivolity, pass by it with dignity;

True servants of God do not strut about arrogantly like haughty tyrants. On the contrary, their gait is gentle, the gait of noble and right people.

[73] who, when they are reminded of the revelations of their Lord, do not fall at them deaf and blind; [74] who are prone to pray: "Our Lord! Grant us that our spouses and our offspring be a joy to our eyes, and do make us the leaders of the God-fearing."[14] [75] They are the ones who will be rewarded for their patience: lofty palaces will be granted to them, and they will be received with greeting and salutation. [76] Therein they shall abide for ever: how good an abode, and how good a resting-place!

[77] Say to them (O Muḥammad): "My Lord would not care for you were it not for your prayer.[15] But now that you have given the lie to (the Message of Allah), an inextricable punishment shall soon come upon you."

14. They prayed that God may enable them to surpass everyone in piety, obedience, righteousness and good deeds; nay, that they may become leaders of the pious, and that they may become a source for the promotion of goodness and virtue and piety in the world. Again, this is stated here to demonstrate that these people do not compete with one another in wealth, power and worldly glory. They rather strive to excel in acts of piety.

15. If one does not worship God, if one does not supplicate to Him for one's needs, and does not seek His help, then one is not worth anything in God's sight. For God does not care for people just because they are His creatures. In this regard, they are no different from stones and quite obviously God stands in no need of them. Hence, if they do not obey Him, this will certainly not endear such persons to God. Nevertheless, were someone to stretch out his hands to Him in supplication, he will instantly find God turning to him in compassion. As for those who arrogantly refuse to worship God or pray to Him, then they are liable to incur God's punishment and He can certainly dispose of them, if He wills, just as one disposes of rubbish.

26
❧❀❧

Al-Shuʿarāʾ [The Poets]
Makkan Period

*In the name of Allah, the Most Merciful,
the Most Compassionate*

[1] *Ṭāʾ. Sīn. Mīm.* [2] These are the verses of the Clear
Book.¹

[3] (O Muḥammad), you will perhaps grieve yourself to
death because these people do not believe. [4] If We will,
We can send down a Sign to them from heaven, so their
necks will be humbled to it.² [5] Never does there come
to them an admonition from the Merciful Lord but they
turn away from it. [6] They will soon come to know the
truth of that which they have been scoffing at.

---

1. That is, the verses of this *sūrah* are from a Clear and Lucid Book.
Everyone who reads or listens to this Book can understand, without
any difficulty, what it is calling people to: what it enjoins and what
it forbids; what it regards as the Truth and what it condemns as
falsehood. To believe or not to believe is a different matter, but
no one has any valid excuse to say that he cannot understand the
teachings of the Book or cannot ascertain what that Book would
like him to act upon and what it urges him to give up.

2. It is not at all difficult for God to send a Sign that would compel
the unbelievers to believe and obey. If God does not send such a
Sign, it is not because this is beyond His power; rather, it is because
He does not want people to believe compulsively.

[7] Do they not look at the earth, how We caused a variety of fine vegetation to grow from it (in abundance)? [8] Surely there is a Sign in this,³ but most of them would not believe. [9] Verily Your Lord is Infinitely Mighty, Most Compassionate.⁴

[10] (Recount to them about the time) when Your Lord called Moses: "Go to the wrong-doing people, [11] the people of Pharaoh: do they have no fear?" [12] He said: "My Lord! I fear that they will brand me a liar. [13] My breast is constricted and my tongue is not fluent, so endow Messengership on Aaron. [14] As for me, they hold the charge of a crime against me. I fear they will put me to death." [15] He said: "Certainly not! So go both of you with Our Signs. We shall be with you listening to everything. [16] Go, then, to Pharaoh and say to him: 'The Lord of the Universe has sent us [17] that you let the Children of Israel go with us.'"

[18] Pharaoh said: "Did we not bring you up among us when you were a child? [19] You spent many years of

---

3. For any seeker of the Truth just a glance at the vegetation on earth tells which of the two worldviews is true: the worldview of the Prophets who affirm God's Unity, or alternatively, the worldview expounded by either atheists or polytheists.

4. God's power is such that He can instantly annihilate anyone. It is out of His Mercy, however, that God does not hasten to punish the guilty; rather, He grants them respite for years and years, possibly extending it to hundreds of years. He gives them time to think, to reflect and to correct themselves. Furthermore, He even forgives the sins of a lifetime if the sinner truly repents, and does so just once.

your life among us and then you committed that deed of yours. You are very ungrateful indeed." [20] Moses replied: "I committed that act erringly. [21] Then I fled for fear of you. Then my Lord bestowed wisdom and authority on me and made me one of the Messengers. [22] Now this is the favour that you tauntingly remind me of: that you enslaved the Children of Israel!"[5] [23] Pharaoh said: "And who is this Lord of the Universe?" [24] Moses answered: "The Lord of the heavens and the earth and of all that is between them, if you were only to believe." [25] Pharaoh said to those around him: "Do you hear (what he says)?" [26] Moses said: "(He is) Your Lord and the Lord of your forefathers of yore." [27] Pharaoh said to the audience: "This Messenger of yours who has been sent to you is simply mad." [28] Moses continued: "(He is) the Lord of the east and the west, and all between them. If you only had any understanding!" [29] Pharaoh said: "If you take any god other than me, I will certainly make you one of those (who are rotting) in prison." [30] Moses said: "Even if I were to bring a Clear Sign to you?" [31] Pharaoh said: "Then bring it if you are truthful at all."

[32] (No sooner had he said this than) Moses threw down his rod and behold, it was a veritable serpent,

---

5. That is, if Pharaoh had not ruthlessly persecuted the Israelites, Moses would not have come to his house and would not have been brought up there. It was only on account of Pharaoh's cruelty that Moses' mother was forced to put him in a chest and cast that chest into the river. But for that, Moses would have been happily brought up in his own home. Therefore, his upbringing in Pharaoh's house was not an act of favour to Moses and it was not appropriate for Pharaoh to mention it as such.

[33] and he drew his hand (out of his armpit) and lo! it had become a shining object to the beholders.[6]

[34] Pharaoh said to the nobles around him: "Surely this man is a skilled magician [35] who wants to drive you out of your land by his magic.[7] Tell us, what do you advise us?" [36] They said: "Detain him and his brother for a while and send forth heralds to the cities [37] to mobilise all skilled magicians." [38] So the magicians were brought together on a particular day at a set time [39] and the people were told: "Will you join the assembly? [40] We may perhaps follow the religion of the magicians if they triumph."[8]

---

6. As soon as Moses took out his hand from his armpit, the whole court became radiant as though the sun had risen.

7. The impact of these two miracles can be judged from the swift change in Pharaoh's attitude. A moment ago he had called Moses a madman because of his claim to be a Prophet and his demand that the Israelites be allowed to leave Egypt with him. Pharaoh had also threatened Moses with imprisonment. But no sooner had he observed these two signs than he was struck with awe and panicked at the prospect of losing all his kingdom.

8. Mere proclamation was not considered enough. Agents were sent all around Egypt to persuade people to come and witness the contest. This shows that the news of Moses' miracles in the court had reached the common people and that Pharaoh was afraid that the masses might have been influenced by it. The faith of the courtiers who had witnessed Moses' miracles had also begun to weaken, as did the faith of those who had only heard about those miracles. The only thing that could possibly strengthen their faith was for the Egyptian magicians to come up with something on a par with Moses' performance. Pharaoh and his nobles, therefore, looked upon the forthcoming contest as an event of crucial importance. It was their own heralds who went around telling people that if the

[41] When the magicians came forth (for the encounter) they said to Pharaoh: "Is there a reward for us if we triumph?" [42] He said: "Yes, you will then become those near-stationed to me." [43] Moses said to them: "Throw down whatever you wish to throw." [44] Thereupon they threw down their ropes and their rods, and said: "By the glory of Pharaoh, we shall prevail." [45] Thereafter, Moses threw down his rod and behold, it went about swallowing up all the false devices they had contrived. [46] Thereupon the magicians fell down in prostration, [47] saying: "We (now) believe in the Lord of the Universe, [48] the Lord of Moses and Aaron." [49] Pharaoh said: "You accepted the word of Moses even before I granted you the leave to do so. Surely he is your chief who has taught you magic. Soon shall you come to know. I shall cut off your hands and feet on opposite sides and shall crucify all of you." [50] They said: "We do not care, for we are bound to return to our Lord, [51] and we surely expect that Our Lord will forgive us our sins for we are the first ones to believe."

[52] We[9] revealed to Moses: "Set forth with My servants by night for you will be pursued." [53] Then Pharaoh sent heralds to the cities (to mobilise troops) [54] saying: "These (Israelites) are only a small band of people [55] who have certainly provoked our wrath. [56] But we are a numerous host, ever on guard." [57] Thus did We drive them out

---

magicians won the day, they would be secure from Moses' religion. If not, their religion would be in trouble.

9. The story is now being resumed from the time when Moses was commanded to emigrate from Egypt.

of their gardens and springs [58] and their treasures and excellent dwellings. [59] This happened with them; (but on the other hand), We enabled the Children of Israel to inherit those bounties.

[60] At sunrise they set off in pursuit of them [61] and when the groups came face to face, the companions of Moses cried out: "We are overtaken!" [62] Moses said: "Certainly not. My Lord is with me; He will direct me." [63] Then We revealed to Moses, (commanding him): "Strike the sea with your rod." Thereupon the sea split up, and then each became like the mass of a huge mount. [64] We also brought the other party close to the same spot, [65] and We delivered Moses and his companions, all of them, [66] then We drowned the others.

[67] Surely there is a Sign in this, but most of them would not believe. [68] Verily your Lord is Immensely Mighty, Ever Compassionate.

[69] And recount to them the story of Abraham: [70] when he asked his father and his people: "What do you worship?" [71] They answered: "There are some idols that we worship and are devoted to them with constancy." [72] He asked: "Do they hear you when you call them [73] or do they cause you any benefit or harm?" [74] They answered: "No; but we found our forefathers doing so." [75] Thereupon, Abraham said: "Have you seen (with your eyes) those whom you have been worshipping, [76] you and your forefathers of yore? [77] They are all enemies to me; all, except the Lord of the Universe [78] Who created me and Who guides me; [79] Who gives me food and drink,

[80] and Who, when I am ill, heals me; [81] Who will cause me to die and then will again restore me to life; [82] Who, I hope, will forgive me my sins on the Day of Judgement." [83] (And then Abraham prayed): "My Lord, endow me with knowledge and wisdom and join me with the righteous, [84] and grant me an honourable reputation among posterity, [85] and make me of those who will inherit the Garden of Bliss, [86] and forgive my father for he is among those who strayed, [87] and disgrace me not on the Day when people will be raised to life, [88] the Day when nothing will avail, neither wealth nor offspring, [89] but only he that brings to Allah a sound heart will (attain to success)."

[90] (On that Day)[10] the Garden will be brought near to the God-fearing, [91] and the Fire will be uncovered for those who strayed, [92] and they will be asked: "Where are the gods that you worshipped [93] beside Allah? Can they be of any help to you, or even be of any help to themselves?" [94] Then the idols and those who strayed will be hurled into the Fire headlong, one upon another, [95] and so too the hosts of *Iblīs*, all of them. [96] There they will quarrel with one another and the erring ones will say (to their deities): [97] "By Allah, we were surely in clear error [98] when we assigned to you a position equal to that of the Lord of the Universe. [99] It is none but those steeped in guilt who led us into this error, [100] and now we have none to intercede on our behalf, [101] nor do we have a truly sincere friend. [102] If only we could return we would be among the believers."

---

10. Verses 90-102 do not seem to be part of Abraham's speech; they are clearly God's Words.

[103] Surely there is a Sign[11] in this, but most of them would not believe. [104] Verily Your Lord is Immensely Mighty, Ever Compassionate.

[105] The people of Noah gave the lie to the Messengers. [106] Recall when their brother Noah said to them: "Do you have no fear? [107] I am a trustworthy Messenger to you; [108] so fear Allah and obey me. [109] I seek of you no reward for this: my reward is with none except the Lord of the Universe. [110] So fear Allah and obey me." [111] They answered: "Shall we accept you even though it is the meanest of people who follow you?" [112] Noah said: "What knowledge do I have about their deeds? [113] It is only for my Lord to take account of them. Would that you made use of your understanding! [114] It is not for me to repel those who choose to believe. [115] I am none but a plain warner." [116] They said: "O Noah! If you do not desist, you will certainly become one of the accursed." [117] He said: "My Lord! My people have branded me a liar. [118] So pass a clear judgement between me and them and rescue me and the believers with me." [119] Thereafter We rescued him and those who were with him in the laden Ark[12] [120] and drowned the rest.

[121] Surely there is a Sign in this, but most of them would not believe. [122] Verily Your Lord is Immensely Mighty, Ever Compassionate.

---

11. That is, the "Sign" in the story of the Prophet Abraham.

12. "Thereafter We rescued him and those who were with him in the laden Ark," means that the Ark contained all the believers and a pair of each of the animal species that God had asked Noah to take along with him. For details see *Hūd* 11: 40.

[123] The ʿĀd gave the lie to the Messengers. [124] Recall, when their brother Hūd said to them: "Have you no fear? [125] I am a trustworthy Messenger to you. [126] So fear Allah and obey me. [127] I seek of you no reward for this; my reward is with none but the Lord of the Universe. [128] What, you build a monument on every hill merely for fun [129] and erect huge palaces as though you will live for ever, [130] and when you strike you strike like tyrants? [131] So fear Allah and obey me. [132] Have fear of Him Who has provided you with all the (good) things you know; [133] Who has provided you with flocks and children [134] and with gardens and springs. [135] I fear for you the chastisement of an Awesome Day." [136] They replied: "It is all the same for us whether you admonish us or not. [137] This has been happening all along. [138] We will not be subjected to any chastisement." [139] Eventually they gave the lie to him and We destroyed them. Surely there is a Sign in this, but most of them would not believe. [140] Verily your Lord is Immensely Mighty, Most Compassionate.

[141] The Thamūd gave the lie to the Messengers. [142] Recall when their brother Ṣāliḥ said to them: "Have you no fear?" [143] "I am a trustworthy Messenger to you. [144] So fear Allah and obey me. [145] I ask of you no reward. My reward is with none but the Lord of the Universe. [146] Do you believe that you will be left here to live securely in the present state [147] amidst gardens and springs [148] and cornfields and date-palms laden with juicy fruits? [149] You hew dwellings in mountains and exult in that. [150] Fear Allah and obey me [151] and do not follow the biddings of those that go to excesses

[152] and spread mischief in the land rather than set things right." [153] They replied: "You are nothing but one of those who are bewitched; [154] you are no different from a mortal like us. So produce a sign if you are truthful." [155] Ṣāliḥ said: "This is a she-camel. There is a day set for her to drink and there is a day set for you to drink. [156] Do not molest her lest the chastisement of an Awesome Day should seize you." [157] But they hamstrung her and then regretted it. [158] So the chastisement seized them. Surely there is a Sign in this, but most of them would not believe. [159] Verily Your Lord is Immensely Mighty, Most Compassionate.

[160] The people of Lot rejected the Messengers, branding them liars. [161] Recall, when their brother Lot said to them: "Have you no fear? [162] I am a trustworthy Messenger to you. [163] So fear Allah and obey me. [164] I seek of you no reward. My reward is with none but the Lord of the Universe. [165] What, of all creation will you go to (fornicate with) the males, [166] leaving aside those whom Allah has created for you as your mates. Nay, you are a people that has transgressed all limits." [167] They said: "O Lot! If you do not desist, you will be one of those expelled (from our towns)." [168] He said: "I am one of those who abhor your practice. [169] My Lord, deliver me and my family from their wicked deeds." [170] Then We delivered him and all his family [171] except an old woman who was among those that stayed behind.[13] [172] Thereafter, We utterly destroyed the rest, [173] and We sent upon them a rain, an evil rain that fell on those who had been warned.

---

13. This is a reference to Lot's wife.

[174] Surely there is a Sign in this, but most of them would not believe. [175] Verily Your Lord is Immensely Mighty, Most Compassionate.

[176] The people of Aykah also gave the lie to the Messengers.¹⁴ [177] Recall, when Shu'ayb said to them: "Have you no fear? [178] I am a trustworthy Messenger to you. [179] So fear Allah and obey me. [180] I ask of you no reward for this. My reward is with none but the Lord of the Universe. [181] Fill up the measure and do not diminish the goods of people, [182] weigh with an even balance [183] and do not deliver short, and do not go about creating mischief in the land, [184] and have fear of Him Who created you and the earlier generations." [185] They said: "You are no more than one of those who have been bewitched, [186] you are only a mortal like us. Indeed we believe that you are an utter liar. [187] So cause a piece of the sky to fall upon us if you are truthful." [188] Shu'ayb said: "My Lord knows well all what you do." [189] Then they branded him a liar, whereupon the chastisement of the Day of Canopy overtook them.¹⁵ It was the chastisement of a very awesome day.

14. The story of the people of Aykah is succinctly mentioned in *Sūrah al-Ḥijr* 15: 78-84.

15. What can be gleaned from the text is this: because these people had asked that a scourge be brought down upon them from the sky, God sent a cloud which hung over them like a canopy until they were destroyed by an evil rain. It should be borne in mind that Shu'ayb's mission extended to both the people of Aykah and the people of Midian and the two communities were visited by different kinds of scourge.

[190] Surely there is a Sign in this, but most of them would not believe. [191] Verily Your Lord is Immensely Mighty, Most Compassionate.

[192] Indeed this is a revelation from the Lord of the Universe;[16] [193] which the truthful spirit[17] has carried down [194] to your heart that you might become one of those who warn (others on behalf of Allah), [195] (a revelation) in clear Arabic language, [196] (a revelation embodied) in the scriptures of the ancients.[18] [197] Is it not a Sign to them – (to wit, the Makkans) – that the learned men of the Children of Israel know that?[19] [198] (But such is their adamance) that had We revealed it to one of the non-Arabs and even if he had recited[20] (this clear Arabic discourse) to them [199] they would still not have believed in it. [200] Thus have We caused this (Admonition) to penetrate the hearts of the culprits (like a hot rod). [201] They will not believe in it until they clearly see the grievous chastisement.

---

16. That is, this Qur'ān whose verses are being recited.

17. That is, Gabriel.

18. The same message, the same Revelation, and the same Divine teachings can be found in all the previous Scriptures.

19. The Jewish religious scholars knew that the Message of the Qur'ān was identical with that of the previous Scriptures. They could not claim that what the previous Scriptures preached was different from the Message of the Qur'ān.

20. The Qur'ān brings peace and tranquillity to the hearts of believers, but not to the hearts of the unbelievers. Instead, the Qur'ān passes through their hearts as though it were a red-hot iron, infuriating them. Hence, instead of reflecting over the contents of the Qur'ān, the unbelievers try to invent pretexts to refute it.

[202] But when it comes upon them suddenly, taking them unawares, [203] they say: "Can we be granted some respite?"

[204] Do they really want Our chastisement to be expedited? [205] Did you consider that if We were to let them enjoy life for many years [206] and then the chastisement of which they were being warned were to come upon them, [207] of what avail will be the provisions of life which they have been granted to enjoy?

[208] We never destroyed any habitation but that it had warners [209] to admonish them. We have never been unjust.

[210] The satans did not bring down this (Clear Book), [211] nor does it behove them, nor does it lie in their power. [212] Indeed they are debarred from even hearing it.[21]

[213] So do not call any other god beside Allah lest you become of those who will be punished, [214] and warn your nearest kinsmen; [215] and be meek to the believers who follow you. [216] Then if they disobey you say to them: "I am quit of what you do." [217] And put your trust in Him Who is Immensely Mighty, Most Compassionate, [218] Who observes you when you rise (to pray)[22] [219] and observes your movements among those who prostrate themselves. [220] He is All-Hearing, All-Knowing.

---

21. Satans are not even given a chance to listen to the Qur'ān when it is revealed to Muḥammad (peace be on him), not to speak of their being aware of is contents.

22. The word "rise" could either refer to Prayers or to the performance of the mission entrusted to the Prophet (peace be on him).

[221] O people, shall I tell you on whom it is that satans descend? [222] They descend on every forgerer steeped in sin, [223] on those who whisper hearsay in the ears of people; and most of them are liars.[23]

[224] As for poets,[24] only the wayward follow them. [225] Do you not see that they wander about in every valley [226] and say things which they do not act upon, [227] except those who believed and acted righteously and remembered Allah much, and when they themselves were subjected to wrong, they exacted retribution no more than to the extent of the wrong?[25] Soon will the wrong-doers know the end that they shall reach.[26]

---

23. This is in answer to the allegation of the unbelievers of Makkah that Muḥammad (peace be on him) was a sorcerer.

24. This, too, is a refutation of their allegation that Muḥammad (peace be on him) was a poet.

25. This verse makes four exceptions to the general condemnation of poets in the previous verse: (i) those who believe in God, in His Prophets, in His Books and in the Hereafter; (ii) those who are pious and virtuous and live within moral bounds; (iii) those who constantly remember God, and (iv) those who do not subject people to satire for personal reasons. However, when the cause of the Truth requires their support against oppressors, they can have recourse to their poetic talent in the manner a warrior uses his sword.

26. The "wrong-doers" here signify those who, merely in order to hurt the cause of the Truth, brazenly resorted to the vile propaganda that the Prophet (peace be on him) was a poet, a soothsayer, a sorcerer, or a lunatic. They deliberately did so in order to arouse misgivings about him and his teachings.

27
❦

Al-Naml [The Ants]
Makkan Period

In the name of Allah, the Most Merciful,
the Most Compassionate

[1] *Ṭā'. Sīn.* These are the verses of the Qur'ān and a Clear Book;¹ [2] a guidance and good tidings for the believers [3] who establish Prayer and give *Zakāh*, and have firm faith in the Hereafter. [4] As for those who do not believe in the Hereafter, We have made their deeds seem attractive to them so they stumble around in perplexity. [5] It is they for whom a grievous chastisement lies in store; it is they who shall be the greatest losers in the Hereafter. [6] As for you, (O Muḥammad), you are receiving the Qur'ān from the Most Wise, the All-Knowing.

[7] (Recount to them) when Moses said to his family: "I perceive something like fire: soon will I bring to you some information from there, or I will bring you a burning brand that you may warm yourselves." [8] But when Moses came to the fire, a call was sounded: "Blessed is He Who is in the fire and whatever is around it. Glory be to Allah, the Sustainer of all in the Universe. [9] O Moses, verily this

---

1. "*Kitāb Mubīn*", a Clear Book which expounds its teachings, instructions and commands in clear terms.

is Me, Allah, the All-Mighty, the All-Wise! [10] Now cast your rod!" But when he saw the rod writhing as though it were a serpent, he turned his back in retreat and did not even look behind. "O Moses, have no fear. Messengers have no fear in My presence, [11] except he who has committed some wrong. But if he substitutes good in place of evil, I am Most Forgiving, Most Compassionate. [12] Now put your hand into your bosom, and it will come forth shining without any blemish. (These are two of the) nine Signs to be carried to Pharaoh and his people. They are surely a wicked people."

[13] But when Our Clear Signs came to them, they said: "This is plain magic." [14] They denied those Signs out of iniquity and arrogance although their hearts were convinced of their truth. So see how evil was the end of those mischief-makers!

[15] (On the other hand), We granted knowledge to David and Solomon and they said: "All praise be to Allah Who has exalted us above many of His believing servants!" [16] And Solomon succeeded David and said: "O people, we have been taught the speech of birds and we have been endowed with all kinds of things.² Surely this is a conspicuous favour (from Allah)." [17] Hosts of *jinn* and humans and birds were marshalled for Solomon and were kept under full control. [18] (Solomon was once on the move with them) until when they reached a valley of ants one of the ants said: "O ants, get into your holes, lest Solomon and his hosts crush you (under their feet) without even knowing." [19] Smiling at the ant's

---

2. That is, God bestowed on them a great many favours.

utterance, Solomon burst into laughter and said: "My Lord! Hold me under (Your) control[3] that I may render thanks for the favour which You have bestowed on me and on my parents, and that I may act righteously in a manner that would please You. Include me, out of Your Mercy, among Your righteous servants."

[20] (On another occasion) Solomon inspected the birds and said: "Why is it that I do not see the hoopoe? Is he among the absentees? [21] I will inflict a severe punishment on him or maybe even slaughter him unless he comes forth with a convincing reason (for his absence)." [22] Not before long the hoopoe came up and said: "I have obtained a knowledge which you could not. I have brought for you sure news about Sheba.[4] [23] I found there a woman ruling over them, one who has been endowed with all things and has a mighty throne. [24] I found that she and her people prostrate themselves before the sun rather than Allah." Satan[5] has made their deeds appear attractive to them and has, thus, debarred

---

3. This prayer of Solomon consists of acknowledging the great gifts and abilities and power that God had bestowed on him which were such that if he were to succumb to negligence even for a moment, he was likely to transgress the bounds of his servitude and fall a prey to excessive arrogance and vanity. So he prayed to God to restrain him from it in order that he might remain grateful to his Lord for His bounties.

4. Saba' was the renowned trading nation of southern Arabia. Their capital city was Ma'ārib, located 55 miles northeast of Ṣan'ā', the present capital of Yemen.

5. The style of this and the next verse suggests that the passage from here till the end of verse 26 is God's addition to the hoopoe's speech.

them from the Right Path so they do not find true guidance [25] that they would prostrate themselves before Allah Who brings to light all that is hidden in the heavens and the earth and knows all that you conceal and all that you reveal. [26] Allah – none is worthy of worship save He; He is the Lord of the Mighty Throne.

[27] Solomon said: "Soon shall we see whether you have spoken the truth or are one of those that lie. [28] Take this letter of mine, deliver it to them, and then draw back from them, and observe what they do."

[29] The Queen said:[6] "Know my nobles that a gracious letter has been delivered to me. [30] It is from Solomon, and it is: "In the name of Allah, the Most Merciful, the Most Compassionate." [31] (It says): "Do not act towards me with defiance, but come to me in submission."[7]

[32] (After reading the letter) the Queen said: "Nobles, let me have your counsel in this matter for I make no firm decision without you." [33] They said: "We are strong and are given to vehement fighting. But the decision is yours. Therefore, consider what you would like to command." [34] The Queen said: "When the kings enter a country they cause corruption in it and abase those of its people who are held in honour. This is what they are wont to do. [35] I will send them a gift and then see with what answer my envoys return."

---

6. The story now resumes from the point where the hoopoe had dropped the letter in front of the queen.

7. That is, go to Solomon as a Muslim, or in the state of submission.

[36] Now, when (the envoy of the Queen) came to Solomon, he said: "Do you want to aid me with wealth? Whatever Allah has granted me is much more than what He has given you. (Keep for yourselves) your gift in which you are exulting. [37] Envoy, go back to those who sent you and we shall certainly come upon them with hosts whom they will be unable to resist. We shall drive them out from there, and they will suffer humiliation and disgrace."

[38] Solomon said: "My nobles, which of you can bring me her throne before they come to me in submission?" [39] A stalwart of the *jinn* said: "I will bring it to you before you rise from your council. Surely I have the power to do so and I am trustworthy." [40] And he who had some knowledge of the Book said: "I will bring it before the twinkling of your eye." When Solomon saw the throne placed firmly beside him, he cried out: "This is by the grace of my Lord so that He may test me whether I give thanks for (His Bounty) or act with ingratitude. Whoever is grateful is so to his own good; and whoever is ungrateful, let him know that my Lord is Immensely Resourceful, Most Bountiful."

[41] Solomon said:[8] "Set the throne before her casually, and let us see whether she gets to the Truth or is one of those who are not guided to what is right." [42] When the Queen arrived, she was asked: "Is your throne like this one?" She said: "It seems as if it is the same. We had already come to

---

8. The narration now turns to the events after the Queen's arrival at Solomon's palace.

know this and we had submitted ourselves."⁹ [43] What prevented her (from accepting the True Faith) was her worshipping deities other than Allah, for she belonged to an unbelieving people.

[44] She was told: "Enter the palace." But when she saw it, she thought it was a pool of water and she bared both her calves (to enter into it). Solomon said: "This is a slippery floor of crystal." Thereupon she cried out: "My Lord, I have been inflicting much wrong on myself. Now I submit myself with Solomon to Allah, the Lord of the whole Universe."

[45] And We sent to Thamūd their brother Ṣāliḥ (with the Message): "Serve Allah," but all of a sudden they became split into two quarrelling factions. [46] Ṣāliḥ said: "My people, why do you wish to hasten that evil rather than good should come upon you? Why should you not seek pardon from Allah so that mercy be shown to you?" [47] They said: "We augur ill of you and those who are with you." Ṣāliḥ replied: "Your augury is with Allah. The truth is that you are a people who are being tried."

[48] Now there were nine ring-leaders in the city who created corruption in the land and never worked to set things right. [49] They said: "Swear to one another in the name of Allah that we shall make a sudden night swoop

---

9. Queen Sheba made it clear that even before observing this miracle, she and her nobles were convinced, on the basis of what they had heard about Solomon (peace be on him), that he was a Prophet, not just a King.

on Ṣāliḥ and his family and will then tell their heirs[10] that we did not witness the destruction of his family. We are indeed truthful." [50] Thus they planned and We too planned, the while they did not know. [51] So see what was the outcome of the plan they made: We utterly destroyed them and their people, all of them. [52] Now behold their houses that lie in utter ruins because of their wrong-doing. Verily there is a Sign in this for the people who know. [53] And We delivered those who believed and were wont to avoid disobeying (Allah).

[54] We also sent Lot, and recall when he told his people: "Do you commit shameless acts with your eyes open?[11] [55] Do you lustfully approach men instead of women? Nay, you engage in acts of sheer ignorance." [56] But this had only one answer from his people. They said: "Expel Lot's folk from your city. They pretend to be absolutely clean." [57] Eventually We saved (Lot) and his family, except his wife. We had decreed that she should be among those who would remain behind. [58] And We rained down upon them a rain. It was an evil rain for those who had already been warned.

---

10. This refers to the chief of Ṣāliḥ's tribe who, according to the ancient tribal usage, would have had the right to claim retaliation for his blood. This was the same position in which Abū Ṭālib, the Prophet's uncle, found himself. The Makkan unbelievers had refrained from killing the Prophet (peace be on him) because if they had done so, Abū Ṭālib, the chief of Banū Hāshim, would have demanded blood revenge on behalf of his clan.

11. They committed this abominable act publicly, as mentioned in *Sūrah al-ʿAnkabūt* 29: 29.

[59] Say, (O Muḥammad): "All praise be to Allah, and peace be on those of His servants whom He has chosen."

(Ask them): "Who is better: Allah or the false gods that they associate with Him as His partners? [60] Who is it that has created the heavens and the earth and sent down for you water from the sky and then We caused to grow therewith orchards full of beauty whose trees you could never grow. Is there any god associated with Allah (in these tasks)?" Nay, they are a people who are veering away from the Right Path.

[61] Who is it Who has made the earth a place of resort, and has caused rivers to flow in its midst, and has placed upon it firm mountains, and has placed a barrier between two masses of water? Is there any god associated with Allah (in these tasks)? Nay; but most of them do not know.

[62] Who is it Who heeds the prayers of the distressed when he calls out to Him and Who removes his affliction? And who is it Who makes you vicegerents of the earth? Is there any god associated with Allah (in this task)? How little do you reflect!

[63] Who is it Who guides you through the darkness on land and sea? And Who sends winds as heralds of good tidings ahead of His Mercy? Is there any god associated with Allah (in this task)? Exalted be Allah above whatever they associate with Him in His Divinity!

[64] Who is it Who creates in the first instance and then repeats it? Who is it Who provides you with sustenance

from the heavens and the earth? Is there any god associated with Allah (in these tasks)? Say: "Bring forth your evidence, if you are truthful."

[65] Say: "None in the heavens or on the earth has knowledge of the Unseen save Allah. They do not know when they will be raised to life."

[66] Nay, but they have lost their knowledge of the Hereafter. They are steeped in doubt and uncertainty about it: rather they are blind to it. [67] The unbelievers say: "When we become dust, we and our forefathers, shall we really be brought out (from our graves)? [68] We were told about this and so were our forefathers before us. But these are no more than fairy tales that have been recounted from ancient times." [69] Say: "Go about through the earth and see what has been the end of the evil-doers." [70] (O Prophet), do not grieve over them, nor be distressed at their designs. [71] They also say: "Tell us when this threat will come to pass, if you are truthful." [72] Say: "The chastisement whose hastening you have been asking for, maybe a part of it has drawn quite near to you." [73] Indeed Your Lord is exceedingly bountiful to mankind. Yet most of them do not give thanks. [74] Verily your Lord knows all that their hearts conceal as well as all that they reveal. [75] There is nothing that is hidden – be it in the heaven or the earth – but is recorded in a Clear Book.[12]

[76] Surely this Qur'ān explains to the Children of Israel most of the matters concerning which they have disagreements [77] and it is a guidance and mercy for

---

12. The expression "Clear Book" means the Book of Destiny.

the believers. [78] Indeed your Lord will decide between them[13] by His judgement. He is All-Mighty, All-Knowing. [79] So put your trust in Allah for you are on the manifest truth. [80] Surely you cannot make the dead hear you,[14] nor can you make the deaf hear your call if they turn back in flight, [81] nor can you direct the blind to the Right Way, preventing them from falling into error. You can make only those who believe in Our verses to hear the call and then submit.

[82] And when the time for the fulfilment of Our Word against them will come, We shall bring forth for them a beast from the earth who will speak to them because people did not believe in Our Signs.[15] [83] Just imagine the Day when We shall muster from every nation a large

---

13. That is, between the Qurayshite unbelievers and the believers.

14. These people are such that their conscience is dead, and they have been rendered incapable of differentiating between truth and falsehood. This because of their obduracy and their propensity to blindly follow inherited customs and usages.

15. According to 'Abd Allāh ibn 'Umar, this will happen when there will remain none on the earth who will bid people to do good and forbid them from evil. Ibn Mardawayh has reported a *ḥadīth* from Abū Sa'īd al-Khudrī in which he says that he, himself, had heard this from the Prophet (peace be on him). This shows that when people stop exhorting others to do good and cease to forbid them from doing evil, God will bring forth a beast just before the resurrection as a final warning. It is not clear whether it will be one animal or a whole species of animals whose members will spread all over the earth. *Dābbah min al-arḍ* could mean both. The time of the coming of this creature was mentioned by the Prophet (peace be on him) in his saying: "The sun will rise from the west and this

group of those who gave the lie to Our Signs, and they shall be duly arranged in ranks [84] until, when all of them have arrived, Allah will say: "Did you give the lie to My Signs even without encompassing them with your knowledge? If that is not so, what did you do?" [85] And the Word will come to pass against them because of their wrong-doing: they will then be able to utter nothing. [86] Did they not perceive that We had made the night so that they may repose in it and made the day clear and shining. Surely there are Signs in this for those who believe.

[87] The Day when the Trumpet will be blown all those who are in the heavens and on the earth shall be terror-stricken – all except those whom Allah wills – and everyone shall come to Him utterly abject. [88] You now see the mountains and consider them firmly fixed, but then they shall pass away even as clouds pass away. That will be the handiwork of Allah Who has created everything with perfect wisdom. He is well aware of what you do. [89] Whosoever comes with good will receive a reward better than his deed, and they will be made secure from the terror of that Day. [90] And whosoever comes with evil, they will be flung upon their faces into the Fire. Will you be recompensed for aught other than what you do?

---

beast will appear in the broad light of the day." As for the question of an animal talking to human beings in their language: this is one of the manifestations of God's Power. God can grant the power of speech to whomsoever He wills. Before the Day of Resurrection, He will grant this power to a beast, but after the Resurrection, He will grant this power to the eyes, ears and skins of human beings and they will speak out and give evidence before God, as clearly stated in *Ḥā' Mīm al-Sajdah* 41: 20-21.

[91] (Tell them, O Muḥammad): "I have been commanded only to serve the Lord of this city that He has made inviolable, to serve Him to Whom all things belong. I have been commanded to be of those that submit to Allah, [92] and to recite the Qur'ān." So, whosoever is guided, his guidance will be to his own good. As for those who stray, tell them: "I am none but a warner." [93] And say: "All praise be to Allah, Who will soon show you His Signs that you will recognize." Your Lord is not unaware of what you do.

28

Al-Qaṣaṣ [The Narration]
Makkan Period

In the name of Allah, the Most Merciful,
the Most Compassionate

[1] *Ṭā'. Sīn. Mīm* [2] These are the verses of the Clear Book. [3] We recount to you with truth some parts of the story of Moses and Pharaoh for the benefit of those who believe.

[4] Indeed Pharaoh transgressed in the land and divided its people into sections. One group of them he humiliated, and slew their sons and spared their daughters. Truly he was among the mischief-makers. [5] We wanted to bestow favour on those who were oppressed in the land. We wanted to make them leaders and heirs [6] and to grant them power in the land, and make Pharaoh and Hāmān and their hosts see what they had feared.

[7] We suggested¹ to the mother of Moses: "Suckle your child, but when you fear for his life cast him into the river and be not fearful nor grieve, for We shall restore him to you and make him one of the Messengers." [8] Then Pharaoh's household picked him up (from the river) that

---

1. It is not explicitly stated here that under these circumstances, a son was born to an Israeli who was to be known by the name of Moses.

he may be their adversary and be a cause of sorrow to them. Surely Pharaoh and Hāmān and their hosts erred (in their scheming). [9] The wife of Pharaoh said: "Here is a delight of the eye to me and to you. Do not kill him. Maybe he will prove useful for us, or we may adopt him as a son." They were unaware of the end of it all.

[10] On the other hand, the heart of Moses' mother was sorely distressed. Had We not strengthened her heart that she might have full faith (in Our promise), she would have disclosed the secret. [11] She told the sister of Moses: "Follow him." So she kept watch over him unperceived (by the enemies). [12] And We had already forbidden the breasts of the nurses for the child. (So seeing the girl) said: "Shall I direct you to the people of a household that will rear him with utter sincerity?" [13] Thus did We restore Moses to his mother that her eyes might be comforted and she might not grieve, and realise that the promise of Allah was true. But most people are unaware of this.

[14] When Moses reached the age of full youth and grew to maturity, We bestowed upon him wisdom and knowledge. Thus do We reward those who do good. [15] Once he entered the city at a time when its people were heedless, and he encountered two men fighting, one of whom belonged to his own people and the other to his foes. Now the man belonging to Moses' own people cried out to him for help against the man from the foes, and Moses struck him with his fist and finished him. Moses said: "This is an act of Satan. Surely he is an enemy who openly misleads." [16] Then he prayed: "My Lord! I have indeed inflicted wrong on myself, so do forgive me," wherefore Allah forgave him for He is Ever Forgiving,

Most Merciful.[2] [17] Thereupon Moses vowed: "My Lord, because of the favour that You have done me[3] I shall never support the guilty."

[18] The next morning he proceeded to the city in fear and looking around as one apprehensive of danger when all of a sudden, the man who had sought his help the day before again called out to him for his help. Moses said to him: "Clearly, you are a very misguided fellow." [19] And when Moses decided to lay his violent hands on the man belonging to the enemy, he cried out:[4] "Moses, do you intend to kill me as you killed a person yesterday?" You simply want to live in the land as a tyrant, and do not wish to set things right." [20] Then a man came running[5] from the farther end of the city and said: "O Moses, the nobles are deliberating about you that they may put you to death. So do be gone. I am one of your well-wishers."

---

2. The word *maghfirah* means to indulge, to forgive as well as to conceal. What Moses (peace be on him) means by this prayer is that God may forgive him his sin which, as He knew, he had not committed intentionally, that He may hide it from others so that his enemies would not be able to trace it.

3. The favour alluded to here consists of God concealing Moses' act of killing and His enabling him to escape.

4. The person who cried out was the same Israelite whom Moses had helped the day earlier. After scolding him, when Moses turned to strike the Egyptian, the Israelite thought he was going to hit him and so he cried out and foolishly divulged the secret.

5. This second incident led to the disclosure of a secret that had hitherto remained unknown, i.e. Moses' involvement in the killing. It first became known to the Copt involved in this particular quarrel, and he then disclosed it to others.

[21] Soon after hearing this Moses departed in a state of fear, looking around as one in apprehension and prayed: "My Lord, deliver me from these unjust people."

[22] When (after his departure from Egypt) Moses headed towards Midian, he said: "I hope my Lord will show me the right Path."[6] [23] When he arrived at the spring of Midian, he found there a crowd of people watering their flocks, and he found apart from them two women holding their flocks back. He asked the women: "What is it that troubles you?" They said: "We cannot water our flocks until the shepherds take their flocks away, and our father is a very old man." [24] On hearing this Moses watered their flocks for them, and then returned in a shaded place and said: "My Lord, I am truly in great need of any good that You might send down to me." [25] Soon thereafter one of the two women came to him, walking bashfully, and said: "My father invites you that he may reward you for your having watered our flocks for us." When Moses came to him and narrated to him the whole of his story, he said: "Have no fear. You are now safe from the iniquitous people."

[26] One of the two women said: "Father, employ this man in your service. The best whom you might employ is he who is strong and trustworthy." [27] Her father said to Moses: "I want to marry one of these two daughters of mine to you if you serve me for eight years. But if you complete ten years, that will be of your own accord (but not an obligation). I do not intend to treat you harshly. If Allah wills, you will find me an upright man."

---

6. That is, the path that would safely take him to Midian.

[28] Moses replied: "So that is agreed between me and you. Whichever of the two terms I fulfil, I trust that I shall not be wronged. Allah is a witness over the covenant we are committing ourselves to."

[29] When Moses had fulfilled the term and was journeying with his family, he perceived a fire in the direction of the Mount (Sinai). He said to his family: "Wait here; I have observed a fire. Maybe I will bring to you some news or a brand of fire from there that you may warm yourselves." [30] But when he came to the fire, a cry was heard from the right bank[7] of the valley, from a tree in the hallowed ground: "O Moses, verily I am Allah, the Lord of all creatures of the Universe." [31] He received the command: "Throw away your rod!" But when he saw the rod writhing as though it were a serpent, he turned back in retreat, and did not even look behind. (He was told): "O Moses, go ahead and have no fear. You are perfectly secure. [32] Put your hand into your bosom, and it will come out shining without any blemish; and draw your hand close to your body to still your fear.[8] Those are the two clear Signs from your Lord for Pharaoh and his chiefs, for truly they are a disobedient people." [33] Moses said: "My Lord, I have killed one person from among them, and I fear that they will kill me. [34] My brother Aaron is more eloquent in speech than I: so send him with me as a helper to confirm my truthfulness for I fear that they

---

7. The side of the valley which was to Moses' right hand.

8. If Moses was ever confronted with a truly dangerous situation, all he had to do was to fold back his arm into himself. This would strengthen his heart and release him from fear.

will reject me as a liar." [35] He said: "We will certainly strengthen you through your brother and will invest both of you with such power that they shall not be able to hurt you. With the help of Our Signs the two of you and your followers will prevail."

[36] But when Moses came to them with Our Clear Signs, they said: "This is nothing but a magic that has been contrived. We never heard anything like it from our ancestors of yore." [37] Moses replied: "My Lord knows best who comes with guidance from Him, and also whose end will be the best in the Hereafter. As for the wrong-doers, they shall not prosper."

[38] Pharaoh said: "O nobles, I do not know that you have any god beside myself. Hāmān, bake bricks out of clay and build a lofty palace for me so that I may mount up and be able to observe the god of Moses, even though I believe that Moses is a liar."

[39] And he and his hosts waxed arrogant in the land without any right, believing that they will never have to return to Us! [40] Eventually We seized him and his hosts and We flung them into the sea. So do see the end of the wrong-doers! [41] And We made them leaders who invite people to the Fire. On the Day of Judgement they shall not find help from any quarter. [42] We have made a curse to pursue them in this world, and on the Day of Judgement they shall be among the despised.

[43] After We had destroyed the earlier generations We bestowed the Book on Moses – a source of enlightenment for people and a guidance and mercy – that they may take heed. [44] (O Muḥammad), you were then not on

the western side[9] when We bestowed this commandment (of Law), and you were not among its witnesses. [45] Thereafter We raised up many a generation and a long time passed. You were then not even present among the people of Midian to rehearse Our verses to them. But it is We Who are sending news about that. [46] Nor were you on the side of the Mount (Sinai) when We called out to Moses (in the first instance). But it is out of Mercy from your Lord (that you are being informed of all this) so that you may warn a people to whom no warner came before you. Maybe they will take heed. [47] (We did so) lest a calamity might seize them because of the misdeeds they committed whereafter they would say: "Our Lord, why did you not send a Messenger to us that we follow Your revelation and become among those who believe?"

[48] But when the Truth reached them from Us, they said: "Why was he not given that which was given to Moses?" But did they not reject before what had been given to Moses?[10] They said: "Both are magic,[11] each supporting the other!" And they said: "We deny each of these." [49] Tell them, (O Prophet): "Then do bring a Book from Allah which is a better guide than either of them, and I will follow it! Do so if you are truthful!"

9. The "western side" here signifies Mount Sinai where Moses was given the Torah. Mount Sinai lies to the west of Ḥijāz.

10. The unbelievers of Makkah had failed to believe in Moses (peace be on him) despite the miracles given to him. What, then, was their justification for asking for the same miracles for Muḥammad (peace be on him)?

11. That is, the Qur'ān and the Torah.

[50] But if they do not hearken to this, know well that they only follow their lusts and who is in greater error than he who follows his lusts without any guidance from Allah? Allah does not guide those given to wrong-doing. [51] We have constantly conveyed them the word (of admonition) that they may take heed.

[52] Those on whom We bestowed the Book before do believe in this (to wit, the Qur'ān).[12] [53] When it is recited to them they say: "We believe in it for it is the Truth from our Lord. Indeed we were already Muslims." [54] These will be granted their reward twice over because they remained steadfast;[13] they repel evil with good, and

---

12. This does not mean that all the People of the Book – the Jews and the Christians – in fact believe in it. This verse actually refers to a particular incident which took place at the time when this *sūrah* was revealed and which was meant to jolt the Makkans into making their ingratitude known: God had done them a great favour by raising someone from among them as a Prophet. It was mentioned in order to make the Makkans realize how thankless it was on their part to reject him while people from far-off places outside Makkah were making their way to the city, recognising the Prophet's true worth, one from whom they derived immense benefit.

The incident alluded to was as follows: After the Migration to Abyssinia when news about the Prophet (peace be on him) had spread to that land, a delegation of 20 Christians came to Makkah and met the Prophet (peace be on him). The Prophet (peace be on him) invited them to Islam and recited a few verses of the Qur'ān. No sooner had they heard the recitation than tears streamed from their eyes. They testified that it was the Word of God and accepted Islam.

13. They would receive double reward: one for their believing in the previous scriptures and the other for believing in the Qur'ān.

spend (in alms) out of the sustenance We provided them, [55] and when they hear any vain talk, they turn away from it, saying: "We have our deeds and you have your deeds. Peace be to you. We do not desire to act like the ignorant."[14] [56] (O Prophet), you cannot grant guidance to whom you please. It is Allah Who guides those whom He will. He knows best who are amenable to guidance.

[57] They say: "If we were to follow this guidance with you, we should be snatched away from our land."[15] Have We not established for them a secure sanctuary to which fruits of all kinds are brought as a provision from Us? But most of them do not know.[16]

[58] And how many a town did We destroy whose inhabitants exulted on account of their affluence. These are their dwellings in which very few dwelt after them. Eventually it is We Who inherited them.[17]

14. This alludes to the mean behaviour of Abū Jahl towards them after they accepted Islam.

15. This is what the Qurayshite unbelievers used to say as an excuse for not accepting Islam. We should bear in mind the position of the Quraysh as religious leaders of all the tribes, a position which they felt would be undermined and earn them the enmity of all Arabs if they were to accept Islam.

16. This is God's first answer to the excuse they offered. This response amounted to asking: "Because of whom has peace and order come to prevail in the sacred territory? Because of whom does their sanctuary enjoy that eminence which is attracting merchandise from all parts of the world? Who has brought this about, you or God?"

17. This is the second answer to their excuse. It suggests that the wealth and prosperity of which they were so proud and for the

[59] Your Lord would not destroy a town until He had sent to its centre a Messenger who would recite to them Our verses. Nor would We destroy any town unless its inhabitants were iniquitous.[18]

[60] Whatever you have been given is a provision for the life of this world and its glitter. But that which is with Allah is better and more enduring. Do you not use your intellect? [61] Now, he to whom We have promised a good which he is going to obtain – can he be like him whom We have given the good things of this life, but who will be brought up for punishment on the Day of Judgement?

[62] (Let them not forget) that the Day when Allah will call unto them, and say: "Where are those whom you imagined to be My associates?" [63] Those against whom the Word will be realised will say: "Our Lord, these are the ones whom we led astray just as we ourselves strayed.[19]

---

sake of which they clung to falsehood and turned away from the Truth, was at one time in the possession of the ʿĀd, the Thamūd and other peoples. Did their wealth and prosperity save them from destruction?

18. This is the third answer to their excuse. Those nations that had been earlier destroyed were steeped in injustice and iniquity. But before destroying them God sent His Messengers to warn them. However, when they did not give up their evil ways, they were totally annihilated. The Makkans now faced the same predicament.

19. This refers to the satans, *jinn* and human beings who were set up as associates of God in His Divinity and whose word they preferred to the word of God and His Messengers. It is these for whose sake people had forsaken the Straight Path. Whether or not people explicitly called them god (*ilāh*) and lord (*rabb*), they

We absolve ourselves before You of all blame. It was not us that they worshipped."[20] [64] They will then be told: "Call upon those for help whom you declared to be Our associates." They will then call upon them but they will not answer them. They will have observed the chastisement in front of them. Would that they were guided!

[65] (Let them not disregard) that the Day when Allah will call out to them saying: "What was the answer you gave to the Messengers?" [66] Then they will not be able to think of any reply, nor will they be able to ask one another. [67] But those who repented and believed and acted righteously, they will perhaps be among those who will prosper there.

[68] Your Lord creates what He will and chooses (for His tasks) whomsoever He will. It is not for them to make the choice. Glory be to Allah. He is exalted far above their associating others in His Divinity. [69] Your Lord knows all that their hearts conceal and all that they reveal. [70] He is Allah; there is no god but He. His is the praise in this world and in the Hereafter. His is the command and to Him will all of you be returned. [71] (O Prophet), tell them: "Did you consider: if Allah were to make the night perpetual over you till the Day of Judgement, is

---

were still guilty of associating them with God if they unreservedly obeyed and followed them in a manner that only God should be obeyed and followed.

20. In other words, they will contend that their followers were not truly worshippers of those gods. Rather, they worshipped their own carnal desires, and, hence, chose the wrong path.

there a god other than Allah who can bring forth light for you? Do you not hear?" [72] Say: "Did you consider: if Allah were to make the day become perpetual over you till the Day of Judgement, is there a god other than Allah who can bring in night for you that you may repose in it? Will you not see?" [73] It is out of His Mercy that He has made for you night and day that you may repose (during the night) and seek His Bounty (during the day) that you might be grateful.

[74] (Let them bear in mind) that on that Day when He will call out to them saying: "Where are My associates, those whom you imagined to be so?" [75] And from each people We shall draw a witness, and shall say to them: "Do produce your evidence now." Then they shall know that the Truth is with Allah alone, and the lies which they had invented will forsake them.

[76] To be sure, Qārūn (Korah) was one of Moses' people; then he transgressed against them. We had bestowed on him such treasure that their very keys would have been raised with difficulty by a whole group of strong people. Once when his people said to him: "Do not exult, for Allah does not love those who exult (in their riches). [77] Seek by means of the wealth that Allah has granted you the Abode of the Hereafter, but forget not your share in this world and do good as Allah has been good to you and do not strive to create mischief in the land, for Allah loves not those who create mischief." [78] He replied: "All this has been given to me on account of a certain knowledge that I have." Did he not know that Allah had destroyed before him those who were stronger in might than he and

were more numerous in multitude? The wicked are not asked about their acts of sin.[21]

[79] Once Korah went forth among his people in full glitter. Those seeking the life of this world said: "Would that we had the like of what Korah has! He truly has a great fortune." [80] But those endowed with true knowledge said: "Woe to you. The reward of Allah is best for those who believe and act righteously. But none except those who are patient shall attain to this."

[81] At last We caused the earth to swallow him and his house. Thereafter there was no group of people that could come to his aid against Allah; nor was he able to come to his own aid. [82] And those who had envied his position the day before began to say on the morrow: "Alas, we had forgotten that it is Allah Who increases the provision of those of His servants whom He will and grants in sparing measure to those whom He will. But for Allah's favour upon us, He could have made us to be swallowed too. Alas, we had forgotten that the unbelievers do not prosper."

[83] As for the Abode of the Hereafter,[22] We shall assign it exclusively for those who do not seek glory on earth nor want to cause mischief. The God-fearing shall have the best end. [84] He who shall bring a good deed shall

---

21. The wicked have always claimed to be good. They never admit to any evil. Their punishment does not depend on their admission that they have been wicked. When they are seized they are not interrogated (in this world) about their acts of sin.

22. That is, Paradise, the seat of true success.

be rewarded with what is better. But those who bring evil deeds shall not be requited more than their deeds.

[85] (O Prophet), surely He Who has ordained the Qur'ān on you[23] will bring you to the best end. Say to them: "My Lord knows best who has brought true guidance and who is in clear error." [86] (O Prophet), you never looked forward for the Book to be revealed to you. It is out of sheer Mercy of your Lord that it was (revealed to you). So do not lend any support to the unbelievers. [87] And let it never happen that the unbelievers might turn you away from the revelations of Allah after they have been revealed to you. Call people to your Lord and never become one of the unbelievers, [88] and do not invoke any god beside Allah. There is no god but He. All will perish but He. To Him belongs the command. And to Him shall all of you return.

---

23. That is, the Prophet (peace be on him) had been entrusted with the responsibility to carry the Qur'ān to people, to instruct them in it, and to reform the world according to its teachings.

29

Al-'Ankabūt [The Spider]
Makkan Period

In the name of Allah, the Most Merciful,
the Most Compassionate

[1] *Alif. Lām. Mīm.* [2] Do people think that they will be let go merely by saying: "We believe," and that they will not be tested, [3] for We indeed tested those who went before them? Allah will most certainly ascertain those who spoke the truth and those who lied.

[4] Do the evil-doers¹ suppose that they will get the better of Us? How evil is their judgement!

[5] Let him who looks forward to meeting Allah know that Allah's appointed term will surely come to pass. He is All-Hearing, All-Knowing. [6] Whosoever strives² (in the cause of Allah) does so to his own good. Surely

---

1. The style of the discourse suggests that the "evil-doers" here signify those who were persecuting the believers. They are the ones who resorted to the worst possible means to harm the message of Islam.

2. The word *mujāhadah* in this verse means that one ought to exert one's utmost in encountering the unbelievers so that the true faith's standard may be raised and kept aloft.

Allah stands in no need of anyone[3] in the whole Universe. [7] Those who believe and do good deeds, We shall cleanse them of their evil deeds and reward them according to the best of their deeds.

[8] We have enjoined upon man kindness to his parents, but if they exert pressure on you to associate with Me in My Divinity any that you do not know (to be My associate), do not obey them.[4] To Me is your return, and I shall let you know all that you have done. [9] As for those who believed and acted righteously, We shall certainly admit them among the righteous.

[10] Among people there are some who say: "We believe in Allah." But when such a person is made to endure suffering in Allah's cause, he reckons the persecution he suffers at the hands of people as though it is a chastisement from Allah. But if victory comes from your Lord, the same person will say "We were with you." Does Allah not know whatever is in the hearts of the people of the world? [11] Allah will surely ascertain who are the believers and who are the hypocrites.

[12] The unbelievers say to the believers: "Follow our way and we will carry the burden of your sins." (They

---

3. The believers were required to engage in this struggle not because God stood in need of their help to attain any of His purposes. On the contrary, they were asked to strive in God's cause because that was conducive to their own moral and spiritual growth.

4. The parents of the Makkan youth who had embraced Islam tried to constrain them to renounce Islam. Here those youngsters are being told that while their parents had rights over them as parents, they certainly had no right to bar them from God's Way.

say so even though) they are not going to carry any part of their sins. Surely they are lying. [13] They will certainly carry their own burdens and other burdens besides their own.⁵ They will assuredly be called to account on the Day of Resurrection concerning the fabrications which they contrived.

[14] We did indeed send Noah to his people and he lived among them a thousand years save fifty. Eventually the Flood overtook them while they were engaged in wrong-doing. [15] Then We rescued Noah together with the people in the Ark and made it (that is, the Ark) a lesson for all people.⁶

[16] We sent Abraham and he said to his people: "Serve Allah and fear Him. This is better for you if you only knew. [17] Those that you worship instead of Allah are merely idols, and you are simply inventing lies (about them). Indeed those whom you worship beside Allah have no power to provide you with any sustenance. So seek your sustenance from Allah and serve only Him and give thanks to Him alone. It is to Him that you will be sent back. [18] And if you give the lie (to the Messenger), then many nations before you also gave the lie (to their Messengers). The Messenger is charged with no other duty than to deliver the Message in clear terms."

---

5. The unbelievers will bear the burden of their own straying from the Truth; additionally, they will bear the burden of prompting or compelling others to go astray.

6. That is, God made Noah's Ark, or the chastisement that visited Noah's people, a lesson and warning for others.

[19] Have they never observed how Allah creates for the first time and then repeats it? Indeed (to repeat the creation of a thing) is even easier for Allah (than creating it for the first time). [20] Say: "Go about the earth and see how He created for the first time, and then Allah will recreate life." Surely, Allah has power over everything. [21] He chastises whom He will and forgives whom He will. To Him all of you will be sent back. [22] You cannot overpower Allah, neither on the earth nor in the heaven. None can protect you from Allah nor come to your aid against Him. [23] Those who disbelieved in Allah's signs and in meeting Him, it is they who have despaired of My Mercy;⁷ it is they for whom a painful chastisement lies ahead.

[24] The people (of Abraham) had no other answer than to say: "Kill him or burn him." But Allah delivered him from the fire. There are many Signs in this for those who believe. [25] He said: "You have taken up idols instead of Allah as a bond of love among yourselves in the present life,⁸ but on the Day of Resurrection you will disown and curse one

---

7. This means that obdurate unbelievers will have no portion of God's Mercy; in fact, they have no reason to entertain any such expectation. The fact is that the unbelievers deny the Hereafter. They do not even recognise that a Day will come when they will have to stand before God's judgement. This clearly means that, to start with, they do not even look forward to God's forgiveness.

8. The nucleus of their collective life was devotion to idols rather than to God. Even devotion to such idols can provide a workable basis for bringing about the cohesion of a people in their worldly life, for people tend to gather around both true and false beliefs. Furthermore, any kind of cohesion and unity, even if it is founded on false propositions, can serve as a means to foster and sustain

another. Your refuge shall be the Fire, and none will come to your aid." [26] Then did Lot believe him, and Abraham said: "I am emigrating unto my Lord. He is All-Powerful, All-Wise," [27] and We bestowed upon him (offspring like) Isaac and Jacob, and bestowed prophethood and the Book on his descendants and granted him his reward in this world; he will certainly be among the righteous in the Hereafter.

[28] We sent Lot and he said to his people: "You commit the abomination that none in the world ever committed before you. [29] What! Do you go to men (to satisfy your lust), engage in highway robbery, and commit evil deeds in your gatherings?" Then they had no answer to offer other than to say: "Bring Allah's chastisement upon us if you are truthful." [30] Lot said: "My Lord, aid me against these mischievous people."

[31] When Our emissaries brought the good news to Abraham, and said (to him): "We are surely going to destroy the inhabitants of this city;⁹ its inhabitants are

---

friendships, family ties, and vocational bonds and also provide a basis for religious, social, cultural, economic and political fellowships.

9. "This city" here alludes to the territory in which Lot's people lived. The Prophet Abraham (peace be on him) then lived in the Palestinian city of Hebron, presently known as al-Khalīl. A few miles to the southeast of this lies that part of the Dead Sea which was once inhabited by Lot's people, and which is now submerged by the sea. This is a low-lying area and is easily visible from the hill-tops of Hebron. This is why the angels pointed in the direction of the city, saying to the Prophet Abraham: "We are surely going to destroy the inhabitants of this city."

immersed in wrong-doing." [32] Abraham said: "But Lot is there." They replied: "We are well aware of those who are there. We shall save him and all his household except his wife." His wife is among those who will stay behind.

[33] When Our emissaries came to Lot he was distressed and embarrassed on their account. They said: "Do not fear nor be distressed. We shall save you and all your household except your wife who is among those that will stay behind. [34] We shall bring down upon the people of this city a scourge from the heaven because of their evil-doing." [35] And We have left a vestige of it in that city as a Clear Sign[10] for a people who use their reason.

[36] And We sent to Midian their brother Shu'ayb. He said: "My people, serve Allah and look forward to the Last Day and do not go about the earth committing mischief." [37] But they denounced him as a liar. So a mighty earthquake overtook them, and by the morning they lay overturned in their houses.

[38] And We destroyed 'Ād and Thamūd, whose dwellings you have observed. Satan had embellished their deeds for them and had turned them away from the Right Path although they were a people of clear perception. [39] And We destroyed Qārūn (Korah) and Pharaoh and

---

10. "A Clear Sign" here refers to the Dead Sea which, owing to its association with Lot, is also called the Sea of Lot. Time and again the Qur'ān told the Makkan unbelievers that there were still Signs of the chastisement that had visited those wicked people. These Signs could still be seen by people, day and night, along the highway in the course of their commercial journeys to Syria.

Hāmān. Moses came to them with Clear Signs but they waxed arrogant in the land although they could not have outstripped (Us). [40] So We seized each for their sin. We let loose upon some a violent tornado with showers of stones; some were overtaken by a mighty Cry; some were caused to be swallowed up by the earth, and some We drowned. Allah would not wrong them, but it is they who wronged themselves.

[41] The case of those who took others than Allah as their protectors is that of a spider who builds a house; but the frailest of all houses is the spider's house; if they only knew. [42] Surely Allah knows fully what they call upon apart from Him. He is the Most Powerful, the Most Wise. [43] These are the parables that We set forth to make people understand. But only those endowed with knowledge will comprehend them. [44] Allah has created the heavens and the earth in Truth. Certainly there is a Sign in this for those who believe.

[45] (O Prophet), recite the Book that has been revealed to you and establish Prayer. Surely Prayer forbids indecency and evil. And Allah's remembrance is of even greater merit.[11] Allah knows all that you do.

[46] Argue not with the People of the Book except in the fairest manner, unless it be those of them that are utterly

---

11. To prevent people from committing acts of indecency is one of the benefits of Prayer, though that is a relatively modest benefit. The true blessings of Prayer – "Allah's remembrance" – is much greater and is of a much higher value.

unjust.[12] Say to them: "We believe in what was revealed to us and what was revealed to you. One is our God and your God; and we are those who submit ourselves to Him." [47] (O Prophet), thus have We bestowed the Book on you.[13] So those on whom We had bestowed the Book before believe in it,[14] and of these (Arabs) too a good many believe in it.[15] It is none but the utter unbelievers who deny Our Signs.

---

12. This verse implies that the attitude one should take in dealing with the "utterly unjust" depends on the attitude those people themselves adopt. If they perpetrate wrongs against Muslims, the latter may depart from the gentle and lenient attitude which they are generally required to observe. In other words, there is no specific mandate that says that Muslims should always remain tender and indulgent regardless of others' attitude towards them. For this might be mistaken for weakness and timidity. Islam certainly teaches its followers to be gracious and affable in their dealings with others, but by the same token this does not mean that Muslims should resign themselves to humiliation and degradation.

13. This can be interpreted in two ways. First, that in the same manner that God revealed scriptures to Prophets in the past, He has now revealed a scripture to the Prophet Muhammad (peace be on him). Second, that God revealed this Book – the Qur'ān – and had directed people to believe in it alongside believing in the earlier scriptures.

14. The context clearly indicates that this statement is not applicable to all the People of the Book. Rather, it applies only to those who were endowed with true knowledge and understanding of the scriptures, and were thus the "People of the Book" in the true sense of the expression.

15. The words "of these" here refer to the people of Arabia. What is meant is that everywhere lovers of the Truth had begun to embrace the Book revealed to the Prophet (peace be on him). Such people comprised those who believed in the scriptures as well as those who did not.

[48] (O Prophet), you did not recite any Book before, nor did you write it down with your hand; for then the votaries of falsehood would have had a cause for doubt. [49] But it is a set of Clear Signs in the hearts of those who have been endowed with knowledge.[16] None except the utterly unjust will deny Our Signs. [50] They say: "Why were Signs from his Lord not sent down upon him?" Say: "The Signs are only with Allah. As for me, I am no more than a plain warner." [51] Does it not suffice for them (as a Sign) that We revealed to you the Book that is recited to them? Surely there is mercy and good counsel in it for those who believe. [52] Say (O Prophet): "Allah suffices as a witness between me and you. He knows whatever is in the heavens and the earth. As for those who believe in falsehood and are engaged in infidelity with Allah, it is they who will be the losers."

[53] They ask you to hasten in bringing chastisement upon them. Had there not been an appointed term for it, the chastisement would have already visited them; in fact it will come down upon them all of a sudden (at its appointed time) while they will not be aware of it. [54] They ask you to hasten the chastisement upon them although Hell encompasses the unbelievers. [55] (They will become aware of it) the Day when the chastisement

---

16. The relevant facts were that an unlettered person had come forward with a scripture as wonderful as the Qur'ān. Moreover, that person had begun to display astounding qualities even though nothing in the early years of his life provided any basis for anticipating such things. These were among the facts that provided some of the most luminous and persuasive Signs of Muḥammad's prophethood to people of knowledge and wisdom.

will overwhelm them from above and from under their feet, and He will say to them: "Taste now the consequence of the deeds that you used to commit."

[56] O My servants who believe, verily My earth is vast; so serve Me alone.[17] [57] Every being shall taste death, then it is to Us that you shall be sent back. [58] We shall house those who believed and acted righteously in the lofty mansions of Paradise beneath which rivers flow. There they shall remain for ever. How excellent a reward it is for those who acted (in obedience to Allah), [59] who remained steadfast and put their trust in their Lord! [60] How many an animal there is that does not carry about its sustenance. Allah provides sustenance to them and to you. He is All-Hearing, All-Knowing.

[61] If you[18] were to ask them: "Who created the heavens and the earth and Who has kept the sun and the moon in subjection?" they will certainly say: "Allah." How come, then, they are being deluded from the Truth? [62] Allah enlarges the sustenance of any of His servants whom He will, and straitens the sustenance of whom He will. Surely Allah has knowledge of everything. [63] If you were to ask them: "Who sent down water from the sky and therewith

---

17. This is an allusion to the *Hijrah*. The purpose of the verse was to impress upon the believers that their supreme duty was to serve God. Now, if it was difficult to do so in Makkah, God's earth was immensely vast and by no means confined to any one particular place. As God's true servants, they should move somewhere else where it would be possible for them to live freely as God's servants.

18. The discourse from this point on is directed to the Makkans.

revived the earth after its death?" they will certainly say: "Allah." Say: "To Allah alone be praise and thanks."[19] But most people do not understand.

[64] The present life is nothing but sport and amusement. The true life is in the Abode of the Hereafter; if only they knew. [65] When they embark in the ships they call upon Allah, consecrating their faith to Him. But when He rescues them and brings them to land, they suddenly begin to associate others with Allah in His Divinity [66] that they may be ungrateful for the rescue that We granted them, and that they may revel in the pleasures (of the present life). Soon they shall come to know. [67] Do they not see that We have given them a sanctuary of safety whereas people around them are being snatched away?[20] So, do they believe in falsehood and ungratefully deny

---

19. The words *al-ḥamdu li Allāh* ("to Allah alone be praise and thanks") here suggest two things. First, if all the great tasks – the creation of the heavens and the earth, the harnessing of the sun and the moon, the bestowal of sustenance on the creatures, and the sending down of water from the sky and therewith reviving the earth after it had become dead were performed by God, then quite obviously, He alone deserves praise and thanks. Second, God should also be thanked in so far as the unbelievers also recognised that all these tasks were performed by God alone.

20. The unbelievers are asked to consider who had brought about such wonderful peace and security that prevails in Makkah. Was it an idol like al-Lāt or Hubal that brought it about? Was it possible for anyone other than God to keep Makkah secure against all kinds of violence and disorder for a period of approximately 2,500 years despite its being located in the strife-ridden country of Arabia? Who could ensure that Makkah's sanctity would remain secure?

Allah's bounties? [68] Who can be more unjust than he who foists a lie on Allah or gives the lie to the Truth after it has come to him? Is Hell not the resort of the unbelievers? [69] As for those who strive in Our cause, We shall surely guide them to Our Ways.[21] Indeed Allah is with those who do good.

_____

21. This is a great assurance from God to those who sincerely strive in His cause and expose themselves to conflicts with the rest of the world. God assures such people that He is not wont to leave them to their fate; instead, He helps and guides such people at every step and constantly opens up new avenues for them which direct them to Him. At every step He instructs them about the ways through which they can achieve His good pleasure. He also constantly illuminates for them the Right Way, making it distinct from the meandering labyrinths of Error. The greater the sincerity of the believers, the greater is the support, guidance and succour that God lavishes upon them.

30

Al-Rūm [The Romans]
Makkan Period

*In the name of Allah, the Most Merciful,
the Most Compassionate*

[1] *Alif. Lām. Mīm.* [2] The Romans have been defeated [3] in the neighbouring land; but after their defeat they shall gain victory in a few years.¹ [4] All power belongs to Allah both before and after. On that day will the believers rejoice² [5] at the victory granted by Allah. He grants victory to whomsoever He pleases. He is the Most Mighty, the Most Compassionate. [6] This is Allah's promise and He does not go back on His promise. But most people do not know.

[7] People simply know the outward aspect of the worldly life but are utterly heedless of the Hereafter.

---

1. This alludes to the war that was then taking place between the Byzantine and Sassanid Empires. The Byzantine forces had been so badly beaten by their adversaries that no one could have imagined that they would recover and rise again. In this verse, however, God prophesied that the Byzantines would emerge victorious within the next few years.

2. This was another prediction. Its meaning was only grasped by people later on. It was grasped first of all when the Muslims gained the upper hand in the Battle of Badr, and thereafter when the Byzantines prevailed over the Sassanids.

[8] Do they not reflect on themselves? Allah created the heavens and the earth and whatever lies between them in Truth and for an appointed term. Yet many people deny that they will meet their Lord.³ [9] Have they not travelled through the earth that they may observe what was the end of their predecessors who were far mightier and tilled the land and built upon it more than these have ever built? And Allah's Messengers came to them with Clear Signs. It was not Allah Who wronged them, but it is they who wronged themselves. [10] Evil was the end of those evil-doers, for they gave the lie to Allah's Signs and scoffed at them.

[11] Allah creates in the first instance and will later repeat it. Thereafter it is to Him that you shall be sent back. [12] On that Day when the Hour will come to pass, the criminals shall be dumbfounded.⁴ [13] None whom they had associated with Allah in His Divinity will intercede on their behalf; rather, they will disown those whom they had set up as Allah's associates in His Divinity.⁵

---

3. If one reflects over the order of the universe, two things stand out as quite evident. First, that the creation of the universe is not the work of someone given to play and frolic; instead, it displays purposiveness. Second, that the order of the universe is not eternal and everlasting; some day at an appointed time, it is bound to come to an end. Both these are pointers to the fact that the Hereafter is bound to come about. Nevertheless, many people deny it.

4. The word *mublisūn* in the verse, which is derived from the verbal form *iblās*, means to be dumbfounded by feelings of utter despair and shock.

5. Those who associate others with God in His Divinity will admit in the Next Life that they were mistaken in taking others as His associates.

[14] On that Day when the Hour will come to pass, people will be split into groups. [15] Then those who believed and acted righteously will be placed in a Garden and will be happy and jubilant. [16] As for those who disbelieved and gave the lie to Our Signs and to the encounter of the Hereafter, they will be arraigned for chastisement.

[17] So glorify Allah in the evening and the morning. [18] His is all praise in the heavens and in the earth; (and glorify Him) in the afternoon and when the sun begins to decline.⁶ [19] He brings forth the living from the dead and brings forth the dead from the living, and revives the earth after it is dead. Likewise will you be raised to life (after you die).

[20] And of His Signs is that He created you from dust and behold, you became human beings, and are multiplying around (the earth).

[21] And of His Signs is that He has created mates for you from your own kind that you may find peace in them and He has set between you love and mercy. Surely there are Signs in this for those who reflect.

[22] And of His Signs is the creation of the heavens and the earth and the diversity of your tongues and colours. Indeed there are Signs in this for the wise.

---

6. Vv. 17-18 clearly indicate the following four times of Prayer: *Fajr* (morning), *Maghrib* (evening), *'Aṣr* (afternoon), *Ẓuhr* (early afternoon when the sun begins to decline). If these verses are read in conjunction with *Hūd* 11: 114, *Banī Isrā'īl* 17: 78 and *Ṭā' Hā'* 20: 130, all the five times of daily Prayer become evident.

[23] And of His Signs is your sleeping at night and your seeking His Bounty during the day. Indeed there are Signs in this for those who hearken.

[24] And of His Signs is that He shows you lightning, arousing both fear and hope, and sends down water from the sky and revives the earth after it is dead. Indeed there are Signs in this for those who use their reason.

[25] And of His Signs is that the sky and the earth stand firm by His command. Then no sooner than He summons you out of the earth you will come forth. [26] To Him belong all who are in the heavens and all who are on the earth. All are in obedience to Him. [27] It is He Who creates in the first instance and it is He Who will repeat the creation, and that is easier for Him. His is the loftiest attribute in the heavens and the earth. He is the Most Mighty, the Most Wise.

[28] He sets forth for you a parable from your own lives. Do you have among your slaves some who share with you the sustenance that We have bestowed on you so that you become equals in it, all being alike, and then you would hold them in fear as you fear each other?⁷ Thus do We make plain the Signs for those who use reason. [29] But the wrong-doers follow their desires without any knowledge. Who, then, can show the way to him whom Allah lets go astray? Such shall have no helpers.

---

7. The verse substantially says the same as was said in *Sūrah al-Naḥl* 16: 62. The argument at both places is as follows: "When people are disinclined to make their slaves partners in their properties, how can they bring themselves to believe that God will make His own creatures partners in His Godhead?"

[30] (O Prophet and his followers), turn your face single-mindedly to the true Faith and adhere to the true nature on which Allah has created human beings. The mould fashioned by Allah cannot be altered.[8] That is the True, Straight Faith, although most people do not know. [31] (Adhere to the True Faith and) turn to Him, and hold Him in awe, and establish Prayer, and do not be of those who associate others with Allah in His Divinity, [32] those who have split up their religion and have become divided into sects, each party exulting in what they have.

[33] (Such are human beings) that when any misfortune befalls them, they cry to their Lord, penitently turning to Him. But no sooner that He lets them have a taste of His Mercy than some of them begin associating others with their Lord in His Divinity [34] so that they may show ingratitude to Us for the favours We had bestowed upon them. So, enjoy yourselves a while; but then you shall soon come to know. [35] Have We sent down any sanction which provides support to their associating others with Allah in His Divinity?

---

8. God has designated man to be His servant and has created him for the sole purpose of serving Him. No one, howsoever hard he might try, can alter this natural pattern on which man was created. Neither can man become anything else than God's servant, nor can anyone become his God even if he chose that person to be so. Man may make for himself as many gods as he pleases, but the fact remains that he is the servant of none but the One True God.

This verse can also be translated as follows: "Do not alter the mould on which man has been fashioned." That is, it is not proper for anyone to try to alter man's natural mould, let alone corrupt and distort it.

[36] When We make people have a taste of Our Mercy, they exult in it; and when any misfortune befalls them in consequence of their deeds, then lo and behold, they despair. [37] Do they not see that Allah enlarges and straitens the sustenance of those whom He pleases? There are Signs in this for those who believe. [38] So give his due to the near of kin, and to the needy, and to the wayfarer.⁹ That is better for those who desire to please Allah. It is they who will prosper. [39] Whatever you pay as interest so that it may increase the wealth of people does not increase in the sight of Allah.¹⁰ As for the *Zakāh* that you give, seeking with it Allah's good pleasure, that is multiplied manifold.

[40] It is Allah Who created you, then bestowed upon you your sustenance, and He will cause you to die and then will bring you back to life. Can any of those whom you associate with Allah in His Divinity! do any such thing? Glory be to Him and exalted be He above whatever they associate with Allah in His Divinity. [41] Evil has become rife on the land and at sea¹¹ because of men's deeds; this

---

9. It is significant that man is not directed in this verse to give charity to his near of kin, and to the needy and the wayfarer. Instead, he has been asked to give them what is their due; to render them the right that they have against him.

10. This is the first verse revealed in the Qur'ān expressing disapproval of interest. For the injunctions on the subject revealed later, see *Āl 'Imrān* 3: 130 and *al-Baqarah* 2: 275-281.

11. This is an allusion to the war that was then taking place between the two great powers of the time, the Byzantines and the Sassanids.

in order that He may cause them to have a taste of some of their deeds; perhaps they will turn back (from evil). [42] (O Prophet), say: "Traverse in the earth and see what was the end of those who went before you: most of them associated others with Allah in His Divinity." [43] So turn your face exclusively towards the True Faith before there comes the Day whose coming from Allah cannot be averted, the Day when people will split into groups. [44] He who disbelieves will suffer the consequence of it and he who acts righteously, they will pave the way for their own good [45] so that Allah may, out of His Bounty, reward those who believe and act righteously. Verily He does not love the unbelievers.

[46] And of His Signs is that He sends winds to herald good tidings and that He may give you a taste of His Mercy, and that ships may sail at His bidding, and you may seek His Bounty and give thanks to Him. [47] We sent Messengers before you to their respective nations, and they brought Clear Signs to them. Then We took vengeance upon those who acted wickedly. It was incumbent on Us to come to the aid of the believers.

[48] Allah sends the winds that stir up clouds and then He spreads them in the sky as He pleases and splits them into different fragments, whereafter you see drops of rain pouring down from them. He then causes the rain to fall on whomsoever of His servants He pleases, and lo, they rejoice at it, [49] although before that they were given to despair. [50] See, then, the tokens of Allah's Mercy: how He revives the earth after it is dead. Verily He is the One Who will revive the dead. He has power over everything. [51] But if We were to send a wind and then their tilth has

become yellow, they would never cease to disbelieve.[12] [52] (O Prophet), you cannot make the dead hear,[13] nor can you make the deaf hear your call when they turn back in retreat, [53] nor can you guide the blind out of their error. You can make none hear (your call) except those who believe in Our Signs and have surrendered themselves (to Him).

[54] It is Allah Who created you in a state of weakness; then after weakness He gave you strength, then after strength He made you weak and old. He creates what He pleases. He is All-Knowing, All-Powerful. [55] On that Day when the Hour will come to pass[14] the wicked shall swear that they had stayed (in the world) no more than an hour. Thus they used to be deceived in the life of the world. [56] But those who had been endowed with knowledge and faith shall say: "According to Allah's Record you have stayed till the Day of Resurrection. Now, this is the Day of Resurrection. But you did not know." [57] So that will be the Day when the excuses of the wrong-doers will not avail them, nor will they be asked to make amends.[15]

---

12. The fact is that the preponderance of evil in the world is due to man's own evil conduct. Ironically, people tend to blame their misfortunes on God even though He always lavishes His favours on them. It is even more strange that when people receive God's bounties in full measure they still fail to be thankful to Him.

13. This refers to those whose conscience has become extinct.

14. This refers to the Resurrection about whose occurrence they are being informed.

15. This could also be translated as follows: "… nor will they be asked to please their Lord."

[58] In the Qur'ān We have explained things to people in myriad ways. But no matter what Sign you bring to them, those who are resolved upon denying the Truth will say: "You are given to falsehood." [59] Thus does Allah seal the hearts of those who have no knowledge. [60] Therefore, (O Prophet), have patience. Surely Allah's promise is true. Let those who lack certainty not cause you to be unsteady.[16]

---

16. The believers should remain firm and steadfast in their attitude. Their enemies should not find them faint-hearted, overpowered by their empty hue and cry, cowed down by their slander campaigns, demoralised by their taunts and ridicules, intimidated by their threats, show of strength and persecution, nor seduced by their allurements.

Luqmān
Makkan Period

In the name of Allah, the Most Merciful,
the Most Compassionate

[1] *Alif. Lām. Mīm.* [2] These are the verses of the Wise Book,¹ [3] a guidance and mercy for the doers of good, [4] who establish Prayer and pay *Zakāh*, and have firm faith in the Hereafter. [5] It is they who are on true guidance from their Lord, and it is they who shall prosper.

[6] There are some human beings who purchase an enchanting diversion² in order to lead people away from the way of Allah without having any knowledge, who hold the call to the Way of Allah to ridicule. A humiliating chastisement awaits them. [7] When Our verses are recited

---

1. That is, these are the verses of the Book immersed in wisdom, a Book every part of which is insightful and judicious.

2. The words in the text are *lahw al-ḥadīth*, which suggest an amusement or diversion that completely absorbs a person, making him oblivious to everything around him. According to traditions, despite all their efforts, the Quraysh failed to prevent the Prophet's Message from spreading around. On seeing this they procured the tales of Rustam and Isfandiyār from Persia and seriously endeavoured to engage people in these tales. They even employed slave-girls skilled in singing and music so that people would not pay heed to the Prophet's teachings. (See al-Bayḍāwī, *Tafsīr al-Bayḍāwī* (Beirut: Dār al-Fikr, 1996], v. 4, pp. 344-5.)

to such a person, he arrogantly turns away, as though he had not heard them, or as though there was a deafness in his ears. So announce to him the tidings of a grievous chastisement. [8] Surely those who believe and do good deeds shall have Gardens of Bliss. [9] They shall abide in them forever. This is Allah's promise that shall come true. He is the Most Powerful, the Most Wise.

[10] He created the heavens without any pillars visible to you and He placed mountains in the earth as pegs lest it should turn topsy turvy with you, and He dispersed all kinds of animals over the earth, and sent down water from the sky causing all kinds of excellent plants to grow on it. [11] Such is Allah's creation. Show me, then, what any others, apart from Allah, have created. Nay, the fact is that the wrong-doers are in manifest error.

[12] We bestowed wisdom upon Luqmān, (enjoining): "Give thanks to Allah." Whoso gives thanks to Allah, does so to his own good. And whoso disbelieves (let him know that) Allah is All-Sufficient, Immensely Praiseworthy.

[13] And call to mind when Luqmān said to his son while exhorting him: "My son, do not associate others with Allah in His Divinity. Surely, associating others with Allah in His Divinity is a mighty wrong." [14] We enjoined upon man to be dutiful to his parents. His mother bore him in weakness upon weakness, and his weaning lasted two years. (We, therefore, enjoined upon him): "Give thanks to Me and to your parents. To Me is your ultimate return. [15] But if they press you to associate others with Me in My Divinity, (to associate) those regarding whom you have no knowledge (that they are My associates), do not obey

them.³ And yet treat them well in this world, and follow the way of him who turns to Me in devotion. Eventually it is to Me that all of you shall return, and I shall then tell you all that you did."

[16] (Luqmān said): "Son, Allah will bring forth everything even if it be as small as the grain of a mustard seed even though it be hidden inside a rock or (anywhere) in the heavens or earth. Allah is Most Subtle, All-Aware. [17] Son, establish Prayer, enjoin all that is good and forbid all that is evil, and endure with patience whatever affliction befalls you. Surely these have been emphatically enjoined.⁴ [18] Do not (contemptuously) turn your face away from people, nor tread haughtily upon earth. Allah does not love the arrogant and the vainglorious. [19] Be moderate in your stride and lower your voice. Verily the most disgusting of all voices is the braying of the donkey."

[20] Have you not seen that Allah has subjected to your service all that is in the heavens and on the earth⁵ and has abundantly bestowed upon you all His bounties, both visible and invisible? Yet some persons dispute regarding Allah without having any knowledge or guidance or any

---

3. "... those regarding whom you have no knowledge," that is, no knowledge about their being God's associates in His Divinity.

4. It could also be translated as follows: "Surely this is a thing requiring great resolve."

5. A thing can be subjected to someone's service in two ways. First, that it is made subservient to him, and he is invested with the power to use it as he wills. Second, that the thing is made part of a system in such manner that it is endowed with utility and so

illuminating Book. [21] When they are told: "Follow what Allah has revealed," they say: "We will rather follow that which we have found our forefathers following." (Will they follow that) even though Satan might invite them to the chastisement of the Blazing Fire?

[22] Whoever surrenders himself to Allah and lives righteously grasps the most firm handle. The ultimate decision of all matters rests with Allah. [23] So let the unbelief of the unbeliever not grieve you. To Us is their return and then We shall inform them of all that they did. Surely Allah knows well even the secrets that are hidden in the breasts (of people). [24] We allow them to enjoy themselves a while in the world and then We shall drive them in utter helplessness to a harsh chastisement.

[25] If you were to ask them: "Who created the heavens and the earth?" they will certainly reply: "Allah." Say: "All praise and thanks be to Allah." Yet most of them do not know. [26] All that is in the heavens and the earth belongs to Allah. Verily He is All-Sufficient, Immensely Praiseworthy. [27] If all the trees on earth become pens, and the sea replenished by seven more seas were to

---

made conducive to serving someone's interests. Now, while it is true that everything in the heavens and the earth has been subjected to man's service, not everything has been subjected to that service in a uniform manner. To illustrate, God has subjected air, water, earth, fire, vegetation, minerals, cattle and many other things to man's service in the sense that he is invested with the power to use them as he wishes. On the other hand, although the sun, the moon, etc. have also been subjected to man's service, this is in the sense that they have been invested with utility and made to serve man's interests.

supply them with ink, the Words of Allah would not be exhausted.[6] Verily Allah is Most Mighty, Most Wise. [28] To create all of you or to resurrect all of you is to Him like (creating or resurrecting) a single person. Verily Allah is All-Hearing, All-Seeing.

[29] Do you not see that Allah makes the night phase into the day and makes the day phase into the night and has subjected the sun and the moon to His will so that each of them is pursuing its course till an appointed time?[7] (Do you not know that) Allah is well aware of all that you do? [30] All this is because Allah, He alone, is the Truth and all that which they call upon beside Him is false. Surely Allah, He alone, is All-High, Incomparably Great.

[31] Do you not see that ships sail in the sea by Allah's Grace that He may show you some of His Signs? Surely there are Signs in this for everyone who is steadfast, thankful. [32] When waves engulf them (in the sea) like canopies, they call upon Allah, consecrating their faith solely to Him. But when He delivers them safely to the land, some of them become lukewarm.[8] None denies Our Signs except the perfidious, the ungrateful.

---

6. We have already come across this very idea in *Sūrah al-Kahf* 18: 109. The purpose of the present statement is to impress upon man that God's creative power is limitless. How can any creature, then, be God's partner in His Godhead?

7. Nothing in the world is eternal and everlasting. Everything has a fixed term of existence. During this term it functions but not after the term's expiry.

8. The word used here is *muqtaṣid*. Were we to take *iqtiṣād* to mean rectitude and uprightness, the verse means that even after a crisis

[33] O people, fear (the wrath) of your Lord, and dread the Day when no father will stand for his child, nor any child stand for his father. Surely Allah's promise is true.[9] So let the life of this world not beguile you, nor let the Deluder delude you about Allah.

[34] Surely Allah alone has the knowledge of the Hour. It is He Who sends down the rain and knows what is in the wombs, although no person knows what he will earn tomorrow, nor does he know in which land he will die. Indeed, Allah is All-Knowing, All-Aware.

---

is over and the person facing it has landed on the shores of safety, he still adheres to *tawhīd*. Alternatively, if the word is considered to signify a moderate, midway course, the verse means that when people encounter a serious difficulty, they become moderate and less rigid in their adherence to atheism and polytheism. It may also mean that after the worst is over, people lose a part of their former fervour and enthusiasm (in devotion to God) which was aroused by the threatening circumstances that enveloped them.

9. "Allah's promise" here signifies the promise of Resurrection.

32

Al-Sajdah [Prostration]
Makkan Period

In the name of Allah, the Most Merciful,
the Most Compassionate

[1] *Alif. Lām. Mīm.* [2] This Book, beyond all doubt, was revealed by the Lord of the Universe. [3] Or do they say: "He has fabricated it?" Nay, it is the Truth from your Lord so that you may warn a people to whom no warner came before you; perhaps they will be guided to the Right Way.

[4] It is Allah Who created the heavens and the earth and all that is between the two, in six days, and then He established Himself on the Throne. You have no guardian or intercessor other than He. Will you, then, not take heed? [5] He governs from the heaven to the earth and then the record (of this governance) goes up to Him in a day whose measure is a thousand years in your reckoning.[1] [6] He knows all that is beyond as well as all that is within

---

1. This means that the annals of a thousand years of man's history are no more than a day's work for God. Whatever tasks God entrusts to His angels today are completed by them before they are entrusted with the tasks for the following day. This day, that we are speaking of, however, is equal to a thousand years according to human computation.

a creature's sense-perception. He is the Most Mighty, the Most Compassionate, [7] He Who excelled in the creation of all that He created. He originated the creation of man from clay, [8] then made his progeny from the extract of a mean fluid, [9] then He duly proportioned him, and breathed into him of His spirit, and bestowed upon you ears and eyes and hearts. And yet, little thanks do you give.

[10] They say: "Shall we be created afresh after we have become lost in the earth?" Nay, the fact is that they deny that they will meet their Lord. [11] Tell them: "The angel of death who has been charged with your souls shall gather you, and then you shall be brought back to your Lord."

[12] Would that you could see the guilty standing before their Lord with their heads downcast, (saying to Him): "Our Lord, we have now seen and heard, so send us back (to the world) that we might act righteously. For now we have come to have firm faith." [13] (They will be told): "If We had so willed, We could have bestowed guidance on every person. But the Word from Me that I will fill Hell with men and *jinn*, all together, has been fulfilled. [14] So taste the chastisement on account of your forgetting the encounter of this Day. We, too, have forgotten you. Taste the eternal chastisement as a requital for your misdeeds."

[15] None believes in Our Signs except those who, when they are given good counsel through Our verses, fall down prostrate and celebrate the praise of their Lord and do not wax proud. [16] Their sides forsake their beds, and they call upon their Lord in fear and hope, and expend

(in charity) out of the sustenance We have granted them. [17] No one knows what delights of the eyes are kept hidden for them as a reward for their deeds. [18] Would a true believer be like him who was an evil-doer? Surely they are not equal. [19] As for those who believe and act righteously, theirs shall be Gardens to dwell in, a hospitality to reward them for their deeds. [20] As for the evil-doers, their refuge shall be the Fire. Every time they want to escape from it they shall be driven back and shall be told: "Taste the chastisement of the Fire which you used to reject as a lie."

[21) We shall certainly have them taste some chastisement in this world in addition to the greater chastisement (of the Hereafter); perhaps they will retract (from their transgression). [22] And who is more unjust than he who is given good counsel through the Signs of his Lord and yet he turns away from them? Surely We will exact full retribution from such criminals.

[23] Verily We bestowed the Book upon Moses. So entertain no doubt if (the Prophet Muḥammad) received the same. We had made that Book a guidance for the Children of Israel, [24] and when they remained steadfast and firmly believed in Our Signs, We created among them leaders who guided people by Our command. [25] Surely your Lord will judge among them on the Day of Resurrection concerning the matters about which the Children of Israel used to differ.

[26] Did (these historical events) not make them realise that We destroyed many nations before them amidst whose dwellings they now move about? Surely there are

many Signs in this. Are they unable to hear? [27] Have they
not seen that We drive water to the parched land, thereby
bringing forth crops which they and their cattle eat? Are
they unable to see? [28] They say: "If you are truthful, (tell
us) when will the Judgement come?" [29] Tell them: "If
the unbelievers were to believe on the Day of Judgement
that will not avail them. For then they will be granted no
respite." [30] So (leave them to themselves and) turn away
from them and wait; they too are waiting.

33

Al-Aḥzāb [The Confederates]
Madīnan Period

In the name of Allah, the Most Merciful,
the Most Compassionate

[1] O Prophet, fear Allah and do not obey the unbelievers and the hypocrites. Verily Allah is All-Knowing, Most Wise. [2] Follow that which is revealed to you from your Lord. Verily Allah is fully aware of all that you do. [3] Put your trust in Allah: Allah is sufficient as Guardian.

[4] Allah has never put two hearts within one person's body; nor has He made your wives, whom you compare to your mothers' backs (to divorce them), your true mothers; nor has He made those whom you adopt as sons your own sons. These are only words that you utter with your mouths.[1] But Allah proclaims the Truth and directs you to the Right Path. [5] Call your adopted sons after their true fathers; that is more equitable in the sight of Allah. But if you do not know their true fathers, then regard them as your brethren in faith and as allies. You will not be taken to task for your mistaken utterances, but you will be taken to task for what you say deliberately. Allah is Most Forgiving, Most Compassionate.

---

1. *Ẓihār* means to declare one's wife to be like one's mother.

[6] Surely the Prophet has a greater claim over the believers than they have over each other, and his wives are their mothers. According to the Book of Allah, blood relatives have greater claim over each other than the rest of the believers and the Emigrants (in the cause of Allah), except that you may do some good to your allies (if you so wish). This is inscribed in the Book of Allah.

[7] And call to mind, (O Prophet), when We took the covenant from all Prophets; and also from you and Noah and Abraham, Moses, and Jesus the son of Mary. We took from them a solemn covenant[2] [8] so that (their Lord) may question the truthful about their truthfulness. As for the unbelievers, He has kept a painful chastisement in store for them.

[9] Believers,[3] call to mind Allah's favour to you when enemy hosts invaded you. Then We sent against them a wind and hosts that you did not see[4] although Allah was

---

2. In this verse God reminds the Prophet (peace be on him) that, like all other Prophets, he too had made a solemn covenant with God, a covenant that he should follow strictly. If one bears in mind the preceding verses, it is evident that the covenant consisted of the Prophet's commitment to obey God's every command and to ask others to do the same. The covenant also comprised the Prophet's commitment to faithfully convey God's commands to others and to spare no effort in putting them into effect. This covenant has also been mentioned at several other places in the Qur'ān, e.g. in *al-Baqarah* 2: 83; *Āl 'Imrān* 3: 187; *al-Mā'idah* 5: 7; *al-A'rāf* 6: 169-171 and *al-Shūrā* 42: 13.

3. From here on until verse 27, the discourse centres on the Battle of the *Aḥzāb* and the expedition against Banū Qurayẓah.

4. The "hosts that you did not see" is an allusion to the angels who fought on the side of the Muslims.

observing all that you were then doing. [10] When they came upon you from above you and from below you, when your eyes were stupefied with horror and your hearts leapt to your throats, and you began to entertain diverse thoughts about Allah. [11] The believers were then put to a severe test and were most violently convulsed.

[12] And call to mind when the hypocrites and all those with diseased hearts said: "All that Allah and His Messenger had promised us was nothing but deceit." [13] And when a section of them said: "(O people of Yathrib), now there is no place for you to stay, so turn back." (And call to mind) when a section of them was seeking permission from the Prophet to leave, saying: "Our houses are exposed (to attack)," although they were not exposed (to attack); they only wished to flee (from the battle-front). [14] If the enemy were to enter the town from various directions, and they were summoned to act treacherously, they would have succumbed to it and would have shown little reluctance in doing so. [15] They had earlier covenanted with Allah that they would not turn their backs in flight. And a covenant made with Allah must needs be answered for.

[16] (O Prophet), tell them: "If you run away from death or slaying, this flight will not avail you. You will have little time after that to enjoy (the pleasures of life)." [17] Say (to them): "Who can protect you from Allah if He desires an evil for you? And who can prevent Him if He desires to show mercy to you?" They shall find none other than Allah to be their protector or helper.

[18] Allah knows well those of you who create obstructions (in war efforts) and say to their brethren: "Come and join

us." They hardly take any part in battle. [19] They are utterly niggardly (in coming to your aid). Whenever there is danger, you will see them looking at you, their eyes rolling as though they were on the verge of fainting at the approach of death. But when the danger passes away, their greed for wealth prompts them to greet you with their sharp, scissor-like tongues. These are the ones who never truly believed, and so Allah has caused their deeds to be reduced to naught. That is easy enough for Allah. [20] They think that the invading confederates have not yet gone. But if the confederates were to mount another assault, they would wish to be in the desert among the bedouins and keep themselves informed about you from there. But even if they remained in your midst, hardly would they fight.

[21] Surely there was a good example for you in the Messenger of Allah,[5] for all those who look forward to Allah and the Last Day and remember Allah much. [22] As for the true believers, when they saw the invading confederates, they cried out: "This is what Allah and His Messenger had promised us, and what Allah and His Messenger said was absolutely true." This only increased their faith and submission. [23] Among the believers there are those who have remained true to the covenant they made with Allah. Among those some of them have fulfilled their vow and others await the appointed time. They have not changed in the least. [24] (All this is) in order that Allah may reward the truthful for their truthfulness, and either punish the hypocrites or, if He

5. It can also be translated as follows: "Surely there *is* (rather than there *was*) a good example for you in the Messenger of Allah …."

so wills, accept their repentance. Verily Allah is Most Pardoning, Most Compassionate.

[25] Allah sent back the unbelievers empty-handed, their hearts seething with rage. Allah sufficed the believers in their fight. Allah is Most Powerful, Most Mighty. [26] Allah brought down from their fortresses those People of the Book who had supported the invading confederates⁶ and cast such terror into their hearts that some of them you kill and some of them you take captive. [27] Allah made you inherit their land, their dwellings, and their goods, and a piece of land on which you had not yet trodden. Verily Allah has power over all things.

[28] O Prophet, tell your wives: "If you seek the world and its embellishments, then come and I will make some provision for you and release you in an honourable way.⁷ [29] But if you seek Allah and His Messenger and the Abode of the Hereafter, then surely Allah has prepared a great reward for those of you who do good."

[30] Wives of the Prophet, if any of you commit flagrant indecency,⁸ her chastisement shall be doubled. That is easy for Allah. [31] But whoever of you is obedient to

6. "The invading confederates" here refers to the Jews of the Qurayẓah tribe.

7. This verse was revealed at a time when the Prophet (peace be on him) was facing severe financial stringency so much so that his household went without food for days. The circumstances that obtained at the time naturally perturbed the Prophet's wives.

8. This does not mean that there was, God forbid, any serious possibility that the Prophet's wives would commit any acts of indecency. The purpose of the statement was to simply make the

Allah and His Messenger and does good deeds, Allah will double her reward. We have prepared for her a generous provision.

[32] Wives of the Prophet, you are not like other women. If you fear Allah, do not be too complaisant in your speech lest those with diseased hearts should covet you; but speak in a straight forward manner. [33] And stay in your homes and do not go about displaying your allurements as in the former Time of Ignorance. Establish Prayer, give *Zakāh*, and obey Allah and His Messenger. Allah only wishes to remove uncleanness from you, O members of the (Prophet's) household, and to purify you completely. [34] Remember the Signs of Allah and the words of wisdom which are rehearsed in your homes. Verily Allah is All-Subtle, All-Aware.[9]

[35] Surely the men who submit (to Allah) and the women who submit (to Allah), the men who have faith and the women who have faith, the men who are obedient and the women who are obedient, the men who are truthful and the women who are truthful; the men who are steadfast and the women who are steadfast, the men who humble themselves (to Allah) and the women who humble themselves (to Allah), the men who give alms and the women who give alms, the men who fast and the women who fast, the men who guard their chastity

---

Prophet's wives conscious of their high station, as the mothers of the believers, and to remind them that they were expected to take due care of their dignity and distinguished position.

9. To say that "Allah is All-Aware" amounts to saying that He has full knowledge of everything, including the most hidden secrets.

and the women who guard their chastity, the men who remember Allah much and the women who remember Allah much: for them has Allah prepared forgiveness and a mighty reward.

[36] It does not behove a believer, male or female, that when Allah and His Messenger have decided an affair they should exercise their choice. And whoever disobeys Allah and His Messenger has strayed to manifest error.

[37] (O Prophet), call to mind when you said to him whom Allah had favoured and you had favoured: "Cleave to your wife and fear Allah,"[10] and you concealed within yourself for fear of people what Allah was to reveal, although Allah has greater right that you fear Him.[11] So when Zayd had accomplished what he would of her,[12]

---

10. The words "… him whom Allah had favoured" allude to Zayd ibn Ḥārithah who was the Prophet's freed slave and adopted son. Zayd's wife at that time was Zaynab, the Prophet's cousin whom he himself had given in marriage to him. The spouses, however, were not maritally well-adjusted. As a result, Zayd felt inclined to divorce Zaynab.

11. God wanted the Prophet (peace be on him) to marry Zaynab, after Zayd would divorce her, the purpose being to put an end to the ancient custom according to which a person's adopted son was regarded, in quite a legal sense, as his own. The Prophet (peace be on him), however, was not inclined to marry Zaynab for he took into account the severe reaction that this might provoke among his people. It was for this reason that he earnestly tried to dissuade Zayd from divorcing Zaynab.

12. That is, Zayd accomplished his desire of definitively divorcing his wife. As a result, all legal relationship between him and his wife was sundered.

We gave her in marriage to you so that there should not be any constraint for the believers regarding the wives of their adopted sons after they had accomplished whatever they would of them. And Allah's command was bound to be accomplished. [38] There could be no hindrance to the Prophet regarding what Allah ordained for him. Such has been Allah's Way (with the Prophets) who went before. Allah's command is a decree firmly determined. [39] (This is Allah's Way) regarding those who deliver the Messages of Allah and who fear Him, and fear no one else than Allah. Allah is Sufficient as a Reckoner.

[40] Muḥammad is not the father of any of your men, but he is the Messenger of Allah and the seal of the Prophets.[13] Allah has full knowledge of everything.

---

13. This one sentence cuts at the root of all objections ventilated by the opponents against the Prophet's marriage. Their first objection was that the Prophet (peace be on him) had married his own daughter-in-law. This was answered by the revelation: "Muḥammad is not the father of any of your men ...." The implication of the statement being that since Zayd was not the Prophet's son, it was not unlawful for him to marry Zayd's divorced wife. The opponents then proferred another objection: even though an adopted son cannot be equated as one's own, there was nevertheless no need to make use of such facilitating permission. In response, the essential position of the Prophet (peace be on him) was explained by saying: "... he is the Messenger of Allah and the seal of the Prophets." The implication of this statement is clear: that as God's Messenger it was incumbent on Muḥammad (peace be on him) to put an end to all unjustified constraints which had encumbered people's lives by prohibiting that which is lawful. In this circumstance it was his duty to restore the lawfulness of the acts that are lawful in God's sight. This aspect of the Prophet's duty was further stressed by saying that he is: "... the seal of the Prophets." The implication being that apart from being God's Messenger, he was also the seal

[41] Believers, remember Allah much [42] and glorify Him morning and evening. [43] It is He Who lavishes His blessings on you and His angels invoke blessings on you that He may lead you out of darkness into light. He is Most Compassionate to the believers. [44] On the Day they meet Him they will be greeted with: "Peace." He has prepared for them a generous reward.

[45] O Prophet, We have sent you forth as a witness, a bearer of good tidings, and a warner, [46] as one who calls people to Allah by His leave, and as a bright, shining lamp. [47] Announce to the believers the good tidings that Allah has kept bounteous blessings in store for them. [48] Do not yield to the unbelievers and the hypocrites, and disregard the hurt that comes from them,[14] and put your trust in Allah. Allah suffices as the Guardian to entrust one's affairs to.

[49] Believers, when you marry believing women and then divorce them before you have touched them, you

---

of the Prophets after whom no other Prophet would come. Hence if anything required reform, either in the legal or social sphere, it was only the Prophet (peace be on him) who could bring that about. The fact of his being the final Prophet made it all the more necessary that he should do away with all the objectionable customs and practices of the Time of Ignorance. This point was even further emphasised by saying: "Allah has full knowledge of everything," meaning that God fully knows why it was necessary that a certain aspect of *Jāhilīyah* should be extirpated through the Prophet (peace be on him) at a given time, and that He also knows the harm of letting the *status quo ante* continue.

14. The Prophet (peace be on him) was asked to disregard the opponents' hostile criticism of his marriage.

may not require them to observe a waiting period that you might reckon against them. So make provision for them and release them in an honourable manner.

[50] O Prophet, We have made lawful for you your wives whose bridal dues you have paid,[15] and the slave-girls you possess from among the prisoners of war, and the daughters of your paternal uncles and paternal aunts, and the daughters of your maternal uncles and maternal aunts who have migrated with you, and a believing woman who gives herself to the Prophet and whom he wants to take in marriage.[16] (O Prophet), this privilege is yours alone to the exclusion of other believers. We know well what restrictions We have imposed upon them as regards their wives and those whom their right hands possess, (and have exempted you from those restrictions) that there may be no constraint upon you. Allah is Most Forgiving, Most Merciful. [51] Of them you may put off any of them you wish, and you may take any of them whom you wish, and you may call back any of those whom you had (temporarily) set aside: there will be no blame on you (on this account). It is likelier that they will thus be comforted, and will not grieve, and every one

---

15. This answered the criticism of those who said that the Prophet (peace be on him) forbade others to keep more than four wives, but he himself had taken a fifth. It is pertinent to mention that at that time the Prophet (peace be on him) already had four wives, namely ʿĀʾishah, Sawdah, Ḥafṣah and Umm Salamah.

16. That is, in addition to these five wives (i.e. Zaynab and the four mentioned in n.15 above) the Prophet (peace be on him) was also permitted to take other wives belonging to the categories mentioned in the present verse.

of them will be well-pleased with what you give them. Allah knows what is in your hearts. Allah is All-Knowing, All-Forbearing. [52] Thereafter women will not be lawful for you, and it will not be lawful for you to take other wives in place of them, even though their beauty might please you,¹⁷ unless they be those whom your right hand owns.¹⁸ Allah is watchful over everything.

[53] Believers, enter not the houses of the Prophet without his permission, nor wait for a meal to be prepared; instead enter when you are invited to eat, and when you have had the meal, disperse. Do not linger in idle talk. That is hurtful to the Prophet but he does not express it out of shyness; but Allah is not ashamed of speaking out the Truth. And if you were to ask the wives of the Prophet for something, ask from behind a curtain. That is more apt for the cleanness of your hearts and theirs. It is not

---

17. This directive has two meanings. First, that except for the women with whom the Prophet's marriage was declared to be lawful in verse 50 above, none else was lawful for him. Second, it was stressed that the Prophet's wives had made up their minds to put up with every kind of straitened circumstance. They had chosen to live with him through thick and thin and had spurned the world and its allurements in order to achieve success and felicity in the Hereafter. They had also clearly indicated their satisfaction with whatever treatment might be meted out to them by the Prophet (peace be on him). In view of all this, it was no longer lawful for him to divorce any of his wives and to replace them with others.

18. This verse makes it clear that it is lawful to have conjugal relations with one's slave-girls in addition to the women whom one has contracted in marriage; furthermore, their maximum number is not specified. This point is also mentioned in *al-Nisā'* 4: 3; *al-Mu'minūn* 23: 6; and *al-Ma'ārij* 70: 30.

lawful for you to cause hurt to Allah's Messenger, nor to ever marry his wives after him. Surely that would be an enormous sin in Allah's sight. [54] (It does not matter) whether you disclose something or conceal it, for Allah certainly knows everything.

[55] It will not be blameworthy for the wives of the Prophet if their fathers, their sons, their brothers, their brothers' sons, their sisters' sons, and the women with whom they have social relations, and the persons whom their right hands possess enter their houses. (O women), shun disobeying Allah. Allah is watchful over everything.

[56] Allah and His angels bless the Prophet. Believers, invoke blessings and peace on him.[19]

[57] Verily those who cause annoyance to Allah and His Messenger – Allah has cursed them in this world and in the Hereafter and has prepared for them a humiliating chastisement. [58] Those who cause hurt to believing men and to believing women have invited upon themselves a calumny and a manifest sin.

---

19. To say that God blesses the Prophet (peace be on him) means that He is extremely benevolent towards him: He praises him immensely, bestows grace on his work, exalts his name, and showers His benedictions on him. Likewise, to say that the angels send their blessings on the Prophet means that they have the highest degree of love and reverence for him and that they pray to God to grant him ever higher ranks. The invocation of God's blessings on the Prophet by believers means that they pray to God to bestow upon him an abundance of His blessings.

[59] O Prophet, enjoin your wives and your daughters and the believing women, to draw a part of their outer coverings around them.[20] It is likelier that they will be recognised and not molested.[21] Allah is Most Forgiving, Most Merciful.

[60] If the hypocrites and those in whose hearts there is a sickness, and the scandal mongers in Madīnah do not desist from their vile acts, We shall urge you to take action against them, and then they will hardly be able to stay in the city with you. [61] They shall be cursed from all around and they shall be ruthlessly killed wherever they are seized. [62] This has been Allah's Way with those who have gone before, and you shall find no change in Allah's Way.

[63] People ask you concerning the Hour (of Resurrection). Say: "Allah alone has knowledge of it. What do you know? Perhaps the Hour is nigh." [64] Allah has cursed

---

20. That is, they should wear their over-garment (*chādar*) and veil. In other words, they should not move about with their faces uncovered.

21. "... It is likelier that they will thus be recognised ..." that is, when people see them dressed in garments exuding simplicity and modesty they will be recognised as honourable and chaste women. They will appear distinct from women of loose character who are ever on the hunt for lewd encounters. These women are unlike those whom immoral men would seek out to gratify their carnal desires. As for the words "and will not be molested," they mean that since those women will be perceived as decent ladies they will not be subjected to teasing and harassment to which men of vile character have recourse when they encounter women not particularly known for their uprightness and firmness of character.

the unbelievers and has prepared for them a Blazing Fire; [65] therein they shall abide for ever. They shall find none to protect or help them. [66] On that Day when their faces shall be turned around in the Fire, they will say: "Would that we had obeyed Allah and obeyed the Messenger." [67] They will say: "Our Lord, we obeyed our chiefs and our great ones, and they turned us away from the Right Way. [68] Our Lord, mete out to them a double chastisement and lay upon them a mighty curse."

[69] Believers, do not be like those who distressed Moses and then Allah declared him quit of the ill they spoke about him; and he had a high standing with Allah. [70] Believers, fear Allah and speak the truth: [71] Allah will set your deeds right for you and will forgive you your sins. Whoever obeys Allah and His Messenger has achieved a great triumph.

[72] We offered the trust[22] to the heavens and the earth and the mountains, but they refused to carry it and were afraid of doing so; but man carried it. Surely he is wrong-doing, ignorant.[23] [73] (The consequence of man's carrying the trust is) that Allah may chastise hypocritical men and hypocritical women and accept the repentance of believing men and believing women. He is Most Forgiving, Most Merciful.

---

22. The word "trust" here signifies the burden of responsibilities which God has placed on man after endowing him with reason as well as power and authority in the earth.

23. That is, even though man is the bearer of a great trust from God, he does not show the requisite sense of responsibility and is wont to wrong himself by committing breach of trust.

34

Saba' [Sheba]
Makkan Period

In the name of Allah, the Most Merciful,
the Most Compassionate

[1] All praise be to Allah to Whom belongs all that is in the heavens and all that is in the earth, and all praise be to Him in the World to Come. He is Most Wise, All-Aware. [2] He knows what penetrates into the earth and what goes forth from it, what descends from the heaven and what ascends to it. He is the Most Merciful, the Most Forgiving.

[3] The unbelievers say: "How come the Hour is not coming upon us!" Say to them: "Yes indeed, by my Lord, by Him Who fully knows the realm beyond the ken of perception, that the Hour shall inevitably come upon you. Nothing escapes Him, not even the smallest particle in the heavens or the earth; nor is anything smaller or bigger than that but is in a Manifest Book." [4] (The Hour shall come) that He may reward those who believe and do righteous deeds. Theirs shall be forgiveness and a generous provision. [5] As for those who worked against Our Signs in order to frustrate them, they shall suffer a painful chastisement. [6] (O Prophet), those who have knowledge see clearly that what has been revealed to you from your Lord is the Truth and directs to the Way of the Most Mighty, the Immensely Praiseworthy Lord.

[7] The unbelievers say: "Shall we direct you to the man who tells you that when you have been utterly broken to pieces, you will be raised to life again? [8] Has he forged a lie against Allah, or is he afflicted with madness?"

Nay, but those who do not believe in the Hereafter are doomed to be chastised and are far gone in error. [9] Do they not see how the heavens and the earth encompass them from the front and the rear? We could, if We so wished, cause the earth to swallow them or let fragments of the sky fall upon them. Verily there is a Sign in this for every servant (of Allah) who penitently turns to Him.

[10] We bestowed Our favour upon David. (We commanded): "O mountains, sing Allah's praises with him"; (and so did We command) the birds. We softened the iron for him, (saying): [11] "Fashion coats of mail and measure their links with care and act righteously. I am watching over whatever you do."

[12] And We subdued the wind to Solomon: its morning course was a month's journey and its evening course was a month's journey. We gave him a spring flowing with molten brass, and We subdued for him *jinn* who, by his Lord's permission, worked before him. Such of them as swerved from Our commandment, We let them taste the chastisement of the Blazing Fire. [13] They made for him whatever he would desire: stately buildings, images,[1]

---

1. An "image" is not necessarily always of men or animals. The Prophet Solomon (peace be on him) was a follower of Mosaic Law in which the making of images of living beings was forbidden just as it is forbidden in the Law of the Prophet Muḥammad (peace be on him).

basins like water-troughs and huge, built-in-cauldrons: "Work, O house of David, in thankfulness (to your Lord).[2] Few of My servants are truly thankful."

[14] When We executed Our decree of death on Solomon, nothing indicated to the *jinn* that he was dead except a worm eating away his staff. So when Solomon fell down, the *jinn* realised that had they known what lies in the realm beyond perception, they would not have continued to be in this humiliating chastisement.

[15] For Sheba there was also a Sign in their dwelling-place: the two gardens to the right and to the left.[3] "Eat of your Lord's provision, and render thanks to Him. Most pleasant is your land and Most Forgiving is your Lord." [16] But they turned away and so We let loose upon them a devastating flood that swept away the dams and replaced their gardens by two others bearing bitter fruits, tamarisks, and a few lote trees. [17] Thus did We retribute them for their ingratitude. And none do We retribute in this manner except the utterly ungrateful.

[18] We placed other prominent towns between them, the towns that We had blessed and had set well-measured

---

2. "Work … in thankfulness (to your Lord)" means to work in the manner God's thankful servants should.

3. This does not mean that there were only two gardens in the whole land. What is meant is that the entire land of Saba' had become a vast garden. Wherever a person stood, he could observe gardens on both sides, to his right as well as to his left.

stages between them.[4] Move back and forth between them, night and day, in perfect security. [19] But they said: "Lord, make the stages of our journeys longer."[5] They wronged their own selves so We reduced them to bygone tales, and utterly tore them to pieces. Verily there are Signs in this for everyone who is steadfast and thankful. [20] *Iblīs* found his estimate of them to be true, and they followed him, except a party of the believers. [21] *Iblīs* had no authority over them and whatever happened was in order that We might know him who believes in the Hereafter as distinct from him who is in doubt about it. Your Lord is watchful over everything.

[22] (O Prophet), say to those who associate others with Allah in His Divinity: "Call upon those whom you fancied to be deities beside Allah. They own not even the smallest particle, neither in the heavens nor on the

---

4. The expression "the towns that We had blessed" signifies the whole region of Syria and Palestine. As for the expression "prominent towns," it denotes those towns located on the highway for which reason they were especially visible. This contrasts with the towns located in the interior regions which were improminent. The statement that God "set well-measured stages between them" refers to the route from Yemen to Syria which traversed the inhabited territory. The distance between any two stages on this route was thus known and determined.

5. This does not necessarily mean that these people prayed using these very words. For sometimes a person acts in a way that seems to say to God that he is not fully worthy of the favour He has bestowed upon him. The following words of the text "Lord, make the stages of our journeys longer" suggest that they considered their large population to be a calamitous misfortune. Hence they wanted the population to shrink so that the stages of their journey would become longer.

earth; nor do they have any share in the ownership of either of them. Nor is any of them even a helper of Allah. [23] No intercession can avail with Allah except for him whom Allah permits (to intercede). When their hearts are relieved of fright they will ask the intercessors: "What did your Lord say?" They will reply: "(He said) what is right, and He is the High, the Great."

[24] Ask them, (O Prophet): "Who provides you sustenance from the heavens and the earth?" Say: "Allah. Now, inevitably only one of us is rightly guided, either we or you; and the other is in manifest error." [25] Tell them: "You will not be called to account about the guilt we committed, nor will we be called to account for what you did." [26] Say: "Our Lord will bring us together and then He will rightly judge between us. He is the Great Judge, the All-Knowing." [27] Say: "Show me those whom you have attached to Him as His associates (in Divinity)." Nay, Allah alone is Most Mighty, Most Wise.

[28] (O Prophet), We have not sent you forth but as a herald of good news and a warner for all mankind. But most people do not know.

[29] They ask you: "When will this promise (of Resurrection) be fulfilled, if what you say is true?" [30] Say: "Your day is appointed, you can neither hold back its coming by an hour, nor hasten it by an hour."

[31] The unbelievers say: "We shall never believe in this Qur'ān, nor in any Scripture before it." If you could only see the wrong-doers arrayed before their Lord, each bandying charges against the other. Those who were

suppressed will say to those who waxed arrogant: "Had it not been for you, we would have been believers." [32] The arrogant ones will retort to those who were suppressed: "What! Did we bar you from the guidance after it came to you? Not at all; rather you yourselves were evil-doers." [33] Those who were suppressed will say to those who waxed arrogant: "By no means; it was your scheming, night and day, when you would enjoin us to disbelieve in Allah and set up others as equals to Him." When they are confronted with the chastisement, they will be remorseful in their hearts. We shall put fetters around the necks of the unbelievers. Can people be requited except for their deeds?

[34] We never sent a warner to any town but its wealthy ones said: "We disbelieve in the Message you have brought." [35] They always said: "We have more wealth and children than you have, and we shall not be chastised." [36] (O Prophet), say to them: "My Lord grants provision abundantly to whomsoever He pleases and straitens it for whomsoever He pleases. But most people do not know this. [37] It is not your riches nor your children that make you near-stationed to Us, except for him who has faith and acts righteously; it is they who will receive double the recompense for their deeds. They shall live in lofty mansions in perfect peace. [38] As for those who work against Our Signs so as to frustrate them, they shall be arraigned into the chastisement.

[39] Say, (O Prophet): "Verily, my Lord grants provision abundantly to whomsoever He pleases and straitens it for whomsoever He pleases. Whatever you spend, He will replace it. He is the Best of all Providers."

[40] And on the Day when He will muster them all and will ask the angels: "Are they the ones who worshipped you?"⁶ [41] They will reply: "Glory to You! You are our Protector, not they. Nay, they rather used to worship the *jinn*. Most of them believe in them." [42] Today none of you has the power to benefit or harm another; and We shall say to the evil-doers: "Taste now the chastisement of the Fire which you used to deny, calling it a lie."

[43] When Our Clear Signs are rehearsed to them they say: "This is a person who wants to turn you away from the deities whom your ancestors worshipped." They say: "This is nothing but an invented falsehood." And when the Truth came to the unbelievers they declared: "This is nothing but plain sorcery," [44] whereas We gave them no Books that they could study nor sent to them any warner before you. [45] Those who went before them also denounced (Allah's Messengers) as liars. They have not attained even a tenth of what We had given them. But when they rejected My Messengers, calling them liars, how terrible was My chastisement!

---

6. The pagans of Arabia used to worship angels. God, therefore, apprises them that He will ask the angels on the Resurrection Day whether these people did in fact worship them. The angels' reply will be: "Glory to You! You are our Protector, not they. Nay, they rather used to worship the *jinn*. Most of them believe in them" (v. 41). The pith of what the angels will say is that although the pagans pretended to be worshippers of angels, they were in fact worshippers of devils. For it is devils who taught them that they should pray to others than God for the fulfilment of their needs and to that end make offerings to them.

[46] Say to them, (O Prophet): "I give you but one counsel: stand up (for heaven's sake), singly and in pairs, and then think: what is it in your companion[7] (to wit, Muḥammad) that could be deemed as madness?" He is nothing but a warner, warning you before the coming of a grevious chastisement. [47] Say to them: "Whatever recompense I might ask of you, it shall be yours. My recompense is with Allah, and He is witness over everything." [48] Say to them: "My Lord hurls down the Truth (upon me). He knows fully all that lies beyond the range of perception." [49] Say: "The Truth has come and falsehood can neither originate nor recreate anything." [50] Say: "If I go astray then the hurt of straying will come only upon me. But if I am rightly-guided, that is only because of the revelation that my Lord makes to me. He is All-Hearing, Ever Nigh."

[51] If you could only see when the unbelievers will go about in a state of terror. They will have no escape and will be seized from a place near at hand. [52] They will then say: "We believe in it"; but whence can they attain it from so far-off a place? [53] They disbelieved in it before and indulged in conjectures from far away. [54] A barrier will be placed between them and what they desire, as was done with the likes of them before. Surely they were in a disquieting doubt.

---

7. The expression "your companion" refers to the Prophet Muḥammad (peace be on him). This expression was used because the Prophet (peace be on him) was no stranger for the Makkans: he was an inhabitant of the same city since his birth and also belonged to the same tribe – Quraysh.

35
❦

Fāṭir [Creator]
Makkan Period

In the name of Allah, the Most Merciful,
the Most Compassionate

[1] All praise be to Allah, the Fashioner of the heavens and earth, Who appointed angels as His message-bearers, having two, three, four wings. He adds to His creation whatever He pleases. Verily Allah has power over everything. [2] Whatever Mercy Allah accords to people, none can withhold; and whatever He withholds, no other will be able to release after Him. He is Most Mighty, Most Wise.

[3] O people, remember Allah's favour upon you. Is there any creator, apart from Allah, who provides you your sustenance out of the heavens and earth? There is no god but He. Whither are you, then, being misdirected? [4] (O Prophet), (there is nothing novel in it) if they cry lies to you; Messengers before you were also cried lies to. To Allah shall all matters be sent back.

[5] O people, assuredly Allah's promise is true. So let the life of the world not delude you, and let not the Deluder delude you concerning Allah. [6] Surely Satan is an enemy to you. Therefore, do take him as an enemy. He calls his followers to his way so that they may be among the inmates of the Fire. [7] A severe chastisement lies in

store for those that disbelieve, but there is pardon and a great reward for those that believe and work righteous deeds.

[8] (How awful is the straying of the person) for whom his evil deed has been embellished so that it looks fair to him? The fact is that Allah causes whomsoever He will to fall into error and shows the Right Way to whomsoever He will. So, (O Prophet), let not your life go to waste sorrowing over them. Allah is well aware of all that they do. [9] It is Allah Who sends forth winds which then set the clouds in motion, which We drive to some dead land giving a fresh life to earth after it had become dead. Such will be the resurrection of the dead.

[10] He who seeks glory, let him know that all glory belongs to Allah alone. To Him do good words go up, and righteous action uplifts them. But those who contrive evil deeds, a severe punishment lies in store for them, and their contriving will come to naught.

[11] Allah created you from dust, then from a drop of sperm, then He made you into pairs. No female conceives, nor delivers (a child) except with His knowledge. None is given a long life nor is any diminished in his life but it is written in a Book. Surely that is quite easy for Allah. [12] The two masses of water are not alike. The one is sweet, sates thirst, and is pleasant to drink from, while the other is salt, bitter on the tongue. Yet from both you eat fresh meat, and extract from it ornaments that you wear; and you see ships cruising through it that you may seek of His Bounty and be thankful to Him. [13] He causes the night to phase into the day and the day into the night, and He has subjected the sun and the moon, each running

its course to an appointed term. That is Allah, your Lord; to Him belongs the Kingdom; but those whom you call upon, apart from Allah, possess not so much as the skin of a date-stone. [14] If you call upon them, they cannot hear your prayer. And if they hear it, they cannot answer it. On the Day of Resurrection they will disown you for associating others with Allah in His Divinity. No one can inform you of the truth save the All-Aware.

[15] O people, it is you who stand in need of Allah; as for Allah, He is Self-Sufficient, Immensely Praiseworthy. [16] If He wishes, He can remove you and put in your place a new creation. [17] That surely is not difficult for Allah. [18] No one can bear another's burden. If a heavily laden one should call another to carry his load, none of it shall be carried by the other, even though he be a near of kin. (O Prophet), you can warn only those who fear their Lord without seeing Him and establish Prayer. Whoever purifies himself does so to his own good. To Allah is the final return. [19] The blind and the seeing are not alike, [20] nor darkness and light; [21] nor cool shade and torrid heat; [22] nor are the living and the dead alike. Allah makes to hear whomsoever He wishes, but you, (O Prophet), cannot cause to hear those who are in their graves.[1] [23] You are no more than a warner.

---

1. As far as God's power is concerned, it is absolute. God can even confer the ability to hear on stones. As for the Prophet (peace be on him), it does not lie in his power to make those whose consciences have become extinct and whose ears have become deaf hear the call to the Truth, and make them imbibe what he would like to convey to them. The Prophet (peace be on him) can only make those who are inclined to give ear to reasonable things hear his message.

[24] We have sent you with the Truth to proclaim good news and to warn. Never has there been a nation but a warner came to it. [25] If they give the lie to you now, those that went before them also gave the lie to their Messengers when they came to them with Clear Proofs, with Scriptures, and with the Illuminating Book. [26] Then I seized those who denied the Truth, and how terrible was My punishment!

[27] Do you not see that Allah sent down water from the sky with which We brought forth fruits of diverse hues? In the mountains there are white and red, of diverse hues, and pitchy black; [28] and human beings too, and beasts, and cattle – diverse are their hues. From among His servants, it is only those who know that fear Allah.[2] Verily Allah is Most Mighty, Most Forgiving.

[29] Surely those who recite the Book of Allah and establish Prayer and spend, privately and publicly, out of what We have provided them, look forward to a trade that shall suffer no loss; [30] (a trade in which they have invested their all) so that Allah may pay them their wages in full and may add to them out of His Bounty. He is Most Forgiving, Most Appreciative. [31] (O Prophet), the Book We have revealed to you is the Truth, confirming the Books that came before it. Verily Allah is well aware of His servants and sees everything. [32] Then We bequeathed the Book to those of Our servants that We chose. Now, some of them wrong themselves and some follow the medium course; and some, by Allah's leave, vie with

---

2. This shows that a truly knowledgeable person is not he who can read books, but he who fears God.

each other in acts of goodness. That is the great bounty. [33] They shall enter the everlasting Gardens, shall be adorned with bracelets of gold and with pearls, and their apparel therein shall be silk. [34] They will say: "All praise be to Allah Who has taken away all sorrow from us. Surely our Lord is Most Forgiving, Most Appreciative; [35] (the Lord) Who, out of His Bounty, has made us dwell in an abode wherein no toil, nor fatigue affects us.

[36] As for those who disbelieved, the Fire of Hell awaits them. There they shall not be finished off and die; nor will the torment (of Hell) be lightened for them. Thus do We requite every thankless being. [37] They will cry out in Hell and say: "Our Lord, let us out so that we may act righteously, different from what we did before." (They will be told): "Did we not grant you an age long enough for anyone to take heed if he had wanted to take heed? Besides, there came a warner to you. So have a taste of the torment now. None may come to the help of the wrong-doers."

[38] Surely Allah knows the Unseen in the heavens and the earth. He even knows the secrets hidden in people's breasts. [39] It is He Who made you vicegerents in the earth. So whoever disbelieves will bear the burden of his unbelief. The unbelievers' unbelief adds nothing but Allah's wrath against them. The unbelievers' unbelief adds nothing but their own loss.

[40] Say to them (O Prophet): "Have you ever seen those of your associates upon whom you call apart from Allah? Show me what have they created in the earth? Or do they have any partnership (with Allah) in the heavens? Or

have We given them a Book so that they have a clear proof (for associating others with Allah in His Divinity)?" Nay, what these wrong-doers promise each other is nothing but delusion. [41] Surely Allah holds the heavens and the earth, lest they should be displaced there, for if they were displaced none would be able to hold them after Him. Surely He is Most Forbearing, Most Forgiving.

[42] Swearing by Allah their strongest oaths they claimed that if a warner came to them they would be better-guided than any other people. But when a warner did come to them, his coming only increased their aversion (to the Truth). [43] They began to wax even more proud on earth and contrived evil designs although the contriving of evil designs only overtakes their authors. Are they waiting, then, for anything except what happened to the nations before them? You shall not find any change in the Way of Allah; and you shall not find anything that can ever alter the Way of Allah. [44] Have they not journeyed in the earth to behold the end of those who went before them though they were stronger than them in might? Nothing in the heavens nor on earth can frustrate Him in the least. He is All-Knowing, All-Powerful. [45] If Allah were to take people to task for their deeds, He would not leave any living creature on earth, but He grants them respite to an appointed time. When their appointed time comes to an end, surely Allah fully observes His servants.

36

Yā' Sīn
Makkan Period

In the name of Allah, the Most Merciful,
the Most Compassionate

[1] *Yā'. Sīn.* [2] By the Wise Qur'ān, [3] you are truly among the Messengers, [4] on a Straight Way, [5] (and this Qur'ān) is a revelation from the Most Mighty, the Most Compassionate [6] so that you may warn a people whose ancestors were not warned before wherefore they are heedless.

[7] Surely most of them merit the decree of chastisement; so they do not believe.¹ [8] We have put fetters around their necks which reach up to their chins so that they are standing with their heads upright,² [9] and We have put a barrier before them and a barrier behind them, and have

---

1. This pertains to those who had become obstinate in regard to the Prophet's Message and had made up their minds not to take heed of his teachings. As regards them, it is declared: "Surely most of them merit the decree of chastisement; so they do not believe."

2. "Fetters" here signify the unbelievers' obduracy which prevented them from believing in the Truth. Owing to the intensity of this obduracy, God has put fetters around their necks so that they "are standing with their heads upright". This refers to a stiffness of the neck that is caused by pride and arrogance.

covered them up, so they are unable to see.[3] [10] It is all the same for them whether you warn them or do not warn them for they shall not believe. [11] You can warn only him who follows the Admonition and fears the Merciful Lord without seeing Him. Give such a one good tidings of forgiveness and a generous reward.

[12] We shall surely raise the dead to life and We record what they did and the traces of their deeds that they have left behind. We have encompassed that in a Clear Book.

[13] Recite to them, as a case in point, the story of the people of the town when the Messengers came to them. [14] We sent to them two Messengers and they rejected both of them as liars. Then We strengthened them with a third (Messenger). [15] They said: "We have been sent to you as Messengers." The people of the town said: "You are only human beings like ourselves, and the Merciful Lord has revealed nothing. You are simply lying."

[16] The Messengers said: "Our Lord knows that we have indeed been sent to you [17] and our duty is no more than to clearly convey the Message." [18] The people of the town said: "We believe you are an evil omen for us. If you do not desist, we will stone you or you will receive

---

3. God has "put a barrier before them and a barrier behind them". This means that the natural consequence of their stubbornness and pride was that they were incapable of learning any lesson from their history and were altogether disinclined to consider the results that would ensue from their attitude in the future. Their biases had covered them from all sides and their misconceptions had so blinded them that they could not even see the glaring realities that were visible to every right-thinking and unbiased person.

a grievous chastisement from us." [19] The Messengers replied: "Your evil omen is with you. (Are you saying this) because you were asked to take heed? The truth is that you are a people who have exceeded all bounds."

[20] In the meantime a man came running from the far end of the town, saying: "My people, follow the Messengers; [21] follow those who do not ask any recompense from you and are rightly-guided. [22] Why should I not serve the One Who created me and to Whom all of you shall be sent back? [23] What! Shall I take any deities apart from Him whose intercession will not avail me the least were the Merciful One to bring any adversity upon me, nor will they be able to rescue me? [24] Surely in that case I should indeed be in evident error. [25] I believe in your Lord; so listen to me."

[26] (Eventually they killed him and he was told): "Enter Paradise." The man exclaimed: "Would that my people knew [27] for what reason Allah has forgiven me and placed me among the honoured ones."

[28] After him, We did not send down any hosts from the heaven; We stood in no need to send down any host. [29] There was but a single Blast and suddenly they became silent and still. [30] Alas for My servants! Never does a Messenger come to them but they mock him. [31] Have they not seen how many nations before them did We destroy? Thereafter they never came back to them. [32] All of them shall (one day) be gathered before Us.

[33] Let the dead earth be a Sign for them. We gave it life and produced from it grain whereof they eat.

[34] We made in it gardens of date-palms and vines, and We caused springs to gush forth [35] that they might eat of its fruits. It was not their hands that made them. Will they not, then, give thanks? [36] Holy is He Who created all things in pairs, whether it be of what the earth produces, and of themselves, and of what they do not know.

[37] And the night is another Sign for them. We strip the day from it and they become plunged in darkness. [38] The sun is running its course to its appointed place. That is the ordaining of the All-Mighty, the All-Knowing. [39] We have appointed stages for the moon till it returns in the shape of a dry old branch of palm-tree. [40] Neither does it lie in the sun's power to overtake the moon nor can the night outstrip the day. All glide along, each in its own orbit.

[41] Another Sign for them is that We carried all their offspring in the laden vessel⁴ [42] and then created for them other vessels like those on which they ride. [43] Should We so wish, We can drown them, and there will be none to heed their cries of distress, nor will they be rescued. [44] It is only Our Mercy (that rescues them) and enables enjoyment of life for a while.

[45] When it is said to such people: "Guard yourselves against what is ahead of you and what has preceded you that mercy be shown to you" (they pay scant heed to it). [46] Never does any Sign of their Lord come to them, but they turn away from it. [47] And when it is said to them: "Spend (in the Way of Allah) out of the sustenance

---

4. The "laden vessel" here alludes to the Prophet Noah's Ark.

that Allah has provided you," the unbelievers say to the believers: "Shall we feed him whom, Allah would have fed, had He so wished?" Say: "You are in evident error."

[48] They say: "When will this threat (of Resurrection) come to pass? Tell us if indeed you are truthful." [49] The Truth is that they are waiting for nothing but a mighty Blast to seize them the while they are disputing (in their worldly affairs), [50] and they will not even be able to make a testament, nor to return to their households. [51] Then the Trumpet shall be blown and lo! they will come out of their graves and be on the move towards their Lord, [52] (nervously) exclaiming. "Alas for us! Who roused us out of our sleeping-place?" "This is what the Merciful One had promised, and what (His) Messengers had said was true."⁵ [53] Then there will simply be one single Blast, and all will have gathered before Us.

[54] Today no one shall suffer the least injustice, and you shall not be recompensed except according to your deeds. [55] Indeed, the people of Paradise will be busy enjoying themselves: [56] they and their spouses shall be reclining on their couches in shady groves; [57] therein there will be all kinds of fruits to eat, and they shall have all that they desire. [58] "Peace" shall be the word conveyed to

---

5. There are several possibilities as regards who would say this. One possibility is that this would be said by the believers. It is also possible that all human beings resurrected on that Day would realise after a while that it was the same Day about which they had been foretold by God's Messengers. It is also possible that the statement might be made by the angels, or that it might be an articulation of the condition prevailing on that Day.

them from their Merciful Lord. [59] "Criminals, separate yourselves from others today! [60] Children of Adam, did I not command you not to serve Satan – he is to you an open enemy [61] and serve Me alone: this is the Straight Way? [62] Still, he misguided a whole throng of you. Did you have no sense? [63] Now this is the Hell of which you were warned. [64] Burn in it on account of your disbelieving.

[65] Today We shall put a seal on their mouths, and their hands will speak to Us and their feet shall bear witness to what they had been doing.

[66] If We so willed, We would have put out their eyes, then they would rush to see the Way, but how would they be able to see? [67] If We so willed, We would have transformed them where they were so that they would not go forward or backward. [68] Whomsoever We grant a long life, We reverse him in his constitution. Do they still not understand?

[69] We did not teach him (to wit, the Messenger) poetry and it does not behove him. This is none but an Admonition, and a Clear Book [70] that he may warn him who is alive and establish an argument against those that deny the Truth.

[71] Do they not see Our handiwork: We created for them cattle which they own? [72] We have subjected the cattle to them so that some of them they ride and eat the flesh of others. [73] They derive a variety of benefits and drinks from them. Will they, then, not give thanks? [74] They set up deities apart from Allah, hoping that they will receive

help from them. [75] Those deities can render them no help. Yet these devotees act as though they were an army in waiting for them. [76] Let not their words grieve you. Surely We know all things about them, what they conceal and what they reveal.

[77] Does man not see that We created him of a sperm-drop, and lo! he is flagrantly contentious? [78] He strikes for Us a similitude and forgot his own creation. He says: "Who will quicken the bones when they have decayed?" [79] Say: "He Who first brought them into being will quicken them; He knows well about every kind of creation; [80] He Who created from a green tree a fire for you, a fire to light your stoves with." [81] Has He Who created the heavens and the earth no power to create the likes of them? Yes, indeed, He is the Superb Creator. [82] Whenever He wills a thing, He just commands it "Be" and it is. [83] Holy is He Who has full control over everything, and to Him you shall all be recalled.

37
❧

Al-Ṣāffāt [The Rangers]
Makkan Period

In the name of Allah, the Most Merciful,
the Most Compassionate

[1] By those who range themselves in rows; [2] by those who reprove severely, [3] and those who recite the Exhortation;¹ [4] surely your God is One, [5] the Lord of the heavens and the earth and of whatever lies between the two, the Lord of the Easts.²

---

1. The majority of the Qur'ān's commentators are agreed that all the three groups mentioned here are groups of angels. Their common characteristic is that they are ever ready to carry out God's commands. This readiness is reflected in their reprimanding and upbraiding those who disobey God, in their asking people in a variety of ways to remember God, and in their rehearsing the Exhortation, that is, the Qur'ān.

2. The sun does not always rise from the same point. Each day it rises from a different angle. Moreover, it does not rise at the same time for the whole world; it rather rises for different places at different times. It is for these reasons that instead of using the word *mashriq* ("east") in the singular, the word *mashāriq* ("easts"), in the plural, has been used. It is also significant that the corresponding word *maghārib* ("wests") has not been used, because *mashāriq* itself implies *maghārib*.

[6] We have adorned the lower heaven³ with the adornment of the stars [7] and have protected it from every rebellious satan. [8] These satans cannot listen to what transpires in the High Council⁴ for they are pelted away from every side [9] and are repelled. Theirs is an unceasing chastisement. [10] And if any is able to snatch a fragment, he is pursued by a piercing flame.

[11] So ask them (that is, human beings): "Were they harder to create than the objects We created?" We created them from sticky clay. [12] You marvel (at the wondrous creations of Allah) and they scoff at it, [13] and when they are admonished, they pay no heed; [14] and if they see any Sign, they laugh it away [15] and say: "This is nothing but plain sorcery. [16] Is it ever possible that after we die and are reduced to dust and (a skeleton of) bones, we will be raised to life? [17] And so also shall our forefathers of yore be raised to life?" [18] Tell them: "Yes; and you are utterly helpless (against Allah)."

[19] There will be a single stern rebuff and lo, they will be observing with their own eyes (all that they had been warned against). [20] They will then say: "Woe for us. This is the Day of Judgement." [21] "Yes, this is the Day of Final Decision that you used to deny as a lie."⁵

---

3. "The lower heaven" in fact means the nearer heaven, one that is visible to the naked eye without the help of any external aids such as telescopes.

4. This refers to the inhabitants of the higher realm; that is, the angels.

5. It is possible that this statement was made by the believers or the angels. It is also possible that this might be a representation of

[22] (Then will the command be given): "Muster all the wrong-doers and their spouses and the deities[6] whom they used to serve [23] apart from Allah, and direct them to the path of Hell, [24] and detain them there; they will be called to account. [25] How is it that you are not helping one another? [26] Indeed, today they are surrendering themselves completely." [27] They will then turn towards each other (and start wrangling). [28] (The followers will say to their leaders): "You used to come to us from the right hand."[7] [29] They will say: "Nay, you yourselves were not the ones who would believe. [30] We had no power over you. You were a rebellious people, [31] and so we became deserving of the Word of our Lord that we shall be made to suffer chastisement. [32] So we led you astray; we ourselves were strayed."

---

the state prevailing on the Day of Resurrection. It is also possible that this might be a reaction of the people themselves; that is, they might, in effect, say to themselves: "We lived in the world as though there would be no Day of Judgement. But our doom has overtaken us. The Day that we used to deny now confronts us in our face."

6. Here the word "deities" does not refer to the angels and saints whom people are wont to deify. Instead, the word denotes, first, those human beings and satans who themselves wanted to be worshipped and even made efforts so that others would worship them rather than God; second, it also denotes those idols and images which were the objects of people's worship.

7. The word *yamīn* in the text may mean, according to Arabic literary usage, strength and power, or good fortune, or swearing. Depending on the sense which the word is considered to convey here, the verse could mean the following: (1) "You pushed us by dint of your strength to error"; (2) "you deceived us by posing to be wishers of good fortune for us"; or (3) "you swore to convince us that what you said was the truth."

[33] On that Day, they will all share the chastisement. [34] Thus do We treat the culprits. [35] Whenever it was said to them: "There is no true deity apart from Allah," they waxed proud [36] and said: "Shall we forsake our deities for the sake of a distracted poet?" [37] (They say so although) he brought the Truth and confirmed the veracity of the Messengers. [38] (They will be told): "You shall taste the grievous chastisement. [39] You will only be recompensed according to your deeds."

[40] But Allah's chosen servants (shall be spared this woeful end). [41] For them awaits a known provision, [42] a variety of delicious fruits; and they shall be honoured [43] in the Gardens of Bliss. [44] They will be seated upon couches set face to face; [45] a cup filled with wine from its springs, will be passed around to them; [46] white, sparkling (wine), a delight to the drinkers. [47] There will neither be any harm in it for their body nor will it intoxicate their mind. [48] Theirs shall be wide-eyed maidens with bashful, restrained glances, [49] so delicate as the hidden peel under an egg's shell.

[50] Then some of them will turn to others, and will ask each other. [51] One of them will say: "I had a companion in the world [52] who used to say: 'Are you also one of those who confirm the Truth (of life after death)? [53] After we are dead and have become all dust and bones shall we still be requited?' [54] He will say: 'Do you wish to know where he is now?' [55] Then he will look downwards, and will see him in the depths of Hell. [56] He will say to him: 'By Allah, you almost ruined me. [57] But for Allah's favour, I should be one of those who

have been mustered here. [58] So,[8] are we not going to die, [59] except for our first death? And shall we suffer no chastisement?'"

[60] Surely this is the supreme triumph. [61] For the like of it should the workers work. [62] Is this a better hospitality or the tree of al-Zaqqūm? [63] We have made this tree a trial for the wrong-doers.[9] [64] It is a tree that grows in the nethermost part of Hell. [65] Its spathes are like the heads of satans. [66] (The people of Hell) will surely eat of it, filling their bellies with it. [67] Then on top of it they will have a brew of boiling water. [68] Then their return will be to the same blazing Hell. [69] These are the ones who found their fathers steeped in error, [70] and they are running in their footsteps. [71] Before them a multitude of people of olden times had erred, [72] and We had sent among them Messengers to warn them. [73] Observe, then, what was the end of those that had been warned, [74] except for the chosen servants of Allah?

[75] Noah had called upon Us (earlier). See, how excellent We were in answering him! [76] We delivered him and

---

8. The style of the discourse clearly indicates that the inmate of Paradise, after talking to his bosom friend in Hell, suddenly begins talking to himself. He utters these sentences in a way that indicates he found himself in a much more felicitous state than he had expected. This realisation overwhelms him with wonder and joy and thus he bursts into soliloquy.

9. The mention of a tree in Hell provides the unbelievers with a pretext to deride the Qur'ān and mock the Prophet (peace be on him). After having a good laugh at the idea of there being a tree in Hell, they say, in effect: "Now listen to another piece of curiosity! A tree will grow in the blazing fire of Hell!"

his household from the great calamity; [77] and made his offspring the only ones to survive, [78] and We established for him a good name among posterity. [79] Peace be upon Noah among all the nations. [80] Thus do We reward all those who do good. [81] Surely he was one of Our truly believing servants. [82] Thereafter We caused the others to be drowned.

[83] Abraham was on the self-same way (as Noah). [84] When he came to his Lord with a pure heart, [85] and said to his father and his people: "Whom do you worship? [86] Is it false deities that you want to serve rather than Allah? [87] What do you think of the Lord of the whole Universe?"

[88] Then he looked carefully at the stars[10] [89] and said: "I am sick."[11] [90] So turning their backs, they went away from him. [91] Then he went quietly to the (temple of the deities) and said: "What is the matter with you, why do you not eat? [92] What is the matter with you, why do you not speak?" [93] Then he turned upon them, striking them with his right hand, [94] whereupon people came to him running. [95] Abraham said to them: "Do you worship what you yourselves have carved with your own hands

---

10. In its idiomatic use, *"naẓara naẓratan ..."* means to "look attentively". In the context of looking at the stars, it means that Abraham thoughtfully observed the stars which led him to deep and serious reflection.

11. We have no means of knowing that at that time the Prophet Abraham (peace be on him) was not in fact suffering from any illness. Therefore, there is no basis to say that his statement was merely a pretext, one contrary to the facts.

[96] while it is Allah Who has created you and all that you make?" [97] They spoke among themselves: "Build him a pyre and then throw him into the furnace." [98] They had contrived an evil plan against him, but We abased them all.

[99] Abraham said: "I am going to my Lord;[12] He will guide me. [100] Lord, grant me a righteous son." [101] (In response to this prayer) We gave him the good news of a prudent boy;[13] [102] and when he was old enough to go about and work with him, (one day) Abraham said to him: "My son, I see in my dream that I am slaughtering you. So consider (and tell me) what you think." He said: "Do as you are bidden. You will find me, if Allah so wills, among the steadfast." [103] When both surrendered (to Allah's command) and Abraham flung the son down on his forehead, [104] We cried out: "O Abraham, [105] you have indeed fulfilled your dream.[14] Thus do We reward the good-doers." [106] This was indeed a plain trial. [107] And We ransomed him with a mighty sacrifice,[15]

---

12. Abraham's statement meant that he was forsaking his own home as well as his homeland in God's cause.

13. This alludes to the Prophet Ishmael (peace be on him).

14. The Prophet Abraham (peace be on him) dreamt that he "*was slaughtering,*" but not that *he had slaughtered* his son. Therefore, when he had made all the preparations to sacrifice his son, it was said: "O Abraham, you have indeed fulfilled your dream."

15. "A mighty sacrifice" here alludes to the ram that God's angels brought before the Prophet Abraham (peace be on him) at that precise moment so that he might slaughter it instead of his son. It is called a "mighty sacrifice" because it served as a ransom from as

[108] and We preserved for him a good name among posterity. [109] Peace be upon Abraham. [110] Thus do We reward the good-doers. [111] Surely he was one of Our believing servants. [112] And We gave him the good news of Isaac,[16] a Prophet and among the righteous ones. [113] And We blessed him and Isaac. Among the offspring of the two some did good and some plainly wronged themselves.

[114] Verily We bestowed Our favours on Moses and Aaron [115] and We delivered both of them and their people from the great calamity. [116] We succoured them, and they gained the upper hand (against their enemies). [117] We granted them a Clear Book, [118] and showed them the Straight Way, [119] and preserved for them a good name among posterity. [120] Peace be upon Moses and Aaron. [121] Thus do We reward the good-doers. [122] Surely both of them were among Our believing servants.

[123] Surely, Elias too was among the Messengers. [124] (Call to mind) when he said to his people: "Will you not fear Allah? [125] Do you call upon Baal and forsake the Best of the Creators? [126] Allah is your Lord and the Lord of your ancestors of yore." [127] But they denounced him

---

faithful a servant of God as Abraham for as patient and obedient a son as Ishmael. Another reason for calling it "a mighty sacrifice" is that God made it incumbent on the believers to offer animal sacrifice on the same day the world over so as to keep fresh the memory of that great event which epitomises fidelity and devotion of the very highest order to God.

16. The good news of Isaac's forthcoming birth was given to the Prophet Abraham (peace be on him) after this "mighty sacrifice".

as a liar, so they will surely be arraigned (for punishment), [128] except Allah's chosen servants. [129] We preserved a good name for him among posterity. [130] Peace be upon Elias. [131] Thus do We reward the good-doers. [132] He was one of Our believing servants.

[133] And Lot too was one of the Messengers. [134] (Call to mind) when We delivered him and all his kinsfolk, [135] except for an old woman who was among those that stayed behind. [136] Then We utterly destroyed the rest of them. [137] You pass by their desolate habitations in the morning [138] and at night. Do you still not understand?

[139] And Jonah too was one of the Messengers. [140] Call to mind when he fled to the laden ship, [141] cast lots, and was among the losers. [142] Then a fish swallowed him, and he was blameworthy.[17] [143] Had he not been one of those who glorify Allah, [144] he would certainly have remained in its belly till the Day of Resurrection.[18]

---

17. If one carefully reflects over what is said here, the following image will emerge: (1) The ship which the Prophet Jonah had boarded was already overloaded. (2) At some time during the voyage when it was realised that the lives of all passengers were endangered due to overloading, lots were drawn to determine who would be thrown overboard. (3) Once the lots were drawn, Jonah was thrown off the ship and was swallowed by a fish. (4) The Prophet Jonah (peace be on him) became a victim of his own misfortune because he had abandoned his post without his Lord's permission. This is supported by the use of the verb *abaqa*, which denotes the unauthorised flight of a slave.

18. That is, the fish's belly would have become the Prophet Jonah's grave till the Day of Resurrection.

[145] But We threw him on a wide bare tract of land while he was ill; [146] and caused a gourd tree to grow over him, [147] and We sent him forth to a nation of a hundred thousand or more,[19] [148] and they believed. So We let them enjoy life for a while.

[149] So ask their opinion: "(Are you convinced) that your Lord should have daughters and you should have sons? [150] Did We create the angels as females the while they witnessed?" [151] Behold, it is one of their fabrications that they say: [152] "Allah has begotten." They are liars! [153] Did He choose daughters rather than sons? [154] What is the matter with you that you make such strange judgements? [155] Will you then not take heed? [156] Do you have any clear authority for such claims? [157] Bring your Book, if you are truthful.

[158] They have established a kinship between Allah and the angels;[20] and the angels know well that these people will be arraigned (as culprits). [159] (They say): "Exalted be Allah above what they attribute to Him, [160] all of them except the chosen servants of Allah. [161] So you and your deities [162] shall not be able to tempt anyone away from Allah [163] except him who shall roast in the Blazing Fire. [164] As for us, there is none but has

---

19. The mention of "a hundred thousand or more" does not mean that God had any doubt as regards their number. What it means is that a casual observer would have surmised that the population of the township was, in any case, more than a hundred thousand.

20. Though the word *jinn* is used here, it actually means angels as becomes evident from the verses that follow. (The word *jinn* literally means a "hidden creature".)

an appointed station. [165] Verily we range ourselves in rows (as humble servants) [166] and we are of those who glorify Allah."

[167] They used to say before: [168] "If only we had the Reminder which had been granted to the people of yore [169] we would surely have been Allah's chosen servants." [170] But when it came to them, they rejected it. They shall soon come to know (the end of such an attitude). [171] We have already given Our promise to Our Messengers [172] that they shall certainly be succoured, [173] and that Our hosts shall triumph. [174] So, (O Prophet), leave them alone for a while, [175] and see, and soon they too shall see. [176] Do they seek to hasten Our chastisement? [177] When that chastisement will descend upon their courtyard, evil shall that Day be for those who had been warned. [178] Leave them alone for a while, [179] and see; and they too shall soon see.

[180] Exalted be your Lord, the Lord of Glory, above what they attribute to Him, [181] and peace be upon the Messengers, [182] and all praise be to Allah, the Lord of the Universe.

38

Ṣād
Makkan Period

In the name of Allah, the Most Merciful,
the Most Compassionate

[1] *Ṣād*, and by the Qur'ān full of exhortation! [2] Nay, but the unbelievers are steeped in arrogance and stubborn defiance.¹ [3] How many a nation did We destroy before them! (When they approached their doom) they cried out (for deliverance), but the time for deliverance was already past.

[4] They wondered that a warner had come to them from among themselves, and the deniers of the Truth said: "This is a sorcerer, and a big liar. [5] Has he made the gods one single God? This is truly astounding." [6] And the elders among them went forth saying: "Go ahead and be steadfast in adhering to your deities. What is being said is with a design."² [7] We have not heard this in the

1. The unbelievers do not disbelieve because of any defect or flaw in the religious faith that was being preached to them. Instead, their disbelief stemmed from their excessive arrogance and obduracy.

2. The nobles of that unbelieving nation asserted that there was something fishy about the whole enterprise. They stressed that the real purpose of the call to Islam was to make people follow Muḥammad (peace be on him), and that this was to be a stepping stone to the establishment of his hegemony over them.

religious community close to our time. This is nothing but a fabrication. [8] Has this Exhortation been sent down among us only to him, to the exclusion of all others?" Nay, they are in doubt regarding My Exhortation,[3] and are saying all this because they have not yet had any taste of My chastisement. [9] Do they possess the treasures of your Lord, the Most Mighty, the Great Bestower? [10] Or do they possess the dominion of the heavens and the earth and of all that is in between them? If so, let them ascend the heights of the realm of causation and see!

[11] This is only a small army out of the several armies that will suffer defeat here.[4] [12] Before them the people of Noah, ʿĀd, and Pharaoh of the tent-pegs gave the lie (to the Messengers) [13] and so did Thamūd and the people of Lot and the people of Aykah. These were all leagued together. [14] Each of them gave the lie to Messengers and My decree of chastisement came upon them. [15] They are waiting for nothing except a single Cry, after which there will be no second Cry. [16] They say: "Our Lord,

---

3. In effect what God says here is that the unbelievers were not simply giving the lie to the Prophet (peace be on him). What is more, they were guilty of giving the lie to God. They were not simply casting doubts about the veracity of the Prophet (peace be on him) but were rather doubting the Truth of God's teachings.

4. "Here" alludes to the city of Makkah. It is stressed here that the very spot where people were engaged in malicious invectives against Islam would be the site where they would suffer utter defeat. The time would soon arrive when those very people, their heads downcast with the infamy of defeat, would stand before the Prophet (peace be on him) whom they had belittled for years, refusing to recognise his genuine prophethood.

hasten to us our share (of chastisement) before the Day of Reckoning."

[17] (O Prophet), bear with patience what they say, and call to mind Our servant David, who was endowed with great strength and who constantly turned (to Allah). [18] With him We had subjected the mountains that they join him in celebrating Allah's glory, evening and morning, [19] and the birds, too, in their flocks, and turn again and again to celebrating Allah's glory. [20] And We strengthened his kingdom and endowed him with wisdom and decisive judgement. [21] Has the story of the litigants reached you – of those who entered his private chambers by climbing over the wall? [22] As they came upon David – and he was frightened of them – they said: "Be not afraid. We are just two litigants: one of us has committed excess against the other. So judge rightly between us, and be not unjust; and guide us to the Right Way. [23] Behold, this is my brother; he has ninety-nine ewes and I have only one ewe." And yet he said: "Give her into my charge," and he got the better of me in argument.[5] [24] David said: "He has certainly wronged you in seeking to add your ewe to his ewes; and indeed many who live together commit excesses, one to the other, except those that believe and act righteously; and they are but few." (While so saying) David realized that it is We Who have put him to test; therefore, he sought the forgiveness of his

---

5. The complainant did not say that the other person had seized his ewe. He rather said that the other person had asked for it, desiring that it should be handed over to him. Now since that person held great power and eminence he was able to exert considerable pressure on the ewe's owner.

Lord, and fell down, bowing and penitently turning (to Him). [25] Thereupon We forgave him[6] his shortcoming and indeed (an exalted position of) nearness awaits him, and an excellent resort. [26] (We said to him): "O David, We have appointed you vicegerent on earth. Therefore, rule among people with justice and do not follow (your) desire lest it should lead you astray from Allah's Path. Allah's severe chastisement awaits those who stray away from Allah's Path, for they had forgotten the Day of Reckoning.

[27] We did not create this heaven and earth and all that lies between them in vain. That is the fancy of those who denied the Truth. So woe from the Fire to all who deny the Truth. [28] Shall We then treat alike those that believe and act righteously and those that create mischief on earth? Or treat alike the God-fearing and the wicked? [29] This is the Blessed Book that We have revealed to you, (O Muḥammad), that people with understanding may reflect over its verses and those with understanding derive a lesson.

[30] We bestowed upon David (an illustrious son), Solomon. How excellent a servant (of Ours he was)!

---

6. What is said here indicates a few things. First, that there had indeed occurred some lapse on David's part. Second, that this lapse somehow resembled the case of the ewes. Hence, while pronouncing his judgement on the case, David instantly thought that he was being tested. Third, the lapse was not so grave that David could not be forgiven; nor that the forgivance be conditional upon David's removal from his high position. According to the Qur'ān, after he "… fell down, bowing and penitently turning (to Him)," he was not only forgiven, but also assured that his high rank in the Hereafter was secure.

Indeed he constantly turned to Us in devotion. [31] And when one evening well-trained and running horses of noble breed were brought to him [32] he said: "Lo! I have come to love this wealth on account of the remembrance of my Lord." And when the horses disappeared, [33] (he ordered): "Bring these horses back to me," and then he began to gently stroke their shanks and necks. [34] Surely We put Solomon to the test and cast upon his throne a mere body. Thereupon he penitently turned (to Us). [35] He said: "My Lord, forgive me and bestow upon me a kingdom such as none other after me will deserve. Surely You are the Bounteous Giver."[7] [36] We subjected the wind to him, so that it blew gently at his bidding,

---

7. It appears from the context that the thrust of the discourse is that even such high-ranking Prophets and God's favourite servants like David and Solomon were not spared being called to account. We do not know for sure the details of the specific ways in which Solomon was put to the test (see v. 34) above. It is pertinent to note, however, that the Qur'ān commentators are not agreed about the ways in which he was tested. It is significant, though, that the Prophet Solomon (peace be on him) prayed as follows: "My Lord, forgive me and bestow upon me a kingdom such as none other after me will deserve." If this prayer is read in the light of Israeli history, one feels that Solomon had probably desired that his son should succeed him so that governmental power and authority in the future would perpetually vest in his progeny. Presumably, it is this temptation that is described by God as a test which Solomon faced. Later on Solomon realised this when his heir Rehoboam grew to be a worthless young man whose life-style clearly showed that he would scarcely be able to hold together the Prophet David's and Solomon's kingdom for any length of time. The statement that: "We … cast upon his throne a mere body …" (v. 34), probably means that his son, whom he sought as his successor, was a good-for-nothing.

wherever he directed it, [37] and We also subjected the devils to him – all kinds of builders and divers; [38] and others that were bound with chains. [39] "This is Our bestowal. So give or withhold as you wish without account." [40] Indeed an exalted position of nearness awaits him and an excellent resort.

[41] And remember Our servant Job: when he cried to his Lord: "Behold, Satan has afflicted me with much hardship and suffering."[8] [42] (We commanded him): "Stamp your foot on earth, and here is cool water to wash with and to drink." [43] And We granted to him his family and also the like of them, as a mercy from Us, and as a reminder to people of understanding, [44] (and We said to him): "Take in your hand a bundle of rushes and strike with it, and do not break your oath."[9] Indeed We found him

---

8. This does not mean that Satan had afflicted Job with illness and had brought distress upon him. It rather means that Job suffered a severe illness as well as lost his wealth, possessions and family, all of which greatly agonised him. What was even more agonising was that Satan began to capitalise on Job's straitened circumstances. He pestered Solomon with insidious promptings, urging him to be ungrateful to God and to eschew his patience.

9. When one reflects on these words it is evident that during his illness Job swore, in a fit of annoyance, that he would strike someone, (according to some reports, his own wife), with a certain number of lashes. After God restored him to health and the annoyance that he had felt during the illness dissipated, he became disconcerted with the idea of honouring that oath. His dilemma being that if he were to fulfil the oath, he would inflict pain on an innocent person; and if he did not, he would commit a sin. God removed this perplexity by directing him to pick up a broom containing as many pieces of straw as the number of lashes he had sworn to deliver and then

steadfast. How excellent a servant (of Ours) he was. Indeed he constantly turned (to his Lord).

[45] And remember Our servants – Abraham, Isaac and Jacob – they were endowed with great strength and vision. [46] Verily We exalted them in consideration of a sterling quality: their remembrance of the Abode of the Hereafter. [47] In Our sight they are among the chosen and excellent ones. [48] And remember Ishmael, Elisha, and Dhū al-Kifl. All were of the best.

[49] This was a remembrance. An excellent retreat awaits the God-fearing [50] – everlasting Gardens with gates wide open for them [51] wherein they shall recline, wherein they shall ask for abundant fruit and drinks, [52] and wherein there shall be with them well-matched, bashful mates. [53] All this is what you are promised for the Day of Judgement. [54] This is Our provision for you, never to end.

[55] All this (is for the God-fearing). But for the transgressors, an evil resort awaits them – [56] Hell, where they will be roasted. An evil place to dwell! [57] All this (is for them); so let them taste boiling water and pus, [58] and other sufferings of the kind. [59] (Observing their followers advancing to Hell they will say, among themselves: "This is a troop rushing in to you. There is no welcome for them. They are destined to roast in the Fire."

---

commanded him to strike the person with the broom just once. This would, on the one hand, enable him to fulfil the oath, and on the other hand it would also make it possible for him to avoid causing unwarranted harm to the innocent.

[60] They will reply: "Rather, no welcome to you. (You will roast in Hell.) It is you who led us to this end. What an evil resort!" [61] They will say: "Our Lord, give two-fold punishment in the Fire to him who has led us to this." [62] They will say to one another: "But why do we not see those whom we considered him among the wicked? [63] Is it that we mistakenly made fun of them; or have they disappeared from our sight?" [64] Verily all this is true. This is how the inmates of the Fire will dispute among themselves.

[65] Tell them, (O Prophet): "I am nothing but a warner. There is no deity but Allah, the One, the Supreme, [66] the Lord of the heavens and the earth and all that is in between them, the Most Mighty, the Most Forgiving." [67] Say: "This is a tiding of tremendous import [68] from which you are turning away."

[69] (Tell them): "I had no knowledge of the High Council when they were disputing. [70] I am told (about matters) by means of revelation only because I am a clear warner." [71] When your Lord said to the angels: "Verily I am creating a human being from clay. [72] After I have created him and breathed into him of My spirit, fall you down, prostrating yourselves to him." [73] Then the angels, all of them, prostrated themselves before Adam [74] except *Iblīs*. He waxed proud and became one of the unbelievers. [75] The Lord said: "O *Iblīs*, what prevented you from prostrating yourself before him whom I created of My Two Hands. Are you waxing proud, or fancy yourself to be too exalted?" [76] He replied: "I am nobler than he. You created me from fire and created him from clay."

[77] He said: "Get out of here; surely you are accursed, [78] and My curse shall remain upon you till the Day of Resurrection." [79] Satan said: "My Lord, then grant me respite till the Day that they are raised up." [80] He said: "You are of those who have been granted respite [81] till the Day whose Hour I know." [82] (*Iblīs*) said: "By Your glory, I shall mislead them all [83] except those of Your servants, the chosen ones from amongst them." [84] He (i.e. Allah) said: "This is the Truth – and I only speak the Truth – [85] I will certainly fill the Gehenna with you and with all those among them who follow you."

[86] (O Prophet), tell them: "I do not ask you for any recompense for the performance of this task; nor am I given to affectation. [87] This is nothing but an Admonition for all people the world over. [88] You will know the truth of the matter after a while."

39

Al-Zumar [Companies]
Makkan Period

*In the name of Allah, the Most Merciful,
the Most Compassionate*

[1] The revelation of this Book is from Allah, the Most Mighty, the Most Wise.

[2] (O Prophet), it is We Who have revealed this Book to you with Truth. So serve only Allah, consecrating your devotion to Him. [3] Lo, religion is exclusively devoted to Allah. Your religion is entirely consecrated to Him. As for those who have taken others than Allah for their guardians, (they say): "We worship them only that they may bring us nearer to Allah." Allah will judge between them concerning what they differ about. Verily Allah does not guide anyone who is given to sheer lying, is an utter unbeliever.

[4] If Allah had wanted to take to Himself a son, He could have chosen anyone He wanted out of those whom He creates. Glory be to Him (that He should have a son). He is Allah: the One, the Overpowering. [5] He created the heavens and the earth with Truth, and He folds up the day over the night and folds up the night over the day. He has subjected the sun and the moon, each is running its course until an appointed time. Lo, He is the Most Mighty, the Most Forgiving. [6] He it is Who created you from a

single being, and He it is Who made from it its mate. He it is Who created for you eight heads of cattle in pairs.[1] He creates you in your mothers' wombs, giving you one form after another in threefold depths of darkness.[2] That, then, is Allah, your Lord. His is the kingdom. There is no god but He. So, whence are you being turned astray?

[7] If you disbelieve, know well that Allah has no need of you. Yet He does not like unbelief in His servants. But if you are thankful, your thankfulness will please Him. No one shall bear another's burden. You are destined to return to your Lord and He will tell you what you used to do. He is well aware even of what lies hidden in your breasts.

[8] When any affliction befalls man, he cries out to his Lord, penitently turning to Him. But when his Lord bestows His favour upon him, he forgets the affliction regarding which he had cried out and sets up compeers to Allah that they may lead others astray from His Path. Say, (O Prophet): "Enjoy your unbelief for a while. Surely you will be among the inmates of the Fire." [9] Is such a person (preferable or he) who is obedient, and prostrates himself in the watches of the night, stands (in Prayer), is fearful of the Hereafter, and looks forward to the mercy of His Lord? Ask them: "Are those who know equal to those who do not know?" Only those endowed with understanding take heed.

---

1. The cattle comprise the camel, the cow, the sheep, and the goat. Four males and four females make a total of eight heads of cattle.

2. The "three-fold depths of darkness" are the belly, the womb, and the membrane enclosing the foetus.

[10] Tell them (O Prophet): "O you servants of Mine who believe, have fear of your Lord. A good end awaits those who did good in this world. Allah's earth is spacious.[3] Verily those who persevere shall be granted their reward beyond all reckoning."

[11] Tell them, (O Prophet): "I am bidden to serve Allah, consecrating my devotion to Him, [12] and I am bidden to be the first of those who surrender to Him." [13] Say: "If I disobey my Lord, I fear the chastisement of an Awesome Day." [14] Say: "Allah alone shall I serve, consecrating my devotion to Him. [15] So serve, apart from Him, whomsoever you please." Say: "Behold, the real losers shall be those who will have lost their own selves and their kith and kin on the Day of Resurrection. Behold, that is the obvious loss. [16] There shall be sheets of fire above them and beneath them. This is the end against which Allah warns His servants. So dread My wrath, O you servants of Mine!" [17] (On the other hand), good tidings await those who eschew serving false gods and penitently return to Allah. (O Prophet), give good tidings to My servants, [18] to those who pay heed to what is said and follow the best of it. They are the ones whom Allah has guided to the Right Way; they are the ones endowed with understanding.

[19] (O Prophet), can you save him (from chastisement) against whom the sentence of chastisement has become due; him who has, (as it were), already fallen into the Fire?"

---

3. If life becomes too constrained for the devotees of the One True God in a particular city, region or country, they should move to another place where they do not have to face such hardships.

[20] But those who fear their Lord shall have lofty mansions built over one another beneath which rivers flow. This is Allah's promise and never does Allah fail to fulfil His promise.

[21] Do you not see that Allah sent down water from the sky, then made it flow on earth as springs and streams and rivers⁴ and then with it He brings forth vegetation of various hues; then this vegetation ripens and dries up, turning yellow, whereafter He reduces it to broken straw? Surely there is a lesson in this for those endowed with understanding. [22] Can he whose breast Allah has opened up for Islam and who is thus (moving along a Path) illumined by a light from Allah (be likened to him who derives no lesson from what he observes)? Woe, then, to those whose hearts were further hardened after Allah's admonition. Such are indeed in obvious error.

[23] Allah has revealed the best teaching, a self-consistent Book which repeats its contents in manifold forms whereat shiver the skins of those that hold their Lord in awe, and then their skins and their hearts soften for Allah's remembrance. That is Allah's Guidance wherewith He guides whosoever He pleases. And he whom Allah does not guide to the Right Path has none to guide him. [24] How woeful is the plight of him who has nothing except his face to shield him from severe chastisement on the Day of Resurrection? Such evil-doers shall be told: "Taste now the consequence of your deeds." [25] Their predecessors gave the lie to the Truth and then

---

4. In this verse the word *yanābī'* is used. It embraces springs, streams and rivers.

chastisement came upon them from whence they could not imagine. [26] So Allah made them taste degradation in the life of this world, and certainly the chastisement of the Hereafter will be much more grievous. Would that they knew!

[27] We have indeed propounded for mankind all kinds of parables in this Qur'ān that they may take heed. [28] It is an Arabic Qur'ān free of all crookedness that they may guard against their evil end. [29] Allah propounds a parable: there is a man whose ownership is shared by several quarrelsome masters, each pulling him to himself; and there is another who is exclusively owned by one man. Can the two be alike? All praise and thanks be to Allah. But most of them are unaware.[5] [30] (O Prophet), you are destined to die and they too are destined to die. [31] Then eventually all of you will contend before your Lord on the Day of Resurrection. [32] Who, then, can be more unjust than he who lied against Allah and denied the Truth when it came to him, calling it a lie? Is there no room for such unbelievers in Hell? [33] But he who brought the Truth, and those who confirmed it as true, such are the ones who shall be guarded against the chastisement. [34] They shall have from their Lord all that they wish for. That is the reward of those that do good, [35] so that Allah

---

5. People fully understand the difference between being the slave of one master and being the slave of several masters. Astonishingly, when it comes to the question of deities, people fail to comprehend the difference between being slaves of the One True God and of being the slaves of a multiplicity of gods. Here they show their utter lack of understanding; here they fail to appreciate the difference even when it is explained to them.

may remit their worst deeds and reward them according to the best of their deeds.

[36] (O Prophet), does Allah not suffice for His servant? They frighten you with others apart from Him, although he whom Allah lets go astray, none can guide him to the Right Way. [37] And he whom Allah guides to the Right Way, none can lead him astray. Is not Allah the Most Mighty, the Lord of Retribution? [38] If you ask them: "Who created the heavens and the earth?" they will surely answer: "Allah." Tell them: "What do you think, then, of the deities whom you call upon instead of Allah? If Allah should will that an affliction befall me, will those deities remove the harm inflicted by Him? Or if Allah should will that I receive (His) Mercy, will they be able to withhold His Mercy from me?" Say: "Allah is sufficient for me; those who have to put their trust, let them put their trust in Him. [39] Tell them: "My people, continue to work in your position as you will, I too will continue with my work. Soon you shall know [40] whom the degrading chastisement will visit and upon whom the everlasting chastisement will alight. [41] (O Prophet), We revealed to you the Book with the Truth for all mankind. So he who follows the Right Way does so to his own benefit, and he who goes astray, shall hurt only himself by straying. You are not accountable on their behalf.

[42] It is Allah Who takes away the souls of people at the hour of their death, and takes away at the time of sleep the souls of those that have not died. Then He retains the souls of those against whom He had decreed death and returns the souls of others till an appointed time. Surely there are Signs in this for a people who reflect.

[43] Or have they taken others instead of Allah as intercessors?[6] Say: "Will they intercede though they may have no power and though they may not even understand?" [44] Say: "All intercession lies with Allah.[7] His is the dominion of the heavens and the earth. And to Him will all of you be sent back."

[45] When Allah alone is mentioned, the hearts of those who do not believe in the Hereafter contract with bitterness, but when deities apart from Allah are mentioned, they are filled with joy.[8] [46] Say: "O Allah, the Originator of the heavens and the earth, the Knower of the unseen and the seen, You it is Who will judge among Your servants

---

6. In the first place, those people had gratuitously assumed that others enjoyed such extraordinary influence with God that He could simply not afford to reject their intercession. They assumed this even though there was no basis to believe that anyone had such an overwhelming ability to intercede with God. God had not indicated this nor had the people concerned claimed that their influence with God was such that they could persuade Him to decide about their favourites in line with their wishes. To cap these follies, the ignorant ones continued to disregard God, their true Lord, and to consecrate all their devotion to those they thought of as intercessors.

7. The fact is that no one has the power to intercede with God, let alone compel God to accept his intercession. God has the sole authority to permit or disallow anyone to intercede. Moreover, if God were to permit anyone to intercede, He might permit that particular person to intercede on behalf of one person but might disallow such intercession on behalf of another.

8. This characteristic is shared by almost all people who have a polytheistic bent of mind. Such people verbally claim that they believe in God, but if anyone happens to mention the One True God their faces exhibit discomfort. This trait is quite widespread, so much so that it has affected the attitude of some Muslims as well.

concerning what they differed. [47] If the wrong-doers possessed the treasures of the earth in their entirety and as much besides, they would gladly offer it on the Day of Resurrection to redeem themselves from the harrowing chastisement. This because there will appear to them from Allah something (exceedingly dismal which) they had never even imagined. [48] The evil consequences of their deeds will become fully apparent to them, and what they had scoffed at will encompass them.

[49] When an affliction befalls man, he cries out to Us; but when We grant him a favour from Us, he says: "I have been granted this on account of my knowledge." Nay; this (favour) is a test; but most of them do not know. [50] Their predecessors also said the same, but their earnings proved of no avail to them, [51] and the evil consequences of their deeds overtook them. The wrong-doers among these will also be overtaken by the evil consequences of their deeds. They will be utterly unable to frustrate (Us). [52] Do they not know that Allah enlarges and straitens the provision of whomsoever He pleases? Therein are Signs for those that believe.

[53] Tell them, (O Prophet): "My servants⁹ who have committed excesses against themselves, do not despair

---

In a fit of anger such people are inclined to say: "This man surely does not believe in saints and holy men and that is why he keeps talking only about God." On the contrary, when someone mentions others than God, their faces are aglow with joy.

9. Some people have come forth with a very strange interpretation of these words. They say that God Himself commanded the Prophet (peace be on him) to address people as "my servants"; therefore,

of Allah's Mercy. Surely Allah forgives all sins. He is Most Forgiving, Most Merciful. [54] Turn to your Lord and surrender yourselves to Him before the chastisement over-takes you; for then you will receive no help. [55] Follow the best of what has been revealed[10] to you from your Lord before the chastisement suddenly comes upon you without you even being aware of it." [56] Lest a person should say: "Alas for me for neglecting my duty towards Allah and for being among those that scoffed"; [57] and lest a person should say: "If only Allah had guided me, I should have been one of the God-fearing"; [58] or lest he should say, when he sees the chastisement: "O that I might return again, and be among those who do good." [59] Yes indeed! But My Signs came to you and you rejected them as lies, and waxed arrogant and were among those who disbelieved. [60] On the Day of

---

all persons are his (to wit, the Prophet's) servants. Such a view can hardly be called an interpretation of the Qur'ān. It rather represents the worst sort of distortion of the Qur'ān's meaning and reducing it to a plaything. If this interpretation were correct, it would falsify and negate the whole of the Qur'ān. For the Qur'ān proclaims, from one end to the other, that human beings are the servants of only the One True God. In fact, the whole Message of the Qur'ān revolves around summoning people to accept the servitude of none except the One True God.

10. "To follow the best of what has been revealed to you from your Lord" means that one should fully devote oneself to carrying out God's commands and refrain from all that He has forbidden, as also to deriving lessons from the Qur'ān's various parables and narratives. As against this, we find that those who turn away from God's commands deliberately commit forbidden acts, pay no heed to God's directives; in short, they adopt an attitude that the Qur'ān utterly denounces.

Resurrection you shall see that the faces of those who had lied against Allah have turned dark. Is Hell not vast enough to provide a room to the vainglorious? [61] But as for the God-fearing, Allah will deliver them on account of their achievements: no harm shall visit them nor shall they grieve.

[62] Allah is the Creator of everything; He is the Guardian over everything. [63] To Him belong the keys of the heavens and the earth. It is those who disbelieve in Allah's Signs who will be the losers. [64] (O Prophet), say: "Ignorant people! Do you bid me to serve any other beside Allah?" [65] (Tell them clearly that) it was revealed to you and to all Prophets before you: "If you associate any others with Allah in His Divinity, your works will surely come to naught and you will certainly be among the losers." [66] Therefore, serve Allah alone and be among those who give thanks.

[67] They did not recognise the true worth of Allah. (Such is Allah's power that) on the Day of Resurrection the whole earth will be in His grasp,[11] and the heavens shall

---

11. This is a metaphorical description of God's absolute sovereignty, dominion, and control of the heavens and earth: "(Such is Allah's power that) on the Day of Resurrection the whole earth will be in His grasp, and the heavens shall be folded up in His Right Hand." We see today that a person encloses a small ball in the hollow of his hand with perfect ease, or another person folds up a handkerchief and then holds it in his hand without the least difficulty. All human beings – and they are presently in no position to have an accurate estimate of God's power and might – will come across a strange spectacle on the Day of Resurrection. They will see that the heavens and the earth are no larger than an ordinary ball or small handkerchief in God's Hand.

be folded up in His Right Hand. Glory be to Him! Exalted be He from all that they associate with Him. [68] And the Trumpet shall be blown and all who are in the heavens and the earth shall fall down dead save those whom Allah wills. Then the Trumpet shall be blown again, and lo! all of them will be standing and looking on. [69] The earth shall shine with the light of its Lord, and the Scroll (of deeds) shall be set in place, and the Prophets and all witnesses shall be brought, and judgement shall be justly passed among them, and they shall not be wronged; [70] and everyone shall be paid in full for all that he did. Allah is best aware of all that they do.

[71] (After the judgement has been passed) the unbelievers shall be driven in companies to Hell so that when they arrive there, its gates shall be thrown open and its keepers shall say to them: "Did Messengers from among yourselves not come to you, rehearsing to you the Signs of your Lord and warning you against your meeting of this Day?" They will say: "Yes indeed; but the sentence of chastisement was bound to be executed against the unbelievers." [72] It will be said: "Enter the gates of Hell. Herein shall you abide." How evil is the abode of the vainglorious!

[73] And those who eschewed disobeying their Lord shall be driven in companies to Paradise so that when they arrive there its gates will have already been thrown open and its keepers shall say to them: "Peace be upon you; you have done well. So enter. Herein you shall abide." [74] They will say: "All thanks and praise be to Allah Who has made His promise to us come true, and Who gave us the earth to inherit. We may now dwell in Paradise

wherever we please." How excellent is the reward of those who laboured!

[75] You shall see the angels surrounding the Throne, glorifying their Lord with His praise, and judgement will have been made among them with fairness, and it will be proclaimed: "All praise and thanks be to Allah, the Lord of the whole Universe."

40
❀

Al-Mu'min [The Believer]
Makkan Period

In the name of Allah, the Most Merciful,
the Most Compassionate

[1] *Ḥā'*. *Mīm*. [2] This Book is a revelation from Allah, the All-Mighty, the All-Knowing; [3] the Forgiver of sins, the Accepter of repentance, the Stern in retribution, the Bountiful. There is no god but He. To Him are all destined to return.

[4] None but the unbelievers dispute regarding the Signs of Allah. So let not their strutting about in the land delude you. [5] Before them the people of Noah also gave the lie (to Messengers), and so did many parties after them. Each nation sallied forth against its Messenger to seize him, and they disputed with false arguments seeking therewith to repudiate the Truth. Then I seized them; and behold, how woeful was My retribution! [6] Thus has the decree of your Lord become due against the unbelievers. They are destined for the Fire.

[7] The angels that bear the Throne and those that are around to extol your Lord's glory with His praise, they believe in Him, and ask forgiveness for the believers, saying: "Our Lord! You encompass everything with Your Mercy and Knowledge. So forgive those that repent and follow Your Path, and guard them against the chastisement of Hell.

[8] Our Lord, admit them to the everlasting Gardens You have promised them and those of their fathers and spouses and progeny that were righteous. Surely You alone are Most Mighty, Most Wise; [9] and guard them against all ills. He whom You guard against ills on that Day, to him You have surely been Most Merciful. That is the great triumph."

[10] It will be announced to the unbelievers (on the Day of Resurrection): "Surely Allah's abhorrence of you when you were called to believe but you disbelieved was greater than is your abhorrence of yourselves today." [11] They will say: "Our Lord, twice have You caused us to die and twice have You given us life.¹ We have now confessed our sins. Is there, then, any way out?" [12] (They will be told): "(The cause of your present state is that) when Allah alone was invoked, you disbelieved; and when others instead of Him were invoked, you believed. Today all judgement lies with Allah, the Most High, the All-Great."

[13] He it is Who shows you His Signs and sends down provision for you from the sky.² Yet none takes heed except he who constantly turns to Allah. [14] So call upon Allah, consecrating all your devotion to Him, howsoever much the unbelievers may dislike it.

---

1. The statement that God twice caused human beings to die and twice He gave them life means substantially the same as was said in *al-Baqarah* 2: 28.

2. God causes rainfall which provides sustenance to mankind. Likewise, God is the source of both heat and cold and they too play a great part in the production of sustenance.

[15] Exalted in Rank, Lord of the Throne: He causes the spirit to descend on whomsoever of His servants He pleases so as to warn them of the Day of Encounter; [16] the Day when they will emerge and nothing of them shall be hidden from Allah. (On that Day they will be asked): "Whose is the kingdom today?" (The whole world will cry out): "It is Allah's, the One, the Overpowering." [17] (It will then be said): "Today shall everyone be fully recompensed for his deeds. None shall be wronged today. Surely Allah is Swift in Reckoning." [18] (O Prophet), then warn them of the Day that has drawn near, the Day when hearts full of suppressed grief will leap up to the throats and the wrong-doers shall neither have any sincere friend nor intercessor whose word will be heeded. [19] He knows even the most stealthy glance of the eyes and all the secrets that hearts conceal. [20] Allah will judge with justice, whereas those whom they call upon beside Him cannot judge at all. Surely Allah – and He alone – is All-Hearing, All-Seeing.

[21] Have they not journeyed in the land that they might observe the end of those who came before them? They were even greater in strength than they and left behind more splendid traces in the land. Then Allah seized them because of their sins and they had none who could protect them from Allah. [22] They came to this end because their Messengers would come to them with Clear Signs[3] and

---

3. The word *bayyināt* ("Clear Signs") in the text means three things: (1) Signs which provided strong proof that the Messengers were appointed by God; (2) convincing arguments which fully establish that the teachings of those Messengers were true; and (3) clear

yet they would refuse to believe. So Allah seized them. He is indeed Strong, Terrible in Retribution.

[23] Verily We sent Moses with Our Signs and a clear authority [24] to Pharaoh and Hāmān and Korah. They said: "(He is) a sorcerer, an utter liar." [25] When Moses brought them the Truth from Us they said: "Kill the sons of all the believers who have joined him, but spare the women." The guile of the unbelievers always ends in vain.

[26] One day Pharaoh said: "Let me go and kill Moses; then let him invoke his Lord. I fear that he will change your religion or cause disruption in the land."

[27] Moses said: "I have taken refuge with my Lord and your Lord from everyone who waxes arrogant and does not believe in the Day of Reckoning."

[28] Then a man endowed with faith, from Pharaoh's folk, who had kept his faith hidden, said: "Do you kill a person simply because he says: 'My Lord is Allah' even though he brought to you clear Signs from your Lord? If he is a liar, his lying will recoil upon him; but if he is truthful, you will be smitten with some of the awesome consequences of which he warns you. Allah does not guide to the Right Way any who exceeds the limits and is an utter liar. [29] My people, today the kingdom is yours, and you are supreme in the land. But if Allah's chastisement were to come upon you, who will come to our help?"

---

directives regarding the problems and affairs of life that would convince every reasonable person that they could not have been given by an impostor or someone driven by selfish interests.

Pharaoh said: "I only counsel what I consider right; I only direct you to the Path of Rectitude."

[30] He who had faith said: "My people, I fear that you will confront a day like that which overtook many parties before you, [31] like the day that overtook the people of Noah and 'Ād and Thamūd, and those who came after them. Allah does not wish to subject His servants to any injustice. [32] My people, I fear that you will encounter a day when there will be much wailing and you will cry out to one another for help, [33] the day when you will turn around to retreat, there will be none to protect you from Allah. He whom Allah lets go astray, none will be able to show him the Right Way. [34] Verily Joseph came to you with Clear Signs before, yet you continued to doubt his Message.⁴ Thereafter when he died, you said: 'Allah shall send no Messenger after him.'" Thus Allah leads astray those who transgress the limits and are given to much doubting; [35] those who contend regarding Allah's Signs without any evidence that might have come to them. That is exceedingly loathsome to Allah and to those that believe. Thus does Allah seal the heart of everyone who is proud and high-handed.

[36] Pharaoh said: "Hāmān, build for me a lofty tower that I may scale the highways – [37] the highways to the heavens – and have a look at the God of Moses, although I am certain that Moses is a liar." Thus Pharaoh's evil

---

4. It seems that the next few sentences were presumably said by God to elaborate and explain the statement of the person belonging to the Pharaonite nation who had been endowed with faith. (See vv. 38 ff. below. Ed.)

deed was made to seem fair to him, and he was barred from the Right Path. Pharaoh's guile only led him to his own perdition.

[38] The person endowed with faith said: "My people, follow me; I shall direct you to the Path of Rectitude. [39] My people, the life of this world is ephemeral, whereas the Hereafter, that is the permanent abode. [40] Whosoever does an evil deed will be requited only with the like of it; and whosoever acts righteously and has attained to faith – be he a male or a female – they shall enter Paradise and be provided sustenance beyond all reckoning. [41] My people, how is it that I call you to salvation while you call me to the Fire; [42] you call me to deny Allah and to associate with Him as His partners those regarding whom I have no knowledge (that they are Allah's partners in His Divinity),⁵ whereas I call you to the Most Mighty, the Most Forgiving? [43] There is no doubt that those whom you call me to have no claim to be called upon in this world and in the Hereafter.⁶ Certainly to Allah

5. That is, to associate with God's Divinity those about whom he did not know they had any share in it.

6. This sentence can be understood to mean several things. [1] That those who were misguided had no right, neither here in this world nor in the Hereafter, to ask people to acknowledge the Godhead of false deities. [2] It is others who had invested those deities with Godhead. As for the deities themselves, they had never laid any claim to Divinity in this world nor will they ever make such a claim in the Hereafter. [3] That it is of no use to invoke those deities either in this world or in the Hereafter because they are absolutely powerless.

shall be our return, and those who exceed the limits are destined to the Fire. [44] Soon you shall remember what I say to you. I entrust my affairs to Allah. Surely Allah is watchful over His servants."

[45] Eventually Allah saved the person endowed with faith from all the evils of their guile, and a woeful chastisement encompassed the Pharaonites.[7] [46] They are exposed to the Fire every morning and evening; and when the Last Hour will come to pass, a command shall be given: "Admit the Pharaonites to an even more severe chastisement." [47] Just imagine when they will remonstrate with one another in Hell. The weak ones will say to those who waxed proud: "We were your followers. Will you, then, lighten for us a part of our suffering of the Fire?" [48] Those who had waxed proud will reply: "All of us are in it. Allah has already passed His judgement among His servants." [49] Those suffering in the Fire will say to the keepers of Hell: "Call upon your Lord to lighten the chastisement for us just for a day." [50] The keepers of Hell will ask: "Did your Messengers not come to you with Clear Signs?" They will say: "Yes (they did)." The keepers of Hell will say: "Then you yourselves should call (upon the Lord). And the call of the unbelievers will end in vain."

---

7. This shows that the "person endowed with faith" was highly important and influential in Pharaoh's realm. This is evident from the fact that although he spoke the Truth in Pharaoh's full court, it was not possible to publicly punish him. Thus Pharaoh and his courtiers had to hatch a plot that he be secretly put to death. But God saw to it that such plans would not take effect.

[51] Surely We shall help Our Messengers and the believers in the life of this world and on the Day when witnesses will rise to testify, [52] the Day when the excuses offered by the wrong-doers shall not avail them. They shall be victims of the curse and a woeful abode. [53] We surely guided Moses and made the Children of Israel the heirs of the Book [54] which was a guidance and good counsel to people endowed with understanding and wisdom. [55] Be steadfast, then, (O Prophet), Allah's promise is true. Seek forgiveness for your shortcomings,[8] and celebrate the praise of your Lord, evening and morning. [56] Verily those who dispute regarding the Signs of Allah without any evidence that might have come to them, nothing but vain pride fills their hearts. Yet they shall never be able to

---

8. This statement should be understood in the context in which it occurs. The context makes it very clear that the "shortcoming" for which the Prophet (peace be on him) was asked to seek forgiveness was one of impatience. Essentially he had become impatient with the severe opposition and cruel treatment which he and his followers encountered. Because of such pressures the Prophet (peace be on him) entertained the desire that some miracle be shown sooner rather than later that would make the unbelievers embrace the True Faith; or that something dramatic should come forth from God that would quell the raging storm of opposition. There was obviously nothing objectionable as far as this desire was concerned. On the other hand, however, God had placed the Prophet (peace be on him) on an exceedingly high pedestal. To live up to the demands made of him required an exceptionally strong will and resolve. It was in consideration of the requirements of the Prophet's exceptional position that even this little show of impatience seemed discordant with his rank and mission. Hence, the Prophet (peace be on him) was asked to seek God's forgiveness and stand his ground in God's cause with the strength of a rock.

satisfy the pride with which they are puffed up. So seek refuge with Allah. Verily He is All-Hearing, All-Seeing.

[57] Surely the creation of the heavens and the earth is a greater act than the creation of human beings. But most people do not know. [58] Never can the blind and the seeing be equal; nor those that believe and act righteously and those that do evil. Little do you understand. [59] The Hour will indeed come; there is no doubt about that. Yet most people do not believe.

[60] Your Lord said: "Pray to Me, and I will accept your prayers.⁹ Surely those who wax too proud to worship Me shall enter Hell, utterly abased."¹⁰

[61] Allah it is Who made the night so that you may seek repose in it, and made the day radiant. Surely Allah is Most Bounteous to people; but most people do not give thanks. [62] Allah (Who bestowed all these favours upon you) is your Lord, the Creator of everything. There is no god but He. Whence are you, then, being led astray?

---

9. Since God alone has the power to accept prayers, it is to God and none else that people should address their prayers.

10. Two things deserve special attention in this verse. First, that prayer (i.e. supplication) and worship are used here as equivalents. What is called "prayer" in the early part of the verse is later called "worship". This shows that prayer is worship; that it is the very heart of it. Second, the words "those who wax too proud to worship Me" are used in regard to those who are not disposed to pray to God. This shows that to pray to God is a requirement of man's servitude and to turn away from praying to Him amounts to being vain and arrogant.

[63] Thus it is only those who had denied Allah's Signs that were led astray.

[64] Allah it is Who made the earth a dwelling place for you and made the sky a canopy, Who shaped you – and shaped you exceedingly well – and gave you good things as sustenance. That is Allah, your Lord; blessed be Allah, the Lord of the Universe. [65] He is the Ever-Living: there is no god but He. So call upon Him, consecrating to Him all your devotion. All praise and thanks be to Allah, the Lord of the whole Universe.

[66] Say, (O Prophet): "I have been forbidden to worship those beside Allah whom you call upon. (How can I worship any beside Allah) when clear Signs have come to me from my Lord and I have been commanded to surrender to Allah, the Lord of the Universe?"

[67] He it is Who created you from dust, then from a sperm-drop, then from a clot; then He brings you out as an infant, then causes you to grow into full maturity, and then causes you to grow further so that you may reach old age, while some of you He recalls earlier. All this is in order that you may reach an appointed term and that you may understand (the Truth). [68] He it is Who gives life and causes death. Whenever He decrees a thing, He only commands to it "Be", and it is.

[69] Did you not see those who dispute concerning Allah's Signs? Whence are they, then, being turned astray? [70] Those who gave the lie to this Book and all the Books which We had sent with Our Messengers shall soon come to know the Truth [71] when fetters and chains shall be

on their necks, and they shall be dragged into [72] boiling water, and cast into the Fire. [73] It will then be said to them: "Where are those whom you [74] associated with Allah in His Divinity?" They will say: "We have lost them; rather, we never used to call upon anyone before." Thus will Allah cause them to stumble in error. [75] (They will be told): "This is because while you were on earth you took delight in untruth and exulted in it. [76] Enter Hell now to abide in it. How woeful is the abode of those who wax proud! [77] So be patient, (O Prophet). Surely Allah's promise is true. Whether We show them a part of the woeful consequences against which We warn them (while you are still in their midst) or We recall you (from this world) before that, eventually it is to Us that they shall be brought back.

[78] Indeed We sent many Messengers before you: of them there are some whose account We have narrated to you and there are others whose account We have not narrated to you. It did not lie in any Messenger's power to bring any Sign except with Allah's leave. So when Allah's decree came, the matter was decided with justice, and those steeped in error courted utter loss, then and there. [79] Allah it is Who has made cattle for you so that you ride some of them and from some of them you derive food. [80] In them there are also other benefits for you, and through them you fulfil your heartfelt need (to reach places), and you are borne along upon them as upon the ships. [81] Allah shows His Signs to you; then which of Allah's Signs will you deny?

[82] Did they not journey in the land that they may behold the end of those who had gone before them? They were

more numerous and greater in strength and left behind
more splendid traces in the land. Yet their attainments did
not avail them. [83] When their Messengers came to them
with Clear Signs, they arrogantly exulted in whatever
knowledge they had. They were then encompassed
by what they had mocked. [84] When they saw Our
chastisement, they said: "We have come to believe in
Allah, the Only One, and we reject all what we had
associated (with Allah in His Divinity)." [85] But their
believing after they had seen Our chastisement did not
avail them. That has been Allah's Way concerning His
servants. And the unbelievers courted utter loss, then
and there.

41

Ḥā'. Mīm. Al-Sajdah
Makkan Period

*In the name of Allah, the Most Merciful,
the Most Compassionate*

[1] *Ḥā'. Mīm.* [2] This is a revelation from the Most Merciful, the Most Compassionate, [3] a Book whose verses have been well-expounded; an Arabic Qur'ān for those who have knowledge, [4] one bearing good news and warning.

Yet most of them turned away and are not wont to give heed. [5] They say: "Our hearts are securely wrapped up against what you call us to, and in our ears is a heaviness, and between you and us is a veil. So act; we too are acting."

[6] Tell them, (O Prophet): "I am only a human being like you. It is revealed to me that your God is One God; so direct yourselves straight to Him, and seek His forgiveness. Woe to those who associate others with Allah in His Divinity, [7] who do not pay *Zakāh*, and who deny the Hereafter. [8] As to those who have faith and do good works, surely theirs shall be a never-ending reward.

[9] Tell them, (O Prophet): "Do you indeed disbelieve in Him and assign compeers to Him Who created the earth in two days? He is the Lord of all beings of the Universe.

[10] (After creating the earth) He set up firm mountains on it, blessed it, and provided it with sustenance in proportion to the needs of all who seek (sustenance).[1] All this was done in four days. [11] Then He turned to the heaven while it was all smoke.[2] He said to the heaven and the earth: "Come (into being), willingly or unwillingly." They said: "Here we come (into being) in willing obeisance." [12] Then He made them seven heavens in two days and revealed to each heaven its law. And We adorned the lower heaven with lamps, and firmly secured it. All this is the firm plan of the All-Mighty, the All-Knowing.

[13] But if they turn away, tell them: "I warn you against a sudden scourge like that which struck 'Ād and Thamūd." [14] When the Messengers (of Allah) came to them from the front and from the rear, saying: "Do not serve any but Allah"; they said: "Had our Lord so willed, He would have sent down angels. So we deny the Message you have brought."

[15] As for 'Ād, they waxed proud in the land without justification and said: "Who is greater than we in

---

1. In His providential scheme God saw to it that there would be enough sustenance to suffice the requirements of all creatures.

2. This does not mean that God created the heavens after having created the earth and after having arranged to provide sustenance for the earth's creatures. The word "then" used in the verse does not denote temporal sequence. Instead, the sequence that we find here is simply for purposes of narration. This is borne out by the statement that immediately follows.

strength?" Did they not see that Allah, Who created them, is greater in strength than they? They continued to deny Our Signs, [16] whereupon We sent upon them a fierce wind on inauspicious days that We might make them taste a degrading chastisement in the life of this world. And surely the chastisement of the Hereafter is even more degrading. There will be none to help them there.

[17] As for Thamūd, We bestowed guidance upon them, but they preferred to remain blind rather than be guided. At last a humiliating scourge overtook them on account of their misdeeds. [18] Yet We delivered those who believed and were God-fearing.

[19] Imagine the Day when Allah's enemies will be mustered to the Fire,³ and the people of the former times will be detained until the arrival of people of the later times,⁴ [20] and when all have arrived, their ears, their eyes, and their skins shall bear witness against them,

---

3. What is meant by this statement is that God's enemies would be mustered so that they stand before God for His final judgement. The actual words, however, are: "… when Allah's enemies will be mustered to the Fire." The reason is obvious: the ultimate destiny of God's enemies is nothing else than Hell-Fire.

4. On the Day of Judgement it will not happen that the people belonging to one generation will be first called to account, followed by the next generation, followed by the next, and so on. What will happen instead is that all human beings will be brought together at one and the same time and all will be so called to account. This is understandable because each generation is affected by the good and evil deeds of the generation that precedes it.

stating all that they had done in the life of the world. [21] They will ask their skins: "Why did you bear witness against us?" The skins will reply: "Allah gave us speech, as He gave speech to all others. He it is Who created you for the first time and it is to Him that you will be sent back. [22] When you used to conceal yourselves (while committing misdeeds) you never thought that your ears or your eyes or your skins would ever bear witness against you; you rather fancied that Allah does not know a great deal of what you do. [23] This thought of yours about your Lord has led to your perdition and you have become among the losers." [24] In this state, whether they bear with patience (or not), Fire alone shall be their abode. And if they seek to make amends, they will not be allowed to do so. [25] We had assigned to them companions who embellished for them all that was before them and behind them. Thus the same decree (of chastisement) which had overtaken the previous generations of *jinn* and human beings (also) became due against them. Surely they became the losers.

[26] The deniers of the Truth say: "Do not give ear to the Qur'ān and cause interruption when it is recited; thus perhaps you will gain the upper hand." [27] We shall certainly make these unbelievers taste a terrible chastisement and shall fully requite them according to the worst deeds that they committed. [28] That is the recompense of the enemies of Allah – the Fire, their abiding home. That will be the re-compense for their denying Our Signs. [29] There the unbelievers will say: "Our Lord, show us those that led us astray, both *jinn* and

humans, and we will trample them under our feet so that they are utterly degraded."

[30] Those who say "Allah is our Lord" and then remain steadfast,⁵ upon them descend angels (and say): "Do not fear nor grieve, and receive good tidings of Paradise which you were promised. [31] We are your companions in this world and in the Hereafter. There you shall have all that you desire and all what you will ask for. [32] This is by way of hospitality from Him Who is Most Forgiving, Most Merciful."

[33] And who is fairer in speech than he who calls to Allah and acts righteously and says: "I am a Muslim"?

[34] (O Prophet), good and evil are not equal. Repel (evil) with that which is good, and you will see that he, between whom and you there was enmity, shall become as if he were a bosom friend (of yours). [35] But none attains to this except those who are steadfast; none attains to this

---

5. This is a major characteristic of those who have true faith in God. When they committed themselves to God, declaring Him to be their Lord, such a declaration was not an accidental utterance. Such people were under no misperception that they could commit themselves to God as their Lord, and then combine this with accepting others as their Lord. On the contrary, once they had made up their minds to accept God as their One True God, they steadfastly stood by that commitment. Such people neither adopted any creed repugnant to their exclusive commitment to the One True God, nor allowed their belief to be adulterated by mixing it with elements drawn from false creeds. Moreover, they also strove hard to translate their belief in the One True God into practice.

except those endowed with mighty good fortune. [36] And if you are prompted by a provocation from Satan,[6] seek refuge with Allah. He, and He alone, is All-Hearing, All-Knowing.

[37] And of His Signs are the night and the day, and the sun and the moon. Do not prostrate yourselves before the sun, nor before the moon, but prostrate yourselves before Allah Who created them, if it is Him that you serve. [38] But if they wax proud (and persist in their attitude, it does not matter, for) the angels near-stationed to your Lord glorify Him night and day, and never grow weary.

[39] And of His Signs is that you see the earth withered, then We send down water upon it, and lo! it quivers and swells. Surely He Who gives life to the dead earth will also give life to the dead. Surely He has power over everything.

[40] Those who pervert Our Signs are not hidden from Us. Is he who will be cast into the Fire better, or he who comes secure on the Day of Resurrection? Do as you wish; He sees all what you do. [41] These are the ones who rejected the Good Counsel when it came to them, although it is certainly a Mighty Book.

---

6. Here the words "provocation from Satan" denote Satan's arousing the believer's anger. When someone becomes infuriated at an opponent's abuse and slander and feels like paying them back in the same coin, he should alert himself to the danger that has set in. He should become conscious that Satan is prompting him to stoop to the level of his ignoble opponents.

[42] Falsehood may not enter it from the front or from the rear.[7] It is a revelation that has been sent down from the Most Wise, the Immensely Praiseworthy.

[43] (O Prophet), nothing is said to you but what was already said to the Messengers before you. Surely your Lord is the Lord of forgiveness and the Lord of grievous chastisement.

[44] Had We revealed this as a non-Arabic Qur'ān they would have said: "Why were its verses not clearly expounded? How strange, a non-Arabic scripture and an Arab audience!"[8] Tell them: "It is a guidance and a

7. The statement that "falsehood may not enter it from the front" means that if someone were to mount a direct, frontal attack on the Qur'ān and try to establish that any of its teachings are erroneous, such an effort will prove abortive. As for the statement that "falsehood may not enter it from the rear," this means that nothing will ever be discovered until the Day of Judgement that will negate the truths propounded by the Qur'ān. No scientific advancement, no expansion of knowledge, no new facts yielded by observation and experiment will ever be able to establish that any guidance furnished by the Qur'ān relating to belief and morality, law and culture, society, economy and polity, is flawed.

8. This illustrates the ill-conceived obduracy which the Prophet (peace be on him) encountered. Since the Qur'ān was couched in the Arabic language and the Prophet (peace be on him) was an Arab, the unbelievers occasionally contended that he himself had authored it and hence there was no basis to claim that it was God's revelation. In other words, they would consider the Qur'ān a revelation from God only if it were couched in a foreign language such as Persian, Latin or Greek and the Prophet (peace be on him) would recite it with absolute fluency despite his being an Arab. Here, this line of argument is being countered. The unbelievers are being told in effect: Now that the Qur'ān has been revealed to them

healing to the believers. But to those who do not believe, it serves as a plug in their ears and a covering over their eyes. It is as if they are being called from a place far away. [45] And in the past We gave Moses the Book and yet it became an object of dispute. If your Lord's decree had not gone forth before, a decisive judgement would have been made among them, once and for all. Surely they are in a disquieting doubt about it.

[46] Whoever does good, does so to his own benefit; and whoever does evil, will suffer its evil consequence. Your Lord does no wrong to His servants.

[47] The knowledge of the Hour rests solely with Him.[9] Not a fruit comes forth from its sheath, nor does any female conceive nor give birth to a child but it is in His knowledge. On that Day He will call out to them: "Where are those associates of Mine?" They will answer: "We have declared to You that none of us can bear witness to that." [48] Then all those deities whom they once used to call upon shall vanish and they will come to know for sure that there is no escape for them.

---

in their own tongue so that they might fully comprehend it, you are casting doubts about its being God's revelation on the grounds that it is in Arabic, the Prophet's own tongue. On the other hand, had it been revealed in a foreign tongue, the same people would have raised a storm of opposition on the grounds that it was odd that the Messenger was raised among the Arabs, but the revelation he brought to them was in a foreign tongue which could be understood neither by the Messenger nor by his people!

9. Knowledge of the Hour means knowledge of the Hour of Resurrection.

[49] Man wearies not of praying for good, but when evil visits him, he despairs and gives up all hope. [50] And if We bestow Our Mercy upon him after hardship, he will surely say: "This is what I truly deserve, and I do not believe that the Hour (of Resurrection) will ever come to pass; and if I am returned to my Lord, there too I shall enjoy the best." Surely We shall fully apprise the unbelievers of what they have done, and We shall certainly make them taste a severe chastisement.

[51] When We bestow Our favour upon man, he turns away and waxes proud; but when a misfortune touches him, he is full of supplication.

[52] Tell them, (O Prophet): "Did you ever consider: if this Qur'ān is indeed from Allah and you still deny it, who can be in greater error than he who goes far in fiercely opposing it?"

[53] Soon shall We show them Our Signs on the horizons and in their own beings until it becomes clear to them that it is the Truth. Is it not enough that your Lord is a witness over everything? [54] Lo, they are in doubt concerning their meeting with their Lord. Surely He fully encompasses everything.[10]

---

10. That is, nothing is beyond God's power, nor is there anything beyond the range of His knowledge.

42
୭୨୨୭

Al-Shūrā [Consultation]
Makkan Period

In the name of Allah, the Most Merciful,
the Most Compassionate

[1] *Ḥā'. Mīm.* [2] *'Ayn. Sīn. Qāf.* [3] Thus does Allah, the Most Mighty, the Most Wise reveal to you even as (He revealed) to those (Messengers) who preceded you.[1] [4] His is all that is in the heavens and all that is in the earth; He is the Most High, the All-Great. [5] The heavens may well nigh rend asunder from above[2] while the angels proclaim the praise of their Lord and ask forgiveness for those on earth. Lo, it is Allah, and He alone, Who is Most Forgiving, Most Merciful. [6] Those who have taken others

---

1. The teachings embodied in the Qur'ān are those that were revealed to the Prophet (peace be on him) as well as to the Messengers of former times.

2. It is not at all trivial in God's sight that any of His creatures be made an associate of His in whatever manner. It is a monstrosity of such magnitude that none should wonder if it caused the heavens to be rent asunder.

than Him as their protectors beside Him,[3] it is Allah Who oversees them; you are no guardian over them.

[7] And thus did We reveal this Arabic Qur'ān to you that you may warn the people of the Mother of Cities (to wit, Makkah) and those who dwell around it; and warn them of the Day of Gathering concerning which there is no doubt: whereon some will be in Paradise, and some in the Blazing Fire.

[8] If Allah had so willed, He could have made them all a single community. But He admits whomsoever He pleases into His Mercy. As to those given to wrong-doing, they shall have none as protector or helper. [9] (Are they so foolish that) they have chosen others rather than Allah as their protectors? Yet it is Allah Who is the Protector and Who resurrects the dead and Who has power over everything.

---

3. The word *awliyā'* (singular, *walī*) used in the text, has wide connotations. A number of beliefs and practices held by people engrossed in error have been characterised in the Qur'ān as "taking other protectors beside Allah." According to the Qur'ān, one who is considered to be a *walī* is: [1] he who is obeyed in all matters, whose instructions are carried out, whose life-styles, customs, rules and laws are followed; [2] he in whose guidance someone has full faith, and who will guide the person to the right path and protect him from erroneous ways; [3] he who is right and will save others from error and protect them from the evil consequences of their ill deeds in the world, and from the torment of God in the Hereafter if God and Hereafter are a reality; and [4] he about whom someone believes that he will come to his aid in worldly matters in supernatural ways, will protect him from calamities and afflictions, will secure jobs for him, bless him with children, and fulfil all of his needs and desires.

[10] The judgement on whatever you differ rests with Allah.[4] Such is Allah, my Lord; in Him I have put all my trust and to Him I always turn in devotion. [11] The Originator of the heavens and the earth, He has appointed for you pairs of your own kind, and pairs also of cattle. Thus does He multiply you. Naught in the universe is like Him. He is All-Hearing, All-Seeing. [12] His are the keys of the heavens and the earth. He enlarges and straitens the sustenance of whomsoever He pleases. Surely He has knowledge of everything.

[13] He has prescribed for you the religion which He enjoined upon Noah and which We revealed to you (O Muḥammad), and which We enjoined upon Abraham and Moses and Jesus, commanding: "Establish this religion and do not split up regarding it." What you are calling to is very hard upon those who associate others with Allah in His Divinity. Allah chooses for Himself whomsoever He pleases and guides to Himself whoever penitently turns to Him.

[14] They did not split up except after knowledge had come to them, and then only because they wished to commit excesses against each other. Had your Lord not already decreed that judgement would be made later at an appointed time, the matter between them would surely

---

4. Although from the present verse until the end of verse 12, the whole discourse is God's revelation, it is as if it is articulated by God's Messenger. To put it differently, it is God Who asked the Prophet (peace be on him) to declare all this on His behalf. In this regard, there is a striking resemblance between this and *Sūrah al-Fātiḥah*. For it is God's Own Words which are couched in the form of a supplication to God by His servants.

have been decided once and for all. Indeed those who were later made the heirs of the Book are in disquieting doubt about it.[5]

[15] (This being so, O Muḥammad), call people to the same religion and be steadfast about it as you were commanded, and do not follow their desires, and say (to them): "I believe in the Book Allah has sent down. I have been commanded to establish justice among you. Allah is our Lord and your Lord. We have our deeds and you have your deeds. There is no contention between us and you.[6] Allah will bring us all together. To Him all are destined to return."

[16] Those who contend concerning Allah (after His call has been responded to), their contention is absolutely void in the sight of their Lord. Allah's wrath is upon them and a grievous chastisement awaits them.

[17] Allah it is Who sent down this Book with the Truth and the Balance.[7] And what would make you know that

---

5. The later generations that followed the Prophets were not fully confident as to what extent the scriptures had remained free from tampering. They were not sure as to what the teachings of their Prophets exactly were; in fact, everything has become subject to doubt and appears perplexing.

6. That is, God did not spare any means to explain His Message along with its supporting evidence. Hence, even if the unbelievers were to engage in contentious argument, the believers should abstain from it.

7. *Mīzān* (Balance) here denotes God's *sharīʿah*. Like a balance it enables one to distinguish between right and wrong, between truth and falsehood, justice and injustice, and righteousness and wickedness.

the Hour (of Judgement) has drawn near? [18] Those who do not believe in it seek to hasten its coming. But those who believe (in it) hold it in dread and know that the Hour (of Judgement) is bound to come. Lo, those who dispute concerning the coming of the Hour are gone far in error.

[19] Allah is Most Gentle to His servants and grants sustenance to whomsoever He pleases. He is All-Strong, Most Mighty. [20] Whoever seeks the harvest of the Hereafter, We shall increase for him his harvest, and whoever seeks the harvest of this world, We shall give him thereof; but he will have no share in the Hereafter.

[21] Do they have any associates (of Allah) who have laid down for them a way pertaining to faith which Allah did not sanction?[8] But for the fact that a decree had already been made, the matter between them would have been decided once and for all. Surely a grievous chastisement awaits the wrong-doers. [22] You will see the wrong-doers fearful of the consequence of their deeds which will certainly overtake them. But those who have faith and

---

8. In this verse the word *shurakā'* (associates of Allah) does not denote beings to whom people address their prayers, or to whom they make offerings, or those to whom their rites of worship are devoted. Instead, it denotes those whom people regard as associates in God's sovereign authority. These are the ones whose ideas and beliefs, ideologies and philosophies people embrace, whose values they recognise as true, whose moral principles, civilization and culture they accept as normative, and whose laws, rules and regulations they adhere to religiously in their practices and rites of worship, in their personal and social lives, in their trade and commerce, in their politics and government as if these were God's Law which they were necessarily required to follow.

do good deeds will be in the meadows of the Gardens,
wherein they shall have whatever they desire from their
Lord; that is the great Bounty. [23] That is the Bounty of
which Allah gives tidings to His servants who have faith
and do good deeds. Tell them, (O Prophet): "I do not ask
you for any recompense for my work except love towards
kinsfolk."⁹ Whoever does a good deed, We shall increase
its merit for him. Surely Allah is Most Forgiving, Most
Appreciative.

---

9. This verse has been interpreted in three ways: [1] That the
Prophet (peace be on him) did not expect any reward from them
for the service he rendered. Instead, he only expected them to show
some regard for the tie of kinship in which they and the Prophet
(peace be on him) were bound. What a pity that the Quraysh not
only showed no consideration for that tie, but acted with enmity.
[2] That the Prophet (peace be on him) did not seek any recompense
for his service except that he wanted his people to develop the
longing to acquire nearness to God. [3] According to some Qur'ānic
commentators, the word "kinsfolk" here refers to all the children of
'Abd al-Muṭṭalib. Others hold the view that "kinsfolk" is confined
to 'Alī and Fāṭimah. This view, however, is not acceptable for a
number of reasons. First, at the time when this *Sūrah* was revealed
in Makkah, 'Alī and Fāṭimah had not yet been joined together by
wedlock and hence the question of their children could not have
arisen. As for the children of 'Abd al-Muṭṭalib, not all of them
followed the Prophet (peace be on him); in fact, some had openly
joined the ranks of his enemies. In this regard, the enmity of Abū
Lahab is all too well known. Second, the "kinsfolk" of the Prophet
(peace be on him) were not only the children of 'Abd al-Muṭṭalib,
but he also had ties with other families of the Quraysh through his
mother and father, and his wife, Khadījah. In all these different clans
the Prophet (peace be on him) had some of his best supporters as
well as his staunchest enemies. Third – and this is most important
of all – in keeping with the high pedestal from which a Prophet
embarks on his mission to call people to God, it does not seem

[24] Do they say: "He has forged a lie against Allah?" If Allah so wanted He could seal up your heart.[10] Allah blots out falsehood and confirms the truth by His Words. He is well aware of all the secrets hidden in the breasts (of people). [25] He it is Who accepts repentance from His servants and forgives sins and knows all what you do, [26] and answers the prayers of those who believe and do good deeds and bestows upon them even more out of His Bounty. As for those who deny (the Truth), a grievous chastisement awaits them.

[27] If Allah were to grant ample sustenance to His servants they would go about transgressing in the land. But He sends down in due measure whatever (sustenance) He

---

befitting that he should ask people to love his kinsfolk in return for the services he renders in connection with his noble mission. It seems inconsistent with good taste that God should have taught His Prophet to publicly ask the Quraysh for something as undignified and lowly as this. Moreover, what makes it even more unlikely for the Prophet (peace be on him) to have said so is that this request is not addressed to the believers but rather to the unbelievers. This is evident from the context because the whole of this discourse, from beginning to end, is addressed to them. Thus, there was no occasion for the Prophet (peace be on him) to ask the unbelievers for this kind of reward. For reward can only be expected from those who have any appreciation for the services that that person has rendered.

10. This means that the opponents seemed to believe that the Prophet (peace be on him) was someone of their ilk. Since they were in the habit of uttering huge lies to promote their interests they perceived that the Prophet (peace be on him) would do the same to achieve worldly success. They further thought that God had been clement to the Prophet (peace be on him) so that unlike what He did to the unbelievers, He did not seal up his heart.

wills. Surely He is Well-Aware and All-Seeing concerning matters that relate to His servants. [28] He it is Who sends down the rain after they despair of it, spreading out His Mercy. He is the Protector, the Immensely Praiseworthy. [29] And of His Signs is the creation of the heavens and the earth and the living creatures that He has spread out in them. He has the power to bring them together when He so wills. [30] Whatever misfortune befalls you is a consequence of your own deeds.[11] But much of it He forgives. [31] You cannot frustrate Him in the earth; you have no protector nor helper against Allah. [32] And of His Signs are the ships that sail in the sea like mountains. [33] If He so wills, He can cause the winds to become still so that they will remain motionless on its surface. Surely there are many Signs in this for those who are wont to be steadfast and give thanks. [34] He may, while forgiving much of the sins of those that ride these ships, drown them on account of some of their misdeeds. [35] Then those who wrangle about Our Signs will come to know that there is no escape for them.

[36] That which has been given to you is only the wherewithal of the transient life of this world. But that which is with Allah is better and more enduring for those who believe and put their trust in their Lord; [37] who eschew grave sins and shameful deeds, and whenever they are angry, forgive; [38] who obey their Lord and establish Prayer; who conduct their affairs by

---

11. "Misfortune" here alludes to the famine which had afflicted Makkah at that time.

consultation, and spend out of what We have bestowed upon them; [39] who, when a wrong is done to them, seek its redress. [40] The recompense of evil is evil the like of it.[12] But he who forgives and makes amends, his reward lies with Allah. Surely He does not love the wrong-doers. [41] There is no blame against him who avenges himself after he has been wronged. [42] Blame attaches only to those who subject people to wrong and commit excesses on earth. A painful chastisement awaits them. [43] But he who patiently endures and forgives, that is a conduct of great resolve.

[44] He whom Allah lets go astray, none after Him can be his protector. You will see that when the wrong-doers observe the chastisement, they will exclaim: "Is there any way to go back?" [45] You shall see them, as they are brought face to face with the chastisement, in a state of abject humiliation, looking with a furtive glance. But the believers will say: "Surely the true losers are they who lose themselves and their kindred on the Day of Resurrection." Lo, the wrong-doers will be in an enduring torment. [46] They shall have no protectors to help them against Allah. For he whom Allah causes to go astray will have no way to save himself.

[47] Accept the command of your Lord before there comes a Day from Allah that cannot be averted. On that Day there shall be no shelter for you, and none may change

---

12. The passage from here until verse 43 is an explanation of verse 39.

your predicament.[13] [48] (O Prophet), if they turn away from the Truth, know that We did not send you to them as their overseer. Your task is only to convey (the Message). Indeed when We give man a taste of Our Mercy, he exults in it. But if any misfortune afflicts them on account of their deeds, man is utterly ungrateful.

[49] The dominion of the heavens and the earth belongs to Allah. He creates whatever He pleases. He grants females to whomever He pleases and males to whomever He pleases, [50] or grants them a mix of males and females, and causes whomever He pleases to be barren. He is All-Knowing, All-Powerful.

[51] It is not given to any human being that Allah should speak to him except through revelation,[14] or from behind a veil,[15] or that a messenger [i.e., an angel] be sent to him

---

13. These words mean several other things as well. First, that the unbelievers will be unable to disown any of their deeds. Second, that they will not be able to take shelter by disguising themselves. Third, that they will be in no position to protest or express their displeasure at the treatment that will be meted out to them. Fourth, that they will not have the power to change the condition to which they will be subjected.

14. *Waḥy* (revelation) here means to inspire someone with something, or to show something to someone in a vision as happened in the case of the Prophets Abraham and Joseph.

15. That is, one may hear a voice without observing the speaker just as it happened to the Prophet Moses when he suddenly heard a voice from a tree on Mount Sinai, while the Speaker remained hidden from sight.

who reveals to him by Allah's leave whatever He wishes.[16] He is All-High, Most Wise. [52] Even so We revealed to you, (O Prophet), a spirit by Our command.[17] (Ere to that) you knew neither what the Book nor what the faith was. But We made that spirit a light whereby We guide those of Our servants whom We please to the Right Way. Surely you are directing people to the Right Way, [53] the Way of Allah, to Whom belongs the dominion of all that is in the heavens and the earth. Lo, it is to Allah that all things ultimately revert.

16. This is the form of *wahy* in which all the scriptures have been communicated to God's Prophets.

17. "Even so" does not only refer to the last form of *wahy* mentioned here, but to all the three forms mentioned above. As for the word "spirit" it means *wahy* (revelation) or the teaching that was communicated to the Prophet (peace be on him) by means of revelation.

43
᪥

Al-Zukhruf [Ornaments]
Makkan Period

In the name of Allah, the Most Merciful,
the Most Compassionate

[1] *Ḥā'. Mīm.* [2] By the Clear Book; [3] verily We have made it an Arabic Qur'ān that you may understand.[1] [4] Indeed it is transcribed in the Original Book[2] with Us; sublime and full of wisdom.

[5] Should We divert this Good Counsel from you because you are a people immersed in extravagance? [6] How many a Prophet did We send to the earlier peoples! [7] Yet never did a Prophet come to them but they mocked him. [8] We utterly destroyed them although they were greater

---

1. The object of the Qur'ānic oath is to affirm that God Himself is the Author of this Book rather than Muḥammad (peace be on him). Moreover, the attribute of the Qur'ān chosen for the oath is its perspicacity. To swear by the Qur'ān with mention of this attribute means to give the following message to the people: "O people, this is an open Book before you. Read it with open eyes. Its themes, its teachings, its language, its diction, are all clear proofs of the fact that none but the Lord of the universe is the Author of this Book."

2. "*Umm al-Kitāb*" means the "Original Book," one that is the prime source of all the Books sent down to the Prophets. In *Sūrah al-Burūj* (85: 22) this is described as *Lawḥ Maḥfūẓ* ("the Preserved Tablet"), that is, the Tablet containing inscriptions that cannot suffer effacement, those that are secure against every sort of tampering.

in might than these. The examples of ancient peoples have gone before.

[9] Yet if you were to ask them: "Who created the heavens and the earth?" they will certainly say: "The All-Mighty, the All-Knowing has created them." [10] He it is Who made this earth for you a cradle and made in it pathways for you³ that you may find the way to your destination; [11] He Who sent down water from the sky in a determined measure, and thereby We revived a dead land: likewise will you be raised up (from the earth) – [12] He Who created these pairs, all of them, and provided you ships and cattle on which you ride, [13] so that when you are mounted upon them you may remember the bounty of your Lord, and say: "Glory be to Him Who has subjected this to Us whereas we did not have the strength to subdue it. [14] It is to our Lord that we shall eventually return."

[15] Yet they have made some of His servants a part of Him. Indeed man is most evidently thankless.

[16] Has Allah taken for Himself daughters out of those whom He creates and has chosen you to have sons? [17] (They believe so although when) any of them is given

---

3. The passes in the mountains and the rivers in the mountainous and plain regions are the natural paths which God has created on the surface of the earth. It is by traversing these paths that human beings have spread over the earth. But God's favour was not confined to this: He did not stamp the whole world with a dull uniformity; instead, He created many landmarks by which people can distinguish between one region and another.

tidings of the birth of a female child the like of which he assigns to the Merciful One, his countenance darkens and he is choked with grief. [18] Do they assign to Allah one who grows up amidst ornaments and is not well-versed in the art of disputation?

[19] They claim that angels, who are Allah's chosen servants, are females. Did they witness how their body is constituted? Their testimony shall be written and they shall be called to account.

[20] They say: "Had the Merciful One so willed, we would never have worshipped these deities."[4] But they have no knowledge of the matter and are simply conjecturing. [21] Or did We bestow upon them a Book before on whose authority they are holding on (to angel-worship)? [22] Nay; they simply claim: "We found our forefathers on a way, and we continue to find guidance in their footsteps." [23] And thus it is: whenever We sent any warner to a city its affluent ones said: "We found our forefathers on a way and we continue to follow in their footsteps." [24] Each Prophet asked them: "Will you do so even if we were to show you a way better than the way of your forefathers?" They answered: "We disbelieve in the religion with which you have been sent." [25] Then We exacted retribution from them. So do consider the end of those who gave the lie (to the Prophets).

---

4. This was the rationale of their straying: that if they had strayed it could not be otherwise, for, after all, that was God's predetermined will. It is significant that those given to erroneous ways have always been wont to put faith in this line of argument.

[26] Call to mind when Abraham said to his father and his people: "I totally disown all whom you serve [27] except the One Who created me; and, behold, it is He Who will direct me to the Right Way." [28] And Abraham left behind this word to endure among his posterity so that they may return to it.[5] [29] (Even when they began worshipping others than Allah We did not destroy them) but bestowed sustenance on them and on their forefathers until there came to them the Truth and a Messenger who clearly expounded things to them. [30] And when the Truth came to them they said: "This is just sorcery and we reject it."

[31] They say: "Why was this Qur'ān not sent down upon some great man from the two (main) cities?"[6] [32] Is it they who distribute the Mercy of your Lord? It is We Who have distributed their livelihood among them in the life of this world, and have raised some above others in rank that some of them may harness others to their

---

5. That is: "Whenever they deviate even a little from the Right Path, this 'Word' should be there to guide them so that they find their way back to it." This event is mentioned here in order to arouse a sense of shame among the Quraysh unbelievers. The thrust of the statement is: "When you decided to follow in the steps of your ancestors, you did not opt to follow the good ones, the likes of the Prophets Abraham and Ishmael. Instead, amongst them that you chose to follow were those that were evil to the core."

6. "The two cities" mentioned here signify Makkah and Ṭā'if. What the unbelievers meant by saying so was that had God really wanted to raise a Messenger and send down a Book to him, He would have selected some truly distinguished person from their major cities.

service. Your Lord's Mercy is better than all the treasures that they hoard. [33] Were it not that all mankind would become a single community (and follow the same way), We would have provided for all those who disbelieve in the Merciful One silver roofs for their houses, and (silver) stairs on which to go up, [34] and (silver) doors to their houses, and couches (of silver) upon which they would recline; [35] or that they be made of gold. Surely all this is only the enjoyment of the life of the world. But (true prosperity) in the Hereafter with Your Lord is only for the God-fearing.

[36] He who is negligent to remember the Merciful One, to him We assign a satan as his boon companion, [37] and these satans hinder them from the Right Path, while he still reckons himself to be rightly-guided. [38] But when he comes to Us, he will say (to his satan): "Would that there had been between me and you the distance as between the East and the West. How evil a companion you were!" [39] (He will then be told): "Today it will not benefit you the least that after your wrong-doing you and your satans now share the chastisement."

[40] Can you, (O Prophet), then make the deaf hear, or direct to the Right Way the blind or one lost in manifest error? [41] We shall inflict retribution on them, whether We take you away from the world (before We do that), [42] or make you see the end that We had promised them, for We have full power over them. [43] So hold fast to what has been revealed to you. Surely you are on the Straight Way. [44] Verily it is a great source of eminence for you and your people, and soon you will be called to

account concerning that.[7] [45] Ask all Our Messengers whom We sent before you whether We had appointed any deities beside the Merciful One to be worshipped.[8]

[46] Indeed We sent Moses with Our Signs to Pharaoh and his nobles. He told them: "I am a Messenger of the Lord of the Universe." [47] Yet when he brought forth Clear Signs from Us, then lo, they burst into laughter. [48] Every Sign that We showed them was greater than its predecessor; and then We seized them with Our chastisement so that they may return (to the Right Way). [49] (Whenever they faced an affliction) they would say: "O magician, pray for us to your Lord according to your station with Him. We shall certainly be guided to the Right Way." [50] But lo, each time We removed Our affliction from them, they would go back on their word. [51] And Pharaoh proclaimed among his people: "My people, do I not have dominion over Egypt, and are these streams not flowing beneath me? Can't you see? [52] Am I better or this contemptible man who is scarcely able to express himself?

---

7. The point stressed here is that no person can have greater luck than that he should be chosen by God to receive His Book. Nor can a nation have greater luck than that it should be chosen by God to raise His Messenger among it to the exclusion of other nations, and that it should have sent down His Book in their tongue, and grant them the opportunity to rise as the standard-bearers of His Message in the world. If the Quraysh and the people of Arabia did not realise how great an honour had been conferred upon them and they were unappreciative of this, then a time will come when they will be called to account for this.

8. "Ask other Messengers" means that they should look into the Books granted to them and find out for themselves.

[53] Why were bracelets of gold not bestowed upon him? Why did a retinue of angels not accompany him as attendants?"

[54] He incited his people to levity and they obeyed him. Surely they were an iniquitous people.[9] [55] So when they incurred Our wrath, We exacted retribution from them, and drowned them all, [56] and made them a thing of the past and an example for those who would come after them.

[57] No sooner the example of the son of Mary was mentioned than, lo and behold, your people raised a clamour [58] and said: "Who is better, our deities or he?"[10] They said so only out of contentiousness. They are a disputatious people. [59] He was no more than a servant (of Ours), one upon whom We bestowed Our favours and whom We made an example (of Our infinite power) for the Children of Israel.

---

9. This short sentence epitomises a great truth. When a person acts despotically in the world and brazenly pursues this with deception and trickery, putting a price on people's conscience and mercilessly oppressing and trampling on those who refuse to sell their conscience, such people, even if they do not say so directly, nevertheless convey by their actions that they take their compatriots' intelligence, moral calibre and worth lightly, that they consider them cowards, a dumb cattle that can be driven in any direction. Eventually when their designs meet with success and the common people become their obedient slaves, this simply confirms that what he had thought was indeed true. The basic reason for their becoming victims of indignity is that they were given to sinful conduct.

10. It was said in verse 45 above that people may ask all the other Messengers who were sent before Muḥammad (peace be on him) if We had appointed any other gods to be worshipped besides the

[60] If We had so willed We could have made some of you into angels to become your successors on earth. [61] Verily he [i.e., Jesus] is a portent of the Hour. So be in no doubt concerning it[11] and follow Me. This is the Straight Way. [62] Let not Satan hinder you (from believing in the Hour), for surely he is your open enemy. [63] When Jesus came with Clear Signs and said: "I have brought wisdom to you that I may make plain to

---

OneTrue God. When this was presented before the people of Makkah, a person put forth the objection: "Is it not a fact that the Christians hold the son of Mary to be the son of God and worship him for that reason? What is wrong, then, with our gods?" No sooner was this said than loud laughter broke out among the crowd who then exerted pressure that an answer be provided to this objection.

11. This can also be translated as follows: "He is a means to the knowledge of the Resurrection." Here a question arises: In what sense has Jesus Christ been called a sign or a means of knowledge of the Resurrection? Many Qur'ānic commentators say that this refers to the second coming of the Prophet Jesus which has been foretold in a large number of traditions, but this meaning is contradicted by the very next verse. For Jesus' second coming can be a means of knowledge of Resurrection only for those who are alive at that time or are born thereafter. So how can he be regarded as a means of knowledge for the Makkan unbelievers who are being asked not to have any doubts about it? Therefore, in our opinion, the true meaning of the verse is the one given by some other Qur'ānic commentators, according to whom the Prophet Jesus' fatherless conception and his making a bird out of clay and his raising the dead back to life are presented as proof of the possibility of Resurrection. So, God's directive here would mean this: "Why do you think it is impossible for God to raise you and all mankind from death, when He can create a child without a father and a servant of His can breathe life into a clay image and raise the dead back to life?"

you some of the things you differ about. So fear Allah and follow me. [64] Allah is my Lord and your Lord; therefore, serve Him. That is the Straight Way."[12] [65] Then the factions fell apart among themselves.[13] So woe to the wrong-doers from the chastisement of a grievous Day.

[66] Are they awaiting anything other than the Last Hour that it should suddenly come upon them without their even perceiving it? [67] On that Day even bosom friends shall become enemies to one another, all except the God-fearing. [68] (It will be said to them): "My servants, today you have nothing to fear or regret, [69] you who believed in Our Signs and had surrendered yourselves (to Us)! [70] Enter Paradise joyfully, both you and your spouses." [71] Platters and cups of gold shall be passed around them, and there shall be all that they might desire and all that their eyes might delight in. (They shall be told): "Herein shall you abide for ever. [72] Such is the Paradise that

---

12. Regardless of what the Christians might have said or done, Jesus did not lay claim to being God or the son of God, nor did he ask anyone to worship him. On the contrary, he called people exactly to what the previous Prophets had called and to which the Prophet Muhammad (peace be on him) was calling, viz. to exclusively serve and worship the One True God.

13. People went to extremes both in supporting and opposing Jesus (peace be on him). Those who opposed him went so far as to blaspheme him, branding him illegitimate. At the other end of the spectrum were those who exaggerated Jesus' status and exalted him to the point of deifying him. But then the question of how a human being could also be God became extremely complicated. The result was that all subsequent efforts to solve the problem have proved futile and all attempts to resolve the issue gave rise to a number of schisms and sects.

you shall inherit by virtue of your good deeds in the life of the world. [73] Herein you will have abundant fruits of which you will eat." [74] But the evil-doers shall abide in the torment of Hell. [75] Never will their torment be lightened for them. They shall remain in utter despair. [76] It is not We Who wronged them; rather, it is they who wronged themselves. [77] They shall call out: "O Mālik,¹⁴ let your Lord put an end to us." He will reply: "You must stay on in it. [78] We brought you the Truth; but to the truth most of you were averse."¹⁵

[79] Have they contrived some scheme?¹⁶ If so, We too will contrive a scheme. [80] Or do they think that We do not hear their secret talks and their whispering counsels? Yes, indeed We do and Our messengers [i.e., angels] are with them, writing.

[81] Say: "If the Merciful One had a son, I would have been the first one to worship him." [82] Exalted be the Lord of the heavens and the earth, the Lord of the Throne, above what they attribute to Him. [83] So leave them alone to indulge in their vanities and to frolic about until they encounter that Day of theirs against which they have been warned.

---

14. Mālik, as is evident from the context, refers to the Keeper of Hell.

15. The Keeper of Hell's statement that "We brought you the truth," resembles an official's use of the pronoun "we" when he speaks on behalf of his government.

16. This hints at the decisive plan that the chiefs of the Quraysh were preparing in their secret assemblies, a plan which aimed at doing away with the Prophet (peace be on him).

[84] He it is Who is God in the heavens and the earth. He is the Most Wise, the All-Knowing. [85] Blessed is He Who has dominion over the heavens and the earth and all that is between them. With Him is the knowledge of the Hour; and to Him you shall all be sent back.

[86] Those whom they call upon, instead of Allah have no power of intercession, except such that testify to the truth based on knowledge.[17]

[87] If you were to ask them: "Who created them?" they will surely say: "Allah."[18] Whence are they, then, being led astray? [88] We call to witness the cry of the Messenger: "O Lord, these are a people not wont to believe!"[19]

[89] Indulge them, (O Prophet), and say to them: "Peace to you." For soon they shall come to know.

---

17. Some people believe that the beings whom they themselves had made into gods possessed the power to intercede with God. They imagined that those deities too wielded such a powerful influence with God that they could secure the forgiveness of whomsoever they wanted. Hence such people are asked a simple, straightforward question: "Can they testify to the truth of that claim on the basis of sure knowledge?"

18. This verse seems to mean two things: (1) "If you were to ask them who has created them, they will say: 'Allah'." (2) "If you were to ask them who is the Creator of their gods, they will say: 'Allah'."

19. In this verse, recourse is made to swearing by the Prophet's statement: "O Lord, these are a people not wont to believe." Indeed how strange it is. These unbelievers admitted that God was the Creator of their gods. Notwithstanding this, they persisted in worshipping God's creatures rather than God Himself.

44
꧁꧂

Al-Dukhān [Smoke]
Makkan Period

In the name of Allah, the Most Merciful,
the Most Compassionate

[1] *Ḥā'. Mīm.* [2] By the Clear Book. [3] We revealed it on a Blessed Night,¹ for We were intent on warning; [4] (We revealed it on the Night) wherein every matter is wisely determined [5] by Our command.² Verily, We were set to send a Messenger [6] as a Mercy from your Lord. Surely He is All-Hearing, All-Seeing, [7] the Lord of the heavens and the earth and of all that is between them: if you would only have sure faith. [8] There is no god but He:³ He gives life and causes death. He is your Lord and the Lord of your forefathers of yore. [9] (But the fact is, they lack certainty) and frolic about in doubt.

---

1. The expression "blessed night" here denotes *Laylat al-Qadr,* the Night of Glory. (See *al-Qadr* 97: 1.)

2. This indicates that this is an extraordinary night under God's sovereign dispensation. This is the night in which He decides the fate of different individuals, nations and countries and entrusts them to His angels for execution.

3. That is, the true deity to whom alone every kind of service and worship ought to be rendered.

[10] So watch for the Day when the sky will come down with a pall of smoke, [11] enveloping people. That will be a grievous scourge. [12] (People will then say): "Our Lord, remove this scourge from us; we shall believe."[4] [13] But how will they take heed? Such are they that a Messenger came to them clearly expounding the Truth,[5] [14] yet they turned away from him and said: "This is a well-tutored madman." [15] Yet We will hold the scourge back for a while, (but no sooner than We will do so) you will revert to your old ways. [16] The Day when We shall seize them with a mighty seizing, that will be the Day on which We shall inflict upon you full retribution.

[17] Indeed before that We subjected the Pharaonites to the same test. A noble Messenger came to them [18] (and said): "Deliver to me Allah's servants. I am a trustworthy Messenger to you, [19] and do not exalt yourselves in defiance of Allah. I have come to you with a clear authority (as a Messenger). [20] I have taken refuge with my Lord and your Lord lest you should attack me with stones. [21] But if you do not believe what I say, leave me alone (and desist from laying hands on me)." [22] Then he called upon his Lord: "These are a criminal people." [23] (He was told): "Set out with My servants by night for you will certainly be pursued. [24] And leave the sea behind you

---

4. The word "scourge" in these verses (i.e. 11 and 12) alludes to the scourge of the Hereafter, whereas "the mighty seizing" mentioned in verse 16, alludes to the famine that had struck Makkah at the time of this *sūrah*'s revelation.

5. That is, a Messenger whose Messengership was self-evident in every possible manner.

as calm as ever. Surely they are an army that is doomed to be drowned." [25] How many gardens did they leave behind, and how many fountains [26] and sown fields and splendid mansions, [27] and the life of ease in which they took delight! [28] Thus it was; and We made another people inherit all that. [29] Then neither the sky shed tears over them nor the earth. They were granted no respite. [30] Thus did We deliver the Children of Israel from the humiliating chastisement, [31] from Pharaoh who was most prominent among the prodigals. [32] We knowingly exalted them (i.e., the Children of Israel) above other peoples of the world [33] and bestowed upon them the Signs wherein lay an evident test for them.

[34] Indeed these people say: [35] "This is our first and only death, and we shall never be raised again. [36] Bring back to us our fathers if you are truthful." [37] Are these better or the people of Tubbaʿ,⁶ and those who went before them? We destroyed them for they were a criminal people. [38] It was not in idle sport that We created the heavens and the earth and all that is between them. [39] We did not create them except in Truth. But most of them do not know. [40] The Day of Final Decision is the appointed time for all; [41] the Day when a friend shall be of no avail to his friend nor shall they be helped, [42] except those to whom Allah shows mercy. He is the Most Mighty, the Most Compassionate.

---

6. Tubbaʿ was the title of the kings of the Ḥimyar tribe. This was similar to the titles of Chosroes, Caesar, Pharaoh, i.e., which were chosen by the sovereigns of various countries. The Ḥimyar had descended from a branch of Sabaʾ and continued to rule over Arabia for many centuries.

[43] The tree of al-Zaqqūm [44] shall be the food of the sinful. [45] Like dregs of oil, it will boil in their bellies [46] like boiling water. [47] "Seize him and drag him to the middle of the Blazing Fire, [48] then pour boiling water over his head as chastisement. [49] Taste this, you are a person mighty and noble! [50] This is what you used to doubt."

[51] Verily the God-fearing shall be in a secure place [52] amidst gardens and springs. [53] Attired in silk and brocade, they shall be arrayed face to face. [54] Thus shall it be: and We shall espouse them to fair, wide-eyed maidens. [55] While resting in security, they shall call for all kinds of fruit. [56] They shall not taste death except the death in this world. And Allah will save them from the chastisement of Hell [57] as a favour from your Lord. That is the great triumph.

[58] (O Prophet), We have made this Book easy in your tongue so that they may take heed. [59] Wait, then; they too are waiting.

45

Al-Jāthiyah [Kneeling]
Makkan Period

*In the name of Allah, the Most Merciful,
the Most Compassionate*

[1] *Ḥā'. Mīm.* [2] This Book is a revelation from the Most Mighty, the Most Wise.

[3] Behold, for those who believe there are (myriad) Signs in the heavens and the earth [4] and in your own creation; and in the animals which He spreads out over the earth too there are Signs for those endowed with sure faith; [5] and in the succession of night and day, and in the provision that Allah sends down from the sky wherewith He gives life to the earth after it had been lifeless, and in the change of the winds: (in all these) there are Signs for people who use reason. [6] These are Allah's Signs that We rehearse to you in Truth. In what kind of discourse after Allah and His Signs will they, then, believe?

[7] Woe to every guilty impostor [8] who hears Allah's Signs being rehearsed to him, and yet persists in his pride, as though he had not heard it. Announce to him, then, the tidings of a grievous chastisement. [9] Whenever he comes to know anything of Our Signs, he makes them an object of jest. For such there awaits a humiliating chastisement. [10] Hell is behind them. Their worldly earnings shall not avail them, nor those whom they took as protectors

instead of Allah. An awesome chastisement lies in store for them.

[11] This (Qur'ān) is the true guidance. Those who deny the Signs of their Lord shall suffer the torment of a woeful scourge.

[12] Allah it is Who has subjected the sea to you so that ships may sail upon it at His bidding and you may seek of His Bounty and give thanks to Him. [13] He has subjected to you all that is in the heavens and the earth, all being from Him.[1] Verily there are Signs in this for those who reflect.

[14] (O Prophet), tell the believers to indulge those who have no fear of any evil days coming upon them from Allah so that Allah may Himself requite them for their deeds. [15] Whoever acts righteously, does so to his own good; and whoever commits an evil will suffer its consequence. All of you will then be sent back to your Lord.

---

1. This has two meanings. First, that the bounties which God bestows on humans is unlike the bounties bestowed by kings and rulers of the world. The latters' bounties, in any case, consist of their granting the wealth which they have wrested from their own subjects to a few chosen persons. On the other hand, the bounties that God grants to His creatures, were all created by Him. None has had any share in either creating these bounties nor in harnessing them to man's use. God alone is their Creator and He alone has granted them to man on His behalf.

[16] Indeed We endowed the Children of Israel with the Book and Wisdom and Prophethood, and provided them with good things as sustenance, and exalted them above the peoples of the whole world. [17] We gave them clear directions in matters pertaining to religion. Yet they differed among themselves (not out of ignorance but) after knowledge had come to them; and they did so out of the desire to commit excesses against one another. On the Day of Resurrection Allah will judge among them regarding what they had differed. [18] And then We set you, (O Prophet), on a clear high road in religious matters. So follow that and do not follow the desires of those who do not know. [19] Surely they will be of no avail to you against Allah.[2] Indeed the wrong-doers are friends of each other, whereas Allah is the friend of the God-fearing. [20] These are the lights of discernment for people and guidance and mercy for those endowed with sure faith.

[21] Do the evil-doers imagine that We shall make them equal to those who believe and do good, making their lives and deaths alike? How vile is their judgement! [22] Allah created the heavens and the earth in Truth that each person may be requited for his deeds. They shall not be wronged.

[23] Did you ever consider the case of him who took his desire as his god, and then Allah caused him to go astray

---

2. That is, "If you make any changes in God's religion merely to please these people, they will not be able to save you from accountability before and chastisement of God."

despite knowledge,[3] and sealed his hearing and his heart, and cast a veil over his sight? Who, after Allah, can direct him to the Right Way? Will you not take heed?

[24] They say: "There is no life other than our present worldly life: herein we live and we die, and it is only (the passage of) time that destroys us. Yet the fact is that they know nothing about this and are only conjecturing. [25] And when Our Clear Signs are rehearsed to them, their only contention is: "Bring back to us our fathers if you are truthful." [26] Tell them, (O Prophet): "It is Allah Who gives you life and then causes you to die, and He it is Who will then bring all of you together on the Day of Resurrection, a Day regarding which there can be no doubt. Yet most people do not know. [27] Allah's is the kingdom of the heavens and the earth, and on the Day when the Hour (of Resurrection) shall come to pass, the followers of falsehood shall be in utter loss.

[28] On that Day you shall see every people fallen on their knees. Every people will be summoned to come forth and see its Record and will be told: "Today you shall be requited for your deeds. [29] This is Our Record which bears witness against you with truth; We used to record all what you did." [30] As for those who believe and act

---

3. The words *aḍallahu Allāh ʿalā ʿilmin* may mean either of the following. [1] That God made that person, although he was endowed with knowledge, go astray. This because he handed himself over to his lusts, so much so that he became virtually enslaved by them. [2] By dint of His knowledge God knew that this person had made his lusts his god. By way of retribution, God then caused him to go astray.

righteously, their Lord shall admit them to His Mercy. That indeed is the manifest triumph. [31] But those who denied the Truth, they shall be told: "Were My Signs not rehearsed to you? But you waxed proud and became a guilty people." [32] And when it was said to them: "Surely Allah's promise is true, and there is no doubt regarding the Hour of Resurrection," you were wont to say: "We do not know what the Hour (of Resurrection) is. We are simply making conjectures and are not at all certain." [33] (On that Day) the evil of their deeds will become apparent to them and what they had mocked at will encompass them, [34] and it will be said: "We will forget you today as you forgot the meeting of this Day of yours. The Fire shall now be your abode, and you shall have none to come to your aid. [35] You reached this end because you made Allah's Signs an object of jest and the life of the world deluded you." So they shall not be taken out of the Fire nor shall they be asked to make amends (and thus please their Lord).[4]

[36] So all praise be to Allah, the Lord of the heavens, the Lord of the earth, the Lord of the whole Universe. [37] His is the glory in the heavens and the earth. He is the Most Mighty, the Most Wise.

---

4. This last sentence seems to portray a master who has been greatly angered by their wicked behaviour. He therefore sternly rebukes them and turns to others, in effect saying: "This is the chastisement that these fellows well deserve."

46
❧❧❧

Al-Aḥqāf [The Sand Dunes]
Makkan Period

In the name of Allah, the Most Merciful,
the Most Compassionate

[1] *Ḥā'. Mīm.* [2] The revelation of this Book is from Allah, the Most Mighty, the Most Wise.

[3] We have created the heavens and the earth and all that is between them in Truth and for an appointed term. But those who disbelieve have turned away from what they were warned against.

[4] Tell them, (O Prophet): "Did you consider those whom you call upon beside Allah? Show me, which part of the earth they created? Or do they have any share in creating the heavens? Bring to me any Scripture earlier than this one, or any vestige of knowledge (in support of your belief) if you are truthful. [5] Who is farther strayed from the Right Path than he who calls upon others than Allah that cannot answer his call till the Day of Resurrection,[1] the while they are not even conscious that callers are

---

1. "… cannot answer his call till the Day of Resurrection" means that these false deities do not have the power and authority by virtue of which they can make decisions as regards the prayers and petitions of their devotees.

calling upon them? [6] When all human beings will be gathered together those who had been called upon will become the enemies to their votaries and will disown their worship.²

[7] When Our Clear Messages are rehearsed to them, the unbelievers exclaim about the Truth when it came to them: "This is plain sorcery." [8] Do they claim that the Messenger himself has fabricated it? (If so), tell them: "If I have fabricated it, then you have no power to protect me from Allah's chastisement. He knows well the idle talk in which you indulge. He suffices as a witness between me and you. He is Most Forgiving, Most Merciful."³

[9] Tell them: "I am not the first of the Messengers;⁴ and I do not know what shall be done with me or with you. I follow only what is revealed to me, and I am nothing

---

2. That is, the deities to whom people addressed their prayers will clearly say that they neither asked people to invoke them for help, nor were they aware that people so invoked them. They did so of their own accord because they assumed such deities could fulfil their needs.

3. This statement conveys two meanings: [1] It is because of God's sheer Mercy and Forgiveness that these people are able to survive in the world. This despite the fact that they declared with impunity God's Own Word as false. Had God been stern and merciless, He would not have allowed such a contumacious people to continue to exist in the world even for a moment. [2] Those steeped in wrong-doing are urged to give up their perverse obduracy. If they do so, they will still find the door to God's Mercy open for them, and their earlier misdeeds will be remitted.

4. The earlier Messengers of God were merely mortal beings who possessed no part of God's attributes and powers.

but a plain warner." [10] Tell them, (O Prophet): "Did you consider (what would be your end) if this Qur'ān were indeed from Allah and yet you rejected it? And this even though a witness from the Children of Israel has testified to the like of it. But he believed, while you waxed arrogant.[5] Verily Allah does not guide such wrong-doers to the Right Way.

[11] The unbelievers say to the believers: "If there was any good in this Book, others would not have beaten us to its acceptance."[6] But since they have not been guided to it, they will certainly say: "This is an old fabrication." [12] Yet before this the Book was revealed to Moses as a guide and a mercy. This Book, which confirms it, is in the Arabic tongue to warn the wrong-doers and to give good tidings to those who do good. [13] Surely those who said: "Our Lord is Allah" and then remained steadfast shall have nothing to fear nor to grieve. [14] They are the people of Paradise. They shall remain in it forever as a reward for their deeds.

---

5. The word "witness" here does not refer to any specific individual but to an ordinary Israelite. The purpose of the statement is to stress that the Qur'ān was not expounding a teaching which could be discarded under the pretext of it being a novelty. In essence, the same teaching was earlier conveyed by means of Revelation. Thus the same teaching was in the Torah, to guide the Israelites, and in other scriptures. Hence as far as the substance of Qur'ānic teaching is concerned, every Israelite subscribes to it.

6. What they meant by saying so is that it is only a few empty-headed people who chose to believe in the Qur'ān. Had believing in it been something truly good, people would have brooked no delay in embracing it.

[15] We have enjoined man to be kind to his parents. In pain did his mother bear him and in pain did she give birth to him. The carrying of the child to his weaning is a period of thirty months. And when he is grown to full maturity and reaches the age of forty, he prays: "My Lord, dispose me that I may give thanks for the bounty that You have bestowed upon me and my parents, and dispose me that I may do righteous deeds that would please You, and also make my descendants righteous. I repent to You, and I am one of those who surrender themselves to You." [16] Such are those from whom We accept their best deeds and whose evil deeds We overlook. They will be among the people of Paradise in consonance with the true promise made to them. [17] But he who says to his parents: "Fie on you! Do you threaten me that I shall be resurrected, although myriad generations have passed away before me (and not one of them was resurrected)?" The parents beseech Allah (and say to their child): "Woe to you, have faith. Surely Allah's promise is true." But he says: "All this is nothing but fables of olden times."

[18] It is against such that Allah's sentence (of punishment) has become due. They will join the communities of humans and *jinn* that have preceded them. Verily all of them will court utter loss. [19] Of these all have ranks according to their deeds so that Allah may fully recompense them for their deeds. They shall not be wronged. [20] And on the Day when the unbelievers will be exposed to the Fire, they will be told: "You have exhausted your share of the bounties in the life of the world, and you took your fill of enjoyments. So, degrading chastisement shall be yours on this Day for you waxed arrogant in the earth without justification and acted iniquitously."

[21] Recount to them the story of (Hūd), the brother of (the tribe of) ʿĀd. Hūd warned his people beside the sand-dunes – and there have been other warners before him and since his time – saying: "Serve none but Allah. Verily I fear that the chastisement of an awesome day shall come upon you." [22] They said: "Have you come to us to turn us away from our gods? Then, bring upon us the scourge that you threaten us with. Do so if you are truthful." [23] He replied: "Allah alone knows about this.[7] I only convey to you the Message that I have been sent with. But I see that you are an ignorant people." [24] When they saw the scourge advancing towards their valleys, they said: "This is a cloud that will bring much rain to us." "By no means;[8] it is what you had sought to hasten – a wind-storm bearing a grievous chastisement [25] that will destroy everything by the command of its Lord." Thereafter nothing was left to be seen except their dwellings. Thus do We requite the wrong-doers. [26] We had established them firmly in a manner We have not established you. We had given them ears and eyes and hearts. But nothing availed them – neither their ears, nor their eyes, nor their hearts, for they denied the Signs of Allah. Then what they had mocked at encompassed them.

---

7. The knowledge as regards when someone will be subjected to chastisement and when they will be granted respite.

8. There is no indication as to who gave this answer. The tenor of the statement, however, seems to suggest that the answer was given by the actual circumstances obtaining at the time. ʿĀd had fancied that a cloud was advancing in their direction to bring them ample rain. In actual fact, it was a wind-storm speedily advancing towards them which was destined to utterly destroy them.

[27] Surely We destroyed many a town around you. We sent Our Messages to them repeatedly and in diverse forms that they may eschew (their evil ways) and return (to Allah). [28] So why did those whom they had set up as gods apart from Allah, hoping that they would bring them nearer to Him, not come to their aid?[9] Instead, they failed them. This was the end of the lie they had fabricated and the false beliefs they had invented.

[29] And call to mind when We sent to you a party of the *jinn* that they may listen to the Qur'ān.[10] When they

---

9. Initially there developed among the ʿĀd a devotion to pious personages under the belief that they were God's chosen ones and through them they could attain nearness to God. However, the ʿĀd gradually deified these beings and began to invoke their help and pray to them. They invented the belief that these beings had the power to change their fate, and that they could answer prayers and remove afflictions. In order to bring people out of such erroneous notions, God sent His revelations to them through His Messengers, thus trying to direct them to the Truth in a variety of ways. They, however, obstinately clung to the worship of their false gods, insisting on their association with them rather than with the One True God. But when God's chastisement struck them down, where were these gods whom they had expected to remove their grievances and afflictions? Why did they not come to their assistance in their hour of need?

10. This refers to the incident that occurred during the Prophet's return journey from Ṭā'if to Makkah. The Prophet (peace be on him) was reciting the Qur'ān in Prayer when a group of *jinn* that was passing by stopped to listen to his recitation. In this connection, all traditions concur that here the *jinn* did not actually appear before the Prophet (peace be on him), nor did he feel their presence. God, however, later informed him, by means of revelation, that they had indeed come and listened to the Qur'ān.

reached the place (where you were reciting the Qur'ān), they said to one another: "Be silent (and listen)." And when the recitation ended, they went back to their people as warners. [30] They said: "Our people, We have heard a Scripture revealed after Moses, verifying the Scriptures revealed before it; it guides to the Truth and to the Straight Way.[11] [31] Our people, respond to the call of him who calls you to Allah and believe in him. Allah will forgive your sins and will protect you from a grievous chastisement." [32] And he who does not respond to the one who calls to Allah will not be able to frustrate Him on earth, nor will they have anyone to protect them from Allah. Such people are in manifest error.

[33] Do they not see that Allah, Who created the heavens and the earth – and creating them did not wear Him out – has the power to bring the dead back to life? Why not! He certainly has the power over everything. [34] On the Day when the unbelievers will be brought within sight of the Fire, they will be asked: "Is this not the Truth?" and they will answer "Yes, by Our Lord (this is the Truth)." Allah will say: "Then suffer the chastisement as a requital for your disbelieving."

---

11. This shows that these *jinn* already believed in the Prophet Moses and the Scriptures. After hearing the Qur'ān, they felt that it expounded the same teachings that the Prophets of yore had expounded. They were, therefore, persuaded instantly to believe in this Book and also in the Prophet who brought it.

[35] So bear with patience, (O Prophet), even as the Messengers endowed with firmness of resolve (before you) bore with patience, and do not be hasty in their regard. The Day when they see what they had been warned against they will feel as though they had remained in the world no more than an hour of a day. (The Truth has been conveyed.) Will any, then, suffer perdition except those who disobey?

47

Muḥammad
Madīnan Period

In the name of Allah, the Most Merciful,
the Most Compassionate

[1] Allah has caused the works of those who disbelieve and hinder people from the way of Allah to go to waste. [2] As for those who attained to faith and did righteous works and believed in what was revealed to Muḥammad – which indeed is the Truth from their Lord – Allah has remitted their evil deeds and has set their condition right. [3] That is because those who disbelieved followed falsehood whereas those who believed followed the Truth that came to them from their Lord. Thus does Allah set forth to people parables showing their true state.

[4] When you meet the unbelievers (in battle), smite their necks until you have crushed them, then bind your captives firmly; thereafter (you are entitled to) set them free, either by an act of grace, or against ransom, until the war ends.¹ That is for you to do. If Allah had so willed,

---

1. The actual words of this verse as well as the context of their occurrence indicate that the verse was revealed during the period when sanction had been given for fighting but before it actually took place. The words "when you meet the unbelievers (in battle)…" imply that the battle had not yet taken place and the Muslims

He would have Himself exacted retribution from them. (But He did not do so) that He may test some of you by means of others.² As for those who are slain in the way of Allah, He shall never let their works go to waste. [5] He will guide them³ and set their condition right [6] and will admit them to Paradise with which He has acquainted them.

[7] Believers, if you aid Allah, He will come to your aid⁴ and will plant your feet firmly. [8] As to those who disbelieve, perdition lies in store for them and Allah has reduced

---

are being directed as to what to do when it does take place. If the encounter were to take place, the Muslims are required to focus their attention on totally destroying the enemy's fighting prowess. Once that task had been accomplished, they may free the prisoners of war either by taking ransom from them or exchanging them for the Muslim prisoners held by the unbelievers. Additionally, they were required to treat such prisoners with due kindness while they are in their custody or release them gratuitously if that was deemed suitable.

2. That is, if Allah had only wanted to suppress the votaries of falsehood, He was in need of their help. He could have achieved this in the twinkling of an eye by means of an earthquake or a tempest. But He had a different purpose in mind: He wanted the devotees of the Truth to enter into conflict with the worshippers of falsehood and strive against them. This in order that the qualities possessed by the two groups would manifest themselves fully in the course of the test to which they would be put. This would then establish the rank and position to which each of them was entitled in consideration of character and conduct.

3. That is, guide them to Paradise.

4. "If you aid Allah" means to participate in the effort to exalt the Word of God and the Truth.

their works to nought. [9] That was because they were averse to what Allah had revealed; so He let their works go to waste. [10] Have they not journeyed through the land to see the end of those who went before them? Allah utterly destroyed them. These unbelievers are doomed to the same end.⁵ [11] That is because Allah is the Protector of the believers whereas the unbelievers have none to protect them. [12] Allah shall admit those who believe and do righteous works to the Gardens beneath which rivers flow. As for the unbelievers, they enjoy the pleasures of this transient life and eat as cattle eat. The Fire shall be their resort.

[13] (O Prophet), how many are the cities that had greater power than your city that drove you out?⁶ We destroyed them and there was none to protect them. [14] Then, can he, who is on a Clear Guidance from His Lord, be like him whose evil deeds have been embellished to him, and who pursued their lusts? [15] Here is the parable of Paradise which the God-fearing have been promised: in it shall be rivers of incorruptible water, rivers of milk unchanging in taste, and rivers of wine, a delight to those that drink;

---

5. This can have two meanings: [1] The devastation that overtook the unbelievers of the past was about to overtake the unbelievers who were unwilling to accept the Prophet Muhammad's Message. [2] The doom of the unbelievers will not be confined to chastisement in this world but will rather extend to the Hereafter.

6. This alludes to Makkah where the Quraysh persecuted the believers to such an extent that the Prophet (peace be on him) was virtually forced to emigrate.

and rivers of pure honey.⁷ In it they will have every kind of fruit as well as forgiveness from their Lord. Can such be like those who will abide in the Fire and will be given a boiling water to drink that will tear their bowels apart?

[16] Among them some give ear to you. But no sooner do they leave your presence than they ask those endowed with knowledge: "What is it that he said just now?"⁸ Such are those whose hearts Allah has sealed and who pursue their lusts. [17] As for those who were led to the Guidance, Allah increases them in their guidance and causes them to grow in God-fearing. [18] Are they waiting, then, for anything else than the Last Hour to suddenly come upon them? Already some of its tokens have come. But when it does actually come upon them, where will any time be left for them to take heed?

---

7. What is stated here has been explained in the *Ḥadīth*. The milk served to the people of Paradise will not have been extracted from the udders of cattle; the wine will not have been obtained by fermenting fruit; and the honey will not have been derived from the nectar of bees. These will rather flow as natural springs flow.

8. This is said in regard to the unbelievers, hypocrites and the People of the Book who refused to believe. They used to seat themselves in the gatherings around the Prophet (peace be on him). They also listened with others when the Prophet (peace be on him) taught people or when the verses of the Qur'ān were recited. However, since they were instinctively disinclined to the substance of his teachings, their listening to what was taught was of no consequence and when they departed from those gatherings they would ask one another what is it that the Prophet (peace be on him) said.

[19] Know, therefore, (O Prophet), that there is no god but Allah, and ask forgiveness for your shortcomings and also for (the shortcomings of) believing men and believing women.[9] Allah knows the places where you move about and where you dwell.

[20] The believers[10] used to say: "Why is a *sūrah* (that would ordain fighting) not revealed?" But when a definitive *sūrah* was revealed wherein fighting was mentioned, you saw that those in whose hearts there was a sickness looked at you as though they were about to faint at the approach of death. Pity on them! [21] (They keep affirming their) obedience and saying good words. But when a course of action was clearly determined, it would have been better for them if they had proved true to Allah. [22] Now, if you were to turn away, what else can be expected but that you will work corruption in the land and fly at each other's

---

9. One of the morals taught by Islam is that even if one does all one can in God's servitude and worship, one should still feel all along that this falls short of what the Lord required one to do. One should, therefore, be ever prone to recognise one's shortcomings and beseech God to forgive any dereliction of duty he owed Him. This is the underlying spirit of the prayer taught by God: "… and ask forgiveness for your shortcomings…"

10. This shows that sincere Muslims were eager that fighting be ordained. On the other hand, however, there were those who had joined the ranks of Muslims only ostensibly but were in fact not imbued with faith. For them, the injunction to fight was viewed as something that only imperilled their lives.

throats?[11] [23] It is these upon whom Allah has laid His curse: so He made them deaf and deprived them of their sight. [24] Do they, then, not reflect on the Qur'ān? Or are there locks on their hearts? [25] Certainly those who have turned their backs on the True Guidance after it became manifest to them, Satan has embellished their ways for them and has buoyed them up with false hopes. [26] This, because they said to those who are averse to the faith that Allah has revealed: "In some matters we shall obey you."[12] Allah has full knowledge of their secret parleys. [27] But how will they fare when angels will take their souls at death and will carry them, striking their faces and backs? [28] That is because they have followed a way that angered Allah, and have been averse to His good pleasure. So He reduced all their works to nought.[13]

---

11. The people concerned are hereby being told that if they shirked from defending Islam and failed to stake their lives and possessions for the sake of the reformative revolution that the Prophet (peace be on him) and his Companions were striving to bring about, then this would have very tragic consequences. If they failed, the people of Arabia would be thrown back to the conditions prevailing in the pre-Islamic Age of Ignorance when for centuries people slit each other's throats and God's earth was filled with injustice and evil-doing.

12. This refers to those who professed faith and were considered part of the Muslim body-politic, but who nevertheless continued to collaborate with Islam's enemies. Such people even promised Islam's enemies that in some matters they would follow them.

13. The word "works" here signifies the works they performed in their state of submission to Allah. Their Prayers, fasting, paying *Zakāh*, and all other acts of worship and good deeds were reckoned

[29] Or do they, in whose hearts there is a sickness, believe that Allah will not bring their failings to light? [30] If We were to so will, We could have shown them to you so that you would recognise them by their faces, and you would certainly know them by the manner of their speech. Allah knows all your deeds. [31] We shall certainly test you until We know those of you who truly strive and remain steadfast, and will ascertain about you.

[32] Those who disbelieved and barred others from Allah's Way and opposed the Messenger after the True Guidance had become manifest to them, they shall not be able to cause Allah the least harm; rather, Allah will reduce all their works to nought. [33] Believers, obey Allah and obey the Messenger and do not cause your works to be nullified.[14] [34] Verily Allah shall not forgive those

---

as righteous acts. In their case, however, these "righteous acts" were rendered void. This because they were bereft of sincerity and loyalty to God, to Islam, and to the Muslim community despite their profession to be Muslims. The fact of the matter was that despite their professed loyalty to Islam and the Muslim body-politic, they conspired with Islam's enemies for trivial worldly gain. Furthermore, as soon as there was any occasion to engage in struggle for God's sake, they took whatever possible precautionary measures they could so as to keep themselves immune from such a risk.

14. In other words, a person's deeds can be beneficial and yield good results only if he fully obeys God and His Prophet (peace be on him). But were he to deviate from this commitment to obey God and His Prophet, he loses his claim to be rewarded for what were ostensibly good deeds.

who disbelieved and barred others from Allah's Way and clung to their unbelief until their death. [35] So, be not faint-hearted and do not cry for peace.[15] You shall prevail. Allah is with you and will not bring your works to nought. [36] The life of this world is but sport and amusement. If you believe and are God-fearing, He will grant you your reward, and will not ask you for your possessions.[16] [37] If He were to ask you for your possessions and press you (in that regard), you would have grown niggardly, and Allah would have brought your failings to light. [38] Behold, you are those who are called upon to spend in Allah's Way, but some of you are niggardly. Whoever is niggardly is in fact niggardly to himself. For Allah is All-Sufficient, whereas it is you who are in need of Him. If you turn away, He will replace you by a people other than you, and they will not be like you.

---

15. The significance of the situational context in which this directive was given needs to be borne in mind. It was revealed when the Muslims consisted of no more than a few hundred *Muhājirūn* and *Anṣār* who lived in the small town of Madīnah. These upholders of Islam were confronted on the one hand by the powerful Quraysh and on the other by the unbelievers and polytheists of the whole of Arabia. Even in these difficult circumstances the believers are being told not to be faint-hearted or seek peace with their enemies. On the contrary, they should prepare themselves to risk their very lives to encounter their foes.

16. God is self-sufficient, possessed of ample resources. If God asks the believers to spend in God's cause He does so for their benefit rather than His Own.

48

Al-Fath [Victory]
Madīnan Period

In the name of Allah, the Most Merciful,
the Most Compassionate

[1] (O Prophet), surely We have granted you a clear victory[1] [2] so that Allah may forgive you your shortcomings, whether earlier or later,[2] and may complete His favours

---

1. When the believers were given the tiding of victory after the Treaty of Ḥudaybīyah, they were left wondering how that treaty could be called a "victory". This because by virtue of the treaty what the unbelievers had asked for had been granted to them. However, it soon became apparent that what could have been superficially perceived as capitulation was indeed nothing but victory for the believers.

2. If we bear in mind the context in which this occurs, it is evident that the shortcomings that God will forgive are those that were related to the struggle in which the Muslims found themselves engaged for the last nineteen years under the Prophet's leadership in order to make Islam operative and triumphant. No human being knows what these shortcomings actually were, and indeed the human intellect finds itself helpless in trying to identify any weaknesses in that struggle. But it seems that God required the highest degree of perfection from His servants during this struggle. Furthermore, it was because of the Muslims' inability to reach these high and exacting standards that they could not achieve a decisive victory against the polytheists of Arabia. What has been said here suggests that had God, in His grace, not decided to overlook such

upon you and guide you to the Straight Way,[3] [3] and that Allah may bestow upon you a mighty help. [4] He it is Who bestowed inner peace on the hearts of the believers[4] so that they may grow yet more firm in their faith. To Allah belong the legions of the heavens and the earth; Allah is All-Knowing, Most Wise. [5] (He did this) to admit the believers, both men and women, to Gardens beneath which rivers flow, wherein they shall abide, and to efface their evil deeds from them. That, in Allah's sight, is the supreme triumph. [6] (He also did this) to chastise the hypocrites, both men and women, and those who associate others in His Divinity, both men and women, and who harbour evil thoughts about Allah. They shall be afflicted with misfortune, Allah is wroth with them. He has laid His curse upon them and has prepared for them Hell. What an evil end! [7] To Allah belong the legions of the heavens and the earth. Allah is Most Mighty, Most Wise.

---

shortcomings, it would have taken a considerably longer time for the Muslims to establish their control over Arabia. But God graciously overlooked these shortcomings and opened the door to victory at Ḥudaybīyah which would have been impossible merely by dint of the Muslims' own efforts.

3. "The Straight Way" here signifies the door leading to victory and success.

4. "*Sakīnah*" (inner peace) denotes a person's mental composure and equanimity. At Ḥudaybīyah the Muslims were confronted with a great many provocations, but they maintained restraint and patience. They also displayed total faith in the Prophet's leadership. That they were able to overcome the provocations and behave with remarkable maturity represents a great favour that God had bestowed on them for even the slightest mistake on this occasion would have caused much harm to the Islamic cause.

[8] (O Prophet), We have sent you forth as a witness,[5] as a bearer of good news, and as a warner [9] so that (all of) you may all believe in Allah and His Messenger, and support him, and revere him, and celebrate Allah's glory, morning and evening.

[10] Those who swore fealty to you,[6] (O Prophet), in fact swore fealty to Allah. The Hand of Allah is above their hands.[7] So whoever breaks his covenant breaks it to his own hurt; and whoever fulfils the covenant that he made with Allah, He will bestow on him a great reward.

[11] (O Prophet), the bedouins who were left behind[8] say to you: "We were occupied with our goods and families.

---

5. Shāh Wāli Allāh has translated into Persian the word *shāhid* as "*iẓhār-i ḥaqq kunandah*," that is, "a bearer of witness to the truth."

6. This alludes to the oath at Ḥudaybīyah after a rumour was spread that 'Uthmān had been martyred in Makkah. The oath being that if 'Uthmān had indeed been martyred, the Muslims would settle their account with the Quraysh immediately even though this might lead to the annihilation of them all.

7. That is, the hand on which the Muslims were swearing fealty was God's Hand rather than simply that of the Prophet (peace be on him). Furthermore, this oath was not simply an oath of fealty to the Prophet (peace be on him) but to God Himself.

8. This refers to the people who lived on the outskirts of Madīnah and whom the Prophet (peace be on him) had asked to accompany him while making preparations for 'umrah. Those people held their lives so dear that they rarely left their homes even though they professed to be people imbued with faith. They thought that travelling to the city of the Quraysh to perform 'umrah amounted to putting themselves in the jaws of death.

So ask forgiveness for us." They say with their tongues what is not in their hearts. Say to them: "Who can be of any avail to you against Allah if He should intend to cause you any harm or confer upon you any benefit?" Allah is well aware of all that you do. [12] (But the truth is not what you say.) You had imagined that the Messenger and the believers would never return to their families, and this notion was embellished in your hearts. You harboured an evil thought, and you are an immensely evil people."

[13] As for those who do not believe in Allah and His Messenger, for such unbelievers We have prepared a Blazing Fire. [14] To Allah belongs the kingdom of the heavens and the earth. He forgives whom He pleases and chastises whom He pleases. He is Most Forgiving, Most Compassionate.

[15] When you press forth for the spoils, those who were left behind will say: "Let us accompany you."⁹ They want to change the command of Allah. Say to them (in clear words): "You shall not accompany us. Thus has Allah already said." Then they will say: "Nay; but you are jealous of us." The truth is that they understand little. [16] Say to the bedouins who were left behind: "You will be called against those who possess great might and be

---

9. This prophesies that the time was not far away when those very people who had shirked accompanying the Prophet (peace be on him) on an ostensibly risky mission would display a very different attitude when they sensed the likelihood of easy victory and an opportunity to obtain abundant booty. They would then zealously make themselves available, requesting that they should be allowed to go along.

asked to fight against them unless they surrender. If you obey (the command to fight), Allah will bestow upon you a goodly reward. But if you turn away, as you turned away before, He shall inflict upon you a grievous chastisement." [17] There is no blame on the blind, nor on the lame, nor on the sick (if they do not go forth to fight). Allah will admit those who obey Allah and His Messenger to the Gardens beneath which rivers flow and will inflict a grievous chastisement on those who turn away.

[18] Allah was much pleased with the believers when they swore fealty to you under the tree. He knew what was in their hearts. So He bestowed inner peace upon them[10] and rewarded them with a victory near at hand [19] and with abundant spoils which they shall acquire.[11] Allah is Most Mighty, Most Wise. [20] Allah has promised you abundant spoils which you shall acquire.[12] He has instantly granted you this (victory)[13] and has restrained

---

10. The word *sakīnah* (inner peace) signifies that on whose strength a man courts dangers with full peace of mind for a great cause. He undertakes the task which is essential for the achievement of the cause to which he is wedded, and this regardless of all risks and dangers he may be exposed to.

11. This alludes to the victory in the Battle of Khaybar and the spoils that they acquired on that occasion.

12. This alludes to the several other victories in quick succession that were attained by the Muslims.

13. This alludes to the Treaty of Ḥudaybīyah which is characterised as "a clear victory" at the beginning of the *sūrah* (see verse 1 above).

the hands of people from you¹⁴ that it may be a Sign for the believers and He may guide you to a Straight Way. [21] He also promises you other spoils which you have not yet taken, but Allah has encompassed them.¹⁵ Allah has power over everything.

[22] Had the unbelievers fought against you at that time, they would have turned their backs (in flight), and would have found none to protect or help them. [23] Such is Allah's Way that has come down from the past. Never shall you find any change in the Way of Allah. [24] He it is Who restrained their hands from you, and your hands from them in the valley of Makkah, even though He had made you victorious against them. Allah was watching all that you did. [25] They are the ones who disbelieved and barred you from the Inviolable Mosque and prevented the animals you had designated for sacrifice from reaching the place of their offering. If it had not been for the believing men and believing women (who lived in Makkah and) whom you did not know, and had there not been the fear that you might trample on them and unwittingly incur blame on their account, (then fighting would not have been put to a stop. It was stopped so that) Allah

---

14. That is, God did not enable the Qurayshite unbelievers to battle with the believers in Ḥudaybīyah. This was despite the fact that apparently they were in a far better position and in terms of military strength seemed to have a clear edge over the Muslims.

15. Presumably this is an allusion to the conquest of Makkah. The upshot of the statement is that even though Makkah did not fall to the Muslims, God has caused it to be surrounded from all directions. As a result of the victory of Ḥudaybīyah, that important city too would soon be theirs.

may admit to His Mercy whomsoever He pleases. Had those believers been separated from the rest, We would certainly have inflicted a grievous chastise-ment on those of them [i.e. the Makkans] who disbelieved. [16] [26] (This is why) when the unbelievers set in their hearts a fierce bigotry – the bigotry of ignorance – Allah bestowed inner peace upon His Messenger and upon the believers [17] and made the word of piety binding on them. They were more deserving and worthier thereof. Allah has knowledge of everything.

---

16. It was because of this consideration that God did not allow fighting at Ḥudaybīyah. At that time there was a considerable number of Muslims, both men and women, living in Makkah some of whom concealed their faith. There were others who were known to be believers but were utterly helpless, were subjected to fierce persecution, and so could not migrate to Madīnah. Had fighting taken place and the Muslims made their way to Makkah, these Muslims might possibly have been unwittingly killed along with the unbelievers by their fellow-Muslims. The other consideration was that God did not want Makkah to capitulate to the Muslims after a bloody conflict. Rather, He wanted to surround the Quraysh from all sides, rendering them utterly helpless within a couple of years. Thus they would be overpowered without putting up any armed resistance. This, in turn, would facilitate the embracing of Islam by the Quraysh. And this is exactly what happened after the conquest of Makkah.

17. The word *sakīnah* here signifies that patience and dignity which characterised the resistance put up by the Prophet (peace be on him) and the Muslims to the unbelievers' chauvinistic rancour. They were never provoked by their bullishness and blatant transgression; nor did they respond to their opponents' behaviour by committing any excesses or acting unrighteously, nor did they act in ways that would unnecessarily complicate matters.

[27] Allah indeed showed His Messenger the true vision, one fully in accord with reality.[18] If Allah so wills you shall certainly enter the Inviolable Mosque, in full security,[19] you will shave your heads and cut your hair short, and do so without any fear. He knew what you did not know, and He granted you a victory near at hand even before (the fulfilment of the vision).

[28] He it is Who sent His Messenger with the True Guidance and the Religion of Truth that He may make it prevail over every religion. Sufficient is Allah as a witness (to this).[20] [29] Muḥammad is Allah's Messenger, and those who are with him are firm with the unbelievers[21] but

---

18. This is the answer to a question that had often perturbed the Muslims. They tended to say: how come they had returned home without having performed *'umrah* when the Prophet (peace be on him) had seen in his vision that he was entering the Inviolable Mosque of Makkah?

19. This promise was fulfilled the following year in Dhū al-Qaʿdah 7 A.H. This *'umrah* is well known in history as *'umrat al-qaḍā'* in so far as it was performed in place of the *'umrah* that had remained incomplete.

20. There is a special reason to state this here. At the time the Treaty of Ḥudaybīyah was being committed to writing, the unbelievers made a fuss about mentioning the Prophet as the Messenger of God. It is affirmed here that his being God's Messenger was a reality regardless of its acceptance or rejection by people. God's Own testimony was sufficient to establish that, whereafter nothing else was needed.

21. The Prophet's Companions are here characterised as being "firm with the unbelievers". What this means is that the believers

compassionate with one another.[22] You see them occupied in bowing and prostrating and in seeking Allah's bounty and good pleasure. They are distinguished from others by the marks of prostration on their faces.[23] Thus are they described in the Torah. And their parable in the Gospel is that of a tilth that puts forth its shoot, then strengthens it so that it becomes stout and stands firmly on its stem. This is a sight pleasing to the sowers and one by which the unbelievers will be enraged. As for those who believe and do righteous deeds, Allah has promised them forgiveness and a great reward.

---

were not lax so that the unbelievers would be able to mould them as they liked either by winning them over or by suppressing them with force. They can neither be overawed nor tempted to change their orientation. The unbelievers simply lacked the ability to throw the believers off their course.

22. While the believers are firm and inflexible in dealing with the unbelievers, their attitude to their fellow-believers is quite different. With them they are kind, compassionate, affectionate, sympathetic and lenient. Being wedded to shared ideals and principles has fostered love, concord and harmony among them.

23. This, in fact, does not refer to the physical mark that one often sees on the foreheads of people owing to prostration. Instead what is being alluded to here are the traces of their being God-fearing; in other words, their magnanimity and purity of character that are manifest in the entire demeanour of the persons who submit to God in all humility. The thrust of this statement is that the Prophet's Companions are a distinguished group of people who are easily marked out for being the best specimens of humanity and whose faces are radiant because of their righteousness.

49

Al-Ḥujurāt [The Apartments]
Madīnan Period

In the name of Allah, the Most Merciful,
the Most Compassionate

[1] Believers, do not advance before Allah and His Messenger,[1] and fear Allah. Verily Allah is All-Hearing, All-Knowing.

[2] Believers, do not raise your voices above the voice of the Prophet and when speaking to him do not speak aloud as you speak aloud to one another, lest all your deeds are reduced to nothing without your even realising it. [3] The ones who lower their voices in the presence of the Messenger of Allah are those whose hearts Allah has tested for God-fearing.[2] Theirs shall be forgiveness and a great reward.

---

1. That is, the believers should remain behind rather than ahead of God and His Messenger; they should follow rather than venture to lead. What this implies is that rather than decide their problems according to their circumstances, they should first look to God's Book and His Prophet's *sunnah* for the guidance that they might have to offer.

2. It is being forcefully asserted here that the truly God-fearing are only those who have constantly stood up to God's tests by showing due reverence to the Prophet (peace be on him). The reverse of this is equally valid: those who lack reverence for the Prophet (peace be on him) are devoid of God-fearing.

[4] Surely most of those who call out to you, (O Prophet), from behind the apartments, are devoid of understanding. [5] If they were patient until you went out to them, that would have been better for them.³ Allah is Most Forgiving, Most Merciful.

[6] Believers, when an ungodly person brings to you a piece of news, carefully ascertain its truth, lest you should hurt a people unwittingly and thereafter repent at what you did.⁴ [7] Know that Allah's Messenger is among you. Were he to follow you in many an affair, you yourselves would suffer. But Allah has endeared faith to you and has embellished it in your hearts, and has made unbelief and evil-doing and disobedience abhorrent to you. Such are those who are rightly guided, [8] by Allah's favour and bounty. Allah is All-Knowing, All-Wise.

---

3. Some of those who came from different parts of Arabia to meet the Prophet (peace be on him) were utterly insolent. On their arrival, they did not care to have him informed through any of his attendants that they would like to see him; instead, they went to his wives' apartments and brashly called him out. This hurt the Prophet's feelings intensely, yet he put up with such behaviour owing to his inherent forbearance. Eventually the matter was taken up by God Himself. He censured such people for their unrefined behaviour and directed them to refrain from calling out the Prophet (peace be on him) but to patiently wait for him to come out to them of his own accord.

4. The Muslims are here being directed that whenever any news touching on a matter of some significance spreads they should ascertain the source of that news. If the person who was the source was ungodly, they should investigate and find out the truth of the matter rather than instantly accept the report and be aroused to action.

[9] If two parties of the believers happen to fight,⁵ make peace between them. But then, if one of them transgresses against the other, fight the one that transgresses until it reverts to Allah's command. And if it does revert, make peace between them with justice, and be equitable for Allah loves the equitable. [10] Surely the believers are none but brothers unto one another, so set things right between your brothers, and have fear of Allah that you may be shown mercy.

[11] Believers, let not a group (of men) scoff at another group, it may well be that the latter (at whom they scoff) are better than they; nor let a group of women scoff at another group, it may well be that the latter are better than they.⁶ And do not taunt one another,⁷ nor revile one

---

5. The actual words of the verse are significant: "If two parties of the believers happen to fight …" The implication of the statement is that inter-Muslim fighting is discordant with Muslim behaviour. If they are people of faith, they would be expected not to fight one another. However, if such an eventuality did arise, they should have recourse to the remedial measure prescribed here.

6. Scoffing is not confined to committing that act by the tongue. One can scoff at another by mimicking him, by pointing at him in ways that make him a laughing-stock; by subjecting another person's words, acts, face or dress to derision, or by playing up any other defects that would make others burst into laughter.

7. This includes, reviling, deriding, jeering, charging somebody falsely or finding faults with him, making him the target of reproach and blame by either open or tacit reference.

another by nicknames.[8] It is an evil thing to gain notoriety for ungodliness after belief. Those who do not repent are indeed the wrong-doers.

[12] Believers, avoid being excessively suspicious, for some suspicion is a sin.[9] Do not spy,[10] nor backbite one

---

8. The purpose of this injunction is that a person should not be given a nickname or called by a title that degrades him. This includes addressing someone as a profligate or hypocrite, calling someone blind or one-eyed, investing someone with a title that highlights any defect in his parents or family, or calling a convert to Islam a Christian or Jew, or causing someone embarrassment and humiliation. However, it does not cover those titles which might appear to be offensive but which in fact are employed to point to a person's distinguishing marks, by titles that do not injure his feelings nor do they subject him to disgrace. For example, to call someone a blind physician is to identify him with a distinct attribute.

9. The believers are being asked here not to be excessively suspicious rather than never to entertain any suspicion at all. The reason for this directive is clearly stated – some kinds of suspicion are sinful. One becomes guilty of this kind of suspicion when one suspects without justified reason; or when in forming one's opinion about another person one suspects him; or one mistrusts a person's words or deeds when apparently he is a good person. It is also sinful to be inclined to negatively interpret a person's words and deeds out of suspiciousness although it is equally possible he has a good intent.

10. "Do not spy" means that believers should not go about prying into the secrets of others, nor should they try to investigate matters that pertain to others. Thus they should refrain from reading others' private letters, eavesdropping, peeping into others' homes and trying to dig out information about others' domestic or private affairs.

another.[11] Would any of you like to eat the flesh of his dead brother?[12] You would surely detest it. Have fear of

---

11. The Prophet (peace be on him) was asked to explain what was meant by backbiting. He said: "It is talking of your brother in a manner that would hurt him." He was further asked: "What if the defect mentioned by me is actually found in him?" The Prophet (peace be on him) replied: "It would be backbiting if the defect that is mentioned exists. But if it does not exist, then it would be slander." This makes it quite clear that talking ill of another person behind his back during his life or after his death is only permissible in a very limited number of situations. One may mention another person's defects only when, according to the standards set by the *Sharīʿah*, it is absolutely necessary to do so, or when not mentioning a person's defect leads to greater evil than backbiting. Elaborating on this exception the Prophet (peace be on him) laid down the following principle: "To attack any Muslim's honour without right is the worst kind of evil." The words "without right" in this tradition imply that in certain circumstances it is permissible to speak ill about another person in his absence. For instance, the person who has been subjected to a wrong by another has the right to lodge a complaint, stating the wrongs the other person did him. To convey the complaint of the wronged against the wrong-doer to a person who, in his opinion, has the power to save him from that wrong. It is also lawful to bring to light the evils of a person or a group to those who can do something to eradicate those evils. It is also lawful to state the facts of someone's misdeeds before a *muftī* to solicit his religious or legal verdict. It is also lawful to warn people against the mischief of a person (or persons) so that they might be on guard. It is also lawful to raise one's voice against those who are spreading immorality, religious heresies or misleading ideas, or who are leading people to irreligiousness, or subjecting them to oppression.

12. Here backbiting is likened to eating the flesh of one's dead brother. The reason for this is that the victim of the act is not even aware that someone has launched an assault on his honour.

Allah. Surely Allah is much prone to accept repentance, is Most Compassionate.

[13] Human beings, We created you all from a male and a female, and made you into nations and tribes so that you may know one another. Verily the noblest of you in the sight of Allah is the most God-fearing of you.[13] Surely Allah is All-Knowing, All-Aware.

---

13. In the verses above, the Muslims are provided with the necessary directives to keep their community immune from evil and corruption. But now through the present verse mankind is being warned about the major erroneous notion that has always led to the spread of evil around the world; namely, the notion of prejudice based on race, colour, language, homeland and nationality. Addressing all human beings, the Qur'ān emphasises three basic points: [1] that all human beings have the same origin, that all of us have arisen originally from the same father and mother. Thus, all ethnic and racial entities that exist today are branches of the same family, their ultimate parents having been the same. [2] That it was natural for mankind to become divided, despite their common origin, into diverse national and tribal entities. While this diversity is quite natural, it does not provide any justification for some people to claim any inherent superiority over others; to consider some on these grounds as high and others as low, some as noble and others as ignoble. Considerations of colour, race or nationality do not warrant people of any particular colour, race or nationality to regard themselves as superior to others. God created such diversities to foster greater cooperation and to enable these different entities to become mutually introduced. [3] There is only one basis for regarding one as better than the other and that is on account of their moral excellence.

[14] The Bedouins say: "We believe."[14] (O Prophet), say to them: "You do not believe; you should rather say: 'We have submitted'"; for belief has not yet entered your hearts. If you obey Allah and His Messenger, He will not diminish anything from the reward of any of your deeds. Surely Allah is Most Forgiving, Most Compassionate. [15] Indeed the ones possessed of true faith are those who believed in Allah and His Messenger and then they did not entertain any doubt and strove hard in the Way of Allah with their lives and their possessions. These are the truthful ones.

[16] Say, (O Prophet), (to these pretenders to faith): "Are you apprising Allah of your faith? Allah knows all that is in the heavens and the earth. Allah has full knowledge of everything." [17] They count it as a favour to you that they accepted Islam. Say: "Do not regard your (accepting) Islam as a favour to me; rather, Allah has bestowed a favour on you by guiding you to faith, if you are truthful (in your claim to be believers). [18] Surely Allah knows every hidden thing of the heavens and the earth. Allah sees all that you do.

---

14. This applies to some specific groups of Bedouins rather than to all bedouins who embraced Islam. Observing that Islam's power was on the rise, some bedouins had converted to Islam merely to remain secure from attack or to derive material benefit ensuing from Islamic conquests. Such people had not become Muslims from the depths of their hearts. They had simply enrolled themselves as Muslims by virtue of verbal profession of faith, a profession which was motivated by utilitarian considerations.

50

Qāf
Makkan Period

In the name of Allah, the Most Merciful,
the Most Compassionate

[1] *Qāf*. By the glorious Qur'ān. [2] Nay; they wondered that a warner should have come to them from among themselves.¹ The unbelievers said: "This indeed is a strange thing. [3] What! When we are dead and reduced to mere dust, (shall we be raised to life)? Such a return is far-fetched."² [4] (Thus do they imagine, although) We know well what the earth takes away from them. With Us is a Record that preserves everything.

---

1. There was no sound rational basis for the Makkans' refusal to recognise Muḥammad (peace be on him) as a Prophet. On the contrary, the cause of their refusal to do so lacked all rhyme and reason. They refused to accept the Prophet's claim to be God's Messenger simply because they found it too incredible for anyone of their kind to be a warner from God. They found it impossible to believe how this could be.

2. This was yet another cause for their wonderment. The first cause of their wonder was that a human being had come as a warner from God. The additional cause for their wonder pertained to his teaching that all human beings will be resurrected after death and be made to face God's judgement.

[5] They gave the lie to the Truth when it came to them. So they are now in a state of great perplexity.

[6] Did they never observe the sky above them: how We built it and beautified it; and it has no cracks; [7] and We have spread out the earth, and have set upon it firm mountains, and have caused it to bring out plants of all beauteous kinds? [8] All these are to serve as eye-openers and as a lesson to every being who is prone to turn (to the Truth). [9] We also sent down blessed water from the heaven, wherewith We caused gardens and harvest-grain to grow, [10] and tall palm-trees with their thickly-clustered spathes; [11] all this as sustenance for Our servants. And thus We do bring the dead land back to life with water. Such shall be the coming forth (of human beings from the earth).

[12] In the past Noah's people, and the people of Rass and Thamūd gave the lie (to Messengers), [13] and so did ʿĀd, and Pharaoh and Lot's brethren, [14] and the people of Aykah, and the people of Tubbaʿ. They all gave the lie to the Messengers. Thereafter My threat of chastisement against them was fulfilled.

[15] Did We, then, become worn out by the first creation? Not at all; but they are in doubt about a fresh creation.

[16] Surely We have created man, and We know the promptings of his heart, and We are nearer to him than even his jugular vein. [17] Moreover, there are two scribes, one each sitting on the right and the left, recording everything. [18] He utters not a word, but there is a vigilant watcher at hand. [19] Lo, the agony of death has indeed come with the Truth. That is what you had sought

to avoid. [20] And then the Trumpet was blown. This is the day of the promised chastisement. [21] Everyone has come, each attended by one who will drive him on, and another who will bear witness. [22] You were heedless of this. Now We have removed your veil and so your vision today is sharp.[3] [23] His companion said:[4] "Here is he who was in my charge." [24] The command was given: "Cast into Hell every hardened, stubborn unbeliever, [25] who hinders good, exceeds the limits, is immersed in doubts, [26] and has set up another deity with Allah. Hurl him into the grievous torment." [27] His companion said:[5] "I did not incite him to rebel; he was far gone into error of his own accord." [28] (It was said): "Do not remonstrate in My presence. I had warned you. [29] My Word is not changed; and never do I inflict the least wrong upon My servants."

[30] On that Day We shall ask Hell: "Are you full?" And it will reply: "Are there any more?"[6] [31] And when

---

3. Man's vision on the Day of Judgement will be very sharp in so far as he will be able to see clearly all that takes place on that Day is as all that was foretold by God's Prophets.

4. The word "companion" here refers to the angel who drove that person to God's Judgement.

5. Here the word "companion" denotes the satan who was attached to that disobedient person as his watchman in this world.

6. This has two possible meanings: (1) That Hell was already filled up and there was no room for any more people. (2) That Hell was very commodious and as such could accommodate all culprits regardless of their number.

Paradise shall be brought close to the God-fearing, and will no longer be far away, [32] it will be said: "This is what you were promised, a promise made to everyone who turned much (to Allah)[7] and was watchful of his conduct,[8] [33] to everyone who feared the Merciful One though He is beyond the reach of perception, to everyone who has come with a heart ever wont to turn (to Him). [34] Enter this Paradise in peace." That will be the Day of Eternity. [35] Therein they shall get whatever they desire; and with Us there is even more.

[36] How many a nation did We destroy before them that were stronger in prowess than these. They searched about the lands of the world. But could they find a refuge? [37] Verily there is a lesson in this for everyone who has a (sound) heart and who listens with an attentive mind.

[38] We created the heavens and the earth and all that is between them in six days, and weariness did not even touch Us. [39] Hence bear with patience whatever they say, and celebrate your Lord's glory before the rising of

---

7. This signifies a person who has abandoned disobedience of God and has bound himself to obeying Him and seeking His good pleasure. It is someone who remembers Him much and turns to Him in all matters that confront him.

8. This suggests a person who takes due care in keeping himself within the bounds set by God and who performs the duties enjoined by Him. It is someone who refrains from all that God has forbidden and critically appraises his own behaviour lest he stumbles into disobeying His Lord.

the sun and before its setting; [40] and in the night, too, celebrate His glory, in the wake of prostration.[9]

[41] Hearken on the Day when the caller will call from a place nearby,[10] [42] the Day when they shall hear the Blast in truth. That will be the Day (for the dead) to come forth. [43] Surely it is We Who give life and cause death, and to Us shall all return [44] on the Day when the earth will be rent asunder and people, rising from it, will hasten forth. To assemble them all will be easy for Us.

[45] (O Prophet), We are well aware of what they say; and you are not required to force things on them. So exhort with the Qur'ān all those who fear My warning.

---

9. To celebrate God's glory here means Prayer. The Prayer "before the rising of the sun" is the *Fajr* Prayer. As for Prayers "in the night" they are the *Maghrib* and the *'Ishā'* Prayers. The *Tahajjud* Prayer is also a part of the Prayers performed at night aimed at celebrating God's glory.

10. Regardless of where a dead person is, the call of God's caller will reach him; his call will summon him to rise and proceed to His Lord and render account to Him. Such will be the call that everyone who rises from the state of death will feel that the caller had called him from a nearby place.

51

Al-Dhāriyāt [The Winds]
Makkan Period

In the name of Allah, the Most Merciful,
the Most Compassionate

[1] By the winds which scatter dust, [2] which carry clouds laden with water, [3] which then smoothly speed along, [4] and execute the great task of apportioning (rainfall): [5] surely what you are being warned against is true, [6] and the Judgement shall doubtlessly take place.[1]

---

1. "Surely what you are being warned against is true, and the Judgement shall doubtlessly take place." This is the point which is being emphasised by stating it on oath. Here attention is especially drawn to the exquisitely ordered and wonderfully functioning phenomenon of rainfall. This system and the wisdom and beneficence underlying it are for anyone to see. All this establishes that this world is not an aimless and absurd play-house; that it is not the stage of a senseless drama being randomly played out over millions of years. On the contrary, it is an immaculate system permeated with wisdom of the highest order, a system through which everything is tied with a purpose and is accompanied by beneficent considerations. Is it at all conceivable, then, that man, who is living under such a system, will first be endowed with authority on earth and then not be called to account for the use he has made of that authority?

[7] By the heaven with its numerous forms: [8] surely you are at variance (about the Hereafter);² [9] though only those who are averse to the Truth will turn away from (believing in it).

[10] Doomed are the conjecturers [11] who are steeped in ignorance and heedlessness.³ [12] They ask: "When will the Day of Judgement be?" [13] It will be the Day when they shall be scourged by the Fire [14] (and be told): "Taste your ordeal! This is what you were seeking to hasten."⁴ [15] As for the God-fearing, they shall be in the midst of gardens and fountains, [16] joyously receiving what their Lord will have granted them. Verily they did good works before (the coming of this Day): [17] they used to sleep but little by night,

---

2. Just as the clouds and the various galaxies in the sky vary in their shape and form, so do the views of people about the Hereafter, each being vastly different from the other. This difference of views is, in itself, an evidence of the fact that the opinions man has formed about his own and the world's end, independently of God's Revelation and Prophecy, are not rooted in true knowledge. For had there been direct access to true knowledge, there would have been no occasion for the rise of numerous and mutually contradictory opinions to emerge.

3. Being devoid of true knowledge and basing themselves merely on conjecture, the unbelievers are unwittingly heading towards a calamitous end. For if one's ideas regarding the Hereafter are flawed, any path that one takes is bound to lead to one's doom.

4. The unbelievers enquired: "When will the Day of Judgement be?" (see v. 12 above). The question is itself suggestive of another query: "If the Day of Judgement is bound to visit us, why is it not visiting us straight away? We have denied the possibility of its occurrence, so why is it not visiting us with all the horrors that are said to be a part of it?"

[18] and would ask for forgiveness at dawn, [19] and in their wealth there was a rightful share for him who would ask and for the destitute.[5]

[20] There are many Signs on earth for those of sure faith, [21] and also in your own selves. Do you not see? [22] And in heaven is your provision and also what you are being promised.[6] [23] So, by the Lord of the heaven and the earth, this is certainly true, as true as the fact of your speaking.

[24] (O Prophet), did the story of Abraham's honoured guests reach you? [25] When they came to him, they said: "Peace"; he said: "Peace also be to you; (you seem to

---

5. This describes the believers. Their behaviour has a two-fold characteristic. On the one hand, they recognise the claims of their Lord against them. On the other hand, they fully realise that whatever has been bestowed upon them by God, whether little or much, does not simply belong to them and their family. Instead, they feel that the needy too have a rightful claim on their wealth.

6. The word "heaven" here denotes the higher realm, and "provision" means all that is given to man to enable him to live and function in the world. As for the words "what you are being promised," they refer to the Resurrection, the Gathering, the Unfolding of the Scrolls, the Accounting, the Reward and Punishment, and Heaven and Hell. These things, according to all heavenly scriptures, and finally according to the Qur'ān, are bound to take place. The present verse thus tells us that the decision regarding the provision we receive in the world is made in the higher realm. Likewise, the decision as to when a person should be recalled to render an account of his deeds to God is also made in the same realm.

be) a group of strangers."⁷ [26] Then he went back to his family and brought a fat roasted calf [27] and laid it before them, saying: "Will you not eat?" [28] Then he became afraid of them. They said: "Fear not," and announced to him the good news of (the birth of) a boy endowed with knowledge.⁸ [29] So hearing his wife went forth shouting. She struck her face and exclaimed: "A barren old woman am I."⁹ [30] They said: "So has your Lord said (that you shall have a boy). Surely He is Most Wise, All-Knowing." [31] Abraham said: "Envoys (of Allah), what is your errand?" [32] They replied: "Behold, we have been sent to a wicked people¹⁰ [33] that we may unleash a shower of clay-stones

---

7. Bearing in mind the context in which this sentence occurs, it might carry either of the following two meanings. First, that the Prophet Abraham (peace be on him) himself told the guests that he had never seen them before, so they were probably newcomers to the area. Second, that after responding to their greeting, Abraham said either to himself, or went inside and told his servants, to arrange a meal for his guests. He said in effect: "These people seem to be strangers for people bearing their demeanour have not been seen around before."

8. According to *Sūrah Hūd* 11: 71, it is specifically said that this was the good news of the birth of the Prophet Isaac (peace be on him).

9. It was hard for Abraham's wife to believe the news for she was both age-stricken and barren. How, then, could any child be born to her? According to the Bible, Abraham was then a hundred years old and Sarah was 90 (Gen. 17: 17).

10. The people referred to here were so wicked that instead of specifically naming them, the angels considered it enough to refer to them as "a wicked people".

[34] marked by your Lord upon those who go beyond the limits."[11] [35] Then We[12] evacuated therefrom all the believers [36] – and We did not find there any, apart from a single house of Muslims – [37] and We left therein a Sign for those who fear the grievous chastisement.[13]

[38] There is also a Sign for you in the story of Moses when We sent him with a clear authority to Pharaoh.[14] [39] But Pharaoh turned away, showing arrogance on account of his power, and said (about Moses): "He is either a sorcerer or a madman." [40] So We seized him and his hosts, and cast them into the sea. He became an object of much blame.

[41] There is also a Sign for you in (the story of) ʿĀd, when We let loose upon them an ominous wind [42] that left nothing that it came upon without reducing it to rubble.

[43] There is also a Sign for you in (the story of) Thamūd. They were told: "Enjoy yourselves for a while."

---

11. Each stone was marked, under God's command, specifically indicating the culprit who would be struck down by it.

12. As to how the angels came to the Prophet Lot (peace be on him) after their meeting with the Prophet Abraham (peace be on him) and what transpired between them and the people of Lot is left unsaid.

13. The word "Sign" here refers to the Dead Sea, the southern part of which still retains vestiges of a great disaster.

14. The words "clear authority" signify those miracles and clear proofs which made it absolutely clear that Moses had been designated by the Lord of the heavens and the earth as His Messenger.

[44] But they brazenly disobeyed their Lord's command, and then a sudden chastisement overtook them while they looked on. [45] They were unable even to stand up or protect themselves.

[46] Before all these We destroyed the people of Noah: they were a wicked people.

[47] And heaven – We made it with Our Own Power and We have the Power to do so.[15] [48] And the earth – We spread it out, and how well have We smoothed it! [49] And of everything We have created pairs;[16] perhaps you will

---

15. The word *mūsi'* (pl. *musi'ūn*) signifies one who possesses abundant power and might. It can, however, also signify: "he who causes expansion". According to the first interpretation, the verse means: "We have built this heaven with Our Own Power and for so doing We did not have to depend on anyone's help, for the task was well within Our power. Since We built this heaven, why should anyone believe that the resurrection of human beings after death is beyond Our power and ability?" According to the second interpretation, the verse means: "We created this immense Universe, but that does not mark the end of Our task of creation. We are constantly expanding the Universe and ever new wonders of Our creation are visible almost every moment. What, then, makes you think that a great Creator such as Us would be unable to resurrect human beings?"

16. Everything in the world has been created on the principle of pairs. The whole universal system runs on the principle that everything matches another with which it is united and this brings into existence a wide variety of forms and combinations. There is nothing in the world that is totally unrelated to everything else and is devoid of a match. For it is by uniting a thing with its matching partner that it becomes productive.

take heed.¹⁷ [50] Flee, therefore, to Allah. Surely I am a clear warner to you from Him; [51] and do not set up any deity with Allah. Surely I am a clear warner to you from Him.¹⁸

[52] Thus has it been (in the past): never did a Messenger come to the nations that preceded them but they said: "(He is) a sorcerer, or a mad-man." [53] Have they arrived at a common understanding concerning this? No; but they are a people given to transgression.¹⁹ [54] So turn your attention away from them; you shall incur no blame. [55] Do, however, keep exhorting them; for exhortation benefits those endowed with faith.

---

17. If one reflects and pays heed, it is clear that the matching partner of the world is the Hereafter. Without the Hereafter the world would be utterly meaningless.

18. Though these sentences are a part of God's speech, the actual speaker here is not God but the Prophet (peace be on him). In other words, it is through the Prophet (peace be on him) that God conveys to human beings the message: "Flee, therefore, to Allah. Surely I am a clear warner to you from Him."

19. It is significant that for thousands of years people of different countries and nations continued to respond to the call of the Prophets in one and the same manner. Obviously, this uniformity did not ensue from mutual deliberation. Instead, such uniformity of response arose from the fact that all those who rejected the call did so out of defiance and transgression. These characteristics are their common denominator.

[56] I created the *jinn* and humans for nothing else but that they may serve Me;[20] [57] I desire from them no provision, nor do I want them to feed Me. [58] Surely Allah is the Bestower of all provision, the Lord of all power, the Strong. [59] The wrong-doers[21] shall receive a portion of the chastisements as their fellows (of yore). So let them not rush Me. [60] Woe, then, betide those who disbelieved in that Day of theirs which they are being asked to hold in dread.

---

20. The point stressed here is that God created man to serve Him to the exclusion of everyone else. Man should serve God by virtue of the fact that He is man's Creator. Now, since God alone is his Creator, what justification can there be for serving others?

21. "The wrong-doers" are those who commit offence against reality as well as their own nature.

52
❧❧❧

Al-Ṭūr [The Mount]
Makkan Period

In the name of Allah, the Most Merciful,
the Most Compassionate

[1] By the Mount, [2] and the Book inscribed [3] on fine parchment; [4] by the much-frequented House, [5] by the elevated canopy; [6] and by the swelling sea: [7] verily your Lord's chastisement shall come to pass, [8] none can avert that.¹ [9] (It shall come to pass) on the Day when the

---

1. "… Your Lord's chastisement" here denotes chastisement in the Hereafter. This because the occurrence of the Hereafter itself is tantamount to the visitation of chastisement on the deniers of the Truth.

Five oaths accompany the statement that the Hereafter will surely come to pass, the implication being that each of these five testifies that the Hereafter is bound to occur. These oaths are as follows: (1) By Mount Sinai where it was decided to exalt an oppressed nation and bring about the downfall of another nation that was immersed in evil-doing. This decision clearly indicates that God's realm is not one of lawlessness and injustice. (2) By the scriptures. These are inscribed on fine parchment from ancient times and testify that the Prophets who came during different epochs stressed on God's behalf the certainty of the Hereafter. (3) "By the much-frequented House," alludes to the Ka'bah, originally built in the sandy desolation of Makkah. However, far from being desolate, God has made it bustle with people, so much so that it excels every shrine on earth in terms of the number of people it attracts. This proves that Prophets do

heaven will convulse in a great convulsion, [10] and the mountains shall violently fly about. [11] Woe, then, on that Day to those who give the lie (to this Message) [12] and amuse themselves with vain argumentation. [13] On the Day when they shall be thrust into Hell with a violent thrust (and shall be told): [14] "This is the Hell which you used to give the lie to." [15] Is this, then, any feat of magic or are you unable to see? [16] Go now and burn in it. It is all the same whether you bear it patiently or do not bear it with patience. You are only being recompensed for your deeds."

[17] Surely the God-fearing shall be in Gardens and bliss, [18] enjoying what Allah will have endowed them with; and their Lord will have saved them from the torment of the Blazing Fire. [19] (They will be told): "Eat and drink to your hearts' content as a reward for your deeds." [20] The God-fearing shall be reclining on couches facing each other, and We shall wed them to maidens with large, beautiful eyes. [21] We shall unite the believers with those descendants of theirs who followed them in their faith, and shall not deny them any part of the reward for their

not engage in loose, baseless talk. After having erected this great shrine in the midst of barren hills, the Prophet Abraham (peace be on him) invited people to proceed to it for Pilgrimage. No one could then have imagined that for thousands of years the world would witness such huge crowds of people pressing forward to this one spot. (4) "By the elevated canopy," here refers to the sky. (5) "By the swelling sea." All these are Clear Signs of God's power, Signs that clearly show that their Creator certainly has the power to make the Hereafter come about.

good deeds. Every person is pledged to what he did.[2] [22] We shall provide them in abundance with all kinds of fruit and meat, whatever they may desire. [23] They shall pass on to one another a cup that will incite neither levity nor sin.[3] [24] Youths as fair as hidden pearls will be set apart to wait upon them; they will be running to and fro to serve them. [25] They will turn to one another and ask (regarding the past events). [26] They will say: "When we were living before among our kinsfolk we lived in constant fear (of Allah's displeasure).[4] [27] Then Allah graced us with His favour and saved us from the

---

2. A person cannot redeem a pledge unless he pays off the debt he owes. In like manner, a person cannot redeem himself from accountability before God unless he discharges the duty he owes Him. Even parents will be unable to redeem their children if the latter are not righteous. In essence, then, the good deeds of the parents will not secure the release of their children from the pledge.

3. This statement is about the wine that will be served in Paradise. This wine will not cause intoxication. Those who drink it will not become drunk, will not lose control over themselves and will not burst into senseless and vulgar babble. Nor will they resort to abusive invectives and obscene expressions or pick a row with others or behave indecently in the manner of drunkards.

4. The believers will describe their life as one lived with the consciousness of being answerable to God. Far from being immersed in hedonistic pursuits and unfettered self-indulgence, they were constantly vigilant lest they did anything that would bring God's wrath upon them. Significantly, it is said that they lived before "among their kinsfolk … in constant fear (of Allah's displeasure)". Living with their kinsfolk is mentioned here for a specific reason. The main reason someone lives a life of sin is that they are driven by the desire to provide ample means of ease and comfort to their immediate dependents.

chastisement of the scorching wind. [28] Formerly we had always prayed to Him. Surely He is Most Benign, Most Compassionate."

[29] So exhort (them, O Prophet), for by your Lord's Grace, you are neither a soothsayer nor a madman.[5]

[30] Or do they say: "He is a poet for whom we await an adverse turn of fortune." [31] Tell them: "Wait; I too am waiting with you." [32] Do their minds prompt them to say such things, or are they a people immersed in transgression?"[6]

---

5. The earlier verses depict a scene of the Hereafter. From here on the discourse turns to berating the intense obduracy with which the Makkan unbelievers resisted the Prophet's Message. Apparently the present verse is addressed to the Prophet (peace be on him), but in fact its true purpose is to disabuse the unbelievers' minds of all false, pre-conceived notions about him, viz. that he was a soothsayer or madman. The unbelievers are in effect being told not to apply these categories to the Prophet (peace be on him) for they do not apply to him.

6. Through these few sentences the hollowness of the opponents' propaganda is fully brought out. The Quraysh notables pretended to be a bunch of smart people. But what was that wisdom that made them dub someone a poet when he was not a poet; to characterise someone as a madman when the entire community acknowledged him to be outstandingly wise; to brand someone a soothsayer when he was not even remotely related to soothsaying? Had they really made use of rational criteria to judge him, they would have arrived at one and the same judgement. But in this case, the Prophet (peace be on him) was declared many things at the same time. Notwithstanding the contradiction involved, he was simultaneously declared a poet, a madman, and a sorcerer.

[33] Do they say: "He has himself fabricated the Qur'ān?" No; the truth is that they are altogether averse to believing. [34] (If they are truthful in this), then let them produce a discourse of similar splendour.

[35] Did they come into being without any creator? Or were they their own creators? [36] Or is it they who created the heavens and the earth? No; the truth is that they lack sure faith.[7]

[37] Or do they have your Lord's treasures in their keeping? Or have absolute authority over them?[8]

[38] Or do they have a ladder whereon they can climb and attempt to listen (to what is transpiring in the Higher Realm)? Then, let any of them who has listened

---

7. The unbelievers verbally admit that God is their Creator as well as the Creator of the whole Universe. But when they are asked to worship only the One True God, they are infuriated to the point of coming to blows about it. This contradiction demonstrates that they simply lack "sure faith".

8. This has been said in response to the objection of the Makkan unbelievers who wondered why, of all people, Muḥammad, son of 'Abd Allāh, was designated God's Messenger? The response suggests that, after all, someone had to be appointed God's Messenger in order to rescue people from the error in which they were wallowing. And if it was necessary to do so, who else was the best judge to decide who should be designated as His Messenger? Now if the Makkans refused to believe that the Messenger had been designated by God Himself, this could only mean one of the two things: either they considered themselves to be invested with Godhead, or that while they accepted God as the Lord of His realm, they nevertheless believed that He should carry out their edicts.

to it produce a clear proof of it. [39] Or does Allah have daughters whereas you have sons?[9]

[40] Or is it that you ask of them any recompense so that they should fear to be weighed down under the burden of debt?

[41] Or is it that they have access to (the Truths in) the realm beyond sense-perception which they are writing down?[10]

[42] Or are they contriving a stratagem against you? If so, that stratagem will rebound against the unbelievers.

[43] Do they have any god other than Allah? Exalted be Allah above whatever they associate (with Him in His Divinity).

---

9. The opponents who denied the Prophet's teaching are being asked if they themselves had any dependable means of knowing the reality. Had any of them travelled to the higher realms and come to know from God, at first hand, that their beliefs on which their religion rested were wholly true? And if such was their claim, let them consider the odd fact that they assigned daughters to God, even though they regarded daughters as a mark of disgrace for themselves.

10. How could the unbelievers feel so sure in denying the Prophet's statements about facts beyond the ken of sense-perception? Had they investigated all this and observed that what the Prophet (peace be on him) said was contrary to the Truth?

[44] (So obstinate are they that) even if they were to see some fragments of the sky falling down they would still say: "It is only a mass of cloud." [45] So leave them alone until they encounter that Day of theirs when they shall be struck down, [46] when their stratagem shall be of no avail to them, nor shall they be succoured. [47] Surely a chastisement awaits the wrong-doers even before the coming of that Day; but most of them do not know.

[48] Be patient, then, (O Prophet), until the judgement of your Lord comes. For surely you are before Our eyes. And celebrate the praise of your Lord when you rise,[11] [49] and also celebrate His praise at night, and at the retreat of the stars.[12]

11. The believers are told that when they commence their Prayers they should glorify God. In compliance with this the Prophet (peace be on him) directed that the following words be recited after saying *"Allāhu Akbar"* to signal the commencement of the Prayer: "Glory and Praise be to You, O Allah, Blessed be Your name, and exalted be Your honour. There is no god apart from You."

12. This signifies the *Fajr* Prayer.

53
❦

Al-Najm [The Star]
Makkan Period

*In the name of Allah, the Most Merciful,
the Most Compassionate*

[1] By the star when it sets:¹ [2] your companion has neither strayed nor is he deluded;² [3] nor does he speak out of his desire. [4] This is nothing but a revelation that is conveyed to him, [5] something that a very powerful one has imparted to him, [6] one endowed with immense wisdom.³ He came forth and stood poised, [7] being on the higher horizon.⁴ [8] Then he drew near and hung above suspended,

---

1. That is, when the bright aurora of the morn appears after the setting of the last star.

2. "Your companion" here refers to the Prophet (peace be on him). He was so called because he was no stranger to the unbelievers of Makkah. He was born among them, spent his childhood and youth in their midst, and attained maturity before their very eyes. The upshot of the verse is that the Makkans knew him in and out. Hence it should be as clear as a resplendent morn that he had neither strayed nor was he deluded.

3. Here the words "one endowed with immense wisdom" are said with regard to Gabriel rather than God. This is quite evident from what follows. (See vv. 5 ff. Ed.)

4. The word "horizon" means the eastern edge of the sky wherefrom the sun rises and the day dawns. This means that when the Prophet

[9] until he was two bows' length away, or nearer.[5]
[10] Then he revealed to Allah's servant whatever he had
to reveal. [11] His heart added no untruth to what he saw.[6]
[12] Are you, then, going to contend with him regarding
what he sees with his eyes?

[13] Indeed he saw him a second time, [14] by the lote-tree
at the farthest boundary,[7] [15] near which is the Garden

(peace be on him) spotted Gabriel for the first time it was on the
eastern edge of the sky.

5. This means that after appearing on the uppermost eastern edge
of the sky, Gabriel kept advancing towards the Prophet (peace be
on him) until he stood suspended in mid-air above him. Then he
leaned towards the Prophet (peace be on him) and reached a point
quite close to him: at just two bows' length or even less. Since all
bows are not of equal length, the approximate distance is expressed:
"he was two bow lengths away, or nearer".

6. The Prophet (peace be on him) had observed all this in broad
daylight when he was fully awake and his eyes were wide open.
It did not occur to him that his observation was a mere illusion.
Nor did he think that the figure he was observing was a *jinn* or
satan. Nor did he think for a moment that his observation was a
hallucination. Far from all this, for his heart fully believed that his
observation was true. He did not entertain any doubt, not even for
a moment, regarding the fact that he had seen Gabriel; nor did he
have the least doubt that the Message which he had delivered was
any other than what God had revealed to him.

7. Literally, *sidrat al-muntahā* means "the lote-tree at the farthest
boundary". It is difficult for us to appreciate what kind of lote-tree
is found at the farthest boundary of this physical world, as also
what the true nature or state of that lote-tree is. All these are hidden
secrets of the Universe which are beyond our comprehension. What
we can feel sure about is that the word "lote-tree" represents God's
own description of that object in the human lexicon.

of Abode. [16] (This was) when the lote-tree was covered with that which covered it. [17] His eye did not waver, nor did it stray, [18] and he certainly saw some of the greatest Signs of His Lord.[8]

[19] Have you ever thought about al-Lāt and al-'Uzzā, [20] and about the third deity, al-Manāt?[9] [21] Shall you have the male issues, and He the female issues?[10] [22] That

---

8. This verse confirms, in categorical terms, that the Prophet (peace be on him) saw God's Great Signs rather than God Himself. This is also evident from the context. For the one whom the Prophet (peace be on him) met on this occasion was the same he had met earlier. Thus there is no escaping the conclusion that neither he whom the Prophet (peace be on him) saw on the "highest horizon" (see v. 7 above) nor he whom he saw "by the lote-tree at the farthest boundary" (see v. 14 above) was God. Had the Prophet (peace be on him) seen God Himself on any of the two occasions the incident would be far too important not to be categorically mentioned here.

9. The unbelievers were wont to denounce the teachings of the Prophet (peace be on him) as false and erroneous. This despite the fact that he had been vouchsafed these teachings by God Who had enabled him to observe at first hand the truths to which he testified. Now it was for them to consider the utter unreasonableness of the beliefs to which they clung with such adamance. It was also for them to think whether they were not hurting their own selves by opposing the person who was directing them to the Right Way.

10. The unbelievers claimed that their goddesses were God's daughters. While inventing this vile untruth they even ignored the fact that they themselves considered the birth of a daughter a matter of disgrace and that they desired instead only male issue. Was it not odd, then, that such people should assign daughters to God?

[792]

is indeed an unfair division! [23] These are nothing but names that you and your forefathers have invented, for which Allah has sent down no authority. They are merely following their conjectures and their carnal desires although guidance has come to them from their Lord. [24] Does man imagine that whatever he wishes for is right for him?[11] [25] To Allah belong both the Next World and the present.

[26] Numerous are the angels in the heavens; yet their intercession shall be of no avail, except in regard to those whom He grants the leave of intercession and whose plea He is pleased to accept. [27] Those who do not believe in the Hereafter give angels the names of females, [28] although they have no knowledge regarding that. They only follow their conjecture and conjecture can never take the place of the Truth. [29] So leave alone those who turn away from the remembrance of Us and who seek nothing but the life of the world – [30] that being the utmost of their knowledge.[12] Surely your Lord fully knows those who have strayed away from His Path and He also fully knows those who are rightly guided. [31] To Allah alone belongs whatever is in the heavens and whatever is in the

---

11. It is possible that this verse contains some other meanings as well. For example: "Does man have the right to take whomsoever he wishes as his deity?" Or: "Can man's desire to have his wishes fulfilled by these deities ever come true?"

12. This is a parenthetical statement. It is inducted here even though it interrupts the current theme in order to elucidate the preceding verse.

earth.[13] He will requite the evil-doers for their deeds and bestow a goodly reward on those who have done good, [32] on those who avoid grave sins and shameful deeds, even if they may sometimes stumble into lesser offences. Surely your Lord is abounding in His Forgiveness. Very well is He aware of you since He produced you from the earth, and while you were still in your mothers' wombs and not yet born. So do not boastfully claim yourselves to be purified. He fully knows those that are truly God-fearing.

[33] (O Prophet), did you see him who turned away (from the Path of Allah), [34] who gave a little, and then stopped?[14] [35] Does he have any knowledge of the world beyond the ken of sense-perception, and therefore, clearly sees (the Truth)? [36] Has he not been informed of what is in the Scrolls of Moses, [37] and of Abraham,

---

13. The earlier theme is resumed here and is connected with v. 29. If one were to disregard the parenthetical statement mentioned above (see n.12 above), the text would read as follows: "So leave alone those who turn away from the Remembrance of Us … so that He may requite the evil-doers for their deeds …."

14. This alludes to Walīd ibn Mughīrah, one of the prominent chiefs of the Quraysh. He initially felt inclined to accept the Prophet's invitation to embrace Islam. But when one of his friends, who was a polytheist, came to know of this, he argued strongly against his renouncing his ancestral faith, enquiring if he was afraid of chastisement in the Hereafter. If that were the case, he said, Walīd should pay him a certain amount of money and he would be ready to suffer the chastisement in his stead. Walīd accepted the offer, choosing thereby not to embrace Islam. Interestingly, Walīd paid his friend only a part of the amount he had agreed to, denying him the rest.

who lived up to the trust?[15] [38] "That no bearer of a burden shall bear the burden of another,[16] [39] and that man shall have nothing but what he has striven for,[17] [40] and that (the result of) his striving shall soon be seen, [41] and that he shall then be fully recompensed, [42] and that the final end is with your Lord, [43] and that He it is Who causes people to laugh and to cry,[18] [44] and that He it is Who causes death and grants life, [45] and He it is Who created the two kinds, the male and the female, [46] from a drop of sperm when it was emitted, [47] and that it is for Him to grant the second life, [48] that He it is Who bestowed wealth and riches,

---

15. The verses that follow (vv. 38-55) contain the gist of the teaching embodied in the Scrolls of the Prophets Moses and Abraham (peace be on them).

16. The point stressed here is that every person is responsible for whatever he does; the responsibility of one person cannot be placed on any other. Even if a person so wishes, it is not possible for him to assume responsibility for others' actions. Nor can a criminal be absolved of his guilt on the grounds that someone else offers himself to suffer chastisement on his behalf.

17. This enunciates some basic points regarding the way man will be recompensed in the Hereafter. Each person will receive the fruit of his deeds. An obvious corollary of this proposition is that a person will not receive the fruit of anyone else's deeds. Still another corollary of it is that no one will receive anything in the Hereafter unless he has some striving and action to his credit.

18. That is, in the ultimate, the causes of happiness and grief are traceable to God. Good luck and misfortune all rest with Him. None other than He has any power to make or mar destinies.

[49] that He is the Lord of Sirius,[19] [50] that He it is Who destroyed the ancient 'Ād, [51] and Thamūd, leaving no trace of them, [52] and that He it is Who destroyed the people of Noah before for they were much given to iniquity and transgression. [53] And He brought perdition upon the subverted cities [54] and caused them to be covered with that which He covered them with.[20] [55] So, which of your Lord's bounties will you doubt?"

[56] This is a warning among the warnings of yore. [57] The imminent Hour has drawn near, [58] and none but Allah can avert it. [59] Will you, then, wonder at this? [60] Will you laugh at it rather than weep? [61] Will you occupy yourselves simply in merriment? [62] Prostrate yourselves before Allah, and serve Him.

---

19. Sirius, (the dog-star), is the brightest star in the sky. The people of Egypt and Arabia believed that this star impacted on people's destinies. Hence Sirius was accepted as one of their deities.

20. "The subverted cities" (v. 53) refer to the settlements of the people of Lot. As for the expression: "He caused them to be covered with that which He covered them with" (v. 54), presumably refers to the water of the Dead Sea which spread over the settlements of Lot's people after they were made to cave in the earth. Interestingly, that water continues to cover the area even now.

54

Al-Qamar [The Moon]
Makkan Period

*In the name of Allah, the Most Merciful,
the Most Compassionate*

[1] The Hour of Resurrection drew near and the moon split asunder.[1] [2] (Regardless of any Signs these people see), they turn away and say: "This is an ongoing sorcery." [3] They also gave the lie to (the splitting asunder of the moon) and only followed their desires. Yet everything is destined to reach an end.

---

1. The splitting asunder of the moon signified that the Day of Resurrection had drawn near. It could now take place at any moment. It appears from this statement and what follows that the moon had actually split asunder. Those who had witnessed the event stated that the moon suddenly split asunder for a short while after its rise on the fourteenth day of a lunar month. As a result, the two separated parts of the moon were visible on the two sides of the mountain in front of them. Soon thereafter, however, the two parts rejoined. If we take into account the relevant traditions from the Prophet (peace be on him), it is evident that there is no substance in the statement made by popular preachers, viz. that the moon's splitting asunder was caused by a gesture made by the Prophet (peace be on him). Nor is there any substance in the statement that this happened in response to the unbelievers' demand for a miracle.

[4] Surely there came to them narratives (of the ancient nations) that should suffice to deter (them from transgression), [5] narratives that are full of consummate wisdom. But warnings do not avail them. [6] So turn away from them, (O Prophet). On the Day when a caller shall call them to a thing most terrible, [7] with down-cast eyes they shall go forth from their graves, as though they were scattered locusts. [8] They shall be hurrying forth towards the caller, and the unbelievers (who had once denied this Day), will say: "This is a woeful Day."

[9] Before them Noah's people also gave the lie (to his Message). They rejected Our servant as a liar, saying: "He is a madman"; and he was rebuffed. [10] Then he called upon His Lord: "Verily I am vanquished; so come You to my aid." [11] Thereupon We opened the gates of the sky for water to pour down, [12] and We made the earth burst forth with springs, and all this water converged to fulfil that which had been decreed. [13] And We bore Noah on the vessel built of planks and nails,[2] [14] which sailed on under Our supervision: a reward for him who had been shown ingratitude. [15] And We left the Ark as a Sign. Is there, then, any who will take heed? [16] So how awesome were My chastisement and My warnings! [17] We have made this Qur'ān easy as a reminder.[3] Is there, then, any who will take heed?

---

2. This alludes to the Ark built at God's behest by the Prophet Noah (peace be on him) before the Deluge.

3. One way of admonishing people was, as happened in the case of several rebellious nations, to visit them with a calamitous scourge. Another means of admonishing them was through the Qur'ān which directs them to the Right Way by means of persuasive

[18] 'Ād also gave the lie (to Hūd). So how awesome were My chastisement and My warnings! [19] We sent a tumultuous wind against them on a day of unremitting misfortune, [20] which tore people away and hurled them as though they were trunks of uprooted palm-trees. [21] So how awesome were My chastisement and My warnings! [22] We have made the Qur'ān easy to derive lessons from. Is there, then, any who will take heed?

[23] Thamūd gave the lie to the warnings, [24] saying: "Are we to follow a single mortal, one from among ourselves? If we do that, we shall surely be in error and folly. [25] Was there none but he to whom the Reminder could be vouchsafed excluding all others? Nay; he is an insolent liar." [26] (We told Our Messenger): "Tomorrow they shall know who is the insolent liar. [27] We shall send the she-camel as a trial for them; so watch their end with patience. [28] Let them know that the water should be divided between them and the she-camel, each availing their turn."⁴ [29] Eventually, they summoned

---

arguments and exhortation. Obviously, the second method is the most convenient. That being the case, why do people choose not to benefit from the Qur'ān instead of waiting for God's scourge? Such an attitude defies all understanding.

4. This explains the verse: "We shall send the she-camel as a trial for them" (v. 27 above). The trial consisted of the following: that a she-camel was sent to the Thamūd who were instructed that they and the she-camel should have access to water on alternate days. The people were directed not to draw water from any well or spring, nor to bring their cattle to the water sources on those days the she-camel was entitled to water. This challenging directive was given by a Prophet about whom they said that he had no armed strength at his command.

their companion, and he undertook the (outrageous) task and hamstrung the she-camel. [30] So how awesome were My chastisement and My warnings! [31] Behold, We sent a single Blast against them, and they became like the trampled twigs of a sheep pen-builder.⁵ [32] Surely We have made this Qur'ān easy as a reminder. Is there, then, any who will take heed?

[33] Lot's people also gave the lie to the warnings, [34] and behold, We let loose upon them a tempest which rained stones upon them, except upon Lot's household whom We rescued in the last hours of the night [35] as a favour from Us. Thus do We reward those who give thanks. [36] Surely Lot warned his people that We shall seize them (with Our chastisement), but they doubted the warnings. [37] Then they even solicited his guests from him, whereupon We blotted out their eyes, (telling them): "Now have a taste of My chastisement and My warnings." [38] Indeed an abiding chastisement came upon them in the morning. [39] So have a taste of My chastisement and My warnings. [40] Surely We have made this Qur'ān easy as a reminder. Is there, then, any who will take heed?

---

5. Those who maintain cattle have to build protective fences around the cattle pens. The fence is usually made of timber and twigs and pieces of bush. The bushes of the fence gradually dry up and in the course of time wither away. Furthermore, the comings and goings of the cattle and other animals trample the fence, and ground the bushes to dust. The crushed and rotten corpses of the Thamūd are here likened to the trampled and trodden twigs and bushes that lie scattered around the cattle pens.

[41] Warnings also came to the Pharaonites, [42] but they gave the lie to Our Signs, to all of them. Thereupon We seized them with the seizing of the Most Mighty, the Most Powerful.

[43] Are your unbelievers (of Makkah) any better than they?[6] Or have you been granted any immunity in the Scriptures? [44] Or do they say: "We are a strong legion, strong enough for victory?" [45] Soon shall this legion be routed and shall turn their backs and flee. [46] Nay; the Hour of Doom is their appointed time, and the Hour shall be more calamitous and bitter. [47] The evil-doers are victims of error and madness. [48] There shall come a Day when they will be dragged on their faces into the Fire and will be told: "Now taste the flame of Hell."

[49] We have created everything in a determined measure.[7] [50] Our command consists of only one Word

---

6. This query – "are your unbelievers any better than they?" – is addressed to the Quraysh. They were plainly told that other nations had been destroyed by God in the past because they disbelieved, gave the lie to the Truth, and acted with obduracy. Now, if the behaviour of the Makkan unbelievers does not differ from the behaviour of other nations, why do they not think they will not be subjected to the chastisement that had visited other iniquitous nations?

7. Nothing in the world is created without a purpose; on the contrary, everything is created according to a determined scheme (*taqdīr*). In keeping with that scheme, everything comes into being at an appointed time, assumes the form determined for it, develops to a given extent, continues to exist until an appointed time, and then comes to its end at an appointed hour.

which is carried out in the twinkling of an eye. [51] We did indeed destroy many like you. Is there, then, any who will heed? [52] All their deeds are recorded in the Scrolls; [53] everything large or small, is duly inscribed.

[54] Surely those who shun disobedience will dwell amidst Gardens and running streams [55] where they will be honourably seated in the presence of a King, Mighty in Power.

55
❦

Al-Raḥmān [The Most Merciful]
Madīnan Period

In the name of Allah, the Most Merciful,
the Most Compassionate

[1] The Merciful One [2] has taught the Qur'ān, [3] has created man, [4] and has taught him articulate speech.

[5] The sun and the moon follow a reckoning, [6] and the stars and the trees all prostrate themselves,[1] [7] and He has raised up the heaven and has set a balance[2] [8] that you may not transgress in the balance, [9] but weigh things equitably and skimp not in the balance.[3]

---

1. That is, the entire Universe is bound in obedience to God. Nothing, not even the sun and the moon, nor the stars and trees may deviate from this even by as much as a hair's breadth.

2. Almost all Qur'ānic commentators have interpreted the word *mīzān* (balance) used here to signify justice. As for the words "… set the balance," they have been interpreted to mean that God made justice embrace the entire Universe.

3. The thrust of the statement is that since man lives in a balanced Universe, one whose entire system is based on justice, he too should adhere to justice. For if he acts unjustly within the sphere in which he has been granted choice, it will be discordant with the very grain of the Universe.

[10] And He has set up the earth for all beings. [11] Therein are fruit and palm-trees with their dates in sheaths, [12] and a variety of corn with both husk and grain. [13] Which of the bounties[4] of your Lord will you twain – you men and *jinn* – then deny?

[14] He has created man from dry, rotten clay like the potter's, [15] and has created the *jinn* from the flame of fire. [16] Which of the wonders of your Lord's power will you twain – you men and *jinn* – then deny?

[17] Lord of the two easts and of the two wests[5] is He. [18] Which of the powers of your Lord will you twain – you men and *jinn* – then deny?

[19] He unleashed the two seas so that they merge together, [20] and yet there is a barrier between them which they may not overstep. [21] Which of the wonders of your Lord will you twain – you men and *jinn* – then deny? [22] From these seas come forth pearls and coral. [23] Which of the wonders of your Lord's power will you twain – you men and *jinn* – then deny?

---

4. The word used here is *ālā'*, which forms part of the refrain that occurs again and again in this *sūrah*. Instead of strictly adhering to one equivalent of this word, we have translated it variously depending on the context in which this word occurs. Thus sometimes we have used the word "wonders" for the word *ālā'* (v. 16); on other occasions we have used "favours" (v. 25), and also "laudable attributes" (v. 30).

5. The expression "Lord of the two easts and of the two wests" possibly means the two points of sunrise and the two points of sunset on the shortest and longest days in winter and summer. Another possible meaning could be the easts and the wests of the two hemispheres of the earth.

[24] His are the ships, towering on the sea like mountains.
[25] Which of the favours of your Lord will you twain – you
men and *jinn* – then deny?

[26] All that is on earth will perish, [27] only the Person
of your Lord, full of majesty and splendour, will endure.
[28] So which of the wonders of your Lord will you
twain – you men and *jinn* – then deny? [29] All in the
heavens and the earth entreat Him for their needs; a new,
mighty task engages Him each day.[6] [30] Which of your
Lord's laudable attributes will you twain – you men and
jinn – then deny?

[31] O you twain, who are a burden (on the earth),[7]
We shall attend to you and call you to account.[8]

---

6. God is continually engaged in the governance of the Universe
and each moment He brings into existence countless beings in
ever-new forms and shapes and with a variety of properties. His
Universe is not a static Universe; it changes moment by moment,
and each time its Creator brings it out in new shapes and forms
that vary from all previous shapes and forms.

7. *Thaqal* denotes the burden placed on a vehicle. *Thaqalān* is in the
dual form and therefore means: "two loaded burdens". Here, this
word is used to signify *jinn* and humans who are both loaded on
the earth. Now, since the present discourse refers to those *jinn* and
humans who are deviant and do not render service and obedience
to their Lord, they are addressed as follows: "O you twain, who
are a burden (on the earth)." In other words, humans and *jinn* are
being warned that God will turn His attention to them and take
them to task.

8. This verse should not be understood to mean that at that time
God was too occupied with other tasks to call His negligent
servants to account. Rather, it means that God has set a specific
time to call humans to their final accounting, and that time has
not yet arrived.

[32] (We shall then see), which of the favours of your Lord will you twain – you men and *jinn* – then deny? [33] O company of *jinn* and men, if you have the power to go beyond the bounds of the heavens and the earth, go beyond them! Yet you will be unable to go beyond them for that requires infinite power.[9] [34] Which of your Lord's powers will you twain – you men and *jinn* – then deny? [35] (If you so venture) a flame of fire and smoke shall be lashed at you, which you shall be unable to withstand. [36] Which of your Lord's powers will you twain – you men and *jinn* – then deny?

[37] (What will happen) when the heaven will be split asunder[10] and will become crimson like leather? [38] Which of your Lord's powers will you twain – you men and *jinn* – then deny?

[39] On that Day there will be no need to ask either men or *jinn* about their sins. [40] (We shall see) which of the favours of your Lord will you twain – you men and *jinn* – then deny?

---

9. The expression "the bounds of the heavens and the earth" in this verse signifies the entire Universe which is a part of God's realm. The purpose of the verse is to stress that it is beyond man's power to escape God's grip. When the time for accountability, about which they are being warned, arrives, they will be seized wherever they might be and will be mustered to God. If they want to escape God's grip, there is only one way to do so: to flee from the Universe itself for the whole of it is entirely under God's control. But doubtlessly man does not have the power to do so and if anyone entertains any vain illusion in that regard, they are challenged to test their power.

10. The splitting asunder of the heaven signifies the loosening of the bonds that hold the celestial system together, the disruption of the cosmic order, and the scattering away of stars and planets.

[41] The culprits shall be known by their marks, and shall be seized by their forelocks and their feet. [42] Which of the powers of your Lord, will you twain – you men and *jinn* – then deny? [43] (It will be said): "This is the Hell that the culprits had cried lies to. [44] They will keep circling around between Hell and boiling water. [45] Which of your Lord's powers will you twain – you men and *jinn* – then deny?

[46] For any who fears to stand before his Lord[11] are two Gardens. [47] Which of your Lord's favours will you twain – you men and *jinn* – then deny? [48] These Gardens will abound in green, blooming branches. [49] Which of your Lord's favours will you twain – you men and *jinn* – then deny? [50] In each of the two Gardens are two flowing springs. [51] Which of your Lord's favours will you twain – you men and *jinn* – then deny? [52] In both these is a pair of every fruit.[12]

---

11. The expression: "For any who fears to stand before his Lord" refers to those who lived in the world being God-fearing, who always worked with the consciousness that they would one Day be made to stand before God and have to render an account of their deeds to Him.

12. This verse can be understood in one of two ways. First, it might be taken to mean that the fruit of each of the two Gardens will be unique. In each Garden there will be fruits of a special quality clustering on branches; and in the other Garden, there will be fruits of a different kind. Second, that a person will find in one Garden one kind of fruit with which he was familiar and had tasted during his worldly life, though in the Hereafter they will be infinitely better. There will, however, also be another kind of fruit with which he was not at all acquainted in the world and which is beyond his imagination.

[53] Which of your Lord's favours will you twain – you men and *jinn* – then deny? [54] They shall recline on couches lined with brocade, and within reach shall hang the fruits of the two Gardens. [55] Which of your Lord's favours will you twain – you men and *jinn* – then deny? [56] In the midst of these shall be maidens with modest, restrained glances;¹³ maidens whom no man or *jinn* has ever touched before.¹⁴ [57] Which of your Lord's favours will you twain – you men and *jinn* – then deny? [58] Lovely as rubies and pearls. [59] Which of the favours of your Lord will you twain – you men and *jinn* – then deny?

[60] Can the reward of goodness be any other than goodness? [61] Which of the laudable attributes of your Lord will you twain – you men and *jinn* – then deny? [62] And besides these two there shall be two other

---

13. This is the true quality of womenfolk: that instead of being immodest and unabashed, they should be bashful. This explains why God, in the course of His depiction of the women of Paradise, accords priority to lauding their modesty and chastity rather than praising them for their beauty and attractiveness. One can find beautiful women the world over: in promiscuous clubs and film studios and carnivals of beauty where none but the most beautiful are able to find their way. Yet such women can only be the favourites of people of decadent taste and depraved character. Women who seek to attract the attention of corrupt men and are ready to jump into every lustful man's lap have no appeal for decent people.

14. This indicates that like righteous humans, upright *jinn* will also be admitted to Paradise and granted female companions of their own species. Furthermore, thanks to God's infinite power, all of them shall be made virgins, "maidens whom no man or *jinn* has ever touched before".

Gardens.[15] [63] Which of the favours of your Lord will you twain – you men and *jinn* – then deny? [64] Two Gardens, dark green and fresh. [65] Which of the favours of your Lord will you twain – you men and *jinn* – then deny? [66] In them will be two gushing springs. [67] Which of the favours of your Lord will you twain – you men and *jinn* – then deny? [68] Therein will be fruits and dates and pomegranates. [69] Which of the favours of your Lord will you twain – you men and *jinn* – then deny? [70] In the midst of these will be maidens, good and comely. [71] Which of the favours of your Lord will you twain – you men and *jinn* – then deny? [72] There shall be maidens sheltered in tents.[16] [73] Which of the favours of your Lord will you twain – you men and *jinn* – then deny? [74] No man or *jinn* ever touched them before. [75] Which of the favours of your Lord will you twain – you men and *jinn* – then deny? [76] They shall be reclining on green cushions and splendid carpets. [77] Which of the favours of your Lord will you twain – you men and *jinn* – then deny?

[78] Blessed be the name of your Lord, the Lord of Majesty and Glory.

---

15. Probably the first two Gardens will serve the purpose of lodging whereas the other two will be for purposes of recreation and entertainment.

16. These tents will possibly resemble those erected in recreational resorts earmarked for the eminent and affluent. Paradise will be full of tents wherein there will be young maidens to provide recreation and delight.

56

Al-Wāqi'ah [The Event]
Makkan Period

*In the name of Allah, the Most Merciful,
the Most Compassionate*

[1] When the Event will come to pass [2] – and then there will be no one to deny its occurrence – [3] (a calamitous Event) that shall turn things upside down: [4] when the earth will suddenly shake with a terrible shaking,¹ [5] and the mountains will crumble [6] and will scatter abroad into fine dust. [7] You shall then become three groups. [8] The People on the Right: and how fortunate will be the People on the Right! [9] And the People on the Left: and how miserable will be the People on the Left! [10] As for the Foremost, they will be the foremost! [11] They shall be near-stationed (to their Lord), [12] in the Gardens of Bliss. [13] A throng of the ancients, [14] and a few from later times. [15] They (will be seated) on gold-encrusted couches, [16] reclining on them, arrayed face to face; [17] immortal youths shall go about them² [18] with goblets and ewers and a cup filled with a drink drawn from a running spring, [19] a drink by

---

1. This earthquake will not be confined to any particular part of the earth; instead, it will shake the whole earth terribly.

2. That is, they will always remain young and will never be subjected to old age.

which their minds will not be clouded nor will it cause drunkenness; [20] they will also go about them with the fruits of which they may choose, [21] and with the flesh of any fowl that they may desire to eat; [22] and there shall be wide-eyed maidens, [23] beautiful as pearls hidden in their shells. [24] All this shall be theirs as a reward for their deeds. [25] There they shall hear no idle talk nor any sinful speech. [26] All talk will be sound and upright.

[27] As for the People on the Right, how fortunate shall be the people on the Right! [28] They shall be in the midst of thornless lote trees,[3] [29] and flower-clad acacias, [30] and extended shade, [31] and gushing water, [32] and abundant fruit, [33] never-ending and unforbidden. [34] They shall be on upraised couches, [35] and their spouses We shall have brought them into being afresh, [36] and shall have made them virgins, [37] intensely loving and of matching age. [38] All this will be for the People on the Right; [39] a large throng from the ancients, [40] and also a large throng from those of later times.

[41] As for the People on the Left: how miserable will be the People on the Left! [42] They will be in the midst of scorching wind and boiling water, [43] and a shade of thick, pitch-black smoke, [44] which will neither be cool nor soothing. [45] Surely they had lived before in luxury, [46] and had persisted in the Great Sin. [47] They used to say: "What! Once we are dead and are reduced to dust

---

3. These will be lote-trees but with a difference: they will be without thorns. It is well known that the more superior the quality of a lote-tree, the fewer are its thorns. The lote-trees being described here will be of the very highest quality, free of thorns.

and bones, shall we still be raised to a new life from the dead? [48] (We) and our fore-fathers of yore?" [49] Tell them, (O Prophet): "The earlier ones and the later ones [50] shall all be brought together on an appointed Day. [51] Then you, the erring ones and those that gave the lie to the Truth, [52] shall all eat from the Tree of al-Zaqqūm, [53] filling your bellies with it; [54] and thereupon you shall drink boiling water, [55] drinking it as thirsty camels do." [56] Thus shall they be entertained on the Day of Recompense.

[57] We have created you, then why would you not confirm it?[4] [58] Did you ever consider the sperm that you emit? [59] Do you create a child out of it, or are We its creators? [60] It is We Who ordained death upon you and We are not to be frustrated. [61] Had We so wished, nothing could have hindered Us from replacing you by others like yourselves, or transforming you into beings you know nothing about. [62] You are well aware of the first creation; then, do you learn no lesson from it?

[63] Have you considered the seeds you till? [64] Is it you or We Who make them grow? [65] If We so wished, We could have reduced your harvest to rubble, and you would have been left wonder-struck to exclaim: [66] "We have been penalised; [67] nay; we have been undone!"

[68] Did you cast a good look at the water that you drink? [69] Is it you who brought it down from the clouds or is

---

4. Since human beings have been created by God, there is no reason why they should not affirm that He is their Lord; that He is the only object of their worship, and that He has the power to restore them to life after death?

it We Who brought it down? [70] If We had so pleased, We could have made it bitter. So why would you not give thanks?

[71] Did you consider the fire which you kindle? [72] Did you make its tree grow or was it We Who made it grow?⁵ [73] We made it a reminder and a provision for the needy.

[74] Glorify, then, (O Prophet), the name of your Great Lord.⁶

[75] No!⁷ I swear by the positions of the stars – [76] and this is indeed a mighty oath, if only you knew – [77] that this indeed is a noble Qurʾān,⁸ [78] inscribed in a well-guarded Book,

---

5. Human beings' attention is drawn to the trees out of whose timber they use to make fire. But the basic question is: who created these trees, man or God?

6. All are urged to celebrate God's blessed name and glorify Him by proclaiming that He is exalted above all the defects, faults and weaknesses which are ascribed by those who associate others with God in His Divinity. These defects, faults and weaknesses in fact underlie every kind of unbelief and polytheism as well as the reasoning of those who deny the Hereafter.

7. The word "no" here suggests that the unbelievers' ideas concerning reality are altogether mistaken. This "no" before the swearing of the oath clearly indicates that the purpose of the oath is to refute the false ideas that people were wont to express about the Qurʾān.

8. The words "the positions of the stars" refer to the positions, stages, and orbits of stars and planets. The purpose of swearing by the positions of stars is to stress that the same excellence found in

[79] which none but the pure may touch;⁹ [80] a revelation from the Lord of the Universe. [81] Do you, then, take this discourse in light esteem, [82] and your portion in it is simply that you denounce it as false?

[83] Why, then, when the soul leaps up to the throat, [84] the while you are helplessly watching that he is on the verge of death, [85] – at that moment when We are closer to him than you, although you do not see (Us) [86] if you are not subject to anyone's authority, [87] why are you then not able to bring them back to life if you are truthful? [88] So if he is one of those who are near-stationed (to Allah), [89] then happiness and delight and Gardens of Bliss are his. [90] And if he is one of the People on the Right, [91] he will be welcomed by the words: "Peace to you" from the People on the Right. [92] And if he is one of those who give the lie (to this Message) and go astray, [93] then he will be served boiling water, [94] and will be scorched by the Fire.

[95] That indeed is the absolute truth. [96] So glorify the name of your Great Lord.¹⁰

---

the system governing celestial bodies also characterises the Qur'ān. The reason for saying so is to emphasise that the same God Who brought the cosmic order into existence also revealed the Qur'ān.

9. The statement that the Qur'ān has been sent down through "pure" angels underscores that it is free from every kind of defilement. This because it has always been beyond the access of satans who have nothing to do with this Book.

10. It was in keeping with this directive that the Prophet (peace be on him) asked the Muslims to say: "*Subḥāna Rabbī al-'Aẓīm*" (Holy is my Lord, the All-Great), when they are in the state of *rukū'* (bowing).

57

Al-Ḥadīd [Iron]
Madīnan Period

In the name of Allah, the Most Merciful,
the Most Compassionate

[1] All that is in the heavens and the earth extols the glory
of Allah. He is the Most Mighty, the Most Wise. [2] His
is the dominion of the heavens and the earth. He gives
life and causes death, and He has power over everything.
[3] He is the First and the Last, and the Manifest and the
Hidden,¹ and He has knowledge of everything. [4] He it
is Who created the heavens and the earth in six days and
then established Himself on the Throne. He knows all that
enters the earth and all that comes forth from it, and all
that comes down from the heaven and all that goes up to
it.² He is with you wherever you are. Allah sees all that
you do. [5] His is the dominion of the heavens and the

---

1. These are some of God's major Attributes: God has always been
even when there was nothing else and He will always be even
when there will be nothing else. Furthermore, God is the Most
Manifest of the manifest, for whatever is manifest is so because
of His Attributes, His Work and His Light. He is also the Most
Hidden of the hidden. This because He cannot be grasped by the
senses. Additionally, His essence and reality defy man's intellect,
thought and imagination.

2. God not only knows the generality of all things, but also their
particulars and details. To illustrate, God knows each seed that

earth, and to Him are all matters referred (for judgement). [6] He causes the night to pass into the day, and causes the day to pass into the night, and He fully knows all that is hidden in the breasts of people.

[7] Believe in Allah and in His Messenger[3] and expend of what He has entrusted to you. A great reward awaits those of you who believe and spend their wealth. [8] How is it that you do not believe in Allah when the Messenger calls you to believe in your Lord[4] and although he has taken a covenant from you,[5] if indeed you are believers? [9] He it is Who sends down Clear Signs to His servant so as to bring you out from darkness into light. Surely Allah is Most Kind and Most Compassionate to you.

---

penetrates the layers of the earth. He also knows all the leaves and buds that open out of the earth, even as He knows the drops of rain that fall from the sky and the vapours that rise from the seas, rivers and lakes and then head towards the sky. So pervasive is God's knowledge that He is well aware of every single seed that lies under the soil, wherever it might be. Thanks to this pervasive knowledge, God causes that seed to split open, sprout and grow. He is also fully aware of the amount of vapour that rises at any given place and the heights to which it reaches. It is again thanks to this knowledge that God is able to merge this vapour into cloud, distribute it and cause it to descend in the form of rain in different parts of the earth according to well-calculated measures.

3. Here the call to believe in God and His Messenger does not signify merely a verbal declaration of faith. The call is rather to believe sincerely, to believe with all one's mind and heart.

4. Here too the call to believe means believing from the depths of one's heart.

5. That is, the covenant to obey God.

[10] How is it that you do not expend in the Way of Allah when to Allah belongs the inheritance of the heavens and the earth?[6] Those who spent their wealth and took part in fighting before the Victory cannot be equated (with those who spent their wealth and took part in fighting afterwards). They are higher in rank than those who spent and fought afterwards. But to each Allah has promised a good reward.[7] Allah is well aware of all that you do.

[11] Who is it that will give Allah a beautiful loan? A loan that Allah will repay after increasing it many times

---

6. This carries two meanings. First, whatever wealth man has will not endure forever. For surely a day will come when he will die and leave all his possessions behind and then God will inherit all that wealth. Second, when a man spends his wealth in God's cause, he need entertain no fear of destitution and poverty on that account. For God on Whom he depends and in Whose cause he spends his wealth is the Lord of the treasures of the heavens and earth. His treasures have not been exhausted by what He has given people so far; there is still an immense amount in His possession which He can bestow on them in the future.

7. At times there might be very strong indications that the balance of power is heavily tilted against Islam. Furthermore, it might appear that the chances of Islam's victory are not within the range of what is possible. Hence, if some people stake their lives and spend their resources to support Islam's cause in such gloomy circumstances before Islam's triumph and victory, they will occupy very high ranks with God, higher than the ranks of those who strive and spend in God's cause after Islam has emerged victorious in its encounter with Unbelief.

and grant him a generous reward.[8] [12] On that Day you will see believing men and women that their light will be running before them and on their right hands.[9] (They will be told): "A good tiding to you today." There shall be Gardens beneath which rivers flow; therein they shall abide. That indeed is the great triumph. [13] On that Day the hypocrites, both men and women, shall say to the believers: "Look at us that we may extract some light from your light." They will be told: "Go back and seek light for yourselves elsewhere." Then a wall shall be erected between them with a door in it. On the inside of it there will be mercy, and on the outside of it there will be chastisement. [14] The hypocrites will call out to the believers: "Were we not with you?" The believers will reply: "Yes; but you allowed yourselves to succumb to temptations, and you wavered and you remained in doubt and false expectations deluded you until Allah's

---

8. This is indicative of God's beneficence and munificence in dealing with people. A person who spends out of his wealth in God's cause in fact spends out of what God Himself has provided him. Nevertheless, God treats this expense as a loan that he has given to God, provided he does so with sincerity. God makes two promises in regard to the loans so given to Him. First, that He will repay them after increasing them several fold. Second, that over and above that, such people will receive "an excellent reward" from Him.

9. This might give rise to a query, namely, that while one can understand the meaning of the light of the believers running before them, but what is meant by saying that this light "will be running ... on their right hands"? Does this imply that there will be darkness on their left hands? The fact, however, is that if a person is walking with a light in his right hand, his left side will also be lit up. This despite the fact that the light is only in his right hand.

command came to pass, and the Deluder deluded you concerning Allah. [15] So no ransom shall be accepted from you today, nor from those who disbelieved. You are destined for the Fire. That will be your guardian. And that indeed is a grievous destination.

[16] Is the time not come that the hearts of the believers[10] should be humbled to Allah's remembrance and to the Truth that He has revealed, and that they should not be like those who were vouchsafed the Book and then a long time elapsed so that their hearts were hardened? A great many of them are now evil-doers. [17] Know well that Allah revives the earth after it becomes lifeless.[11] We have clearly shown Our Signs to you, perchance you will use your reason.

[18] Verily those who give alms – be they men or women,[12] – and give Allah a beautiful loan shall be repaid after

10. The word "believers" here does not embrace all Muslims. It refers here only to those who had become a part of the Prophet's community after their verbal declaration of faith although their hearts were devoid of any true identification with and sympathy for Islam.

11. The context in which this statement is made needs to be fully grasped. At several places in the Qur'ān, prophethood and revelation of the Book are likened to rainfall. This because the effect produced by them for humanity is similar to the effect of rainfall on the soil. Rainfall causes fertile soil to bloom and blossom. On the contrary, a tract of barren land remains barren even after rainfall.

12. Ṣadaqah, in Islamic parlance, signifies whatever is given in charity with sincerity and with the intent to please God. It is required that this be done without flaunting it and without impressing upon its recipients that it was given to them as a favour.

increasing it many times; and theirs shall be a generous reward. [19] In Allah's sight only those who truly believe in Allah and His Messengers are utterly truthful[13] and true bearers of witness[14] (for the sake of Allah). For them is their reward and their light. As for those who gave the lie to Our Signs, they are the people of Hell.

[20] Know well that the life of this world is merely sport and diversion and adornment and an object of your boasting with one another, and a rivalry in the multiplication of riches and children. Its likeness is that of rain: when it produces vegetation it delights the tillers. But then it withers and you see it turn yellow, and then it crumbles away. In the Hereafter there is (either) grievous chastisement (or) forgiveness from Allah and (His) good pleasure. The life of this world is nothing but delusion. [21] So vie with one another in seeking to attain your Lord's forgiveness and a Garden whose width is as the width of the heaven and the earth,[15] one

13. *Ṣiddīq* ("the most truthful") is the intensive form of *ṣādiq* ("the truthful"). It denotes a truthful person who is free from every taint of falsehood, a person who never diverges from the course of truth and righteousness, one about whom it is inconceivable that he will ever say even a word against his conscience. He is the kind of person who, when he believes in something, does so with utter sincerity and remains faithful to his commitment in all circumstances, a person whose truthfulness of faith is fully testified to by his actions.

14. *Shahīd* is he who bears witness to the Truth both by his word and deed.

15. If this verse is read alongside *Āl ʿImrān* 3: 133, it will be evident that the gardens and palaces that will be granted to people in

which has been prepared for those who believe in Allah and His Messengers. That is Allah's bounty which He bestows upon those whom He pleases. Allah is the Lord of abounding bounty.

[22] No misfortune ever befalls on earth, nor on yourselves but We have inscribed it in the Book before We make it manifest. Surely that is easy for Allah. [23] (We do so) that you may not grieve over the loss you suffer, nor exult over what He gave you. Allah does not love the vainglorious, the boastful, [24] those who are niggardly and bid others to be niggardly. And he who turns away, (should know that) Allah is Self-Sufficient, Immensely Praiseworthy.

[25] Indeed We sent Our Messengers with Clear Signs, and sent down with them the Book and the Balance that people may uphold justice.[16] And We sent down iron, wherein

---

Paradise will be provided to serve as their dwellings. However, the inmates of Paradise will not be confined to these gardens and palaces, but will be able to traverse about the entire Universe (which will also be turned into Paradise).

16. Here we find a succinct statement describing the essence of all Prophets' Mission. All God's Messengers brought along with them three things: (1) *bayyināt*: that is, Clear Signs, strong and persuasive arguments and lucid directives; (2) a Book embodying the teachings needed for mankind's guidance so that people could turn to it for enlightenment; and (3) *mīzān*, that is, the criterion of right and wrong that might precisely indicate, as does a balance, the golden mean of justice that eschews extremes in thought, moral conduct and inter-human relationships.

there is awesome power and many benefits for people,[17] so that Allah may know who, without even having seen Him, helps Him and His Messengers. Surely Allah is Most Strong, Most Mighty.

[26] Indeed We sent forth Noah and Abraham and established in their line Prophecy and the Book. Then some of them embraced the guidance and many of them are wicked. [27] In their wake, We sent a succession of Our Messengers, and raised Jesus, son of Mary, after all of them, and bestowed upon him the Evangel, and We set tenderness and mercy in the hearts of those that followed him. As for monasticism,[18] it is they who invented it; We did not prescribe it for them. They themselves invented it in pursuit of Allah's good pleasure, and then they did not observe it as it ought to have been observed. So We gave their reward to those of them that believed. But many of them are wicked.

---

17. The statement that God "sent down iron" immediately after stating the Prophets' Mission clearly indicates that the word "iron" is not used here in its literal sense; instead, it is used figuratively to signify political and military power. The purpose of the verse, therefore, is to stress that God did not raise His Messengers simply to put forward a scheme to establish justice. It was also a part of the Messengers' Mission to strive to put that scheme into effect. Likewise, it was a part of their Mission to acquire the power needed to establish justice and to render powerless all those who would try to disrupt or resist that scheme.

18. *Rahbānīyah* (monasticism) signifies world-renunciation, withdrawal from the affairs of mundane life, and retreat to mountains and forests or to a life of seclusion and solitude.

[28] Believers, have fear of Allah and believe in His Messenger, and He will grant you a two-fold portion of His Mercy, and will appoint for you a light whereby you shall walk; and He will forgive you. Allah is Most Forgiving, Most Compassionate. [29] (You should do this) so that the People of the Book know that they have no control over Allah's Bounty, and that all bounty is in Allah's Hand; He bestows it on whomsoever He pleases. Allah is the Lord of abounding bounty.

58

Al-Mujādalah [The Contention]
Madīnan Period

In the name of Allah, the Most Merciful,
the Most Compassionate

[1] Allah has surely heard the words of her who contends with you concerning her husband and complains to Allah.[1] Allah hears what both of you say. Verily Allah is All-Hearing, All-Seeing. [2] Those among you who divorce their wives by declaring them to be their mothers,[2] such

---

1. These verses were revealed in connection with the problems faced by a lady, Khawlah bint Tha'labah, whose husband had repudiated the marital tie with her by resorting to *ẓihār*. Khawlah enquired of the Prophet (peace be on him) what the legal position was in that regard. The reason for the enquiry was that no clear injunction on the issue had until then been sent down by God. The Prophet (peace be on him) declared that conjugal relations had become unlawful for the husband on account of *ẓihār*. On hearing this, Khawlah wailed and cried, and said that that would bring utter ruin upon her and her children. At the very same moment that she was entreating the Prophet (peace be on him) to suggest some way out of the impasse, God revealed these verses which embody the injunction relevant to the question. (See vv. 2 ff.)

2. It was common in Arabia that when a quarrel took place between the spouses, the husband would say to his wife in a fit of rage: "You are to me like my mother's back." This expression meant that sexual intercourse with her would amount to having sexual intercourse with his own mother. Such words are still uttered by ignorant and

are not their mothers; none are their mothers except those who gave birth to them. Indeed what they say is highly contemptible and false. Verily Allah is Most Pardoning, Most Forgiving.[3] [3] Those who declare their wives to be their mothers and thereafter go back on what they have said[4] shall free a slave before they may touch each other. That is what you are exhorted to do. Allah is fully aware of all your deeds.[5] [4] And he who does not find a slave

---

foolish people who, in the heat of a family quarrel, declare their wife to be like their mother or sister. This means that she ceases to be his wife and becomes like one of those women with whom marriage is unlawful. Such a pronouncement is called *zihār*. In pre-Islamic times, the Arabs considered this to be a form of divorce; in fact it was considered an even more emphatic statement than the simple pronouncement of divorce.

3. Such a statement is highly reprehensible and calls for severe punishment of the person who pronounces it. Out of sheer benevolence, however, God abrogated this pre-Islamic law and thus saved people from the devastating consequences of *zihār*. Moreover, God laid down a punishment for those guilty of *zihār* (see vv. 3-4). If we bear in mind the enormity of the guilt, the punishment that is laid down should indeed be considered light.

4. This can mean either of the following two: (1) if they wish to rescind their previous statement in order to offset its harmful effects, or (2) if they wish to restore the lawfulness of their marital tie with their spouse which had become unlawful because of their declaring their wife was, to them, like their mother.

5. It is possible that somebody might resort to *zihār* with his wife without publicly announcing it. He might also resume his conjugal relations with his wife later on without atoning for the sin he had committed (by having resorted to *zihār*). It is stressed here that no matter how hard the person concerned might try to keep all this hidden from the rest of the world, God will doubtlessly know it and it will be impossible for him to escape God's chastisement.

(to free), shall fast for two months consecutively before they may touch each other;[6] and he who is unable to do so shall feed sixty needy people.[7]

All this is in order that you may truly believe in Allah and His Messenger.[8] These are the bounds set by Allah; and a grievous chastisement awaits the unbelievers. [5] Verily those who oppose Allah and His Messenger shall be brought low even as those before them were brought low. Surely We have sent down Clear Signs; and a humiliating chastisement awaits the unbelievers; [6] a chastisement that shall come upon them on the Day when Allah will raise them all to a new life and will inform them of their deeds. Allah has recorded it all while they have forgotten it. Allah is a witness over everything.

[7] Are you not aware[9] that Allah knows whatever is in the heavens and whatever is in the earth? Never is there

---

6. That is, it is imperative that such a person should fast consecutively for two months before resuming conjugal relations with his wife. It is mandatory that during these two months there should be no interruption in fasting.

7. The person concerned is required to feed 60 needy people to their fill twice a day. He, however, has the option to provide them cooked food or uncooked food. Moreover, he may feed 60 people all in one day, or feed one person daily for 60 days.

8. Here "believing" signifies believing truthfully and sincerely rather than merely making a formal declaration of faith.

9. From here onwards (vv. 7-10), the hypocrites are censured for the attitude they adopted in the Muslim society. Although they appeared to be a part of the Muslim collective entity, they had secretly formed a group of their own apart from the community of believers. Whenever the Muslims saw them, they would find

any whispering among three but He is their fourth; nor among five but He is their sixth; nor fewer nor more but He is with them wherever they may be. And then He will tell them on the Day of Judgement all that they have done. Surely Allah knows everything. [8] Have you not seen those who were forbidden to whisper and yet they engaged in what they had been forbidden? They secretly converse among themselves concerning sin and transgression and disobedience to the Messenger. And when they come to you, they greet you in a manner that Allah does not greet you,¹⁰ and say to themselves: "Why does Allah not chastise us for these utterances of ours?" Hell it is that shall suffice them, and in it will they burn. How woeful is their destination!

[9] Believers, when you converse in secrecy, let that not be concerning sin and transgression and disobedience to the Messenger; rather, converse concerning virtue and piety. And fear Allah to Whom all of you shall be mustered.

---

them conferring among themselves in hushed tones. It is in the course of these secret deliberations that they came up with ideas as to how to sow discord and spread panic in the ranks of Muslims. In order to accomplish this, they contrived ever-new schemes and invented as well as disseminated all kinds of mischievous rumours.

10. This practice was common among the Jews and the hypocrites. According to a number of traditions, some Jews came to the Prophet (peace be on him) and said: "*Al-Sām ʿalayka yā Abā al-Qāsim.*" They pronounced these words in such a way that people might be led to think that they were pronouncing the well-known greeting: "*al-salām ʿalayka.*" But in fact they used the word *sām* which means death, instead of using the word *salām* which means peace. (The actual meaning of the greeting they used: "*Al-Sām ʿalayka ...*" was: "Death be upon you.")

[10] Whispering is an act of Satan, one that aims at causing grief to the believers; yet without Allah's leave no harm can be caused to them. So in Allah should the believers put all their trust.

[11] Believers, when you are told: "Make room for one another in your assemblies," then make room; Allah will bestow amplitude on you.[11] And when it is said: "Rise up," then rise up;[12] Allah will raise to high ranks those of you who believe and are endowed with knowledge. Allah is well aware of all that you do.

[12] Believers, when you come to the Messenger for private consultation, offer some charity before your consultation with him.[13] That is better for you and more conducive to purity. But if you find nothing to offer in charity, then know that Allah is Most Merciful, Most Compassionate.

---

11. One of the rules of decent behaviour which God and His Messenger (peace be on him) had taught the Muslims was that when any newcomer arrives, those sitting in an assembly should show deference to him and squeeze themselves a bit to make room for him. On the other hand, newcomers were required to act with grace and were asked not to forcefully press their way into any assembly nor should they try to occupy other's seats and thus make them leave the assembly.

12. That is, when people are asked to disperse, they should indeed get up and leave rather than keep sitting.

13. 'Abd Allāh ibn 'Abbās mentioned the reason which led to the promulgation of this injunction. According to him, it was promulgated because people had begun to request the Prophet (peace be on him) to grant them private audiences a little too frequently and without any genuine reason.

[13] Are you afraid that you will have to offer charity when you hold private conversation with the Prophet? But if you are unable to do so and Allah pardons you, then establish Prayer and pay *Zakāh*, and obey Allah and His Messenger. Allah is well aware of all that you do.[14]

[14] Do you not see those who took for friends a people whom Allah is wroth with? They neither belong to you nor you to them. They swear to a falsehood, and they do so knowingly. [15] Allah has prepared for them a grievous chastisement. Indeed, evil are the acts in which they are engaged. [16] They have taken their oaths as a shield by means of which they hinder people from the Way of Allah. Theirs shall be a humiliating chastisement. [17] Neither their possessions nor their offspring will be of any avail to them against Allah. They are the people of the Fire; therein they shall abide. [18] On the Day when Allah will raise them all from the dead they will swear before Him as they swear before you today, thinking that this will avail them. Behold, they are utter liars. [19] Satan has gained mastery over them and has made them neglect remembering Allah. They are the party

---

14. This is the second injunction that was revealed sometime after the first one. The second injunction abrogated the first injunction which had made it mandatory to give some form of charity before a private audience with the Prophet (peace be on him). There is disagreement, however, as regards how long the first injunction remained in force. Qatādah says that it remained in force for less than a day after which it was abrogated. On the other hand, Muqātil ibn Ḥayyān says that it remained in force for ten days, which is the longest period mentioned in any tradition.

of Satan. Behold, the party of Satan will be the losers. [20] Verily those who oppose Allah and His Messenger will be among the most abject beings. [21] Allah has written: "Surely I will prevail; I and My Messengers." Verily Allah is Most Strong, Most Mighty.

[22] You shall not find a people who believe in Allah and the Last Day befriending those who oppose Allah and His Messenger even though they be their fathers or their sons or their brothers or their kindred. He has inscribed faith in their hearts and has strengthened them with a spirit from Him, and He shall make them enter Gardens beneath which rivers flow. Therein they shall abide. Allah is well-pleased with them, and they are well-pleased with Him. They belong to Allah's party. Verily Allah's party shall prosper.

59
༺᭗༻

Al-Ḥashr [The Gathering]
Madīnan Period

*In the name of Allah, the Most Merciful,
the Most Compassionate*

[1] All that is in the heavens and all that is in the earth
extols Allah's Glory: He is the Most Mighty, the Most Wise.
[2] He it is Who in the first assault drove forth the People
of the Book that disbelieved from their homes at the first
gathering of forces.[1] You did not believe that they would
leave; while they too thought that their fortresses would
defend them against Allah. Then Allah came upon them

---

1. "The People of the Book that disbelieved" refers to the Jewish
clan, the Banū al-Naḍīr, who lived in a quarter of Madīnah. The
Prophet (peace be on him) had a treaty of alliance with them which
they repeatedly violated. As a result, the Prophet (peace be on him)
eventually notified them in Rabīʿ al-Awwal 4 A.H. either to leave
Madīnah or to fight. Initially, they declined to leave Madīnah.
Thereupon the Prophet (peace be on him) amassed an army and
launched an attack upon them. However, before any actual battle
could commence, the Banū al-Naḍīr agreed to go into exile. They
did so even though they had very strong fortresses to protect them,
their numbers were larger than the Muslims' and they were well-
equipped militarily.

from whence they did not even imagine,[2] casting such terror into their hearts that they destroyed their homes by their own hands and their destruction was also caused by the hands of the believers. So learn a lesson from this, O you who have perceptive eyes!

[3] If Allah had not decreed banishment for them, He would certainly have chastised them in this world.[3] As for the Hereafter, the chastisement of the Fire awaits them. [4] That is because they set themselves against Allah and His Messenger; and whoever sets himself against Allah should know that Allah is surely Most Stern in retribution.

---

2. The verse reads: "Then Allah came upon them from whence they did not even imagine." Obviously this does not mean that God was previously elsewhere and that later on He launched an attack upon them from a specific location. What is said here is a figurative statement. It means that the Banū al-Naḍīr had thought that they would be able to use their fortresses to defend themselves when an attack came. But when the events unfolded they were taken by surprise. The real attack under whose pressure they collapsed, did not come from outside. Instead, they capitulated because they were left with no will to fight and their morale simply failed them. As a result, neither their army nor their fortresses availed them.

3. "He would certainly have chastised them in this world" means that God would simply have effaced them. Had they chosen to fight rather than surrender, they would have been totally wiped out.

[5] The palm-trees that you cut down or those that you left standing on their roots, it was by Allah's leave that you did so.[4] (Allah granted you this leave) in order that He might humiliate the evil-doers.[5]

---

4. This alludes to the fact that at the very outset of laying siege on the Banū al-Naḍīr's hamlet, the Muslims cut down or burnt many of the palm-trees that stood in the oasis around it. This was obviously done to facilitate the siege. However, the Muslims refrained from cutting down those trees which did not obstruct the movement of troops. Yet the hypocrites and Jews of Madīnah raised a storm of protest against this. They vociferously protested that the Prophet's conduct was self-contradictory. On the one hand he condemned creating disorder in the world. Yet on the other hand, lush green trees laden with fruit were being axed down at his behest. They asked: if that is not spreading disorder in the world, what is? It was in this context that this verse was revealed, stating that the believers' actions – cutting down some trees and letting others stand – could not be declared unlawful, for both acts enjoyed God's sanction.

5. The purpose of the verse is to emphasise that both these acts – cutting down some trees and letting others stand – were meant to humiliate the evil-doers. In the first instance, they were humiliated when the trees, which they themselves had planted and which had been in their possession for a long time, were cut down and they could do nothing but helplessly watch it happen. In the second instance, they also suffered humiliation because whilst leaving Madīnah they could see their green orchards, which they had owned until then, were now in the hands of the Muslims. If they had the power to do so, they would have laid all those orchards to waste so that not a single tree would pass to the Muslims. But the fact was that they were fleeing their home town in utter helplessness. They could do no more than watch, in a state of sheer grief and desperation, their properties slip out of their hands.

[6] Whatever Allah has taken away from them[6] and bestowed (as spoils) on His Messenger[7] for which you spurred neither horses nor camels; but Allah grants authority to His Messengers over whomsoever He pleases. Allah has power over everything.[8] [7] Whatever (from the possessions of the towns people) Allah has bestowed on His Messenger belongs to Allah, and to

---

6. Here mention is being made of the lands and properties that came to be possessed by the Islamic state after Banū al-Naḍīr's exile. From the present verse onwards till verse 10, God lays down a set of directives as to how these properties should be managed.

7. The words suggest that the earth and whatever is on it does not truly belong to God's rebels. The true position of the properties whose ownership passed on to the Muslims from the unbelievers as a result of a lawful and just war is that God, the true Owner of those properties, withdrew them from His disobedient and rebellious servants and granted or restored them to His loyal and faithful servants. This is why, in Islamic parlance, such properties are called *fay'* (restored properties).

8. The Muslims were able to take possession of these properties not because of their army's fighting prowess, but because of the overall strength that God had bestowed upon His Messenger and his community and the wholesome system that it had established. Therefore, the position of these properties was quite different from that of the spoils of war and hence they could not be distributed among the soldiers. It is for this reason that the Islamic law makes a distinction between *ghanīmah* (spoils) and *fay'* (restored properties). *Ghanīmah* consists of those transferable properties which are seized from the enemy in the course of actual fighting. All other transferable and non-transferable goods of the enemy are excluded from the definition of *ghanīmah* and are treated as *fay'*.

the Messenger, and to his kinsfolk,[9] and to the orphans, and to the needy, and to the wayfarer so that it may not merely circulate between the rich among you.[10] So accept whatever the Messenger gives you, and refrain from whatever he forbids you. And fear Allah: verily Allah is Most Stern in retribution.[11] [8] It also belongs to the poor

9. The "kinsfolk" of the Prophet (peace be on him) signify the Banū Hāshim and Banū al-Muṭṭalib. Their portion was laid down in order to enable the Prophet (peace be on him) to use it to meet his own expenses and those of his immediate family as well as to fulfil his obligations towards those of his relatives who stood in need or whom he himself wanted to help. After the Prophet's demise, however, the portion earmarked for his kinsfolk ceased to be a separate and independent apportionment. This because, like the rights of the rest of the orphans, wayfarers and needy, providing for the needy ones of the Banū Hāshim and Banū al-Muṭṭalib became the responsibility of the public treasury. It was, however, recognised that the claims of the needy among the Prophet's kinsfolk had priority over others' claims.

10. This is one of the major guiding principles expounded by the Qur'ān. This verse spells out a basic principle of the Islamic state's economic policy, viz., that wealth should circulate in the whole community rather than only among the rich, this in order to prevent the rich from getting richer and the poor poorer.

11. Although this injunction was revealed in connection with the distribution of the properties of Banū al-Naḍīr, the terms in which it is couched are of a general character. The verse directs the Muslims to obey the Prophet (peace be on him) in all matters. The purpose of the injunction becomes even clearer if we were to consider the words that are used here: "So accept whatever the Messenger gives you, and refrain from whatever he forbids you." It is significant that the words used in opposition to "whatever the Messenger gives you" are not "whatever he does not give". Instead, the words are: "… and refrain from whatever he forbids you."

Emigrants who have been driven out of their homes and their possessions, those who seek Allah's favour and good pleasure and help Allah and His Messenger. Such are the truthful ones. [9] It also belongs to those who were already settled in this abode (of *Hijrah*) having come to faith before the (arrival of the) *Muhājirūn* (Emigrants).[12] They love those who have migrated to them and do not covet what has been given them; they even prefer them above themselves though poverty be their own lot. And whosoever are preserved from their own greed, such are the ones that will prosper. [10] (And it also belongs to) those who came after them,[13] and who pray: "Lord, forgive us and our brethren who have preceded us in faith, and do not put in our hearts any rancour towards those who believe. Lord, You are the Most Tender, the Most Compassionate."[14]

---

12. The people meant by this expression are the *Anṣār*. The purpose of this injunction was to drive home the fact that not only the *Muhājirūn* but also those Muslims who had been living in the Abode of Islam (i.e. Madīnah) before the *Hijrah*, were also entitled to a share in *fay'*.

13. A share in *fay'* was not only meant for the present generation, for the future generations also had a claim on it.

14. Through this verse the Muslims were provided with an important moral directive: that they should nurse no feelings of spite and rancour in their hearts towards other Muslims, and that they should pray for the forgiveness of other Muslims rather than lavish curses and abuse upon them.

[11] Did you[15] not see the hypocrites say to their brethren, the unbelievers among the People of the Book: "If you are banished we too will go with you and will not listen to anyone concerning you; and if war is waged against you, we will come to your aid." But Allah bears witness that they are liars. [12] To be sure, if they are banished, they will not go with them and if war is waged against them, they will not aid them; and even if they provide any aid to them, they will still turn their backs, and thereafter no aid will be forthcoming to them. [13] Surely they have greater dread for you in their hearts than for Allah. That is because they are a people who are devoid of understanding.[16] [14] They will never fight against you as

---

15. The whole passage (vv. 11–17) is a commentary on the hypocrites' attitude and behaviour. This relates to the time when the Prophet (peace be on him) served notice on the Banū al-Naḍīr to leave Madīnah within ten days but had not yet laid siege to the district in which they lived. At this stage the chiefs of the hypocrites sent the Banū al-Naḍīr a message that they would assist them with two thousand men. They also informed them that the Qurayẓah and the Ghaṭafān too would come to their aid. They were, therefore, urged to confront the Muslims courageously and not to lay down their arms. They assured the Banū al-Naḍīr that if the Muslims attacked them, they would fight side by side with them; and if things came to such a pass that the Banū al-Naḍīr were banished, they too would share their exile.

16. The statement that the hypocrites were "devoid of understanding" succinctly epitomises a great truth. Anyone who is granted true understanding of things is aware that it is God Who ought to be held in awe rather than human beings. Hence a wise person will strive to avoid all acts that make him liable to God's censure, regardless of whether any human censures him for that action or not. In like manner, if God enjoins him to perform

a body (in an open battlefield); and if they fight against you they will fight only in fortified townships or from behind walls. Intense is their hostility to one another. You reckon them united while their hearts are divided. That is because they are a people devoid of reason.

[15] They are like those who tasted the evil consequences of their deeds a short while before.[17] A grievous chastisement awaits them. [16] Their parable is that of Satan when he says to man: "Disbelieve," but when he disbelieves, he says: "I am quit of you. Verily I fear Allah, the Lord of the Universe." [17] In the end both will be in the Fire, and will abide in it. That is the recompense of the wrong-doers.

---

a duty, he rises to perform it even if he faces the whole world's opposition in that regard. The person who lacks true understanding and wisdom is he who takes into account how other humans perceive his actions and is not at all concerned about how God sees them. If he avoids doing something he does not do so because he believes that he will be held to account by God; instead, it is because of his fear that human authority will bring him to book. Likewise, if he does something, it is not because God enjoined that action on him, but rather because there existed an authority whose order either commanded or commended it. It is this understanding or lack of it which marks out the attitude and character of a believer from that of an unbeliever.

17. This alludes to the pagans of the Quraysh, and the Jews of the Qaynuqāʿ tribe. As we know, despite their superiority in numbers and weapons, they were vanquished by a handful of ill-equipped Muslims because of these very weaknesses of theirs.

[18] Believers, fear Allah and let every person look to what he sends forward for the morrow.[18] Fear Allah; Allah is well aware of all that you do. [19] And be not like those who forgot Allah and so He made them oblivious of themselves.[19] They are the wicked ones. [20] Those destined for the Fire and those destined for Paradise cannot be alike. Verily it is those destined for Paradise who shall triumph.

[21] Had We sent down this Qur'ān upon a mountain you would indeed have seen it humbling itself and breaking asunder out of fear of Allah.[20] We propound such parables to people that they may reflect.

---

18. The words "for the morrow" refer to the Hereafter. In other words, the assumption is that the life of this world constitutes "to-day" whose "morrow" is the Day of Resurrection.

19. If one forgets God, this inevitably leads one to forget one's true self. When man forgets that he is God's servant, he assigns to himself a position that is basically wrong. Thus his whole life is oriented in the wrong direction because of this misconception on his part. The same happens when he forgets that he is the servant of none else except the One True God. When this happens, he refrains from serving Him whose born servant he is and serves instead many others whose servant he is not.

20. This parable stresses the awesomeness of the responsibility symbolised by the Qur'ān's revelation. The Qur'ān extols God's greatness and states in clear and emphatic terms how immense man's responsibility towards God is. Had any mountain been endowed with the understanding granted to man, it would have trembled and shivered with fear.

[22] He is Allah: there is no god but He;[21] the Knower of the unseen and the manifest, He is the Most Merciful, the Most Compassionate. [23] He is Allah: there is no god but He: the King, the Holy,[22] the All-Peace,[23] the Giver of security,[24] the Overseer,[25] the Most Mighty, the Overpowering, the All-Great. Exalted be He from whatever they associate with Him. [24] He is Allah, the Planner, Executer and Fashioner of creation. His are the names most beautiful. Whatever is in the heavens and the earth extols His Glory.[26] He is the Most Mighty, the Most Wise.

---

21. None other than God has the status and position that entitles him to be served and worshipped. None other than God is possessed of the attributes and powers that justify regarding them as an object of worship and service.

22. God is above any defect or shortcoming; nor is it possible that He has any demerit. On the contrary, He is the Most Holy, One about Whom no imperfection is conceivable.

23. God is far above being liable to any harm, weakness or deficiency; nor can His Perfection ever suffer decline.

24. God's creatures are secure from the possibility that He will ever subject them to injustice, or deny them their rights, or nullify the reward of their deeds, or commit a breach of promise.

25. The word used in the text is *muhaymin* which signifies that God is: (1) the Guardian and Protector; (2) the One Who observes all what others do; and (3) the Provider.

26. This means that all that exists proclaims either by words or by the very fact of its existence that the Creator is immune from every kind of flaw or deficiency, weakness or mistake.

60

Al-Mumtaḥinah [The Examining]
Madīnan Period

In the name of Allah, the Most Merciful,
the Most Compassionate

[1] Believers,[1] if you have left (your homes and) have come forth to struggle in My Way and to seek My good pleasure, do not make friends with My enemies and your enemies. You befriend them whereas they have spurned the Truth that has come to you; and (such is their enmity that) they expel the Messenger and yourselves for no other reason than that you believe in Allah, your Lord. You send to them messages of friendship in secrecy, although I know well whatever you do, be it secretly or publicly. And whosoever of you does so has indeed strayed far away from the Straight Path. [2] If they could overcome you, they would act as your foes and would hurt you by their hands and tongues, and would love to see you become unbelievers.

---

1. Commentators on the Qur'ān are agreed that these verses were revealed at the time when a letter by Ḥāṭib ibn Abī Balta'ah addressed to the unbelievers of Makkah was intercepted. This letter contained information about the Prophet's preparations to launch an attack on Makkah.

[3] On the Day of Resurrection neither your blood-kindred nor your own offspring will avail you.[2] (On that Day) He will separate you.[3] Allah sees all that you do.

[4] You have a good example in Abraham and his companions: they said to their people: "We totally dissociate ourselves from you, and from the deities that you worship instead of Allah. We renounce you[4] and there has come to be enmity and hatred between us and you until you believe in Allah, the One True God." (But you may not emulate) Abraham's saying to his father: "Certainly I will ask pardon for you, although I have no power over Allah to obtain anything on your behalf."[5]

---

2. Ḥāṭib ibn Abī Balta'ah had written this letter to ensure that the members of his family in Makkah remained safe in the event of war. It was, therefore, pointed out: "On the Day of Resurrection neither your blood-kindred nor your own offspring will avail you."

3. This means that all worldly relationships, all ties, all bonds of friendship will be sundered and every person will present himself and render his account in his individual capacity. No one should do anything that is unfair or impermissible in deference to blood kinship, personal friendship or group loyalty for one will have to face the harmful consequences of one's actions in the Hereafter and none will share one's responsibility.

4. That is, the believers renounce them; they neither consider them nor their religious faith to be in the right.

5. In other words, there is an excellent example in Abraham who disavowed his people and broke off relations with them because they disbelieved and associated others with God in His Divinity. This deserves to be emulated. At the same time, one action by Abraham does not merit emulation: namely, his promise to pray for his parents' forgiveness which he later fulfilled.

(And Abraham and his companions prayed): "Our Lord, in You have we put our trust, and to You have we turned, and to You is our ultimate return. [5] Our Lord, do not make us a test for the unbelievers,[6] and forgive us, our Lord. Surely You are Most Mighty, Most Wise."

[6] Indeed there is a good example for you in them; a good example for anyone who looks forward to Allah and the Last Day. As for him who turns away, Allah is All-Sufficient, Immensely Praiseworthy.

[7] It may well be that Allah will implant love between you and those with whom you have had enmity.[7] Allah is Most Powerful; and Allah is Most Forgiving, Most Compassionate.

---

6. There are several ways in which believers can become a test for unbelievers. (1) The unbelievers might establish their dominance over the believers and then claim this to be proof of their being right and of believers being wrong. (2) They may persecute the believers to an unendurable extent with the result that the believers might yield and be ready to compromise their religious faith. (3) The believers, in spite of being representatives of the true faith, should be lacking in the moral excellence that ought to characterise their lives. As a consequence, others might notice in them the flaws that are commonly found in societies rooted in Ignorance. This might provide the unbelievers with an opportunity to claim that the believers' faith had nothing that makes it superior to their unbelief.

7. After asking the Muslims to distance themselves from their unbelieving relatives, they are now being told that a time might come when those same relatives might embrace Islam. If that happens, the strained relations that once prevailed between the Muslims and their unbelieving relatives might be replaced by amity and friendship.

[8] Allah does not forbid that you be kind and just to those who did not fight against you on account of religion, nor drove you out of your homes. Surely Allah loves those who are equitable.[8] [9] Allah only forbids you to be friends with those who have fought against you on account of religion and who have driven you out of your homes and have abetted in your expulsion. And any who make friends with them, they are the wrong-doers.

[10] Believers, when believing women come to you as Emigrants (in the cause of faith), examine them. Allah fully knows (the truth) concerning their faith. And when you have ascertained them to be believing women, do not send them back to the unbelievers.[9] Those women

---

8. Justice demands that Muslims should not be inimical to those who have not been inimical to them. Evidently, it is not fair for Muslims to treat their enemies and non-enemies alike. Muslims have a right to be severe with those who opposed them, drove them out of their homes, and thereafter pursued them with hostility simply because they were Muslims. As for those who do not persecute the Muslims, fairness demands that the Muslims too should treat them well and render them the rights that arise from blood kinship or other kinds of fellowship.

9. After the Treaty of Ḥudaybīyah, the Muslim men who fled Makkah for Madīnah were sent back to Makkah in deference to the terms of the Treaty. Later, Muslim women also began to arrive in Madīnah and the unbelievers demanded that they too should be repatriated. At this stage the question arose as to whether the Treaty also applied to women. God answers the question here, and the essence of the directive that He gives is that if those women were truly Muslims and it was ascertained that they had migrated only for their faith's sake, then they should not be sent back to Makkah. This directive was given because the text of the Treaty, according to a tradition in *Bukhārī*, contained the word *rajul* (man),

are no longer lawful to the unbelievers, nor are those unbelievers lawful to those (believing) women. Give their unbelieving husbands whatever they have spent (as bridal-dues); and there is no offence for you to marry those women if you give them their bridal-dues.[10] Do not hold on to your marriages with unbelieving women: ask for the return of the bridal-due you gave to your unbelieving wives and the unbelievers may ask for the return of the bridal-due they had given to their believing wives. Such is Allah's command. He judges between you. Allah is All-Knowing, Most Wise. [11] And if you fail to receive from the unbelievers a part of the bridal-due of your disbelieving wives, and then your turn comes, pay to those who have been left on the other side an amount the like of the bridal-due that they have paid. And have fear of Allah in Whom you believe.

[12] O Prophet, when believing women come to you and pledge to you[11] that they will not associate aught with

which suggests that the Muslims' commitment to repatriate was confined to the males only.

10. This means that a Muslim who wants to marry any of those women should pay a fresh bridal-due. The bridal-due that would be returned to the unbelieving husbands of Muslim women would not, however, dispense with the need for a fresh payment.

11. This verse was revealed sometime before the conquest of Makkah. Thereafter, the Quraysh started coming to the Prophet (peace be on him) in large numbers to take the oath of allegiance. The Prophet (peace be on him) himself took the oath from men on Mount Ṣafā. As for women, he appointed 'Umar to administer the oath on his behalf. By this oath, the women were asked to pledge that they would refrain from the things mentioned in this verse. Then, on his return to Madīnah the Prophet (peace be on him)

Allah in His Divinity, that they will not steal, that they will not commit illicit sexual intercourse, that they will not kill their children, that they will not bring forth a calumny between their hands and feet,[12] and that they will not disobey you in anything known to be good,[13] then accept their allegiance and ask Allah to forgive them. Surely Allah is Most Forgiving, Most Compassionate.

---

asked the Muslim women of that city to gather in a house and sent 'Umar to take the oath from them.

12. This implies two kinds of calumny: (1) that a woman should accuse another woman of having had unlawful relations with someone and then spreads such rumours around; and (2) that a woman should give birth to a child by someone other than her husband and then assures the latter that the child was his.

13. In this succinct statement two important points of law are enunciated. (1) That obedience even to the Prophet (peace be on him) is limited to "what is known to be good". This despite the fact that there never was any doubt that he would ever order anyone to do anything that was evil. It is evident from this that no one should obey anyone in contravention of God's law. For if obedience even to God's Messenger is contingent upon its being limited to matters "known to be good," who else can claim that people should obey him unconditionally, so that all his commands, laws, rules and practices be necessarily followed even when they are opposed to God's law? (2) This verse also has a constitutional implication. After laying down five prohibitions, the present verse enjoins only one positive command – to obey the Prophet (peace be on him) in all things that are good. As for evils, mention was made of the main evils in which women of the Time of Ignorance were generally involved, and they were asked to pledge that they would refrain from them. As for good actions, these are neither mentioned here nor was any pledge taken in regard to them. The only pledge that they were required to take was that they would obey the Prophet (peace be on him) in the good actions he enjoined.

[13] Believers, do not make friends with those against whom Allah is wrathful and who are despaired of the Hereafter, as despaired as are the unbelievers lying in their graves.

61
꧁꧂

Al-Ṣaff [Battle Formation]
Madīnan Period

*In the name of Allah, the Most Merciful,
the Most Compassionate*

[1] All that is in the heavens and all that is on earth extols Allah's glory. He is the Most Mighty, the Most Wise.

[2] Believers, why do you profess that which you do not practise? [3] It is most loathsome in the sight of Allah that you should profess what you do not practise. [4] Allah indeed loves those who fight in His Way as though they are a solid wall cemented with molten lead.¹

[5] And call to mind when Moses said to his people: "O my people, why do you torment me when you know well that I am Allah's Messenger to you?"² So when they deviated,

---

1. This elucidates two things. First, that God is truly pleased only with those believers who are ready to fight and risk their lives in His Way. Second, that the army of believers whom God loves is possessed of three qualities: (1) It should fight with full consciousness that it is fighting in God's cause alone. (2) It should fight as a well-organised and well-arrayed force rather than as a disorganised and undisciplined mob. (3) It should be possessed of full unity in its ranks and be like "a solid wall cemented with molten lead" against the enemy.

2. This is said as a warning to the Muslims lest they behave towards their Prophet (peace be on him) in the manner the Israelites had

Allah made their hearts deviant. Allah does not direct the evil-doers to the Right Way.[3]

[6] And call to mind when Jesus, son of Mary, said: "O Children of Israel, I am Allah's Messenger to you,[4] I verify the Torah which has come before me, and I give you the glad tiding of a Messenger who shall come after me, his name being Aḥmad."[5]

Yet when he came to them with Clear Signs they said: "This is sheer trickery."[6] [7] Who would be more unjust

---

behaved towards their Prophets. For if they did so, they would inevitably meet the same fate that overtook the Israelites.

3. God does not direct to the Straight Way those who are bent upon following crooked ways. Nor does He forcibly dignify those who are intent upon disobeying Him by enabling them to embrace true guidance and tread the path of righteousness.

4. This refers to the second instance of Israel's disobedience. The first instance belongs to the early period of their glory, whereas the second belongs to a time that marks the end of that period whereafter they were overtaken by God's enduring scourge. The main purpose of narrating these instances is to warn the Muslims against the dire consequences of behaving in the manner the Israelites had behaved.

5. This refers to an unambiguous prediction by Jesus (peace be on him) regarding the coming of the Prophet Muḥammad (peace be on him). We have elaborately substantiated this prediction elsewhere. See my comments on this verse in *Tafhīm al-Qur'ān* (Lahore: Idārah-'i Tarjumān al-Qur'ān, 1971), II edition, Vol. 5, *al-Ṣaff* 61: n. 8, pp. 461-476.

6. The actual word used is *siḥr* which signifies, in the present context, trickery and fraud rather than magic or sorcery. It may be noted that in the Arabic literary usage the meaning of the word

than he who invents a lie about Allah[7] the while he is being called to Islam?[8] Allah does not direct such evil-doing folk to the Right Way. [8] They seek to extinguish Allah's light (by blowing) with their mouths, but Allah shall spread His light in all its fullness, howsoever the unbelievers may abhor this.

[9] He it is Who has sent forth the Messenger with the Guidance and the True Religion that He may make it prevail over all religion, however those that associate aught with Allah in His Divinity might dislike this.

[10] Believers, shall I direct you to a commerce[9] that will deliver you from a grievous chastisement?

---

sihr is not confined to magic. The use of this word in the sense of deceit is also well-established. The verse, therefore, means that when the Prophet Muḥammad (peace be on him), whose coming had been foretold by Jesus, did indeed come, his claim to prophethood was denounced as sheer fraud and deception by the Israelites and the followers of the Prophet Jesus (peace be on him).

7. In other words, it is highly iniquitous to give the lie to the claim made by a Prophet who had been so designated by God and to dismiss God's revelation to him as his own contrivance.

8. In the first place, it is outrageously unjust to declare a true Prophet to be an imposter. But it is even more monstrous to hurl abuses and slanders at a true Prophet who calls people to worship and obey God, and then to resort to such ignoble means as lies, false accusations and slander to thwart his Mission.

9. "Commerce" represents a venture wherein a person employs his wealth, time, effort, intelligence and ability to obtain profit. It is in consideration of this that faith and *jihād* are here called "commerce". The point that is being made here is that only when a person devotes all his possessions to God's cause will he be able to obtain the profit that is mentioned hereinafter.

[11] Have faith in Allah and His Messenger and strive in the Way of Allah with your possessions and your lives. That is better for you if you only knew. [12] He will forgive you your sins and will admit you to Gardens beneath which rivers flow. He will lodge you in excellent mansions in the Gardens of eternity. That is the supreme triumph. [13] He will also grant you the other favour that you desire: help from Allah and a victory that will come soon. Give glad tidings of this to the believers.

[14] Believers, become Allah's helpers, as Jesus, son of Mary, said to the disciples: "Who is my helper in (calling people) to Allah?" The disciples had responded by saying: "We are Allah's helpers." Then a section of the Children of Israel believed and a section rejected the call. Thereafter We aided the believers against their enemies, and they prevailed.[10]

---

10. Those who do not believe in Jesus Christ are Jews. As for those who believe in him, they are Christians as well as Muslims. God first made the Christians prevail against the Jews, and later that Muslims too prevailed against them. Thus, those who disbelieve in Jesus (peace be on him) were overcome by both Christians and Muslims. The purpose of mentioning this fact is to deliver a message of assurance to the Muslims that in the same manner that Muslims and believers in Jesus Christ (peace be on him) had triumphed over those who disbelieved in him in the past, so will the believers in the Prophet Muḥammad (peace be on him) triumph over those who would disbelieve in him.

62
❊❊❊

Al-Jumuʿah [Friday]
Madīnan Period

In the name of Allah, the Most Merciful,
the Most Compassionate

[1] All that is in the heavens and all that is in the earth extols the glory of Allah, the Sovereign, the Holy, the All-Mighty, the All-Wise.

[2] He it is Who has sent to the gentiles¹ a Messenger from among themselves, one who rehearses to them His verses, purifies their lives, and imparts to them the Book and the Wisdom although before that they were in utter error; [3] and (He has also) sent him to those others who have not yet joined them.² He is the Most Mighty, the

---

1. Here the word *ummī* (gentile) is used as a Jewish term. Implicit in its use is a subtle irony. In order to appreciate this we ought to recall that the Jews used to look down upon the Arabs and disdainfully called them gentiles. These very Jews are now being told that God the Most Mighty and the Most Wise had raised His Messenger from the ranks of these contemptible gentiles. Since that Messenger did not rise of his own accord but was raised instead by the Mighty and Wise Sovereign of the Universe, the Jews will only harm themselves rather than the Prophet (peace be on him) if they decide to clash with him.

2. Muḥammad's Messengership is not confined to the Arabs but embraces all other nations and races of the world as well, including those who have not yet joined the ranks of believers but who will do so in the future.

[852]

Most Wise.³ [4] Such is Allah's favour: He bestows it on whomsoever He pleases. Allah is the Lord of abounding favour.

[5] The parable of those who were charged with the Torah and then they failed to live up to it is that of a donkey laden with books. Even more evil is the parable of the people who gave the lie to the Signs of Allah.⁴ Allah does not direct such wrong-doers to the Right Way.

[6] Tell them: "O you who have become Judaised,⁵ if you arrogantly fancy that you are Allah's favourites to the

---

3. It is a portentous manifestation of God's power and wisdom that He raised a Prophet of immense greatness in a nation of uncultivated gentiles. His greatness is evidenced by the fact that his teachings are so immensely revolutionary and comprise universal principles of such abiding value that they can unify humanity for all times into one community and serve as the nucleus of its guidance and inspiration.

4. Those who gave the lie to God's Signs are even worse than donkeys. For donkeys are excusable on the grounds that they are devoid of all understanding. On the contrary, those who were given the Torah as a guidance are possessed of understanding. Moreover, they read as well as teach the Torah and, hence, are well aware of its teachings. Despite this, they had deviated from its teachings and deliberately refused to accept Muḥammad (peace be on him) as God's Prophet. They did so even though according to their own scripture – the Torah – he was absolutely right in claiming to be a Prophet. Thus their guilt did not consist of not comprehending but of wittingly giving the lie to God's Revelation.

5. The words used here are significant. The audience is not addressed with the words: "O Jews"; they are rather addressed as: "O you who have become Judaised." This because the religion entrusted to the Prophet Moses and to the other Prophets before and after him (peace be on all of them) was none else than Islam.

[853]

exclusion of all people, then wish for death, if you are truthful in your claim."⁶ [7] But they shall never wish for death because of the (evil) deeds they have committed. Allah is well aware of these evil-doers. [8] Tell them: "The death from which you flee will certainly overtake you. Then you will be returned to Him Who fully knows what is hidden and what is manifest. Thereupon He will let you know all that you used to do."

[9] Believers, when the call for Prayer is made on Friday, hasten to the remembrance of Allah and give up all trading.⁷ That is better for you, if you only knew.

None of these Prophets was a Jew, nor did Judaism exist in their time. The emergence of a distinct religion called Judaism relates to a period long after Moses' time.

6. The Jews of Arabia were not inferior to the Muslims in respect of their numbers and strength; as for their resources, they were vastly superior. Despite all this the Muslims prevailed against them. This can be explained mainly by the fact that far from being afraid to die in God's cause, the Muslims simply yearned to lay down their lives. In sharp contrast, the Jews were not committed to any cause for which they would be prepared to fight and, if need be, to die: neither for God's cause, nor for the sake of their nation, nor for the sake of their life, property and honour. They only wished to live, and live regardless of the quality of that life. This excessive love for life had generated cowardice in their ranks.

7. The word "remembrance" here signifies the Friday Sermon. This is because the first thing to which the Prophet (peace be on him) paid attention after the *adhān* (Call to Prayer) was not Prayer itself but the Friday Sermon which always preceded the Friday Prayer. Furthermore, the words "hasten to the remembrance of Allah," mean that one should proceed to the Friday Sermon with a sense of urgency and importance, and not that one should literally run to it. The directive "to give up all trading" means that after the Call to Friday Prayer has been made, one should not only give up trading

[10] But when the Prayer is ended, disperse in the land and seek Allah's Bounty,[8] and remember Allah much so that you may prosper.[9]

---

but also concern oneself solely with the Friday service and shun every other occupation. It is also pertinent to mention that Muslim jurists are agreed that every kind of business transaction after the Call to Friday Prayer is forbidden. It is also pertinent to note that according to a *ḥadīth*, children, women, slaves, sick people, and travellers are exempt from the obligation to perform Friday Prayer.

8. This does not mean that everybody is *obligated* to disperse in the land and engage in seeking their livelihood after the Friday Prayer is over. What is meant is that people *may* disperse in the land and proceed with their economic activities. It is important to bear in mind the context in which these words occur. The words "disperse in the land and seek Allah's Bounty" follow the directive to stop all business activities after the Call to the Friday Prayer is made. Therefore, when the Prayer is over, it is natural that believers be told that they *may* proceed with whatever economic activities they wish to.

This is similar to what was said in the Qur'ān on another occasion. People were ordered not to engage in hunting when they were in the state of *iḥrām*. But once they had completed the obligatory requirements of Pilgrimage: "… then hunt" (*al-Māʾidah* 5: 2). This does not mean at all that it was *obligatory* for such people to hunt; rather, what is meant is that the restrictions on hunting were now terminated and so they *may* hunt if they so wanted.

Those who argue on the basis of this verse that there is no holiday on Friday in Islam, however, put forward a flawed argument. For if the Muslims have to have a weekly holiday it should obviously be on Friday in the same manner that the Jews have it on Saturday and the Christians on Sunday.

9. We have translated this verse as follows: "… so that you may prosper." If we take the Arabic word *laʿalla* used in the verse literally, we would have translated it as: "… perhaps you will prosper." Our present translation, however, is appropriate because here the word *laʿalla* is not used to indicate any doubt. In order to comprehend

[11] Yet no sooner than they saw some trading or amusement, they flocked to it and left you standing by yourself.[10] Tell them: "That which is with Allah is far better than amusement and trading.[11] Allah is the Best Provider of sustenance."[12]

---

the true purport of *la'alla* (literally, "perhaps") it should be borne in mind that the statement here is analogous to a royal declaration and is couched in terms befitting royalty. The statement is like a boss saying to his subordinates: "Carry out this duty well, and perhaps you will be promoted." The tenor of the address subtly implies a promise in expectation of which subordinates will perform their tasks with full devotion.

10. This refers to an incident that took place in the early Madīnan period of the Prophet's life. A trading caravan had arrived in Madīnah from Syria exactly at the time of Friday Prayer and its arrival was announced by the beating of drums. The Prophet (peace be on him) was then delivering his Friday Sermon. The sound of the drums made people impatient with the result that all but 12 persons left the mosque and headed for the caravan.

11. These words indicate a kind of lapse on the part of the Companions. Had the underlying cause of this lapse been their weakness of faith or their wilful preference for worldly benefits over the Hereafter, God's reproach would have been couched in much sterner terms. But what caused the incident was the fact that the Muslims had not yet received any extensive training to live according to Islamic principles. In view of this, the rules pertaining to the Friday Prayer were enunciated much in the manner a teacher would do. This was followed by expressing disapproval of the Companions' actions after which it was declared that the reward they would receive by listening to the Friday Sermon and offering the Friday Prayer would be far greater than anything they could gain from engaging in business and recreation.

12. God is a much better Provider of sustenance than all those who are ostensibly a means to provide sustenance to God's creatures.

63

Al-Munāfiqūn [The Hypocrites]
Madīnan Period

In the name of Allah, the Most Merciful,
the Most Compassionate

[1] (O Prophet), when the hypocrites come to you, they say: "We bear witness that you are certainly Allah's Messenger." Allah certainly knows that you are His Messenger. But Allah also bears witness that the hypocrites are utter liars![1] [2] They shelter behind their oath, and thus hinder their own selves and others from the Path of Allah. Evil indeed is what they do. [3] All that is because they first believed and then disbelieved, and therefore a seal was set on their hearts; as a result they understand nothing.[2]

---

1. The hypocrites' statement about the Prophet (peace be on him) that he was God's Messenger was intrinsically true. They were, however, simply uttering something with their tongues without truly believing in it. In this sense, they were guilty of lying even though their statement itself was factually correct.

2. In this verse, the statement that they "believed" merely signifies a verbal declaration of faith in order to join the ranks of Muslims. As for the statement "and then disbelieved," this means that those people did not believe with sincerity. In other words, they continued to persist in their former state of unbelief despite their verbal declaration of faith.

This is one of those verses of the Qur'ān in which the meaning of the notion of sealing a person's heart has been clearly explained. The

[4] When you look at them, their persons are pleasing, and when they speak, you pay heed to what they say. But in truth they are (merely) beams of timber propped-up (against a wall).[3] They consider every shout they hear to be directed against them. They are your utter enemies; guard against them. May Allah do away with them! How are they being turned away (from the Truth)?[4]

[5] When it is said to them: "Come, Allah's Messenger will seek forgiveness for you," they (contemptuously) shake their heads and you see them holding back in pride. [6] It is all the same for them whether you ask forgiveness for

---

hypocrites' present state had not come about because God first sealed their hearts and then, as a result of His sealing, faith could not enter into them, and hence why they were forced to become hypocrites! The fact, however, is quite contrary to this. God sealed their hearts after they themselves had decided to cling to their unbelief despite their verbal declaration of faith. It was only then that they were deprived of the ability to believe sincerely and were enabled to embrace the hypocrisy which they chose for themselves.

3. Those whom one saw sitting propped-up against a wall were, in truth, not humans but beams of timber. They were considered to be like timber because they were altogether devoid of the moral spirit which is the essence of humanity. Again, the simile of beams of timber propped-up against a wall was used to underscore their utter worthlessness. For beams of timber propped-up against a wall can do no good. For if timber has any worth it is only when it is used in a ceiling, or door, or furniture. But timber placed in the manner described above is totally devoid of any use.

4. It is not clear who turned them away from the true faith to hypocrisy. This ambiguity itself would suggest that their perversion was caused not by one but by a combination of factors. One of these factors was Satan himself; another was evil companions; still

them or not; for Allah shall never forgive them. Surely Allah does not direct the transgressing folk to the Right Way.

[7] It is they who say: "Give nothing to those who are with the Messenger of Allah so that they may disperse." (They say so although) the treasures of the heavens and the earth belong to Allah. But the hypocrites do not understand. [8] They say: "When we return to Madīnah, the honourable ones will drive out from it those that are abject."⁵ In truth, all honour belongs to Allah, and to His Messenger, and to the believers. But the hypocrites do not know.

[9] Believers, let your possessions and your offspring not make you negligent of Allah's remembrance. For whoso does that, they will be the losers. [10] And spend of what Allah has granted you by way of sustenance before death should come to any of you and he should say: "Lord, why did You not defer my return for a while so that I might give alms and be among the righteous?" [11] But when a person's term comes to an end, Allah never grants any respite. Allah is well aware of all that you do.

---

other factors were their own evil selves, their spouses, their children, or the evil ones in their community. Likewise, some people were driven to the path of evil by envy, spite and arrogance. All these factors contributed to their turning away from the True Faith.

5. Such people do not simply fail to approach the Prophet (peace be on him) with the request that he seek God's forgiveness on their behalf. What is more, no sooner is such a suggestion made to that effect than they arrogantly shake their heads, considering it an affront to go to the Prophet (peace be on him) and ask him to seek God's forgiveness on their behalf. They, therefore, abstained from going to him altogether. This was a clear indication of their hypocrisy.

64

Al-Taghābun [Mutual Gains and Losses]
Madīnan Period

*In the name of Allah, the Most Merciful,
the Most Compassionate*

[1] All that is in the heavens and all that is in the earth extols Allah's glory. His is the sovereignty and to Him is all praise due; He has power over everything.¹ [2] He it is Who has created you: and among you are those that deny the Truth and among you are those that believe in it. Allah observes all that you do. [3] He created the heavens and the earth with Truth and shaped you, giving you excellent shapes. And to Him is your ultimate return. [4] He knows what is in the heavens and the earth, and knows what you conceal and what you disclose.² Allah even knows what lies hidden in the breasts of people.

[5] Has the news of the unbelievers of the past not reached you? (They disbelieved) and then tasted its evil consequence. A grievous chastisement awaits them. [6] This was because their Messengers would come to them with Clear Signs, but they would say: "Shall mortals

---

1. God is All-Powerful and can do whatever He pleases. It is beyond anyone's ability to limit His power.

2. This can also be translated as follows: "He knows whatever you do secretly and whatever you do publicly."

(like ourselves) guide us to the Right Way?" They rejected the Truth and turned away. Thereupon Allah became unconcerned with them, for Allah is Self-Sufficient, Innately Praiseworthy.

[7] The unbelievers have vehemently contended that they shall not be raised to life. Say to them: "Yes, by my Lord, you shall surely be raised to life,[3] and you shall certainly be fully informed of all that you did. That is easy enough for Allah."

[8] So believe in Allah and in His Messenger and in the Light that We have sent down.[4] Allah is fully aware of what you do. [9] (You shall come to know that) when

---

3. The affirmation of the Hereafter by stating it on oath gives rise to the question: what difference will it make for anyone who denies the Hereafter, whether they affirmed it on oath or not? Since they do not believe in the Hereafter, how can we expect them to believe in it simply because someone states its veracity on oath. The answer to the question is that the audience of the Prophet (peace be on him) – thanks to their personal knowledge and experience of him – were well aware that he never said anything untrue in all his life. Hence, notwithstanding the slanderous allegations they fabricated against him, they knew in the depths of their hearts that such an utterly truthful person could never state on oath anything about which he was not absolutely sure.

4. The context itself indicates that the "Light" which is mentioned here is the Qur'ān itself. A light is itself manifest and it also makes other things manifest which were hidden by the darkness around it. The same is the case with the Qur'ān. In the first place, the Qur'ān is a light which makes its own Truth manifest. Moreover, through this light human beings can comprehend all that they are unable to comprehend through the usual means of knowledge and intellection available to them.

He will assemble you on the Day of Gathering.[5] That shall be the Day (to determine) mutual gains and losses.[6] Whoever believes in Allah and acts righteously, Allah will have his evil deeds expunged and will admit him to Gardens beneath which rivers flow. Therein they shall abide forever. That is the supreme triumph. [10] As for those who disbelieved and gave the lie to Our Signs: they shall be the inmates of the Fire, and will abide in it. That is a woeful resort!

[11] No misfortune ever befalls unless it be by Allah's leave. And whosoever has faith in Allah, Allah directs his heart along the Right Path. Allah has knowledge of everything. [12] Obey Allah and obey the Messenger. But if you turn away from obedience, (then know that) Our Messenger has no other duty than to clearly convey the Truth. [13] Allah there is no god but He; in Allah should the believers put all their trust.[7]

---

5. "The Day of Gathering" means the Day of Resurrection when all humans ever born in the world from the beginning of creation until the Last Day will be gathered together at the same time.

6. Whether one has made a gain or incurred a loss will only be known on the Day of Resurrection. It is only then that it will become clear as to who has acted foolishly and who has acted sensibly; who devoted his resources to a worthless enterprise and is thus a pauper and who directed his energies, ability, wealth and time to a gainful bargain and will thus obtain immense riches. These gains could also have been obtained by others had they not failed to know the Truth.

7. All power of overlordship belongs exclusively to God. No one else has the power to make or mar anyone's destiny. God alone can make someone prosper and He alone can avert adversity and suffering. Hence anyone who sincerely believes in the One True God has no

[14] Believers, there are enemies to you from among your spouses and your off-spring, so beware of them. But if you forgive and overlook their offences and pardon them, then surely Allah is Most Forgiving, Most Compassionate.[8] [15] Your possessions and your offspring are nothing but a trial for you. And there awaits a great reward for you with Allah. [16] So hold Allah in awe as much as you can, and listen and obey, and be charitable. This is for your own good. And whoever remains safe from his own greediness, it is such that will prosper. [17] If you give Allah a goodly loan, He will increase it for you several fold and will forgive you. Allah is Most Appreciative, Most Forbearing. [18] He knows that which is beyond the ken of perception as well as that which can be perceived. He is the Most Mighty, the Most Wise.

---

option but to put all his trust in Him and continue to perform his duty as a person of faith, fully convinced that good lies only in following the Way which God Himself has directed His creatures to.

8. In terms of worldly relationships, a person is wont to regard his spouses and offspring as his dearest. But seen from the vantage-point of religious faith, they could also be considered his enemies. This enmity might manifest itself in myriad ways. Some people might be enemies because they prevent him from goodness and urge him to evil. Others might be enemies because they prevent him from proceeding along the Path of True Faith and push him towards unbelief. Still others might be enemies in so far as their sympathies lie with the unbelievers. Whatever the case might be, he needs to be on guard against them and not overly attuned to these bonds to the point of ruining one's prospects in the Hereafter. On the other hand, this does not mean that he should be harsh in his dealings with his immediate family on the grounds that they are his enemy. The upshot of this directive is that if he does not succeed in reforming his nearest and dearest, he should at least try to save himself from being deflected from the right course.

65
༜༻༺

Al-Ṭalāq [Divorce]
Madīnan Period

In the name of Allah, the Most Merciful,
the Most Compassionate

[1] O Prophet, when you divorce women, divorce them
for their waiting-period,¹ and compute the waiting period
accurately, and hold Allah, your Lord, in awe.² Do not

---

1. The injunction "to divorce them for their waiting-period"
means two things, and both are meant here. First, it means that a
person should not divorce his wife during her menstrual period;
he should rather pronounce his divorce at a time when her *'iddah*
(waiting-period) might commence. (That is, the divorce should be
pronounced in the clear period.) Second, the divorce should be of
a kind wherein it would be possible for the husband and the wife
to reconcile themselves during the waiting-period. According to
the traditions which explain this injunction, whenever a person
decides to pronounce divorce he should adopt the following
procedure: (i) that he should pronounce the divorce during his
wife's clear period wherein he did not have sexual intercourse
with her; (ii) that he should not pronounce it if it is known that the
wife is pregnant; and (iii) that he should not pronounce the three
divorces together.

2. The directive to "compute the waiting-period accurately"
means that divorce should not be treated lightly, and that the
people concerned should be exactly aware of when the divorce
was pronounced, when the waiting-period commenced, and
when it came to an end. In other words, due care should be taken

turn them out of their homes (during the waiting period) – nor should they go away (from their homes)[3] – unless they have committed a manifestly evil deed.[4] Such are the bounds set by Allah; and he who transgresses the bounds set by Allah commits a wrong against himself. You do not know: maybe Allah will cause something to happen to pave the way (for reconciliation). [2] And when they reach the end of their term (of waiting), then either honourably retain them (in the bond of wedlock) or honourably part with them, and call two persons of known probity as witnesses from among yourselves,[5] and (let these witnesses) give upright testimony for the sake of Allah.

to remember the date and time and the state of the woman upon whom the divorce was pronounced.

3. In those circumstances the husband should not allow his anger to make him expel his wife from the house nor should the wife leave the house in a state of annoyance and disgust. The house in which she had been living is hers during the waiting-period. Both the spouses should stay in that house during the waiting-period for this might bring about reconciliation between them. It is obvious that if they stay in the same house for a duration of three months, or three menstrual cycles, or until child-birth in the case of pregnancy, many an occasion for reconciliation is likely to arise.

4. "… have committed a manifestly evil deed" refers either to an act of sexual immorality, excessively quarrelsome behaviour, or recourse to abusive language by the divorced woman during the waiting-period.

5. That is, to call two persons of known probity as witnesses to the pronouncement of divorce or to its revocation.

That is to what all those that believe in Allah and the Last Day are exhorted.[6] Allah will find a way out for him who fears Allah, [3] and will provide him sustenance from whence he never even imagined. Whoever puts his trust in Allah, He shall suffice him. Surely Allah brings about what He decrees; Allah has set a measure for everything.

[4] The waiting period of those of your women who have lost all expectation of menstruation shall be three months in case you entertain any doubt; and the same shall apply to those who have not yet menstruated.[7] As for pregnant

---

6. These words clearly indicate that the instructions given above were by way of good counsel and moral exhortation rather than as mandatory legal commands. Now it is possible that someone might pronounce divorce in disregard of the procedure prescribed above, or he might not compute the waiting-period accurately, or might expel his divorced wife from the house without justification, or revoke his divorce and return to his wife with the intent to vex her, or part company with her after an acrimonious quarrel rather than in a graceful manner, or fail to call anyone to witness his pronunciation of divorce. Even though all these acts constitute violations of the instructions given above, this fact still does not nullify his divorce or its revocation. However, the fact that a person acts in contravention of God's directive will indicate that his heart is devoid of true faith in God and the Last Day. It is primarily for this reason that he had acted in a manner that does not behove a good believer.

7. Those women may not have experienced menstruation either because they are too young, or because their menstrual cycle was delayed (as does happen in the case of some women), or because they never experienced menstruation at all (which happens rarely). In any event, the waiting-period of such women is the same as for the women who are divorced after menopause; namely, three months from the time of the pronouncement of divorce.

women, their waiting period shall be until the delivery of their burden.[8] Allah will create ease for him who fears Allah. [5] This is the commandment of Allah that He has revealed to you. Whoever fears Allah, He will expunge his evil deeds and will richly reward him.

[6] (During the waiting period) lodge them according to your means wherever you dwell, and do not harass them to make them miserable.

And if they are pregnant, provide for them maintenance until they have delivered their burden. And if they suckle your offspring whom they bore you, then give them due recompense, and graciously settle the question of compensation between yourselves by mutual understanding. But if you experience difficulty (in determining the compensation for suckling) then let another woman suckle the child. [7] Whoever has abundant means, let him spend according to his means; and he whose means are straitened, let him spend out of what Allah has given him. Allah does not burden any human being beyond the means that He has bestowed upon him. Possibly Allah will grant ease after hardship.

---

8. The waiting-period of a widow comes to an end with the delivery of the child in her womb. This is regardless of the time lapse between the death of her husband and the child's birth. If she happens to deliver the child immediately after her husband's death, the time of delivery still marks the end of her waiting-period. However, her waiting-period will not end even after the lapse of four months and ten days if she has not yet given birth to the child in her womb.

[8] How many⁹ towns rebelled against the commandment of their Lord and His Messengers. Then We called them to a stern accounting, and subjected them to a harrowing chastisement. [9] So they tasted the evil fruit of their deeds; and the fruit of their deeds was utter loss. [10] Allah has laid in store for them a grievous chastisement. So fear Allah, O people of understanding who have attained to faith. Allah has sent down to you an Exhortation, [11] a Messenger¹⁰ who rehearses to you Allah's verses that clearly expound the Guidance so that He may bring out those that believe and act righteously, from every kind of darkness into light. He will admit whosoever believes in Allah and acts righteously to Gardens beneath which rivers flow. They shall abide in them forever. For such has Allah made an excellent provision.

---

9. Here the Muslims are being warned of dire consequences both in this world and in the Next if they disobey the commands conveyed to them through God's Messenger and His Book. On the other hand, they are also being apprised of the great rewards that will be theirs if they obey God and His Messenger.

10. Some commentators on the Qur'ān are of the opinion that "Exhortation" here signifies the Qur'ān, and the word "Messenger" (see v. 11) signifies the Prophet Muḥammad (peace be on him). Some other commentators believe that "Exhortation" here refers to the Prophet (peace be on him) because he was the personification of "exhortation". We are inclined to this second view.

[12] Allah it is He Who created seven heavens, and, like them, the earth.[11] His commandment descends among them. (All this is being stated so that you know) that Allah has power over everything, and that Allah encompasses all things in His knowledge.

---

11. The expression "like them" does not mean that God has created the same number of earths as He has created the heavens. What it really means is that in the same way that God has created several heavens, He has also created several earths. Here the words "like them, the earth" are used with a purpose. God has made the earth to serve as a bed and a cradle for the creatures living on it. In like manner, God has also made the other earths in the Universe to serve the same purpose – to provide a bed and a cradle to the creatures living on them. In other words, the innumerable stars and planets that we see in the sky are not empty and desolate; a great many of them are as vibrant with life as the earth is.

66

Al-Taḥrīm [Prohibition]
Madīnan Period

In the name of Allah, the Most Merciful,
the Most Compassionate

[1] O Prophet, why do you forbid what Allah has made lawful for you?¹ Is it to please your wives?² Allah is Most

---

1. Although this sentence is couched in the form of a question, it is in fact a statement of disapproval. These words are not said in order to enquire about why the Prophet (peace be on him) acted in the manner described here, but to let him know that God does not approve of his act of making unlawful for himself that which God had made lawful. The Prophet (peace be on him) was, in any case, not an ordinary person. When he made something unlawful for himself, this could influence his followers to regard it as unlawful, or at least as something religiously disapproved. God censures the Prophet (peace be on him) on this account and asks him to refrain from prohibiting for himself whatever God has made lawful. It clearly follows from this that the Prophet (peace be on him) did not have the authority *per se* to declare things of his own accord lawful or unlawful.

2. It is evident from this particular event that the Prophet's act of making a lawful thing unlawful was not actuated by desire; instead, he did so in deference to some of his wives' desires. According to authentic traditions, someone had sent honey to one of his wives (viz. Zaynab). The Prophet (peace be on him) being fond of honey then started staying in her house for a longer time than usual, which incited the other wives' jealousy. They, therefore, joined hands in creating in him a dislike for honey so much so that he promised to give up its consumption altogether.

Forgiving, Most Compassionate. [2] Allah has prescribed for you a way for the absolution of your oaths.[3] Allah is your Guardian. He is All-Knowing, Most Wise.

[3] The Prophet confided something to one of his wives and then she disclosed it (to another); so after Allah revealed to the Prophet (that she had disclosed that secret), he made a part of it known to her and passed over a part of it. And when he told her about this [i.e., that she had disclosed the secret entrusted to her], she asked: "Who informed you of this?" He said: "I was told of it by He Who is All-Knowing, All-Aware."[4]

---

3. That is, the Prophet (peace be on him) should free himself of the constraint that he had imposed upon himself by breaking the oath and offering expiation as laid down in *al-Mā'idah* 5: 89. [The expiation for breaking oaths, as laid down in this verse, is as follows: either "… to feed ten needy persons with more or less the same food as you are wont to give to your families, or to clothe them, or to set free from bondage the neck of one man; and he who does not find the means to do so shall fast for three days." Ed.]

4. No tradition precisely indicates what secret it was that one of the Prophet's wives disclosed to another and which God subsequently revealed to the Prophet (peace be on him). It may be noted, however, that in order to comprehend the purpose for which this verse was revealed, it is not at all important to know what that secret was. The true purpose for which this incident is narrated in the Qur'ān is to warn the Prophet's wives, and through them, the wives of responsible Muslims not to be negligent in guarding their secrets. The higher a person's position of responsibility in the community the more dangerous it is that secrets should leak out of his household. Regardless of whether a matter is important or not, once a person becomes careless in guarding his secrets it is likely that he will disclose important matters along with those that are unimportant.

[4] If the two of you turn in repentance to Allah (that is better for you), for the hearts of both of you have swerved from the Straight Path.[5] But if you support one another against the Prophet, then surely Allah is his Protector; and after that Gabriel and all righteous believers and the angels are all his supporters.[6] [5] Maybe if he were to divorce you, your Lord might grant him in exchange wives better than you[7] – those who truly submit to Allah, are full of faith, obedient, disposed to repentance, and given to worship and fasting – both previously wedded ones and virgins.

---

5. According to a tradition narrated by 'Umar, "both of you" here alludes to 'Ā'ishah and Ḥafṣah. The meaning of the words "swerved from the Straight Path" is also explained by 'Umar who stated that both these ladies had begun taking a degree of liberty with the Prophet (peace be on him). God did not approve of this and therefore warned them.

6. The Prophet's wives were told that if they entered into a league against him they would only hurt themselves because the Prophet (peace be on him) enjoyed God's protection and support. Moreover, Gabriel and God's other angels and also all righteous believers too stood by him. How, then, would their binding together against him be able to cut any ice?

7. This shortcoming did not only apply to 'Ā'ishah and Ḥafṣah but to some of the Prophet's other wives as well. Therefore, after admonishing these two, the other wives are also admonished. Traditions indicate that in those days the Prophet (peace be on him) was so unhappy with his wives that he distanced himself from them for a month which gave rise to the rumour that he had divorced them.

[6] Believers, guard yourselves and your kindred against a Fire whose fuel is human beings and stones,[8] a Fire held in the charge of fierce and stern angels who never disobey what He has commanded them, and always do what they are bidden. [7] (It will then be said): "Unbelievers, make no excuses today. You are being recompensed for nothing else but your deeds."

[8] Believers, turn to Allah in sincere repentance; maybe your Lord will expunge your evil deeds and admit you to the Gardens beneath which rivers flow. This will be on the Day when Allah will not disgrace the Prophet and those who have embraced faith and are with him;[9] their light will be running before them and on their right hands, and they will say: "Our Lord, perfect for us our light and forgive us. Surely You have power over everything."

[9] O Prophet, strive against the unbelievers and the hypocrites, and be severe with them. Hell shall be their resort. What a grievous end!

---

8. This verse indicates that a person is required, first of all, to strive to guard himself against God's chastisement. Over and above that, he should also do whatever he can, to raise the members of his family who are under his care as righteous people so that they win God's pleasure. But if they are inclined to follow a course that is likely to land them in Hell, he should try, as far as he can, to prevent them from proceeding along that path. As for the words "whose fuel is human beings and stones," they probably signify coal. Ibn Masʿūd, Ibn ʿAbbās, Mujāhid, Muḥammad al-Bāqir and al-Suddī are all of the opinion that Hell's fuel will be brimstone.

9. That is, God will not deprive them of the reward of their good deeds; He will not provide the unbelievers and the hypocrites with an occasion to taunt the believers that they had gained nothing despite their sincere devotion to God. On the contrary, disgrace will be the lot of those who do not believe in and do not obey God.

[10] Allah has set forth for the unbelievers the parable of the wives of Noah and Lot. They were wedded to two of Our righteous servants, but each acted treacherously with her husband,[10] and their husbands could be of no avail to them against Allah. The two of them were told: "Enter the Fire with all the others who enter it." [11] Allah has set forth for the believers the parable of Pharaoh's wife. She prayed: "My Lord, build for me a house with You in Paradise and deliver me from Pharaoh and his misdeeds; and deliver me from the iniquitous people." [12] Allah has also set forth the parable of Mary, the daughter of 'Imrān,[11] who guarded her chastity,[12] and into whom We breathed of Our Spirit,[13] and who testified to the words of her Lord and His Books. She was among the obedient.[14]

---

10. The statement that "each acted treacherously" does not mean, God forbid, that the wives of the Prophets Noah and Lot succumbed to any act of indecency. What is meant is that instead of lending support to the efforts of their husbands – Noah and Lot – to uphold the Truth, they lent support to the opponents of the True Faith.

11. It is possible that the name of Mary's father was 'Imrān, or that she was called "daughter of 'Imrān" because she belonged to 'Imrān's family.

12. This refutes the Jews' allegation that Jesus' birth was, God forbid, the result of a sin committed by his mother. The Qur'ān refutes this charge and calls it "a monstrous calumny". (See *al-Nisā'* 4: 156.)

13. That is, Mary conceived Jesus without there having been any physical contact between her and any male. It took place simply because God breathed into her womb a spirit from Himself.

14. Mary's case is mentioned here to emphasise a point: although God tested her by causing her to become miraculously pregnant, despite her virginity, she still exercised great patience and willingly submitted to God's will.

Al-Mulk [Dominion]
Makkan Period

In the name of Allah, the Most Merciful,
the Most Compassionate

[1] Blessed is He in Whose Hand is the dominion of the Universe, and Who has power over everything;[1] [2] Who created death and life that He might try you as to which of you is better in deed.[2] He is the Most Mighty, the Most Forgiving; [3] Who created the seven heavens one upon another. You will see no incongruity in the Merciful One's creation.[3] Turn your vision again, can you see any flaw?[4] [4] Then turn your vision again, and then again; in the end your vision will come back to you, worn out and frustrated.

---

1. God can do whatever He pleases; there is no way to strip Him of His power or to prevent Him from doing what He wills.

2. The purpose underlying the whole system of human beings' life and death is to ascertain who of them are best in their deeds.

3. Literally, *tafāwut* means disharmony, a thing's discordance with something else.

4. The word *fuṭūr* denotes crack, rift, fissure, cleaving, or breaking apart. The verse means that the whole Universe is so well-knit together and everything in it, from a particle on the earth to the enormous galaxies, is so coherent and so well connected that no matter how hard one might try one can find neither flaw nor crack in the system.

[5] We have adorned the lower heaven⁵ with lamps, and have made them a means to drive away the satans. We have prepared for them the chastisement of the Blazing Fire.

[6] The chastisement of Hell awaits those who disbelieve in their Lord. What a wretched destination! [7] When they will be cast into it, they will hear it roar⁶ as it boils, [8] as though it will burst with rage. Every time a multitude is cast into it, its keepers will ask them: "Did no warner come to you?" [9] They will say: "Yes, a warner came to us, but we gave the lie to him and said: 'Allah has revealed nothing. You are surely in huge error.' [10] They will say: 'If we had only listened and understood, we would not be among the inmates of the Blazing Fire.'" [11] Thus will they confess their sins. Damned are these inmates of the Blazing Fire.

[12] Surely forgiveness and a mighty reward await those who fear Allah without seeing Him. [13] Whether you speak in secrecy or aloud, (it is all the same to Allah). He even knows the secrets that lie hidden in the breasts of people. [14] Would He not know, He Who has created,⁷ when He is All-Subtle, All-Aware?

---

5. "The lower heaven" denotes the heaven whose stars and planets can be observed with the naked eye without recourse to any mechanical aid such as a telescope.

6. This might refer either to the sound of Hell itself, to the sound rising from it, or to the sound of those who were cast in it and who would therefore be crying and screaming.

7. An alternative translation could be: "Would He not know His Own creatures?"

[15] He it is Who made the earth subservient to you. So traverse in its tracks and partake of the sustenance He has provided. To Him will you be resurrected. [16] Do you feel secure that He Who is in the heaven will not cause the earth to cave in with you, and then suddenly it will begin to rock violently? [17] Do you feel secure that He Who is in the heaven[8] will not let loose upon you a storm of stones? Then shall you know what My warning is like! [18] Those who came before them also gave the lie (to the Messengers): then how awesome was My chastisement! [19] Have they not seen birds above them spreading and closing their wings, with none holding them except the Merciful One? He oversees everything. [20] Which is your army that will come to your aid against the Merciful Lord?[9] But the unbelievers are in utter delusion.

---

8. This does not mean that God lives, literally, in the heavens. The present verse reflects the fact that when man wants to turn to God, he instinctively looks up to the heavens. Furthermore, when he prays to God, he raises his hands towards the heaven. Likewise, when he is overpowered with affliction and feels helpless, he again turns upwards to the heavens to convey his grievance to God; or when a misfortune suddenly befalls him, he tends to say that it has descended on him from heaven. In the same way, when he receives something in an extraordinary way, he says that it has come from heaven. Again, the scriptures revealed by God are called heavenly books. All this indicates that it is a part of man's nature that when he thinks of God, he associates Him with the heavens above rather than with the earth below.

9. An alternative translation would be: "Who is there other than the Merciful Lord Who comes to your aid as would your own army?"

[21] Who shall provide for you if He withholds His sustenance? Nay; but they persist in rebellion and aversion. [22] Who is better guided: he who walks grovelling on his face,[10] or he who walks upright on a Straight Path? [23] Say: "He it is Who has brought you into being, and has given you hearing and sight, and has given you hearts to think and understand. How seldom do you give thanks!"[11]

[24] Say: "Allah it is Who multiplied you in the earth and to Him you will be mustered." [25] They say: "If you are truthful, tell us when will this promise (of the Hereafter) be fulfilled?" [26] Say: "Allah alone knows about that; and I am no more than a plain warner." [27] When they will see it near at hand, the faces of all those who had denied it will be distraught, and then they will be told: "This is the doom which you used to ask for."

[28] Say to them: "Did you ever consider: whether Allah destroys me and those that are with me, or shows mercy to us, who can protect the unbelievers from a grievous

---

10. The expression "… who walks grovelling on his face" brings to mind an image of cattle with their heads cast down, trudging along the course on which they have been put.

11. God has endowed human beings with knowledge and intelligence, sight and hearing so that they might arrive at the Truth. But they are ungrateful in so far as they use these endowments for all kinds of purposes except the one for which they were supposed to be used – to know the Truth!

chastisement?"[12] [29] Say to them: "He is Merciful, and it is in Him that we believe, and it is in Him that we put all our trust. Soon will you know who is in manifest error." [30] Say to them: "Did you even consider: if all the water that you have (in the wells) were to sink down into the depths of the earth, who will produce for you clear, flowing water?"

---

12. When the Prophet (peace be on him) embarked on his mission in Makkah and the members of the different Quraysh families started embracing Islam, the people of many a household began to curse him and his Companions. They even resorted to the use of magic and charms in their bid to exterminate him. They also hatched conspiracies designed to assassinate him. It was in this context that they were told that it was not really important for them whether the Prophet (peace be on him) died or continued to live. They should rather be concerned with themselves, thinking about how they will save themselves from God's chastisement.

Al-Qalam [The Pen]
Makkan Period

*In the name of Allah, the Most Merciful,
the Most Compassionate*

[1] *Nūn.* By the pen and what the scribes write.¹ [2] By your Lord's Grace, you are not afflicted with madness,² [3] and surely yours shall be a never-ending reward,³ [4] and you are certainly on the most exalted standard

---

1. The great commentator on the Qur'ān, Mujāhid, says that the word "pen" here signifies the pen with which the Qur'ān was being inscribed. From this it automatically follows that what was being inscribed was the Qur'ān.

2. These words are apparently addressed to the Prophet (peace be on him), but the real purpose of the statement is to refute the unbelievers' slanderous utterances imputing madness to him. The thrust of the verse is that the Qur'ān, which was being written down by scribes, was itself sufficient refutation of such slanderous statements.

3. It is being asserted that the Prophet's reward will be boundless and that it will never cease. This because he strove to direct man to the Right Way, but in return had to suffer bitter and heart-rending remarks from a great many people. Admirably enough, the Prophet (peace be on him) disregarded all this, patiently performing his duty with unabated dedication.

of moral excellence.[4] [5] So you will soon see, and they too will see, [6] which of you is afflicted with madness. [7] Surely your Lord knows well those who have strayed from His Way just as He knows well those who are on the Right Way. [8] Do not, then, yield to those who reject the Truth, decrying it as false; [9] they would wish you to be pliant so that they too may be pliant.[5] [10] And do not yield to any contemptible swearer, [11] the fault-finder who goes around slandering, [12] the hinderer of good, the transgressor, the sinful; [13] the coarse-grained, and above all mean and ignoble; [14] (who so acts) simply because he has wealth and sons,[6] [15] and whenever Our verses are rehearsed to him, he says: "These are fairy-

4. In addition to the Qur'ān, the Prophet's excellent character also falsified the charge of madness that was directed at him. This because madness and high morals are mutually inconsistent.

5. The unbelievers approached the Prophet (peace be on him) with the offer that if he would slacken a bit in his drive to preach his teachings, they would relax their opposition to him. Another nuance of the offer was that if the Prophet (peace be on him) were to modify his religious stance in deference to the unbelievers' beliefs and practices, they would be willing to come to terms with him.

6. This statement can relate to the themes that both precede and follow it. In the first instance, it would mean that the Prophet (peace be on him) should not yield to such a person simply because he has an abundance of wealth and children. In the second instance, these words would mean that this person has become exceedingly arrogant because he has much wealth and numerous sons. It is because of such arrogance that when the Revelation is rehearsed to him such a person says: "These are fairy-tales of times gone by."

tales of times gone by." [16] Soon shall We brand him on his snout.[7]

[17] We have put them [i.e., the Makkans] to test even as We put to test the owners of the orchard when they vowed that they would gather the fruit of their orchard in the morning, [18] without making any allowance (for the will of Allah).[8] [19] Thereupon a calamity from your Lord passed over it while they were asleep, [20] and so by morning the orchard lay as though it had been fully harvested. [21] At daybreak they called out to one another: [22] "Hurry to your orchard if you would gather its fruit." [23] So off they went, whispering to one another: [24] "No destitute person shall enter it today." [25] They went forth early, believing that they had the power (to gather the fruit). [26] But as soon as they beheld the orchard, (they cried out): "We have certainly lost the way; [27] rather, we are utterly ruined." [28] The best among them said: "Did I not say to you: why do you not give glory to (your Lord)?"[9] [29] They cried out: "Glory be

---

7. Such a person considered himself to be possessed of extraordinary greatness and eminence. To controvert this arrogance, his nose is called a "snout". To say that "We shall brand him on his snout" means that God will disgrace him both in this world and the Hereafter, and will do so in such a way that the disgrace he is subjected to will endure.

8. The owners of the orchard were exceedingly confident about their power and authority. Hence they swore that they would gather the fruit of their orchard the next morning, without feeling any need to say: "We shall do so if God so wills."

9. That is, why do they not remember God? Why have they forgotten that above them is their Lord?

to our Lord! Certainly we were sinners." [30] Then they began to reproach one another. [31] They said: "Woe to us! We had indeed transgressed. [32] Maybe our Lord will give us a better orchard in its place; to our Lord do we penitently turn." [33] Such is the chastisement; and the chastisement of the Hereafter is assuredly even greater, if only they knew.

[34] Surely[10] the God-fearing shall have Gardens of bliss with their Lord. [35] What! Shall We treat those who have submitted (to Our command) like those who have acted as criminals? [36] What is the matter with you? How ill do you judge! [37] Or do you have a Book[11] wherein you read [38] that (in the Hereafter) you shall have all that you choose for yourselves? [39] Or have We sworn a covenant with you which We are bound to keep till the Day of Resurrection, (a covenant requiring that whatever you ordain for yourselves shall be yours)? [40] Ask them: "Which of them can guarantee that? [41] Or has something been guaranteed by any of those whom they associate with Allah in His Divinity?" If so, let them bring forth their associates, if they are truthful.

---

10. This is a rejoinder to the Makkan nobility who teased the Muslims by saying that they enjoyed a great many blessings thereby indicating that they were God's favourites. Conversely, that the Muslims' lot was a miserable one which only proved that God was wroth with them. They further argued that if there were life after the present one, it would be they, the unbelievers, who would enjoy bliss in much the same way that they did in the present world; as for the Muslims, they would suffer in the Hereafter as well. The present verse as well as the verses that follow refute this claim.

11. That is, the Book revealed by God.

[42] On the Day when the dreadful calamity will unfold, when people will be summoned to prostrate themselves, and yet they will not be able to prostrate. [43] Their eyes shall be downcast and ignominy shall overwhelm them. For when they were safe and sound, they were summoned to prostrate themselves, (and they refused).

[44] So leave Me, (O Prophet), to deal with him who gives the lie to this Discourse. We shall draw them little by little (to their undoing) in a way that they will not know. [45] I am giving them a respite. Great is My scheme!

[46] Or are you asking them for some compensation so that they feel burdened with debt? [47] Or do they have any knowledge of the Unseen which they are now writing down? [48] So bear with patience until the Judgement of your Lord comes, and do not be[12] like the man in the fish (i.e., Jonah) who called out, choking with grief: [49] had his Lord not bestowed His favour upon him, he would have been cast upon that barren shore (and would have remained there) in disgrace. [50] But his Lord exalted him, and included him among His righteous servants.

[51] When the unbelievers hear this Exhortation, they look at you as though they would knock you off your feet with their (hostile) glances. They say: "Surely he is afflicted with madness"; [52] although this is nothing but an Exhortation (to goodness) for everyone in the world.

---

12. The directive is that they should stop behaving with the impatience that was displayed by the Prophet Jonah (peace be on him). For it was on account of Jonah's impatience that he was consigned to the belly of a fish.

69

Al-Ḥāqqah [The Indubitable Event]
Makkan Period

In the name of Allah, the Most Merciful,
the Most Compassionate

[1] The indubitable event!¹ [2] And what is that indubitable event? [3] And what do you know what that indubitable event is?

[4] The Thamūd and the ʿĀd denied the (possibility of a) sudden calamity,² calling it false. [5] Then the Thamūd were destroyed by an awesome upheaval; [6] and the ʿĀd were destroyed by a furiously raging wind-storm [7] which He let loose upon them for seven nights and eight days in succession; so that (if you had been there) you might have seen people lying prostrate, as though they were uprooted trunks of hollowed palm trees. [8] Do you now see any trace of them?

---

1. Literally, *al-ḥāqqah* denotes something that is bound to take place. The significance of using this word is to convey to the unbelievers that their denial of the Inevitable Event, howsoever vehement, will fail to avert its occurrence.

2. The word "calamity" is used here to emphasise that the coming event is not only inevitable, but also extremely horrendous.

[9] Pharaoh and those before him and the people of the overturned habitations[3] all engaged in the same great sin. [10] They did not follow the Messenger of their Lord, and so He seized them with a severe grip.

[11] Verily when the water rose to great heights,[4] We bore you upon a floating vessel (i.e. the Ark)[5] [12] so that We might make it an instructive event for you, and retentive ears might preserve its memory.

[13] So when the Trumpet is blown with a single blast [14] and the earth and the mountains are carried aloft and are crushed to bits at one stroke, [15] on that Day shall that indubitable event come to pass; [16] when the sky will be rent asunder, the grip holding it together having loosened on that Day, [17] and the angels will stand on the sides, with eight of them bearing aloft the Throne of your Lord on that Day.[6] [18] That will be the Day when you shall be brought forth (before Allah) and no secret of yours shall remain hidden.

---

3. This is an allusion to Lot's people who were struck by God's chastisement, causing their dwellings to be overturned.

4. This alludes to Noah's Deluge.

5. The whole human race that exists today consists of the descendants of those who boarded the Ark several thousand years ago. Hence it is being said that: "We bore you upon a floating vessel."

6. This is a *mutashābih* (ambiguous) verse of the Qur'ān, one whose meaning is hard to determine. We can neither know the reality of the Throne, nor fully comprehend how it will be held aloft by eight angels on the Day of Resurrection. It is, however, hardly conceivable

[19] On that Day, he whose Record is given to him in his right hand will say: "Lo! Read my Record! [20] Verily I was sure that I would be handed over my account."[7] [21] Then he shall find himself in a life of bliss; [22] in a lofty Garden [23] the clusters of whose fruit will be hanging low to be within reach (of the inmates of Paradise). [24] (They will be told): "Eat and drink with good cheer as a reward for the good deeds you did in the days that have passed by."

[25] As for him whose Record will be given to him in his left hand, he will exclaim: "Would that I had never been given my Record, [26] and had not known my account.[8]

---

that on that Day God will be seated, (literally speaking), on the Throne that will be held up by eight angels. Not insignificantly, the present verse too does not say that at that moment God will be *seated* on the Throne. Besides, the overall concept of God as expounded by the Qur'ān, also prevents one from accepting such a notion. For how can it be imagined that God, Who is above the limitations of corporeality, space and direction, will be seated on a certain object with His creatures holding Him aloft? Hence, it is futile to probe into the matter attempting to know about the pith of things in definite terms; in fact it exposes one to totally erroneous ideas.

7. Such a person will explain the reason behind his good fortune: that it lay in the fact that he was never heedless of the Hereafter and spent his whole life believing that one Day he will be made to stand before God and be called to account by Him.

8. Another possible translation could be: "Would that I had known what accounting is!" This emphasises that the evil-doers will be faced with something they had not even imagined – that they will be required to render an account of all their deeds and that the whole record of their lives will be placed before them.

[27] Oh! Would that the death that came to me in the world had made an end of me! [28] My riches have not availed me, [29] and my authority has vanished."⁹ [30] (A command will be issued): "Seize him and shackle him, [31] then cast him in the Fire, [32] then fasten him with a chain, seventy cubits long. [33] He would not believe in Allah, the Most Great; [34] nor would he urge the feeding of the poor.¹⁰ [35] Today he has been left here friendless; [36] and has no food except the filth from the washing of wounds, [37] which only the sinners will eat."

[38] But no;¹¹ I swear by what you see, [39] and by what you do not see, [40] that this is the speech of an honourable Messenger, [41] not the speech of a poet. Little do you believe! [42] Nor is this the speech of a soothsayer. Little do you reflect! [43] It has been revealed by the Lord of the Universe. [44] And if he [i.e., the Prophet] had forged this Discourse and thereafter ascribed it to Us, [45] We would surely have seized him by the right hand, [46] and then severed his life vein; [47] and not one of you would have

---

9. On that Day he will see that the power he once had and which had turned his head has vanished. Unaided by an army or by those who once obeyed him, he will stand as a miserable and powerless creature lacking even the power to defend himself.

10. Let alone feeding a hungry person, he does not even ask others to do so.

11. That is, the reality is quite different from what they fancy.

been able to withhold Us from doing so.[12] [48] Surely it is a Good Counsel for the God-fearing. [49] We certainly know that some among you will give the lie to it, [50] and surely it will be a cause of regret for the unbelievers. [51] Certainly it is a Truth of absolute certainty. [52] So glorify the name of your Lord Most Great.

---

12. The true purpose of the statement is to stress that the Prophet (peace be on him) had no authority whatsoever to alter the Revelation; if he did so, he would be liable to God's severe chastisement. The tone and tenor of the statement brings to mind how a king might react on knowing that his officials had forged a document and had then ascribed it to him. It should not be surprising if such persons are subjected to a grievous punishment. Some people put forward an altogether false assertion on the basis of this verse. They claim that if anyone declared that he was a Prophet and his life-vein was not then immediately severed, it would prove that his claim was true. The fact, however, is that what is said here in this verse pertains to Prophets and not to false claimants of prophethood. For as we know, there have been claimants even to Godhead who lived long years despite the absolute falsity of their claims. Their longevity was no proof that their claim to Godhead was true.

70
❧❧❧

Al-Maʿārij [The Ascending Steps]
Makkan Period

In the name of Allah, the Most Merciful,
the Most Compassionate

[1] A beseecher besought the visitation of chastisement, [2] (a chastisement meant) for the unbelievers, one which none can avert; [3] a chastisement from Allah, the Lord of the ascending steps, [4] by which the angels and the Spirit¹ ascend to Him² in one Day the duration of which is fifty thousand years.³ [5] So, (O Prophet), persevere

---

1. The word "Spirit" here denotes Gabriel who is mentioned independently from the angels on account of his eminence.

2. By the nature of things, any statement about ascension to God belongs to the category of ambiguous Qurʾānic statements, statements whose meaning cannot be determined precisely. To take this particular case, it is evident that we do not fully know the reality of the angels, nor how they will ascend to God; nor can our minds comprehend what "the ascending steps" are like. Likewise, we cannot even imagine that God lives (literally) in a particular place for the Supreme Being transcends all limitations of time and space.

3. In *al-Ḥajj* 22: 47 and *al-Sajdah* 32: 5, the measure of a day is stated to be a thousand years. But here, in response to an unbeliever's challenging demand that God's chastisement visit them, one day of God's reckoning is stated to measure fifty thousand years. In order to grasp the two statements it is necessary that we relinquish our

with gracious perseverance.[4] [6] Verily they think that the chastisement is far off, [7] while We think that it is near at hand. [8] It shall befall on a Day whereon the sky will become like molten brass,[5] [9] and the mountains will become like dyed tufts of wool, [10] and no bosom friend will enquire about any of his bosom friends [11] although they shall be within sight of one another. The guilty one would fain ransom himself from the torment of that Day by offering his children, [12] and his spouse and his brother, [13] and his kinsfolk who had stood by him, [14] and all persons of the earth, if only he could thus save himself. [15] By no means! It will be the fierce flame [16] that will strip off the scalp. [17] It shall insistently summon him who turned his back and retreated, [18] and amassed wealth and covetously hoarded it.

[19] Verily man is impatient by nature:[6] [20] bewailing when evil befalls him, [21] and tight-fisted when good fortune visits him, [22] except those that pray, [23] and are constant in their Prayer; [24] and those in whose wealth

---

own, restricted scales of measurement when we speak of time with reference to God. When we speak of a hundred or even 50 years with reference to human beings, that is a fairly long time span. But when we speak of time durations with reference to God, each chunk of time consists of a thousand or even fifty thousand years; and even these figures are for purposes of illustration only.

4. That is, he should exercise the kind of perseverance that befits a dignified and gracious person.

5. That is, the sky will constantly change its colour.

6. The statement that "man is impatient by nature" means that he is naturally predisposed to impatience.

there is a known right [25] for those that ask and those that are dispossessed, [26] those who firmly believe in the Day of Recompense, [27] and fear the chastisement of their Lord – [28] surely the chastisement of their Lord is a thing none can feel secure from – [29] and those who guard their private parts, [30] except in regard to their spouses and those whom their right hands possess, for in regard to them they are not reproachable, [31] but any who seeks to go beyond that, it is indeed they who are the transgressors, [32] and those who fulfil their trusts and their covenants, [33] and those who are upright in their testimonies; [34] and who take due care of their Prayer: [35] all these shall live honourably in the Gardens.

[36] But what is the matter with the unbelievers who are hurrying towards you⁷ [37] in crowds, both on the right and on the left? [38] Does everyone of them wish to enter the Garden of Bliss? [39] By no means! They know that which We have created them from. [40] I swear by the Lord of the easts and the wests⁸ that We have the power [41] to replace them by others who would be better than they; and We shall certainly not be overpowered.

---

7. This refers to those unbelievers who, whenever they heard the Prophet (peace be on him) recite the Qurʾān or saw him invite people to embrace his teachings, rushed towards him, subjecting him to ridicule and banter.

8. The words "east" and "west" are used in the plural for good reason. Each day the angle of the rise and setting of the sun varies; furthermore, the angles at which it rises and sets in different parts of the earth vary. In this sense, there is not one but many easts; there is not one but many wests.

[42] So leave them to engage in vain talk and to amuse themselves until they come face to face with the Day which they are promised, [43] the Day on which they will hastily come forth from their graves, as though they were hurrying on to the altars of their deities. [44] Their eyes will be downcast and disgrace will overwhelm them. Such is the Day that they were promised.

71

Nūḥ [Noah]
Makkan Period

In the name of Allah, the Most Merciful,
the Most Compassionate

[1] We sent Noah to his people (and directed him): "Warn your people before a grievous chastisement comes upon them." [2] Noah said: "My people, I have certainly been sent as a clear warner to you, [3] that you serve Allah and fear Him, and follow me; [4] He will forgive your sins and will grant you respite until an appointed term.¹ Indeed when Allah's appointed term comes, it cannot be deferred;² if you only knew!"

---

1. Noah asked his people that if they accepted the three above-mentioned directives – to serve God, to fear Him, and to follow Noah, God's Messenger – then God would grant them respite to live until the time that He had determined for their natural death. In other words, God would not subject them to any collective scourge.

2. The expression "Allah's appointed term" signifies the time determined by God to send His scourge on a people. In this context, the Qur'ān has clearly stated on many an occasion that once God resolves to strike a nation down with His scourge, that nation is not spared the scourge even if they embrace the true faith.

[5] He[3] said: "My Lord, I called my people by night and by day, [6] but the more I called, the farther they fled. [7] And every time I called them so that You might forgive them, they thrust their fingers into their ears and wrapped up their faces with their garments[4] and obstinately clung to their attitude, and waxed very proud. [8] Then I summoned them openly, [9] and preached to them in public, and also addressed them in secret. [10] I said to them: "Ask forgiveness from your Lord; surely He is Most Forgiving. [11] He will shower upon you torrents from heaven, [12] and will provide you with wealth and children, and will bestow upon you gardens and rivers. [13] What is amiss with you that you do not look forward to the majesty of Allah[5] [14] when He has created you in

---

3. These verses briefly mention the main points of Noah's teaching and his early efforts to convey his Message. Thereafter no detailed account is given of the greater part of Noah's life involving his continuous efforts to teach and admonish his people. Leaving all that aside, the *sūrah* goes straight to the last phase of his life and brings to the fore Noah's entreaty to God. See vv. 5 ff.

4. There could be several reasons why those unbelievers "wrapped up their faces with their garments". One reason could be that owing to their disgust at his preachings they could not even stomach looking at Noah and so kept their faces, including their eyes, covered. Another reason for so doing could have been to prevent Noah from recognising them. They resorted to this measure probably to forestall Noah from communicating his teachings to them.

5. People are generally cognizant that it is dangerous to say or do anything that is offensive to the majestic sensibilities of even the petty chiefs and nobles of this world. But they are scarcely concerned with showing deference to God's majesty. In fact they do a great deal that should offend Him: they rebel against Him,

stages?[6] [15] Do you not see how Allah has created seven heavens, one upon the other, [16] and has placed the moon in them as a light, and the sun as a radiant lamp? [17] And Allah has caused you to grow out of the earth so wondrously,[7] [18] and He will later cause you to return to it and will then again bring you out of it. [19] Allah has made the earth a wide expanse for you [20] so that you may tread its spacious paths."

[21] Noah said: "My Lord, they did not pay heed to what I said, and followed those (nobles) whose possession of wealth and children has led them to an even greater loss. [22] They contrived a plot of great magnitude. [23] They said: "Do not abandon your deities; do not abandon Wadd, nor Suwāʿ, nor Yaghūth, nor Yaʿūq, nor Nasr.[8]

---

associate others with Him in His Divinity, disobey His commands. Furthermore, they are not truly afraid of His wrath which they invite upon themselves by their actions.

6. That is, God has brought man to the present stage of his existence: he has passed through the various earlier stages of the creation process.

7. Here a simile is drawn between man's creation out of the different elements taken from the earth, and the growth of vegetation. There was a time when there was no vegetation on earth and then God caused vegetation to appear. In like manner, there was a time when man did not exist on earth and then God planted him on it.

8. Here only some deities of the Prophet Noah's people are mentioned. These were the deities that were also worshipped by the Arabs and their temples and shrines were scattered across the expanse of Arabia at the time of Islam's advent.

[24] They have misled many. So do not enable these evil-doers to increase in anything except straying (from the Right Way)."⁹

[25] And so they were drowned on account of their sins, and then cast into the Fire, and did not find any other than Allah, to come forth to their help. [26] Noah said: "My Lord, do not leave out of these unbelievers even a single dweller on earth, [27] for certainly if You should leave them (alive), they will mislead Your servants, and will beget none but sinners and utter unbelievers. [28] My Lord, forgive me and my parents, and whoever enters my house as a believer, and forgive all believers, both men and women, and do not increase the wrong-doers in anything except perdition."

---

9. The Prophet Noah (peace be on him) did not invoke this curse simply out of impatience on his part. He did so after he had tried extremely hard to reform his people by constantly preaching his message and only then reached a point of utter desperation.

72

Al-Jinn [The *Jinn*]
Makkan Period

In the name of Allah, the Most Merciful,
the Most Compassionate

[1] Say, (O Prophet), it was revealed to me that a band of *jinn* attentively listened to (the recitation of the Qur'ān)[1] and then (went back to their people) and said: [2] "We have indeed heard a wonderful Qur'ān which guides to the Right Way; so we have come to believe in it, and we will not associate aught with Our Lord in His Divinity"; [3] and that "He – exalted be His Majesty – has not taken to Himself either a wife or a son"; [4] and that "the foolish among us[2] have been wont to say outrageous things about Allah"; [5] and that "we had thought that men and *jinn* would never speak a lie about Allah", [6] and that "some

---

1. This shows that the *jinn* on this occasion were not visible to the Prophet (peace be on him) nor did he know that they were listening to the Qur'ān's recitation. Instead, he was informed of the incident later by revelation. In connection with this ʿAbd Allāh ibn ʿAbbās has stated the following: "The Prophet (peace be on him) had not recited the Qur'ān before the *jinn* nor did he see them." (See Muslim, Tirmidhī, Aḥmad ibn Ḥanbal, Ibn Jarīr al-Ṭabarī.)

2. The words "foolish among us" here could have both singular and plural meaning. If we take the word "foolish" to refer to an individual, it would denote *Iblīs*. Alternatively, if it is considered to be a plural, it would denote a group of foolish *jinn* who made such statements.

from among the humans used to seek protection of some among the *jinn*, and thus they increased the arrogance of the *jinn*"; [7] and that "they thought, even as you thought, that Allah would never raise anyone (as a Messenger)"; [8] and that "we tried to pry (the secrets of) the heaven, but we found it full of terrible guards and shooting meteors"; [9] and that "we would take up stations in the heaven to try to hear but anyone who now attempts to listen finds a shooting meteor in wait for him"; [10] and that "we do not know whether evil is intended for those on the earth, or whether their Lord intends to direct them to the Right Way";[3] [11] and that "some of us are upright and some of us are otherwise for we follow widely divergent paths"; [12] and that "we thought that we will neither be able to frustrate Allah on earth, nor frustrate Him by flight";[4] [13] and that "when we heard the teaching of the Right Way we came to believe in it; he who believes in His Lord shall have no fear of suffering loss or being subjected to any injustice";

---

3. This shows that these *jinn* noticed that strict measures had been taken in the heavens to prevent the spread of any news. They therefore tried to find out what was about to happen on earth that required such strict secrecy to be maintained. However, the arrangements they found were too stringent to allow them any opportunity to eavesdrop. For whenever anyone makes such an attempt, he finds a "shooting meteor in wait for him" (v. 9].

4. The *jinn*'s belief that they could neither frustrate God on earth nor flee from it, led them to be saved. They feared God and were also conscious that if they disobeyed, they would not be able to avert His chastisement. Therefore, when they heard God's Word which directed them to the Right Way, they did not have the audacity to cling to erroneous beliefs that had been spread among them by the ignorant persons of their society. They could not do so because they had come to know the Truth.

[14] and that "among us some are Muslims [those who have submitted to Allah], and some of us are deviant. So those who became Muslims found the Right Course; [15] but those who deviated from the Truth, will be the fuel for Hell."[5]

[16] If people were to keep firmly to the Right Way, We would have vouchsafed them abundant rain [17] so that We might try them through this bounty. Whoso turns away from the remembrance of his Lord, He will cause him to suffer a grievous chastisement; [18] and that "mosques belong to Allah, so do not invoke anyone with Him";[6] [19] and when Allah's servant stood up to call on Him, they well-nigh swarmed him. [20] Say, (O Prophet): "I call on my Lord alone, and I do not associate aught with Him in His Divinity." [21] Say: "Surely neither it is in my power to hurt you nor to bring you to the Right Way." [22] Say: "None can protect me from Allah, nor can I find a refuge apart from Him. [23] (My task is no more than) to deliver Allah's proclamation and His messages. And whoever disobeys Allah and His Messenger, surely the Fire of Hell awaits him; therein he will abide in perpetuity."

[24] (They shall not change their ways) until they see that against which they had been warned, and then they will know whose helpers are weaker and whose supporters

---

5. This might prompt one to ask: "The *jinn*, according to the Qur'ān itself, were created out of fire. How, then, can Hell-fire torment them?" In response, one can point to a parallel case. Man, according to the Qur'ān, was created out of the earth, and yet he is hurt if a brick (which is made from earth), is hurled at him.

6. That is, one may not worship, pray to, or invoke anyone for help.

are fewer in number.[7] [25] Say: "I know not whether what you are promised is near or whether my Lord will prolong its term. [26] He is the Knower of the Unseen, and He does not disclose His Unseen to anyone [27] other than to a Messenger whom He chooses (for the bestowal of any part of the knowledge of the Unseen),[8] whereafter He appoints guards who go before him and behind him,[9] [28] so that He may know that they have delivered the messages of their Lord.[10] He encompasses in His knowledge their surroundings and keeps a count of all things."[11]

---

7. Those of the Quraysh who were wont to attack the Prophet (peace be on him) as soon as they heard him call people to God, entertained a false notion about the strength of their supporters. Compared to their imposing host, the force at the Prophet's command was quite feeble. They, therefore, succumbed to the illusion that they could easily prevail against the Prophet (peace be on him) and his followers.

8. That is, Messengers do not have access to the Unseen as such; but when God decides to designate anyone as His Messenger, He bestows upon him whatever portion of the truths of the Unseen He pleases.

9. The word "guards" denotes angels. The purpose of the verse is to affirm that when God communicates any knowledge of the truths belonging to the realm of the Unseen through revelation, He appoints angels to safeguard that knowledge. This is done to ensure that it reaches the Messengers safely, untarnished by adulteration.

10. This shows that Messengers are endowed with the knowledge of only that portion of the Unseen that is needed by them to perform their mission as God's Messengers. Further, God appoints angels to see to it that this knowledge reaches them in its pristine form and also that the Messengers faithfully transmit it to His creatures.

11. God's power firmly encompasses the Messengers and the angels. Hence, if they deviate even slightly from God's directives, they will be instantly taken to task. A strict count is kept of every letter of God's Message. Hence neither the Messengers nor the Prophets can tamper with even a single letter of His Message.

73

Al-Muzzammil [The Enwrapped One]
Makkan Period

In the name of Allah, the Most Merciful,
the Most Compassionate

[1] O you the (sleeping) enwrapped one! [2] Stand up in Prayer by night, all but a small part of it; [3] half of it, or reduce it a little; [4] or add to it a little; and recite the Qur'ān slowly and distinctly. [5] Behold, We shall cast upon you a Weighty Word. [6] Surely getting up at night is the best means of subduing the self and is more suitable for uprightness in speech. [7] You are indeed much occupied during the day with the affairs of the world. [8] So remember the name of your Lord and devote yourself to Him with exclusive devotion. [9] He is the Lord of the East and the West; there is no god but He. So take Him alone for your Guardian,¹ [10] And bear patiently

---

1. The word *wakīl* is used for someone to whom one entrusts all one's affairs on account of one's complete trust in him. In Urdu, too, we use this word in more or less the same sense; it is used to denote the legal expert to whom one entrusts one's judicial case, which one does because of one's confidence that the advocate will present his case on one's behalf in the best possible manner, dispensing with the need that one plead it for oneself.

the vain things they utter, and gracefully forsake them.[2]
[11] Leave it to Me to deal with the affluent ones who
give the lie (to the Truth), and bear with them for a while.
[12] We have heavy fetters and a blazing Fire in store
for them; [13] and a food that chokes, and a grievous
chastisement. [14] (They will come across all this) on
the Day when the earth and the mountains shall tremble
violently and the mountains shall crumble into heaps of
scattered sand.

[15] Surely We have sent to you[3] a Messenger as a witness
over you, just as We had sent a Messenger to Pharaoh.
[16] But Pharaoh disobeyed Our Messenger, so We
seized him with a terrible seizing. [17] If you persist in
disbelieving, how will you guard yourself against the
(woe of the) Day that will turn children grey-haired,
[18] the Day whose severity shall cause the heaven to split
asunder? Allah's promise is ever bound to be fulfilled.
[19] Indeed this is nothing but a Good Counsel; so let him
who will take a way leading to his Lord.

---

2. The directive to "gracefully forsake them" does not mean to
sunder all relations with such people and to give up addressing
God's Message to them. It simply means that the Prophet (peace
be on him) should graciously disregard his opponents' depraved
behaviour, should not stoop to their level, and should abstain from
responding to their vile acts. It is essential that this "forsaking"
should not be accompanied by expressions of injury, anger or
irritation. The "forsaking" should, instead, be of the kind to which
a decent person resorts when a rustic hurls an obscene abuse:
one should ignore it so that it does not leave a bad taste in one's
mouth.

3. The discourse now turns to the Makkan unbelievers who were
vehemently decrying the Prophet (peace be on him) as a liar.

[20] (O Prophet),[4] your Lord knows that you sometimes stand up in Prayer nearly two-thirds of the night, and sometimes half or one-third of it, and so does a party of those with you; Allah measures the night and the day. He knows that you cannot keep an accurate count of it, so He has shown mercy to you. So now recite as much of the Qur'ān as you can.[5] He knows that there are among you those who are sick and others who are journeying in the land in quest of Allah's bounty, and still others who are fighting in the cause of Allah. So recite as much of the Qur'ān as you easily can, and establish Prayer, and pay *Zakāh*,[6] and give Allah a goodly loan. Whatever good you send forth for yourselves, you shall find it with Allah. That is better and its reward is greater. And ask for Allah's forgiveness; surely He is Most Forgiving, Most Compassionate.

---

4. The last verse (v. 20) was revealed in Madīnah some ten years after the first nineteen verses of the *sūrah*.

5. Prayers become lengthy if the amount of the Qur'ānic recitation in them is lengthy. Hence the Prophet (peace be on him) was directed to "recite as much of the Qur'ān as you can" in the *Tahajjud* Prayer. This was said in order to lighten the burden of his exacting Prayer schedule. For by shortening the recitation, the length of the Prayer would also be automatically reduced.

6. Commentators on the Qur'ān are agreed that "Prayer" here denotes the five daily Prayers which are obligatory. Likewise, *Zakāh* denotes the obligatory alms.

74

Al-Muddaththir [The Cloaked One]
Makkan Period

In the name of Allah, the Most Merciful,
the Most Compassionate

[1] O you enveloped in your cloak![1] [2] Arise, and warn, [3] and magnify the glory of your Lord, [4] and purify your robes, [5] and shun uncleanness, [6] and bestow not favour in order to seek from others a greater return, [7] and persevere for your Lord's sake.

[8] When the Trumpet shall be sounded,[2] [9] that will surely be a hard day, [10] not an easy day for the unbelievers.

---

1. The first seven verses of this *sūrah* are those in which the Prophet (peace be on him) was directed for the first time ever to preach Islam's Message to others. The very first revelation of the Qur'ān consisted of the verses of *Sūrah* 96 (*Sūrah al-'Alaq*). Vv. 1-7 of this *sūrah* are the first verses to be revealed after the revelation of that *sūrah*.

2. These verses were revealed a few months after the revelation of the initial verses of the present *sūrah* at the time of the first *Ḥajj* following the commencement of Islam's public preaching. This was on the occasion when the chiefs of the Quraysh held a conference wherein they decided to launch a vigorous propaganda campaign designed to poison the minds of the Pilgrims who came from outside Makkah against the Qur'ān and the Prophet (peace be on him).

[11] Leave Me with him whom I alone have created,[3] [12] whom I have endowed with abundant riches, [13] and sons ever present with him, [14] and for whom I have smoothed the way (to power and riches), [15] and who still greedily desires that I should bestow upon him more. [16] By no means; he is stubbornly opposed to Our Signs. [17] I shall soon constrain him to a hard ascent. [18] He reflected and then hatched a scheme. [19] Ruin seize him, how did he hatch a scheme? [20] Again, ruin seize him, how did he hatch a scheme? [21] He looked (at others); [22] then frowned and scowled; [23] then he retreated and waxed proud, [24] and said: "This (Qur'ān) is merely a sorcery of yore; [25] this is nothing but the word of a mere mortal!" [26] Him shall I soon roast in Hell. [27] And what do you know what Hell is? [28] It spares nothing; it leaves nothing intact;[4] [29] it scorches (even) the skin. [30] Over it are nineteen keepers. [31] We[5]

---

3. This refers to Walīd ibn Mughīrah. In his own heart Mughīrah was convinced that the Qur'ān was the Word of God. But in order to retain his position as a tribal chief of Makkah he counselled during that conference (see n. 2 above) that the Prophet (peace be on him) was a sorcerer and the Qur'ān no more than a piece of sorcery.

4. Hell will not spare anyone who deserves to be chastised; and once it seizes anyone, it will not let him escape chastisement.

5. The whole passage commencing from the present verse until "And none knows the hosts of your Lord but He" (v. 31) is a parenthetical statement which has been introduced here to respond to the unbelievers' objection that God had appointed only 19 angels as Hell's keepers. They instantly began to ridicule this statement. They considered it quite bizarre that on the one hand it was said that all people from the time of Adam till the end of time who had rejected the true faith and had committed mortal sins would be cast into Hell. Yet, it was also being claimed that Hell would

have appointed none but angels as the keepers of the Fire, and We have not made their number but as a trial for the unbelievers so that those who have been endowed with the Book will be convinced and the believers' faith will increase, and neither those who have been endowed with the Book nor the believers will fall into any doubt.[6] As for those in whose hearts there is a sickness as well as the unbelievers, they will say: "What did Allah aim at by this strange parable?" Thus does Allah let whomsoever He pleases to go astray, and directs whomsoever He pleases to the Right Way. And none knows the hosts of your Lord but He. (And Hell has only been mentioned here) that people may take heed. [32] Nay,[7] by the moon, [33] and by the night when it recedes, [34] and by the day when it dawns (with its radiance), [35] surely (Hell) is one of the greatest Signs,[8] [36] a warning to humankind, [37] a warning to everyone of you whether he would like to come forward or lag behind.

[38] Each one is a hostage to one's deeds, [39] save the People of the Right Hand [40] who shall be in the Gardens,

---

have no more than 19 keepers to chastise such enormous hordes of people.

6. The People of the Book and the believers were well acquainted with the extraordinary abilities of angels. It was evident to them, therefore, that it was perfectly feasible for the 19 keepers to cope efficiently with Hell's administration.

7. That is, what is being said here is not baseless prattle or irresponsible gossip. There was no occasion, therefore, to subject it to ridicule.

8. In the same way that the moon and the night and the day are all among the Great Signs of God's power, so also is Hell.

and shall ask [41] about the guilty ones:⁹ [42] "What drove
you to Hell?" [43] They will answer: "We were not among
those who observed Prayer, [44] and we did not feed the
poor, [45] and we indulged in vain talk with those who
indulged in vain talk, [46] and we gave the lie to the Day
of Judgement [47] until the inevitable event overtook us."
[48] The intercession of the intercessors shall then be of
no avail to them.

[49] What is the matter with people that they are turning
away from this Exhortation, [50] as though they were
frightened wild asses, [51] fleeing from a lion?¹⁰ [52] No
indeed; each one of them desires that open letters be
sent to each of them.¹¹ [53] No indeed; the truth is that
they have no fear of the Hereafter. [54] Nay;¹² this is an
Exhortation. [55] So, whoever wills may benefit from it.
[56] But they will not benefit from it unless Allah Himself
so wills. He is worthy to be feared; and He is worthy to
forgive (those that fear Him).

---

9. This implies that the inmates of Paradise will be able, even while
remaining there, to communicate with the inmates of Hell.

10. This is an idiomatic Arabic expression. No sooner do wild asses
sense danger than they are totally stupefied and flee in fright in a
manner that no other animals do.

11. The Makkan chiefs were of the opinion that if God had indeed
designated Muḥammad (peace be on him) as a Prophet, He should
have sent a letter to each of the chiefs and elders of Makkah
informing them of this. (Only then would they accept him as a
Prophet.)

12. "No indeed" is said here to stress that God will not accede to
any such requests.

75

Al-Qiyāmah [The Resurrection]
Makkan Period

In the name of Allah, the Most Merciful,
the Most Compassionate

[1] Nay,¹ I swear by the Day of Resurrection;² [2] and nay, I swear by the self-reproaching soul!³ [3] Does man imagine that We will not be able to bring his bones together again? [4] Yes indeed; We have the power to remould even his

---

1. To open a discourse with "nay" itself indicates that this *sūrah* was revealed in order to refute something. "Nay" in the present context signifies that the unbelievers' notions about Resurrection are altogether false. This is followed by a sworn statement enunciating what the Truth really is.

2. Ironically, the occurrence of the Resurrection is being affirmed here by recourse to swearing by the Day of Resurrection itself. This swearing emphasises that it is beyond every doubt that Resurrection is bound to occur. The entire Universe testifies that it has neither always been in existence nor will it always remain so. It came into existence at a given moment of time from nothingness and a time will come when it will come to an end.

3. "The self-reproaching soul" here means conscience, for conscience reproaches man whenever he commits evil deeds. The very existence of conscience bears testimony to the fact that man is answerable for his deeds.

finger-tips. [5] But man desires to persist in his evil ways.⁴
[6] He asks: "When will the Day of Resurrection be?"
[7] When the sight is dazed, [8] and the moon is eclipsed,
[9] and the sun and the moon are joined together, [10] on
that Day will man say: "Whither the refuge?" [11] No,
there is no refuge. [12] With your Lord alone will be the
retreat that Day. [13] On that Day will man be apprised
of his deeds, both the earlier and the later. [14] But lo,
man is well aware of himself, [15] even though he might
make up excuses.⁵ [16] (O Prophet),⁶ do not stir your
tongue hastily (to commit the Revelation to memory).
[17] Surely it is for Us to have you commit it to memory
and to recite it. [18] And so when We recite it, follow its
recitation attentively; [19] then it will be for Us to explain it.

---

4. The true reason for a person's denial of Resurrection is not that
he really has rational or scientific proof establishing that it is beyond
the range of the possible; instead, the true reason for this denial is
his proclivity to engage in evil.

5. Man's Record will be placed before him on the Judgement-Day.
This will be done not in order that the evil-doers become acquainted
with their evil deeds, for each person is already aware of the evil
deeds he has committed. The Record will, nevertheless, be brought
forward so as to fulfil the requirements of justice which demand
that proof of a culprit's offence be placed before the court.

6. The whole passage from here to "then it will be for Us to explain
it" (vv. 16-19) is a parenthetical statement which interrupts the
discourse to bring an important matter to the Prophet's attention.
The need to do so arose because when Gabriel was communicating
this *sūrah* to the Prophet (peace be on him), the latter kept repeating
it so that he could firmly commit it to his memory.

[20] Nay;[7] the truth is that you love ardently (the good of this world) that can be obtained hastily, [21] and are oblivious of the Hereafter. [22] Some faces on that Day will be fresh and resplendent, [23] and will be looking towards their Lord; [24] and some faces on that Day will be gloomy, [25] believing that a crushing calamity is about to strike them. [26] Nay;[8] when a man's soul reaches up to the throat, [27] and it is said: "Is there any enchanter who can step forward and help (by his chanting)?" [28] and he realises that the hour of parting is come, [29] and calf is inter-twined with calf. [30] On that Day you will be driven to your Lord.

[31] But he did not verify the Truth, nor did he observe Prayer; [32] on the contrary, he gave the lie to the Truth and turned his back upon it, [33] then he went back to his kinsfolk, elated with pride. [34] This (attitude) is worthy of you, altogether worthy; [35] again, it is worthy of you, altogether worthy.

---

7. This marks the resumption of the original subject that was interrupted by the parenthetical statement. The word "nay" here emphasises that the true reason for denying the Hereafter was not that they were truly convinced that it was beyond God's power to raise the dead to life. The true reason, instead, was that they ardently loved this world (and denial of Resurrection came handy for if there were no Resurrection and After-Life, they could pursue their worldly interests with full impunity).

8. This "nay" relates to the basic subject under discussion. It underlines that they were mistaken in fancying that death would bring about their final extinction and that they would not return to their Lord for His reckoning.

[36] Does man think that he will be left alone, unquestioned?[9] [37] Was he not a drop of ejaculated semen, [38] then he became a clot, and then Allah made it into a living body and proportioned its parts, [39] and then He made of him a pair, male and female? [40] Does He, then, not have the power to bring back the dead to life?

---

9. The word used here is *sudā*. When this word is used about a camel it denotes the camel that wanders about aimlessly, grazing at will, one whom there is none to oversee.

Al-Dahr [Time]
Madīnan Period

In the name of Allah, the Most Merciful,
the Most Compassionate

[1] Was there a period of time when man was not even worthy of a mention?[1] [2] Verily We created man out of a drop of intermingled sperm so that We might try him, and We therefore endowed him with hearing and sight.[2] [3] Surely We showed him the Right Path, regardless of whether he chooses to be thankful or unthankful (to his Lord).[3]

[4] For the unbelievers, We have kept ready chains and fetters and a Blazing Fire.

[5] The virtuous shall drink from a cup tempered with camphor water. [6] This will be a gushing spring

---

1. While this statement is couched in the form of a query, its true purpose is to make man confirm that there indeed was a time when he was not "even worthy of a mention". This should also make him realise that if he was brought into existence from non-existence, why then he cannot be restored to life after death?

2. That is, God endowed man with certain abilities which made him a significant species.

3. God bestowed upon man the capacity to choose between giving thanks to God and being thankless to Him. Moreover, He also clearly indicated the landmarks of both the alternative ways.

wherefrom Allah's servants shall drink wine, a spring from which they will take out channels wherever they wish. [7] These will be the ones who fulfil their vows[4] and dread the Day whose woe shall be spread far and wide; [8] those who, for the love of Him, feed the needy, and the orphan, and the captive, [9] (saying): "We feed you only for Allah's sake; we do not seek of you any recompense or thanks, [10] we fear from our Lord a Day that shall be long and distressful." [11] So Allah shall guard them against the woe of that Day, and will procure them freshness and joy, [12] and will reward them for their steadfastness[5] with Paradise and robes of silk. [13] There they will recline on elevated couches and will be subjected neither to the burning heat of the sun nor to bitter cold. [14] The shades of Paradise will bend over them, and its fruits will be brought within their easy reach; [15] and there shall be passed around them vessels of silver and goblets of crystal,[6] [16] goblets bright as crystal but made

4. The word *nadhr* (vow) denotes the firm promise that a person makes to God to perform certain supererogatory acts of goodness over and above those he is obligated to perform.

5. Here righteous believers are being promised a great reward for their steadfastness. They have been steadfast in so far as they observed God's commands and tried their best to avoid disobeying Him ever since they committed themselves to faith.

6. According to *al-Zukhruf* 43: 71, "vessels of gold" shall be passed around the God-fearing. Now we find instead that "vessels of silver" will be passed around. All this shows is that on some occasions vessels of gold will be passed around to the people of Paradise, and on others, vessels of silver.

of silver,[7] filled to exact measure. [17] Therein they shall be served a cup flavoured with ginger,[8] [18] drawn from a spring (in Paradise) called Salsabīl. [19] There boys of everlasting youth shall go about attending them: when you see them, you would think that they are scattered pearls. [20] Whitherto you look around, you will see an abundance of bliss and the glories of a great kingdom. [21] They [i.e., the virtuous] shall be attired in garments of fine green silk and rich brocade and will be adorned with bracelets of silver.[9] Their Lord will give them a pure wine to drink. [22] Behold, this is your recompense and your endeavour has been appreciated.

[23] (O Prophet), indeed We have revealed the Qur'ān to you in portions.[10] [24] So persevere with the command of

---

7. That is, although those vessels will be of silver they will be as transparent as crystal.

8. The Arabs were fond of drinks blended with a ginger-flavoured water.

9. It is stated in *al-Ḥajj* 22: 23 and *Fāṭir* 35: 33 that the righteous would be adorned with bracelets of gold. (Here, however, they are being promised bracelets of silver.) This shows that they will be made to wear bracelets of gold or silver, variously as well as in combination.

10. Apparently this is addressed to the Prophet (peace be on him). However, the purpose of this statement is to refute the unbelievers' contention that the Qur'ān represents the Prophet's own thoughts. They used to argue that had it been from God, it would have come down in one piece, rather than in fragments.

your Lord[11] and do not pay any heed to the wicked and the unbelieving, [25] and remember the name of your Lord, morning and evening; [26] and prostrate yourself before Him at night, and extol His Glory during the long watches of the night.[12] [27] Verily they love (the good of this world) that is hastily obtainable and are oblivious of the burdensome Day ahead of them. [28] We created them and strengthened their joints; and whenever We wish, We can change their faces entirely. [29] Verily this is an Exhortation; so let him who so will take a way to his Lord. [30] But your willing shall be of no avail until Allah Himself so wills. Surely Allah is All-Knowing, Most Wise. [31] He admits to His Mercy whomsoever He pleases. As for the wrong-doers, He has prepared for them a grievous chastisement.

---

11. This was said to impress upon the Prophet (peace be on him) the need to remain steadfast in pursuing his Mission, to patiently endure the hardships and difficulties that he might encounter in that regard, and not to allow anything to make him waver in his resolve.

12. Whenever there is an injunction to remember God alongside the mention of a specific time, such injunctions refer to the prescribed Prayers (as distinguished from prayer in the sense of supplication to God or voluntary Prayer). In the present verse, two words are used: (1) *bukrah* which denotes "morning" and (2) *aṣīl*, which denotes the span of time beginning with the sun's decline till sunset. This covers the time for *Ẓuhr* and *'Aṣr* Prayers. This is followed in the next verse by the injunction to "prostrate yourselves before Him at night." Now "night" starts from sunset. Thus the injunction to prostrate "at night" covers the *Maghrib* and *'Ishā'* Prayers. Next comes the injunction in the same verse to "extol His glory during the long watches of the night." This clearly refers to the *Tahajjud* Prayers.

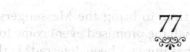

77

Al-Mursalāt [Those Sent Forth]
Makkan Period

In the name of Allah, the Most Merciful,
the Most Compassionate

[1] By the (winds) sent forth in quick succession, [2] which then blow tempestuously [3] and raise (clouds) and scatter them around, [4] then winnow them thoroughly, [5] and then cast (Allah's) remembrance (in people's hearts), [6] to serve as an excuse or a warning.¹ [7] Surely what you are promised shall come to pass.²

[8] So when the stars are extinguished, [9] and the sky is rent asunder, [10] and the mountains are blown away,

---

1. The winds serve several important purposes. Sometimes when they cease to blow they give rise to the frightful prospect of a famine which tends to soften people's hearts. This leads people at times to sincerely turn to God and repent. On other occasions, winds bring plentiful rainfall, filling people's hearts with gratitude to God. On still other occasions they blow tempestuously, inspiring all, including the sordid-hearted, with fear. As a result, many turn to God, dreading His chastisement that would play havoc with them.

2. The system underlying the blowing of the winds, etc., testifies that a time will surely come when Resurrection will take place. For although the winds are an important means to nourish God's creatures that live on earth, God can, and occasionally does, direct them to cause devastation and strike wicked people down.

[11] and the appointed time to bring the Messengers together arrives,³ (then shall the promised event come to pass). [12] To which Day has this task been deferred? [13] To the Day of Judgement. [14] What do you know what the Day of Judgement is? [15] Woe on that Day to those that give the lie to the Truth!

[16] Did We not destroy many a nation of the earlier times? [17] And We shall cause those of later times to follow them. [18] Thus do We deal with the guilty. [19] Woe on that Day to those that give the lie to the Truth!⁴

[20] Did We not create you of a mean fluid, [21] which We then placed in a secure repository [22] until an appointed time? [23] See that We had the power to do so. Great indeed is Our power to do what We will. [24] Woe on that Day to those that give the lie to the Truth!⁵

[25] Did We not make the earth a receptacle, [26] for the living and the dead, [27] and did We not firmly fix

---

3. It is mentioned quite often in the Qur'ān that when God will examine mankind's Record on the Judgement Day, the Messenger of each nation will be summoned to testify that he conveyed God's Message to his people. See for instance *al-Nisā'* 4: 41.

4. This is said to emphasise that howsoever woeful a person's lot might be in this world, it does not represent the full measure of the chastisement that might lie in store for him. It is only on the Day of Judgement that each person will come to know the full extent of the chastisement that awaits him.

5. These are the people who deny the possibility of life after death, calling such a notion an utter lie. They do so despite the overwhelming evidence in support of it. On the Judgement Day such people will certainly encounter a woeful chastisement.

towering mountains on it and give you sweet water to drink? [28] Woe on that Day to those that give the lie to the Truth![6]

[29] Proceed[7] now towards that which you were wont to deny as false; [30] proceed towards the three-pronged shadow,[8] [31] which neither provides (cooling) shade nor protection against the flames; [32] it indeed throws up sparks like castles, [33] which seem as though they are yellow-coloured camels. [34] Woe on that Day to those that give the lie to the Truth!

[35] That will be the Day on which they will not (be able to) utter a word, [36] nor will they be allowed to proffer excuses.[9] [37] Woe on that Day to those that give the lie to the Truth!

---

6. People decry the Hereafter as false, calling it both impossible and irrational. They do so in spite of the stunning manifestations of God's power and wisdom. If they wish, they may remain immersed in their puerile fancies. But a Day will certainly come when they will see that many a thing quite contrary to their expectation will come to pass. It is then that they will fully realise how foolish they were in precipitating such devastation upon themselves.

7. After proffering evidence that the Hereafter is bound to occur, the deniers of the Truth are being told about the treatment that will be meted out to them after the Hereafter becomes a reality.

8. "Shadow" here denotes the shadow caused by smoke. What is meant by its being "three-pronged" can be grasped by observing a thick pall of smoke when it splits into numerous branches.

9. That is, the case against them will be established by such solid evidence that they will be left utterly speechless and will be unable to put up any defence whatsoever.

[38] That is the Day of Judgement on which We have assembled you as well as all those who went before you. [39] So if you have any ploy, try it against Me! [40] Woe on that Day to those that give the lie to the Truth!

[41] Behold, today the God-fearing will be amidst shades and springs, [42] and the fruits that they desire (will be ready at hand). [43] Eat and drink and may every joy attend you as a reward for your deeds. [44] Thus do We reward those that do good. [45] Woe on that Day to those that give the lie to the Truth!

[46] Eat[10] and enjoy yourselves for a while. Surely you are evil-doers. [47] Woe on that Day to those that give the lie to the Truth! [48] When it is said to them: "Bow down (before Allah)," they do not bow down. [49] Woe on that Day to those that give the lie to the Truth! [50] In what discourse after this (Qur'ān) will they, then, believe?

---

10. The *sūrah* concludes by addressing these words not only to the Makkan unbelievers of the time, but to the unbelievers of all times, wherever they may be.

78

Al-Naba' [The Tiding]
Makkan Period

In the name of Allah, the Most Merciful,
the Most Compassionate

[1] About what are they asking one another? [2] Is it about the awesome tiding [3] that they are in utter disagreement? [4] No indeed;¹ soon will they come to know; [5] again, no indeed; soon will they come to know.

[6] Have We not spread the earth like a bed, [7] and fixed the mountains like pegs, [8] and created you in pairs (as men and women), [9] and made your sleep a means of repose, [10] and made the night a covering, [11] and made the day to seek livelihood, [12] and built above you seven strong firmaments, [13] and placed therein a hot, shining lamp,² [14] and sent down abundant water from the clouds [15] so that We may thereby bring forth grain and vegetation, [16] and gardens dense with foliage?

1. "No indeed" here purports to negate the unbelievers' utterances concerning the Hereafter, declaring them to be utterly false. The upshot of the expression "no indeed" is that the concepts which the unbelievers entertain about the Hereafter are all untrue.

2. The expression "a hot, shining lamp" denotes the sun. The word used here is *"wahhāj"* which at once connotes the qualities of being very hot and very shining.

[17] Surely the Day of Judgement has an appointed time; [18] the Day when the Trumpet shall be blown, and you will come forth in multitudes; [19] and when the sky shall be opened up and will become all doors; [20] and the mountains will be set in motion and become a mirage.

[21] Surely the Hell is an ambush,[3] [22] a resort for the rebellious; [23] therein they shall abide for ages,[4] [24] they shall taste in it no coolness, nor any pleasant drink [25] save boiling water and wash of the wounds; [26] a befitting recompense for their deeds. [27] For indeed they did not look forward to any reckoning, [28] and roundly denied Our Signs as false. [29] And everything have We recorded in a Book. [30] So taste (the fruit of your deeds). We shall only increase your torment.

[31] Surely the state of triumph awaits the God-fearing: [32] gardens and vineyards, [33] and youthful maidens of like age, [34] and an overflowing cup. [35] Therein they shall hear no idle talk, nor any falsehood;

---

3. The word *mirṣād* (ambush) denotes a spot which is especially chosen to entrap the game; a spot where it is caught unawares. Hell is described as an ambush because God's rebels, being unaware, are fearless of it. As a result, they strut about, considering the world to be simply a den for their self-indulgence, altogether incognizant of the possibility of being caught and punished. Thus Hell, being hidden from their eyes, is like an ambush wherein they are likely to be entrapped.

4. The word *aḥqāb* used here denotes long periods of time, each period following the other in succession.

[36] a recompense from your Lord and an ample reward[5]
[37] from the Lord of the heavens and the earth and of
that which is between them; the Most Merciful Lord before
Whom none dare utter a word.[6]

[38] The Day when the Spirit[7] and the angels are ranged
row on row. None shall speak save he whom the Merciful
Lord will permit; and he too will speak what is right.
[39] That Day is sure to come. So let him who will seek a
resort with his Lord.

[40] Lo! We warn you of a chastisement near at hand; the
Day when a man will look on what his own hands have
sent forth, and the unbelievers shall say: "Oh would that
I were utter dust."

---

5. The words "a recompense from your Lord and an ample reward"
convey the sense that the God-fearing will not simply receive
due recompense for their good deeds; in addition, God will also
bestow upon them a special reward, one that will be "ample".

6. This refers to what will happen on the Day of Judgement when
all have been brought to the "Plain of Gathering," and Reckoning
will be in progress. Awe will overwhelm everyone. So much so
that none – whether they dwell on earth or heavens – will be able
to utter a word in God's presence, nor will they dare to interfere
in the Reckoning to which all will be subject.

7. The word "Spirit" here stands for Gabriel. The very high position
which God invested him with called for his being mentioned
independently of all the other angels.

79

Al-Nāziʿāt [The Soul Pluckers]
Makkan Period

In the name of Allah, the Most Merciful,
the Most Compassionate

[1] By those (angels) that pluck out the soul from depths, [2] and gently take it away;¹ [3] and by those that speedily glide along (the cosmos),² [4] and vie with the others³ (in carrying out their Lord's behests); [5] and then manage the affairs of the Universe⁴ (according to their Lord's commands). [6] The Day when the quaking will cause a violent convulsion, [7] and will be followed by another quaking. [8] On that Day some hearts shall tremble (with fright), [9] and their eyes shall be downcast with dread.

---

1. Here the allusion is to the angels of death who descend to the depths of a person's being in order to draw out his soul from every fibre of his body.

2. The words "speedily glide along" portray the promptness and swiftness which characterise the actions of the angels in carrying out God's commands.

3. That is, as soon as the angels receive any indication of what God wants them to do, they begin to vie with one another in carrying out His commands.

4. This shows that the angels are God's functionaries who are appointed by Him to administer the affairs of the Universe according to His commands.

[10] They say: "Shall we indeed be restored to life, [11] even after we have been reduced to bones, hollow and rotten?" [12] They say: "That will then be a return with a great loss!"⁵ [13] Surely they will need no more than a single stern blast, [14] and lo, they will all be in the open plain.

[15] Has Moses' story reached you? [16] When his Lord called him in the sacred valley of Ṭuwā, [17] and directed him: "Go to Pharaoh, he has rebelled, [18] and say to him: 'Are you willing to be purified, [19] that I may direct you to your Lord and then you hold Him in awe?' " [20] Then Moses (went to Pharaoh and) showed him the Great Sign;⁶ [21] but he denied it as false and disobeyed, [22] and then he turned back to have recourse to his craftiness, [23] and gathered his people and declared: [24] "I am the supreme lord of you all." [25] Thereupon Allah seized him for the chastisement of the World to Come as well as of the present. [26] Surely there is a great lesson in it for whoever would fear (Allah).⁷

---

5. In response to the query from the deniers of the Hereafter (see vv. 10-11 above), it was made clear that they would certainly be restored to life even "after they have been reduced to bones, hollow and rotten." On hearing this they gave full vent to jest and irony, saying to one another that such a return would mean courting a very substantial loss (for they would then be skeletons, simply rotten bones).

6. "The Great Sign" demonstrated by Moses consisted in his staff becoming a serpent. It is mentioned at several places in the Qur'ān. See, for instance, *Ṭā' Hā'* 20: 19-20, *al-Naml*, 27: 10-13.

7. The lesson behind Pharaoh's story is that one should be fearful of the abhorrent consequences which stem from decrying God's Messengers as liars.

[27] Is it harder to create you or the heaven? But Allah built it, [28] and raised its vault high and proportioned it; [29] and covered its night with darkness and brought forth from it its day; [30] and thereafter spread out the earth, [31] and brought out of it its water and its pasture, [32] and firmly fixed in it mountains; [33] all this as provision for you and your cattle.

[34] But when the great calamity will come about[8] [35] on the Day when man will recall all his strivings, [36] and Hell will be brought in sight for anyone to see: [37] then he who transgressed [38] and preferred the life of this world, [39] most surely his abode shall be Hell. [40] But he who feared to stand before his Lord, and restrained himself from evil desires, [41] most surely his abode shall be Paradise. [42] They ask you about the Hour: "When will it be?" [43] What concern do you have to speak about that? [44] Its knowledge rests with your Lord. [45] You are only a warner to him who has a fear of it. [46] On the Day they see it, they will feel as though they had stayed (in the grave) no more than one evening or one morning.

---

8. That is, Resurrection.

80

'*Abasa* [He Frowned]
Makkan Period

In the name of Allah, the Most Merciful,
the Most Compassionate

[1] He frowned and turned away [2] that the blind man came to him.¹ [3] How could you know? Perhaps he would cleanse himself, [4] or he might be mindful and good counsel might avail him. [5] Now he who waxes indifferent, [6] you attend to him, [7] though you are not to blame if he would not cleanse himself. [8] But he who comes to you running, [9] and fears (Allah), [10] you pay no heed to him. [11] No indeed;² this is only a Reminder.

---

1. As the sentences that follow indicate, he "who frowned and turned away" was the Prophet (peace be on him) himself. As for the "blind man," this was Ibn Umm Maktūm, a cousin of the Prophet's wife, Khadījah. Ibn Umm Maktūm, came to the Prophet (peace be on him) at a time when he was deeply engrossed in conveying Islam's message to the most influential people of Makkah, the heads of the different clans. Ibn Umm Maktūm had wanted to ask him a few questions, but the Prophet (peace be on him) was irked by this intrusion.

2. The words "no indeed" are here indicative of God's directive to the Prophet (peace be on him) not to show undue deference to those who are heedless of Him on account of their worldly eminence. For Islam's teachings should not be presented as though the Prophet (peace be on him) were abjectly begging those who had spurned

[12] So whoso wills may give heed to it. [13] It is contained in scrolls highly honoured, [14] most exalted and purified,[3] [15] borne by the hands of scribes, [16] noble and purified.[4]

[17] Accursed[5] be man! How stubbornly he denies the Truth. [18] Out of what did Allah create him?

---

it to now honour him by accepting it. It also did not become the Prophet (peace be on him) to invite such arrogant people to Islam in such manner for this might give rise to the misconception that their acceptance of Islam would serve the Prophet's own interests. Nor was it appropriate that they be made to feel so important that if they accepted Islam, it would prosper as a result; and if they did not, then Islam would court disaster. Islam cares as little for them as they care for it.

3. This is to stress that the scrolls which embody the Revelation were free of impurity. These scrolls expound nothing but unadulterated Truth because false or corrupt ideas and doctrines have not been able to find their way into them.

4. The scribes mentioned here denote the angels who were charged under God's Own guidance with writing down the scrolls of the Qur'ān. This so as to safeguard them and faithfully convey them to the Prophet (peace be on him).

5. From here on God's reprimand is addressed directly to the unbelievers who were disregarding the Truth. Prior to this, from the opening verse of the *sūrah* to v. 16, the discourse seems to be addressed to the Prophet (peace be on him), but it was in actual fact meant to reprimand the unbelievers. This reprimand, however, was implicit. It consisted of asking the Prophet (peace be on him) why he paid scant attention to a genuine seeker of the Truth and instead directed his entire focus on those who were worthless from the point of view of his Mission. These unbelievers had gone too far in opposing the Truth to merit that the Prophet (peace be on him) should present before them something as exalted as the Qur'ān.

[19] Out of a sperm-drop did He create him and then determined a measure for him, [20] and then made the course of life easy for him, [21] then He caused him to die and brought him to the grave, [22] and then, whenever He wishes, He will raise him back to life. [23] Nay, but man did not fulfil what Allah had enjoined upon him. [24] So let man just consider his food: [25] We poured water, pouring it in great abundance,[6] [26] and cleaved the earth, cleaving it asunder; [27] then caused the grain to grow out of it, [28] together with grapes and vegetables, [29] and olives and palms, [30] and dense orchards, [31] and fruits and pastures – [32] all this as a provision for you and your cattle.

[33] But when the deafening cry shall be sounded[7] [34] on the Day when each man shall flee from his brother, [35] and his mother and his father; [36] and his consort and his children; [37] on that Day each will be occupied with his own business, making him oblivious of all save himself. [38] Some faces on that Day shall be beaming with happiness, [39] and be cheerful and joyous. [40] Some faces on that Day shall be dust-ridden, [41] enveloped by darkness. [42] These will be the unbelievers, the wicked.

6. Water here means rainwater.

7. This refers to the final and very horrendous sound of the Trumpet. After it has been blown all the dead will rise to life again.

81

Al-Takwīr [The Folding Up]
Makkan Period

In the name of Allah, the Most Merciful,
the Most Compassionate

[1] When the sun shall be folded up,[1] [2] when the stars shall scatter away, [3] when the mountains shall be set in motion, [4] when the ten-months pregnant camels shall be abandoned,[2] [5] when the savage beasts shall be brought together, [6] when the seas shall be set boiling, [7] when the souls shall be rejoined (with their bodies),[3] [8] and when the girl-child buried alive shall be asked: [9] for what offence was she killed? [10] and when the scrolls of (men's) deeds shall be unfolded, [11] and when Heaven is laid bare;

---

1. That is, when the light that is emitted by the sun and then spreads all around the world will be folded around the sun so that it will cease to radiate thereafter.

2. The Arabs held nothing as valuable as a pregnant she-camel on the verge of giving birth. When she reached that stage she received every possible protection and care. Hence, to say that people would abandon such she-camels meant that some extraordinary calamity had occurred that would totally occupy their attention, making them oblivious to the protection of their most precious property.

3. To say that "souls shall be rejoined (with their bodies)" means that human beings shall be restored to the state in which they lived in the world before their death.

[12] and Hell is stoked, [13] and Paradise brought nigh: [14] then shall each person know what he has brought along.

[15] No indeed;[4] I swear by the alternating stars [16] that hide, [17] and by the night as it recedes, [18] and the morn as it breathes. [19] Verily this is the word of a noble message-bearer;[5] [20] one mighty and held in honour with the Lord of the Throne; [21] there he is obeyed[6] and held trustworthy. [22] (O people of Makkah), your companion is not mad;[7] [23] he indeed saw the message-bearer on the clear horizon; [24] nor does he grudge (conveying this knowledge about) the Unseen; [25] nor is it a word of an accursed Satan. [26] Where to are you then heading? [27] It is nothing but Good Counsel for everyone in the world, [28] for everyone of you who wishes to follow the Straight Way; [29] but your wishing will not avail unless Allah, the Lord of the Universe, so wishes.

---

4. This represents an emphatic denial of their false notions about the Qur'ān, viz. that it merely consists of the musings of a lunatic or the evil suggestions of Satan.

5. The expression "noble message-bearer" here refers to the angel who carried the revelation to the Prophet (peace be on him). This is evident from the verses that follow (see vv. 20 ff. below). The statement that "this is the word of a noble message-bearer," however, does not mean that the contents of the Message stem from the noble angel. In fact, the use of the expression "message-bearer" itself indicates that it is the Word of the Being Who made that angel the bearer of that Message.

6. This means that he is at the head of those angels who work under his supervision.

7. The expression "your companion" here refers to the Prophet (peace be on him).

82

Al-Infitār [The Splitting Asunder]
Makkan Period

In the name of Allah, the Most Merciful,
the Most Compassionate

[1] When the heaven is split asunder, [2] when the stars
are scattered, [3] when the seas are made to burst forth,
[4] and when graves are laid open,[1] [5] everyone shall
know all his deeds, both the earlier and the later.

[6] O man! What has deceived you about your
generous Lord [7] Who created you, shaped you,
and made you well-proportioned, [8] and set you in
whatever form He pleased? [9] No indeed;[2] (the fact
is that) you deny the Reckoning, declaring it a lie;[3]

---

1. "When the graves are laid open" alludes to the resurrection of
the dead.

2. This is meant to negate the unbelievers' opinion about the
Hereafter and to vehemently stress that there is no reason why
human beings will be raised to life after death and that there will
be anything like a Next Life.

3. People who miscomprehend the Hereafter do so not because of
any persuasive rational argument in support of their standpoint.
They entertain the false notion that reward and punishment will
not follow people's actions. This false and baseless assumption has
made them heedless of God, impervious to the fact that He will call
them to account and mete out justice, and has fostered in them an
irresponsible moral attitude.

[10] you do so the while there are watchers over you; [11] noble scribes, [12] who know what you do.

[13] Surely the virtuous shall be in Bliss, [14] and the wicked shall be in the Blazing Fire. [15] They shall enter it on the Day of Recompense [16] and then shall never come out of it. [17] What do you know what the Day of Recompense is? [18] Again, what do you know what the Day of Recompense is? [19] It is the Day when no one shall have the power to do anything for another, and all command shall be Allah's.

83

Recompense ... ... what the
shall have the power to do anything for another and all
command shall be Allah's.

Al-Muṭaffifīn [The Stinters]
Makkan Period

*In the name of Allah, the Most Merciful,
the Most Compassionate*

[1] Woe to the stinters; [2] those who, when they take from others by measure, take their full share; [3] but who, when they measure or weigh for others, give less than their due. [4] Do they not realise that they will be raised to life [5] on a Great Day,¹ [6] a Day when mankind will stand before the Lord of the Universe?

[7] No indeed!² Verily the deeds of the wicked are in the Record locked up in the prison-house! [8] And how would you know what the Record of the prison-house is? [9] It is a Book inscribed. [10] Woe, then, to those that give the lie, [11] those that give the lie to the Day of Recompense. [12] Yet none gives the lie to it except the transgressor immersed in sin; [13] who, when Our verses

---

1. The Day of Resurrection has been called a "Great Day" because on that Day all humans and *jinn* will be called to account and God Himself will judge them all. Furthermore, on that Day hugely important decisions will be made about whom to reward and whom to punish.

2. Those who believe that they will not be held to account after they engaged in evil during their worldly life are certainly mistaken.

are recited to him,[3] says: "Mere tales of olden times!" [14] No indeed! The truth is that their hearts have become rusted on account of their evil deeds.[4] [15] No indeed! On that Day they will be screened off from seeing their Lord, [16] and then they shall enter Hell, [17] whereafter they will be told: "This is what you used to give the lie to."

[18] No indeed![5] Verily, the deeds of the virtuous shall be in the record of the exalted ones. [19] And what do you know what the Record of the exalted ones is? [20] It is a Book inscribed, [21] which the angels placed near Allah to safeguard. [22] Verily the virtuous shall be in Bliss; [23] resting on couches, looking around. [24] You shall see upon their faces the glow of bliss. [25] They will be served a drink of the finest sealed wine, [26] whose seal is musk – so let all aspirants aspire after that – [27] a wine whose mixture is *Tasnīm*,[6] [28] a fountain at which the chosen ones shall drink.

---

3. "Our verses" here refers to the verses that contain information about the Day of Recompense.

4. There was no good reason for anyone to say that the notions regarding reward and punishment in the Next Life were simply "tales of olden times" (v. 13). What makes people say so, however, is that their hearts have become rusted on account of the sins they have committed. Hence, an idea that is wholly reasonable appears to them as merely fanciful "tales of olden times".

5. This is said to contradict those who believe that no one will be rewarded or punished in the Life-to-Come.

6. The word *tasnīm* contains the nuance of "height". To call a spring *tasnīm* carries the connotation of a spring that flows down from a great height.

[29] Behold, the wicked were wont to laugh at the believers: [30] when they passed by them they winked, [31] and when they went back to their families, they went back jesting, [32] and when they saw the believers, they said: "Lo! These are the erring ones"; [33] (they said so although) they had not been appointed watchers over them. [34] But today the believers are laughing at the unbelievers; [35] seated upon their couches, they are looking around. [36] Have the unbelievers been duly rewarded for their deeds?[7]

---

7. These words have a subtle, ironic note about them. The unbelievers looked upon their persecution of the believers as an act of virtue. In this context it is stated that in the Life-to-Come the believers will be enjoying the delights of Paradise and will observe the woeful state of the unbelievers, wallowing in Hell. This will certainly make them say to themselves: "Have the unbelievers been duly rewarded for their deeds?"

84

Al-Inshiqāq [The Rending Asunder]
Makkan Period

In the name of Allah, the Most Merciful,
the Most Compassionate

[1] When the sky is rent asunder [2] and hearkens to the command of its Lord, doing what it should; [3] and when the earth is stretched out¹ [4] and casts out what is within it and is emptied,² [5] and hearkens to the command of its Lord, doing what it should. [6] O man, you are striving unto your Lord and you will meet Him. [7] Whoever is given the Record in his right hand [8] shall be called to an easy accounting,³ [9] and shall return to his people

---

1. "When the earth is stretched out" refers to the time when the seas and rivers will be filled up, the mountains will be reduced to particles of dust that will be made to dissipate, and the earth will be levelled and turned into a flat plain.

2. This refers to the fact that the earth will throw up the dead that had lain buried within it. This will bring to the surface all evidence pertaining to their deeds that had thus far remained hidden from sight. Nothing regarding them will then remain unknown.

3. That someone should be given the Record in his right hand is indicative of his being a righteous person. As a result, he will be subjected to a relatively light reckoning. In other words, such people will not be subjected to strict interrogation as to why they committed certain deeds; nor will they be asked to produce extenuating explanations for their misdeeds. Likewise, even

joyfully.[4] [10] But he who is given the Record behind his back,[5] [11] shall cry for "perdition," [12] and will enter the Blazing Fire. [13] He used to live joyfully among his people, [14] thinking he would never revert (to Us). [15] But no; (how would he not revert)? His Lord was ever watching him.

[16] Nay; I swear by the twilight; [17] and by the night and what it enfolds, [18] and by the moon, when it reaches its fullness: [19] you shall proceed onwards from stage to stage.[6] [20] So, what is the matter with them that they

---

though there will be evil along with good deeds in their Record, forbearance will be shown to them because their good deeds will outweigh their evil deeds, and they will be forgiven.

4. "His people" denotes those members of a person's family and those relatives and companions who will be forgiven in the same manner that he himself was forgiven.

5. It is stated in *al-Ḥāqqah* 69: 25 that the Record of an unrighteous person will be handed over to him in his left hand. Here, however, it is stated that such people will be given the Book behind their backs. What will probably happen is that when a person's Record will be given to people to hold it in their left hand, they will be greatly embarrassed. They will, therefore, put their hand behind their back so as to receive their Record. But this effort to hide will not be of much avail, for in any case they will still be handed their Record. What difference will it then make whether they receive their Record with their hand outstretched, and hence in the full sight of others, or behind their backs?

6. Man's life does not remain in one state; instead, it goes through various stages: from youth to old age, from old age to death, from death to *barzakh* (the transitory stage between death and Resurrection), from *barzakh* to resurrection, from resurrection to the Plain of Gathering, then to Reckoning and then to the meting out of

do not believe, [21] and when the Qur'ān is recited to them, they do not prostrate themselves? [22] Instead, the unbelievers reject it, calling it a lie. [23] Allah knows best what they are accumulating (in their Record).[7] [24] So give them the good news of a painful chastisement, [25] except for those who believe and do good deeds. Theirs shall be an unending reward.

---

reward and punishment. It is emphasised here that all this is bound to happen. This is reinforced by a sworn statement mentioning (1) the twilight, (2) the darkness of the night and the gathering together in it of those humans and animals that remain scattered during the day, and (3) the moon's passing through different phases from being a mere crescent until becoming full. These are among the phenomena that testify to the fact that the Universe in which man lives is not static. On the contrary, incessant changes occur all over it. Thus, there is no basis to support the view that everything ends with a person's breathing his last.

7. This could also mean that God knows well the unbelief, the hostility to and the rancour against the Truth, and the evil intentions with which some people have filled their hearts.

85

Al-Burūj [The Castles]
Makkan Period

In the name of Allah, the Most Merciful,
the Most Compassionate

[1] By the heaven with its impregnable castles;[1] [2] by the Promised Day, [3] and by the witness and what is witnessed:[2] [4] the people of the pit were destroyed [5] with fire abounding in fuel, [6] while they sat around it, [7] and were witnessing what they did to the believers.[3] [8] Against these they had no grudge except that they believed in Allah, the Most Mighty, the Most Praiseworthy, [9] to Whom belongs the dominion of the heavens and the earth. Allah witnesses everything.

---

1. The expression "impregnable castles" refers to the massive stars and planets of the heavens.

2. The word "witness" here refers to the person who will be present on the Day of Resurrection to observe it. As for the expression "what is witnessed," it signifies the Resurrection itself whose harrowing scenes will be witnessed by all.

3. The "people of the pit" were those who had stuffed pits with believers and then set them ablaze, intensely enjoying this carnival. To say that the "people of the pit were destroyed" amounts to saying that they invited God's curse upon themselves and were overtaken by His chastisement.

[10] Surely those who tormented the believing men and the believing women and then did not repent, theirs shall be the chastisement of Hell, and theirs shall be the chastisement of burning. [11] As for those who believed and acted righteously, theirs shall be Gardens beneath which rivers flow. That is the great triumph.

[12] Stern indeed is your Lord's punishment. [13] He it is Who creates for the first time and He it is Who will create again, [14] and He is the Ever Forgiving, the Most Loving [15] – the Lord of the Glorious Throne, [16] the Executor of what He wills. [17] Has the story of the armies reached you, [18] the armies of Pharaoh and Thamūd? [19] The unbelievers are indeed engaged in denying it, calling it a lie, [20] although Allah surrounds them. [21] Nay; but this is a glorious Qur'ān, [22] inscribed on a well-guarded Tablet.[4]

---

4. This signifies that the Qur'ān's writ is bound to come about for it is inscribed on God's Well-Guarded Tablet and hence cannot be subjected to alteration.

86
❧

Al-Ṭāriq [The Night Visitor]
Makkan Period

In the name of Allah, the Most Merciful,
the Most Compassionate

[1] By the heaven, and the night-visitor, [2] what do you
know what the night-visitor is? [3] It is the piercing star.
[4] There is no living being but there is a protector over it.¹
[5] So let man consider of what he was created. [6] He was
created of a gushing fluid, [7] emanating from between
the loins and the ribs.² [8] Surely He (the Creator) has the
power to bring him back (to life). [9] On the Day when

---

1. The word "protector" here signifies God Himself Who is looking
after and protecting all the creatures of the earth and the heavens,
be they large or small. The thrust of the verse is that the countless
stars and planets that glisten in the sky at night bear witness that
there certainly is a Being Who created them, illuminated them,
suspended them in space, and Who protects them in such manner
that they neither fall from their locations nor collide with the other
countless stars in the course of their movement, nor do any other
stars and planets collide with them. In like manner, God looks after
and protects each and every object in the Universe.

2. The life-generating fluid of both men and women issues from
that part of their body that lies between the back and the breast. It
is being said, therefore, that man was created of a "gushing fluid
emanating from between the loins and the ribs."

man's deepest secrets shall be put to the test[3] [10] he shall have no power, and no helper. [11] By the heaven with its recurring cycle of rain, [12] and by the earth ever bursting with verdure, [13] this (Qur'ān) is surely a decisive Word, [14] not a flippant jest.[4] [15] They are devising a guile, [16] and I too am devising a guile. [17] So leave the unbelievers to themselves; respite them awhile.

---

3. "Man's deepest secrets" signify those actions that are unknown to others. They also signify those matters about whom some people might know about, but whose underlying intent and motive are hidden from others.

4. Just as the downpour from the heaven and the vegetation that pierces through the earth's crust is a serious reality rather than a jest, so is the Qur'ān's teaching that man is bound to return to his Lord.

87

Al-Aʿlā [The Most High]
Makkan Period

In the name of Allah, the Most Merciful,
the Most Compassionate

[1] Glorify the name of your Lord, the Most High, [2] Who created all things and fashioned them in good proportion;[1] [3] Who determined[2] and guided them,[3] [4] Who brought forth the pasture, [5] and then made it into a blackish straw.

---

1. God created everything in the Universe from the earth to the heavens and endowed each with right proportion and balance, giving it the best possible form.

2. "… your Lord … determined," that is, before creating anything God decided what its role would be in the world, and what would be its size, its shape, its qualities, and its location. God also decided the means and opportunities that should be provided to it for its existence, sustenance and function; how it should come into existence, how long it should remain in existence, and how, after accomplishing its task, its existence should come to an end. This scheme in its totality is known in Arabic as *taqdīr*, meaning God's determination of all things.

3. That is, God did not simply bring a thing into existence and then abandon it. On the contrary, God informed each created object what the mode of its function would be.

[6] We shall make you recite and then you will not forget,[4] [7] except what Allah should wish.[5] He knows all that is manifest and all that is hidden.

[8] We shall ease you to follow the way of Ease. [9] So render good counsel if good counsel will avail.[6] [10] He who fears (Allah) shall heed it, [11] but the wretched will turn away from it. [12] He will be cast into the Great Fire. [13] Then he will neither die in it, nor live.

---

4. This refers to the early period of revelation. At times the Prophet (peace be on him) would start rehearsing the verses while Gabriel was in the process of communicating them to him. He did so lest he might forget them. For this reason God asked him not to rehearse the Revelation while it was being communicated to him; he should rather do no more than listen attentively. He was assured that after a portion of revelation had been made, God would make him recite it after which he would then never forget.

5. True, if the Prophet (peace be on him) had committed the entire Qur'ān to memory this was not because of his own capacity to do so. It was rather because of God's special grace and succour. For, if God had so wanted, He could have erased from the Prophet's memory, either wholly or partially, whatever had been revealed to him.

6. This is to stress that God does not want to place any undue burden on the Prophet (peace be on him) as regards preaching the Message of the True Faith. He does not want him to embark on such impossible tasks as making the deaf hear and the blind see. Instead, God wants the Prophet (peace be on him) to engage in the relatively easier task of giving good counsel to those who, in his opinion, are capable of benefiting from it. However, he need not pursue those whom he knows, on the basis of personal experience, to be incapable of benefiting from good counsel.

[14] He who purified himself shall prosper, [15] remembering his Lord's name and praying. [16] No; but you prefer the present life, [17] whereas the Hereafter is better and more enduring. [18] This, indeed, was in the ancient Scrolls, [19] the Scrolls of Abraham and Moses.

88

◦◦◦◦◦

Al-Ghāshiyah [The Overwhelming Event]
Makkan Period

In the name of Allah, the Most Merciful,
the Most Compassionate

[1] Has the news of the overwhelming event reached you? [2] Some faces[1] that Day shall be downcast with fear, [3] be toiling and worn-out; [4] they shall burn in a Scorching Fire; [5] their drink shall be from a boiling spring. [6] They shall have no food except bitter dry thorns [7] that will neither nourish nor satisfy their hunger. [8] On that very Day some faces shall be radiant with joy, [9] well-pleased with their striving. [10] They will be in a lofty Garden [11] wherein they shall hear no vain talk. [12] In it there shall be a flowing spring, [13] and couches raised high, [14] and goblets laid out, [15] and cushions arrayed in rows, [16] and rich carpets levelled out.

---

1. The expression "some faces" means "some people". The word "faces" is used to denote people because the face is the most conspicuous part of a person's body.

[17] Do (these unbelievers) not observe the camels: how they were created? [18] And the sky: how it was raised high? [19] And the mountains: how they were fixed? [20] And the earth: how it was spread out?[2]

[21] So render good counsel, for you are simply required to counsel, [22] and are not invested with the authority to compel them. [23] But whoever will turn away (from the Truth), [24] Allah will chastise him with the most terrible chastisement. [25] Surely to Us is their return; [26] and then it is for Us to call them to account.

---

2. Those who deny the Hereafter on the grounds that it is beyond the range of possibility should look around and consider some well-known facts pertaining to God's creation of the camels, to the establishment of the mountains, to His raising the heavens to very lofty heights, and to the spreading out of the earth. They should also ponder on how all this was brought about. If it was possible to bring all these things into existence – and their existence is a tangible reality –what, then, are their grounds for believing that Resurrection cannot take place? Why can a new world not come about, and what is the basis for thinking that Hell and Heaven are beyond the range of what is possible?

89

Al-Fajr [The Dawn]
Makkan Period

In the name of Allah, the Most Merciful,
the Most Compassionate

[1] By the dawn, [2] and the ten nights, [3] and the even and the odd, [4] and by the night when it departs. [5] Is there in this an oath for one endowed with understanding?[1]

[6] Have you not seen how your Lord dealt with 'Ād [7] of Iram, known for their lofty columns, [8] the like of whom no nation was ever created in the lands of the world? [9] And how did He deal with Thamūd who hewed out rocks in the valley? [10] And with Pharaoh of the tent pegs [11] who transgressed in the countries of the world

---

1. Reflection on the verses that follow (see vv. 6 ff.) makes it clear that the Prophet (peace be on him) and the unbelievers were contending over the question of reward and punishment in the Next Life. The Prophet (peace be on him) sought to establish that the Hereafter was bound to take place whereas the unbelievers denied it. In this context we encounter an oath referring to four things: (i) the dawn, (ii) the ten nights, (iii) the even and the odd, and (iv) the night when it departs. The implication being that the testimony contained in this oath dispensed with the need for any other evidence to establish that the Next Life was bound to occur.

[12] spreading in them much corruption? [13] Then their Lord unloosed upon them the lash of chastisement. [14] Truly your Lord is ever watchful.[2]

[15] As for man, when his Lord tests him by exalting him and bestowing His bounties upon him, he says: "My Lord has exalted me." [16] But when He tests him by straitening his sustenance, he says: "My Lord has humiliated me."[3] [17] But no; you do not treat the orphan honourably, [18] and do not urge one another to feed the poor, [19] and greedily devour the entire inheritance, [20] and love the riches, loving them ardently. [21] But no;[4] when the earth is ground to powder, [22] and when your Lord appears

---

2. The verse depicts God as One Who lays an ambush. Whoever lays an ambush remains in hiding, waiting to surprise the enemy with a sudden attack. Unaware of the ambush, the victim is likely to come but when he exceeds a certain point, he falls prey to the ambush. This analogy applies to the wrong-doers of the world who are spreading all kinds of mischief and corruption, unaware that God is watching their misdeeds. Thanks to their heedlessness, they commit ever more misdeeds with impunity. Thus they reach a limit which God does not let them exceed. At this point they are suddenly seized by His scourge.

3. This, then, is man's materialistic concept of life. Man equates wealth, position and power in the world with the bestowal of honour; and when he is deprived of these, he thinks that God has humiliated him. The fact which he fails to grasp is that whatever God gives anyone in this world is by way of a test. One is tested both when one has wealth and power as well as when one is in a state of poverty and destitution.

4. It is stressed here that it is quite erroneous for man to fancy that he can act as he wishes and not be called to account thereafter.

with rows upon rows of angels, [23] and when Hell is brought near that Day. On that Day will man understand, but of what avail will that understanding be? [24] He will say: "Would that I had sent ahead what would be of avail for this life of mine!" [25] Then on that Day Allah will chastise as none other can chastise; [26] and Allah will bind as none other can bind.

[27] (On the other hand it will be said): "O serene soul!⁵ [28] Return to your Lord well-pleased (with your blissful destination), well-pleasing (to your Lord). [29] So enter among My (righteous) servants [30] and enter My Paradise."

---

5. The expression "serene soul" signifies the person who accepts, with full conviction, the One True God as his Lord and Sustainer, and recognizes the religious faith expounded by the Prophets as the True Faith.

90

Al-Balad [The City]
Makkan Period

*In the name of Allah, the Most Merciful,
the Most Compassionate*

[1] Nay!¹ I swear by this city [2] – this city wherein you have been rendered violable² – [3] and I swear by the parent and his offspring: [4] Verily We have created man into toil and hardship.³ [5] Does he think that no one can overpower him? [6] He says: "I have squandered enormous wealth." [7] Does he believe that none has seen him?⁴ [8] Did We not grant him two eyes,

---

1. The word "nay" is used here to stress that the unbelievers' ideas were altogether devoid of reality.

2. The irony was that in Makkah even animals, let alone human beings, were inviolable and enjoyed security. Astonishingly, in that very city, every kind of wrong and injustice was perpetrated against the Prophet (peace be on him) as though it were lawful to do so only in this particular case.

3. That is, this world is essentially not a place of fun and frolic; instead, here one has to pass through the rigours of toil and hardship, something which no human being can escape.

4. There are people who boastfully flaunt that they are great squanderers of wealth. Are such people too foolish to take any note of the fact that there is, after all, God above them Who takes note of how they had acquired wealth and the purposes on which they spent it?

[9] and a tongue and two lips?[5] [10] And did We not show him the two highroads (of good and evil)? [11] But he did not venture to scale the difficult steep. [12] And what do you know what that difficult steep is? [13] It is freeing someone's neck from slavery; [14] or giving food on a day of hunger [15] to an orphan near of kin; [16] or to a destitute lying in dust; [17] and, then besides this, he be one of those who believed, and enjoined upon one another steadfastness and enjoined upon one another compassion. [18] These are the People of the Right Hand. [19] As for those who rejected Our Signs, they are the People of the Left Hand.[6] [20] Upon them shall be a Fire that will hem them in.

---

5. The purpose of this query is to impress upon us that God has endowed man with the means to acquire knowledge and wisdom.

6. To comprehend what is meant by "the People of the Right Hand" and "the People of the Left Hand," see *al-Wāqiʿah* 56: 8, 9, 27–40 and 41–56.

91

Al-Shams [The Sun]
Makkan Period

In the name of Allah, the Most Merciful,
the Most Compassionate

[1] By the sun and its heat and brightness, [2] and by the moon as it follows it; [3] and by the day as it displays the sun's glory, [4] and by the night as it envelopes the sun; [5] and by the sky and by Him Who made it; [6] and by the earth and by Him Who stretched it out; [7] and by the soul and by Him Who perfectly proportioned it,¹ [8] and imbued it with (the consciousness of) its

---

1. That is, God has invested man's body and mind with special characteristics and has also equipped him with senses and other powers and abilities by means of which he can perform the task that is required of him.

evil and its piety:² [9] He who purifies it will prosper, [10] and he who suppresses it will be ruined.³

[11] In their presumptuous insolence the Thamūd called the Truth a lie [12] when their arch-criminal rose up in rage. [13] Then Allah's Messenger warned them: "Hands off the she-camel and her drink!" [14] But they rejected his statement as a lie and hamstrung the she-camel. For that crime their Lord rumbled down upon them, utterly razing them to the ground.⁴ [15] He has no fear of its sequel.

---

2. This has two meanings. First, that the Creator has imbedded in man's nature tendencies and inclinations towards both good and evil. Second, that God has impregnated every person's subconscious with certain notions of good and evil: that good and evil deeds are intrinsically different, and are not of equal worth; that while *fujūr* (immorality) is condemnable, *taqwā* (avoidance of evil) is praiseworthy, etc. These ideas are not foreign to man. On the contrary, his nature is quite profoundly acquainted with them. This is because man's Creator has endowed him with an innate capacity to distinguish between good and evil.

3. "To purify the self" means to cleanse oneself of evil and to nurture good qualities in oneself instead. On the contrary, "to suppress the self" means to develop one's evil potentialities.

4. The wicked person hamstrung the she-camel not simply with the consent and approval of his people, but also at their behest. See *al-Qamar* 54: 29. The whole nation, therefore, invited God's wrath upon itself.

92

Al-Layl [The Night]
Makkan Period

In the name of Allah, the Most Merciful,
the Most Compassionate

[1] By the night when it enshrouds, [2] and by the day when it breaks in its glory, [3] and by Him Who created the male and the female: [4] surely your strivings are divergent.¹ [5] As for him who gave out his wealth (for Allah's sake) and abstained (from disobeying Him), [6] and affirmed the Truth of goodness: [7] We shall facilitate for him the Way to Bliss.² [8] As for him who was a miser and behaved with aversion (to Allah), [9] and denied the Truth of goodness:

---

1. We observe that the night and the day, and the male and the female are different from one another, and that they give rise to mutually divergent results. Likewise, human beings strive in a variety of ways and for a variety of purposes. Similarly, the results of their striving too are greatly at variance.

2. The statement that "We shall facilitate for him the Way to Bliss" means that God will facilitate man to tread the path that is in sync with his true nature.

[10] We shall facilitate for him the way to Hardship,[3] [11] and his wealth shall be of no avail to him when he perishes.

[12] Surely it is for Us to show the Right Way, [13] and to Us belong the Next Life and the present. [14] I have now warned you of a Blazing Fire, [15] where none shall burn except the most wicked, [16] who rejected the Truth, calling it falsehood and turned his back on it. [17] But the God-fearing shall be kept away from it, [18] the God-fearing who spends his wealth to purify himself; [19] not as payment for any favours that he received, [20] but only to seek the good pleasure of his Lord Most High. [21] He will surely be well-pleased (with him).

---

3. "We shall facilitate for him the way to Hardship" means that God will facilitate those who choose the path that is discordant with their true nature to tread that very same path, and that will lead them to Hardship.

93

Al-Ḍuḥā [The Forenoon]
Makkan Period

In the name of Allah, the Most Merciful,
the Most Compassionate

[1] By the bright forenoon, [2] and by the night when it covers the world with peace: [3] (O Prophet), your Lord has neither forsaken you, nor is He displeased. [4] Indeed what is to come will be better for you than what has gone by. [5] Verily your Lord will soon give you so amply that you will be well-pleased. [6] Did He not find you an orphan and then gave you shelter? [7] Did He not find you unaware of the Right Way, and then directed you to it? [8] And did He not find you in want, and then enriched you? [9] Therefore, be not harsh with the orphan; [10] and chide not him who asks, [11] and proclaim the bounty of your Lord.

94

Alam Nashraḥ [The Opening Up]
Makkan Period

In the name of Allah, the Most Merciful,
the Most Compassionate

[1] (O Prophet), Did We not lay open your breast[1] [2] and relieve you of the burden [3] that had well-nigh broken your back?[2] [4] And did We not exalt your fame?

---

1. The expression "to open the breast" occurs at several places in the Qur'ān. See, for instance, *al-An'ām* 6: 125, *Ṭā' Hā'* 20: 25, *al-Zumar* 39: 22. If one reflects on its use on different occasions, it is evident that it denotes two things: (1) the state of a person when he overcomes every kind of mental perturbation and reluctance and attains the conviction that Islam is the right Way of life, and (2) the state of a person who has become imbued with the spirit to embark on any task, howsoever arduous, for the sake of Islam and acquires the nerve to shoulder the great responsibilities of prophethood.

2. The word "burden" here signifies the burden of sorrow and grief and of anxiety and concern which had weighed heavily on the Prophet (peace be on him). Being of a sensitive disposition, he was immensely distressed to see that his people were immersed in ignorance and followed ways far removed from righteousness. He agonised over all this but in the early stage of his life did not know how to bring his people out of this state. At that time of his life the burden of this anxiety virtually broke his back. God removed this burden by directing him to Divine Guidance. Henceforth, the Prophet (peace be on him) felt relieved, enjoyed inner peace and

[5] Indeed, there is ease with hardship. [6] Most certainly, there is ease with hardship.[3] [7] So, whenever you are free, strive in devotion, [8] and turn to your Lord with longing.[4]

was fully convinced that he could liberate not only the people of Arabia, but all humanity from the evils that afflicted them.

3. This is repeated twice in order to fully assure the Prophet (peace be on him) that the hard times through which he was passing would not endure; that good times would soon follow.

4. The Prophet (peace be on him) is being directed here to devote his free hours to acts of worship and to focus his attention exclusively on God.

95

Al-Tīn [The Fig]
Makkan Period

In the name of Allah, the Most Merciful,
the Most Compassionate

[1] By the fig and the olive;¹ [2] and by the Mount Sinai, [3] and by this city (of Makkah), a haven of peace: [4] surely We created man in the best mould; [5] then We reverted him to the lowest of the low, [6] except those who have faith and do righteous deeds. Theirs is a never-ending reward. [7] Who, then, can give the lie to you, (O Prophet), about the Reward and the Punishment? [8] Is not Allah the Greatest of all sovereigns?²

---

1. "The fig and the olive" here refer to the regions where figs and olives are grown in great abundance and where a large number of Prophets were raised; that is, Syria and Palestine.

2. Human beings both want and expect ordinary judges to mete out justice, to punish the criminals and reward the righteous. If such is their expectation from worldly judges, what should their expectation be from God, the Greatest of all judges? Is it proper to believe that God will treat the righteous and the wicked alike? Is it credible that He will let both the righteous and the wicked to simply end up in dust, without rewarding those who merit it for their good deeds and without punishing those who deserve it for their evil deeds?

96

Al-'Alaq [The Clot]
Makkan Period

In the name of Allah, the Most Merciful,
the Most Compassionate

[1] Recite in the name of your Lord Who created, [2] created man from a clot of congealed blood. [3] Recite: and your Lord is Most Generous, [4] Who taught by the pen, [5] taught man what he did not know.[1]

[6] Nay,[2] surely man transgresses; [7] for he believes himself to be self-sufficient. [8] Surely to your Lord is your return. [9] Did you see him who forbids [10] a servant (of Allah) when he prays? [11] Did you consider: what if he is on the Right Way, [12] and enjoins piety? [13] Did you consider: what if he gives the lie (to the Truth) and turns away (from it)? [14] Does he not know that Allah sees everything? [15] No indeed; if he does not desist, We shall drag him by the forelock; [16] by the lying forelock steeped in sin. [17] So let him summon his helpmates; [18] We too shall summon the guards of Hell. [19] No, not at all. Never obey him. But prostrate yourself and become nigh (to your Lord).

---

1. These are the very first verses of the Qur'ān that were revealed to the Prophet (peace be on him).

2. The present verse and the ones that follow were revealed while the Prophet (peace be on him) was praying in the sacred sanctuary of Makkah after being designated a Prophet.

97

Al-Qadr [Power]
Makkan Period

In the name of Allah, the Most Merciful,
the Most Compassionate

[1] Behold, We revealed this (Qur'ān) on the Night of Power. [2] And what do you know what the Night of Power is? [3] The Night of Power is better than a thousand months. [4] The angels along with the Spirit descend in it by the permission of their Lord with all kinds of decrees. [5] All peace is that night until the rise of dawn.

98

Al-Bayyinah [The Clear Proof]
Madīnan Period

*In the name of Allah, the Most Merciful,
the Most Compassionate*

[1] Those who disbelieved – be they from the People of the Book or from those who associated others with Allah in His Divinity – will not desist from unbelief until the Clear Proof should come to them; [2] a Messenger from Allah,¹ reciting from Purified Scrolls; [3] in writings wherein are scriptures, absolutely true and unerring.²

[4] Nor did those to whom the Book had been given split up until after the Proof (of the Right Way) had come to them.³ [5] Yet all that they had been commanded was that they serve Allah, with utter sincerity, devoting themselves exclusively to Him, and that they establish Prayer and pay *Zakāh*. That is the Right Faith.

---

1. The words "Clear Proof" here refer to the Prophet (peace be on him).

2. That is, the Prophet (peace be on him) brought a revealed message unblemished from falsehood, error or any taint of moral corruption.

3. The People of the Book had for long been victims of a great many errors. As a consequence, they were split into several sects. This was not because of any inadequacy in God's arrangements to guide

[6] Those who disbelieved – be they from among the People of the Book or among those who associated others with Allah in His Divinity[4] – shall be in the Fire, and will abide in it. They are the worst of creatures. [7] But those that believe and work righteous deeds, they are the best of creatures. [8] Their recompense lies with their Lord: Gardens of eternity beneath which rivers flow; therein they shall dwell, forever and ever. Allah is well-pleased with them, and they are well-pleased with Him. All this is for him who fears his Lord.

---

them. It was rather because they followed erroneous ways after God had made True Guidance available to them. Hence, they themselves were responsible for wallowing in misguidance.

4. "Those who disbelieved" refers to those who refused to accept the Prophet Muḥammad (peace be on him) as God's Prophet and Messenger.

99

Al-Zilzāl [The Earthquake]
Madīnan Period

In the name of Allah, the Most Merciful,
the Most Compassionate

[1] When the earth will be shaken with a mighty shaking, [2] and the earth will throw up all her burdens, [3] and man will cry out: "What is the matter with her?" [4] On that Day it will relate all her news, [5] for your Lord will have commanded her (to do so). [6] On that Day people will go forth in varying states so that they be shown their deeds. [7] So, whoever does an atom's weight of good shall see it; [8] and whoever does an atom's weight of evil shall see it.

100

❧

Al-ʿĀdiyāt [The Chargers]
Makkan Period

In the name of Allah, the Most Merciful,
the Most Compassionate

[1] By (the horses) that charge snorting, [2] then raise sparks of fire (by their hoofs), [3] then raid by the dawn, [4] and blaze a trail of dust, [5] and penetrate deep into a host. [6] Verily man is most ungrateful to his Lord;¹ [7] and he himself is a witness to that,² [8] and surely he loves riches with a passionate loving. [9] Is he not aware that when whatever lies (buried) in the graves is overthrown; [10] and the secrets of the hearts are laid bare (and examined)?³ [11] Surely on that Day will their Lord be fully informed about them.⁴

---

1. That is, man uses the powers that God had bestowed on him to perpetrate injustices and oppress others.

2. Man's conscience as well as his deeds bear witness that he tends to be ungrateful to God. Many unbelievers act in ways that betray their ungratefulness to God; moreover, they even verbally express their ingratitude.

3. On the Judgement Day even the intentions and motives underlying people's actions, which had thus far remained hidden, will be laid bare.

4. That is, on the Judgement Day God will be well aware of each person's standing and know fully the reward and punishment that each deserves.

101

Al-Qāri'ah [The Calamity]
Makkan Period

In the name of Allah, the Most Merciful,
the Most Compassionate

[1] The Calamity! [2] What is the Calamity? [3] And what do you know what the Calamity is? [4] On that Day human beings shall be like scattered moths, [5] and the mountains shall be like fluffs of carded wool in varying colours. [6] Then he whose scales weigh heavier [7] shall have a blissful life; [8] but he whose scales weigh lighter, [9] his shall be the deep pit for a dwelling. [10] And what do you know what that is? [11] A Blazing Fire!

102

Al-Takāthur [Acquisitiveness]
Makkan Period

*In the name of Allah, the Most Merciful,
the Most Compassionate*

[1] The craving for ever-greater worldly gains and to excel others in that regard keeps you occupied [2] until you reach your graves. [3] Nay, you will soon come to know;¹ [4] nay, again, you shall soon come to know. [5] Nay, would that you knew with certainty of knowledge (what your attitude will lead to, you would never have acted the way you do). [6] You will surely end up seeing Hell; [7] again, you shall most certainly end up seeing it with absolute certainty. [8] Then, on that Day, you will be called to account for all the bounties you enjoyed.

---

1. The word "soon" here refers to the Hereafter as well as death. This because everyone learns no sooner than he dies whether the occupations in which he engaged himself throughout life were a means of happiness and success or of misfortune and failure.

103

Al-'Aṣr [The Time]
Makkan Period

*In the name of Allah, the Most Merciful,
the Most Compassionate*

[1] By the time!¹ [2] Lo! Man is in a state of loss; [3] save
those who have faith and do righteous deeds, and counsel
each other to hold on to truth and counsel each other to
be steadfast.

---

1. "Time" here refers both to the present and the past. To swear
by time amounts to saying that both man's past and present bear
witness that the statement which follows is absolutely true.

104

Al-Humazah [The Fault-finder]
Makkan Period

In the name of Allah, the Most Merciful,
the Most Compassionate

[1] Woe to every fault-finding backbiter; [2] who amasses wealth and counts it over and again. [3] He thinks that his wealth will immortalise him forever.¹ [4] Nay, he shall be thrown into the Crusher. [5] And what do you know what the Crusher is? [6] It is the Fire kindled by Allah, [7] the Fire that shall rise to the hearts (of criminals). [8] Verily it will close in upon them, [9] in outstretched columns.²

---

1. Another possible meaning of the verse is: "He thinks that his wealth will endure with him." He never realises that a time will come when he will have to say adieu to this world with empty hands, leaving behind whatever he might have of worldly possessions.

2. The words *"fī 'amadin mumaddadah"* can mean several things: [1] that the gates of Hell will be closed and lofty columns will be erected on them; [2] that the culprits will be tied to those lofty columns; and [3] that the flames of the Fire shall rise to great heights appearing as though they were lofty columns.

105

Al-Fīl [The Elephant]
Makkan Period

*In the name of Allah, the Most Merciful,
the Most Compassionate*

[1] Have you not seen how your Lord dealt with the people of the elephants? [2] Did He not bring their plan to naught? [3] And He sent against them swarms of birds [4] which smote them with stones of baked clay, [5] and made them like straw eaten up (by cattle).[1]

---

1. This refers to an incident that took place only 50 days before the Prophet's birth. Abrahah, the Christian ruler of the Abyssinian kingdom of Yemen, led an expedition to Makkah with 60,000 troops. He was fired with the resolve to destroy the Ka'bah. His army had also brought along some elephants. When Abrahah reached a place that lies between Muzdalifah and Minā, there suddenly appeared swarms of birds carrying stones in their beaks and claws, which they pelted upon the Abyssinian army. Anyone who was hit by these stones soon started to rot, his flesh would start falling away from his bones. Thus the whole army was destroyed. This incident was well known in Arabia. At the time of the revelation of this *sūrah* there were still thousands of people in Makkah who had personally witnessed this incident. The Arabs accepted that the destruction of the "people of the elephants" had been brought about by God's will and power.

106
❧

Quraysh [The Quraysh]
Makkan Period

In the name of Allah, the Most Merciful,
the Most Compassionate

[1] Since the Quraysh became accustomed, [2] accustomed to the journey of winter and summer,¹ [3] therefore, let them worship the Lord of this House;² [4] Who fed them against hunger, and secured them against fear.³

---

1. These allude to the trade journeys undertaken by the Quraysh. In summer the Quraysh travelled northwards carrying merchandise to Syria and Palestine, and in winter they travelled southwards to southern Arabia. Their journeys had given rise to great prosperity.

2. "This House" here means the Ka'bah.

3. As Makkah was an inviolable city, the Quraysh had no fear of being attacked by any of the Arab tribes. Also, as keepers of the Ka'bah, their trade caravans passed freely throughout Arabia and no one molested them.

107
⚜️

Al-Māʿūn [Articles of Common Necessity]
Makkan Period

In the name of Allah, the Most Merciful,
the Most Compassionate

[1] Did you see him who gives the lie to the Reward and Punishment of the Hereafter? [2] Such is the one who repulses the orphans away, [3] and urges not the feeding of the needy.[1] [4] Woe, then, to those who pray, [5] but are heedless in their Prayers,[2] [6] those who do good (in order) to be seen, [7] and deny people the articles of common necessity.

---

1. That is, he neither persuades himself to feed the needy, nor urges his kinsfolk to do so, nor asks others to assist the poor.

2. This does not mean forgetting something during Prayer, but being heedless of Prayer itself.

108
༺❀༻

Al-Kawthar [Abundance]
Makkan Period

In the name of Allah, the Most Merciful,
the Most Compassionate

[1] (O Prophet), We have surely bestowed upon you good in abundance.¹ [2] So offer Prayer and sacrifice to your Lord alone. [3] Verily your enemy alone has been cut off from the roots.²

---

1. *Kawthar* signifies abundant good both in this world and the Hereafter. This includes the Fountain of *Kawthar* on the Day of Resurrection and the Stream of *Kawthar* in Paradise.

2. The unbelievers called the Prophet *abtar* (cut off from the roots). They said so to stress that he had been alienated from his people and that none of his male issue survived. They therefore believed that in the course of time no trace would be left of him. Here it is being pointed out that such a fate will overtake the Prophet's enemies rather than him.

109
❧

Al-Kāfirūn [The Unbelievers]
Makkan Period

In the name of Allah, the Most Merciful,
the Most Compassionate

[1] Say: "O unbelievers!"¹ [2] I do not worship those that you worship;² [3] neither do you worship Him Whom I worship;³ [4] nor will I worship those whom you have worshipped;⁴ [5] nor are you going to worship Him Whom I worship. [6] To you is your religion, and to me, my religion.⁵

---

1. "O unbelievers!" These words are addressed to those who had refused to believe in the Prophethood and teachings of the Prophet Muḥammad (peace be on him).

2. The unbelievers of Arabia worshipped God alongside other gods. The Prophet (peace be on him) is here made to disclaim the unbelievers' worship because worshipping God alongside other deities does not constitute worship at all.

3. The unbelievers are being told that they do not worship the One True God Who has the attributes possessed by Him Whom the Prophet (peace be on him) worshipped.

4. That is, the Prophet (peace be on him) would not worship the unbelievers' and their forefathers' deities.

5. This made it quite clear that in the matter of religion there was nothing in common between the Prophet (peace be on him) and the unbelievers.

110
❦

Al-Naṣr [Help]
Madīnan Period

*In the name of Allah, the Most Merciful,
the Most Compassionate*

[1] When¹ the help comes from Allah, and victory (is granted), [2] and you see people entering Allah's religion in multitudes, [3] then extol the praise of your Lord and pray to Him for forgiveness.² For He indeed is ever disposed to accept repentance.

---

1. According to reliable traditions, this was the last *sūrah* of the Qur'ān that was revealed some three months before the Prophet's demise. Thereafter, only a few verses were revealed but not any complete *sūrah*.

2. Traditions also indicate that after the revelation of this *sūrah*, the Prophet (peace be on him) began to pay markedly greater attention to celebrating God's praise and seeking His forgiveness.

111

Al-Lahab
Makkan Period

In the name of Allah, the Most Merciful,
the Most Compassionate

[1] Destroyed were the hands of Abū Lahab,[1] and he lay utterly doomed.[2] [2] His wealth did not avail him, nor his acquisitions. [3] Surely, he will be cast into a Flaming Fire [4] along with his wife,[3] that carrier of slanderous tales; [5] upon her neck shall be a rope of palm-fibre.

---

1. This refers to an uncle of the Prophet (peace be on him) who was commonly known as Abū Lahab.

2. Much though Abū Lahab tried to obstruct the forward march of Islam, his efforts ended in utter failure. What is said here is in fact a prediction but is couched in terms that convey the impression of an event that had already taken place.

3 The woman concerned was called Umm Jamīl. She was a sister of Abū Sufyān and was as staunch an enemy to Islam as her husband.

112

Al-Ikhlāṣ [Sincerity]
Makkan Period

In the name of Allah, the Most Merciful,
the Most Compassionate

[1] Say:[1] "He is Allah,[2] the One and Unique;[3] [2] Allah, Who is in need of none and of Whom all are in need; [3] He neither begot any nor was He begotten, (4) and none is comparable to Him."

---

1. The unbelievers often asked the Prophet (peace be on him) to describe the Lord in Whom he asked them to believe to the exclusion of all other deities. What kind of God is He? What is His pedigree? What is He made of? From whom did He inherit this Universe and who will later inherit it from Him? It is in response to such questions that this *sūrah* was revealed.

2. The Prophet (peace be on him) informed the unbelievers that his Lord was no other than He Whom the unbelievers themselves called Allah, and Whom they regarded as their own Creator as well as the Creator and Sustainer of the entire Universe. For the Arabian polytheists' beliefs regarding Allah see *Yūnus* 10: 22, 23, 31; *Banī Isrā'īl* 17: 67; *al-Mu'minūn* 23: 84-89; *al-'Ankabūt* 29: 61-63; *al-Zukhruf* 43: 87.

3. The word used here is *aḥad* rather than *wāḥid*. Though both the words mean "one," the word *wāḥid* is used for things that have the potential of plurality; for example, one man, one nation, one country, one world. The implication in all these cases is that here there is one man out of a number of men; and so on and so forth. Contrary to this, *aḥad* is used for Him Who is One and Unique in every respect, Who has no connection whatsoever with plurality. That is why *aḥad* is used in Arabic exclusively for God.

113

Al-Falaq [The Rising Day]
Makkan Period

In the name of Allah, the Most Merciful,
the Most Compassionate

[1] Say: "I seek refuge with the Lord of the rising day;[1] [2] from the evil of all that He created; [3] from the evil of night's darkness when it spreads around;[2] [4] from the evil of the women who blow on knots;[3] [5] and from the evil of the envier when he envies."[4]

---

1. That is, "I seek refuge with God Who brings out the light of dawn from the darkness of the night."

2. Refuge is sought from night's darkness because most of the crimes and acts of injustice and oppression are committed at night. Moreover, most dangerous animals also come out of their hiding places and go around at night.

3. This refers to magicians and sorcerers, both male and female.

4. Refuge is sought from envy because it prompts people to harm others.

114

Al-Nās [Mankind]
Makkan Period

In the name of Allah, the Most Merciful,
the Most Compassionate

[1] Say: "I seek refuge with the Lord of mankind;
[2] the King of mankind, [3] the True God of mankind,
[4] from the mischief of the whispering, elusive
prompter who returns again and again,[1] [5] who
whispers in the hearts of people; [6] whether he be from
the *jinn* or humans."[2]

---

1. That is, when this prompter to evil does not succeed in deluding
someone by his whisperings, he withdraws. But then he returns
over and over again, whispering to him that which is evil.

2. That is, one ought to seek refuge with God from such whisperers,
regardless of whether they belong to the human species or *jinn*.

Glossary of Terms

Adhān, the Islamic call to prayer.

Aḥad is used for Him Who is One and Unique in every respect, He Who has no connection whatsoever with plurality.

Aḥbār, religious jurists.

Aḥqāb, (sing. *ḥuqb*), denotes long periods of time, each period following the other in succession.

Anfāl is the plural of *nafl*, which stands for that which is extra, that which is over and above the obligatory. If this extra is from the servant, it denotes that additional service which he voluntarily renders over and above what is obligatory. But if this extra is from the master, it denotes the additional reward which the master awards his servant over and above what he deserves.

A'rāf (Heights). The people of *A'rāf* (Heights) will be the people who are neither righteous enough to enter Paradise nor wicked enough to be cast into Hell. They will, therefore, dwell in *al-A'rāf* situated between the two and will look forward to God's Mercy to be allowed to enter Paradise.

'Arafāt is the name of a plain in the north of Makkah. On the ninth day of Dhū al-Ḥijjah, Pilgrims gather there and are required to stay there for a part of the day praying and

invoking Allah. This stay in 'Arafāt is the most essential requirement of the *Ḥajj*.

Aṣīl denotes the span of time beginning with the sun's decline till sunset.

Awliyā', (sing. *walī*), has a wide range of connotation. A *walī* is: (1) he who is obeyed in all matters, (2) he in whose guidance someone has full faith, (3) he who is right and will save others from error and protect them from the evil consequences of their ill deeds in the world, and from the torment of God in the Hereafter, and (4) he about whom someone believes that he will come to his aid in worldly matters in supernatural ways.

Āyah, (pl. *āyāt*), means sign (or 'token'), that which directs one to something significant. In the Qur'ān the word has been used in five different meanings: (1) sign or indication; (2) the phenomena of the universe (called *āyāt* of God for the reality to which they point is hidden behind the veil of appearances); (3) miracles performed by the Prophets; (4) God's major acts of punishing the wicked such as the Flood which inundated and destroyed the people of Noah; and (5) the individual units (i.e. verses) of the Qur'ān.

Ayyām, (sing. *yawm*), literally means days. The word *ayyām*, as a technical term, signifies events of great historical significance. The expression *Ayyām Allāh* (literally, "the Days of Allah") (see, e.g., *Sūrah Ibrāhīm* 14: 5), refers to those major events in human history which show that God treated the evil-doing nations and personalities of the past by subjecting them to exemplary punishment.

Āzar, the Prophet Abraham's (peace be on him) father.

Baḥīrah was the name of a female camel which had already borne five offspring the last of which was a male. The practice was to slit the ear of such a camel and let her loose.

Bakkah, name for Makkah.

Burhān denotes an argument or proof.

Chādar, an over-garment or big shawl which is used to cover the head and the body.

Dār al-Islām, (Domain of Islam), denotes the territories wherein Islam and Islamic religious law prevail.

Fajr denotes the first light of the morning; daybreak.

Faqīr, (the poor). In the Qur'ānic usage this term applies to those who depend for their subsistence on others.

Faskh means annulment. In Islamic parlance it is commonly used to denote annulment of a sale or purchase or contract of marriage.

Fay' literally denotes restored properties. In Islamic parlance it signifies the goods of the enemy, whether transferable or non-transferable, which the Muslims have seized without engaging in actual warfare.

Fisq: transgression; disobeying God's command.

Fitnah means 'trial', 'test', 'temptation', 'civil strife' and 'insurrection'.

Fujūr, immorality.

Futūr denotes crack, rift, fissure, cleaving, or breaking apart.

Ghanīmah consists of those transferable properties which are seized by the Muslims from the enemy in the course of actual fighting.

Ḥabl Allāh, literally 'the cable of Allah', refers to the 'religion of God'. The reason for the use of the word 'cable' (*ḥabl*) is that it establishes a nexus between man and God and also between one believer and the other.

Ḥām: if the young of camels in the second degree of descent became worthy of riding they were let loose and called *ḥām*. Likewise, if ten offspring had been borne by a female camel she was also let loose and called *ḥām*.

Ḥanīf denotes the person who turns his face away from all other directions in order to exclusively follow a particular course. In Islamic parlance it signifies the person who exclusively devotes himself to God.

Ḥujjāj, (sing. *ḥājj*), denotes those who perform the *Ḥajj*.

Ilāh: god, deity.

Ilḥād, deviation, heresy.

Ilqā', literally means 'to throw'. In the Qur'ānic usage it means to put something in someone's heart.

Īmān literally means faith and belief.

Isrā' signifies the nocturnal journey of the Prophet (peace be on him) from the Holy Mosque (in Makkah) to the Farther Mosque (in Jerusalem). (See *Sūrah Banī Isrā'īl* 17: 1.) This nocturnal journey, which was itself of a miraculous nature, was a prelude to the Prophet's ascension to Heaven (*mi'rāj*).

Ka'bah, literally cube. It is a large cubic stone structure covered with a black cloth which stands in the centre of al-Masjid al-Ḥarām. It is also known as *al-bayt al-ḥarām* and *al-bayt al-'atīq*. It marks the direction to which the Muslims should turn in their Prayers.

Kalimāt, (sing. *kalimah*), 'Words'.

Khalīfah or vicegerent is one who exercises the authority delegated to him by his principal.

Khātam al-nabīyīn (the Seal of the Prophets), i.e. the Prophet Muḥammad (peace be on him) after whom no Messenger or Prophet would be raised.

Khawf, fear.

Kitāb, literally a thing on which something is written; a book or inscription; also a writ or command.

Kursī, literally that on which one sits. God's *Kursī* signifies His dominion and authority. Scholars differ, however, as to whether the Qur'ānic usage of this word with reference to God should be understood literally or figuratively.

Lahw al-ḥadīth, literally idle talk. In the Qur'ānic usage this signifies an amusement or diversion that completely absorbs a person, making him oblivious to things around him, making him even forget his duties to God.

Lawḥ Maḥfūẓ, literally the Guarded Tablet; the repository of destiny (*al-qadr*).

Laylat al-Qadr, the Night of Power. It refers to the night when the Qur'ān was first revealed to the Prophet (peace be on him).

Majnūn, literally one possessed by the *jinn*, but used by the Arabs to denote the insane.

Al-Mash'ar al-Ḥarām refers to al-Muzdalifah.

Mīzān means balance. It is also the Qur'ānic symbol of eschatological justice and retribution for deeds in this life.

Al-Mu'allafat qulūbihim is derived from the expression *ta'līf al-qalb* which literally means to soften someone's heart or induce sympathy in it. In its Qur'ānic usage it refers to those whom the Muslims seek to win over to the cause of Islam. The rule derived from the verse in which this expression occurs (see *Sūrah Tawbah* 9: 60) is that a part of *Zakāh* funds may be used to soften the hearts of those who are hostile to Islam or are in the unbelievers' camp, or to assist the new converts to Islam to make them feel at home in their new fraternity of faith.

Muftī is a jurist who is entitled to respond to legal queries or issue decisions of general religious import called *fatwā*.

Muhājirūn: Emigrants; those who migrated from Makkah to Madīnah in the way of God when it had become extremely

[986]

difficult for them to live in their home town according to the requirements of their faith.

Muḥkam means that which has been made firmly and perfectly. The *muḥkam* verses mentioned in the Qur'ān are those which are embodied in clear and lucid language and whose meaning is not liable to any ambiguity or equivocation. (See *Sūrah Āl 'Imrān* 3: 7.)

Mujāhadah literally means to strive, to make continuous effort to do good deeds, especially to devote oneself to acts of worship and remembrance of God.

Munāfiq, pl. *munāfiqūn*, means hypocrite.

Mutashābih, ambiguous. When used with reference to the Qur'ānic verses (see *Āl 'Imrān* 3: 7), it signifies the Qur'ānic verses whose meaning is ambiguous.

Nadhr denotes the firm promise that a person makes to God to perform certain supererogatory acts of goodness over and above those he is obliged to perform.

Naḥr, the ritual sacrifice of a camel.

Naqīb denotes supervisor and censor.

Nār, literally fire. It has been used in the Qur'ān to mean Hell.

Nuṣub signifies the place consecrated for offerings to others than the One True God.

Nusuk (pl. *manāsik*), signifies ritual sacrifice as well as other forms of devotion and worship.

Qarn usually denotes 'the people of a given age'. However, the word in its several usages in the Qur'ān connotes a 'nation' which, in its heyday, was ascendant in the world.

Qārūn, the Korah of the Bible and the Talmud, was Moses' cousin. According to his lineage given in Exodus (6: 18-21), his father and Moses' (peace be on him) father were brothers. In spite of his being an Israelite, Qārūn had allied himself with Pharaoh and was one of the most vocal opponents of Moses (peace be on him).

Qitāl, war, fighting.

Rabbānī has been used in the Qur'ān to denote Jewish religious scholars and functionaries who were supposed to provide true religious guidance to establish their rites of worship, implement religious laws, and so on. The same word occurs in *Sūrah al-Mā'idah* 5: 44 and 63. In the Christian tradition, the word 'divine' is an equivalent of the word *rabbānī*.

Rahbānīyah signifies monasticism, world-renunciation, withdrawal from the affairs of mundane life, and retreat to mountains and forests or to a life of seclusion and solitude.

Rajm is the stoning to death of a person who has committed fornication after having entered the fold of wedlock.

Rizq, sustenance.

Rūḥ, literally spirit, embraces all the possible meanings of 'spirit'.

Ru'yā, literally vision. The word is often used metaphorically for intellectual understanding or psychic visions or intuitions. It also refers to the dreams of the Prophets.

Ṣābi'ah, a people named in the Qur'ān along with Christians, Jews and Magians as having a religion rooted in revelation.

Ṣadaqah signifies whatever is given in charity with sincerity and the intent to please God. It is required that those who give charity should do so without flaunting it, without impressing upon its recipients that it was given to them as a favour, and without causing them any hurt.

Al-Ṣafā is the name of one of the two hillocks in the Holy Mosque of Makkah, the other being al-Marwah, between which Pilgrims run in remembrance of Hājar, the Prophet Ishmael's (peace be on him) mother. To run between these two hillocks was among the rites which God had taught Abraham (peace be on him) in connection with *Ḥajj* and which the Muslims continue to practise.

Sā'ibah was the name of either a male or female camel which had been let loose after consecration as a mark of gratitude in fulfilment of a vow taken for either recovery from some ailment or delivery from some danger. Likewise, the female camel that had borne ten times, and each time a female, was let loose and called *sā'ibah*.

Sakīnah means inner peace. It denotes mental composure and equanimity. It also signifies that serene state of mind on whose strength a man courts danger for a great cause with peace of mind.

Sha'ā'ir Allāh. This expression refers to all those rites which, in opposition to polytheism and outright unbelief and atheism, are the characteristic symbols of exclusive devotion to God.

Shahādah, literally the act of witnessing, is the declaration of belief in the unity of God and the Prophethood of the Prophet Muḥammad (peace be on him). Its pronouncement is considered one of the Five Pillars of Islam. When one proclaims it aloud, one is considered to have officially declared oneself to be a Muslim.

Ṣiddīq denotes someone who is utterly honest and veracious, someone who is conspicuous in his devotion to truth.

Sidrat al-muntahā is literally the lote-tree at the farthest boundary (see *al-Najm* 53: 14). However, as to what kind of tree it is and what its true nature is, all these are the hidden secrets of the universe which are beyond our comprehension.

Sunnah means a way, course, rule, mode or manner of acting or conduct of life. In Islamic terminology it denotes the way of the Prophet Muḥammad (peace be on him) as evidenced by his authentic precepts and practices.

Sūrah, literally a row or fence, refers to any of the 114 chapters of the Qur'ān.

Tadhakkur conveys the sense that somebody who had been either heedless or negligent suddenly wakes up and takes heed.

Tafāwut: disharmony, discordance.

Tafrīq is repudiation of the marital tie as a result of judicial decision.

Taqdīr means God's determination of all things, that is, before creating anything God decided what the role of each thing would be in the world, what would be its size, its shape, its qualities, and its location. God also decided the means and opportunities that should be made available to it for its existence, sustenance and function; how it should come into existence, how long it should remain in existence, and how, after accomplishing its task, its existence should come to an end.

Taqdīs means (1) to celebrate and proclaim holiness, and (2) to purify.

Taqīyah is the prudent concealment of faith in order to save one's life. This concealment should, however, remain within reasonable limits. The most one is permitted to do is to save one's life and property without causing harm either to the interests of Islam or of the Muslim community as a whole.

Taqwā is one of the many words in the Islamic terminology whose exact equivalent is hard to find in English. It has been translated as 'fear of Allah', 'God fearing', 'piety', 'righteousness', 'dutifulness', and 'God-consciousness'.

Glossary of Terms

Tasbīḥ has two meanings: (1) to proclaim God's glory, and (2) to exert oneself earnestly and energetically to do God's will.

Al-Tashrīq. The 11th, 12th and 13th of Dhū al-Ḥijjah are called *Ayyām al-Tashrīq.* The Pilgrims are required to spend these days in Minā.

Tasnīm is a fountain in Paradise at which the chosen ones shall drink. The word *tasnīm* has the nuance of 'height'. To call a spring *tasnīm* carries the connotation of a spring that flows down from a great height.

Ta'wīl al-aḥādīth (see *Sūrah Yūsuf* 12: 101) does not simply signify explaining of the true meaning of dreams, as people are wont to believe. What it really signifies is that God will bless Joseph, in whose context this expression occurs, with the capacity to grasp complicated matters, to comprehend the true nature of things.

Tayammum literally means 'to turn to', 'to aim at', 'to head for'. As an Islamic terminology, however, it is the symbolic ablution attained through wiping one's face and hands with clean earth when water is not available for washing.

Thawr is the name of the cave in the vicinity of Makkah in which the Prophet (peace be on him) took refuge with his Companion Abū Bakr *en route* to Madīnah.

Ṭuwā is the valley in which God spoke to Moses.

Ulū al-amr are those invested with authority. The expression embraces all those entrusted with directing Muslims in matters of common concern. They include the intellectual and political leaders of the community as well as administrative officials, judges of the courts, tribal chiefs, and regional representatives.

Wāḥid means 'one'. It is used, however, for objects that have the potential of plurality; for example, one man, one nation, one country, one world. The implication in all these cases is that here there is one man out of a number of men; and so on and so forth.

Wakīl signifies one upon whom a person totally relies; one in whom full trust is reposed; one to whose care one entrusts one's affairs, to whom one looks for guidance and support.

Walāyah denotes the relationship of kinship, support, succour, protection, friendship, and guardianship.

Waṣīlah. When twins were born to a goat and one of them was a male and the other a female, the male goat was not slaughtered but was rather let loose in the name of the deities. This male goat was called *waṣīlah*.

Yamīn, according to Arabic literary usage, means strength and power, or good fortune, or swearing.

Zaqqūm is the name of the tree that will grow in the depths of Hell and the inmates of Hell will be obliged to eat of it.

Zīnah, literally adornment, denotes in the Qur'ān (see *al-Aʿrāf* 7: 31) full and proper dress. While performing Prayer people are required not only to cover the private parts of their body but also to wear a dress that serves the two-fold purpose of covering the body and giving them a decent appearance.

Ẓuhr means early afternoon when the sun begins to decline. This word is used in Islamic parlance to denote one of the five daily Prayers which is offered at this particular time.

Biographical Notes

'Abd Allāh ibn 'Abbās, d. 68 A.H./687 C.E., a Companion of the Prophet (peace be on him), was the most outstanding scholar of Qur'ānic exegesis in his time.

'Abd Allāh ibn 'Abd al-Muṭṭalib, d. 571 C.E., the last and most beloved son of 'Abd al-Muṭṭalib and the Prophet's father who died a few months before his birth. He was known for his noble character.

'Abd Allāh ibn Mas'ūd, d. 32 A.H./653 C.E., one of the most learned Companions of the Prophet (peace be on him) who was noted especially for his juristic calibre. He was held by the Iraqi school of law as one of its main authorities.

'Abd Allāh ibn Ubayy ibn Salūl, d. 9 A.H./630 C.E., was the foremost enemy of the Prophet (peace be on him) and the ringleader of the hypocrites in Madīnah.

'Abd Allāh ibn 'Umar, d. 73 A.H./692 C.E., a famous Companion and son of the second Caliph, was famous for his piety and for transmitting many traditions from the Prophet (peace be on him).

'Abd Allāh ibn Umm Maktūm, d. 14 A.H./635 C.E., was a blind Companion of the Prophet (peace be on him). It was in regard to him that the first few verses of *Sūrah 'Abasa* 80: 1 ff. were revealed. He was one of the *mu'adhdhin*s who used to call the *adhān* in Madīnah.

'Abd al-Muṭṭalib ibn Hāshim ibn 'Abd Manāf, d. 579 C.E., was the grandfather of the Prophet (peace be on him). He was a leading figure of the Quraysh in pre-Islamic times and was highly respected in Makkah.

Abrahah, d. 570 C.E., was the Christian ruler of Yemen who tried to demolish the Ka'bah but failed. *Sūrah al-Fīl (Sūrah* 105) relates how God dealt with him and his army.

Abū Bakr, 'Abd Allāh ibn 'Uthmān, d. 13 A.H./634 C.E., was the most trusted Companion of the Prophet (peace be on him) and the first Caliph of Islam. Abū Bakr's wisdom and indomitable will ensured the survival of Islam after the death of the Prophet (peace be on him).

Abū Ḥanīfah, al-Nu'mān ibn Thābit, d. 150 A.H./767 C.E., was a theologian and jurist who dominated the intellectual life of Iraq in the later part of his life and became the founder of a major school of law in Islam known after his name.

Abū Hurayrah, d. 59 A.H./679 C.E., was a Companion of the Prophet (peace be on him) who transmitted a very large number of traditions.

Abū Jahl, 'Amr ibn Hishām ibn al-Mughīrah, d. 2 A.H./624 C.E., was an arch-enemy of Islam throughout his life. He was killed during the Battle of Badr in which he was the leading commander on the side of the Quraysh.

Abū Lahab, 'Abd al-'Uzzā ibn 'Abd al-Muṭṭalib ibn Hāshim, d. 2 A.H./624 C.E., was an uncle of the Prophet (peace be on him). He was, however, one of the staunchest enemies of Islam and the Prophet.

Abū Sufyān, Ṣakhr ibn Ḥarb ibn Umayyah, d. 31 A.H./652 C.E., was one of the foremost opponents of Islam and the Prophet (peace be on him) until the conquest of Makkah, when he embraced Islam. In subsequent military encounters, Abū Sufyān fought on the Muslim side.

Abū Ṭalḥah, Zayd ibn Sahl ibn al-Aswad, d. 34 A.H./654 C.E., was a Companion noted for his courage and skill as an archer. He participated in the battles of Badr, Uḥud, Khandaq, and in several other military expeditions.

Abū Ṭālib, 'Abd Manāf ibn 'Abd al-Muṭṭalib, d. 620 C.E., was an uncle of the Prophet (peace be on him) and father of the fourth Caliph 'Alī. He continued to provide effective protection and support to the Prophet (peace be on him) till his death.

'Adī ibn Ḥātim, d. 68 A.H./687 C.E., was a Companion who took a prominent part in the military expedition against the apostates during the caliphate of Abū Bakr.

Aḥmad ibn Ḥanbal, d. 241 A.H./855 C.E., was the founder of one of the four Sunnī schools of law in Islam. He valiantly suffered persecution for the sake of his religious convictions.

'Ā'ishah, d. 58 A.H./678 C.E., daughter of Abū Bakr, was a wife of the Prophet (peace be on him). She has transmitted a wealth of traditions, especially those concerning the Prophet's personal life. She was also highly regarded for her mature and sharp understanding of the teachings of Islam.

'Alī ibn Abī Ṭālib, d. 40 A.H./661 C.E., was a cousin and son-in-law of the Prophet (peace be on him) and the fourth Caliph of Islam. He was known for his many qualities, especially piety and juristic acumen.

Al-Bukhārī, Muḥammad ibn Ismā'īl, d. 256 A.H./870 C.E., is regarded as the most famous traditionist of Islam whose work is recognised as one of the six most authentic collections of *Ḥadīth*. Bukhārī's work is generally considered the 'soundest book after the Book of Allah'.

Fāṭimah bint Muḥammad was the last daughter of the Prophet Muḥammad (peace be on him) from Khadījah. She was married to 'Alī ibn Abī Ṭālib and gave birth to al-Ḥasan, al-Ḥusayn, Umm Kulthūm and Zaynab. She died within a year after the death of the Prophet (peace be on him).

Ḥafṣah, d. 45 A.H./665 C.E., daughter of the second Caliph, 'Umar ibn al-Khaṭṭāb, was one of the wives of the Prophet (peace be on him).

Al-Ḥasan al-Baṣrī, d. 110 A.H./728 C.E., known primarily for his piety, was a major theologian of Baṣrah during the last decades of the first century of Hijrah/seventh century C.E.

Ḥāṭib ibn Abī Balta'ah, d. 30 A.H./650 C.E., embraced Islam quite early and was known for his bravery as well as poetic skills. The Prophet Muḥammad (peace be on him) sent him as his envoy to Muqawqis, the governor of Alexandria, inviting him to Islam.

Hilāl ibn Umayyah ibn 'Āmir was one of the three Companions who stayed behind in Madīnah instead of joining the expedition to Tabūk. Like the other two Companions, Hilāl also repented and his repentance was accepted by God. (See Sūrah al-Tawbah 9: 118).

Hūd was an Arabian Prophet of the 'Ād, a people who lived in al-Ahqāf in northern Ḥaḍramawt. Hūd has been mentioned in the Qur'ān several times. For the Qur'ānic references to Hūd see especially Sūrah al-A'rāf 7: 65-72.

Ibn Kathīr, Ismā'īl ibn 'Umar, d. 774 A.H./1373 C.E., was a famous traditionist, historian and jurist and the author of one of the best-known commentaries on the Qur'ān.

Ibn Mājah, Muḥammad ibn Yazīd, d. 273 A.H./887 C.E., was a famous traditionist whose collection of traditions, Kitāb al-Sunan is one of the six most authentic collections of Ḥadīth.

Ibn Sa'd, Muḥammad, d. 230 A.H./845 C.E., historian, traditionist and the secretary of al-Wāqidī, is known for his al-Ṭabaqāt al-Kubrā, a major biographical dictionary of the early period of Islam.

Ibn Sīrīn, Muḥammad, d. 110 A.H./729 C.E., was a noted second generation scholar of Baṣrah, who was especially prominent as a traditionist.

Jābir ibn Zayd, d. 93 A.H./712 C.E., was a Successor and a leading jurist. He was a disciple of 'Abd Allāh ibn 'Abbās and was highly respected for his knowledge.

Ja'far al-Ṣādiq ibn Muḥammad al-Bāqir ibn 'Alī Zayn al-'Ābidīn ibn al-Ḥusayn ibn 'Alī, d. 148 A.H./765 C.E., is considered by the Twelver Shī'ites to be their sixth *imām*. He was a great scholar and a pious man. Noted scholars of his time such as Abū Ḥanīfah and Mālik ibn Anas benefited from his knowledge.

Ka'b ibn Mālik al-Anṣārī, d. 50 A.H./670 C.E., was a Companion of the Prophet (peace be on him) and a noted poet. He took part in many battles and was one of the strongest supporters of 'Uthmān when the latter faced opposition.

Khadījah bint Khuwaylid, d. 620 C.E., was the first woman whom the Prophet (peace be on him) married. She gave birth to several sons and daughters including Fāṭimah, Zaynab, Umm Kulthūm and Ruqayyah.

Al-Khudrī, Abū Sa'īd Sa'd ibn Mālik ibn Sinān al-Anṣārī, d. 74 A.H./693 C.E., was a Companion of the Prophet (peace be on him) who tried to keep the Prophet's company to the maximum. He narrated a large number of traditions. As many as 1,170 traditions narrated by him are extant in the *Ḥadīth* collections.

Mālik ibn Anas, d. 179 A.H./795 C.E., was a famous second Islamic century/eighth century C.E. traditionist and jurist of Madīnah, and the founder of one of the four Sunnī schools of law. His *al-Muwaṭṭa'*, a collection of traditions as well as legal opinions of the jurists of Madīnah, is one of the earliest extant works of *Ḥadīth* and *Fiqh*.

Muḥammad al-Bāqir ibn 'Alī Zayn al-'Ābidīn ibn al-Ḥusayn, d. 114 A.H./732 C.E., was the father of Ja'far al-Ṣādiq. He is considered the fifth *imām* by the Twelver Shī'ites.

Mujāhid ibn Jabr, d. 104 A.H./722 C.E., was a Successor and among the foremost Qur'ān commentators of Makkah in his time. His *Tafsīr*, which is now published, is one of the earliest extant works of that genre.

Muqātil ibn Sulaymān, d. 150 A.H./767 C.E., was one of the distinguished scholars in the field of *Tafsīr*. He has left behind a number of works in the field of Qur'ānic sciences.

Mūrārah ibn Rabī' al-Anṣārī, a Companion of the Aws tribe, was one of the three Companions who stayed behind in Madīnah instead of joining the expedition to Tabūk. He, like the other Companions, repented and his repentance was accepted by God. (See *Sūrah al-Tawbah* 9: 118.)

Muslim ibn al-Ḥajjāj al-Nisābūrī, d. 261 A.H./875 C.E., was one of the greatest scholars of *Ḥadīth* whose *Ṣaḥīḥ Muslim* is one of the six most authentic collections of *Ḥadīth* and ranks second in importance only to that of al-Bukhārī.

Al-Nasā'ī, Aḥmad ibn 'Alī, d. 303 A.H./915 C.E., was one of the foremost scholars of *Ḥadīth* whose *Kitāb al-Sunan* is one of the six most authentic collections of traditions.

Qatādah ibn Di'āmah, d. 118 A.H./736 C.E., was an erudite scholar of *Sīrah* who was also known for his knowledge of Qur'ānic exegesis, *Ḥadīth*, Arabic language and Arabic genealogy.

Rabī' ibn Anas, d. 139 A.H./757 C.E., was a Successor who narrated *aḥādīth* from Umm Salamah and Anas ibn Mālik. 'Abd Allāh ibn Mubārak has reported from him quite a number of *aḥādīth*.

Ṣāliḥ was an Arabian Prophet of the Thamūd, a people who have been mentioned many a time in the Qur'ān. Ṣāliḥ lived before the Prophets Moses and Shu'ayb. His mission was to direct his people to righteousness, but they refused to respond to his call whereupon they were destroyed.

Sawdah bint Zamʿah ibn Qays, d. 54 A.H./674 C.E., was the first woman whom the Prophet (peace be on him) married after the death of Khadījah. She was among the first converts and had migrated to Abyssinia before settling in Madīnah.

Al-Shāfiʿī, Muḥammad ibn Idrīs, d. 204 A.H./820 C.E., was the founder of one of the four Sunnī schools of law in Islam.

Shāh Walī Allāh, d. 1214 A.H./1762 C.E., was the most celebrated theologian, scholar and expounder of the Qurʾān produced in Muslim India. His greatest contribution was his popularising of Qurʾānic education. He was among the first translators of the Qurʾān into Persian. He stood for reform in social customs, beliefs and practices.

Shuʿayb, an Arabian Prophet of Madyan, was from the progeny of the Prophet Abraham. He lived in the period before Moses and after the Prophets Hūd and Ṣāliḥ. His tomb is said to be in Ḥiṭṭīn in Palestine.

Al-Suddī, Ismāʿīl ibn ʿAbd al-Raḥmān, d. 128 A.H./745 C.E., was one of the early scholars of *Tafsīr* who has left behind a work in that field.

Al-Ṭabarī, Muḥammad ibn Jarīr, d. 310 A.H./923 C.E., was a distinguished historian, jurist and Qurʾān commentator. His major extant works include his commentary *Jāmiʿ al-Bayān fī Tafsīr al-Qurʾān* and his *Annals*, viz. *Taʾrīkh al-Rusul wa al-Mulūk*.

Al-Tirmidhī, Muḥammad ibn ʿĪsā, d. 279 A.H./892 C.E., was a famous traditionist whose collection of traditions, *Kitāb al-Sunan*, is one of the six most authentic collections of *Ḥadīth*.

ʿUmar ibn al-Khaṭṭāb, d. 23 A.H./644 C.E., was the second Caliph of Islam under whose Caliphate the Islamic state became increasingly organized and its frontiers vastly expanded.

Umm Jamīl, was Abū Lahab's wife and as inveterate an enemy of Islam as her husband. She used to carry thorns and sharp wood and place them in the Prophet's path and throw dirt on him.

Umm Salamah, Hind bint Abī Umayyah, d. 62 A.H./681 C.E., was one of the wives of the Prophet (peace be on him) who has reported several hundred traditions from him.

'Uthmān ibn 'Affān, d. 35 A.H./656 C.E., was a son-in-law of the Prophet (peace be on him) and the third Caliph of Islam under whose reign vast areas were conquered and the Qur'ān's present codex was prepared.

Walīd ibn Mughīrah, was the chief of the Banū Makhzūm clan of the Quraysh. His clan was responsible for warfare, and he was very well off. These two factors combined to make him proficient in warfare and fighting. Initially, he wanted to embrace Islam but didn't do so out of arrogance. He was killed in the Battle of Badr. His vile characteristics have been mentioned in more than one chapter in the Qur'ān. (See *Sūrah al-Najm* 53: 33-35 and *al-Muddaththir* 74: 11-26.)

Zayd ibn Ḥārithah ibn Sharāḥīl (or Shuraḥbīl) al-Kalbī, was a Companion of the Prophet (peace be on him) and one of the earliest converts to Islam. The Prophet (peace be on him) adopted him as his son and held him in considerable affection. He also appointed him commander of different military expeditions. He was martyred in the battle of Mu'tah in 8 A.H./630 C.E.

Zaynab bint Jaḥsh al-Asadīyah, d. 20 A.H./641 C.E., was a cousin of the Prophet (peace be on him) who was first married to Zayd ibn Ḥārithah. This marriage, however, broke up whereafter the Prophet (peace be on him) married her.

Subject Index

247, 252, 254, 255, 262, 303, 321, 324, 332, 333, 334, 346, 364, 366, 369, 382, 385, 391, 394, 395, 398, 399, 403, 408, 422, 425, 427, 429, 431, 443, 448, 452, 454, 459, 477, 483, 492, 508, 511, 539, 540, 541, 592, 615, 616, 620, 627, 630, 639, 641, 651, 654, 655, 656, 660, 663, 672, 685, 686, 699, 702, 703, 707, 716, 720, 724, 725, 727, 729, 751, 772, 778, 779, 793, 814, 822, 872, 873, 886, 887, 890, 901, 906, 907, 923, 924, 928, 931, 935, 951, 963

Anger, 89, 242, 399, 681, 703, 865, 903

Animals of sacrificial offering (see Ritual sacrifice, Sacrificial offering)

Anṣār, 76, 291, 295, 753, 836

Apes, 13, 170, 245

Apostasy, 272, 437

Apostates, 272

Appointed Time, 8, 90, 96, 196, 493, 494, 500, 514, 596, 601, 613, 622, 646, 674, 679, 709, 731, 801, 918, 922

Ascendancy, 300

Astray, 1, 6, 78, 82, 126, 135, 140, 157, 173, 194, 198, 207, 211, 212, 221, 224, 247, 248, 249, 278, 286, 314, 325, 367, 369, 372, 377, 378, 396, 406, 428, 431, 437, 444, 451, 471, 472, 474, 478, 495, 541, 543, 583, 590, 603, 640, 656, 668, 675, 679, 690, 694, 695, 701, 715, 728, 735, 736, 814, 907

Atheism, 151, 499, 614

Awliyā' (see Saint(s))

Balance, 28, 219, 424, 558, 710, 803, 817, 821, 944

Barzakh, 519, 938

Battle of Badr, 89, 94, 253, 255, 256, 260, 263, 265, 502, 600

Battle of Ḥunayn, 274, 275

Battle of Khaybar, 758

Battle of the *Aḥzāb*, 620

Battle of Uḥud, 88, 89, 95, 96, 123, 254

Bedouin(s), 290, 296, 756, 757, 769

Bedouin Arabs, 289, 290, 291, 296

Believers, 4, 6, 15, 18, 22, 31, 34, 35, 37, 43, 44, 48, 55, 59, 60, 63, 64, 65, 66, 69, 71, 75, 84, 85, 86, 87, 88, 89, 90, 91, 93, 94, 95, 97, 98, 100, 108, 112, 116, 121, 122, 123, 126, 127, 129, 130, 132, 134, 138, 139, 140, 141, 144, 150, 152, 155, 156, 163, 165, 168, 169, 170, 174, 175,

176, 177, 178, 180, 188, 190, 214, 218, 223, 230, 232, 253, 254, 255,
256, 257, 258, 261, 262, 264, 267, 271, 272, 273, 274, 275, 277, 279,
281, 284, 285, 287, 292, 293, 294, 295, 296, 297, 298, 317, 329, 340,
368, 377, 379, 382, 388, 389, 407, 409, 425, 434, 439, 441, 460, 462,
491, 497, 508, 509, 522, 525, 526, 527, 530, 534, 535, 537, 540, 545,
554, 555, 559, 560, 562, 571, 588, 589, 597, 599, 600, 606, 608, 620,
621, 622, 623, 624, 626, 627, 628, 629, 630, 631, 632, 636, 638, 651,
655, 661, 686, 689, 693, 705, 710, 713, 715, 734, 740, 747, 748, 752,
753, 754, 755, 757, 758, 759, 760, 761, 762, 763, 764, 765, 766, 769,
777, 779, 784, 785, 789, 816, 818, 819, 823, 826, 827, 828, 832, 833,
839, 841, 842, 843, 844, 847, 848, 850, 851, 852, 854, 855, 859, 862,
863, 872, 873, 874, 897, 907, 914, 936, 940

Bequest, 105, 106, 180

Birth control, 135

Blasphemy, 196, 436

Blessing(s), 19, 31, 62, 83, 85, 201, 209, 234, 239, 328, 333, 455, 489,
594, 627, 630, 883

Blood money, 35, 36, 128, 420

Book of Allah, 2, 20, 71, 166, 268, 620, 644

Bridal-due, 102, 111, 155, 845

Bridal gift, 52

Brothers, 47, 85, 94, 105, 106, 107, 110, 148, 149, 272, 274, 341, 342, 350,
351, 353, 354, 355, 358, 359, 386, 419, 466, 529, 536, 630, 765, 830

Brotherhood, 267, 268

Cattle, 34, 65, 70, 128, 135, 150, 177, 179, 209, 211, 248, 303, 392, 401,
404, 468, 498, 500, 501, 511, 543, 544, 612, 618, 644, 652, 675, 696,
709, 719, 724, 748, 749, 799, 800, 878, 926, 929, 972

Celestial system, 806

Celibacy (see Monasticism)

Charity (see *Ṣadaqah*)

Chastisement, 3, 17, 18, 19, 21, 23, 25, 32, 33, 34, 36, 41, 42, 67, 70, 71,
77, 80, 82, 85, 96, 98, 99, 107, 108, 115, 120, 126, 129, 132, 139, 141,
142, 144, 147, 162, 163, 165, 173, 174, 177, 180, 182, 186, 188, 191,
192, 195, 196, 201, 207, 213, 216, 228, 230, 243, 245, 255, 258, 259,
270, 277, 281, 287, 289, 291, 299, 301, 307, 308, 309, 311, 315, 316,
317, 320, 321, 323, 324, 325, 326, 328, 330, 331, 333, 335, 336, 337,
345, 359, 360, 363, 366, 368, 369, 372, 373, 375, 376, 379, 386, 394,
397, 400, 405, 407, 408, 409, 410, 411, 415, 416, 417, 425, 426, 428,

Name Index